INTERNATIONAL
HUMAN
RESOURCE
MANAGEMENT

Praise for the third edition

'The third edition of *International Human Resource Management* firmly cements its place as the leading, research-based text on the subject, both in terms of its content and its authors.'

Mick Marchington, Professor of Human Resource Management, Strathclyde Business School

SAGE was founded in 1965 by Sara Miller McCune to support the dissemination of usable knowledge by publishing innovative and high-quality research and teaching content. Today, we publish more than 750 journals, including those of more than 300 learned societies, more than 800 new books per year, and a growing range of library products including archives, data, case studies, reports, conference highlights, and video. SAGE remains majority-owned by our founder, and on her passing will become owned by a charitable trust that secures our continued independence.

Los Angeles | London | Washington DC | New Delhi | Singapore

INTERNATIONAL HUMAN RESOURCE MANAGEMENT

FOURTH EDITION

ANNE-WIL HARZING AND ASHLY H. PINNINGTON

Los Angeles | London | New Delhi
Singapore | Washington DC

Los Angeles | London | New Delhi
Singapore | Washington DC

SAGE Publications Ltd
1 Oliver's Yard
55 City Road
London EC1Y 1SP

SAGE Publications Inc.
2455 Teller Road
Thousand Oaks, California 91320

SAGE Publications India Pvt Ltd
B 1/I 1 Mohan Cooperative Industrial Area
Mathura Road
New Delhi 110 044

SAGE Publications Asia-Pacific Pte Ltd
3 Church Street
#10-04 Samsung Hub
Singapore 049483

Editor: Kirsty Smy
Assistant editor: Nina Smith
Production editor: Sarah Cooke
Copyeditor: Gemma Marren
Proofreader: Lynda Watson
Indexer: Silvia Benvenuto
Marketing manager: Alison Borg
Cover design: Lisa Harper
Typeset by: C&M Digitals (P) Ltd, Chennai, India
Printed and bound in Great Britain by
CPI Group (UK) Ltd, Croydon, CR0 4YY

Library of Congress Control Number: 2014933555

British Library Cataloguing in Publication data

A catalogue record for this book is available from the British Library

ISBN 978-1-4462-6730-1
ISBN 978-1-4462-6731-8 (pbk)

At SAGE we take sustainability seriously. Most of our products are printed in the UK using FSC papers and boards. When we print overseas we ensure sustainable papers are used as measured by the Egmont grading system. We undertake an annual audit to monitor our sustainability.

Contents

List of Figures and Tables

Tables

List of Contributors

Phil Almond is Professor of Comparative Employment Relations at De Montfort University, Leicester, UK. He has published widely on the relations between multinationals and business and employment institutions. He is the editor, with Anthony Ferner, of *American Multinationals in Europe* (Oxford University Press, 2006). He also has published research on comparative industrial relations and human resource management, comparative methodology, and the varieties of capitalism debate.

Ingmar Björkman is Professor and Dean of Aalto University School of Business (Finland). Most of his work deals with issues related to people management in multinational corporations. His latest books are *Global Challenge: International Human Resource Management* (2011), co-authored with Paul Evans and Vladimir Pucik, and *Handbook of Research in International Human Resource Management* (2012), co-edited with Günter K. Stahl and Shad Morris.

Chris Brewster is Professor of International Human Resource Management at Henley Business School, University of Reading, UK, and also holds similar appointments at Radboud University, Nijmegen, the Netherlands, the University of Vaasa in Finland and at ISCTE, Lisbon in Portugal. He has conducted extensive research in the field of international and comparative HRM, and has published 25 books and almost 200 articles on these topics.

Pawan S. Budhwar is Professor of International Human Resource Management at Aston Business School, UK. Pawan has published over 80 articles on people management related topics for the Indian context in leading journals. He has also written and co-edited 11 books on HRM in different regions. Pawan is a Fellow of the British Academy of Management and an Academician of the Academy of Social Sciences. He is also the editor-in-chief of *British Journal of Management*.

Fang Lee Cooke is Professor of Human Resource Management and Asia Studies at Monash University, Melbourne, Australia. Fang's research interests are in strategic HRM, outsourcing and shared services, diversity management, employment and labour market studies and employment relations. Fang's current research projects include:

Chinese firms in Africa and their employment practices and labour relations; employee resilience; HRM practices and performance in the finance sector in the Asian region.

Yaw A. Debrah is Professor of Human Resource and International Management at Swansea University (University of Wales), UK. He has published numerous articles and edited books on HRM, IHRM and International Business and Management in Asia and Africa, including: FDI, technology and knowledge management; organizational failure; CSR; employment relations in SMEs in the MENA region; informal sector employment in developing countries; FDI and employment issues in sub-Saharan Africa.

Tony Edwards is Professor of Comparative Management and Head of the Department of Management at Kings College, London. His research focuses on the management of labour in multinational companies, including the diffusion of practices across countries, the influence of the domestic business system in international HR policies and the management of human resources during and after international mergers and acquisitions.

Paul A.L. Evans is Shell Professor of Human Resources and Organizational Development, Emeritus, and Emeritus Professor of Organizational Behavior at INSEAD. His research focuses on leadership development, international human resource management and global talent management (he is Academic Director of INSEAD's Global Talent Competitiveness Index). His most recent book, with Vladimir Pucik and Ingmar Björkman, is *The Global Challenge: International Human Resource Management* (2010).

Damian Grimshaw is Professor of Employment Studies, Manchester Business School, University of Manchester, UK. He has published widely on comparative employment systems, including on wage systems and IT outsourcing. He is author of *Pay Equity, Minimum Wages and Comparative Industrial Relations* (2013) and joint author with Jill Rubery of *The Organisation of Employment: An International Perspective* (2003).

Anne-Wil Harzing is Research Professor and Research Development Advisor at ESCP Europe, London. Anne-Wil's research interests include IHRM, HQ-subsidiary relationships, transfer of HRM practices, the role of language in international business, the international research process, and the quality and impact of academic research.

K. Galen Kroeck is an industrial and organizational psychologist, and Professor and Chairman of the Department of Management and International Business at Florida International University (FIU), USA. Professor Kroeck has served as a federal court expert witness in numerous discrimination cases and has authored many book chapters, textbooks and articles in top academic journals.

Miguel Martínez Lucio is a Professor at the Manchester Business School, University of Manchester, UK. He has worked on various projects and published on issues related to regulation and employment. He is concerned with the question of how marketization, privatization and new forms of managerialism impact on employment relations and their regulation. In addition he has published on the impact of globalization on industrial relations, migrant networks and social movements.

Robert MacKenzie is Professor of Work and Employment at Leeds University Business School, UK. His research interests are restructuring, labour market change, contingent contracts and the regulation of the employment relationship. These issues have been studied in various national and sectoral contexts, including telecommunications and construction, and through the social and economic experiences of migrant workers.

Wolfgang Mayrhofer is full Professor of Management and Organizational Behaviour at WU Vienna, Austria. His research interests focus on international comparative research in human resource management, leadership and careers. He has co-edited, authored and co-authored 27 books and more than 170 book chapters and peer reviewed articles.

Dana Minbaeva is Professor of Strategic and Global Human Resource Management at the Department for Strategic Management and Globalization, Copenhagen Business School, Denmark. Dana's research on strategic IHRM, knowledge sharing and transfer in multinational corporations has appeared in leading international academic journals.

Alan Nankervis is Professor of HRM at Curtin University, Perth, Australia. He is the author or co-author of more than a hundred books, book chapters, journal and conference papers. His research interests include comparative Asian HRM, comparative management, links between performance management and firm effectiveness, skills shortages and the ageing workforce.

Ashly H. Pinnington is Dean, Faculty of Business and Professor of Human Resource Management, The British University in Dubai, United Arab Emirates. He has published extensively on the management of professionals, chiefly institutionalist perspectives in HRM, IHRM and organizational change. His recent work concentrates on careers, ethics and social responsibility.

Vladimir Pucik is Visiting Professor of Management and Strategy at CEIBS, Shanghai. He received his PhD from Columbia University in New York and taught for many years at the University of Michigan, Cornell University and IMD. His research focuses on international management and HR strategies in global firms. He is a founding partner of several IT start-ups and has consulted and conducted workshops for major corporations worldwide.

Christopher J. Rees is a Senior Lecturer in Human Resources at the Institute for Development Policy and Management, University of Manchester, UK. He is a Chartered Psychologist and Chartered Fellow of the Chartered Institute for Personnel and

Development. His teaching and research interests focus upon HR-related organizational change and development initiatives and he has published widely on this subject.

B. Sebastian Reiche is Associate Professor in the Department of Managing People in Organizations at IESE Business School in Barcelona, Spain. His research focuses on international assignments and international HRM, knowledge transfer, employee retention and careers, global leadership and cross-cultural management. He is associate editor of *Human Resource Management Journal* and regularly blogs on topics related to expatriation and global work (http://blog.iese.edu/expatriatus).

Laurence Romani is Associate Professor at the Center for Advanced Studies in Leadership, Stockholm School of Economics, Sweden. Her research investigates how to recognize and respect cultural differences (cultures, ethnicities, genders, etc.) through ethical leadership. Laurence adopts a critical and feminist perspective to study cross-cultural and diversity management.

Professor Chris Rowley is Director of Research and Publications at the HEAD Foundation, Singapore and also Professor of Human Resource Management at Cass Business School, City University, London, UK. He is editor of the *Asia Pacific Business Review* and series editor of both *Asian Studies* (Elsevier) and *Working in Asia* (Routledge). He researches in a range of areas, including HRM and Asian business and has published over 500 articles, books and chapters.

Jill Rubery is Professor of Comparative Employment Systems, Manchester Business School, University of Manchester, UK. She has published widely on comparative employment systems. Recent books include *European Employment Models in Flux* (2009) with Gerhard Bosch and Steffen Lehndorff, *Welfare States and Life Course Transitions* (2010) with Dominique Anxo and Gerhard Bosch, and *Women and Austerity* (2014) with Maria Karamessini.

Günter K. Stahl is Professor of International Management at WU Vienna, Austria, and Adjunct Professor of Organizational Behavior at INSEAD, France and Singapore. His research and teaching interests include socio-cultural processes in teams, alliances, mergers and acquisitions; and how to manage people and culture effectively in those contexts.

Arup Varma is Professor of Human Resource Management at the Institute of Human Resources and Employment Relations at Loyola University Chicago's Quinlan School of Business, USA. His research interests include performance appraisal, expatriate issues and HRM in India.

Mary Ann Von Glinow is the Knight Ridder Eminent Scholar Chair in International Management and the CIBER Director at Florida International University. Mary Ann is former President of the Academy of International Business (2010), past President of the Academy of Management, and has authored 11 books and over 100 journal articles.

Malcolm Warner is Professor and Fellow Emeritus, Wolfson College, Cambridge and Judge Business School, University of Cambridge. He is the author/editor of many books and articles on Asian management, OB and HRM, particularly on China. His latest work has been recently published: *Understanding Management in China: Past, Present and Future* (2014). He is currently co-editor of the *Asia Pacific Business Review.*

Jean Qi Wei is a Lecturer in the Department of Management and Business Systems at University of Bedfordshire, UK. She is also an academic member of the Chartered Institute of Personnel and Development (CIPD). Her specialist areas of interest include IHRM, rewards and performance management. Her work has been published in referred academic journals, HRM text books, and national and international academic conferences.

Abbreviations

AA	affirmative action
CSR	corporate social responsibility
DM	diversity management
DPE	domestic private enterprises
EEOL	Equal Employment Opportunity Law
EI	employee involvement
EO	equal opportunity
EU	European Union
FDI	foreign direct investment
FOE	foreign-owned enterprise
GLOBE	The Global Leadership and Organizational Behavior Effectiveness research project
HCN	host country nationals
HRD	human resource development
HRIS	Human Resource Information Systems
HRM	human resource management
IA	international assignment
ICT	information and communication technologies
IHRM	international human resource management
ILO	International Labour Organization
JSC	joint stock companies
M&A	merger and acquisition

MNC	multinational company
MNE	multinational enterprise
NGO	non-governmental organization
OECD	Organisation for Economic Co-operation and Development
OEM	original equipment manufacturer
OJT	on-the-job training
PCN	parent country nationals
PMS	performance management system
PRP	performance-related pay
R&D	reseach and development
SOE	state-owned enterprise
T&D	training and development
TCN	third country nationals
TQM	total quality management
UN	United Nations
WLB	work–life balance
WLC	work–life conflict
WTO	World Trade Organization

Guided Tour

Learning objectives

After reading this chapter you

- Understand the validity of and critical
- Explain the major points of management knowledge de
- analyse a situation using e

Learning Objectives
Outline what you can expect to learn from each chapter.

Chapter outline

The chapter provides an a culture in IHRM. This analyt on culture, and the resulting rich understanding and, conse cultural environments.

Chapter Outlines
Highlight the main issues and topics that will be covered in each chapter.

Box 1.5 Stop and reflect

Interpretive research gives us a local an
construct (e.g. how is 'good leadership' p
terms of generalization, this perspective
ferability, this perspective is very help
een (a) generalization and (b) tr

Stop and Reflect Boxes Challenge you to reflect on key theories and ideas discussed in the chapter.

Summary and Conclusions Summarize the chapters and draw important conclusions.

Summary and conclusions

IHRM is intrinsically international and
quent component of issues IHR man
ted in this chapter are an analytic
e comprehensively, situations
argument in the pursuit

Discussion questions

1. 'With globalization, people's beh
    similar, and especially so in organ
    the IHRM of multinational organiza
    on this statement.
    sing multiple views on culture (posi
    ituation is only making thing

Discussion Questions Encourage in-class discussion and debate.

CASE STUDY

'Not the way we do business arou

Please note: this case is based on original email m
seudonym). The English translation reflects the o
hors of the emails.

Case Studies From real
organizations help you
to relate theory and
real-world practice.

Case study questions

Use the analytical framework
cal research in cross-cultural man
Table 1.5 and you will progressively

1. Which cultural dimensions (Table
   between Tapio and Per? What is
   ral profile of Finland? What lead
   ish employees? Draft a few

Case Study Questions
Encourage you to apply
particular theories or ideas from
the chapter to the case study.

Further reading

- Hofstede, G. (2001) *Cultu*
  and Organizations Across
  This is the second edition
  1980. It presents five cultura
  masculinity/femininity, u
  orientation). Each dimensi

Further Reading Brief
outlines of key books and
academic journal articles
to help deepen your
understanding.

Internet resources

- www.cranet.org. Cranetis
  HRM in more than 40 cou
  about the network as well
- www.epp.eurostat.ec.europa
  Union, offers a wealth of da

Internet Resources
Useful and relevant websites that will aid your research and further reading.

Self-assessment Questions Test your understanding of key concepts, ideal for revision.

Self-assessment questions

Indicative answers to these questions c
study.sagepub.com/harzing4e.

...en facing a situation involving cultu
...f questions to use the different
...le questions that are help

Companion Website

International Human Resource Management, 4th edition, edited by Anne-Wil Harzing and Ashly H. Pinnington, is supported by a companion website.

Visit study.sagepub.com/harzing4e to access the following resources:

For Lecturers

- Instructors' Manual: including indicative answers to the questions within each chapter.
- PowerPoint Slides: including key points and tables and figures from each chapter.

For Students

- Annotated Web Links: including links to resources on IHRM and HRM in different countries and on key themes such as globalization, migration and international labour relations.
- SAGE Online Journals: free access to full text SAGE Online journal articles.

Introduction

Ashly H. Pinnington and Anne-Wil Harzing

International human resource management (IHRM) is a new and rapidly changing area of specialist and generalist practice. It is also a lively and growing academic subject having links with many different disciplines including economics, international business, strategy, communications, political science and public policy. Its origins can be traced back to the growth of international business operations and the development of multinational companies (MNCs) with their formal and informal approaches to staffing, personnel administration and personnel management. IHRM as a field of study has changed substantially over the years.

From the early beginnings to the present

Herbert Perlmutter (1969) is one of a small group of people who had a major influence on the early stages of development of IHRM (see Chapter 5). His three different approaches to MNC staffing (ethnocentric, polycentric and geocentric) are a mainstream method of conceptual analysis in much the same way that Michael Porter's generic strategies have profoundly shaped the field of strategy. The tendency of publications during the 1970s and 1980s was to concentrate on MNCs with headquarters based in a parent country in Europe, the US or Japan. This has created a substantial theoretical and empirical IHRM literature on parent country nationals (PCN), host country nationals (HCN) and third country nationals (TCN). One of the key research

1

questions debated during those decades (e.g. Morgan, 1986) on topics such as staffing policies, differences between countries, types of employees, and the MNCs human resource management (HRM) activities was, 'What exactly are the best policies and practices when procuring, allocating and utilizing international human resources?'

Since the 1980s the volume of material specifically produced addressing issues of IHRM has grown and journals such as the *International Journal of Human Resource Management* have established a strong position alongside other business and management journals and in journal rankings. There is a lively community of academics specializing in areas of IHRM research employed in universities across many different countries. The subject is constantly changing in relation to new ideas and a variety of issues such as cultural differences (see Chapter 1), new approaches to IHRM (see Chapter 4), alternative ways of managing mergers and acquisitions (see Chapter 8), increasingly sophisticated approaches to knowledge management in MNCs (see Chapter 9), diversity management, corporate social responsibility (CSR) and sustainability (see Chapters 14 and 15).

Interestingly, the opportunities and problems in IHRM since the 1990s have become on the one hand more straightforward and on the other hand more complex. Clearly, videoconference multimedia and simple email facilities on desktop computers offer a wealth of opportunities for virtual working and rapid communication across massive distances. There again when we talk about MNCs, there are now a greater number of parent countries and their HRM policies and practices in host countries are more diverse (see Chapters 2 and 3). Their regulation has become more straightforward with the reduction of national barriers to trade, but has also at the same time become more complex with the growth of industry quality standards and different forms of global business regulation including the area of employment regulation (see Chapter 7). The characteristics of HRM in developed and developing countries often differ so that, for example, in developing countries there may be less comprehensive legislation and less effective enforcement than is practised in the developed countries. These and other political, economic, institutional and cultural differences between nations can all influence the local relevance and acceptability of HR practices. They are also likely to affect the extent of transfer of HR practices between the parent company and its various subsidiaries (see Chapter 6).

Intellectual roots

In addition to the early development of the field through Perlmutter's work, the intellectual roots of the field of IHRM can be traced back to three main strands of research.

Cross-cultural management

The first strand of research is the area of cross-cultural management. In this field, Geert Hofstede's work (1980, 2001) has had a tremendous influence on the development of

IHRM. It is also highly cited in research studies on culture, cross-cultural communication, international and global management. Although his empirical survey study of many IBM subsidiaries has been criticized on various conceptual and methodological grounds, his ideas are now commonly understood jargon terms in academic and practitioner discourses on culture (see Chapters 1 and 2). Hofstede argues that there are substantial differences in national culture. He subdivided the major differences into: power distance, individualism versus collectivism, masculinity/femininity, uncertainty avoidance, and long-term versus short-term orientation. Many other studies focusing on cross-cultural management (e.g. Kluckhohn and Strodtbeck, 1961; Hampden-Turner and Trompenaars, 1997; House et al., 2004) present very similar dimensions (see Chapter 1 for a summary and integration).

A striking example of national culture differences is related in the case study of Lenovo (see Chapter 14) explaining some of the tensions it faces in different countries with achieving a uniform corporate culture and consistent approach to equal opportunities and diversity management. In common with many other research studies on diversity management in MNCs, Western domestic diversity programmes globally often fail to achieve their objectives and meet with strong resistance in the host country operations because these programmes fail to reflect other countries' specific demographic profile and the varied legal, historical, political and cultural contexts.

Comparative management

Academic debate and modes of theorizing in IHRM have also been very influenced by comparative approaches such as are adopted in research on comparative HRM and comparative employment relations. Studies set within these schools of thought concentrate on similarities and differences that exist between countries in policies and practices adopted by a wide range of stakeholders including the government, political and public sector institutions, professional groups, employers and employee associations, and private and non-profit sector organizations. Comparative IHRM researchers tend to be sensitive towards geographical and historical differences and often will pay attention to distinctions between regions and organizations within a country as well as between countries (see Chapters 2 and 11).

A large volume of theoretical critique and research studies have adopted institutional approaches when comparing and contrasting countries. One major strand of this work has been the neo-institutional theory (e.g. DiMaggio and Powell, 1983), which is based on the assumption that institutions and their structures, systems, policies and practices are subject to a range of general forces. Institutions may find themselves being pushed to follow a particular direction (coercive) or they may elect to copy others (mimetic) or they may simply feel the pressure to conform to what is socially accepted as the normal way of doing things (normative). One of the key distinguishing features of MNCs is that due to their size, scale, scope and reach, they have the capacity to implement expertise in their operations in one country that was developed in another. Exactly how individual MNCs proceed with the transfer of expertise depends on a range of political, economic, social and legal factors, for example, their actual transfer of employment practices depends on how they are embedded in distinctive national contexts (see Chapters 10 and 11).

International management and HQ subsidiary relationships

Another group of researchers concentrate less on the institutional and cultural contexts and adopt more of a specifically organizational focus, focusing primarily on its markets and the firm's strategy, structure and alignment of human resources. Major influences on this way of looking at things include Bartlett and Ghoshal's (1989) *Managing Across Borders*. These authors argue that MNCs are evolving towards a new form of management and organizational form typified in the concept of the 'transnational firm' which is understood to have global networks of managers, global projects and international mobility. In these transnational firms, competitiveness in global markets is argued to be based more on managers possessing a global mindset. Their organizations survive and grow by having the flexibility and capability to transfer knowledge and expertise across global networks (see Chapter 9).

One of the main problems executives must deal with when seeking to create a transnational management approach is how to integrate the organization on a global scale and simultaneously, how to differentiate it to fit in with variations in the local conditions. The growth of global markets, reduction of trade barriers and increased activity across state boundaries have all had a major impact stimulating the long-term growth of international merger and acquisition (M&A) activity. A significant challenge for IHRM practitioners and researchers concerns dealing effectively with the integration processes in cross-border M&As. It requires understanding and managing cultural differences between organizations, successfully implementing the appropriate strategy and managing the process through its various stages of integration (see Chapters 4 and 8).

A brief overview of the chapter contents

This book is divided into three sections. The first section (Cultural, Comparative and Organizational Perspectives on IHRM) introduces the prevalent ways of thinking about IHRM. The second section (International Assignments and Employment Practices) deals with the fundamental area of multinational companies and how they manage their workforce with specific reference to IHRM as well as national forms of HRM. The third and final section (IHRM Policies and Practices) focuses more on particular areas of policy and practice in IHRM commencing with contemporary advances in knowledge management and global training and development, and then moving on to the topics of employee-resourcing, performance management and employee rewards. The final two chapters concentrate on central strands of thought and innovation in IHRM, considering a number of core areas of responsibility and accountability that are likely to continue in significance throughout future decades, notably matters of equal opportunities, diversity management, corporate social responsibility, sustainability and ethical work practices.

Part 1 Cultural, comparative and organizational perspectives on IHRM

This section presents various ways of thinking about IHRM theory and practice. Chapter 1 – Culture and Cross-Cultural Management (Laurence Romani) – offers a critique of several of the traditional approaches to culture and cultural difference and presents a new way of thinking more flexibly about culture and culture management as seen from distinct stakeholder perspectives. Chapter 2 – Comparative Human Resource Management (Chris Brewster and Wolfgang Mayrhofer) – explores the differences between countries in their management of human resources. It presents a comparative perspective on HRM and within the context of MNCs considers the challenges of integration and differentiation. Chapter 3 – The Transfer of Employment Practices across Borders in Multinational Companies (Tony Edwards) – examines more closely the internal context of MNCs. It explores MNCs' motivations for international transfer of expertise and presents a framework of four key influences. These are the country of origin effect, dominance effects, international integration and host country effects. Chapter 4 – Approaches to International Human Resource Management (Chris Rowley, Jean Qi Wei and Malcolm Warner) – charts the development of HRM as a background for IHRM. It considers five distinctive frameworks of HRM and IHRM: 'matching model', 'Harvard model', 'contextual model', '5-P model' and 'European model'. It then evaluates the extent that these models apply in theory and practice to different firms, country business systems, institutional contexts and cultural environments, and concludes by offering an integrative framework for IHRM.

Part 2 International assignments and employment practices

This section concentrates on MNCs, IHRM and country approaches to HRM. Chapter 5 – International Assignments (B. Sebastian Reiche and Anne-Wil Harzing) – reviews the staffing options in MNCs and corporate motives for international transfers and then discusses the available forms of international assignment assessing the various processes and their success criteria. Chapter 6 – Multinational Companies and the Host Country Environment (Damian Grimshaw, Jill Rubery and Phil Almond) – explores the diverse environments for MNCs' overseas subsidiaries and appraises the extent that host countries will influence pay systems, work organization and collective representation. In contrast, and with a greater emphasis placed on external and global regulatory environments, Chapter 7 – Regulation and Multinational Corporations: The Changing Context of Global Employment Relations (Miguel Martínez Lucio and Robert MacKenzie) – studies wider debates on the regulation of businesses and raises questions of power, control and democracy. The concepts of de-regulation and re-regulation are discussed in detail and in relation to ideas on human rights. Chapter 8 – Human Resource Management in Cross-Border Mergers and Acquisitions (Vladimir Pucik, Ingmar Björkman, Paul Evans and Günter K. Stahl) – examines one of the most important contemporary organizational change phenomena in IHRM. It reviews the meaning and activities of integration in M&As, highlighting various challenges to MNC growth by M&A that may occur during different stages of the process.

Part 3 IHRM policies and practices

This section reviews the traditional and newer approaches to IHRM policies and practices. Chapter 9 – Managing Knowledge in Multinational Firms (Ingmar Björkman, Paul Evans, Vladimir Pucik and Dana Minbaeva) – addresses issues of knowledge management in MNCs and contends that knowledge sharing is facilitated by such things as collaborative values and global mindsets. It assesses how MNCs can access and retain knowledge. Chapter 10 – Training and Development: Developing Global Leaders and Expatriates (Ashly H. Pinnington, Yaw A. Debrah and Chris Rees) – presents an overview of the global situation of training and development (T&D) and then examines its potential in more detail, focusing on the development of global leaders and expatriates. It discusses the competencies and tasks associated with global leaders' work and global Leadership development programmes. Finally, it covers issues surrounding cross-cultural training for expatriates which include activities such as international assignments, participation in global teams and cross-cultural sensitivity training. Chapter 11 – Global and Local Resourcing (Chris Rowley, Alan Nankervis and Malcolm Warner) – considers IHRM recruitment and retention, discussing changes in labour market policy and regulations to assess their impacts. Four Asian economies (Japan, Taiwan, China and Vietnam) are examined for their degree of continuity and change in HRM policy and practice. Chapter 12 – Global Performance Management (Arup Varma and Pawan S. Budhwar) – discusses performance evaluation in IHRM and presents the key features of performance management systems (PMSs) in four major national economies (USA, UK, China and India). Chapter 13 – Total Rewards in the International Context (K. Galen Kroeck and Mary Ann Von Glinow) – provides comprehensive examples of rewards policies and practices for expatriates and short-term and long-term international assignments, drawing primarily on data from US MNCs where many of these IHRM approaches were first developed. It provides a thorough account of the issues (including international taxation and cost of living), components (base salary, hardship premium, allowances and benefits) and available methods (going rate and balance sheet) for designing total rewards systems. Chapter 14 – Equal Opportunity and Diversity Management in the Global Context (Fang Lee

Cooke) – attends to the global challenges facing MNCs in developing and implementing equality and diversity management strategies. It describes how the concepts of equal opportunity, work–life balance and diversity management gain popularity as part of strategic human resource management in firms seeking competitive advantage. It then critically analyses how different societal contexts may influence the way these ideas are valued and dealt with in workplaces. Chapter 15 – Corporate Social Responsibility and Sustainability through Ethical HRM Practices (Fang Lee Cooke) – provides an overview of the emergence of the concepts of ethics, labour standards and corporate social responsibility. It examines how national and international organizations have been promoting ethical employment and labour standards as important areas of corporate social responsibility and IHRM. It evaluates how different societal contexts may affect firms' level of motivation and accountability in fulfilling their social responsibility through ethical HRM practices.

What makes this book different?

This book provides an *integrated* research-based perspective of the consequences of internationalization for the management of people across borders. The book's comprehensiveness is evidenced by its broad and global coverage. We commence with a thorough overview of the main ways that IHRM has been conceptualized to date. IHRM has been linked to strategy, viewed through comparative HRM research, and seen from cultural, institutional, market and organizational perspectives. The second section of this book addresses expatriate management and employment practices seen from both their external environment and the internal environment of the MNC. In the third section we consider the current state of the field on IHRM policies and practices, which attends to the role of globalization and the extent to which HRM differs between countries, and the underlying reasons for these differences. The last two chapters consider how IHRM appears to be developing and changing in relation to issues of equal opportunities, diversity management, gender, work–life balance, regulation of employment, social responsibility and sustainability.

A second distinctive feature of this book is its *solid research base*. All chapters have been specifically commissioned for this book and all authors are experts and active researchers in their respective fields. Rather than having a final chapter with 'recent developments and challenges in IHRM', we have given all authors the clear brief to supplement classic theories and models with cutting-edge research and developments.

A third and final distinctive characteristic of this book is that it is *truly international*, both in its outlook and in its author base. Authors use examples from all over the world and their research base extends beyond the traditional American research literature. Although many authors are currently working at American, European and Australian universities, virtually all have extensive international experience and their countries of origin are very varied.

Who is this book for?

As a textbook this book will appeal to advanced undergraduate students and Masters students wanting a comprehensive and integrated treatment of IHRM that includes the most recent theoretical developments. As a research book, it provides PhD students and other researchers with a very good introduction to the field and an extensive list of references that will allow them to get an up-to-date overview of the area. Finally, practitioners looking for solutions to their international HR problems might find some useful frameworks in Parts 1 and 2, while the chapters in Part 3 will allow them to gain a better understanding of country differences in managing people.

In the following chapters of this book the authors contribute numerous worthwhile theoretical ideas and empirical observations on IHRM policy and practice. We hope that you will enjoy reading the fourth edition of *International Human Resource Management*. As we work and live in changing local and global contexts, inevitably there is much that we can learn from each other.

References

Bartlett, C.A. and Ghoshal, S. (1989) *Managing Across Borders: The Transnational Solution*. Boston, MA: Harvard Business School Press.

DiMaggio, P.J. and Powell, W. (1983) '"The iron cage revisited": institutional isomorphism and collective rationality in organizational fields', *American Sociological Review*, 48: 147–160.

Hampden-Turner, C. and Trompenaars, F. (1997) *Riding the Waves of Culture: Understanding Diversity in Global Business*. Maidenhead: McGraw-Hill.

Hofstede, G. (1980) *Culture's Consequences: International Differences in Work Related Values*. Beverly Hills, CA: Sage Publications.

Hofstede, G. (2001) *Culture's Consequences: Comparing Values, Behaviors, Institutions and Organizations across Nations*, 2nd edn. London: Sage.

House, R.J., Hanges, P.J., Javidan, M., Dorfman, P.W. and Gupta, V. (eds) (2004) *Leadership, Culture, and Organizations: The GLOBE Study of 62 Societies*. Thousand Oaks, CA: Sage.

Kluckhohn, F.R. and Strodtbeck, F.L. (1961) *Variations in Value Orientations*. Evanston, IL: Row, Peterson and Co.

Morgan, P.V. (1986) 'International human resource management: fact or fiction?', *Personnel Administrator*, 31(9): 43–47.

Perlmutter, H.V. (1969) 'The tortuous evolution of the multinational corporation', *Columbia Journal of World Business*, 4(1): 9–18.

Part 1
Cultural, Comparative and Organizational Perspectives on IHRM

Part 4

Cultural, Comparative
and Organizational
Perspectives on HRM

Culture and Cross-Cultural Management[1]

Laurence Romani

Contents

[1]This chapter is part of the research project 'The hidden side of cross-cultural management', financed by the Swedish Research Council, Vetenskapsrådet (412-2009-2020).

Learning objectives

After reading this chapter you will be able to:

- Understand the validity of three different views on culture: positivist, interpretive and critical
- Explain the major points of difference between these views. Present the different management knowledge developed by each view
- Analyse a situation using each of the three views
- Combine each mode of analysis to reach an enriched understanding of culture and cross-cultural management in IHRM

Chapter outline

The chapter provides an analytical method useful for dealing with situations involving culture in IHRM. This analytical method derives from the combination of three views on culture, and the resulting knowledge they create. Together, these views provide a rich understanding and, consequently, can be advantageous when dealing with cross-cultural environments.

1 Introduction

What is culture? A set of norms, beliefs and values shared by a group? Rather, is it how people make sense of the world around them? Or even a rhetorical device used by those in power to reproduce inequalities in organizations? In management research,

Table 1.1   The three views on culture and their related knowledge

Positivist views: Culture and values	Interpretive views: Culture and meanings	Critical views: Culture and power
• Researchers search for laws and regularities • Instrumental knowledge, predictions, development and test of models	• Researchers search for meanings: how people make sense of their situation • Knowledge on sense-making and cognitive processes, on social constructions	• Researchers' investigation reveals silenced voices and hidden structures of inequality and domination • Knowledge that questions and challenges, exposing power relationships and inequalities
Example: Cultural dimension constructs such as 'Power Distance' or 'Assertiveness', value-dimensions valid across many countries	Example: Meaning systems associated to notions such as 'leadership', 'job description' or 'competence'. Local and specific knowledge	Example: Talks about 'culture differences' can be used to masquerade another issue (of power). Unveils structures of domination with local and specific examples

views on what culture is, and its implications for management, differ strongly. The aim of this chapter is to present an analytical method for understanding IHRM situations involving culture. This method is based on the combination of three major views on culture used in cross-cultural management research. Combining these three views, and their respective forms of knowledge, develops a rich analysis which can be advantageous in IHRM when dealing with culture.

2 Studies on culture in management

Studies on culture and management are prolific and diverse. It is a challenging task to gain a clear overview since one needs to take multiple research streams into consideration. Cross-cultural management encompasses studies from a variety of research literatures including comparative management (Redding, 1994; Child, 2000), cross-cultural management (e.g. Søderberg and Holden, 2002; Leung et al., 2005; Kirkman et al., 2006; Lowe et al., 2007; Tsui et al., 2007), international management (e.g. Boyacigiller et al., 2004; Sackmann and Phillips, 2004) and cross-cultural psychology of organizational behaviour (e.g. Gelfand et al., 2007). While many reviews of culture tend to consider only one of these streams of research, Primecz et al. (2009) and Romani et al. (forthcoming) offer a broad presentation considering major research paradigms. By following a broad-based approach, this chapter addresses the diversity of studies in cross-cultural management and identifies three main viewpoints rooted in different research paradigms (see Romani, 2010a). The next three sections of this chapter briefly explain and discuss the positivist and then the interpretive and critical viewpoints on culture, cross-cultural management and IHRM.

3 Positivist views: 'Culture and values'

Within the positivist paradigm, the functionalist group of studies are the most prolific in cross-cultural management. In the functionalist approach, culture is seen as providing answers to the basic needs that human beings have to fulfil and this is the foundation for what are known as cultural dimensions (e.g. Hofstede, 1980). The idea is that there are distinct ways in which culture can fulfil these human needs, thus creating variations in the cultural dimensions. These variations are linked to different values. For instance, human societies are compelled to deal with their environment (see Kluckhohn and Strodtbeck, 1961) and the different ways in which they can do this are claimed to be variations (e.g. harmony, mastery or subjugation) within the cultural dimension 'Relation to broad environment' (see, for example, Trompenaars, 1993; Maznevski et al., 2002). Each variation is embedded in a set of values, that 'people carry around in their heads', thus giving to positivist researchers the possibility of investigating culture through values.

The functionalist approach substantially influenced seminal contributions by Hofstede (see Hofstede, 2001) and by Schwartz (1994), the works by Maznevski et al. (2002), as well as by the GLOBE (Global Leadership and Organizational Behavior Effectiveness) research project (House et al., 2004). Likewise, the legitimacy of searching for social axioms (beliefs endorsed and used by people to guide their behaviour in different work situations) is also based on the functionalist argument: they are important for human survival and functioning (see Leung et al., 2002: 288). It is a similar foundation that supports the investigation of 'sources of guidance' (see Smith et al., 2002). In sum, culture is said to fulfil the function of meeting human needs. Since they are universal human needs, they are universal (etic) aspects to culture (the cultural dimensions) and to human behaviour. The etic approach is viewed as general, and it often focuses on previously developed constructs or concepts that are then investigated, for example, in a number of different countries. Cultural dimension constructs such as 'individualism-collectivism' are argued to be etic: the concept is understood to be valid and coherent across countries. This means that the influence of this dimension on IHRM practices can be compared across countries.

An impressive amount of studies have used the cultural dimensions to test the relationship between culture and various aspects of management, such as motivation, reward allocation, hierarchy, preferred forms of training and leadership (see review by Kirkman et al., 2006). For example, in a cultural environment scoring high on Power Distance, organizations are likely to have centralized decision-making structures, tall hierarchies, a large proportion of supervisory personnel, privileges and status symbols for managers that are both expected and accepted, and a wide salary range between employees at the top and the bottom of the organization pyramid (Hofstede, 2001: 107–108). Hofstede describes representative behaviour for low scores on Power Distance as 'decentralized decision structures; less concentration of authority. The ideal boss is a resourceful democrat and subordinates expect to be consulted' (Hofstede, 2001: 107–108).

Table 1.2   Sample of argued representative behaviour linked to Hofstede's cultural dimensions and examples of country positioning

Dimension	High score	Low score
Power Distance Extent to which the less powerful members of a society expect and accept unequal distribution of power	• Centralized decision structures; more concentration of authority • The ideal boss is a well-meaning autocrat or good father; sees self as benevolent decision maker • Subordinates expect to be told • Malaysia, Mexico, Singapore, France	• Decentralized decision structures; less concentration of authority • The ideal boss is a resourceful democrat; sees self as practical, orderly and relying on support • Subordinates expect to be consulted • Denmark, New Zealand, Sweden, Canada

Dimension	High score	Low score
Masculinity When emotional gender roles are clearly distinct, this is a masculine society; it is feminine when they overlap	• Live in order to work • Stress on equity, mutual competition, and performance • Career ambitions are compulsory for men, optional for women • Japan, Austria, Venezuela, Mexico, Germany	• Work in order to live • Stress on equality, solidarity and quality of work life • Career ambitions are optional for both men and women • Sweden, Denmark, Costa Rica, Finland, Thailand
Uncertainty Avoidance Extent to which the members of a culture feel threatened by ambiguous or unknown situations	• Strong loyalty to employer • Appeal of hierarchical control role • Top managers involved in operations • Power of superiors depends on control of uncertainties • Greece, Belgium, Japan, Peru, Argentina	• Weak loyalty to employer • Appeal of transformational leader role • Top managers involved in strategy • Power of supervisors depends on position and relationships • Singapore, Denmark, Sweden, Malaysia, USA
Individualism Individualism pertains to societies in which the ties between the individuals are loose, Collectivism pertains to societies in which people are integrated into strong, cohesive in-groups	• Employees supposed to act as 'economic men' • Hiring and promotion decisions should be based on skills and rules only • Employer–employee relationship is a business deal in a 'labour market' • USA, Australia, Netherlands, South Africa	• Employees act in the interest of their in-group, not necessarily of themselves • Hiring and promotion decisions take employees' in-group into account • Employer–employee relationship is basically moral, like a family link • Ecuador, Panama, Indonesia, Pakistan, Peru
Long-term Orientation Long-term orientation stands for the fostering of virtues oriented towards future rewards	• Persistence, perseverance • Relationships ordered by status, and this order is observed • Leisure time not so important • China, Hong Kong, Japan, Brazil, India	• Status not major issue in relationships • Leisure time important • Quick results expected • Pakistan, Nigeria, Canada, USA
Indulgence versus Restraint Indulgence stands for a tendency to allow relatively free gratification of needs related to enjoying life and having fun	**Indulgence** • Personal life control • Importance of leisure, enjoying life, having fun • Freedom of speech viewed as relatively important • Mexico, Colombia, Sweden, Australia, UK	**Restraint** • Moral discipline • Gratification needs to be curbed and regulated by strict social norms • Thrift is important • Freedom of speech not primary concern • Egypt, Pakistan, Iraq, Russia, China, India

Source: based on Hofstede (2001) and Hofstede et al. (2010)

In an environment scoring high on Uncertainty Avoidance, there is a tendency for more formal conceptions of management, hierarchical controls and roles. There is also a tendency for a stronger belief in specialists and in expertise (see Hofstede, 2001: 169–170).

In the GLOBE project (House et al., 2004), additional cultural dimensions are developed and existing dimensions are further refined (see Table 1.3). For example, GLOBE considers the dimension 'Humane Orientation' that encourages and rewards individuals for being fair, altruistic, generous, caring and kind to others (Kabasakal and Bodur, 2004). In an environment scoring low on Humane Orientation, there will tend to be greater use of IHRM for control and coordination of organizations, than in an environment scoring high on Humane Orientation, where 'organizations are relatively autonomous in their employee relations' (Kabasakal and Bodur, 2004: 584). Assertiveness is found to have a positive relationship with an 'autonomous' leader (independent and individualistic), and a negative relationship with a leader who is team-oriented and participative (Den Hartog, 2004).

Cross-cultural management research largely adopts a mainstream psychological approach (see Smith and Bond, 1998), that tends to define culture as an independent variable influencing human cognition or behaviour. Values, and consequently the study of values across countries, are a fundamental part of cross-cultural comparison studies. The Rokeach Value Survey (Rokeach, 1973) is the point of departure for the seven value-types (similar to cultural dimensions) devised by Schwartz and colleagues (see Schwartz and Bilsky, 1987). He distinguishes the same seven types of values in each country (Smith and Schwartz, 1997; Schwartz, 2004) and assesses their implications for management (see Table 1.4).

For example, in the dimension Egalitarianism, voluntary cooperation is emphasized, 'leaders motivate by enabling', and members 'flexibly enact their roles' (Sagiv and Schwartz, 2000: 420). Role overload and role conflicts are more likely to be reported by managers working in a cultural environment where values of 'Mastery' and 'Hierarchy' are praised, and where values linked to 'Harmony' have a low priority (Sagiv and Schwartz, 2000: 427). In environments where values of 'Embeddedness' are important for individuals, it is less likely that managers will choose pay levels exclusively based on their employees' work productivity. They tend to also take employees' family situation into account (Sagiv and Schwartz, 2000: 432).

Another important contribution made by psychologists to cross-cultural management research is the work of Triandis (1995) on individualism and collectivism. This dimension is the most researched and documented of the cultural dimensions. It has been investigated regarding its direct or moderating impact on, for example, motivation, job attitudes and group processes (see reviews by Earley and Gibson, 1998; Gelfand et al., 2004).

In complement to the etic investigations of culture with the search for universals and cultural dimensions, Gannon (2004, 2009) proposes to use a metaphor to describe and make sense of the cultural profile of a country. He defines a cultural metaphor as a 'unique or very distinct institution, phenomenon, or activity of a nation's culture that most or all of its citizens consider to be very important and with which they identify

Table 1.3 Sample of argued representative behaviour for the societal practices (as is) of the cultural dimensions of the House et al. (2004) study and examples of country positioning

Dimension	High score	Low score
Power Distance is the degree to which people expect and agree that power should be stratified and concentrated at higher levels of an organization or government	• Different groups have different involvement, and democracy does not ensure equal opportunities • Society differentiated into classes on several criteria • Information is localized • Argentina, Turkey, Germany	• All the groups enjoy equal involvement, and democracy ensures parity in opportunities and development for all • Society has large middle class • Information is shared • Denmark, Qatar, Israel
Uncertainty Avoidance members strive to reduce uncertainty by relying on established social norms, rituals, bureaucratic practices	• Show less tolerance for breaking rules • Be orderly, keeping meticulous records • Rely on formalized policies and procedures, establishing and following rules, verifying communication in writing • Switzerland, Finland, Singapore	• Show more tolerance for breaking rules • Rely on informal interactions and informal norms rather than formalized policies, procedures and rules • Show less resistance to change • Greece, Hungary, Russia
Future Orientation relates to engagement in future-oriented behaviour such as planning and delaying gratification	• Individuals are more intrinsically motivated • View materialistic success and spiritual fulfilment as an integrated role • Organizations with longer strategic orientation • Canada, Malaysia, Singapore	• Value instant gratification and place higher priorities on immediate rewards • See materialistic success and spiritual fulfilment as dualities, requiring trade-offs • Argentina, Russia, Guatemala
Gender Egalitarianism minimizes gender-role differences while promoting gender equality	• More women in positions of authority • Higher percentage of women in the labour force • Afford women a greater role in community decision making • Less occupational sex segregation • Sweden, Canada, Norway	• Fewer women in positions of authority • Lower percentage of women in the labour force • Afford women no or a smaller role in community decision making • More occupational sex segregation • Japan, India, Kuwait
Humane Orientation encourages and rewards individuals for being fair, altruistic, generous, caring and kind to others	• Mentoring and patronage support • Practices reflect individualized considerations • Need for belonging and affiliation to motivate people • Members of society are urged to be sensitive to all forms of racial discrimination • Thailand, Zambia, Malaysia	• Supervisory support • Practices reflect standardized considerations • Formal welfare institutions replace paternalistic norms and patronage relationships • Welfare state guarantees social and economic protection of individuals • Germany, South Africa, Italy

(Continued)

Table 1.3   (Continued)

Dimension	High score	Low score
Assertiveness is the degree to which individuals are assertive, confrontational and aggressive in their relationships with others	• Stress equity, competition and performance • Expect demanding and challenging targets • Value assertive, dominant and tough behaviour. Positive associations with the term 'aggression' • Believes anyone can succeed if s/he tries hard enough • Hong Kong, US, Australia	• Stress equality, solidarity and quality of life • Have sympathy for the weak • Value who you are more than what you do • Associate competition also with defeat and punishment. More negative associations with the term 'aggression' • Value cooperation • New Zealand, Sweden, Switzerland
Performance Orientation Encourages and rewards performance improvement and excellence	• Emphasize results more than people • Attach little importance to age in promotional decisions • Believe that schooling and education are critical for success • Value training and development • Expect demanding target • Singapore, Iran, Taiwan	• Have high respect for quality of life • View merit pay as potentially destructive to harmony • Performance appraisal systems that emphasize integrity, loyalty and cooperative spirit • Regard being motivated by money as inappropriate • Hungary, Argentina, Qatar
In-Group Collectivism is the degree to which individuals express pride, loyalty and cohesiveness in their organizations or families	• Members assume that they are highly interdependent with the organization and believe it is important to make personal sacrifices to fulfil their organizational obligations • Employees tend to develop long-term relationships with employers from recruitment to retirement • Jobs are designed in groups to maximize social and technical aspects of the job • Iran, Philippines, Zimbabwe	• Members assume that they are independent of the organization and believe it is important to bring their unique skills and abilities to the organization • Employees develop short-term relationships, and change companies at their own discretion • Compensation and promotions based on equity model, in direct relationship to the employee's contribution to success • Sweden, Netherlands, US
Institutional Collectivism encourages and rewards collective distribution of resources and collective action	• Organizations take responsibility for employees' welfare • Obliging, compromising and accommodating conflict resolution tactics are preferred • Sweden, South Korea, China	• Direct and solution-oriented conflict resolution tactics are preferred. • Jobs are designed individually to maximize autonomy • Greece, El Salvador, Morocco

Source: inspired by similar tables made by House et al. (2004) and Romani (2010b)

Table 1.4   Sample of argued representative behaviour for Schwartz's value structures and examples of country positioning

Dimensions	Examples of implications for organizational behaviour
Egalitarianism: people are socialized to internalize a commitment to voluntary cooperation with others and to feel concern for everyone's welfare	• Organizations acknowledge the legitimacy of cooperative negotiation among members who flexibly enact their roles and try to affect organizational goals • Leaders motivate by enabling participation in goal-setting • Positive relationship to the societal norm 'entitlement' • Positive relationship to the work value 'social' • Finland, Sweden, Spain, Germany
Mastery: encourages active self-assertion in order to master, change and exploit the natural and social environment to attain goals	• Organizations are likely to be competitive and strongly oriented towards achievement and success • Positive relationship to the work value 'power' • Work centrality • USA, South Korea, Japan
Harmony: accepts the world as it is, trying to comprehend and fit in rather than change or exploit	• Organizations are likely to be viewed holistically as systems to be integrated with the larger society, which should minimize competition • Leaders are likely to try to understand the social and environmental implications of organizational actions and to seek non-exploitive ways to work towards organizational goals • Chile, Estonia, Slovenia, Hungary
Affective Autonomy: individuals are seen as autonomous. Affective autonomy encourages individuals to pursue affectively positive experience for themselves	• Organizations are open to change and diversity • Organizations treat their members as independent actors with their own interests, preferences, abilities and allegiances • Positive relationship with the work value 'intrinsic' • UK, New Zealand, Ireland, Canada (English speaking)
Intellectual Autonomy: individuals are seen as autonomous. Intellectual autonomy encourages individuals to pursue their own ideas and intellectual directions independently	• Organizations are open to change and diversity • Organizations treat their members as independent actors with their own interests, preferences, abilities and allegiances • Positive relationship to the societal norm 'entitlement' • Positive relationship with the work values 'intrinsic', 'curiosity', 'broad-mindedness', 'creativity' • France, French speaking Canada and Switzerland, Denmark
Hierarchy: relies on hierarchical systems of ascribed roles to ensure responsible behaviour. It defines the unequal repartition of power, roles and resources as legitimate	• Emphasis on chain of authority • Well-defined roles in a hierarchical structure • Demand of compliance in the service of goals set from the top • Positive relationship with the societal norm 'obligation' • Positive relationship to the work value 'power' • Zimbabwe, India, Hong Kong, Thailand
Embeddedness: people are viewed as entities embedded in the collective. Meaning in life comes through social relationship, identifying with the group, a shared way of life and shared goals	• Organizations tend to take responsibility for their employees in several domains of life • Employees' loyalty to the organization is expected • Positive relationship with the work value 'extrinsic' • Philippines, Nigeria, Malaysia, Georgia

Source: based on Schwartz (1999) and Sagiv and Schwartz (2000)

closely' (Gannon and Audia, 2000: 91). There is not a total parallel between the metaphor and culture, but with a metaphor, the different components of national culture are integrated into a coherent image rather than being a set of scores on independent cultural dimensions. For example, Nielsen et al. (2009) use the metaphor of the 'Fado' (a popular form of song) to describe the Portuguese culture. Using the rich metaphor of a social institution in a given country, cultural metaphors explain the complexity of a local culture in an intuitive way. Cultural metaphors can contribute to the preparation of employees for expatriation, as well as assist with making sense of the cultural differences between two partners in a merger.

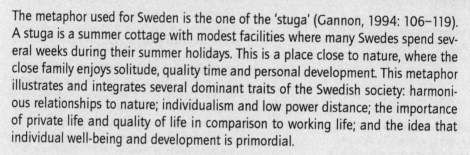

Box 1.1   Example: The metaphor of the Swedish stuga

The metaphor used for Sweden is the one of the 'stuga' (Gannon, 1994: 106–119). A stuga is a summer cottage with modest facilities where many Swedes spend several weeks during their summer holidays. This is a place close to nature, where the close family enjoys solitude, quality time and personal development. This metaphor illustrates and integrates several dominant traits of the Swedish society: harmonious relationships to nature; individualism and low power distance; the importance of private life and quality of life in comparison to working life; and the idea that individual well-being and development is primordial.

Most recently, the work of Tony Fang (e.g. 2003, 2012) is gaining popularity as a value-based understanding of culture, not using cultural dimensions, but the observation of cultural paradoxes and tensions in all societies. The Yin Yang model illustrates that there are conflicting values in each society (rather than a set of dominating ones as cultural dimension frameworks sustain), and that these values are expressed at different times or in different situations. This model accounts for cultural change in societies.

Box 1.2   Stop and reflect

All individuals do not act in accordance with a set of average scores for cultural dimensions of a particular country. In addition, the cultural dimension frameworks were not developed for an individual level of analysis. However, in what ways do you think we can use the cultural dimension frameworks to explicate (and predict) individual employees' behaviour in organizations?

4 Interpretive views: 'Culture and meanings'

Interpretive views on culture posit that people use meaning systems to organize their actions. In other words, people act and interact in a way that makes sense to them and it is the actor's point of view that is seen as most relevant to explain behaviour. It is therefore an emic positioning in strong contrast to the etic constructs such as cultural dimensions. From an emic position, meaning exists within the context of its experience. The emic approach is seen as situated and focused on the particular meanings given by a specific group of individuals, thus implying that there are implicit aspects to knowledge and understanding. For example, the idea of statistical theory that was applied to product quality control in the United States in the 1920s was further made sense of in a comprehensive way by Japan in the post Second World War period. Quality was not interpreted as the feature of a finalized product, but rather as the outcome of a process. The focus expanded from quality of products to quality of numerous other aspects of organizations, leading to what became later internationally known as total quality management (TQM). Similarly, the same IHRM tool can lead to distinct practices in the various (cultural) environments where it is implemented, since the local interpretations and the local views will vary. Emic studies are reflected in an interpretive approach to science that emphasizes the interpretations of individuals and the significance of the local context in the development of these meanings. In interpretive views researchers such as Geertz (1973), Schutz (1962), Garfinkel (1967) or Berger and Luckmann (1966) are key inspirational figures in societal and organization culture studies.

Within each society, there are tremendous variations between individuals, social groups or genders in possible ways of making sense of situations. At the same time, some claim that through socialization, in generation cohort groups, in gender groups and in other social groups, individuals tend to develop similar frames of interpretation or similar interpretations of symbols. A unique stream of studies in cross-cultural management, inspired by the works of d'Iribarne (1989, 2009), argues that it is possible to identify similar national patterns of interpretation within countries, called 'frames of meanings'.

Box 1.3   Stop and reflect

A French multinational had repeatedly tried to implement TQM in its Moroccan subsidiary, without success, and then it suddenly worked. The origin of the success was attributed to a combination of elements that enabled employees to make sense

(Continued)

(Continued)

of TQM, and thus to implement it. The new CEO adopted an 'exemplary' leadership attitude, combining it with a new form of TQM training that articulated parallels between the key principles of TQM and verses of the Quran. This ability to relate the values of TQM in a culturally meaningful way meant that employees could make sense of the implementation of TQM with the emic concept of the *Zaouia*. They drew a semantic parallel between the community of the Zaouia, with its exemplary leader and its religious connotations, and their own organization, now including an exemplary leader, a community of employees, and TQM principles associated with moral guidance (see d'Iribarne, 2002).

The association of meanings that are present in societies around the notions of 'good work', a 'good organization' or even a 'good boss' are very useful to know about, since they influence what is perceived as desirable behaviour. For example, leadership studies inform us that an ideal of idea-oriented leadership tends to be shared between Swedish top and middle managers.

Box 1.4   Example: Meanings associated with good leadership in Sweden

'Idea-oriented leadership means that leaders bring about involvement, commitment and motivation through skilfully communicating inspiring [ideas] ... The relationship to the supervised is built on confidence and trust (rather than coercion) and openness' (Åkerblom, 1999: 48). Leaders are seen as visionary, team-oriented and favouring collaboration and consultation, and supervision and instructions are considered as the opposite to a desirable leadership style. An informal style and frequent communication between superiors and subordinates is the preferred approach to leadership.

Meanings systems are not rigid; they can be adapted to new situations or altered depending on the circumstances. In the study of a large Tunisian corporation, Yousfi (2011) reveals first how the association of the organization with the theme of 'a family' is frequently used in Tunisian organizations, leading to potential dysfunctions (absence of explicit rules, favouritism, etc.). She shows that this metaphor is also used in the exceptional Tunisian organization she studies, but it is used with a twist: written rules. The introduction of an 'American management model' (e.g. performance assessment) did not replace the metaphor of the family, but rather consolidated it because it could control its dysfunctions. Managers and employees built on a meaning system linking an organization with a family (a personal place, where one grows and receives support, etc.) when dealing with the rules of performance assessment. In other words, there is a Tunisian meaning system linking the notions of family and organization, and this meaning system is flexible and dynamic: it can encompass new items, reinforce others and keep its role of sense making for the employees in the organization even when management practices change.

Knowing what local meaning systems are associated to organizational practices is primordial. Resistances, failures or difficulties in the transfer of HRM processes have been linked to disparate understandings and cultural practices occurring between, for example, the headquarters and foreign subsidiaries. Henry (2007) investigates the resistance of a French consulting firm to the implementation of detailed job descriptions in the Société d'Electricité du Cameroun, when these job descriptions were in fact explicitly requested and thus were part of the consultants' brief. After the analysis of the cultural meanings associated with job descriptions by the French consultants (e.g. lack of freedom, disempowerment) and the Cameroonian employees (e.g. protection against arbitrary and pervasive use of power, clarification and delimitation of tasks) the people working in the consulting firm and in Société d'Electricité du Cameroun were then able to come to an agreement and move forwards with the specification of acceptable job descriptions.

Interpretive views on culture are not solely linked to investigating shared meanings in organizations; they also include the study of meanings developed by institutions and their implications for organizations' practices. Child (2000) explains that management and business have distinctive institutional foundations in different societies. These institutions (e.g. state, legal system, etc.) and the roles they play shape different 'national business systems' (Whitley, 1992a, 1992b; Redding, 2005; Hasegawa and Noronha, 2009). Local systems of ideas (political, religious, etc.) influence the ideology, structure and culture of institutions, which themselves influence organizations, organizational behaviour, HRM and IHRM. Budhwar and Sparrow (2002) report how different contextual variables (such as industrial relations, labour markets, business systems) in India and the United Kingdom shape different logics of actions for managers, even when they are aiming to achieve the same goal of improving integration between HRM and business strategy. Institutional influences are presented in this book (see Chapter 2) to explain differences across countries regarding HRM practices (Ferner et al., 2001).

Box 1.5   Stop and reflect

Interpretive research gives us a local and specific understanding of a situation or a construct (e.g. how is 'good leadership' perceived) in a given environment. Therefore, in terms of generalization, this perspective is weak, but if you think instead in terms of transferability, this perspective is very helpful. Investigate and reflect on the distinction between (a) generalization and (b) transferability of knowledge about culture.

5 Critical views: 'Culture and power'

Postmodern, critical and postcolonial perspectives have much internal diversity, just like the other two views presented above. Works adopting these perspectives can be said to share in common their conceptualization of societal structures as processes and outcomes of power struggles. They also focus on the influence of societal and structural elements in the explanation of (work) interactions. Such elements are social, political and historical contexts that affect how, for example, employees consider and evaluate their colleagues coming from a different culture (Muhr and Salem, 2013).

Critical perspectives can contribute to diversity management for international human resource (IHR) managers by encouraging more questioning on their views on diversity. Respecting cultural diversity for IHR managers goes beyond the consideration of 'traditional' forms of diversity (such as gender, age, people with a disability) to include, for example, religious belonging, professional training and sexual preferences. IBM and Volvo group, for example, are actively managing this multi-faced diversity of their international workforce through programmes such as 'Diversity and inclusive leadership'. In their investigation, critical scholars pay attention to power imbalance between organizational members and sometimes highlight surprising results. For example, Zanoni and Janssens (2003) assert that IHR managers' discourse on diversity may reflect dominant views and reaffirm management practices and underlying inequalities. Likewise, Omanović (2013) reveals how an organization 'closed the door' to diversity with a programme designed precisely to establish a diversity initiative. Critical perspectives can thus help IHR managers to realize that they may involuntarily be reproducing the inequalities they intend to address.

Cultural differences are also shown by critical researchers to be used as 'excuses'. Organizational or national culture differences are shown, for example by Riad (2005) or Vaara (2002), as a narrative construction (in other words a story) to explain the success or the failure of mergers and acquisitions. Discourses on cultural differences between organizations present suitable narratives for explaining incompatibility between organizations and legitimizing partial actions, or making sense of failures. In the study of mergers between several banks in the Nordic European region, researchers show how the discussions about cultural differences (between, for example, Danish, Finnish and Swedish) were not as neutral as it first seemed. The way the national identities were constructed in these conversations, the examples that were chosen, contributed to exclude females from top management positions (Vaara et al., 2003; Tienari et al., 2005).

In consequence, the critical approach urges us to pay attention to how discourses are constructed, and how 'cultural differences' can be used in these discourses to hide another aspect or to masquerade an issue. For example, Mahadevan (2011) studied an organization where HRM attempted to train engineers based in Germany in cross-cultural management, in view of their future collaboration with Indian engineers. The analysis of the case progressively reveals that the will to impose a training intervention (using the excuse that engineers are low on social and cultural skills and therefore need such education) is coupled with the will to gain more power over the conflictual areas of relationships between different professional groups in the organization.

Ybema and Byun (2009) provide the example of a study that shows how discourses on culture are constructed and mobilized in individual power struggles in the case of Japanese–Dutch interactions. The researchers realized that each national group was not consistent in its description of cultural differences. For example, Japanese managers assert that Dutch culture is egalitarian, compared to the Japanese one, but Japanese subordinates see their Dutch superiors as hierarchical with top-down decision-making styles. This highlights that talking about cultural differences is not an objective depiction of reality, otherwise the argued cultural differences would be the same. Consistency is found when one looks at the hierarchical levels. In both countries, people who have a superior of a different nationality argue that their boss's national culture is hierarchical. This means that the power inequalities are important in determining what cultural differences people see as relevant. In other words, the cultural differences are talked about in a way that creates two different groups: 'the Japanese' and 'the Dutch' who are essentialized as different, especially when they are connected to different hierarchical levels. These boundaries serve the reproduction of power and status inequalities in their organizations.

Critical views address the discourse about the other and about concepts of difference. They contribute to shedding a new light on cross-cultural management knowledge that is used, for example, for expatriation training (e.g. Jack and Lorbiecki, 2003; Szkudlarek, 2009). Pre-expatriation training may implicitly reproduce stereotypes about non-Western cultures, thereby justifying the transfer of HRM practices from the headquarters to subsidiaries in developing countries. For example, the use of discourse essentializing others and presenting them as culturally determined and 'backward' (Kwek, 2003; Fougère and Moulettes, 2011) may lead to IHRM policies and practices in favour of bureaucratic control mechanisms rather than cultural ones based on training – since the assumption is that 'they' are not going to change or that any change will be difficult. Peltonen (2006) argues that the relationship between head-quarters and subsidiaries is embedded in political, economic and symbolic power inequalities that tend to favour the views of the headquarters. Likewise, expatriates sent to subsidiaries can be on a mission that tends to prioritize the interests of the group or the global operations of the group, rather than the local subsidiary (Gersten and Søderberg, 2011).

Box 1.6   Stop and reflect

The critical perspectives tell us, among other things, that the cross-cultural knowledge that we develop about the (cultural) others is biased by the power relationship we have with them. Does it mean that there are no absolute cultural differences?

6 Summary and conclusions

IHRM is intrinsically international and multi-cultural, contributing to making culture a frequent component of issues IHR managers deal with in their work. The three views presented in this chapter are an analytical tool to better investigate, and then to under-stand more comprehensively, situations that are influenced by culture, or that employ culture as an argument in the pursuit of certain goals.

The positivist analysis is frequently employed in the management literature and provides an answer to a central question: What are the value discrepancies that can be identified in this situation? And consequently: What are the external influences of culture on what is happening? This investigation is especially useful for identifying culture as a central consideration in any analysis of IHRM.

The interpretive view regards management as cultural. In other words, culture is the way that people make sense of their situation, thus the meanings attached to it by actors are at the core of the investigation. A main question of this analysis is: What does the situation mean to each of the people involved? This investigation is especially useful for explicating how people experience the situation, why they react the way they do, and how new processes are adopted or rejected.

The critical view considers, for example, that culture can be a rhetorical device serving the stake of parties involved in power struggles. A central question is: What is at stake? What are the (hidden) structures that impact the reality we need to deal with? It is especially useful to unmask the tensions and struggles at play in a situation and to expose it in a new light, leading to more possibility for change.

Together, these three views compose a flexible method for performing a complex analysis of a situation, and consequently, can lead to more effective IHRM. Table 1.5 proposes questions to guide your analysis in each of the three views.

Table 1.5   Sample questions to use in the analysis of a situation dealing with culture

Positivist views Culture and values	Interpretive views Culture and meanings	Critical views Culture and power
How does culture influence this situation?	What does this situation mean to those involved?	Is there a struggle between two camps?
Which are the cultural dimensions that can explain people's behaviour?	What do they associate with the situation/elements of the situation?	Who is in a position of power? Who is silenced? What is at stake?
Which are the cultural dimensions' score differences between the two countries/organizations?	What does the situation remind them of?	Are people collaborating? What are the risks for each camp?
What are the characteristics of an environment scoring high/low on these dimensions?	Which terms, which metaphors do people use when talking about it?	What is said to be 'normal' (status quo or stated situation)? And by whom? Is culture talked about explicitly?
How does it apply here?	What are the arguments advanced, how do the arguments make sense for the participants involved?	Which stake/camp does talking about cultural differences serve?

Discussion questions

1. 'With globalization, people's behaviour and values are increasingly becoming similar, and especially so in organizations. Therefore, in about ten years' time, the IHRM of multinational organizations will be conducted globally.' Comment on this statement.

2. 'Using multiple views on culture (positivist, interpretive and critical) for the analysis of a situation is only making things more complicated. Models should simplify reality, so that we can act upon it.' Explain why this comment is limited in potential and discuss the differences between a rich analysis and an over-complicated one.

3. Every researcher tends to do research mainly within one paradigm. Similarly, you, as a manager, will also tend to spontaneously make one type of analysis of the situations

(Continued)

(Continued)

you encounter. Which one is it? The positivist, the interpretive or the critical one? Reflect on your view, and its inherent limitations. Then, discuss how you can develop a way of thinking which will bring to your analysis the other two views.

4. An etic view on culture reflects a positivist position, whereas an emic view reflects an interpretive position. What view of culture is reflected by the critical position?

CASE STUDY

'Not the way we do business around here'

Please note: this case is based on original email material in Swedish, from Nickell Sweden (Nickell is a pseudonym). The English translation reflects the original proficiency of Swedish and writing style of the authors of the emails.

Introduction

Robin hangs up the phone, it's almost 11 p.m. and tomorrow will be a long day. Today was spent visiting an important client and Robin was out of reach most of the time, while installing a new system. The phone call that just ended with Tapio Mäkelä, the managing director of the Nordic area, is worrying. If Tapio does what he threatens to do, Robin will lose one of the most important members of the Swedish team: the technical specialist, Per Jonson. How can things go so wrong in just one afternoon? Robin decides that a good night of sleep is needed before writing – or not – a report to the European HR manager.

Background

Robin works as the sales director of Sweden, for a European company called Nickell, specialized in the development, production and sales of cleaning chemicals and dosing systems for the food-processing industry (cleaning of pipes, tanks, etc.). The Swedish operations of Nickell are a subsidiary of Nickell Nordic Area, located in Finland. The problem started last year, when Bekvema (a pseudonym), one of the most important international customers of Nickell, established a subsidiary in Sweden. Bekvema is a centrally run corporation, with headquarters in Finland where its activities make about 70 per cent of the turnover of Nickell Finland. Tapio Mäkelä is personally in charge of the relationships with Bekvema and will not tolerate Per Jonson continuing with his attacks on his work.

Robin is sceptical. Is Per right in saying that the system used by Bekvema in all its subsidiaries is not appropriate, thereby criticizing the solution developed together with Nickell Finland? On the other hand, Tapio often said that Bekvema does not always follow his recommendations and that they tend to do what they think is right, or enough. Bekvema now wants to have a new system installed for its Swedish subsidiary during the holiday weekend of Midsummer. This is the most important holiday here in Sweden! Robin understands the importance given to the midsummer celebrations. They mark the beginning of the summer break for very many people in the country. But what is the most upsetting for Per? Is it really that Tapio said 'yes' to Bekvema, which means that they are going to have to work during Midsummer? But Per will not even be there! Robin scrolls down the email inbox searching for the first email sent by Per.

EMAIL #1

From: Per Jonson
Sent: Thursday, June 21, 2007 12:17 PM
To: Tapio Mäkelä
Cc: Robin; Bengt Karlson; Göran Söderberg
Subject: Bekvema Sundbyberg

Dear Tapio,
To my consternation I hear that we are going to install the system Propre at Bekvema in Sundbyberg.

I must decisively protest against this coward attitude towards Bekvema and its demand to start up Propre in Sweden.

To accept this was not good to any party involved, in view of the circumstances.

The success we have reached through the years in Sweden depends to a large extent to the fact that we have demands on our customers, as much as they have demands on us.

Many times, a No from us was positively perceived by the Swedish customers.

By acting like puppet dolls we have never reached any success in Sweden, but it is maybe different in Finland?

As you certainly remember, I was from the start of Bekvema Sweden in Sundbyberg strongly critical to the inferior (the least we can say) cleaning system they use.

To dose 1,2 g PXX at 60° is like doing nothing, because this brings no significant disinfection.

(Continued)

(Continued)

Besides this remarkable recommendation, the cleaning process is performed without FGcs?? What is it for process??

Your answer was that it is Bekvema's decision and that we don't have anything to say as far as processes are concerned.

In my eyes this sounds like a coward attitude to the client!!!!

If the processes were right from the start we probably would not have ended in that situation.

The fact that Bekvema Finland experiences an awesome good result with Propre does prove that the earlier processes were not good?

You also said that we, in Sweden, don't know anything since we don't have experience with PXX.

Nothing can be more wrong!!

Long before you started using PXX in Finland, we had an extensive international project where we investigated the PXX processes and disinfection in ClientX in Karlstad. The fact that it has never been a success in Sweden is linked to the too high costs it implies.

Unfortunately, all the documentation was lost in the three moves.[1]

Without doubts, the best in this case would have been to install instead of Propre *a real PXX process* during the month of July ...

If the client were Client Y, they had applauded such a clear decision, especially when one knows that the service resources are limited during the summer vacations. We did so with Client Z and they were thankful for it.

Someone must learn to say no now and then to Bekvema too, and maybe learn to motivate why one says no.

Next time we have a common meeting, I think that we must discuss in detail how we are going to do in the future, because we cannot successfully continue in this way.

Note that my criticisms are about actions, not persons.

Best regards and best wishes for a nice Midsummer.

Per Jonson

Technical Specialist

---

[1]Per refers to the recent changes that occurred in the company. Both Finnish and Swedish activities of Nickell were part of a larger multinational corporation, itself the result of a merger between business units of other companies. Previously, another ownership change had taken place.

Robin remembers the criticisms that Per Jonson made loudly to the other members of the sales team during their last meeting. His convincing arguments had gained the agreement of the other sales technicians. It is true that Per is the only technical specialist in the Nordic area. His influence on the Swedish sales team is clear and Robin already wondered whether this could be a problem. Robin searches for Tapio's answer.

EMAIL #2

From: Tapio Mäkelä
Sent: Thursday, June 21, 2007 12:36 PM
To: Per Jonson
Cc: Robin; Bengt Karlson; Göran Söderberg
Subject: RE: Bekvema Sundbyberg

My dearest Per,
You think you can just like that criticize the case of Bekvema although you don't even taken part in the work for the last months. How can you think that you would know better?

Unfortunately, you don't have now enough information to judge the situation. For this reason I cannot either answer to your assertive email. In case you want to learn more about the situation, you are welcome to call me today or next week (although I don't understand why you are so interested in a client you did not even work with for the last months). If you call you'll get answers.

I wish you a nice holiday and hope at the same time that you can get some rest. In the future, please learn more about the background before you start sending emails that can be seen as written with a negative attitude. I rather have this kind of discussion on the phone since emails are a much too powerful media for sensitive matters and often opinions are polarized unnecessary. Same wishes to the others as well. I hope this will become a habit in the future.

Best wishes
Tapio
    PS. I would love to know why you have so many feelings in regard to everything that has to do with Bekvema. I could almost believe that this has something to do with Sweden versus Finland ... could that be the case?

Robin wonders whether Tapio has a point. It seems that the feelings of competition between Sweden versus Finland are there. In Nordic sports, very often the finalists

(Continued)

(Continued)

are Sweden and Finland, and both countries tend to see the other as the eternal adversary. It appears to Robin that whatever comes from Nickell Finland is received negatively. On the other hand, it seems that Tapio does not know much about the situation here, since he believes that Per does not work much with Bekvema. This is not the case. Per's response came two hours later.

EMAIL #3

From: Per Jonson
Sent: Thursday, June 21, 2007 14:33 PM
To: Tapio Mäkelä
Cc: Robin; Bengt Karlson; Göran Söderberg
Subject: RE: Bekvema Sundbyberg

Tapio,
- If I was involved or not has nothing to do with the matter, and nothing to do with knowing better. You don't know much of my commitment to Bekvema. However, I know that it was a bad decision, at this point of time, to start the installation of a project like Propre.
- I have enough information to see that this is a stupid decision, and furthermore, I know very well how the processes they use today (don't) work.
- No one in Sweden is interested in working in a company where they cannot (or should not) write their true opinion in emails. The coming situation with Bekvema touches us all to a great deal. In this country, it is a habit to circulate one's opinion, via mail or phone. I assume this will continue in the future. To insinuate that we should not do so in the future is weak and pure dangerous leadership.
- I don't understand what you mean with 'first learn about the background'. The background facts I have are more than enough to judge that starting up a Propre project at this point of time is risky.
- It is not about feelings, don't you understand the problem? If not, I'd be happy to explain again.
- The cleaning processes used so far are hardly professional and I suppose, this is why it is so urgent to start Propre.

I repeat point 3 in other words, just to be sure because this is important:
   To suggest that we should go quiet and carefully with our opinions is not only stupid, it is also wrong. I cannot even see that this would polarize into something negative.

In Sweden, it was a long time ago that man stood with the hat in the hand, and we are never going to go back to that time.

Your wish that we should not write down our opinion in mail does not scare only me …

I can also mention that most of the decisions that we make in Sweden are based on consensus.

This is not about Sweden versus Finland, it is just that business and management are fundamentally different in our countries, well, one could say incompatible☺

It would never occur to a Swede to implement a system that was wrongly developed by the client. In this case, you have to have good arguments to explain where the mistake lies. We are good at that. To say No, too.

Of course I will rest during the holiday, but this does not imply that I will tie me a muzzle. On the contrary. Tremble should the ones I'll meet.

Honestly, I was expecting a better, actually a much better answer from you Tapio. Your answer felt empty. A bit unpleasant.

Best regards, with the hope that you too will get the possibility to rest during the holiday, and maybe reflect about life.

Per Jonson

Technical specialist

Per called around the other sales technicians and even Robin during the afternoon. Robin remembers how upset Per was, saying that Tapio is some kind of Stalinist dictator, and that keeping one's head down in front of the hierarchy, or clients, is unacceptable. It may be the usual way in Finland, but 'this is not the way we do business around here!' Robin tried to calm him down. The afternoon was tense and Robin spent also some time with Tapio on the phone, trying to calm him down too. That afternoon, another sales technician reacted.

EMAIL #4

From: Bengt Karlson
Sent: Thursday, June 21, 2007 17:55 PM
To: Tapio Mäkelä; Per Jonson
Cc: Robin; Göran Söderberg
Subject: RE: Bekvema Sundbyberg

Tapio and Per!
Without going into detail in your exchange on whether things are done this way or that way, whether one does this or that in Sweden or Finland, I consider too that

(Continued)

(Continued)

this is crazy to start a new project just before the holidays. This shows imprudence and a big faith that everything is going to happen the way we want. In my world there is a guy call Murphy (the devil's assistant) and we meet him quite often. Free translation: If something can go wrong, then it goes wrong. And especially because we purposefully did not take any safety measure. And then the fact that if something goes wrong, someone has to go to the client and fix the problem when we are on holiday. Is this going to give trust to the client?

If you see that as a criticism from Per, you need to know that it was I who first was upset about all this. I am not as much in touch with all the technical details as Per, but it does not mean that I don't have an opinion.

Finally, I want to say that I agree with Per, we have it good in Sweden. We basically discuss everything. Even your behaviour in the Bekvema related matters. You have to understand that what you decide on the other side of the Baltic Sea, we have to implement it on this side. So I think this is more than right that we should be in the decision process too.

And yes, Bekvema touches us all in Sweden. Not just Göran who is responsible for the client. Every one of us feels responsible, and will get mobilized if for some reason Göran is not available.

All in all, I want to calm down this storm a bit with wishing you a happy Midsummer. We'll sort things out in the future.

Best regards,
Bengt

The conversation Robin just ended with Tapio was mostly about Per's latest email (see below). Tapio found Per's attitude unacceptable and disrespectful. He said he could no longer tolerate such an attitude from one of his subordinates. And since whatever he says to Per is misinterpreted, he'd rather meet Per next time with a lawyer, to serve as a witness. Tapio wants Robin to translate the emails and to send them to Jaap van der Dorp, the European Human Resource Manager. He asked Robin to send along a note to Jaap van der Dorp, in order to give a third party's opinion on the matter. Tapio wants to use this note, together with the emails, as material in his case against Per. If Per continues like that, he wants him to go.

EMAIL #5

From: Per Jonson
Sent: Thursday, June 21, 2007 20:06 PM

To: Bengt Karlson; Tapio Mäkelä
Cc: Robin; Göran Söderberg
Subject: RE: Bekvema Sundbyberg

Unlike Bengt, I don't see all this as a storm, in fact just an illustration of how things go wrong when one tries processes with a quasi science and let the client take over knowledge,* and at the same time, a lack of ability to say No.

Tapio's nonanswer (!) to me gave no explanation as why it could not have worked with a normal PXX-process during the month of July (which would have been easier and more cost effective in time).

This would have been much safer, but instead Tapio came with an answer asking us to shut up with our cap in the hand and bow, which is never going to happen, this we have, in this country, left behind us for a long time (circa 1950s). I indicated this in my previous answer.

Now I don't only think that Tapio's answer was unpleasant, it was even alarming (I get vibes from the old East block).

In general, I agree with Bengt. Business and application decisions must, in the future, be made in consensus, this way is accepted with thankfulness.

The current decision measure with Bekvema is what we call in Sweden, in a modern language, something low, and even very low.

Regards
Per Jonson, who will be available most of the holidays
Technical specialist
*Like the 1,2g PXX/m which is according to the book *not authorized* by our company, Bekvema made it up!

Robin was out of email reach for the entire day and thought to react to this email exchange in writing now. What am I going to answer? wonders Robin. What is the situation really about? Why are they so upset? How could the situation go so wrong within a few hours? Of course tensions have occurred before … The communication between the Swedish sales team and Tapio usually goes all right; he makes the effort to speak Swedish although his mother tongue is Finnish. 'What am I going to write to Jaap van der Dorp?' wonders Robin. Robin has met Jaap only once, and got the impression of an old and conservative manager, clearly from another generation, and certainly not used to trying to understand that there are different ways of managing people in Sweden than in Belgium.

(Continued)

(Continued)

Case study questions

Use the analytical framework of this chapter with positivist, interpretive and critical research in cross-cultural management. Conduct each analysis with the help of Table 1.5 and you will progressively uncover the depth of the problem.

1. Which cultural dimensions (Tables 1.2–1.4) can help explicate the interaction between Tapio and Per? What is Tapio's leadership style? Does it fit to the cultural profile of Finland? What leadership style is expected from Per and the other Swedish employees? Draft a few recommendations to Robin on the basis of this analysis.
2. Note in the text of the emails the words and meaning associations used by Tapio, Per and Bengt in their description of good (versus bad) leadership. How are these views reconcilable? What are the distinct areas of expertise claimed by Tapio and Per? What would you recommend Robin to do, in light of this further analysis?
3. Why are Tapio and Per not collaborating? Is Per using the argument of cultural differences to impose a certain view? Which one? Why? What are the consequences of the PXX system not functioning properly? What do you recommend Robin to do now?

Further reading

- Hofstede, G. (2001) *Culture's Consequences: Comparing Values, Behaviors, Institutions, and Organizations Across Nations* (2nd edn). Thousand Oaks, CA: Sage.
  This is the second edition of the seminal work of Geert Hofstede first published in 1980. It presents five cultural dimensions (power distance, individualism collectivism, masculinity/femininity, uncertainty avoidance and long-term or short-term orientation). Each dimension is comprehensively introduced and discussed in its implications for, among others, work situations and IHRM.

- House, R.J., Hanges P.J., Javidan M., Dorfman, P.W. and Gupta, V. (eds) (2004) *Culture, Leadership and Organizations: The GLOBE Study of 62 Societies*. Thousand Oaks, CA: Sage.
  This edited volume is becoming the major source of reference regarding cultural dimensions and thus positivist and etic studies on culture. It investigates how 62

societies compare on nine cultural dimensions, in practice and in value preferences. Each dimension is richly introduced and discussed in its implications for, among others, work situations, but especially leadership. The GLOBE database is more recent than the one used by Hofstede.

- Hofstede, G., Hofstede, G.J. and Minkov, M. (2010) *Cultures and Organizations: Software of the Mind*, 3rd edn. New York: McGraw Hill.
  This volume is a practitioner version of the 2001 study and presents the addition of the latest cultural dimension (Indulgence versus Restraint).

- d'Iribarne, P. (2002) 'Motivating workers in emerging countries: universal tools and local adaptations', *Journal of Organizational Behavior*, 23(3): 243–256.
  This publication illustrates an interpretive analysis of important changes in the human resource management of the subsidiaries of two multinationals, Sgs-Thomson and Danone, in Morocco and in Mexico. The interpretive analysis shows how the same situation, which was workers' lack of motivation, had dissimilar origins, and thus had to be addressed differently. It explains how motivation is introduced by changing the system of meanings that employees used to associate with their work, in other words, how they were accustomed to making sense of their work.

- Primecz, H., Romani, L. and Sackmann, S.A. (eds) (2011) *Cross-cultural Management in Practice: Culture and Negotiated Meanings*. Cheltenham: Edward Elgar.
  This edited volume gathers ten short interpretive case studies on cultural influences in collaboration, in management practices and on organizations (internationalization, mergers, implementation of new HRM practices, etc.). It illustrates the contributions achieved with a focus on meanings for the understanding of cross-cultural interactions. The edited volume starts with a presentation of what interpretive theories and methods stand for.

- Gersten, M.C. and Søderberg, A.-M. (2011) 'Intercultural collaboration stories: on narrative inquiry and analysis as tools for research in international business', *Journal of International Business Studies*, 42: 787–804.
  Using an interpretive analysis of interviews about a collaboration between a Danish expatriate manager and his Chinese CEO in the Shanghai subsidiary of a multinational enterprise (MNE), the authors of this article demonstrate the benefit of narrative analysis for the understanding of cross-cultural competence development. They make it clear how the partners overcame most of their differences and established common ground through mutual learning.

- Zanoni, P. and Janssens, M. (2003) 'Deconstructing differences: the rhetoric of human resource managers' diversity discourses', *Organization Studies*, 25(1): 55–74.
  This article is an illustration of the type of knowledge and the mode of analysis performed by research using critical discourse analysis. Through critical examination

of verbatim interviews with HR managers of Flanders (Belgium), the authors show how discourses essentialize the others (those who are seen as 'different': persons with a disability, migrant workers, etc.), how their discourses devalue or value diversity, and also reaffirm management practices.

- Jack, G. and Westwood, R. (2009) *International and Cross-cultural Management Studies: A Postcolonial Reading*. Basingstoke: Palgrave Macmillan.
  This volume systematically examines research in cross-cultural management and points to the limitations of these studies in light of a postcolonial analysis. The authors demonstrate that this discipline is a Western and Eurocentric discourse that echoes the colonial project. They urge us to reconsider our theoretical frameworks and common understandings of culture to include more local, emic and alternative understandings and research. The author's positioning is in strong contrast to the positivist views using cultural dimensions and etic constructs and models.

- Javidan, M. and Dastmalchian, A. (2009) 'Managerial implications of the GLOBE project: a study of 62 societies', *Asia Pacific Journal of Human Resources*, 47(1): 41–58.
  This article gives an overview of the GLOBE project and discusses the practical implications of this research for managers and leaders.

- Peterson, M.F. and Pike, K. (2002) 'Emics and etics for organizational studies. a lesson in contrast from linguistics', *International Journal of Cross-Cultural Management*, 2(1): 5–19.
  This article provides a comprehensive explanation and discussion of emic and etic concepts of culture.

- Fang, T. (2003) 'A critique of Hofstede's fifth national culture dimension', *International Journal of Cross Cultural Management*, 3(3): 347–368.
  This critique of Hofstede's fifth dimension serves also to introduce Fang's Yin Yang model of culture.

- Gannon, M.J. (2009) 'The cultural metaphoric method: description, analysis, and critique', *International Journal of Cross Cultural Management*, 9(3): 275–287.
  In this article, Martin Gannon presents the cultural metaphor as an alternative to the cultural dimension frameworks to describe a country's cultural profile.

- McSweeney, B. (2009) 'Dynamic diversity: variety and variation within countries', *Organization Studies*, 30(9): 933–957.
  Brendan McSweeney has written some of the most read critiques on the work of Hofstede. In this piece, he examines point-by-point the limitation of the cultural dimension frameworks research on culture.

- Chevrier, S. (2008) 'Is national culture still relevant to management in a global context? The case of Switzerland', *International Journal of Cross Cultural Management*, 9(2): 169–183.

This article is in the (interpretive) tradition of the works by d'Iribarne in cross-cultural management that study frames of meanings. It illustrates the method and strength of the approach and implications for managers.

- Mahadevan, J. (2012) 'Are engineers religious? An interpretative approach to cross-cultural conflict and collective identities', *International Journal of Cross Cultural Management*, 12(1): 133–149.
  This article views culture from an interpretive, sense-making perspective. It analyses religion-based cross-cultural conflict through the example of two ethnographic studies of multicultural high-tech organizations undergoing change.

- Ybema, S. and Byun, H. (2009) 'Cultivating cultural differences in asymmetric power relations', *International Journal of Cross Cultural Management*, 9(3): 339–358.
  This article illustrates how power (hierarchical) discrepancies between Dutch and Japanese employees influence their respective perceptions of cultural differences. It adopts a critical viewpoint on cross-cultural management.

- Woong, L. (2010) 'Postcolonial interventions and disruptions: contesting cultural practices', *International Journal of Cross Cultural Management*, 10(3): 345–362.
  This article suggests that the integration of postcolonial perspectives into cross-cultural management and its theorizing enhances and enriches its discursive import. Postcolonial studies illustrate a stream of research with a critical viewpoint.

Internet resources

- www.geert-hofstede.com. This website provides visitors with comparative tools, country profiles and other valuable information to those who want to access Hofstede's research and outcomes. This is currently the official page for the diffusion of Geert Hofstede's research and tools.
- www.Harzing.com. This website contains multiple references and resources linked to IHRM. In the section 'resource' a spreadsheet with the scores of 98 countries on Hofstede's and/or GLOBE's dimensions is free to download.
- www.sietareu.org or www.sietarusa.org. The Society for Intercultural Education, Training and Research (SIETAR) is the world's largest interdisciplinary network for professionals working in the field of intercultural relations. You find on SIETAR Europa's and SIETAR USA's pages information about trainings, publications and cross-cultural management and cross-cultural communication tools. SIETAR organizations have close links with the Intercultural Communication Institute (ICI). It is a private, non-profit foundation designed to foster an awareness and appreciation of cultural differences in both the international and domestic arenas (www.intercultural.org). It provides, for example, education and professional development in intercultural communication.

- www.dialogin.com. The mission of the Delta Intercultural Academy is to act as a global knowledge and learning community on culture, communication and management in international business. The website provides information or reviews of a large range of books, articles and commentaries on cross-cultural activities. It advertises conferences, training and job offers and regularly organizes e-conferences between Dialogin members (open membership) and influential researchers in the field of culture and management.

Self-assessment questions

Indicative answers to these questions can be found on the companion website at study.sagepub.com/harzing4e.

1. When facing a situation involving culture, you will need to ask yourself different kinds of questions to use the different views presented in this chapter. Can you state sample questions that are helpful to adopt positivist, interpretive and critical views?
2. Each view is best suited to develop a certain kind of knowledge. Can you provide an example of knowledge achieved by the positivist view?
3. Can you provide an example of knowledge achieved by the interpretive view?
4. Can you provide an example of knowledge achieved by the critical view?

References

Åkerblom, S. (1999) *Delade meningar om ledarskap? En enkätstudie av mellanchefers föreställningar om framstående ledarskap.* Stockholm: EFI.

Berger, P. and Luckmann, T. (1966) *The Social Construction of Reality: A Treatise in the Sociology of Knowledge.* London: Penguin Books.

Boyacigiller, N.A., Kleinberg, M.J., Phillips, M.E. and Sackmann, S.A. (2004) 'Conceptualizing culture: elucidating the streams of research in international cross-cultural management', in B.J. Punnett and O. Shenkar (eds), *Handbook for International Management Research*, 2nd edn. Ann Arbor: University of Michigan Press, pp. 99–167.

Budhwar, P.S. and Sparrow, P.R. (2002) 'Strategic HRM through the cultural looking glass: mapping the cognition of British and Indian Managers', *Organization Studies*, 23(4): 599–638.

Child, J. (2000) 'Theorizing about organization cross-nationally', in L.C. Cheng Joseph and R.B. Peterson (eds), *Advances in International Comparative Management*, Vol. 13. Greenwich, CT: JAI Press, pp. 27–75.

Den Hartog, D. (2004) 'Assertiveness', in R.J. House, P.J. Hanges, M. Javidan, P.W. Dorfman and V. Gupta (eds), *Culture, Leadership and Organizations: The GLOBE Study of 62 Societies.* Thousand Oaks, CA: Sage, pp. 395–436.

d'Iribarne, P. (1989) *La Logique de l'honneur.* Paris: Le Seuil.

d'Iribarne, P. (2002) 'Motivating workers in emerging countries: universal tools and local adaptations', *Journal of Organizational Behavior*, 23(3): 243–256.

d'Iribarne, P. (2009) 'National cultures and organizations in search of a theory: an interpretative approach', *International Journal of Cross-Cultural Management*, 9(3): 309–321.

Earley, P.C. and Gibson, C.B. (1998) 'Taking stock in our progress on individualism-collectivism: 100 years of solidarity and community', *Journal of Management*, 24(3): 265–304.

Fang, T. (2003) 'A critique of Hofstede's fifth national culture dimension', *International Journal of Cross-Cultural Management*, 3(3): 347–368.

Fang, T. (2012) 'Yin Yang: a new perspective on culture', *Management and Organization Review*, 8(1): 25–50.

Ferner, A., Quintanilla, J. and Varul, M.Z. (2001) 'Country-of-origin effects, host-country effects, and the management of HR in multinationals: German companies in Britain and Spain', *Journal of World Business*, 36(2): 107–127.

Fougère, M. and Moulettes, A. (2011) 'Disclaimers, dichotomies and disappearances in international textbooks: a postcolonial deconstruction', *Management Learning*, 1–20.

Gannon, M.J. (2004) *Understanding Global Cultures: Metaphorical Journeys Through 28 Nations, Clusters of Nations, and Continents*, 3rd edn. Thousand Oaks, CA: Sage.

Gannon, M.J. (2009) 'The cultural metaphoric method: description, analysis, and critique', *International Journal of Cross-Cultural Management*, 9(3): 275–287.

Gannon, M.J. and Audia, P.G. (2000) 'The cultural metaphor: a grounded method for analyzing national cultures', in P.C. Earley and H. Singh (eds), *Innovations in international and cross-cultural management*. Thousand Oaks, CA: Sage, pp. 91–106.

Garfinkel, H. (1967) *Enthnomethodology*. Englewood Cliffs, NJ: Prentice-Hall.

Geertz, C. (1973/1993) *The Interpretation of Cultures*. London: Fontana Press.

Gelfand, M.J., Bhawuk, D.P.S., Nishii, L.H. and Bechtold, D.J. (2004) 'Individualism and collectivism', in R.J. House, P.J. Hanges, M. Javidan, P.W. Dorfman and V. Gupta (eds), *Culture, Leadership and Organizations: The GLOBE Study of 62 Societies*. Thousand Oaks, CA: Sage, pp. 437–512.

Gelfand, M.J., Erez, M. and Aycan, Z. (2007) 'Cross-cultural organizational behaviour', *Annual Review of Psychology*, 58(1): 479–514.

Gersten, M.C. and Søderberg, A.-M. (2011) 'Intercultural collaboration stories: on narrative inquiry and analysis as tools for research in international business', *Journal of International Business Studies*, 42: 787–804.

Hasegawa, H. and Noronha, C. (eds) (2009) *Asian Business and Management*. Houndmills: Palgrave.

Henry, A. (2007) 'Revolution by procedures in Cameroon', in P. d'Iribarne and A. Henry (eds), *Successful Companies in the Developing World: Managing in Synergy with Cultures*. Paris: Agence Française de Développement, pp. 95–126.

Hofstede, G. (1980) *Cultures' Consequences*. Beverly Hills, CA: Sage.

Hofstede, G. (2001) *Culture's Consequences: Comparing Values, Behaviors, Institutions, and Organizations Across Nations*, 2nd edn. Thousand Oaks, CA: Sage.

Hofstede, G., Hofstede, G.J. and Minkov, M. (2010) *Cultures and Organizations: Software of the Mind*, 3rd edn. New York: McGraw Hill.

House, R.J., Hanges, P.J., Javidan, M., Dorfman, P.W. and Gupta, V. (eds) (2004) *Culture, Leadership and Organizations: The GLOBE Study of 62 Societies*. Thousand Oaks, CA: Sage.

Jack, G. and Lorbiecki, A. (2003) 'Asserting possibilities of resistance in the cross-cultural teaching machine: re-viewing videos of others', in A. Prasad (ed.), *Postcolonial Theory and Organizational Analysis: A Critical Engagement*. New York: Palgrave Macmillan, pp. 213–231.

Kabasakal, H. and Bodur, M. (2004) 'Humane orientation in societies, organizations, and leader attributes', in R.J. House, P.J. Hanges, M. Javidan, P.W. Dorfman and V. Gupta (eds), *Culture, Leadership and Organizations: The GLOBE Study of 62 Societies*. Thousand Oaks, CA: Sage, pp. 564–601.

Kirkman, B.L., Lowe, K.B. and Gibson, C.B. (2006) 'A quarter century of culture's consequences: a review of empirical research incorporating Hofstede's cultural values framework', *Journal of International Business Studies*, 37(3): 285–320.

Kluckhohn, F. and Strodtbeck, F. (eds) (1961) *Variations in Value Orientations*. Evanston, IL: Row, Peterson and Company.

Kwek, D. (2003) 'Decolonizing and *re*-presenting culture's consequences. a postcolonial critique of cross-cultural studies in management', in A. Prasad (ed.), *Postcolonial Theory and Organizational Analysis: A Critical Engagement*. New York: Palgrave Macmillan, pp. 121–146.

Leung, K., Bhagat, R.S., Buchan, N.R., Erez, M. and Gibson, C. (2005) 'Culture and international business: recent advances and their implications for future research', *Journal of International Business Studies*, 36(4): 357–378.

Leung, K., Bond, M.H., Reimel de Carrasquel, S., Muñoz, C., Hernández, M., Murakami, F., Yamaguchi, S., Bierbrauer, G. and Singelis, T.M. (2002) 'Social axioms: the search for universal dimensions of general beliefs about how the world functions', *Journal of Cross-Cultural Psychology*, 33(3): 286–302.

Lowe, S., Moore, F. and Carr, A.N. (2007) 'Paradigmapping studies of culture and organization', *International Journal of Cross-Cultural Management*, 7(2): 237–251.

Mahadevan, J. (2011) 'Engineering culture(s) across sites: implications for cross-cultural management of emic meanings', in H. Primecz, L. Romani and S. Sackmann (eds), *Cross-cultural Management in Practice: Culture and Negotiated Meanings*. Cheltenham: Edward Elgar, pp. 89–100.

Maznevski, L.M., DiStefano, J.J., Gomez, C.B., Noorderhaven, N.G. and Wu, P.-C. (2002) 'Cultural dimensions at the individual level of analysis', *International Journal of Cross-Cultural Management*, 2(3): 275–295.

Muhr, S.L. and Salem, A. (2013) 'Spectres of colonialism: illusionary equality and the forgetting of history in a Swedish organization', *Management and Organizational History*, 8(1): 62–76.

Nielsen, C.S., Soares, A.M. and Páscoa Machado, C. (2009) 'The cultural metaphor revisited: exploring dimensions, complexities and paradoxes through the Portuguese Fado', *International Journal of Cross-Cultural Management*, 9(3): 289–308.

Omanović, V. (2013) 'Opening and closing the door to diversity: a dialectical analysis of the social production of diversity', *Scandinavian Journal of Management*, 29: 87–103.

Peltonen, T. (2006) 'Critical theoretical perspectives on international human resource management', in G. Stahl and I. Björkman (eds), *Handbook of Research in International Human Resource Management*. Cheltenham: Edward Elgar, pp. 523–535.

Primecz, H., Romani, L. and Sackmann, S.A. (2009) 'Multiple perspectives in cross-cultural management', *International Journal of Cross-Cultural Management*, 9(3): 267–274.

Primecz, H., Romani, L. and Sackmann, S.A. (eds) (2011) *Cross-cultural Management in Practice: Culture and Negotiated Meanings*. Cheltenham: Edward Elgar.

Redding, S.G. (1994) 'Comparative management theory: jungle, zoo or fossil bed?', *Organization Studies*, 15(3): 323–360.

Redding, S.G. (2005) 'The thick description and comparison of societal systems of capitalism', *Journal of International Business Studies*, 36(2): 123–155.

Riad, S. (2005) 'The power of organizational culture as a discursive formation in merger integration', *Organization Studies*, 26(10): 1529–1554.

Rokeach, M. (1973) *The Nature of Human Values*. New York: Free Press.

Romani, L. (2010a) 'Culture in international human resource management', in A.W. Harzing and A. Pinnington (eds), *International Human Resource Management*, 3rd edn. Sage: London, pp. 79–118.

Romani, L. (2010b) *Relating to the Other: Paradigm Interplay in Cross-cultural Management Research*. Saarbrucken: LAP publishing.

Romani, L., Primecz, H. and Bell, R. (forthcoming) 'There is nothing so practical as four good theories', in B. Gehrke and M.-T. Claes (eds), *Advanced Cross-Cultural Management: Developing Deep Intercultural Competencies for a Globalized World*. Basingstoke: Palgrave MacMillan.

Sackmann, S.A. and Phillips, M.E. (2004) 'Contextual influences on culture research: shifting assumptions for new workplace realities', *International Journal of Cross-Cultural Management*, 4(3): 370–390.

Sagiv, L. and Schwartz, S.H. (2000) 'A new look at national culture: illustrative applications to role stress and managerial behaviour', in N.M. Ashkanasy, C.P.M. Wilderom and M.F. Peterson (eds), *Handbook of Organizational Culture and Climate*. Thousand Oaks, CA: Sage, pp. 417–435.

Schutz, A. (1962) *Collected Papers, Volume 1, The Problem of Social Reality* (edited and introduced by Maurice Natanson). The Hague: Martinus Nijhoff.

Schwartz, S.H. (1994) 'Beyond individualism/collectivism: new cultural dimensions of values', in U. Kim (ed.), *Individualism and Collectivism: Theory, Method, and Applications*. London: Sage, pp. 85–119.

Schwartz, S.H. (1999) 'A theory of cultural values and some implications for work', *Applied Psychology: An International Review*, 48(1): 23–47.

Schwartz, S.H. (2004) 'Mapping and interpreting cultural differences around the world', in E. Vinken, J. Soeters and P. Ester (eds), *Comparing Cultures. Dimensions of Culture in a Comparative Perspective*. Leiden: Brill.

Schwartz, S.H. and Bilsky, W. (1987) 'Towards a psychological structure of human values', *Journal of Personality and Social Psychology*, 53: 550–562.

Smith, P.B. and Bond, M.H. (1998) *Social Psychology Across Cultures*, 2nd edn. Harlow: Prentice Hall, Pearson Education.

Smith, P.B., Peterson, P.F. and Schwartz, S.H. (2002) 'Cultural values, sources of guidance, and their relevance to managerial behaviour: a 47-nation study', *Journal of Cross-Cultural Psychology*, 33(2): 188–208.

Smith, P.B. and Schwartz, S.H. (1997) 'Values', in J. Berry, M.H. Segall and C. Kagitcibasi (eds), *Handbook of Cross-Cultural Psychology, Vol. 3 Social Behavior and Applications*, 2nd edn. Boston: Allyn and Bacon, pp. 77–118.

Søderberg, A.-M. and Holden, N. (2002) 'Rethinking cross-cultural management in a globalizing business world', *International Journal of Cross-Cultural Management*, 2(1): 103–121.

Szkudlarek, B. (2009) 'Through Western eyes: insights into the intercultural training field', *Organization Studies*, 30(9): 975–986.

Tienari, J., Søderberg, A.-M., Holgersson, C. and Vaara, E. (2005) 'Narrating gender and national identity: Nordic executives excusing for inequality in a cross border merger context', *Gender, Work and Organization*, 12(3): 217–247.

Triandis, H.C. (1995) *Individualism and Collectivism*. Boulder: Westview Press.

Trompenaars, F. (1993) *Riding the Waves of Culture: Understanding Cultural Diversity in Business*. London: Nicholas Brealey Publishing Limited.

Tsui, A.S., Nifadkar, S.S. and Yi Ou, A. (2007) 'Cross-national, cross-cultural organizational behavior research: advances, gaps, and recommendations', *Journal of Management*, 33(3): 426–478.

Vaara, E. (2002) 'On the discursive construction of success/failure in narratives of post-merger integration', *Organization Studies*, 23(2): 211–248.

Vaara, E., Risberg, A., Søderberg, A.-M. and Tienari, J. (2003) 'Nation talk: the construction of national stereotypes in a merging multinational', in A.-M. Søderberg and E. Vaara (eds), *Merging Across Borders: People, Cultures and Politics*. Copenhagen: Copenhagen University Press, pp. 61–86.

Whitley, R.D. (1992a) *Business Systems in East Asia*. London: Sage.

Whitley, R.D. (1992b) *European Business Systems: Firms and Markets in their National Contexts*. London: Sage.

Ybema, S.B. and Byun, H. (2009) 'Cultivating cultural differences in asymmetric power relations', *International Journal of Cross-Cultural Management*, 9(3): 339–358.

Yousfi, H. (2011) 'When American management system meets Tunisian culture: the Poulina case', in H. Primecz, L. Romani and S. Sackmann (eds), *Cross Cultural Management in Practice: Culture and Negotiated Meanings*. Cheltenham: Edward Elgar, pp. 64–76.

Zanoni, P. and Janssens, M. (2003) 'Deconstructing differences: the rhetoric of human resource managers' diversity discourses', *Organization Studies*, 25(1): 55–74.

Comparative Human Resource Management[1]

Chris Brewster and Wolfgang Mayrhofer

Contents

[1]Much of the evidence reported in this chapter is taken from Cranet (www.cranet.org). The authors acknowledge the work of colleagues in the network in collecting the data and discussing the issues and the role of the Cranfield School of Management in the UK in coordinating the network.

Learning objectives

After reading this chapter you will be able to:

- Appreciate the importance of comparative HRM for IHRM
- Understand the difference between best practice and best fit models of HRM
- Identify the reasons why countries remain different in the ways that they conceptualize and conduct HRM
- Discuss some of the ways in which HRM differs between countries
- Understand how MNCs have to balance between being globally effective and fair while appreciating and benefiting from national differences

Chapter outline

This chapter explores the differences between countries in the ways that they manage their human resources. Within a context of increasing globalization, the chapter argues that context is crucial: what the term HRM means, how it is understood, what would be considered 'good' HRM and the way that people management is practised, all vary from country to country. As such, these differences form the backdrop against which MNCs must manage the integration/differentiation paradox, and against which all IHRM must be measured. Comparative HRM is a challenge to the universalist paradigm of HRM, generally expressed in the notion of 'best practice'.

Fundamental to understanding these differences between countries are two concepts: the ideas of cultural and institutional differences, and the notions of convergence and divergence. The chapter argues that we need to gain a better understanding of both pairs of concepts. They constitute important means of understanding what is actually happening in HRM. On the first issue, we argue that both cultural and institutional explanations are valuable; on the second we argue that convergence of trends is apparent, but final convergence remains unrealistic.

We provide more detail, as examples, of differences between countries in the configuration of HRM, flexible working practices and communications and consultation. Finally, we outline some of the key theoretical, empirical and practical challenges posed by a comparative approach to HRM.

1 Introduction

A major problem for those who study and practise HRM is that much of our understanding and most of our knowledge about the topic comes from the USA and are assumed to apply universally. The version of HRM propounded in most books on

HRM and published in most of the HRM journals, the lessons taught in most business schools around the world, the recommendations put forward by the major consultancy companies and the whole best practice movement in HRM, are all based on the US model. This creates built-in cultural assumptions and contextual limitations for HRM specialists and for those working in organizations operating internationally. The fact that HRM differs from country to country should not be read as implying that some countries are just 'backward' or need to 'catch up' to more modern ways of doing things. The fact that some of the richest countries in the world manage their HRM in different ways, and that there are world-beating MNCs from an ever-increasing number of countries, reminds us that 'different' does not mean 'worse'.

If we want to run effective HRM policies in an internationally operating organization, we have to understand the different national cultures and institutional constraints – at least in terms of their importance for organizations, restrictions or limited room for manoeuvre in imposing corporate policies and practices, and their opportunities and limitations when managing an international workforce (see Chapter 5). Organizations operating across national and cultural borders will need to bridge the divide between being globally coherent and consistent in their HRM policies and practices for reasons of cost-effectiveness and equity with the imperative of being sensitive to local variations in national, cultural and institutional requirements. Arguably, this dilemma is best summarized in an early statement by Laurent:

> The challenge faced by the infant field of international human resource management is to solve a multidimensional puzzle located at the crossroad of national and organisational culture. (Laurent, 1986: 101)

From its beginnings, IHRM (see Introduction) was aware of these requirements. Dealing with an international workforce, especially expatriates, looking at HRM specifics of MNCs and comparing HRM policies and practices constituted the fundamentals for IHRM in the early 1980s (Dowling, 1999). Various developments at the global level such as economic globalization and the rising significance of MNCs have not only quickened the development of IHRM as an established part of HRM, but also paved the way for more detailed discussions on the topic. In this sense, comparative HRM has become an established part of IHRM, and a major perspective on how to look at HRM in an international setting (see, for example, contributions taking an explicitly comparative angle in HRM such as Harzing and van Ruysseveldt, 2004; Brewster et al., 2007c; or the Routledge Global Human Resource Management series edited by Schuler, Jackson, Sparrow and Poole). European researchers in particular have made significant contributions to theoretical, empirical and methodological advances in the field of comparative HRM (e.g. Poole, 1990; Brunstein, 1995; Gooderham et al., 1999; Brewster et al., 2000, 2004). There have also been important contributions from other parts of the world such as Asia (e.g. Zanko, 2002; Zanko and Ngui, 2003; Budhwar, 2004), Africa (Kamoche et al., 2003) and the developing countries (Budhwar and Debrah, 2001).

Box 2.1   Stop and reflect

Look up the table of contents of the following books and analyse:

1. In which book does comparative HRM play a major role?
2. Is comparative HRM a central theme around which the book is organized or is it just one element among many others?
3. Where applicable: what are the underlying dimensions of the comparative perspective?

Brewster, C. and Mayrhofer, W. (eds) (2012) *Handbook Of Research On Comparative Human Resource Management*. Cheltenham: Edward Elgar.

Briscoe, D., Schuler, R. and Tarique, I. (2012) *International Human Resource Management: Policies and Practices for Multinational Enterprises* (4th edn). New York: Routledge.

Dickmann, M., Brewster, C. and Sparrow, P.R. (eds) (2008) *International HRM: A European Perspective*. London: Routledge.

Dowling, P.J., Festing, M. and Engle Sr., A.D. (2013) *International Human Resource Management*. London: Cengage Learning EMEA.

Parry, E., Stavrou, E. and Lazarova, M.B. (eds) (2013) *Global Trends in Human Resource Management*. Houndsmills and New York: Palgrave Macmillan.

Sparrow, P.R. (ed.) (2009) *Handbook of International Human Resource Management: Integrating People, Process, and Context*. Chichester: Wiley.

Stahl, G., Björkman, I. and Morris, S. (eds) (2012) *Handbook of Research in International Human Resource Management*, 2nd edn. Cheltenham and Northampton, MA: Edward Elgar.

The way that people think about HRM and the way it is practised vary from country to country. Managers have their own approaches to managing their people, each unit manages differently, as does each function within the company – and each organization has its own unique form of HRM. There is commonality too in so far as organizations of a similar size or in a particular sector tend, other things being equal, to have similar forms of HRM. Both common and distinctive social institutions exist and are nested at a range of levels in societies (Hollingsworth and Boyer, 1997). Each country has its own generic recipes for HRM and there are general approaches to the subject that draw universal conclusions about HRM. The differences, often linked to a named country as the 'nutshell' for cultural, institutional or regional specifics, are one of the fundamental reasons why IHRM is more difficult than HRM in one country since, out of all of the aspects of management, HRM is most subject to local influences (Rosenzweig and Nohria, 1994).

Any discussion of IHRM, therefore, needs to include an understanding of comparative HRM. Despite this, comparative research in HRM has been somewhat rare. The main reason for this is that comparative IHRM research work is difficult: there are 'noble and not so noble' (Mayrhofer and Brewster, 2005) problems, including questions of conceptualization such as finding an adequate theoretical frame, and practical difficulties such as bringing together international research teams and sustaining working relationships between researchers of different nationality, culture or scientific tradition. In contrast, comparative research in the fields of industrial and employment relations has been more common (see Barry and Wilkinson, 2011). 'Referring to both a field of study and material practices, the analytical core of employment relations is … the employment relationship and the exchange between employer and employee centred on the reward–effort bargain. This relationship is complex, contextual and dynamic' (Nienhüser and Warhurst, 2012: 216). Closely related to HRM, employment relations research focuses on different levels of analysis. At the individual and firm levels one looks at (implicit) contracts between employer and employee or within institutions governing the effort–reward bargain. At the country level, issues such as means of power and exploitation or the analysis of the contextual conditions for supplying an adequate workforce are at the heart of the analyses. Theoretically, employee relations research borrows from disciplines such as economics, sociology, political sciences and social psychology, using frameworks such as transaction cost theory, labour process theory, institutional theory or the psychological contract (Nienhüser and Warhurst, 2012: 217).

Drawing the previous paragraphs together encapsulates a key issue: to understand and analyse the complexity of IHRM requires a comparative approach and an understanding of comparative HRM. This chapter concentrates on comparative HRM. We mention (briefly because it is also covered in Chapters 3, 4, 6 and 14) the issues of globalization and MNCs as major reasons for the importance of IHRM in general and comparative HRM in particular; we examine the importance of context and look at some of the different ways that it has been analysed, how it is changing and whether HRM is converging; we look at country-related differences of core HRM elements; and finally we comment on the drive to standardize HRM practices and simultaneously to deal with the need to adapt these practices to the local environment.

2 Globalization and HRM

IHRM continues to attract interest, which is not surprising. At the time of writing, the long-term effect of the global recession that began in 2008 is still uncertain. Figures from the World Investment Report by UNCTAD (various years), the United Nations'

(UN) body measuring the extent of international trade and development, show that the growth of international trade had been patchy in the first years of the twenty-first century, after a long period of almost exponential growth towards the end of the twentieth century. The economic crisis during the end of the first decade of the new century exacerbated that trend and some governments have been forced to react to the severe economic downturn with austerity policies and in some cases even with protectionist measures.

The term 'globalization' is widely used but often harbours different meanings. Generally it refers to processes of unification that have taken place in markets and consumer tastes, increasingly mobile investment capital, and the rapid spread of technology. Within and between firms, actions are increasingly grounded in an overall perspective that views the whole world as nationless and borderless (Ohmae, 1990, 1995). Globalization theories hold that economies are becoming globally integrated, resulting in the proliferation of global management structures and the convergence of management techniques around shared notions of 'best practice' (Sera, 1992). MNCs are exposed to the forces of globalization and, so, are most likely to comply with dominant worldwide practices aimed at enhancing competitiveness in world markets. Hence, they attempt to promote integrated international standards and resist pressures to be locally responsive (Hamel and Prahalad, 1986; Ashkenas et al., 1995; Yip, 1995; Kim and Gray, 2005). These global strategies encourage greater homogenization to create greater efficiency (Kostova and Roth, 2002). Grounded in the rational choice tradition, this global perspective assumes that firms pursue economic advantage through choices 'guided by unambiguous preferences and bounded rationality' (Gooderham et al., 1999: 507). While the diffusion process may be slow or uneven, it will eventually make for inter-industry and international practices that are to a large degree uniform. Firms will either attempt to enforce their own view of the most efficient ways of handling HRM in other countries; or they will all gradually drift towards HRM policies that mirror the most rational and efficient approach, as propounded in the US model of management (Smith and Meiksins, 1995; Jain et al., 1998; McDonough, 2003). The main argument and prediction of this set of theories is increasing convergence.

Global competition can encourage increasing levels of coordination of resources, equipment, finance and people (Sparrow et al., 2004). For example, it is important to coordinate pricing, service and product support worldwide since multinational customers can compare prices in different regions. Through global trade, traditional and domestic business boundaries become increasingly permeable, accelerating the rate of convergence of business practices and firms face more risk in becoming decoupled from familiar settings, thus challenging national mindsets and assumptions (Sparrow and Hiltrop, 1997).

Sceptics and critics of the globalization thesis (see, for example, Dunning, 1997; Whitley, 1999; Rugman, 2005) have contested even the assumption that globalization is new (Parker, 1998). Others have suggested on the contrary that even multinational firms are extremely local in terms of key areas such as employment practices: 85 per cent of multinationals produce more than two-thirds of their output in their home market, with two-thirds of their employees being nationals of their home country (*The Economist*, 2000). Indeed, most MNCs cannot easily be defined as stateless (Hu, 1992); a long-term analysis of the United Nations Conference on Trade and Development (UNCTAD, 2007) using the index of transnationality shows that between 1993 and 2003 the Top 100 transnational companies have only moderately increased their transnational characteristics. Partly, the index has decreased, reflecting a concentration on local or regional markets.

The effects of globalization – as far as it exists – are hotly debated, both empirically and theoretically. Whitley (1999) offers a well-received analysis, pointing towards three major consequences influencing national business systems which are a major contextual factor for organizations (see also Edwards and Rees, 2006). First, globalization may influence organizations strongly involved in international operations which can have effects on the national environment, for example by transferring international standards into the national context; second, foreign direct investment (FDI) flowing into a country may influence the competitive structure and processes within the national business system, for example by increasing the level of competition when a global chain such as Starbucks enters a traditionally organized coffee consumer market such as Austria; and third, globalization can lead to a new supra-national systems level of economic organization and competition which will, in the long run, be as important as the nation state, as is the case for example with the European Union (EU). All this affects organizations and their HRM. For example, the four freedoms of the European Union – free movement of labour, capital, services and goods – have an impact on HRM issues such as recruitment policies and practices, wage level or expected standards of education and training.

For our purposes, it is worthwhile reminding ourselves that human resources are, in most organizations, the largest single element of operating costs. That is why MNCs locate many of their operations in low-wage economies. Although there is little thought, either in the literature or in practice, given to the idea that firms should equalize wages globally, there is a widespread assumption, as we shall see, that the rest of HRM can be standardized to match the global reach of MNCs (Brewster et al., 2008).

3 The importance of context

HRM viewed through a comparative lens is always contextualized, such that how HRM works, what is covered by HRM, what is regarded as good HRM, etc., depends heavily on the respective context. Context in this sense includes the internal context (e.g. organizational size, structure and demography) as well as the external context, which covers national culture and values, as well as elements of the institutional environment such as legal regulations, the respective industry and the type of economy.

Contextualizing HRM prompts us to ask at least three questions. First, can HRM in different contexts be conducted in a similar way or does it have to adapt to the respective circumstances? Behind this question lies the discussion on best practice versus best fit, which asks whether there is one best model of HRM as is often assumed in US-based HRM concepts, or whether alternatively it is necessary to take into account specific contextual issues in order to achieve the best outcome? Second, what are the crucial forces leading to relevant contextual differences in HRM? Two major factors often treated as mutually exclusive are culture and institutions. Third, how do similarities and differences between various contexts develop over time? Taking a temporal perspective, the issues of convergence, divergence or stasis arise, and so the question is: will the different contexts – most often countries – become more alike, more different or stay relatively stable? This section explores all three questions consecutively.

Best practice versus best fit

It can be argued that an organization's HRM policies and practices should be tightly connected to the organization's corporate strategy and should be coherent in all its operations. However, for companies operating in more than one country the question arises as to whether that is sensible or even possible.

There are some advantages for MNCs in adopting 'best practice' – that is, choosing to apply the practices with which they are most familiar, or those that appear to promise high returns in performance, regardless of the location of their subsidiary (Gooderham and Nordhaug, 2003). In most companies and in most circumstances, it appears to the firm's leaders that best practice is the one used in the headquarters country. It is common for an MNC based in the USA to insist that its policies are best practice and could and should be applied in Venezuela whereas it is very rare for such companies to find an example of excellent practice in Venezuela and insist that it is applied by managers in the USA.

The advantages of a best practice approach include mutual learning, so that an effective practice discovered in one location can be spread across the world, without the costly and often ineffective need for each subsidiary to 're-invent the wheel'. In addition, global alignment of systems will facilitate an internal labour market and make expatriation and other forms of cross-border movement of personnel less complicated (Almond et al., 2003). Common systems of HRM may then be easier to control and monitor from headquarters. Alongside these benefits, there are ethical considerations of equity and fair treatment for all employees – why should the organization treat people differently just because they come from or are located in different countries?

Besides these benefits there are disadvantages, too. Companies' policies and practices may not be seen as legitimate, or even be legal, in some countries and the approaches of companies from around the world in relation to issues of gender, ethnic or age discrimination will be very different. Some countries have legislation requiring companies to discriminate in favour of certain ethnic groups; equality legislation in the USA encourages positive discrimination but that is illegal in the European Union. Therefore, some degree of adaptation to local circumstances is inevitable.

As a result, researchers increasingly acknowledge that HRM is one of the management subjects in which organizations are most likely to maintain a national flavour and have a strong contextual interface. This switches the focus from best practice to best fit, especially related to different contexts. Many studies reveal substantive differences between various aspects of HRM in European countries (e.g. Brewster et al., 2004; Scholz and Böhm, 2008; Morley, 2009; Parry et al., 2013). A large survey of HRM directors of the biggest firms in Germany, the USA and Japan found that HRM practices differ widely (Pudelko, 2004). There is considerable evidence that, even in the most centralized MNCs, forms of control (Harzing and Sorge, 2003), work systems (Geppert et al., 2003) and team work (Woywode, 2002) vary by country and that, in practice, the form of implementation of 'worldwide' policies is negotiated or varied at the national level (Ferner, 1997; Wächter et al., 2003).

The background for these two views is the distinction between the universalist and the contextual paradigms in HRM research (Brewster, 1999). The universalist paradigm is dominant in the USA but also widely applied elsewhere. It assumes that the purpose of the study of HRM is to improve the way that human resources are managed strategically within organizations. The ultimate aim of this approach is to improve organizational performance, as judged by its impact on the organization's declared corporate strategy (Huselid, 1995), the customers (Ulrich, 1989) or shareholders (Becker et al., 1997). It is implicit in these writings that this objective applies to all cases: the aim is, by analogy with the physical sciences, to test 'yes/no' hypotheses with the objective of identifying universal rules.

In contrast, the contextual paradigm searches for an overall understanding of what is contextually unique and why it is different. It is focused on understanding what is distinctive between and within HRM in various contexts, and identifying what the antecedents of those differences are. The policies and practices of 'leading-edge' companies, something of a value-laden term in itself, which are often the focus of universalist HRM research, are of less interest than identifying ways that labour markets work and examining what the more typical organizations are doing. For most researchers working within this paradigm, it is the explanations that matter and links to company performance are secondary. It is assumed that HRM applies to societies, governments or regions as well as to companies. At the level of the organization (and not just the 'firm' because public-sector and not-for-profit organizations should be included), even the organization's objectives and strategy are not necessarily assumed to be 'good' either for the organization or for society (Mayrhofer and Brewster, 2012).

Box 2.2　Best practices or best fit?

An MNC applied a diversity policy across its worldwide operations. It issued polices to enforce non-discrimination, changed its recruitment and promotion procedures and set up online support groups and meetings opportunities for disadvantaged workers. It found that its Japanese subsidiary (based in an ethnically remarkably homogenous country) was not interested in 'blacks and so on' but was enthusiastic about gender equality. Japan is a country in which people prefer to work for indigenous rather than foreign firms but in which those indigenous firms expect their female employees to give up work when they get married, as did many Western countries up until as late as the 1960s. This Japanese subsidiary of a foreign company thought that it would be able to recruit top quality female graduates who were looking for a lifetime career. But when they asked for financial support for crèche facilities and child care this proved too much for HQ, who had not intended to spend a lot of cash on these policies (Sparrow and Brewster, 2009).

It is not that either HRM paradigm is necessarily correct or more instructive than the other, but that the level and focus needs to be specified to make the analysis meaningful (Brewster, 1999). Comparative HRM falls decidedly within the contextual paradigm.

Culture versus institutions

Comparative HRM should attempt to provide explanation as well as give description (Boxall, 1993). So what are the reasons for the differences in the way that countries conceive of and practise HRM? There are, broadly, two competing sets of theoretical explanation: the cultural and the institutional.

Cultural explanations

One reason for the variation between countries in the way they think about and undertake HRM can be found in the concept of cultural differences (see Chapter 1 for a cultural view on differences in communication). Culture is, as one of the classic texts put it, 'one of those terms that defy a single all-purpose definition and there are almost as many meanings of culture as people using the term' (Ajiferuke and Boddewyn, 1970: 154). Related to management issues, three approaches to culture have become prominent over recent decades.

- Hofstede's view of culture as consisting of five cultural dimensions – power distance, individualism, masculinity/femininity, uncertainty avoidance, complemented by long-term versus short-term orientation, which was added later (Hofstede, 1980, 2001) – is widely known and dominated much of the discussion in the 1980s and 1990s. Its great success can be attributed to a very straightforward approach to culture, regarding it as 'the software of our minds'. Ready-made data that was conveniently applicable in econometric analyses proved particularly helpful for those who believe in the illusion of rigour in quasi-quantitative management research.
- Schwartz's concept of culture as value oriented and reducible to systemic cultural dimensions (Schwartz, 1992, 2010). Values are beliefs, refer to desirable goals, transcend specific actions and situations, serve as standards or criteria, and are ordered by importance. Schwartz's most recent model has three cultural dimensions: mastery versus harmony (which addresses the issue of economic and social viability), hierarchy versus egalitarianism, and embeddedness versus autonomy (intellectual and affective autonomy).
- The Global Leadership and Organizational Behavior Effectiveness (GLOBE) project (House et al., 2004) shares with Hofstede and Schwartz the perception that culture is something rather stable. It provides an integrated theory of the relationship between culture and societal, organizational and leadership effectiveness. Looking at modal practices ('how things are done in a culture') and modal values ('the way things should be done'), the study uses nine culture dimensions, partly overlapping with other models such as Hofstede: uncertainty avoidance, power distance, institutional collectivism, intra-group collectivism, gender egalitarianism, assertiveness, future orientation, performance orientation and social orientation. Against this backdrop, the GLOBE study focused on actual and ideal leadership.

National cultures will, typically, reflect national boundaries, but this is by no means always the case. Thus, countries like Belgium, Spain and Switzerland contain communities speaking different languages and following different religions and legislation, seeming, at least to the resident citizens, profoundly different in their approach to life. Cultural groups in the Middle East and Africa were divided by the colonial mapmakers and in many instances may have more in common with groups in countries across the national border than they do with many citizens of their own country. In many countries, however, especially the longer established ones and those within coherent geographical boundaries, such as islands, culture in many spheres of social life equates to country – and that is certainly the conclusion of the research into workplace values (e.g. Spony, 2003) or the world-value studies (see, for example, Welzel and Inglehart, 2005).

The 'culturalist' school is an extremely broad one. It covers many different approaches and addresses the interaction between national culture and the behaviour of organizations and individuals. Cultural differences will inevitably be reflected in differences in the ways people are managed and HRM is conducted.

Institutional explanations

The institutional perspective sees the institutions of a society as environments that maintain their distinctiveness. All transactions are assumed to be embedded in specific social settings (Hollingsworth and Boyer, 1997) and organizations are understood to adhere to formal rules and unwritten social norms in the interests of efficiency and legitimacy (DiMaggio and Powell, 1983; Marsden, 1999). The institutionalist line of argument runs broadly as follows. There are a number of different and equally successful ways of organizing economic activities (and management) in any capitalist economy (Whitley, 1999; Hall and Soskice, 2001; Amable, 2003). These different patterns of social and economic organization tend to be a product of the particular institutional environments occurring within the various nation states.

Neo-institutional theory (Powell and DiMaggio, 1987) argues that organizations are subject to a range of forces – coercive, mimetic and normative – that require them to develop an HRM approach that is perceived to be legitimate to influential stakeholders within each context. Coercive mechanisms include the influence of trade unions, works councils, employment legislation and the government; mimetic mechanisms refer to the benchmarking and imitation of strategies and practices of successful competitors; and normative mechanisms include the impact of professional bodies and employers associations, the impact of business schools, consultancies and pressure groups and the expectations of public opinion (Paauwe and Boselie, 2003). Organizations need to achieve legitimacy within the environment in which they operate, since they have to work with other bodies such as employees, trade unions, governments, shareholders, financial institutions and other influential stakeholders who can refuse or restrict access to necessary resources (Deephouse, 1999). As these institutional bodies and their views of what is legitimate vary from country to country, MNCs have to adapt their HRM policies in each location (Farndale et al., 2008).

From a pragmatic perspective, this means that the types of organizations that are dominant, the shape of customer–supplier relationships, and the work systems and employment practices differ significantly from society to society despite the pressures of globalization. The institutions are likely to shape the social construction of any organization within the society. Thus, the specific patterns of ownership within a society, general and vocational education systems, the way labour markets work, employment legislation and the industrial relations system will all impact on the way that HRM can be conducted in particular states (Brewster, 2004).

Box 2.3 Variety of contexts

Clearly, for an internationally operating organization, it does not make much sense to have the same HRM policies all over the world: in Uganda, where most of the working population is unemployed, and Denmark, where employers have a shortage of labour; in Japan, where women are generally expected to leave the workforce on marriage and Canada, where women expect a lifetime career; in Finland where the great majority is well-educated, in Columbia, where only a minority are, and in the United States where a highly educated elite and functionally non-literate millions live side by side. Such organizations would, properly, not dream of having identical recruitment strategies or pay levels in these countries.

It is evident that HRM is at least partly a function of the country's particular institutional arrangements – the 'societal effect' (Maurice et al., 1986). As with the culture effects, there seems to be a kind of societal recipe that it is possible to go against or even ignore, but only at some social cost. Most people, and the majority of organizations, in general, do not do so.

Combining the two

While proponents of these two streams of thought often give no more than a passing nod to the others' viewpoint, it seems that neither an exclusively culturalist nor an exclusively institutionalist approach are satisfactory accounts. Many of the 'culturalist' writers treat institutions as being key artefacts of culture reflecting deep underlying variations in the values that they see between societies. Likewise many 'institutionalist' writers include culture as one of the institutional elements explaining differences. These two forms of theoretical explanation are not necessarily mutually exclusive. Organizations are not entirely rational and issues of history and personality play a great part. In addition, just as individual behaviour and social structure are reciprocally constituted, so too are cultures and institutions. Thus, institutions cannot survive without legitimacy, but individual perspectives are partially created and sustained by their institutional context. Arguably, the two schools of thought examine and explain the same factors from different points of view (Brewster, 2004; Sorge, 2004), encouraging one to draw the conclusion that 'both institutional and cultural dimensions … have an important impact on HRM practices in different countries' (Romani, 2004: 163). It may be that organizations have more choice in relation to cultures (they can select staff carefully to be atypical of the culture of that country for example or argue that certain norms are inappropriate for their business) but they have more limited options in relation to institutional differences (they cannot ignore the effects of the labour market or legislation). Whatever the balance, both factors need to be taken into account.

Static versus dynamic

Comparing HRM in different contexts inevitably leads to questions about developments over time and changes in the actual similarities and differences. Given the underlying dynamic developments of the current political, economic and social systems across the globe, static 'snapshot' analyses using cross-sectional designs do have some value, but leave many questions unanswered. While it is important to analyse the status quo, it is of equal importance to be able to estimate future developments in the light of past events and processes. For example, comparing the relative size of HRM departments at the country level and at a given point in time provides valuable information about the relative position of each country. However, further information about the development path through observing changes over time would help to answer questions such as: Is this an increase compared to a decade ago? Do we see a pendulum swing in all countries? Do countries move in the same direction? Has there been a general increase or decrease of the relative size of HRM departments over time? This matters because if the differences between countries are being reduced as countries change their practices then it makes sense to study 'best practice' and to help other countries to 'catch up'. If, on the other hand, the differences persist then we need to be aware of them and to adapt our understanding of HRM accordingly.

From a comparative HRM angle, this raises the question of convergence and, by implication, divergence and stasis. The concept of convergence is worth examining. The meaning most commonly assumed in the literature (even if it is rarely stated explicitly) is movement towards greater similarity. At the comparative national level of HRM this would mean countries becoming more like each other in the way that they manage their human resources. Much of the evidence that is adduced for this (found in the literature cited above), however, comes from research conducted either at a single point in time or from the identification of similar trends across countries. Logically, these research assumptions and study designs cannot prove movement towards greater similarity. An attempt has been made, therefore, to disaggregate the notion of convergence in comparative HRM so that we can consider three forms of convergence (Mayrhofer et al., 2002). These forms are:

- *directional convergence*, in which the trends go in the same direction but commence from different starting points and may mean that countries remain in parallel, maintaining the same relationship to each other, or even diverge
- *final convergence*, where the practice of HRM in these countries becomes more similar even though that might, on occasion, mean that different countries are heading in different directions, and
- *majority convergence*, where organizations within one country become more alike, again perhaps by some countries heading in opposite directions to others.

The convergence debate in comparative HRM is dominated by two major issues: first, and linked with the best practice versus best fit debate, there is the question of whether a more or less common global model of HRM is emerging; second, within global regions or selected groups of countries, do we see convergence, divergence or stasis when we follow the development of HRM in these countries over time?

Box 2.4 Stop and reflect

In which areas of HRM would you expect final convergence, i.e. HRM practices moving towards a common ground? And where would you assume directional convergence, i.e. practices moving towards the same direction without necessarily coming closer together or further apart? Why?

Regarding the emergence of a global model of HRM, an assumption frequently made is that there is an optimal set of strategies, decisions and practices at any specific time (Kostova and Roth, 2002) and that global markets promote greater homogenization as companies compete with similar products and under a similar rate of technological change (Duysters and Hagedoorn, 2001). Hence, it is argued, HRM practices, especially through MNCs and their global as well as local effects, are likely to converge towards an emerging global paradigm, or, perhaps, towards the US model that is often held up as an example of the success of lightly regulated markets (Smith and Meiksins, 1995). The best practice debate and thinking around high-performance work systems (US Department of Labor, 1993) follows this route and makes the established normative claim that these practices should be a universal benchmark.

The empirical evidence for a one-world model is certainly mixed. While undoubtedly MNCs have a strong influence on local HRM practices and policies with their sophisticated policies and practices rolled out internationally and policed by a central HRM function, it also is quite clear that there are no simple homogenizing effects at work. Rather, HRM practices and policies are reshaped, resisted and redeployed by the socially embedded processes of the host locale, emphasizing country-level distinctiveness (Ferner, 1997; Ferner and Quintanilla, 1998; D'Aunno et al., 2000). In this sense, national differences are strong, robust and deeply embedded and are unlikely to change significantly. Recent research on the role of MNCs, using the large-scale Cranet database rather than case studies, argues that MNCs do indeed manage their people differently from indigenous companies and that this applies to indigenous MNCs as well as foreign ones: but, overall, country of location rather than country of origin is still the most convincing explanation of differences in HRM (Brewster et al., 2008; Farndale et al., 2008). The role of MNCs seems to be a mixture of bringing in new practices, adapting to local ones and developing hybrid forms.

In terms of converging or diverging developments over time within a group of countries or a region, the best evidence comes from the European section of the longitudinal set of Cranet studies. Cranet shows conclusively that there are significant differences between the countries in all major functional areas of HRM (Brewster et al.,

2004). What is widespread or standard practice in one country plays much less of a role in others. More significantly in relation to the convergence/divergence debates, HRM in these countries tends not to change very much and countries tend to sustain their relative positions. For example, the presence of HRM at Board level (or equivalent) changes very little and the countries retain their positions, with the single exception of a clear trend in Germany towards more organizations having an HRM director appointed to the Board. To take a completely different example; the number of companies with more than 10 per cent of their workforce on part-time contracts shows more fluctuation, but less sign of any overall pattern or trend (Tregaskis and Brewster, 2006; Richbell et al., 2011).

These examples could be multiplied, but overall there are consistent developments towards directional convergence in Europe to be found in three areas of HRM configuration (the strategic potential of the HRM department; the assignment of HRM responsibilities to line managers; and HRM professionalization) and four areas of HRM practices (the increasing use of more sophisticated practices in recruitment and selection; increased individualization of employee relations; increased information to employees; and increased use of contingent compensation systems). These common trends are limited: the ratio of HRM specialists to the rest of the organization, or the size of the HRM department, varies considerably and mainly with country, but it also differs according to the size of the organization (Brewster et al., 2006) but overall it has no clearly discernible direction. Neither does training and development reveal much clarity regarding its pathway (Goergen et al., 2012), so although it is given high priority in many countries it nonetheless seems to be the first area selected for cutbacks whenever finances become tight.

In terms of final convergence, however, the overall evidence, for all of the HRM practices analysed, is unequivocal: there is no trend towards final convergence (Mayrhofer et al., 2004, 2011). Countries continue to manage their people in markedly different ways. Despite the similarities in trends, there is very little evidence of globalization of HRM. '[N]ational contexts ... exert a strong influence on local developments. Even in the light of overarching global or at least regional forces ... [there is a] lack of final convergence' (Mayrhofer et al., 2011: 62).

It is clearly evident therefore that we need a more nuanced view and in-depth understanding of convergence in HRM policies and practices than has been apparent hitherto. While, on the basis of the available evidence, things appear to change slowly in HRM, there does seem to be at least some clear indication of directional convergence in a few areas. However, the country recipes remain powerful. HRM varies by country, sector and size of organization; by subjects within the generic topic of HRM; and by the nature of the organization, for example, life-stage, governance or market. Further, we should distinguish the policy intentions of those at the top of organizations from practice on the ground. Overall, then, the evidence overwhelmingly supports the continuing importance of an internationally comparative dimension of HRM due to national differences.

4 Differences in HRM practice

Context-related differences in HRM abound, as we have noted above. Reasons of space mean that it is impossible here to examine all the international variations in HRM so this section provides three typical examples, one of which relates to the more strategic aspects of HRM, the representation of HRM in formal top decision-making bodies and the role of line managers in HRM, and another two relating to HRM practices, flexible working patterns and communications.

HRM department and role of line managers

The role of the HRM function varies considerably across countries. Most commentators argue that HRM has become more important to organizations in the last two decades. Since human resources and the knowledge and skills they incorporate are difficult to replicate, they offer organizations the opportunity of obtaining a sustained competitive advantage, at a time when traditional ways of obtaining competitive advantage become ever easier to copy (Collins and Clark, 2003). Some experts have argued that we should expect to see the influence of the human resource function on corporate decision making increasing over time (e.g. Pfeffer, 1998; Ulrich and Brockbank, 2005). Arguably, where the human resource function is represented at the key decision-making forums of the organization, and becomes closely involved in strategic decision making, awareness of the problems or opportunities that effective HRM might provide will be raised and decision making in increasingly knowledge-reliant organizations consequently will be improved.

One perceptive commentator on HRM made the point some time ago that the rhetoric of integration of the HRM specialist function at Board level and its position of influence has outpaced reality (Legge, 1995). In terms of membership of the Board, the Cranet research data show considerable stability over time set alongside large variation between countries (Brewster et al., 1997; Mayrhofer and Brewster, 2005; see also Cranet, 2006). France, Spain, Sweden and Japan, for example, consistently report seven or eight out of ten organizations having an HRM director on the main decision-making body of the organization (the Board in shareholder companies). In the Central and Eastern European countries and Israel the figures are much lower. Many other European countries, including the UK and Germany, and Australia, show a little less than half of the organizations with HRM departments being directly represented at the top decision-making level. In the Netherlands and Germany employees have rights to have representatives at the supervisory Board level: presumably the employee representatives ensure that the HRM implications of corporate strategy decisions are taken into account. Germany is a particularly interesting case, as it is one of the few countries where HRM representation on the Board has increased significantly over the stages of the study, and at a time that human resources have become more critical for organizations and the function itself has become less administrative in focus. In terms of HRM influence on the corporate strategy, there is more uniformity: in most countries the personnel departments are involved from the outset in strategy formulation in approximately half of the organizations. A recent analysis deals with the effects of feminization at the top of HRM departments on the strategic importance of HRM. It shows a continuous gap in the status of top HRM jobs so that, despite the increasing feminization of the profession generally, men still retain the top positions. However, having women in top HRM positions does not automatically have a negative effect on the strategic importance of the HRM department (Brandl et al., 2013).

What about the size of the HRM department (or, more precisely, its ratio to the rest of the organization)? Against the backdrop of organizations becoming smaller over a decade of downsizing, the introduction of new technology leading to Human Resource Information Systems (HRIS) or electronically enabled HRM (e-HRM), the pressure on 'overhead' departments to prove themselves, and line management taking over some HRM tasks, one would expect HRM departments to have become smaller. However, its size relative to the total organization hardly changed at all during the 1990s and early 2000s (Brewster et al., 2006).

The role of line managers has been seen as a touchstone for HRM (Storey, 2001). The notion is that people can only be managed cost-effectively and well when their immediate superiors have a substantial responsibility for that management. In Europe, the trend during the 1990s was to give line managers more responsibility for the management of their staff and to reduce the extent to which HRM departments control or restrict line management autonomy in this area (Brewster et al., 1997) but this trend has since reversed (Mayrhofer and Brewster, 2005; Mayrhofer et al., 2011). Seemingly regardless of the overall trend, countries tend to hold their positions relative to each other. On a range of personnel issues, it is the Italians who are most likely to lodge responsibility with the personnel department; the British come next. This stands in sharp contrast to the Danes, for example, who, on all issues, tend to give much greater responsibility to line managers. These country differences in responsibility for HRM persist over time.

Flexible working practices

Flexibility in labour patterns is now widely accepted as a critical issue in HRM, although it is bedevilled with problems of terminology: what is called 'flexibility' among European employers and academics is known as 'atypical working' by the European Commission, 'vulnerable work' among trade unionists and 'contingent working' in the USA. Research conducted by the Cranet network, comparing organizations at national level across Europe (Tregaskis and Brewster, 2006; Richbell et al., 2011) is consistent with the national labour market statistics (European Commission Eurostat, 2008) and workplace level data (Kersley et al., 2006) in showing extensive use of flexible working across Europe. Furthermore, some of these forms of flexibility – temporary employment and self-employment – are more widespread in Europe than in the USA. In part-time work the USA has fallen behind the European Union since the mid-1990s to about a median position on a ranking with the European countries. Japan has a different pattern of flexible working from these two continents, with considerable part-time and temporary working (Buddelmeyer et al., 2005).

The Cranet data shows that despite differences within countries and between sectors, particularly, flexible working practices are growing in both extent and coverage almost everywhere. This is so in nearly all countries in Europe, in Japan and Australasia, in all sectors, in organizations both large and small, and whatever the form or origin of ownership. 'Atypical' work patterns or contracts, such as temporary, casual, fixed-term, home-based and annual hours contracts, are spreading, despite differing legal, cultural and labour traditions.

However, organizations where these forms of flexibility cover the majority of their workers continue to be in a clear minority. Furthermore, the increase in the use of flexible contracts tends to be significantly higher among those organizations already making comparatively high use of such contracts. The result is to confirm patterns of difference: countries like the Netherlands and the UK with a substantial proportion of part-time contracts among their workforce (more than 25 per cent) tend to increase usage; countries with very few part-timers continue to have very few. And the same applies to the other forms of flexible working. Between countries, there are clear preferences for different kinds of flexibility. No country or organization makes extensive use of the full range of flexible working patterns and contracts. Thus, in Spain there is a high level of short-term employment with low levels of part-time work. Countries such as Austria, the Netherlands, Sweden and the UK have a third or more of organizations with over 5 per cent of the workforce on temporary contracts. Most of the other countries in Europe have far fewer. By contrast, the Netherlands, Sweden and the UK all have more than a quarter of their working population employed in part-time jobs. These differences correlate with differences in the institutional environment of these countries. Similarly, analyses of the extent of flexible working in Japan need to take into account the Japanese practice of generally restricting employment to women after they are married. Overall, although the trends are similar, there are still varied situations, assumptions and practices occurring in the different countries. Flexibility is dependent upon a complex, interlocking web of national culture, history, institutions, trade union approaches and strength, governmental policies and practices (including legislation) and managerial tradition (Tregaskis and Brewster, 2006).

Communications

Effective communication is a requirement for all organizations and is vital to those seeking commitment from workers to the objectives of the enterprise. Yet there is less clarity about the most effective form and content of communication for these purposes and whether it varies by country. Much of the literature associates the concept of HRM with the individualization of communication and a move away from, or even antagonism towards, communication and consultation which is collective and particularly that which is trade-union based. This non-union implication sits uneasily with the history and circumstances of not just Europe but of a number of other countries around the world. Trade unionism remains widespread and important in places like Japan and Korea, for example, which have extensive, legally backed, systems of employee communication. In Europe, consultation with employees is required by law. These arrangements give considerable (legally backed) power to the employee representatives and, unlike consultation in the USA for example, they tend to supplement rather than supplant the union position (Brewster et al., 2007a, 2007b). In relatively highly unionized countries it is unsurprising that many of the representatives of the workforce are, in practice, trade union officials (for example, four-fifths of them are in Germany). The balance between individual and collective communication is a matter for empirical investigation.

Research shows that there have been increases in all forms of communication: through representative bodies (trade unions or works councils), as well as through direct verbal and written communication (Brewster et al., 2004, 2013). The latter two channels have expanded considerably.

When upward communication is examined, the two most common means, by a considerable margin, are through immediate line management and through the trade union or works council channel. The evidence tends to support the analyses of those researchers (Hollingsworth and Boyer, 1997) who focus on the presence or absence within countries of communitarian infrastructures that manifest themselves in the form of strong social bonds, trust, reciprocity and cooperation among economic actors. There are clear differences between countries, with more communication being apparent in, broadly, the richer countries and less in, for example, the southern European countries. In addition, increases in communication, both up and down, appear to be greater in the countries where most communication goes on (Mayrhofer et al., 2000).

Furthermore, access to financial and strategic information is clearly hierarchical: if you are in a higher position in the organization you are more likely to be briefed regularly about the strategy or the financial performance of the organization. While the hierarchy still persists, the information gap appears to have narrowed during the 1990s as an increasing number of organizations make sure that their administrative employees are informed about the organization's plans and performance. Unionized organizations are more likely than non-union ones to provide such information. There are noticeable differences in average 'slopes' in the distribution of this information: lower level employees in the Nordic countries, for example, receive considerably more information than those working elsewhere.

5 Summary and conclusions: future issues in comparative HRM

Comparative HRM exposes significant differences in the way the concept of HRM is understood, managed and implemented in different countries. For researchers and for organizations operating internationally this raises crucial academic and practical issues.

Theoretical issues

In many areas of comparative HRM we lack adequate theory to explain the complexity of the differences between the meaning, policies and practices of HRM in different countries (Boxall, 1995). For the future, three groups of theories seem especially fruitful for meaningful contributions to knowledge on IHRM.

First there is a group of theories focusing on differences. The theoretical arguments run along the broad line of identifying crucial differences occurring at the macro-level that lead to distinct differences at the level of organizations or individual behaviour. Examples include concepts such as varieties of capitalism (Hall and Soskice, 2001), national business systems (Whitley, 1999) or culture theories (House et al., 2004; Schwartz, 2004). There are an increasing number of analyses of HRM using these approaches (see e.g. Goergen et al., 2009; Croucher et al., 2012). Second, there is theoretical thinking that predicts that the strong logic of global capitalism is ultimately leading to similar approaches at the organizational level. Rational choice theory (e.g. Becker, 1976; March and Simon, 1993) is a major example of this type of argument. Third, and in a somewhat middle-position, is the world polity approach (e.g. Meyer et al., 1997). It argues that there is an ongoing worldwide replacement of traditional particularistic schemes through universal standards associated with modernity. Global myths such as rationality or equality exist that exert considerable influence on all kinds of actors, be it individual or collective, economic or political. However, these global myths do not lead to uniformity. On the contrary, due to specific local conditions there is a great variety of difference in how these global myths are actually realized. All three groups of theories may contribute towards fruitful answers to core questions of comparative HRM such as reasons for contextual differences, mechanisms for translating contextual conditions into organizational and individual action or the long-term development of country differences and their effects on HRM.

Empirical issues

Empirically, a rich, if somewhat daunting, empirical research agenda exists since there are many countries in the world about which we still have little information; and in many cases the information we have is stereotyped, inadequate or non-comparable. At this point in our knowledge we still need the deep, but narrow, understanding of meaning and process that can be provided by detailed comparative case studies; the wide, but shallow, evidential base that large-scale surveys can bring; and access to secondary data provided by governments and international organizations for further analysis and exploration. And if our evidence about and understanding of national differences remains a research gap, there is a research chasm in our knowledge of developments in HRM over time that can only be filled by longitudinal research studies. Comparative HRM research is both more complex and more difficult than research that is based in one country or focuses solely on the practices of MNCs, more complex and difficult but equally exciting and informative (Mayrhofer and Brewster, 2012). As the world becomes more global, so must our research.

Practical issues

For HRM practice, the task is daunting: if an organization covers more than just a few countries even the experts at the centre cannot know the details of HRM expectations and common practice in each local context. They are highly dependent on the information they obtain from their expatriate managers and the (usually local) HRM practitioners in each country – and they may have different agendas and understandings. The fact that most companies manage to cope with this complexity at all is perhaps more noteworthy than are the times they make mistakes. Comparative HRM can contribute to better HRM practice by providing and improving the information base that HRM practitioners rely on when deciding on operational HRM practices as well as strategic issues. Working together with practitioners in organizations operating across national and cultural borders as well as with international professional HRM organizations increases the potential impact of comparative HRM as it leads research and theory building towards practically relevant issues, especially when new phenomena appear that are first detected by people involved in HRM practice rather than from academia.

Concluding remarks

As we pointed out at the beginning of this chapter, HRM differences between countries should not be read as implying that some countries must 'catch up': 'different' does not mean 'worse'. This means that IHRM has an additional layer of complexity. The academic study may be slow to produce conclusions and recommendations but this additional complexity of IHRM has always been a problem for MNCs. Research that is thorough and informed provides a rich opportunity to learn. The more we know about HRM in other countries, the way it is conceived, what good practice there implies, and how it is conducted, then the more we can learn. That is one of the major challenges for students of HRM today and an increasingly pertinent issue for students of IHRM.

Discussion questions

1. Discuss the pros and cons of a 'best practice' type of HRM rolled out in a globally operating company. Focus specifically on the consequences for employees and organizational performance.
2. What do you regard as the most pressing practical questions comparative HRM should tackle? Why do you see them as the most urgent?
3. Give one example each for a cultural and an institutional determinant of HRM practice and discuss how HRM practitioners are restricted by these factors in their practical action.
4. Discuss potential tensions between taking into account cultural and institutional drivers supporting differentiation in HRM and standardization tendencies leading to integration in the areas of recruitment and compensation. How would you handle these tensions?
5. What five core competencies do you see as essential for an HRM practitioner working in a globally operating company that is sensitive to various contexts? Why? How could you train and develop these competencies?

CASE STUDY

Flextronics University – qualifying line managers for leadership and HRM tasks

Founded in 1969 and headquartered in Singapore, Flextronics (www.flextronics.com) is a leading Electronic Manufacturing Services (EMS) provider operating in 30 countries on three continents with a total workforce of about 162,000 employees and revenues in 2008 of US\$ 27.6 billion. The majority of its manufacturing capacity is located in low-cost regions such as Brazil, China, Hungary, India, Malaysia, Mexico, Poland and Ukraine. It offers the broadest worldwide EMS capabilities, from design resources to end-to-end vertically integrated global supply chain services. Flextronics operates in seven distinct markets: infrastructure (e.g. networking equipment; mobile communication devices); computing (e.g. handheld computers); consumer digital devices (e.g. cameras); industrial, semiconductor and white goods (e.g. plastics injection moulding); automotive, aerospace and marine (e.g. bar code

(Continued)

(Continued)

readers); and medical devices, which includes, among others, telemedicine devices. Flextronics designs, builds and ships complete packaged products for its original equipment manufacturer (OEM) customers such as Microsoft for consumer electronics products such as the X-box, Hewlett Packard for its inkjet printers and storage devices, or Sony-Ericsson for cellular phones, and provides after-market and field services to support customer end-to-end supply chain requirements.

In early 2000, Flextronics Central and Eastern European (CEE) operations were headquartered in Vienna, Austria, and covered primarily Austria and Hungary, with plans to expand into the Ukraine. The Austrian sites consisted of an experienced workforce and had well-functioning work routines. The newly established Hungarian plants, by contrast, were characterized by typical start-up problems such as insufficiently experienced personnel, high fluctuation and, because of a highly volatile sales market, significant needs to adapt production capacity to consumer demand. As part of the response to this situation, Peter Baumgartner, then CEE Executive HR Director, lobbied internally for a Flextronics Academy in the CEE region and finally implemented it. As an effort to increase qualifications of Flextronics CEE employees, it covered both technical qualifications as well as soft skills. Together with an external consultancy, Flextronics also developed a high-potential programme for a future cadre of line managers that specifically was designed to offer the selected individuals a broad range of activities and equip them with leadership and HRM qualifications. In the mixed groups from different countries, cultural specifics soon turned out to be important elements for the long-term success of this programme. For example, Hungarian participants were much less likely to fully complete the programme or stay with Flextronics for some time after the end of the programme. Due to a greater readiness to 'jump ship' even in the light of only minimal pay increases, Flextronics often was faced with a higher rate of fluctuation compared to Austrian employees and sunk costs when individuals left the company and joined a competitor or changed industry. Likewise, learning and communication styles were quite different between Hungarian and Austrian participants. For example, in terms of directness and interpersonal distance, typical differences between Austria and Hungary occur with Austrians being more direct and more concerned with formal and distant behaviour.

At the overall Flextronics level, training of line managers was strongly influenced by the introduction of the corporate-wide Flextronics University. Originally, this programme started as a web-based learning platform and knowledge-management tool for the US and Mexican operations. As e-learning got more and more popular, the idea to use this platform throughout the corporation took hold. The goal was to use the 'collective intelligence' of a global corporation in the most effective way. However, in practice the realization of this idea turned out to be much more time-consuming than was anticipated. It took off only after it was integrated with a second initiative within Flextronics: the Flex Factory. After a decade of rapid growth in the 1990s with a substantial number of acquisitions, factories within Flextronics varied widely in terms of production processes, quality standards and service orientation. After increasing customer complaints about Flextronics being not reliable enough, an initiative to create 'ONE Flextronics' started. It was aiming at standardizing production relevant processes to make the 'ONE Flextronics' idea effective in practice and visible to customers, suppliers and employees. Globally, various teams collected worldwide best practice ideas in the areas of SixSigma, quality and material management, production, programme management, engineering, finances and training. Soon it became obvious that a common platform was needed for sharing these ideas and for training individuals along these lines. This led to a new drive for the Flex University idea and to an integration of both Flex University and Flex Factory. Flex University offered the possibility to have immediate and global access to standardized training content, technical as well as related to leadership and HRM, which could be tailored to the needs of employees in general and line managers in particular. It offered a tailored system for training administration which included supervisors as well as users and a learning management system that allowed the definition of specific training packages.

In the context of a globally operating company with employees coming from 30 countries, a number of issues emerged due to cultural idiosyncrasies. For example, handing out certificates on the basis of a successfully accomplished training module led to quite different reactions. Whereas in Eastern European countries as well as in the US certificates are generally welcomed and regarded as a sign of one's achievement, many Western Europeans are more cautious. They see certificates not primarily as a positive feedback, but as an appraisal with the danger of being 'boxed in'. Employees from these countries prefer a sober, stripped down feedback without too many frills seen as artificial. Although Flex University worked with such certificates, the varying degree of acceptance of certification programmes across employees from different countries illustrated the emerging difficulties. In a similar vein, controlling learning progress in such a system can be interpreted as being

(Continued)

(Continued)

interested in a person's development and as a valuable source for feedback. At the same time, especially in Western Europe this was also regarded as a means of control, observation and surveillance that employees tend to see in a negative light.

Case study questions

1. What were the major cultural and institutional forces which Flextronics had to take into account in this situation?
2. What was the implicit underlying assumption about how HRM should be done – 'best practice' or 'best fit'? Why do you think that?
3. What differences would national cultural and institutional specifics make for a company intending to implement a similar solution in a country of your choice?
4. What influence will the emergence of ever more powerful information and communication technologies have on projects similar to the Flextronics' effort described above? Do you expect divergence, convergence or stasis? Why?

Further reading

Basics of comparative management

- Warner, M. (ed.) (2004) *Comparative Management.* London: Routledge.
  An edited volume offering access to the material that has shaped this field. It includes articles on principles and methods of comparative management, and a wide range of country-based studies, covering North America, Europe, Asia and the developing world. The topics range from leadership to HRM and contributions written by scholars from a great number of countries discuss the impact of cultural, institutional and societal variables across countries.

Comparative HRM

- Brewster, C. and Mayrhofer, W. (eds) (2012) *Handbook Of Research On Comparative Human Resource Management.* Cheltenham: Edward Elgar.
  This handbook provides a theoretical, practical and regional analysis of comparative HRM. It collects leading experts on each topic and from each region, explores the range of different approaches to conceptualizing HRM, and highlights HRM policy and practice that occur in the various regions of the world. As such, the volume

provides a challenge to the typical assumption that there are consistent problems in managing human resources around the globe that call for standardized solutions. Instead, the contributors emphasize the importance of institutional and cultural factors that make HRM a most context-sensitive management task.

- Parry, E., Stavrou, E. and Lazarova, M.B. (eds) (2013) *Global Trends in Human Resource Management*. Houndsmills and New York: Palgrave Macmillan.
  This edited volume looks at the demands of managing people in different national contexts and to develop HRM policies and practices that are appropriate for their specific location. These demands require an understanding of how HRM policies and practices may differ across countries and how the development of management practice may be affected by different institutional and cultural contexts. This volume, compiled of contributions from a range of well-respected HRM scholars worldwide, offers such an understanding and is based upon data from a unique research project, Cranet, that have been collected from more than 40 countries and over a period of 23 years.

- Boxall, P. (1995) 'Building the theory of comparative HRM', *Human Resource Management Journal*, 5(5): 5–17.
  This article outlines the basic requirements for building a theory of comparative HRM. It also argues that it is important to identify dominant models of HRM in each country, recognizing that there is significant variation both within and between nations. The article points towards the array of stakeholders that play a role when explaining HRM. While management in firms plays a critical role in shaping models of HRM, analyses must also take account of the impact of other actors such as state and labour.

- Brewster, C. (1995) 'Towards a "European" model of human resource management', *Journal of International Business Studies*, 26(1): 1–21.
  This article examines the concept of HRM from a European perspective and arguably is the starting point for an extensive discussion about regional models of HRM deviating from the 'generic' models provided by US authors. It builds on the criticism related to the US bias and goes beyond general critiques by addressing the core of the concept and proposing a more internationally applicable model. Drawing on data collected in Europe, the article analyses major characteristics of European HRM.

- Budhwar, P.S. (ed.) (2004) *Managing Human Resources in Asia-Pacific*. London: Routledge.
  This edited volume presents an HRM scenario in a number of South East Asian and Pacific Rim countries and highlights the growth of the personnel/HRM function in these countries, their dominant HRM system(s), along with the influence of different factors on their HRM and the challenges faced by HR functions in these nations.

- Budhwar, P.S. and Mellahi, K. (eds) (2006) *Managing Human Resources in the Middle-East*. London: Routledge.
  The edited volume presents the HRM scenario in a number of countries in the Middle East, highlighting rapid developments in the fields of HRM and IHRM and giving the reader an understanding of the dynamics of HRM in the area. The text moves from a general overview of HRM in the Middle East to an exploration of the current status, role and strategic importance of the HR function in a wide range of country-specific chapters, before highlighting the emerging HRM models and future challenges for research, policy and practice.

- Kamoche, K., Debrah, Y., Horwitz, F. and Muuka, G.N. (eds) (2003) *Managing Human Resources in Africa*. London: Routledge.
  This edited volume looks at the HRM challenges in countries right across Africa, examining the impact of contextual factors on the development of HRM practices in Africa. Taking a regional approach to the subject, and featuring chapters on South Africa, Botswana, Zambia, Mauritius, Tanzania, Kenya, Ethiopia, Ghana, Ivory Coast, Tunisia and Libya, this comprehensive study offers a fresh perspective on a growing subject area that shows readers not only how to develop techniques and practices that reflect the real needs of workers in Africa, but also provides a more balanced analysis of the area than they might be used to.

- Mayrhofer, W., Brewster, C., Morley, M. and Ledolter, J. (2011) 'Hearing a different drummer? Evidence of convergence in European HRM', *Human Resource Management Review*, 21(1): 50–67.
  This article explores the notion of convergence in managerial practice as a result of globalization. Focused on convergence at the national level, it offers a more nuanced exposition of convergence than has been evident in previous literature and draws upon a study that empirically analyses the development of HRM in larger private sector firms in 13 European countries between 1992 and 2004 to examine any evidence of HRM practices becoming more alike. The article finds considerable evidence of directional similarity – practices increasing or decreasing in the same way across the countries – but no evidence of final convergence – countries becoming more alike in the way they manage people.

Internet resources

- www.cranet.org. Cranetis a global academic network studying the development of HRM in more than 40 countries worldwide since 1990, and contains information about the network as well as a list of publications.
- www.epp.eurostat.ec.europa.eu. Eurostat, the statistical arm of the European Union, offers a wealth of data about various aspects relevant to HRM such as labour

market data, living conditions or population, information about economic data in general, e.g. gross domestic product (GDP) per capita or GDP growth as well as a number of EU policy indicators.

- www.ilo.org. The International Labour Organization (ILO) is a tripartite UN agency that brings together governments, employers and workers of its member states in common action to promote decent work throughout the world. It provides a number of statistics, e.g. official core labour statistics and estimates for over 200 countries since 1969, and databases such as Labordoc which contains references to a wide range of print and electronic publications, including journal articles, from countries around the world, on all aspects of work.
- www.worldvaluessurvey.com. World Values Survey investigating values and cultural changes in societies all over the world; allows access to the complete Values Studies results online and tailored analyses.

Self-assessment questions

Indicative answers to these questions can be found on the companion website at study.sagepub.com/harzing4e.

1. A multinational corporation is planning to implement a common set of performance management practices throughout its global subsidiaries. What advice would you offer to the HRM director of the firm in relation to this plan and why?
2. Show how the local environment influences a firm's approach to flexible working practices, taking the example of a country you know.
3. What would be the best way for multinational companies, operating across borders, to ensure that their human resource policies were applied equitably throughout the organization in order to generate company-wide thinking?
4. Compare and contrast the role of HRM departments in your country and one other you know about, critically appraising the impact on firm competitiveness.
5. Evaluate whether cross-cultural differences in HRM practices are increasing or decreasing and why. You may want to use examples to illustrate your argument.

References

Ajiferuke, M. and Boddewyn, J. (1970) '"Culture" and other explanatory variables in comparative management studies', *Academy of Management Journal*, 13: 153–163.

Almond, P., Edwards, T. and Clark, I. (2003) 'Multinationals and changing national business systems in Europe: towards the "shareholder value" model?', *Industrial Relations Journal*, 34(5): 430–445.

Amable, B. (2003) *The Diversity of Modern Capitalism*. Oxford: Oxford University Press.

Ashkenas, R., Ulrich, D., Jick, T. and Kerr, S. (1995) *The Boundaryless Organization: Breaking the Chains of Organizational Structure*. San Francisco: Jossey-Bass.

Barry, M. and Wilkinson, A. (eds) (2011) *Research Handbook of Comparative Employment Relations*. Northampton, MA: Edward Elgar.

Becker, B., Huselid, M., Pickus, P. and Spratt, M. (1997) 'HR as a source of shareholder value: research and recommendations', *Human Resource Management Journal*, 36(1): 39–47.

Becker, G.S. (1976) *The Economic Approach to Human Behavior*. Chicago, IL: University of Chicago Press.

Boxall, P. (1993) 'The significance of human resource management: a reconsideration of the evidence', *International Journal of Human Resource Management*, 4(3): 645–665.

Boxall, P. (1995) 'Building the theory of comparative HRM', *Human Resource Management Journal*, 5(5): 5–17.

Brandl, J., Reichel, A. and Mayrhofer, W. (2013) 'New captain but a sinking ship? The influence of HR director's gender on the status of the HR department – a longitudinal study', in E. Parry, E. Stavrou and M.B. Lazarova (eds), *Global Trends in Human Resource Management*. Houndsmills and New York: Palgrave Macmillan, pp. 35–53.

Brewster, C. (1999) 'Strategic human resource management: the value of different paradigms', *Management International Review*, 39(9): 45–64.

Brewster, C. (2004) 'European perspectives on human resource management', *Human Resource Management Review*, 14(4): 365–382.

Brewster, C., Brookes, M., Croucher, R. and Wood, G. (2007a) 'Collective and individual voice: convergence in Europe?', *International Journal of Human Resource Management*, 18 (7): 1246–1262.

Brewster, C., Brookes, M., Johnson, P. and Wood, G. (2014) 'Direct involvement, partnership and setting: a study in bounded diversity', *International Journal of Human Resource Management*, 25(6): 795–809.

Brewster, C., Larsen, H.H. and Mayrhofer, W. (1997) 'Integration and assignment: a paradox in human resource management', *Journal of International Management*, 3(1): 1–23.

Brewster, C., Mayrhofer, W. and Morley, M. (eds) (2000) *New Challenges in European Human Resource Management*. London: Macmillan.

Brewster, C., Mayrhofer, W. and Morley, M. (eds) (2004) *Human Resource Management in Europe. Evidence of Convergence?* Oxford: Elsevier/Butterworth-Heinemann.

Brewster, C., Sparrow, P. and Vernon, G. (2007c) *International Human Resource Management*, 2nd edn. London: Chartered Institute of Personnel and Development.

Brewster, C., Wood, G. and Brookes, M. (2008) Similarity, isomorphism or duality: recent survey evidence on the HRM policies of multinational corporations', *British Journal of Management*, 19 (4): 320–342.

Brewster, C., Wood, G., Brookes, M. and van Ommeren, J. (2006) 'What determines the size of the HR Function? A cross-national analysis', *Human Resource Management*, 45(1): 3–21.

Brewster, C., Wood., G., Croucher, R. and Brookes, M. (2007b) 'Are works councils and joint consultative committees a threat to trade unions? A comparative analysis', *Economic and Industrial Democracy*, 28 (1): 53–81.

Brunstein, I. (ed.) (1995) *Human Resource Management in Western Europe*. Berlin: de Gruyter.

Buddelmeyer, H., Mourre, G. and Ward-Warmedinger, M.E. (2005) 'Part-time work in EU countries: labour market mobility, entry and exit', IZA Discussion Paper No. 1550.

Budhwar, P.S. (ed.) (2004) *Managing Human Resources in Asia-Pacific*. London: Routledge.

Budhwar, P.S. and Debrah, Y.A. (eds) (2001) *Human Resource Management in Developing Countries*. London: Routledge.

Collins, C.J. and Clark, K.D. (2003) 'Strategic human resource practices, top management team social networkers, and firm performance: the role of human resource practices in creating organizational competitive advantage', *Academy of Management Journal*, 46(6): 740–751.

Cranet (2006) *Cranet Survey on Comparative Human Resource Management – International Executive Report 2005*. Cranfield, UK: Cranfield University.

Croucher, R., Wood, G., Brewster, C. and Brookes, M. (2012) 'Employee turnover, HRM and institutional contexts', *Economic and Industrial Democracy* 33(4): 605–620.

D'Aunno, T., Succi, M. and Alexander, J. (2000) 'The role of institutional and market forces in divergent organisational change', *Administrative Science Quarterly*, 45: 679–703.

Deephouse, D.L. (1999) 'To be different, or to be the same? It's a question (and theory) of strategic balance', *Strategic Management Journal*, 20(2): 147–166.

DiMaggio, P.J. and Powell, W.W. (1983) '"The iron cage revisited": institutional isomorphism and collective rationality in organizational fields', *American Sociological Review*, 48: 147–160.

Dowling, P.J. (1999) 'Completing the puzzle: issues in the development of the field of international human resource management', *Management International Review*, 39(4): 27–43.

Dunning, J.H. (1997) *Alliance Capitalism and Global Business*. London: Routledge.

Duysters, G. and Hagedoorn, J. (2001) 'Do company strategies and structures converge in global markets? Evidence from the computer industry', *Journal of International Business Studies*, 32(2): 347–356.

The Economist (2000) 'The world's view of multinationals', *The Economist*, 354 (29 January): 21–22.

Edwards, T. and Rees, C. (2006) *International Human Resource Management: Globalization, National Systems and Multinational Companies*. Harlow: Financial Times Prentice Hall.

European Commission Eurostat (2008) *Europe in Figures: Eurostat Yearbook 2008*. Luxembourg: Office for Official Publications of the European Communities.

Farndale, E., Brewster, C. and Poutsma, E. (2008) 'Co-ordinated vs liberal market HRM: the impact of institutionalisation on multinational firms', *International Journal of Human Resource Management*, 19(11): 2004–2023.

Ferner, A. (1997) 'Country of origin effects and HRM in multinational companies', *Human Resource Management Journal*, 7(1): 19–38.

Ferner, A. and Quintanilla, J. (1998) 'Multinationals, national business systems and HRM: the enduring influence of national identity or a process of "anglo-saxonisation"', *International Journal of Human Resource Management*, 9(4): 710–731.

Geppert, M., Williams, K. and Matten, D. (2003) 'The social construct of contextual rationalities in MNCs: and Anglo-German comparison of subsidiary choice', *Journal of Management Studies*, 40(3): 617–641.

Goergen, M., Brewster, C. and Wood, G. (2009) 'Corporate governance regimes and employment relations in Europe', *Relations industrielles/Industrial Relations*, 64(4): 620–640.

Goergen, M., Brewster, C., Wood, G.T. and Wilkinson, A. (2012) 'Varieties of capitalism and investments in human capital', *Industrial Relations*, 51(2): 501–527.

Gooderham, P.N. and Nordhaug, O. (2003) *International Management. Cross-Boundary Challenges*. Oxford: Blackwell.

Gooderham, P.N., Nordhaug, O. and Ringdal, K. (1999) 'Institutional and rational determinants of organizational practices: human resource management in European firms', *Administrative Science Quarterly*, 44: 507–531.

Hall, P.A. and Soskice, D. (eds) (2001) *Varieties of Capitalism: The Institutional Foundations of Comparative Advantage*. Oxford: Oxford University Press.

Hamel, G. and Prahalad, C.K. (1986) 'Do you really have a global strategy?', *Harvard Business Review* (July): 139–148.

Harzing, A.-W. and Sorge, A. (2003) 'The relative impact of country of origin and universal contingencies on internationalization strategies and corporate control in multinational enterprises: worldwide and European perspectives', *Organization Studies*, 24(2): 187–214.

Harzing, A.-W. and van Ruysseveldt, J. (2004) *International Human Resource Management*. London: Sage.

Hofstede, G. (1980) *Culture's Consequences: International Differences in Work-Related Values*. Newbury Park: Sage Publications.

Hofstede, G. (2001) *Culture's Consequences: Comparing Values, Behaviors, Institutions and Organizations Across Nations*. London: Sage.

Hollingsworth, J.R. and Boyer, R. (1997) 'Coordination of economic actors and social systems of production', in J.R. Hollingsworth and R. Boyer (eds), *Contemporary Capitalism*. Cambridge: Cambridge University Press, pp. 1–5.

House, R.J., Hanges, P.J., Javidan, M., Dorfman, P.W. and Gupta, V. (eds) (2004) *Culture, Leadership, and Organizations: The GLOBE Study of 62 Societies*. Thousand Oaks, CA: Sage.

Hu, Y.-S. (1992) 'Global or stateless corporations', *California Management Review*, 34(2): 107–126.

Huselid, M.A. (1995) 'The impact of human resource management practices on turnover, productivity, and corporate financial performance', *Academy of Management Journal*, 38(3): 635–672.

Jain, H., Lawler, J. and Morishima, M. (1998) 'Multinational corporations, human resource management and host-country nationals', *International Journal of Human Resource Management*, 9(4): 533–566.

Kamoche, K., Debrah, Y., Horwitz, F. and Muuka, G.N. (eds) (2003) *Managing Human Resources in Africa*. London: Routledge.

Kersley, B., Alpin, C., Forth, J., Bryson, A., Bewley, H., Dix, G. and Oxenbridge, S. (2006) *Inside the Workplace: Findings from the 2004 Workplace Employment Relations Survey*. London: Routledge.

Kim, Y. and Gray, S.J. (2005) 'Strategic factors influencing international human resource management practices: an empirical study of Australian multinational corporations', *International Journal of Human Resource Management*, 16(5): 809–830.

Kostova, T. and Roth, K. (2002) 'Adoption of an organizational practice by subsidiaries of multinational corporations: institutional and relational effects', *Academy of Management Journal*, 45(1): 215–233.

Laurent, A. (1986) 'The cross-cultural puzzle of international human resource management', *Human Resource Management*, 25(1): 91–102.

Legge, K. (1995) 'HRM: rhetoric, reality and hidden agendas', in J. Storey (ed.), *Human Resource Management: A Critical Text*. London: Routledge, pp. 33–59.

March, J.G. and Simon, H.A. (1993) *Organizations*, 2nd edn. Oxford: Blackwell.

Marsden, D. (1999) *A Theory of Employment Systems*. Oxford: Oxford University Press.

Maurice, M., Sellier, F. and Silvestre, J. (1986) *The Social Foundations of Industrial Power*. Cambridge, MA: MIT Press.

Mayrhofer, W. and Brewster, C. (2005) 'European human resource management: researching developments over time', *Management Revue*, 16(1): 36–62.

Mayrhofer, W. and Brewster, C. (2012) 'Comparative human resource management: an introduction', in C. Brewster and W. Mayrhofer (eds), *A Handbook of Research into Comparative Human Resource Management Practice*. Cheltenham: Edward Elgar, pp. 1–23.

Mayrhofer, W., Brewster, C. and Morley, M. (2000) 'Communication, consultation and the HRM debate', in C. Brewster, W. Mayrhofer and M. Morley (eds), *New Challenges for European Human Resource Management*. London: Macmillan, pp. 222–245.

Mayrhofer, W., Brewster, C., Morley, M. and Ledolter, J. (2011) 'Hearing a different drummer? Evidence of convergence in European HRM', *Human Resource Management Review*, 21(1): 50–67.

Mayrhofer, W., Morley, M. and Brewster, C. (2004) 'Convergence, stasis, or divergence?', in C. Brewster, W. Mayrhofer and M. Morley (eds), *Human Resource Management in Europe. Evidence of Convergence?* London: Elsevier/Butterworth–Heinemann, pp. 417–36.

Mayrhofer, W., Müller-Camen, M., Ledolter, J., Strunk, G. and Erten, C. (2002) 'The diffusion of management concepts in Europe – conceptual considerations and longitudinal analysis', *Journal of Cross-Cultural Competence and Management*, 3: 315–349.

McDonough, T. (2003) 'What does long wave theory have to contribute to the debate on globalization', *Review of Radical Political Economics*, 35(3): 280–286.

Meyer, J.W., Boli, J., Thomas, G.M. and Ramirez, F.O. (1997) 'World society and the nation-state', *The American Journal of Sociology*, 103(1): 144–181.

Morley, M. (ed.) (2009) *Managing Human Resources in Central and Eastern Europe*. London: Routledge.

Nienhüser, W. and Warhurst, C. (2012) 'Comparative employment relations: definitional, disciplinary and development issues', in C. Brewster and W. Mayrhofer (eds), *Handbook of Research on Comparative Human Resource Management*. Cheltenham, UK and Northampton, MA: Edward Elgar, pp. 211–238.

Ohmae, K. (1990) *The Borderless World*. New York: Harper Collins.

Ohmae, K. (1995) *The End of the Nation State: The Rise of Regional Economies*. New York: Free Press.

Paauwe, J. and Boselie, P. (2003) 'Challenging "strategic HRM" and the relevance of the institutional setting', *Human Resource Management Journal*, 13(3): 56–70.

Parker, B. (1998) *Globalization and Business Practice: Managing Across Boundaries*. London: Sage.

Parry, E., Stavrou, E. and Lazarova, M.B. (eds) (2013) *Global Trends in Human Resource Management*. Houndsmills and New York: Palgrave Macmillan.

Pfeffer, J. (1998) *The Human Equation: Building Profits by Putting People First*. Harvard: Harvard Business School Press.

Poole, M. (1990) 'Human resource management in an international perspective', *International Journal of Human Resource Management*, 1(1): 1–15.

Powell, W. and DiMaggio, P.J. (eds) (1987) *The New Institutionalism in Organizational Analysis*. Chicago: University of Chicago Press.

Pudelko, M. (2004) 'HRM in Japan and the West: what are the lessons to be learnt from each other?', *Asian Business and Management*, 3(3): 337–361.

Richbell, S., Brookes, M., Brewster, C. and Wood, G. (2011) 'Non-standard working time: an international and comparative analysis', *International Journal of Human Resource Management*, 22 (4): 945–962.

Romani, L. (2004) 'Culture in management: the measurement of differences', in A.-W. Harzing and J. van Ruysseveldt (eds), *International Human Resource Management*. London: Sage.

Rosenzweig, P.M. and Nohria, N. (1994) 'Influences on human resource development practices in multinational corporations', *Journal of International Business Studies*, 25(1): 229–251.

Rugman, A. (2005) *The Regional Multinationals: MNEs and 'Global' Strategic Management*. Cambridge: Cambridge University Press.

Scholz, C. and Böhm, H. (eds) (2008) *Human Resource Management in Europe: Comparative Analysis and Contextual Understanding*. London: Routledge.

Schwartz, S.H. (1992) 'Universals in the content and structure of values: theoretical advances and empirical tests in 20 countries', *Advances in Experimental Social Psychology*, 25: 1–65.

Schwartz, S.H. (2004) 'Mapping and interpreting cultural differences around the world', in H. Vinken, J. Soeters and P. Ester (eds), *Comparing Cultures, Dimensions of Culture in a Comparative Perspective*. Leiden: Brill, pp. 43–73.

Schwartz, S.H. (2010) 'Values: cultural and individual', in S.M. Breugelmans, A. Chasiotis and F.J.R. van de Vijver (eds), *Fundamental Questions in Cross-cultural Psychology*. Cambridge: Cambridge University Press, pp. 463–493.

Sera, K. (1992) 'Corporate globalization: a new trend', *Academy of Management Executive*, 6(1): 89–96.

Smith, C. and Meiksins, P. (1995) 'System, societal and dominance effects in cross-national organisational analysis', *Work, Employment and Society*, 9(2): 241–268.

Sorge, A. (2004) 'Cross-national differences in human resources and organization', in A.-W. Harzing and J. van Ruysseveldt (eds), *International Human Resource Management*. London: Sage, pp. 117–140.

Sparrow, P. and Brewster, C. (2009) *Global HRM in Practice*. London: Chartered Institute of Personnel and Development.

Sparrow, P.R., Brewster, C. and Harris, H. (2004) *Globalizing Human Resource Management*. London: Routledge.

Sparrow, P.R. and Hiltrop, J.-M. (1997) 'Redefining the field of European human resource management: a battle between national mindsets and forces of business transition?', *Human Resource Management*, 36(2): 201.

Spony, G. (2003) 'The development of a work–value model assessing the cumulative impact of individual and cultural differences on managers' work–value systems: empirical evidence from French and British managers', *International Journal of Human Resource Management*, 14 (4): 658–679.

Storey, J. (ed.) (2001) *Human Resource Management: A Critical Text*, 2nd edn. London: Thomson Learning.

Tregaskis, O. and Brewster, C. (2006) 'Converging or diverging? A comparative analysis of trends in contingent employment practice in Europe over a decade', *Journal of International Business Studies*, 37(1): 111–126.

Ulrich, D. (1989) 'Tie the corporate knot: gaining complete customer commitment', *Sloan Management Review*, 30(4): 19–28.

Ulrich, D. and Brockbank, W. (2005) *The HR Value Proposition*. Cambridge, MA: Harvard Business School Press.

UNCTAD (various years) *World Investment Report*. New York: United Nations.

UNCTAD (2007) *The Universe of the Largest Transnational Corporations*. New York and Geneva: United Nations.

US Department of Labor (1993) *High Performance Work Practices and Firm Performance*. Washington DC: US P.M. Wright, Government Printing Office.

Wächter, H., Peters, R., Tempel, A. and Müller-Camen, M. (2003) *The 'Country-of-Origin-Effect' in Cross-national Management of Human Resources*. München, Mering: Hampp.

Welzel, C. and Inglehart, R. (2005) *Modernization, Cultural Change, and Democracy*. New York: Cambridge University Press.

Whitley, R. (1999) *Divergent Capitalisms: The Social Structuring and Change of Business Systems*. Oxford: Oxford University Press.

Woywode, M. (2002) 'Global management concepts and local adaptations: working groups in the French and German manufacturing industry', *Organization Studies*, 23(4): 497–524.

Yip, G.S. (1995) *Total Global Strategy*. Englewood Cliffs, NJ: Prentice-Hall.

Zanko, M. (ed.) (2002) *The Handbook of Human Resource Management Policies and Practices in Asia-Pacific Economies – Volume 1*. Cheltenham: Edward Elgar.

Zanko, M. and Ngui, M. (eds) (2003) *The Handbook of Human Resource Management Policies and Practices in Asia-Pacific Economies – Volume 2*. Cheltenham: Edward Elgar.

The Transfer of Employment Practices across Borders in Multinational Companies

3

Tony Edwards

Contents

Learning objectives

After reading this chapter you will be able to:

- Appreciate how employment practices are embedded in distinctive national contexts
- Understand the different theoretical perspectives concerning why multinationals transfer practices across borders
- Evaluate the competing influences on the inclination and ability of multinationals to engage in transfer
- Explore the process of transfer in practice through studying case studies

Chapter outline

This chapter addresses the issue of how multinational companies transfer expertise that was developed in one country to their international operations. It explores why multinationals seek to do this and develops a framework of four key influences that can help to analyse transfer practices.

1 Introduction

One of the key distinguishing features of multinational companies is that they have the capacity to implement expertise in their operations in one country that was developed in those in another. One element of this is the transfer of employment practices across borders. This capacity can be seen as a potential source of higher efficiency in MNCs compared with firms based solely at the national level. However, many of those who work for MNCs, including some managers, may see the transfer of practices as a challenge since the process can cause a shift away from practices accepted in their country. Employee representatives, in particular, might see their interests as being threatened and attempt to block the introduction of practices originating from elsewhere. Thus the process of transfer can be contested, even subverted in some cases, and may also create fraught relations between different organizational groups.

The problematic nature of transfer of employment practices arises in part from the way in which they are 'embedded' in distinctive national contexts. Employment practices, like any other social custom, are strongly influenced by the context in which they operate. The political system and the dominant political traditions within it shape several key aspects of employment relations, notably the strength of organized labour and the nature of employment regulations. The legal system, itself partly the product of the political system, not only constrains the range of options open to management when devising procedures in areas such as employee representation, but also plays a part in conditioning the expectations of organizational actors. Related to this, the nature of key institutions in the labour market also limits the options available to management in employment relations and further contributes towards the creation of a set of norms and values. The existence of a set of values concerning work and organizations – often referred to as culture – is the most commonly cited source of national distinctiveness in employment relations (e.g. Tayeb, 1996; Schuler and Rogovsky, 1998). The dominant values in societies emerge from specific political, legal and institutional contexts and these contexts and values are central to the character of the employment relationship. Since context and the values differ markedly from country to country, transferring practices across diverse social systems is bound to be complicated.

In this chapter we tackle several of the key aspects of the transfer of employment practices within MNCs. An initial question is that given that such practices are embedded in particular national contexts, why do many MNCs seek to transfer practices to quite different national contexts? Three broad explanations of MNCs' motives to transfer employment practice are reviewed and the strengths and weaknesses of each are assessed. Identification of the weaknesses implies the need for a more integrated approach which can explain a number of aspects of the transfer of employment practices, such as the likely geographical origins of the practices that are transferred, variations between MNCs in the extent of transfer, and the likely nature of the relations between different groups within MNCs in the transfer process. To this end, the fourth approach elaborated here consists of an integrative framework of four key influences. The chapter concludes by examining the consequences of the transfer of practices for national systems, addressing in particular whether it contributes to the convergence of these systems.

2 Why transfer employment practices?

The complications involved in the transfer of employment practices raises a key management question: why do many senior managers look to engage in such transfer at all? Why do they not simply take a highly decentralized approach, allowing actors in the various countries in which the firm has subsidiaries to determine the type of employment practices that are compatible with the particular national context? Some do, of course, seeing the pressures of 'multi-culturalism' (Ghoshal and Bartlett, 1998) as significant enough to warrant a hands-off approach to employment practice from senior management. This nationally responsive style was termed 'polycentric' by Perlmutter (1969) more than 30 years ago. Perlmutter (1969: 13) argued that the polycentric style recognizes that 'since people are different in each country, standards for performance, incentives and training methods must be different'. Indeed, some writers have argued that these pressures to adapt, often referred to as 'host country effects', are significant and arise from the necessity of going with the grain of the rules and norms in the various host countries in which the firm operates. Over-riding local norms entails significant costs, even for large internationalized firms. These costs can be tangible in the form of penalties for contravening laws and regulations, but more commonly they are intangible in the form of losing the goodwill of local actors, for example, a widely cited survey study (Rosenzweig and Nohria, 1994) on foreign-owned affiliates in the US found that HR practices in these workplaces 'tend to resemble local practices' (1994: 248) in the US and that 'adherence to local practices is the dominant influence' (1994: 250). This is also in evidence in Gamble's (2003) study of a British retail firm in China in which he argued that local institutions and cultural features of the host environment offered a better explanation of the nature of employment practices than did a focus on the country of origin. A further example is Lunnan et al.'s (2005) study of a Norwegian MNC in which they revealed the range of ways in which local factors inform the operation of global policy.

Three broad categories of explanation – *market, cultural* and *political* – have been used to explain the attractiveness of transfer (Edwards et al., 2007b). The first, known as the 'market-based' approach, sees the transfer of employment practices as a potential source of enhanced efficiency. For many writers on HRM in MNCs, the strength of competition in the global product markets that multinationals tend to inhabit means that a firm is missing opportunities to enhance its own efficiency if it does not engage in the sharing of 'best practice'. One particularly influential book about the multinational company that emphasizes the power of market forces is Ghoshal and Bartlett's (1998) *Managing Across Borders*. The authors argue that the mature stage of evolution for a firm which spans many different countries is the 'transnational' form, which is based on an 'integrated network' of plants sharing expertise and knowledge with each other. The transfer of employment practices is a central part of such a firm. The authors go so far as to claim that 'in the future, a company's ability to develop a transnational organizational capability will be the key factor that separates the winners from the mere survivors in the international competitive environment' (1998: 299). Some models of IHRM exhibit a strong element conceptualizing how MNCs respond to market pressures. For example, a key element of the 'resource-based' model of IHRM developed by Taylor et al. (1996) is the idea of 'organizational competencies' and how MNCs can enhance their competitive position by transferring these competencies across their operations. Some empirical studies of MNCs also exhibit assumptions based on the market-based approach. Schmitt and Sadowski's (2003) study of MNCs in Germany, for instance, emphasized the influence of commercial imperatives on transfer arguing that a 'rationalistic cost-minimization' approach is well equipped to explain the transfer of practices across borders.

The contribution of this approach stems from the recognition of the potential advantages that can arise from transferring employment practices, especially to senior management, owners and shareholders. However, the market-based approach risks downplaying the contested nature of transfer. The balance between adopting policies that are both globally integrated and locally sensitive tends to be portrayed as a technical matter, on which senior managers simply need to make a reasoned decision.

Where some recognition is given to the possibility that there will be differences of viewpoints on the desirability of transferring practices, as in Ghoshal and Bartlett's (1998) work, senior managers are seen as having the capacity to resolve any problems through communication, persuasion and creating an appropriate 'management mentality'. However, as a range of studies of MNCs has revealed, the process of transfer across borders is an intensely political process, in which a number of organizational actors have some influence. Belanger et al.'s (1999) study of ABB, a company cited by Ghoshal and Bartlett themselves as a 'classic transnational organization', emphasizes the political nature of transfer. Belanger and his colleagues argued that Ghoshal and Bartlett's account of ABB downplays the tensions between groups that are a key feature of organizational life in multinational companies, and demonstrated in their research that international coordination is strongly contested within the firm. A further illustration of the potential for conflict is evident in Kristensen and Zeitlin's (2005) longitudinal study of the British multinational APV in which they likened the firm to a 'battleground' between different factions.

The 'cultural' approach is the second form of explanation for why MNCs transfer practices across their sites in different countries. Many argue that the transfer of practices is not so much a process governed by the forces of competition as one shaped by the legacy of national and corporate cultures. That is, the incentives that MNCs have to develop a global approach must be balanced against the requirements to be sensitive to local conditions. This is evident in some of the research concerned with the transfer of Japanese employment practices in MNCs from Japan as they expanded into Europe and North America during the 1980s and 1990s. Abo (1994), for example, saw the dilemma facing senior managers in Japanese firms concerning the management of employment relations in their foreign subsidiaries as essentially a trade-off between the competitive pressure to utilize those practices that formed a part of successful production at home on the one hand, and the need to adapt to the exigencies of local conditions on the other.

Writers adopting the cultural approach commonly draw on Hofstede's (2001) much cited work, originally published in 1980 with updated versions, in which he distinguished four and later five dimensions along which national cultures differ. The culturalist approach raises two important points concerning the transfer of practices. First, it provides an explanation, albeit partial, for why MNCs must adapt their desired practices to local conditions rather than implement common practices across their operations. Hofstede's own study of IBM showed that even in a company with a strong company culture, there were marked variations in employee values at the local level. Second, an extension of this idea is that national cultures influence MNCs' behaviour by encouraging them to take aspects of national culture with them when they go abroad. In other words, their corporate culture is informed by the national culture in the country of origin. Thus some researchers have sought to explain the transfer of home country practices to foreign subsidiaries through this cultural lens (e.g. Ngo et al., 1998).

The value of this approach is in recognizing that transfer is more than just a question of competition and rationality. Rather, national cultures differ and their distinguishing characteristics endure. This argument though has a number of problems. The key shortcoming arises from heavy reliance on the small number of available typologies in the literature on culture – primarily Hofstede's but also Trompenaars and Hampden-Turner (1994) – which means these studies are open to the same criticisms as the original works themselves. In particular, these typologies tend to fail to locate cultural values in a convincing social context. As noted above, dominant values and attitudes in a society emerge in a specific political, legal and institutional environment, yet the culturalist approach fails to acknowledge the full force of these contextual and institutional influences. Moreover, while the culturalist approach says something about how tensions can arise during the process of transfer, it says little about how political activity is played out within organizations and this is worthy of consideration in its own right.

The third approach, which can be termed the 'political' approach, is one that looks at the way that actors in organizations can be willing to engage in the process of transfer as a way of gaining legitimacy and advancing their own interests. A range of actors can seek to protect or advance their own positions by initiating or engaging in the transfer of practices. For example, those at the HQ may look to raise their status within the organization by portraying themselves as key agents in controlling the transfer of practices. For those in senior positions in firms producing a component or providing a service to other organizations, ensuring that their operational units and subsidiaries are sharing practices with one another may also assist senior managers in their quest to obtain legitimacy – and consequently orders – from potential customers, since creating an image of a networked 'transnational' is likely to be viewed favourably by potential customers. Those in key managerial positions in the subsidiaries may be keen to engage in sharing practices with their counterparts in order to portray themselves as key contributors to the MNC's networks. Acting as 'good corporate citizens' in this way may be a way of advancing an individual's claims for promotion or for a pay rise (Edwards, 1998). Others who work in the subsidiaries of MNCs, particularly employees and their representatives, may be willing to comply with transferring practices if they fear that failing to cooperate will result in their unit being less likely to receive future investment from the HQ. In contrast, as we noted at the outset, some actors may seek to block diffusion if they perceive it as challenging their interests (see Broad, 1994, for a case study of a Japanese transplant in the UK). Hence, diffusion is a contested and political process (Dorrenbacher and Geppert, 2011).

A key contribution of this approach is to recognize that the motivation that organizational actors have to engage in the transfer of practices is more than just a rational assessment of the potential gains to the organization as a whole. However, the focus on the micro-politics of the organization on its own does not tell us much about the influence of the wider 'national business systems' which MNCs transcend and, consequently, is not particularly revealing in generating an understanding of where the imperative to transfer practices comes from, nor does it tell us much about constraints on transfer that are external to the firm.

These three approaches (market, cultural and political) each make a contribution to understanding the transfer of practices across borders, but on their own each of these offers only a partial understanding. What is required is an integrated approach which does three things: first, it should recognize the competitive pressures on firms in international markets and the commercial interests in transferring practices (the market-based approach); second, it should analyse the influence of contexts and institutions as well as cultures in shaping the behaviour of MNCs (an amended version of the cultural approach); and, third, it should examine the role of organizational actors in initiating, engaging in or obstructing the transfer of practices (the political approach). This integrated approach, which is based on four sets of influences, is explained in the next section.

3 The four influences framework

The framework outlined here consists of four key influences – *country of origin, dominance, international integration* and *host country* – on the nature and form of the transfer of practices across borders. The influences arise from the combination of, first, the differences between national business systems and, second, the growing internationalization of economic activity. In some cases the impact of the particular influences is contrary to those of others, creating a tension; in others, however, the impact is for one influence to reinforce another. Each of the four influences is now considered in turn.

Country of origin effect

The first influence is an enduring 'country of origin' effect in MNCs. This is where the country in which the multinational originates creates a distinctive national effect on management style in general and on the nature of employment practices in particular. A range of sources indicates that even the largest MNCs retain strong roots in their home country (Ferner, 1997). Ruigrok and van Tulder (1995: 168), for instance, examined the geographical distribution of the operations of the biggest 100 MNCs in the world (ranked by foreign assets) and concluded that 'not one of these can be dubbed truly global, footloose or borderless'. Analysis of data from the United Nation's *World Investment Report* (2012) suggests that there have been some changes in this respect since Ruigrok and van Tulder's study was published but that the links with the home country remain strong. The Transnationality Index, which condenses the ratios of foreign assets to total assets, foreign sales to total sales and foreign employment to total employment into one ratio, shows that on average close to 40 per cent of the operations of the largest 100 MNCs are located in the home base. While there are some MNCs which have a high degree of global spread – mainly those originally based in small countries such as Nestlé and those formed through a string of mergers and acquisitions such as Vodafone – many of the largest MNCs still have well over half of their operations in their home country. This is true for some of the largest firms including by employment, such as Wal-Mart and Hitachi.

The influence of the home country over an MNC stems not just from the concentration of assets, sales and employment but also from other ways in which MNCs are 'embedded' in the country of origin. One such source of a country of origin effect is the dominance of home country nationals in senior managerial positions. The CEO of the vast majority of MNCs is a citizen of the original country of the firm, while the management boards are disproportionately filled with home country nationals. The significance of the effect of country of origin lies in the way that the managerial traditions of the country of origin shape the nature of key decisions. Another source of the country of origin effect relates to the way that firms are financed and governed. We know that financial systems differ markedly and that MNCs retain close links with banks, stock markets and other financial institutions at home (Doremus et al., 1998). For example, the fluid and arm's length relationship between shareholders and management in Britain and the USA contrasts with the stable and close relationship between the two groups in Germany (O'Sullivan, 2000). The consequence of this is that the differing pressures on firms that the divergent financial systems create are carried over to the international level in MNCs. A further source of the country of origin effect is the concentration of key activities in the home base. In particular, research and development (R&D) activities tend to be concentrated in the home country and since national innovation systems differ this will lead to differences by nationality in the nature of innovations found in MNCs.

There is considerable evidence of the way in which the 'institutional configurations' (Hall and Soskice, 2001) in the country of origin of MNCs influence the style the firm adopts in managing its international workforce. For instance, the primacy of the rights of shareholders in the financial system in the USA and the hostility of management to trade unions have created a clear orientation at the international level towards shareholder interests and a related hostility to unions among US-owned MNCs (Almond and Ferner, 2006). Also, US-owned firms adopt a more centralized mode of decision making on HR issues, reflecting the extension of domestic structures of control to the international level (Ferner et al., 2013). In contrast, other evidence testifies to the link between the way that the German system of corporate governance accords rights to a range of 'stakeholders' and the more consultative management style and pragmatic approach to dealing with unions in German MNCs (Ferner and Varul, 1999). Crucially, the influence of the country of origin also arises in the preferences of MNCs of different nationalities for particular employment practices. Many Japanese MNCs in the 1980s and 1990s, for example, made strenuous attempts to transfer the practices associated with 'lean production', such as team-working, functional flexibility and 'single status' (e.g. Oliver and Wilkinson, 1992). American MNCs, on the other hand, appear to have transferred 'human resource management' practices, such as performance-related pay (PRP) and forms of direct communication, to their foreign subsidiaries (Muller, 1998). In the conclusion to a major survey of employment practice in Britain, Edwards et al. (2007a) noted the 'persistent influence of nationality' and argued that the data confirm 'that national ways of doing things continue to inform the behaviour of multinationals in the world economy' (2007a: 100).

In terms of relations between different groups of organizational actors, the logic of the strength of the country of origin effect is that actors in and from the home country are likely to be key players in the transfer of practices. Thus transfer is characterized by a strong authority flow from the centre to the subsidiaries in different countries. Actors in the subsidiaries may adopt a variety of approaches in responding to this central influence: some may be very willing to learn from the parent company and implement the practices enthusiastically; others may question the appropriateness of 'foreign' practices being transferred but grudgingly accept that they should go along with the demands of the HQ; while others may seek to resist the transfer altogether or insist on practices being adapted. Thus the focus on the role of the country of origin is also revealing in understanding the political nature of transfer.

The nature of the country of origin effect evolves over time. It tends to reduce in significance as a firm engages in international expansion, such as in the case of a cross-border merger which significantly extends the global reach of a firm. Moreover, many actors in MNCs, including some at the HQ, will not see a strong influence from the home country as necessarily advantageous for the firm and, consequently, may look outside the country of origin for 'best practice'. In other words, MNCs do not possess a fixed and rigid national identity which imposes a straightjacket on organizational actors; rather, country of origin shapes and constrains the actions of these actors but leaves scope for them to draw on practices operating in other countries.

Dominance effects

Given that actors have scope to observe and implement practices from countries other than the country of origin, what influences how they go about this process? A key factor in this respect is their perceptions of the strengths and weaknesses of economic performance across countries. Strong performance in one country gives rise to interest from firms in other countries in 'borrowing' elements of that business system. Smith and Meiskins (1995: 255–256) argue that the hierarchy of economies within the international system gives rise to 'dominance effects'; at any one time, they argue, countries 'in dominant positions have frequently evolved methods of organizing production or the division of labour which have invited emulation and interest'. In terms of the impact on the transfer of employment practices, the logic of the dominance effects argument is that such transfer is not solely created by the legacy and force of institutions, but is also shaped by competitive pressures at the international level.

For much of the post-war period it was the American economy which appeared to be the most influential. In a context of US political hegemony and with industry in the USA emerging from the war relatively unscathed compared to its counterparts elsewhere, the American business system exerted a significant, albeit contested, influence over the form of restructuring in Europe and Japan (Djelic, 1998). During the 1980s and early 1990s, however, the Japanese economy was widely perceived to be the dominant power, and writers and practitioners alike referred to the Japanese model in general, and lean production in particular, as providing the solutions to common organizational problems. Towards the end of the twentieth century and into the twenty-first, however, the prolonged stagnation in Japan and the resurgence of the US economy have arguably led to a renewal of the influence of the American business system.

In its simplest form the concept of dominance is open to a number of lines of criticism. First, it rests on an assumption that there exist marked differences in rates of economic growth between the major developed economies; in fact, these differences are not so great as often is assumed. For instance, while the 1970s and 1980s was seen as a period of economic decline by many in the US, the growth rate of the American economy was actually higher than that in Germany, Sweden and the UK. Only compared with the Japanese economy was there a marked difference and even this was less significant than is often supposed (see, for example, Hall and Soskice, 2001). Second, even where there are significant differences in economic performance between countries, only a part of these differences can be explained by divergences in forms of economic organization. Some of the explanation lies in the process of 'convergence and catch-up'. Very rapid economic growth in an economy is often due in large part to recovery from an adverse shock or the more intensive use of existing resources rather than the result of key features of the national business system. It is widely accepted that this factor explains part of the rapid rates of economic growth found in the so-called 'Asian Tiger' economies prior to 1997. Third, the notion of dominance might imply that a national business system is characterized by a homogeneous set of structures and practices that operate across firms, and that companies in other countries can identify and seek to emulate these. This is, of course, not the case; all national business systems are characterized by a degree of intra-national variety.

Despite these criticisms, the concept of dominance retains some utility. When thought of as an approximate measure of management ideology and the way that the perceptions of actors create a dynamic for change and diffusion, it adds to the understanding of the process of transfer. Indeed, Pudelko and Harzing (2007) demonstrate that dominance effects are of great importance in how MNCs manage their international workforces. As they put it, they came to 'the surprising conclusion that a function (HR) generally considered to be the most local of business functions shows very strong signs of converging to a dominant model, regardless of the home or host countries involved' (2007: 536). Paul Edwards and colleagues also found some evidence of dominance effects in their study of MNCs in four countries (Edwards et al., 2013a).

Actors within MNCs can perceive the diversity of employment practices that they experience across national systems as an opportunity to advance the competitive position either of the firm as a whole in relation to other firms, or of the unit in which they work in relation to other units and subsidiaries within the firm. Actors can utilize the notion of dominance to advance their own positions within a firm. For instance, managers in the American operations of European MNCs may use their knowledge and familiarity with the current dominant business system to develop an international role within the firm. In other words, dominance effects also shape the politics of transfer.

Part of the idea of dominance effects is that the flow of practices can arise from different places and is not solely from the home country to the firm's operations in other countries. As we saw in the previous sub-section, there certainly is evidence of the country of origin effect leading to transfer occurring in this direction, and we might expect this to be most common in MNCs from a dominant country since the two effects reinforce one another. However, in the case of MNCs from a developing economy, or a developed economy which has been performing poorly, dominance effects will challenge the country of origin effect. The possible result is that practices that are transferred across a multinational may originate in the foreign subsidiaries. Indeed, there is a growing body of evidence that such 'reverse' transfer does occur and that it is shaped by the notion of dominance (Edwards and Ferner, 2004). The case study illustrates this process, and demonstrates the dynamic and competing influence of the country of origin effect and dominance effects.

International integration

The third element to the framework concerns the extent to which MNCs are internationally integrated, defined as the generation of inter-unit linkages across borders. A number of recent developments have created scope for MNCs to build stronger linkages between their international operations. In relation to product markets, differences in consumer tastes appear to have narrowed – a process in which the advertising and marketing strategies of MNCs themselves have contributed – while there has also been a trend towards de-regulation of many markets, making it easier for firms to realize synergistic linkages between their subsidiaries.

Coupled with these changes, improvements in communications and transportation have facilitated international coordination and many MNCs have strengthened inter-unit linkages by developing new structures for their international operations (Edwards et al., 2013b). Typically, they have moved away from country-based structures towards organizing themselves around global divisions or regional blocks, so that comparable operations are linked together. The survey of MNCs in Britain by Edwards et al. (2007a) found that 'relatively few are characterized by a straightforward hierarchical relationship between HQ and operating units. Instead, in most MNCs there are intermediate levels within complex, multi-layered corporate structures' (2007a: vi). Indeed, among those MNCs that had multiple dimensions to how they were organized, only 4 per cent identified the 'national subsidiary' as the most important aspect of the structure. For example, IBM's operations are not structured along the lines of the various countries in which the firm operates, such as IBM China or IBM Canada; rather they are organized into both global divisions, such as software and services, and regional blocks, such as Europe, Middle East and Africa (EMEA) and North America.

The replacement of country-based structures with these types of international management structures appears to have been most developed within Europe. The process of European integration has created a product market which is largely free from formal barriers to trade, while aspects of the regulation of other issues, such as competition, industrial and social policies, have also become harmonized. Perhaps most significantly, the single currency has increased the transparency of costs and prices across Europe and created a large Euro capital market. Thus Marginson (2000: 11) has argued that Europe is 'an economic, political and regulatory space whose character and dynamic is distinctive when set against wider, global, developments or those in the other two "triad" regions'. Consequently, many MNCs have created an influential European aspect to the structure, with the potential to develop Europe-wide policies in HRM.

The developments described above in relation to markets are uneven, however, and many sectors remain localized in that they are strongly influenced by nationally distinct tastes or regulations. Commonly, these sectors are ones in which MNCs are generally absent, such as the provision of personal care and hairdressing. In some other sectors which are still influenced by national tastes or regulations, MNCs are present but tend to adopt management structures based around the countries in which they operate, and there are few inter-linkages between their operations. Examples are electricity provision, auditing and retail banking. In contrast, the scope for achieving a high degree of international integration is much stronger in sectors like textiles, automotive, IT services and investment banking, where units are strongly integrated with their counterparts in other countries.

This integration can take various forms, each of which has important implications for employment relations. International integration can take the form of the *outsourcing* of operations across countries, with those in one country providing components or services to those in another. Examples of international integration through outsourcing are the producers of branded sports and fashion wear which subcontract production to nominally independent, but in fact closely controlled, firms mainly in South East Asia. These arrangements, through which production is both internationalized and externalized, are often referred to as 'global value chains' (Gereffi et al., 2005). A different form of integration is for MNCs to keep production or service provision in-house but to use *segmentation* in which the roles of operations within the multinational in different countries are quite distinct from one another. Survey evidence shows that around 80 per cent of MNCs conduct some form of cross-border trade within the firm (Edwards et al., 2013b). For instance, Wilkinson et al. (2001)

showed how Japanese electronics manufacturers use segmentation as a production strategy within Asia, retaining high value-added functions such as design and testing in Japan and locating low value-added functions such as assembly in countries such as Malaysia. In this scenario, the various units across the world are performing quite distinct functions, leading to variations in the type of HR practices that the firm deploys and there is little incentive for such firms to transfer practices across their sites. International integration can also take the form of the *standardization* of operations, with the units in different countries carrying out very similar activities. Examples of sectors in which this is the case are heavy engineering, pharmaceuticals production, some food manufacturing, auditing and fast-food, which have developed increasingly standardized products and, relatedly, similar production or service provision techniques but where there are technical or market factors that prevent the firms from servicing standard markets through exporting. Given that the operations in different countries have important similarities, there is considerable scope for such firms to transfer practices across borders (Edwards and Zhang, 2008).

In sum, the pressures to achieve international integration reflect the nature of competition and the structure of operations in particular sectors. We have seen that the scope for transfer is constrained in MNCs which operate in sectors that are characterized by nationally specific tastes or regulations. Moreover, in MNCs which have outsourced or segmented their international operations, there will be little incentive to transfer practices across borders. In contrast, in those sectors in which MNCs have developed standardized operations the transfer of employment practices is likely to be more feasible and thus attractive to management. It is in such 'standardized' MNCs in which the forces of the country of origin and of dominance will be felt most acutely, whereas sectors constrained by national differences and those in which MNCs have developed 'segmented' international operations the influence of the country of origin and of dominance is likely to be more muted. The strength of these forces though is not determined exclusively by the extent and form of international integration, but also by the characteristics of the various host country employment systems in which MNCs operate.

Host country effects

There are a number of aspects of a national business system which can limit the scope a multinational has to transfer practices. The system of employment law to a greater or lesser degree poses constraints on employers implementing practices in the workplace. Moreover, the nature of key labour market institutions, such as unions and works councils, presents similar limitations, both directly through affecting the form of employee representation, and indirectly through the impact these institutions are able to exert on other areas of employment relations. There are also cultural barriers to transferring practices to host environments. Broad's (1994) study of a Japanese transplant in the UK, for instance, found that the parent company's insistence that the plant operate the system termed 'High Involvement Management' clashed with the expectations of British managers who were not used to devolving responsibility for operating decisions to shop-floor workers. Similarly, the policy in many US MNCs of insisting that managers across countries adopt a 'forced distribution' in appraisals and ensure that negative consequences, such as a pay freeze or even dismissal, follow for those in the bottom category has been subjected to resistance by some managers who feel that such an approach clashes with the expectations of local workforces (Edwards et al., 2007b). This illustrates the way in which the institutional and cultural features of national business systems constrain the scope for transfer, and the way in which actors in host countries may be able to block transfer when they see it as challenging their culture and interests.

In other cases, however, the constraints may be only partial. A practice may be adapted to fit the new national business system as it is transferred. In this way, a particular practice 'may not operate in the same fashion in the recipient as in the donor unit but, rather, may undergo *transmutation* as actors in the recipient seek to adapt it to pre-existing models of behaviour, assumptions and power relations' (Edwards and Ferner, 2004: 64). One example is the adoption by many US MNCs of Japanese-style lean production. These practices have been implemented in a distinctive system of employment relations, involving a reliance on the external labour market and a pronounced hierarchy within work organization. Maccoby (1997: 165) argues that US companies have concentrated on the use of lean production to eliminate waste and defects, and downplayed the Toyota-style emphasis on the creation of 'trust' and facilitating 'learning'.

While the peculiarities of the host business systems may exercise constraints on transfer, be they absolute or partial, these constraints will often be malleable to the influence of large MNCs. By appearing to be globally mobile rather than dependent on a particular set of geographical operations, senior managers in large MNCs can pressurize governments to relax regulations and pressurize unions into making concessions during collective bargaining. Accordingly, Muller's (1998) study of American and British MNCs in Germany found that a significant number had opted out of the systems of sector-wide collective bargaining and vocational training. In this way, actors in the HQ may be able to break down resistance to transfer from those at national or plant level. Indeed, some writers have argued that local constraints are weaker than is commonly perceived, with MNCs in a strong position to over-ride them where they endeavour to do so (Kostova et al., 2008).

However, the role of host country effects in the transfer of practices is not simply a matter of managers at HQ trying to break down resistance. To operate effectively, a particular practice may be dependent on workers possessing a high level of skills and knowledge. In the absence of these, organizational actors may lack the ability to operate the practice in question. In this case, the host country is not 'receptive' to transfer, but this lack of receptiveness is not due to any opposition. An example of this is the implementation by Japanese MNCs of amended versions of lean production in Brazil;

the amendments reduced the requirements for workers to rotate across a range of tasks since the Brazilian workers tended to lack the breadth of skills necessary for this form of flexible working (Humphrey, 1995).

When resistance to transfer occurs it will not necessarily be confined to the implementation of practices. Resistance can also appear at an earlier stage, namely during the search for practices that have the potential to be diffused. Where those at the HQ set up mechanisms designed to identify practices in one part of the firm that can be implemented in another, and combine this with establishing competitive relations between different units, actors at plant level may be reluctant to share their expertise with their counterparts for fear of undermining their performance within the group. Instead of letting other plants which are their internal competitors use the practices they have developed, some will prefer to keep to themselves specific practices they perceive give them an advantage. In doing so, they may also draw on the peculiarities of the national business system concerned to obfuscate the nature of employment practice in their plant.

Thus since the transfer of practices entails the crossing of 'institutional divides' (Morgan et al., 2001), the process of transfer is evidently a highly political one. Actors at the centre of MNCs may find that the distinctiveness of host country systems of employment relations present constraints to the transfer of practices, although these will sometimes be malleable. Actors at subsidiary level, on the other hand, may be able to use host country distinctiveness to block either the implementation of practices or the initial search for them. The way in which the features of host countries complicate MNCs' initiatives to achieve international integration is clearly demonstrated in the case study of General Motors in Spain.

4 Summary and conclusions

The framework set out in this chapter provides a mechanism with which to analyse the transfer of employment practices across borders within MNCs. This approach based on the framework of 'four key influences' has sought to integrate elements of the three approaches outlined at the beginning of the chapter. It recognizes the strength of the competitive pressures on MNCs to engage in transferring practices across their operations. In particular, the notion of 'dominance' and the extent of the pressures for firms to achieve international integration capture this dynamic. The four influences framework also attaches great significance to the institutional and cultural aspects of national business systems in shaping and constraining the nature of transfer. The legacy of institutions shows up most clearly in the concepts of country of origin and host country effects. Moreover, the framework accords importance to the political nature of transfer by recognizing the way in which organizational actors can use a range of resources – relating for example to 'dominant' ideas in the international economy or to characteristics of the particular systems in which they are located – to initiate, engage in or obstruct the process of transfer. Thus this fourth, integrated approach has sought to use elements of the market-based, cultural and political approaches.

By way of conclusion, what do the arguments made in this chapter tell us about the consequences for national systems of employment relations? One clear consequence is the way in which the transfer of practices within MNCs will lead to change within national systems as the practices introduced are spread throughout an economy. Some argue that the development of standardized policies on employment practice within many MNCs is a key factor in the convergence of national systems. Cases such as the move by GM towards establishing teamworking as the norm throughout the company's international operations appears to lend some weight to this argument. Yet the logic of this chapter has been that while transfer will lead to change, it will not necessarily lead to convergence because transferred practices often go through a process of transmutation, in that they operate differently in the recipient unit from the way they had operated in the donor unit. While it may be possible to operate some practices in a more or less identical way in different countries, many others will be adapted by management to 'fit' the new environment or will be interpreted in a different way by actors in the recipient country. Indeed, in this respect, the effects of the transfer of practices within MNCs is similar to the more general impact of the internationalization of economic activity; national systems of employment relations evolve in response to these pressures, but do not necessarily converge.

Discussion questions

- Select between two and six countries and, based on different ideas and research findings reported in this book, compare and contrast these countries for distinctive national practices in: employee relations, employee resourcing, rewards, performance management, training and development, and managing organizational change.
- Taking each of the four key influences – *country of origin, dominance, international integration* and *host country* – discuss and suggest ways that senior executives can seek to reduce the influence of each through corporate policy. Then, discuss and recommend ways that employees can work to increase the positive advantages of each of these four key influences.
- Based on the four key influences – *country of origin, dominance, international integration* and *host country* – discuss different practical ways of increasing management knowledge, skills and competences in MNCs.

CASE STUDY

Swedco

The issue of the direction in which practices are diffused across a multinational's operations is particularly interesting in the case of Swedish MNCs. The small size of the domestic economy has meant that in order to grow, many firms became multinational at a relatively early stage in their development and subsequently became highly internationalized. Thus, compared to MNCs of most other nationalities, the domestic operations of Swedish MNCs comprise a small proportion of their total sales, assets and employment. Moreover, the nature of the Swedish system of employment relations – the historically highly centralized system of bargaining; the strength of union organization and high level of density; the structures promoting co-determination and tradition of cooperation between management and labour – raises the issue of how such a distinctive system influences a firm's approach at the international level where the cultural and institutional supports for such practices frequently will be much weaker.

The issue of the transfer of employment practices is at the heart of a case study of a Swedish multinational. Swedco is a highly internationalized firm providing IT and communications services and equipment for other firms. It employs tens of thousands of employees, with approximately 50 per cent based outside Sweden, while 95 per cent of the firm's sales are abroad. The case study involved research into the Swedish, Belgian and British units of the firm and sought to address the influence of the Swedish business system over employment relations in the firm and the role of the transfer of practices in reinforcing or eroding the effect of the home country.

There was evidence of a distinctively Swedish element to the management of the firm's international workforce, something which was evident in a number of respects. First, in the international context, Swedish workers operate with relatively little direct supervision; indeed, there is no direct translation in Swedish for the word 'supervisor' (Anderson, 1995: 72). Managers at the HQ of Swedco described attempts to spread a 'democratic' approach to decision making throughout the organization. As one put it: 'I want to let my guys loose. I don't want to control them and stand behind their backs. This is typically Swedish, to be a coach.' Second, Hedlund (1981) has argued that in Swedish firms it is acceptable to 'bypass the hierarchy', in that organizational actors do not feel constrained by formal authority relationships. Accordingly, one of the British managers claimed that: 'the company encourages a Nordic approach to openness. Swedes think nothing of jumping the hierarchy to put forward their ideas.'

Third, the tradition of seeking agreement through compromise and negotiation – what Anderson (1995: 76) refers to as the 'quest for accord' – was also evident at the international level in Swedco. One of the Belgian managers argued that this style clashed with what he was used to: 'You cannot always agree or compromise. Sometimes you have to say no. In Belgium, we raise our voices, we explode sometimes. But Sweden says this is something you must not do.'

Fourth, the Swedishness of the firm shows up in the stability of ownership. Unlike most big American and British firms which have fluid ownership structures involving a large number of shareholders each holding a small proportion of the total stock, Swedco has three large shareholders who control nearly three-quarters of the voting shares and have done so for decades. Consequently, in an industry characterized by significant restructuring in recent years, involving a number of 'hostile' take-overs, Swedco has expanded internationally by 'greenfield' investments and through a series of collaborative joint ventures and 'friendly' acquisitions.

This evidence of a country of origin effect is very significant; even in a highly internationalized MNC the nature of the domestic business system shapes the management of the international workforce. However, the evidence also indicated that the country of origin effect is being eroded as senior management seek to draw more actively on practices originating in other business systems. This process was most evident in compensation and management development practices. The first of these is the development of 'flexible' or 'variable' compensation systems. An international policy working group involving HR managers from across Swedco has recently introduced bonus systems that are linked to individual and company performance. In addition, for very senior managers, there is a 'Short Term Incentive Plan' which rewards the achievement of immediate goals. Moreover, four years ago all employees were given the right to subscribe to a convertible debenture scheme, something that about 40 per cent of staff world-wide have joined. Perhaps most significantly, an individual performance-related pay scheme, in which an employee's performance is assessed against specified targets, affects all employees across the group worldwide. These variable forms of compensation appear to have much in common with practices which have become popular in America and Britain during the last two decades.

A similar process of adopting 'Anglo-American' style practices was evident in relation to management development. In recent years the HQ has made a

(Continued)

(Continued)

concerted effort to develop a cadre of international managers from across the multinational. Subsidiaries have been encouraged to submit suggestions for individuals who should be considered for promotion to positions elsewhere in the firm, a group known as 'high potentials'. The identification of such 'high potentials' as part of an international cadre of managers is, according to Ferner and Varul (1999), a common trait of British and American MNCs. More generally, in Swedco the British operations appear to have been particularly influential in the formation of policy on management development. The manager of the firm's 'Management Institute' indicated that the UK subsidiary and UK universities have been influential in developing policy on training programmes and management development:

> When I am developing a training programme for managers, I always include the UK. Firstly, it ensures I get the language right but, secondly, there are a lot of good training and management development ideas in the UK that I would like to benefit from. I always bring someone in from the UK site onto the team. We are also developing links with the UK universities such as Cranfield and LSE.

In sum, while there is evidence of the country of origin being influential over the way Swedco manages its international workforce, there is also evidence that senior managers in the firm perceive the USA and the UK as providing practices in the areas of compensation, performance management and management development that were seen as being desirable. This process of reverse transfer – arguably reflecting the perceptions of key actors of dominant systems – can be seen as constituting an erosion of the country of origin effect.

For more detail, see Hayden and Edwards (2001).

Case study questions

1. How did the Swedish context affect the approach of management to managing their international workforce?
2. In what ways was the country of origin effect being eroded?
3. How does the notion of dominance effects shape our understanding of the transfer of employment practices?

CASE STUDY

General Motors in Spain

During the 1980s and 1990s many large American firms experimented with the practices that appeared to exist at the heart of the strong performance of their Japanese counterparts. In the case of General Motors (GM), a principal way in which the firm learned about these practices was through the collaboration with Toyota which began in the early 1980s. The joint venture between the two firms, termed NUMMI, was significant because it was seen by the management of GM as a way of facilitating learning about Japanese management practices, and through joint venture a means of moving away from those practices which had characterized the company's North American plants. One important aspect of this cooperation was the emphasis on teamwork, involving groups of operators working flexibly within teams and taking on shared responsibility for the quality of their work (see O'Sullivan, 2000). Apparently persuaded by the idea that teamwork had potential benefits across its operations, senior managers sought to transfer it to other locations across the world as part of a standardized production system within GM.

In its Spanish subsidiary, as in many others, GM was faced with overcoming the potential resistance of its trade unions. There are two main union confederations in Spain: the UGT, which has enjoyed close links with the Socialist Party (PSOE), and is considered to be moderate; and the communist-oriented CCOO which has its roots in workplace resistance to Franco's dictatorship (Martínez Lucio, 1998). In addition to union representation, there exists another channel of worker representation known as the *comité de empresas*, or works committees. While formally separate from unions, in many cases the delegates elected by workers to these committees are also union representatives. The dual system of unions and works committees had to be confronted by GM's managers in attempting to implement teamwork.

The form of teamwork favoured by management for its Spanish plant had many common elements with that in other GM plants. The key aspects included: work being organized into teams of between 8 and 15 people; operators rotating across jobs within a team; members of a team meeting regularly to discuss possible improvements to their work; and 'the usual rhetoric about fostering a "team spirit" between workers and the company' (Ortiz, 1998: 46). The initial proposals envisaged maintenance workers being required to engage in 'mixed teams' with production workers. Moreover, the appointment of a team leader by the company was significant since he or she was to have a role in the appraisal and promotion of members of the team.

(Continued)

(Continued)

Managers and unions began the process of negotiations concerning the introduction of teamwork. The unions were initially sceptical, expressing concerns about potential job losses, the prospect of work becoming intensified, the danger of unions being marginalized by the identification of workers with their teams, and the possibility that workers would not share in the benefits of higher productivity gains.

Despite these concerns, and a history of division between the UGT and the CCOO, the two main union groups did cooperate with management and negotiated a number of concessions. For instance, teamworking was to be piloted for a year in the first instance, workers would only join the experiment voluntarily, and maintenance workers were excluded from teamwork. While these concessions ameliorated the concerns of many union representatives, they also saw some possible advantages of the scheme: job rotation could help relieve monotony and avoid the danger of repetitive strains; many workers (particularly those in low grades) could be promoted; teamwork could increase the autonomy that workers enjoyed from supervisors; and it could also result in more information being provided to workers and unions. Possible opposition from unionists was further eroded by pressure from the company, since managers stressed the multinational character of the company and the competitive position of the plant within it. Many union leaders had been taken to visit other plants operating teamwork, creating a sense of it being an inevitable development in Spain too. For the leaders of the CCOO, now controlled by more 'moderates', opposing teamwork seemed futile and risked marginalizing the union since the UGT would probably go along with management. In this context, an agreement was reached at the works committee.

This shows the way that a powerful company can exert influence over the constraints of national business systems. By instilling competitive relations between plants, and by making concessions on some aspects of their plans, managers were able to break down resistance from unions, resulting in the constraints becoming partial rather than absolute. However, this was not the end of the story. At the end of the pilot scheme there was a call from the minority union, the USO, for a workforce ballot to decide on whether to continue with teamwork. Despite a campaign for ratification from all the unions the workers voted narrowly to reject the proposal. There appeared to be a number of reasons why employees were more hostile to teamwork than were their unions. Some workers, particularly those with scarce skills, were reluctant to engage in job rotation if this meant moving to less desirable jobs, and related to this was a concern at a loss of status for these workers. More generally, the adversarial industrial relations traditions of the plant meant that many workers were sceptical about management's motives. While it is likely that many workers in GM's plants in other countries shared such concerns, the Spanish system of employment law presented a distinctive constraint.

Ortiz concludes that many characteristics of national systems of industrial relations shape the attitudes of unions and workers to teamwork, such as the organizational strength of unions and the legal support that they enjoy. He argues, for example, that the British unions were more opposed to teamwork than their Spanish counterparts because it endangered the important role of the shop steward. The peculiarities of these aspects of national systems of industrial relations are key forces on the nature of transfer of practices across borders, particularly for those MNCs seeking to use this as a way of developing internationally integrated operations. Yet, these are not set in stone; in subsequent research in VW in Spain, Ortiz argues that after two unsuccessful attempts to introduce teamwork the multinational was eventually successful in implementing the practice. His interpretation of this was that host country constraints had become less influential and that management had found ways round what had appeared at first sight to be tight constraints.

For more details, see Ortiz (1998) and Ortiz and Llorente-Galera (2008).

Case study questions

1. Why did the management of GM seek to standardize its production system?
2. How can we understand the approach of unions to management's plans for teamwork?
3. What are the lessons for firms seeking to introduce teamwork into new countries?

Discussion questions

Indicative answers to these questions can be found on the companion website at study.sagepub.com/harzing4e.

1. Does the transfer of practices result in MNCs from various countries becoming more like one another?
2. You have been hired as a consultant to three firms: a British retail bank setting up in Spain; a German textiles firm relocating its production to Vietnam; and an American high-tech electronics firm opening a new site in Britain. You have been asked by all three firms to advise them on the desirability and feasibility of transferring practices to their new locations. How would your advice differ?
3. You have been appointed as an adviser to an international federation of national unions in the oil industry. The member unions are concerned at the growing tendency on the part of the major companies in the sector to transfer

(Continued)

> *(Continued)*
>
> practices across their operations. You have been asked to advise them on how they might seek to block or amend those practices they see as challenging their interests. What would you tell them?

Further reading

- Edwards, T., Colling, T. and Ferner, A. (2007) 'Conceptual approaches to the transfer of employment practices in multinational companies: an integrated approach', *Human Resource Management Journal*, 17(3): 201–217.
  The market-based, cultural and political approaches to studying transfer are described and the benefits of integrating these are highlighted through analysis of an American multinational.

- Edwards, T. and Ferner, A. (2002) 'The renewed "American challenge": a review of employment practice in US multinationals', *Industrial Relations Journal*, 33(2): 94–111.
  This article provides a comprehensive description of the four influences framework. It also illustrates the uses to which the four influences can be applied, in this case to analyse the strengths of previous research in a particular area.

- Lunnan, R., Lervik, J., Traavik, L., Nilson, S., Amdam, R. and Hennestad, B. (2005) 'Global transfer of management practices across nations and MNC subcultures', *Academy of Management Executive*, 19(2): 77–80.
  A case study of a multinational in a number of countries, demonstrating the range of ways in which global policy is adapted to national contexts.

- Pudelko, M. and Harzing, A. (2007) 'Country-of-origin, localization or dominance effect? An empirical investigation of HRM practices in foreign subsidiaries', *Human Resource Management*, 46(4): 535–559.
  The article considers the relative influence on the way MNCs operate of the legacy of the country of origin, the pressures to adapt to local contexts and the influences of 'dominant' ideas in the global economy. It draws on survey data from US, Japanese and German MNCs.

Internet resources

- www.cipd.co.uk/communities/forums/inter. The CIPD is the professional association representing HR professionals in the UK and the link takes you to its international forum.
- www.shrm.org/hrdisciplines/global/Pages/default.aspx. SHRM (Society for Human Resource Management) is the equivalent organization to the CIPD in the USA and it has news items on global HR matters.
- www.internationalhradviser.co.uk. A magazine that caters for international HR professionals.

Indicative answers to these questions can be found on the companion website at study.sagepub.com/harzing4e.

1. How would you assess the contribution of each of the three perspectives on transfer that are outlined in this chapter? Can elements of the three be combined into one `eclectic' perspective?
2. What are the origins of the `four influences' framework?
3. How useful is the concept of `dominance' effects?
4. What is the range of ways in which a global HRM policy may be adapted to national contexts?
5. If MNCs engage in the transfer of employment practices to an increasing extent does this mean that national business systems will converge?

Acknowledgements

Some of the ideas in this paper have been developed with colleagues, and I would particularly like to thank Trevor Colling and Anthony Ferner, and have featured in co-authored articles with the two of them (Edwards et al., 2007b; Edwards and Ferner, 2002). I am grateful to Trevor and Anthony for encouraging me to use the ideas in this chapter.

References

Abo, T. (1994) *Hybrid Factory: The Japanese Production System in the United States*. Oxford: Oxford University Press.

Almond, P. and Ferner, A. (2006) (eds) *American Multinationals in Europe: Managing Employment Relations Across Borders*. Oxford: Oxford University Press.

Anderson, B. (1995) *Swedishness*. Stockholm: Positiva Sverige.

Belanger, J., Berggren, C., Björkman, T. and Kohler, C. (1999) *Being Local Worldwide: ABB and the Challenge of Global Management*. Ithaca: Cornell University Press.

Broad, G. (1994) 'The managerial limits to Japanization: a manufacturing case study', *Human Resource Management Journal*, 4(3): 52–69.

Djelic, M. (1998) *Exporting the American Model: The Post-War Transformation of European Business*. Oxford: Oxford University Press.

Doremus, P., Keller, W., Pauly, L. and Reich, S. (1998) *The Myth of the Global Corporation*. Princeton, NJ: Princeton University Press.

Dorrenbacher, C. and Geppert, M. (2011) *Politics and Power in the Multinational Corporation: The Role of Institutions, Interests and Identity*. Cambridge: Cambridge University Press.

Edwards, P., Edwards, T., Ferner, A., Marginson, P. and Tregaskis, O. (2007a) 'Employment practices of MNCs in organisational context: a large scale survey', Survey Report (June), www2.warwick.ac.uk/fac/soc/wbs/projects/mncemployment/conference_papers/full_report_july.pdf (accessed 14 May 2014).

Edwards, P., Sanchez-Mangas, R., Tregaskis, O., Levesque, C., McDonnell, A. and Quintanilla, J. (2013a) 'Human resource management practices in the multinational company: a test of system, society and dominance effects', *Industrial and Labor Relations Review*, Special Issue on Multinational Companies, Article 2, 66(3): 587–617.

Edwards, T. (1998) 'Multinationals, work organisation and the process of diffusion: a case study', *International Journal of Human Resource Management*, 9(4): 696–709.

Edwards, T., Colling, T. and Ferner, A. (2007b) 'Conceptual approaches to the transfer of employment practices in multinational companies: an integrated approach', *Human Resource Management Journal*, 17(3): 201–217.

Edwards, T. and Ferner, A. (2002) 'The renewed "American challenge": a review of employment practice in US multinationals', *Industrial Relations Journal*, 33(2): 94–111.

Edwards, T. and Ferner, A. (2004) 'Multinationals, national business systems and reverse diffusion', *Management International Review*, 44(1): 49–79.

Edwards, T., Marginson, P. and Ferner, A. (2013b) 'Multinational companies in cross-national context: integration, differentiation and the interactions between MNCs and nation states', *Industrial and Labor Relations Review*, 66(3): 547–587.

Edwards, T. and Zhang, M. (2008) 'Multinationals and national systems of employment relations: innovators or adapters?', *Advances in International Management*, 21: 33–58.

Ferner, A. (1997) 'Country of origin effects and HRM in multinational companies', *Human Resource Management Journal*, 7(1): 19–37.

Ferner, A., Belanger, J., Tregaskis, O., Morley, M. and Quintanilla, J. (2013) 'US MNCs and the control of subsidiary human resource and employment practice', *Industrial and Labor Relations Review*, 66(3): 645–669.

Ferner, A. and Varul, M. (1999) *The German Way? German Multinationals and the Management of Human Resources in their UK Subsidiaries*. London: Anglo-German Foundation for the Study of Industrial Society.

Gamble, J. (2003) 'Transferring human resource practices from the United Kingdom to China: The limits and potential for convergence', *International Journal of Human Resource Management*, 14(3): 369–387.

Gereffi, G., Humphrey, J. and Sturgeon, T. (2005) 'The governance of global value chains: an analytical framework', *Review of International Political Economy*, 12(1): 78–104.

Ghoshal, S. and Bartlett, C. (1998) *Managing Across Borders: The Transnational Solution*. London: Random House.

Hall, P. and Soskice, D. (2001) *Varieties of Capitalism: The Institutional Foundations of Comparative Advantage*. Oxford: Oxford University Press.

Hayden, A. and Edwards, T. (2001) 'The erosion of the country of origin effect: a case study of a Swedish multinational company', *Relations Industrielles*, 56(1): 116–140.

Hedlund, G. (1981) 'Autonomy of subsidiaries and formalization of headquarters-subsidiary relationships in Swedish MNCs', in L. Otterbeck (ed.), *The Management of Headquarters–Subsidiary Relationships in Multinational Corporations*. Aldershot: Gower, pp. 25–78.

Hofstede, G. (2001) *Culture's Consequences: Comparing Values, Behaviors, Institutions and Organizations*. London: Sage.

Humphrey, J. (1995) 'The adoption of Japanese management techniques in Brazilian industry', *Journal of Management Studies*, 32(6): 767–787.

Kostova, T., Roth, K. and Dacin, M. (2008) 'Institutional theory in the study of MNCs: a critique and new directions', *Academy of Management Review*, 33(4): 994–1006.

Kristensen, P. and Zeitlin, J. (2005) *Local Players in Global Games: The Strategic Constitution of a Multinational Company*. Oxford: Oxford University Press.

Lunnan, R., Lervik, J., Traavik, L., Nilson, S., Amdam, R. and Hennestad, B. (2005) 'Global transfer of management practices across nations and MNC subcultures', *Academy of Management Executive*, 19(2): 77–80.

Maccoby (1997) 'Just another car factory? Lean production and its discontents', *Harvard Business Review*, 75(6): 161–168.

Marginson, P. (2000) 'The Eurocompany and Euro industrial relations', *European Journal of Industrial Relations*, 6(1): 9–34.

Martínez Lucio, M. (1998) 'Spain: regulating employment and social fragmentation', in A. Ferner and R. Hyman (eds), *Changing Industrial Relations in Europe*. Oxford: Blackwell, pp. 426–458.

Morgan, G., Kristensen, P. and Whitley, R. (2001) *The Multinational Firm: Organizing Across Institutional and National Divides*. Oxford: Oxford University Press.

Muller, M. (1998) 'Human resource and industrial relations practices of UK and US multinationals in Germany', *International Journal of Human Resource Management*, 9(4): 732–749.

Ngo, H., Turban, D., Lau, C. and Lui, S. (1998) 'Human resource practices and firm performance of multinational corporations: influences of country origin', *International Journal of Human Resource Management*, 9(4): 632–652.

Oliver, N. and Wilkinson, B. (1992) *The Japanization of British Industry: New Developments in the 1990s*. Oxford: Blackwell.

Ortiz, L. (1998) 'Unions' response to teamwork: the case of Opel Spain', *Industrial Relations Journal*, 29(1): 42–57.

Ortiz, L. and Llorente-Galera, F. (2008) 'Two failed attempts and one success: The introduction of teamwork at SEAT – Volkswagen', in J.J. Lawler and G. Hundley (eds) 'The Global Diffusion of Human Resource Practices: Institutional and Cultural Limits', *Advances in International Management*. Emerald Group Publishing Limited, 21: 59–87.

O'Sullivan, M. (2000) *Contests for Corporate Control: Corporate Governance and Economic Performance in the United States and Germany*. Oxford: Oxford University Press.

Perlmutter, H.V. (1969) 'The tortuous evolution of the multinational corporation', *Columbia Journal of World Business*, 4(1): 9–18.

Pudelko, M. and Harzing, A. (2007) 'Country-of-origin, localization or dominance effect? An empirical investigation of HRM practices in foreign subsidiaries', *Human Resource Management*, 46(4): 535–559.

Rosenzweig, P. and Nohria, N. (1994) 'Influences on human resource management practices in multinational corporations', *Journal of International Business Studies*, Second Quarter: 229–251.

Ruigrok, W. and van Tulder, R. (1995) *The Logic of International Restructuring*. London: Routledge.

Schmitt, M. and Sadowski, D. (2003) 'A cost-minimisation approach to the international transfer of HRM/IR practices: Anglo-Saxon multinationals in the Federal Republic of Germany', *International Journal of Human Resource Management*, 14(3): 409–430.

Schuler, R. and Rogovsky, N. (1998) 'Understanding compensation practice variations across firms: the impact of national culture', *Journal of International Business Studies*, 29(1): 159–177.

Smith, C. and Meiskins, P. (1995) 'System, society and dominance effects in cross-national organisational analysis', *Work, Employment and Society*, 9(2): 241–267.

Tayeb, M. (1996) *The Management of a Multicultural Workforce*. Chichester: Wiley.

Taylor, S., Beechler, S. and Napier, N. (1996) 'Toward an integrative model of strategic international human resource management', *Academy of Management Review*, 21(4): 959–985.

Trompenaars, F. and Hampden-Turner, C. (1994) *The Seven Cultures of Capitalism*. London: Piatkus.

United Nations (2012) *World Investment Report*. New York: UN.

Wilkinson, B., Gamble, J., Humphrey, J., Morris, J. and Anthony, D. (2001) 'The new international division of labour in Asian electronics: work organization and human resources in Japan and Malaysia', *Journal of Management Studies*, 38(5): 675–695.

Approaches to International Human Resource Management

Chris Rowley, Jean Qi Wei and Malcolm Warner

4

Contents

Learning objectives

After reading this chapter you will be able to:

- Describe and analyse the characteristics, contributions and limitations of prominent models of human resource management
- Explain the differences between contingency and divergence theories of HRM and different institutional and cultural factors
- Understand how and why HRM approaches in the Asian context are similar to, or different from, those in the West
- Evaluate the applicability of HRM approaches and discuss the implications of change for HRM

Chapter outline

This chapter examines the varieties of IHRM approaches, identifies the development and transformation of HRM, and explores some basic questions on the universality of HRM. Contemporary research on IHRM has considerable variation in its theoretical perspectives, HRM approaches and types of organization included. This chapter compares and contrasts the dominant IHRM approaches in the US and Europe, namely the matching model, the Harvard model, the contextual model, the 5-P model, the European model and the integrative IHRM framework. The outcome of the comparison is then reviewed in the light of their key aspects and current practices in different organizations and countries. The chapter evaluates whether various HRM approaches are applicable and can be transferred to different firms, business systems, institutional contexts and cultural environments. It shows that HRM practices developed in one context cannot simply be assumed to work in the same way in other countries. The chapter concludes that though differences in HRM approaches exist, they are often subject to dynamic change over time. The evolutionary nature of change in organizations and approaches to IHRM is illustrated using ideas and examples from Asia.

1 Introduction

Globalization effects, such as the expansion of overseas markets, aided by information and communication technologies (ICT) and the growing importance of multinational companies, has encouraged a proliferation of IHRM research. With the growth of new markets such as in China, India, South East Asia and Eastern Europe and an increased level of competition among firms at both national and international levels, there is a clear need to develop an understanding of how to manage human resources working in different parts of the world (see Chapters 14 and 15).

Academics have responded positively to the challenges of internationalization proposing different HRM approaches (Warner et al., 2005). The majority of IHRM scholars are concerned with the design of HRM processes in global organizations/ MNCs, interactions between institutions, societal norms and government regulations and comparative analysis of HRM approaches across economies (Metcalfe and Rees, 2005). There is also substantial interest in issues of culture and acculturation. Yet, many of the prominent theoretical models and concepts of HRM were developed based on American or European countries. The relevance of such American or European ('Anglo-Saxon') experience to other institutional and cultural contexts, as well as the applicability of these approaches to dynamic, emerging economies, such as some Asian countries, is questionable (Rowley and Warner, 2005). Some argue that IHRM is a recent subject discipline and that its roots are not explicitly accounted for nor fully explained (Rowley and Warner, 2007b). Besides, there is a series of questions pursued by comparative HRM researchers that require further attention (See Box 4.1).

Box 4.1 Questions to be considered by comparative HRM researchers

- How much are existing HRM approaches that are based on Western ways of thinking relevant and applicable to other parts of the world?
- What evidence is there for one model or set of 'best' HRM practices?
- What are the similarities and differences in HRM systems across different countries?
- What are the reasons for these similarities and differences in HRM?
- As business becomes more global, to what extent is HRM becoming more uniform?
- To what extent will different regions retain their own distinctive approaches to HRM?
- Is HRM converging or diverging at the cross-national level?
- What is the influence of institutional and cultural factors on the HRM approaches of global firms?
- What are the changes in HRM approaches over time?

A starting point for investigating such questions is to examine the key characteristics of different HRM approaches developed so far. This can assist with answering some of the basic questions about the universality of HRM. In the next section, five models of HRM are analysed. These models are well documented in the literature and have wide-ranging implications for contemporary research. Based on the comparison of key characteristics, contributions and limitations of these models, the second part of the chapter then evaluates whether various HRM approaches can be transferred to different business systems, institutional contexts and cultural environments. In the final section, some cases and examples of firms in Asia are used to show the dynamic changes in HRM approaches over time. The chapter then draws its conclusions and outlines some future directions for IHRM.

2 Review of IHRM approaches

This section compares and contrasts the dominant paradigm of HRM in North America and Western Europe. The literature contains many theoretical models of HRM. However, due to limitations of space, only six major models of HRM are addressed. These are the: matching model (Tichy et al., 1982), Harvard model (Beer et al., 1984), contextual model (Hendry and Pettigrew, 1990), 5-P model (Schuler, 1992), European model of HRM (Brewster, 1995) and integrative IHRM framework (Shen, 2005). The reason for analysing these models is to identify their principal contributions to the development of HRM and their application in the international environment to IHRM. In addition, many of these models exemplify particular cultural characteristics of their country of origin which can help readers to reflect on the transferability of Western-oriented models to other contexts and institutional environments (Hsu and Leat, 2000).

Matching model

Characteristics

The main contributors to the matching model of HRM come from the Michigan and New York schools. Tichy and colleagues (1982) propose this model which highlights the 'resource' aspect of HRM and emphasizes a 'tight fit' between organizational strategy, organizational structure and HRM system (see Box 4.2). On the surface the matching model bears a strong resemblance to earlier ideas, such as scientific management (Taylor, 1911), in so far as it promotes the idea of 'best fit' or 'best practice'. The model shares similarities with Galbraith and Nathanson (1978) who link different personnel functions to an organization's strategy and structure, and emphasize the significance of the HR function for achieving an organization's mission.

Contributions

Despite the many criticisms, the matching model deserves credit for providing a framework for subsequent theory development in the field of HRM. When working within this model, a company is concerned with performance systems that exercise tight control over individual activities, with the ultimate goal of securing a competitive advantage (Guest, 1995).

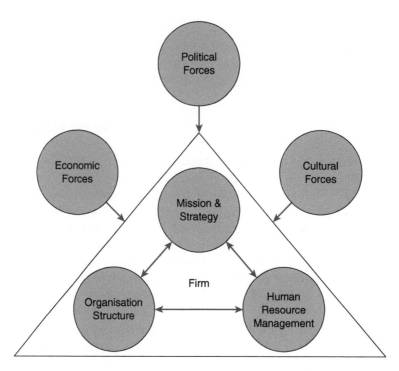

Figure 4.1   Matching model

Source: from MIT Sloan Management Review. © 1982 by Massachussetts Institute of Technology. All rights Distributed by Tribune Media Services

Limitations

The matching model is based on a classical view of strategy formulation which assumes that design and implementation are separate activities and that HR policies and practices can simply be 'matched' to business strategies at the formulation stage. It fails to acknowledge the complexities within and between concepts of strategy and HRM (Dyer, 1985) and underestimates the difficulties inherent to obtaining a reciprocal relationship between strategy and HRM (Boxall, 1992). The model also overlooks the 'human' aspect of HRM and does not take account of significant variations in power, politics and culture (Purcell and Ahlstrand, 1994) and therefore has been categorized as a 'hard' model of HRM (Legge, 1995; Storey, 1995; Guest, 1997).

Box 4.2   Example 1: Theoretical perspectives on HRM fit

The SHRM literature distinguishes between what has been termed vertical or external fit and horizontal or internal fit. While external fit denotes the alignment between

HRM practices and the specific organizational context (e.g. organizational strategy), internal fit refers to the coherent configuration of individual HRM practices that support each other (Becker et al., 1997; Delery, 1998) and the arrangement of HRM activities (e.g. HRM policies and practices) that work in concert.

Contingency perspective

This predicts that the relationship between HRM practices and organizational effectiveness is contingent upon an organization's strategy (Delery and Doty, 1996). It proposes that organizations which have HR policies and practices that are more responsive to external factors will report superior performance.

Configurational Perspective

This takes a more holistic view that is aligned with the concept of equifinality and highlights the importance of fit and complementarity among HRM practices in predicting organizational effectiveness (Delery and Doty, 1996). According to the concept of equifinality, 'different HRM practices that fit together can yield identical outcomes' (1996: 386–387). Internal fit of HRM activities (e.g. HRM policies or practices) that work in concert, researchers have called 'systems' (e.g. Delery and Doty, 1996), 'bundles' (e.g. MacDuffie, 1995), or 'clusters' (e.g. Arthur, 1992).

Harvard model

Characteristics

During the same period that the 'hard' oriented matching model was developed, the Harvard model (Beer et al., 1984) with more 'soft' characteristics was produced. It pays attention to the 'human' aspect of HRM and is more concerned with the employer–employee relationship (Zhu et al., 2007). This model highlights the interests of different stakeholders in the organization and links their interests with the objectives of management. It regards people as the single most important asset of the organization and emphasizes employee's needs and societal well-being. In short, it comprises a broader area of focus than the 'hard model' and aims to increase the sum of human satisfaction at a variety of interrelated levels (Zhu et al., 2007). Some people have equated this model with the concept of a 'high commitment work system' (Walton, 1985). The Harvard model conceives HRM as a series of policy choices, comprising (a) HR flows (selection, appraisal, development and outflows), (b) reward systems, (c) work systems, and (d) employee influence (through trade unions and work councils). The outcomes of these four HR policies are commitment, competence, congruence and cost effectiveness.

Contributions

This model provides a broad classification of the content of HRM and a range of outcomes at the individual, organizational and societal levels, and hence it can provide a useful basis for comparative analysis of HRM (Poole, 1990). It also encourages useful holistic thinking about the sources of skill supply and draws attention to skill as an important concept for HRM (Hendry and Pettigrew, 1990).

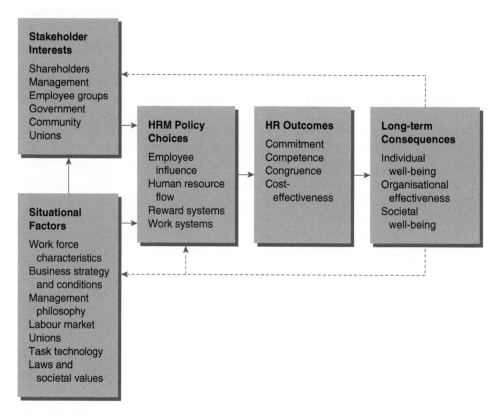

Figure 4.2   Harvard model

Source: reprinted with kind permission from Michael Beer (Beer et al., 1984)

Limitations

However, this model has been criticized for not explaining the complex relationships between strategic management and HRM (Guest, 1991). By outlining a range of policy choices and not recommending specific approaches, this model is descriptive rather than prescriptive and therefore does not predict the relationships between HRM policies and outcomes (Guest, 1997).

Contextual model

Characteristics

In reality, both hard and soft elements are present in organizations. The interactive process within the HRM system can be complex and is heavily influenced by a variety of contextual and historical factors. Hendry and Pettigrew (1990) argue that the existence of a number of linkages between the outer environmental context (socio-economic, technological, political-legal and competitive) and inner organizational context (culture, structure, leadership, task technology and business output) form the content of HRM. To analyse this contextual model, past information related to the organization's development and management of change is essential (Sparrow and Hiltrop, 1994). Organizations may follow different pathways to achieve positive results and there is no straightforward flow from business strategy to HRM (Budhwar and Debrah, 2001).

Contributions

Under this model, changes in HR practices can be conceived as a response to business strategy, and the scope of the HRM function to respond effectively depends on the contextual factors. This implies that two firms facing the same set of external circumstances may not respond in the same way or evolve in HRM to the same degree, and hence their HR practices will remain different. The model can be used for detailed contextual analysis and case study research.

Limitations

A potential problem that can arise from this approach is that personnel policy and practice become the dependent variable of the analysis and outcomes such as company performance become the independent variable (Guest, 1991). Besides, different views and interests of management and employees (Purcell and Ahlstrand, 1994) can influence the interactive process. The issues of lagged response, emergent business strategy and limited resources (Brewster, 1993) can also complicate the relationship of HR practices and contextual factors.

5-P model

Characteristics

The field of IHRM became substantially more important in the early 1990s due to globalization and accelerated changes in economic, social, legal, technological and workforce conditions. One result was that MNCs became more concerned to integrate

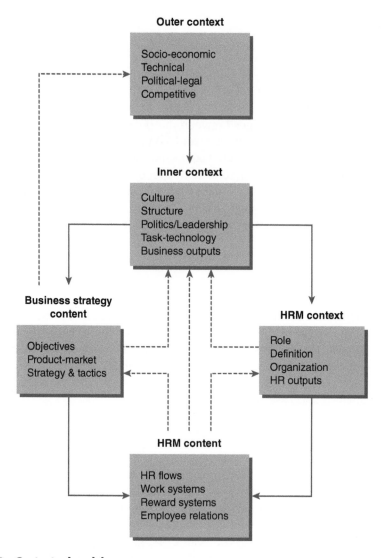

Figure 4.3   Contextual model

Source: from Hendry and Pettigrew (1990). Reprinted by permission of the publisher (Taylor and Francis Group, www. informaworld.com)

HRM into business strategy on an international or global platform. Schuler (1992) proposes a 5-P model which combines various HR activities with strategic needs. These activities are philosophy, policies, programmes, practices and processes. Whether they are categorized as strategic or not depends on (a) if the HR activities are systematically linked to the strategic needs of the business or the operational needs, or (b) if they occur over the long term or in the short term, or (c) if they focus on senior managers or non-managerial employees (Schuler, 1992).

Contributions

This model shows the interrelatedness of activities (see Box 4.3) that were often treated separately in the earlier literature and provides an understanding of the complex interaction between organizational strategy and strategic HRM activities (Adler and Ghadar, 1990; Budhwar and Debrah, 2001). Another contribution is that it demonstrates the influence of both internal characteristics (organizational culture and nature of the business) and external characteristics (economy and industry) on the strategic business needs of an organization.

Limitations

This model, however, suffers from being over-prescriptive and too hypothetical in nature and is difficult to implement in practice (Budhwar and Debrah, 2001). It may be of interest to scholars, but it is limited in its applications for management practitioners. HR managers who have not had to align HR activities with strategic needs will find that the process takes time and developing a detailed understanding of the needs requires extra effort (Schuler, 1992).

Box 4.3   Example 2: Strategy and HR activities link

One benefit of the 5-P model is that it highlights the complex interaction of the strategy–HR activity link.

- Philosophy: makes statements to define business values and culture
- Policies: expresses as shared values and guidelines for action the people-related business issues and HR programmes
- Programmes: articulates as HR strategies for coordinating effort and facilitating change to address major people-related business issues
- Practices: motivates needed role behaviours, e.g. leadership, managerial and operational roles
- Processes: defines how HR activities are carried out.

Source: Schuler, 1992.

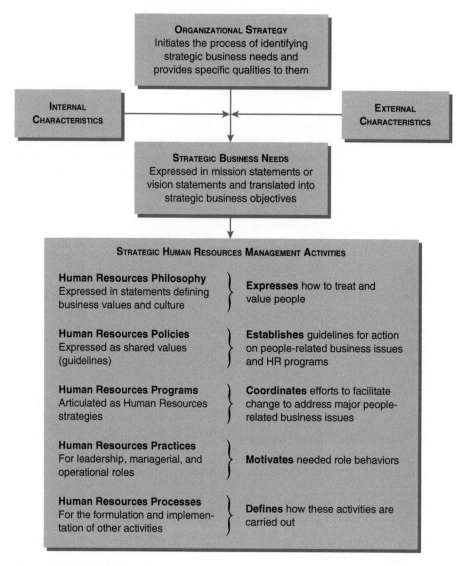

Figure 4.4   5-P model

Source: Schuler (1992). Reprinted with permission from Elsevier

European model

Characteristics

While various approaches to IHRM were proposed in the 1980s and 1990s, an international comparison of HR practices indicates that the basic functions of HRM are given different value in different countries and implemented differently (Gaugler, 1988).

Surveying European management, Pieper (1990: 11) concludes that 'a single universal model of HRM does not exist'. What is needed is a model of HRM that explains country differences in the context of national culture and its diverse manifestations in history, law, institutions and organization structures (Filella, 1991). Hence, Brewster (1993, 1995) proposes a European model of HRM to reflect increasing European Union integration and the adoption of common EU labour legislation. His model assumes that European organizations operating with restricted autonomy are constrained: (a) at the international and national level by national culture and legislation, (b) at the organization level by patterns of ownership, and (c) at the HRM level by trade union involvement and consultative arrangements. In addition, Brewster (1995) emphasizes the need for a more comprehensive understanding of the role of different players in developing the concept of HRM and testing its applications in the international environment.

Contributions

The European model moves beyond countries' borders and enables analysis of HRM at a broader geographical and continental level. This places HRM concepts firmly within the cross-national border context and allows better understanding of situations in Europe (Budhwar and Debrah, 2001). Significantly, factors that in the previous models of HRM were seen as external to organizations become a part of the HRM model, rather than understood as a set of external influences. This can reveal differences in HRM practices between nations and across clusters of similar countries and can provide an understanding of how MNCs may attempt to adopt or reject local practices (Brewster, 1995).

Limitations

Within Europe, large differences exist between countries with more labour regulations, for example the Scandinavian and German countries, and countries that are comparatively less regulated, like Ireland or the UK (Mayrhofer and Brewster, 2005). Hence, there exists considerable variety across countries in the single European model and even within clusters of similar countries. Besides, a number of subsequent studies have argued that differences in HRM might be due to factors not included in the model, such as skill-level and available types of qualifications in the workforce, the role of HR and employees' participation in decision making.

Integrative IHRM framework

Characteristics

This model reflects that the transfer of HRM policies and practices to international contexts are contingent on a set of intervening factors which are from three broad sources: the effect of country of origin, host political, legal, economic and socio-cultural environments and firm characteristics (Shen, 2005).

Cultural, Comparative and Organizational Perspectives

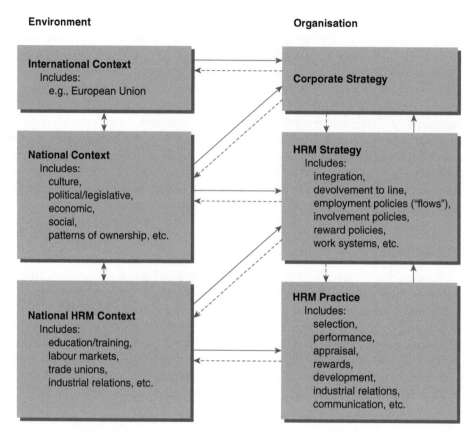

Figure 4.5   European model

Source: Brewster (1995). Reprinted by permission from Macmillan Publishers Ltd, Copyright 1995

Contributions

The model integrates the division of intervening factors and their impact on IHRM from the previous models by Evans and Lorange (1989), Schuler et al. (1993), Paauwe and Dewe (1995) and Taylor et al. (1996). The model also indicates the differential impact of intervening factors on IHRM policies and practices.

Limitations

The model is developed from theories and frameworks on MNCs which are mostly in the Western context. Apart from some Chinese MNCs, the model has not been widely tested in other developing and transforming economies in the IHRM area (Shen, 2005).

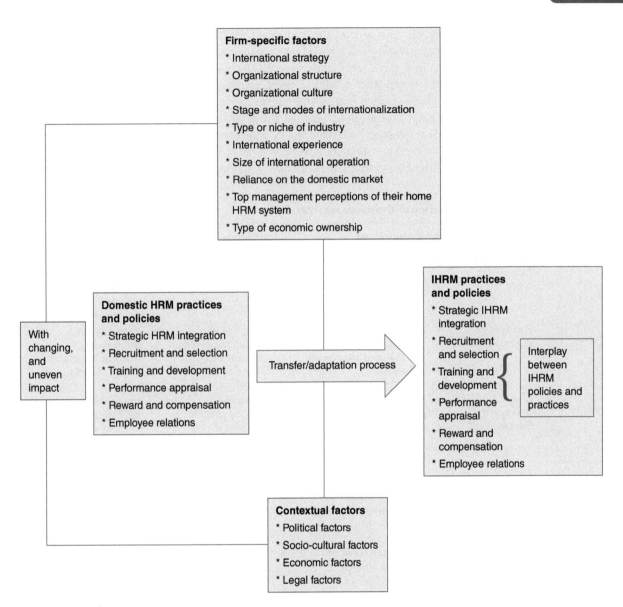

Figure 4.6 Integrative HRM framework

Source: Shen (2005: 373)

Implications of HRM models

The above discussion presents an outline of theoretical developments in HRM and compares and contrasts the characteristics of six models of HRM. Whereas these six models in no way provide a complete picture of the field of HRM, the comparison reviews certain patterns of formation and development of the HRM paradigm in North America and Western Europe. This leads us to three conclusions and sets of questions.

First of all, HRM as a field of academic study is primarily of North American/Anglo-Saxon origin and for this reason may be inappropriate for other cultures. Despite the fact that research into HRM is now taking place in many countries around the world, current IHRM research that is genuinely international in orientation remains limited (Rowley and Warner, 2007a). Among these six models, is there one (or a set of) best HRM approaches? And if so, what is the conceptualization of HRM in the international context?

Table 4.1   Comparison of five dominant HRM models

HRM model	Basic assumptions	Contributions	Limitations
Matching model (Tichy et al., 1982)	• Existence of best HRM practices • Does not consider synergies, interdependencies or integration mechanisms	• Demonstration of the importance of HRM in organizations	• Excessive emphasis on 'fit' issues • Does not take account of power, politics and culture aspects
Harvard model (Beer et al., 1984)	• No best HRM practices • Effects depend on variables such as internal and external environment	• Inclusion of other variables that mediate the relationship between HRM and performance	• Narrow objectives, non-prescriptive • Difficult to apply to complex relationships
Contextual model (Hendry and Pettigrew, 1990)	• Consideration of HRM as part of a bigger social macro-system that both influence and is influenced by HRM strategy	• Introduction of social and processual dimensions of HRM	• Personnel policies and practices as dependent variables
5-P model (Schuler, 1992)	• Combination of various elements that create the HRM system and consideration of those elements that may be equally efficient	• Consideration of synergy and interdependence between different elements of the system	• Definition of management patterns is a simplification of reality • Difficult to implement in practice
European model (Brewster, 1995)	• Consideration of national culture and legislation, in addition to organizational characteristics	• Integration of the HRM system in a macro-institutional context and revealing differences between nations	• Differences in HRM model may be due to factors other than national culture and external influences
Integrative IHRM framework (Shen, 2005)	• Consideration of intervening factors from home and host country environments, as well as MNCs' characteristics	• Integration of the complex set of intervening factors • Interplay between intervening factors and IHRM policies and practices	• Little empirical research evidence

Second, as management and organizational writers have noted the field of HRM has expanded beyond the management of HR to include a strong connection with corporate strategy, regional integration, extension into cross-cultural management, knowledge management and transnational organizations. Consequently, scholars are steadily extending their knowledge of HRM beyond specific national boundaries with information about HRM in many other countries. Can any of these HRM approaches be applicable to other national contexts, such as the Asian economies? If so, is there a difference between the larger examples of the latter and the smaller ones, known as the Little Dragon economies?

Finally, a large number of factors may affect HRM approaches in an international environment. What might these be? What are the implications of change to IHRM approaches? The following sections will explore these questions in detail and concentrate on examples from Asia.

3 The concept of HRM

Despite an extensive and growing body of literature addressing the HRM paradigm in North America and Western Europe and the increasing importance of an international perspective (Stahl and Björkman, 2006), there remains limited consensus as to the substance, nature and implications of IHRM concepts. First, of the six models reviewed, there is an identifiable difference between the way in which HRM is conducted and understood in North America and in Western Europe, and probably elsewhere too. This, in part, reflects theoretical developments in debates about how HRM should be conceived.

The word 'HRM' can simply be used as an updated word for 'personnel management', and can also be used to cover other concepts, such as what is now known as 'employee relations'. Many researchers (e.g. Easterby-Smith et al., 1995) have criticized HRM for being a culturally bound and Anglo-American biased concept that cannot be divorced from its institutional context and indeed its individualistic, capitalist background. To apply the HRM concept in other countries, it is important to understand the differences between domestic HRM and IHRM (Wei and Rowley, 2011). Western notions of HRM might not be present in organizations in Asia (Warner, 1995, 2009b) because the roles of personnel management common in Asia can be far removed from the concept of HRM as understood in Western business management theory due in part to the cultural differences that exist between the East and the West. Traditional practices predominately used in Asia, for example lifetime employment, seniority-based pay and organizational specific/technical skills training, can be very different from those practices used in the West. These may, however, vary between different cultures within Asia itself, such as between China and Japan (Rowley and Warner, 2005).

The notion of IHRM was defined by Morgan (1986) as the administration and development of HR policies and practices such as HR planning, staffing, performance evaluation, training and development, compensation and benefits, and labour relations in the international context – each practice has its own social, cultural, legal, economic, political and historical characteristics. More recently, Peltonen (2006) and Dowling and Welch (2004) further note that IHRM explores the added complexity in HRM due to a diversity of national contexts of operation, such as more broader external influences, risk exposure, as well as the mix of expatriates and locals in the workforce. Nevertheless, Caldas et al. (2011) also highlight the current issues of IHRM in developing countries.

4 Are IHRM models applicable to other contexts?

In understanding the concepts of HRM and IHRM, some key questions arise: Is HRM becoming more uniform as business becomes more global? Or will HRM remain distinct in different regions? If so, are the differences increasing or decreasing? This leads us to questions concerning possible divergence in HRM. To locate these questions within an international context, the analysis should include consideration of factors such as the differential impact of globalization upon organizations operating within different geographical regions, the role of MNCs in promoting global HRM practices, and the variety and different forms of national business system. However, there is also the issue of indigenous MNCs, such as those emerging in China, which may be closer to convergence than domestic enterprises.

Universalist view

On one side of the coin, globalization, internationalization and technological advancement are some of the factors thought to push national systems towards uniformity (Kerr et al., 1960) such as when copying, benchmarking and transferring of practices are encouraged. Competition and market development may encourage international companies to adopt some 'best practices' in order to survive and compete. The best practice argument (Pfeffer, 1994) and international best practice research suggest that proactive management strategies significantly affect business outcomes and that the search for a 'transnational solution' (Bartlett and Ghoshal, 1992) will lead to the convergence of structural forms and processes, and can be cost-effectively and fairly adopted across the organization worldwide. Such 'isomorphism' may be of theoretical interest in this debate.

The forces of globalization and search for optimal management practices by MNCs have the potential to make a significant impact on the field of IHRM. For example, firms tend to adopt broadly similar policies towards their staff and in their relations with other stakeholders within specific national contexts (Whitley, 1999). When universalist viewpoints that there is 'one best way' of managing are influential on MNCs or when simplified ideas of strategic alignment and fit are prevalent, such as in the matching model, then one might assume emulation of universally identified 'best practice' will lead to greater convergence in management approaches (Rowley et al., 2004).

Contingency versus divergence

On the other side of the coin, the forces of globalization and socio-economic integration imply increased cultural diversity in management composition as well as more varied influences on the contextual development of cross-national organizations. The differentiation or 'best fit' approach concentrates on the need to fit HRM practices to local conditions, rejecting the notion of one best way of doing things in all contexts (Delery and Doty, 1996; Brewster, 1999).

As proposed by the contextual model and the 5-P model, the right mix of HRM strategies depends on a complex variety of critical environmental and internal contingencies. Thus, under a contingency view, international organizations should constantly adjust and change their IHRM strategies to fit with different sets of external and internal factors. They must consider external factors such as host country variables (Jackson et al., 1989; Heenan and Perlmutter, 1990; Smale 2008) and internal factors such as corporate lifecycle or HRM fit and their influences on subsidiaries (Becker and Gerhart, 1996; Delery and Doty, 1996; Smale, 2008). Hence, there is a need to develop an understanding of how to manage IHRM when working in different parts of the world.

Nevertheless, various IHRM models, regardless of whether a 'hard model' or 'soft model' is applied, can be constrained at international, national and organizational levels. Similar to the difficulty of applying the North American matching model to Europe, the degree to which IHRM approaches are applicable elsewhere may vary. Turbulent, competitive and changing environments can limit the case for one best way (Guest, 1991). There may be factors pulling in contradictory directions, such as towards greater globalization but at the same time placing new restrictions on trade in order to protect employment during an economic crisis.

Besides, structural variations and interactions in terms of social, political, economic systems, culture and history, and the dominance of different economic sectors, produce distinctive forms of national business system, as claimed by the divergence view (Valiukonyte and Parkkonen, 2008). For instance, different varieties of capitalist economic organizations in North America, Western Europe and Asia have been developing over some time interdependently within dominant societal institutions. Their implications for existing forms of capitalism are by no means straightforward. The ways in which different types of internationalization operate are path dependent and reflect their historical legacies as well as current institutional linkages (Whitley, 1998). Distinctive and homogenous cultures in Asia have developed their own integrated business systems. This in turn generates significant variations in how firms in Asia operate. Hence, the 'best' IHRM approach in one situation may not be the 'best' approach in another business system given that institutional forces and structural factors are very different between countries and organizations (Zhu et al., 2007).

Crossvergence and hybridization

Some duality theorists (Evans et al., 2002) argue that organizations need to be effective simultaneously at both standardization and differentiation. This duality has also been described as hybrid localization (Poutsma et al., 2006). The concept of crossvergence has been operationalized and studied among developing economies and newly industrialized economies (see Priem et al., 2000; Jackson, 2004). Commenting on the characteristics of HR practices in East Asia, Zhu et al. (2007) conclude that a hybridization of the people management system has been developed in Asia. The hybrid system has the characteristics of maintaining indigenous management value and practices while being highly adaptive and flexible to utilizing 'good' practices developed in other countries. This concept challenges the conventional wisdom of the contingency approach and helps to overcome the tension and contradiction created by Western HRM systems. We may well continue to see a coexistence of both globalization and localization (see Warner, 2012).

5 What factors affect HRM approaches internationally?

Developing management models that are universally applicable in all contexts presents a considerable challenge. Practice, norms and concepts from different countries, whatever their origin, tend to show some cultural specificity and contextual and institutional factors often vary from country to country.

Institutional theory

Institutional forces of coercion and imitation play an important role in IHRM. Norms and expectations shared by members of a society or a particular industry influence how organizations should be structured and the kinds of managerial behaviour that are considered legitimate (Meyer and Rowan, 1977). International organizations, as social entities, are affected by domestic, regional and global forces. They tend to seek approval for their behaviours in a socially constructed environment (Jackson and Schuler, 1995) which is constituted by a range of institutional forces including local governments (Walder, 1995), social networks (Child, 1994) and regional economic policy (Tse et al., 1997) (see Box 4.4). Hall and Soskice (2001) argue that societal institutions (such as market, culture and history), together with the complementarities among them, mould the specific institutions of corporate governance, management practice, inter-firm relations and labour markets. This 'varieties of capitalism' framework for analysis has been applied to Asia, such as Vietnam (Truong and Rowley, 2014). Thus there exist a large number of institutional ways of organizing economic activity rather than one best way and they create many alternative, distinctive national business systems within the parameters of capitalism (Tempel and Walgenbach, 2007).

Social forces can act as constraints on the degree of international transfer of HRM when MNCs adopt local institutional norms and rules for structuring companies and managing activities. Summarizing the institutional perspective, Hoffman (1999: 351) states that the HRM model an MNC adopts 'is seen not as a choice among an unlimited array of possibilities determined by purely internal arrangements, but rather as a choice among a narrowly defined set of legitimate options'.

Box 4.4   Example 3: What roles do institutional forces play in HRM change in Asia?

Institutionalists argue that assumptions, beliefs and expectations existing within society determine how firms should be organized and which functions they do and do not perform. In some Asian economies, the opening up of markets to MNCs in China and Vietnam as well as implementation of economic reforms in Malaysia and Korea to match the standards of global competition have created a new institutional environment and exerted pressure on indigenous Asian companies to adopt new ways of working. Joining the World Trade Organization (WTO) accelerated economic development but at the same time pressurized China's state-owned enterprises (SOEs) to imitate the practices of Western MNCs to demonstrate that they are in step with international markets. The popularity of business schools in many Asian economies (such as Hong Kong, Singapore and Taiwan) also promotes the transfer of business ideas and managerial practices prevalent in the West.

Source: Walsh and Zhu, 2007; Rowley and Poon, 2008; Poon, 2010.

Cultural approach

Another factor affecting the approach to HRM in an international environment is national culture. Hofstede (1984) identifies different approaches in collectivistic and individualistic cultures in his classic study. HRM practices in culturally diverse workforces in twenty-first-century organizations are inevitably imprinted with their home country's culture and traditions (Plessis, 2010). For instance, 'national difference in collectivism and orientation towards providing for and protecting employees suggests that Asian merit pay allocators in both Indonesia and Singapore may give larger merit raises than merit pay allocators in the US' (Gully et al., 2003: 1371).

Two paradoxical trends run through HRM in international businesses. First, there are clear cross-country differences which can be understood and explained in the context of each national culture and its manifestations in history, regulations (Florkowski and Nath, 1993), political systems (Carroll et al., 1988) or socialization factors (Lockett, 1988; Rowley and Yukongdi, 2009). Second, cultural distance from the home country can create problems for MNCs operating in, and adapting to, a host setting (Davidson, 1980) because change in decision making, communication and personnel practices are difficult (Child and Markoczy, 1993) and concepts of ideal management practice are different.

Furthermore, traditional philosophies embedded in Asian societies have an influence on the transfer and adoption of international managerial approaches (Child, 1994; Noronha, 2002; Rowley and Ulrich, 2012a, 2012b). Evidence has shown that, for example, Japanese firms operating in the Asian context tend to adapt to local conditions (Rodgers and Wong, 1996; Wong, 1996) as a consequence of the similarity of cultural values between Japan and Asian countries (Ngo et al., 1998). It is, therefore, important to extend previous research by investigating whether practices brought by companies from different nationalities, and hence different cultural contexts, are likely to be compatible and hence adopted. It has been suggested (Braun and Warner, 2002) that some HRM approaches are more cross-cultural and hence transferable than others. For instance, many recruitment and training practices are less culture-bound because they are often characterized by the technical skills, roles and responsibilities attached to various positions (Anderson, 1992; Watson, 1994).

Box 4.5   Stop and reflect

The media and practitioner journals often focus on the importance of a particular 'leader' and 'leadership style', less so on so-called 'followers'. Also, they often verge on hagiography – the organization is the person and its success is due to their leadership of various types and forms. Think of examples such as Apple with Steve Jobs, Virgin with Richard Branson, the Tata Group, etc.

In light of this and your reading of this chapter so far and after particularly reading Rowley and Ulrich (2012a, 2012b), stop and reflect on the following:

1. What are the implications of these perspectives and frameworks for IHRM?
2. To what extent can there be international leadership styles?
3. How useful are the 3Cs (country context, competence, corporate culture) in analysing effective leadership internationally?
4. What do you think are the implications of your reading for both (a) indigenous and (b) non-local leaders?
5. Think of a well-know leader and their style and read up on them, say in the *Financial Times* or practitioner journals. How well do they fit in with the models in this chapter and your readings?

6 What are the implications of change for IHRM approaches?

Approaches to management, including IHRM, can be subject to systematic reform and change. Transfer and adoption of international management and employment practices (see Chapters 2 and 3) demonstrates change in both directions towards greater similarity and difference. The degree of acceptance of change can vary, but there are a number of general implications that change holds for IHRM approaches.

First, in Asia there is a strong foreign influence on the process of change, in particular the North American approach (Rowley and Ulrich, 2013). The more dependent the economy on foreign capital and MNCs' activities (e.g. Taiwan, Malaysia and Thailand), the more Western HRM approaches may be adopted and greater change in management approach can be expected. For example, West European or North American-owned firms tend to have more individualist values and hence are more accustomed to individualized rewards schemes. These schemes are different from rewards policies and practices prevalent among Asian firms, such as residual 'iron rice bowl' policies in China (Warner, 2009a), seniority based wage systems in Japan, or 'collective equality' in South Korea (Zhu et al., 2007; Rowley et al., 2011).

Economic restructuring in East Asia has led to relocation of some production processes from developed to developing countries, such as China, Cambodia, Malaysia, the Philippines, Thailand and Vietnam (Rowley and Abdul-Rahman, 2008; Rowley and Paik, 2009; Rowley and Quang, 2009; Rowley et al., 2010). Such liberalization of the economy has created more opportunity for domestic enterprises to adopt some of the widely used Western and Japanese HR practices (Benson and Zhu, 1999; Rowley and Ulrich, 2013). Thus, key HRM practices, such as individualized employment contracts, individual performance evaluation, individual career development and strategic roles for HRM have become more apparent in the East Asian approaches to HRM (Rowley et al., 2011).

The state has played a major role during the change process. 'State-led development' has impacted not only on processes of modernization but also on the role of active labour market practice in Asia (Lee and Warner, 2007; Rowley et al., 2010). Among the Asian economies, China and Vietnam have undergone a period of state-led economic reform and change in their people management systems, transforming from the traditional personnel management model into a hybrid model combining personnel management and HRM (Zhu et al., 2007; Rowley and Quang, 2009).

However, other factors can generate some resistance towards change and certainly slow down the speed of diffusion of HRM approaches in Asia. The role of the state can hinder change in HRM as well. For instance, bureaucratic control and inertia in Japan means that change has been difficult. This, combined with the sophistication of sub-contractor networks, has meant that change can be resisted. In South Korea, direct government involvement has exemplified the business–government relationship while the network links of the chaebol have often made change more difficult to implement (Rowley et al., 2004).

Moreover, the HRM approach may be opposed by the country's specific culture and institutions. Some Asian values, such as emphasis on hard work, respect for elders, strong family ties and passion for learning, mean that any imported HRM approach will be subject to change and adaptation to these cultural preferences (Rowley et al., 2004). HRM approaches and ideas tend to be more readily assimilated in different cultures when developed and tested in culturally compatible settings. Likewise, history is an important factor requiring due consideration in the adoption and implementation of HRM policies and practices and success is related to the 'fit' of the historical path of change with general societal norms in a particular local setting.

In short, reform, evolution and transformation each have different implications for HRM approaches since there is no homogeneous universal approach to IHRM. HRM practices and ideas from different countries tend to possess some cultural specificity, whatever their origin, and may run into difficulty when transplanted into other countries. To sum up, one may emphasize that there is no one best way.

Box 4.6   Stop and reflect

The development of IHRM research can be divided into three categories (Wei and Rowley, 2011): (1) studies that look at the management of firms in a multinational context, that is, the international aspects of management that do not exist in domestic firms, such as the internationalization processes, entry mode decisions, foreign subsidiary management and expatriate management; (2) comparison of management practices across different cultures; and (3) studies that look at management in specific countries within the domain of international management. More recent research into IHRM has acknowledged the link between strategy–structure configuration in MNEs and the demands for global integration

In light of this and your reading of this chapter so far, and after particularly reading Wei and Rowley (2011) and Brewster et al. (2005), stop and reflect on the following:

1. Globalization is generally seen as an economic process, but is not one that is well defined. Is there a distinction between IHRM and global HRM?
2. How can international HR professionals adopt a broad view of globalization?
3. Where does the added value of the HR function in global HRM lie?

7 Summary and conclusions

This chapter reviews some dominant IHRM approaches in North America and Western Europe and then explores the questions about the universality of HRM in other contexts. There are a number of factors affecting the applicability of HRM to different institutional contexts and international environments, particularly in the context of globalization. HRM's transfer and application to the Asian economies can be affected by the traditional philosophies embedded in Asian societies, the role the state plays during the change process and the degree of Western influence (Warner, 2009b; Rowley and Ulrich, 2013). Hence, the degree of acceptance of change in any HRM approach can vary. This chapter has examined and focused on HRM with an international dimension, indicating scope for diversity in IHRM approaches, and has argued in favour of making HRM more relevant and accessible to different economies.

First, IHRM is complex and multi-faceted and brings together a variety of approaches and factors. Practices developed in one context, for example in the West, cannot simply be assumed to work in the same way in other countries, such as Asian economies, which have substantially different value-sets. One of the future challenges for IHRM researchers is to synthesize national and comparative studies in developing economies and develop and clarify the field of IHRM (see Chapter 2). Future research should also integrate research across countries and regions, and access the complex interaction of culture, institutions, societal norms and values.

Second, MNCs are competing not only on a global level, but also on a regional or local level (Ghemawat, 2005). Local conditions relevant to HRM practices vary greatly. MNCs usually find themselves having different HRM practices across localities (Schuler and Tarique, 2007; Cox et al., 2014). In order to obtain consistency across all subsidiaries, some MNCs may develop common corporate values that guide the development of local HR policies while leaving the detailed plans to be designed by local branches or offices (see Case Study on HSBC in Asia). This practice requires MNCs to have a good understanding of the issues in the global context and, in turn, requires an understanding of their local environments.

Third, understanding the environment requires that MNCs adjust their IHRM approach continually towards the external and internal contextual factors. Even though differences in HRM approaches exist, they are often subject to dynamic change over time; and the direction of change is not necessarily towards some final destination or universal model of best practice. This chapter has illustrated the evolutionary nature of change in organizations' approaches to IHRM.

Above all, IHRM research should move beyond exploring practices and approaches that are exclusively organization-bound, to examine the socio-cultural contexts, varieties of business systems and political and economic environments in which the global workforce is managed. The turbulence in the firms' environments due to downturns as well as upswings in the business cycle, given the current global crisis and varied paths of economic recovery, should also be considered in IHRM research.

Discussion questions

1. Discuss the different IHRM approaches that have contributed to the development of HRM.
2. Universalistic and contingent theorists have differing views on how IHRM is used in the international context. Discuss the core arguments on both sides.
3. How do you think HRM practices might be transferred between countries?
4. What might be some of the constraints on the transfer of Western HRM approaches to Asian economies?
5. Choose a country and discuss the implications of the latest change in that country to the 'best practices' in HRM approach.

CASE STUDY

HSBC in East Asia (before the 2008 credit crisis)

(Data are extracted from companies' websites, industry reports and authors' long-term research and work experience in this region)

The forces in the world economy have necessitated many financial institutions to become more international in outlook in order to survive in the global industry. Noticeable changes, for example mergers and acquisitions, emergence of new players, de-regulation, and application of modern technology, have all been influencing the structure of the global financial industry (Qing, 2001). These changes have intensified competition among financial institutions in many countries, such as East Asian economies. Rapid changes in the industry can pose serious challenges even for the giant financial institutions and their approaches to HRM. Three areas of HRM that have been concerning the banks most in their Asian operations are recruitment, rewards, training and development. The following case considers HSBC's HRM policies and practices in East Asia and discusses how relevant and applicable existing IHRM approaches are to other parts of the world, what institutional and cultural factors influence HRM approaches in global firms, and what the implications of change are for HRM approaches in the finance and banking industries.

Company background

HSBC Holdings plc, number one in the Fortune Global 500 in 2007, is the world's largest company and bank. The Holdings was established in 1991 to become the parent company to the Hong Kong and Shanghai Banking Corporation. It has a significant presence in the major financial markets. By 2008, HSBC operated a network of around 600 offices in 20 countries in the Asia-Pacific region. Its long history in East Asia can be traced back to the nineteenth century. It has been the largest note-issuing bank in Hong Kong since the 1880s, handled the first public loan in China in 1874 and was the first bank to be established in Thailand in 1888.

Recruitment

When entering the Asian market, many MNCs have adopted an ethnocentric approach to their recruitment policies. Key top positions were often filled by expatriates from home countries although a number of MNCs have used a geocentric staffing policy to search for the best people. A key issue, however, for many Asian economies, such as China and Vietnam, which have had a large pool of unskilled and semi-skilled workers, is they have local labour market shortages of sufficient numbers of well-trained managers and technical people. Furthermore, recruiting qualified bankers in these local markets can be very difficult.

Business expansion during recent years has fuelled a talent war in the labour market. For instance, HSBC had planned to double its number of branches in China over the next few years. According to its manpower planning policy, there has always been 'a need to recruit managers to oversee new branches and handle new services, but experienced and talented bankers are limited in the market'. Consequently, HSBC implemented a global talent management process to attract, motivate and retain its employees. HR professionals first visited all countries to describe key principles and nomination guidelines for talent assessment to ensure employees 'buy in' to the recruitment process. Multiple sources of data, including interviews, panel interviews and 360 degree feedback, were then used to review capability ratings for all global talent nominees. A list of potential leaders and specialists were identified to fill future positions planned for the next three to seven years (Gakovic and Yardley, 2007).

Nevertheless, cultural and social influences played a key role in talent decisions in HSBC. The globally consistent talent nomination criteria and instructions were subject to local interpretations (Gakovic and Yardley, 2007). Cross-cultural differences further impacted on the consistency of the talent management processes.

(Continued)

(Continued)

Besides, the panel members who reviewed nominations were not equally comfortable with challenging one another or voicing negative criticisms because such views often can mean that people 'lose face', which is not acceptable in East Asian cultures (McGreal, 1995).

Rewards

The intensified competition resulting from the enhanced globalization of the Asian market created high demand for qualified bankers and finance and banking professionals. In competing for human talent, compensation has been increasingly used as an effective means to recruit, motivate and retain much needed professionals. According to some salary surveys, financial institutions witnessed the biggest salary increases among all industries in most Asian economies during the period 2005 to 2007.

Interestingly, HSBC adopted an ethnocentric approach to its rewards practices. Its grading structure, salary adjustment and bonus scheme were inherited from its head offices. For example, to encourage employees to have a direct interest in the bank, an employee share option saving plan was offered to employees in most countries. Global bonus schemes designed to align employees more closely with the achievement of long-term strategic objectives were introduced in Asia.

The implementation of standardized rewards practice might imply that the head office was concerned with consistent HRM approaches across its overseas operations, and that it was interested in having the ability to compare performance across countries. However, the connection between global rewards schemes and local performance evaluation involved lengthy delays and consequently failed to keep employees highly motivated.

Training and development

Due to their large size and extensive networks, most MNCs can leverage their training resources across the Asian region. In HSBC, training programmes were organized by regional training teams and launched by local offices. Typically, managers with one to two years company service would attend fundamental management skills training and those with three to five years company service would attend advanced courses. Some managers also went through job shadowing of their counterparts in other Asian countries (Poon and Rowley, 2008). In addition, similar to other financial institutions, HSBC launched online training programmes and learning resource centres which enabled geographically dispersed staff to gain access to learning materials and packages. The use of more flexible training and development methods provided wider choice and better access to development opportunities for employees.

Nonetheless, the high level of training investment could at times generate negative returns whenever the trainees 'job-hopped', were 'poached' or became misaligned with organizational objectives. Moreover, these changes pressurized HR departments and practitioners to manage increased diversity and utilize different systems to cope with employees' increasingly diverse needs and demands (Rowley and Poon, 2008).

Discussion

Transferring the bank's global HRM approach without making any adaptation to the local market was not without pain. Past success or 'best practice' in the head office did not automatically guarantee its effective transfer and adoption in local subsidiaries. In summary, there is no single management model available that can prescribe the way companies are organized and their people are managed, regardless of their Asian or Western origin (Warner, 2003). To make a global HRM approach work, often involves modifying global HRM or IHRM approaches and blending them with Asian characteristics. Consequently, the resultant characteristics of the corporate IHRM approach may be difficult to predict for each country and region and so there needs to be a greater appreciation of cultural and institutional contexts as well as more understanding of the dynamics of HRM change in international markets.

Case study questions

1. Will HSBC's HRM policies and practices become more uniform as business expands in Asia? Or will HSBC adopt distinct HRM policies and practices in different Asian economies?
2. Discuss the advantages and disadvantages of the following IHRM policies and practices: (a) global talent management process; (b) standardized corporate rewards; and (c) high level of training investment.
3. What alternative IHRM policies and practices would you recommend to HSBC for its operations in East Asia?

Case study questions for further reflection

1. Imagine you are offered the opportunity to propose new IHRM policies and practices for a multinational company starting in Asia. What are your suggested IHRM policies and practices?
2. Imagine you are given a task to harmonize HRM policies and practices among three operations in US, Europe and Asia. What would you propose? And why?

Further reading

- Rowley, C. and Benson, J. (2002) 'Convergence and divergence in Asian HRM', *California Management Review*, 44(2): 90–109.
  This article discusses how globalization of HRM has led to some common changes in IHRM practices. It suggests that many differences in HRM remain due to a variety of limiting factors, ranging from economic stages of development to business strategies, national culture and fixed enterprise mindsets.

- Mayrhofer, W. and Brewster, C. (2005) 'European HRM: researching developments over time', *Management Revue*, 16(1): 36–62.
  The article studies HRM developments in Europe to explore the notion of 'European HRM' and the meanings of convergence and divergence in HRM. It presents a more nuanced view of the notions of convergence and divergence, finding evidence of directional convergence, but national differences remain a key factor in HRM.

- Rowley, C., Benson, J. and Warner, M. (2004) 'Towards an Asian model of HRM? A comparative analysis of China, Japan and South Korea', *International Journal of HRM*, 15(4/5): 917–933.
  This study examines China, Japan and South Korea to see if a degree of convergence is taking place and if it is towards an identifiable 'Asian' model of HRM. A model of change is presented that distinguishes between levels of occurrence and acceptance. The development and practice of HRM in each country is analysed.

- Zhu, Y., Warner, M. and Rowley, C. (2007) 'HRM with "Asian" characteristics: a hybrid people-management system in East Asia', *International Journal of HRM*, 18(5): 745–768.
  This study illustrates the similarity and difference of people management system among the key economies in East Asia. It concludes that HRM is in a process of reform moving towards hybrid forms of people management in East Asia. A large number of factors are shaping the outcome of the process of reform.

- Brewster, C., Morley, M. and Mayrhofer, W. (2004) *HRM in Europe: Evidence of Convergence*. Oxford: Butterworth-Heinemann.
  A highly informative investigation of the empirical evidence for convergence of HRM in Europe. This book covers concepts and theoretical issues, trends in relation to these issues and comparisons between individual countries, and summaries and conclusions on the issue of convergence and divergence.

- Hall, P.A. and Soskice, D. (2001) *Varieties of Capitalism: The Institutional Foundations of Comparative Advantage*. Oxford: Oxford University Press.
  This book proposes comparative institutional advantage to explain differences among national political economies and distinguish between 'liberal' and 'coordinated' market economies.

- Rowley, C. and Warner, M. (eds) (2007) *Globalising International HRM*. London and New York: Routledge.

This book covers a wide range of regional and national cultures. It explores how cultures might shape both theory and practices in the field of IHRM.

- Rowley, C. and Warner, M. (eds) (2005) *Globalisation and Competitiveness*. London and New York: Routledge.
  This book evaluates the evolution of 'Big Business in Asia'. It focuses on recent issues affecting large corporations, both indigenous and foreign owned, such as multinational companies and international joint ventures, as well as key events such as the Asian crisis and its aftermath, China's entry into the WTO, and the downturn in the world economy.

- Warner, M., Edwards, V., Polansky, G., Pucko, D. and Zhu, Y. (2005) *Management in Transitional Economies: Central/Eastern Europe, Russia and China*. London: Taylor and Francis.
  This book examines the past, present and future management in several transitional economies, discusses the nature of the transition process and outlines a number of theoretical approaches.

Internet resources

- www.cipd.org.uk. The Chartered Institute of Personnel and Development is a professional institute for HRM professionals.
- www.berr.gov.uk. The Department for Business, Innovation and Skills is the UK government's department responsible for developing a remit for higher and professional/vocation education and training.
- www.worldatwork.org. World at Work is a US-based community specializing in research into compensation and rewards at work.
- www.hrmthejournal.com. HRM The Journal is an association of discussion forum and publication networks for researchers and practitioners in HRM and IHRM.

Self-assessment questions

Indicative answers to these questions can be found on the companion website at study.sagepub.com/harzing4e.

1. What are some key questions to be considered when conducting a comparative HRM study?
2. What are the pros and cons of the Harvard model in explaining HRM approaches?
3. What does 5-P stand for?

(Continued)

(Continued)

4. What are the three broad intervening factors that influence IHRM in terms of the transfer of HRM overseas and adaptation of HRM to local practices for Shen (2005)?
5. What roles do institutional forces play in HRM change?

References

Adler, N.J. and Ghadar, F. (1990) 'Strategic HRM: a global perspective', in R. Pieper (ed.), *Human Resource Management: An International Comparison*. Berlin: Walter de Gruyter, pp. 235–260.

Anderson, G. (1992) 'Selection', in B. Towers (ed.), *Handbook of Human Resource Management*. Oxford: Blackwell, pp. 167–185.

Arthur, J.B. (1992) 'The link between business strategy and industrial relations systems in American steel minimills', *Industrial and Labour Relations Review*, 45(3): 488–506.

Bartlett, C. and Ghoshal, S. (1992) *Transnational Management*. Boston, MA: Irwin.

Becker, B. and Gerhart, B. (1996) 'The impact of HRM on organisational performance: progress and prospects', *Academy of Management Journal*, 39(4): 779–802.

Becker, B., Huselid, M., Pickus, P. and Spratt, M. (1997) 'HR as a source of shareholder value: research and recommendations', *Human Resources Management*, 36(1): 39–47.

Beer, M., Spector, B., Lawrence, P.R., Mills, D.O. and Walton, R.E. (1984) *Managing Human Assets*. New York: Free Press.

Benson, J. and Zhu, Y. (1999) 'Market, firms and workers: the transformation of HRM in Chinese manufacturing enterprises', *HRM Journal*, 9(4): 58–74.

Boxall, P.F. (1992) 'Strategic HRM: beginning of a new theoretical sophistication?', *HRM Journal*, 2(2): 60–79.

Braun, W. and Warner, M. (2002) 'The "culture-free" versus "culture-specific" management debate', in M. Warner and P. Joynt (eds), *Managing across Cultures: Issues and Perspectives*, 2nd edn. London: Thomson Learning, pp. 13–25.

Brewster, C. (1993) 'Developing a "European" model of HRM', *International Journal of HRM*, 4(4): 765–784.

Brewster, C. (1995) 'Towards a European model of HRM', *Journal of International Business Studies*, 26(1): 1–21.

Brewster, C. (1999) 'Different paradigms in strategic HRM: questions raised by comparative research', in P. Wright, J.B.L. Dyer and G. Milkovich (eds), *Research in Personnel and HRM*. Greenwich, CT: JAI Press Inc., pp. 213–238.

Brewster, C., Sparrow, P. and Harris, H. (2005) 'Towards a new model of globalizing HRM', *International Journal of Human Resource Management*, 16(6): 949–970.

Budhwar, P.S. and Debrah, Y. (2001) 'Rethinking comparative and cross-national HRM research', *International Journal of HRM*, 12(3): 497–515.

Caldas, M.P., Tonelli, M.J. and Lacomba, B.M.B. (2011) IHRM in developing countries: does the functionalist vs critical debate make sense south of the equator? *Brazilian Administration Review*, 8(4): 433–453.

Carroll, G.R., Delacroix, J. and Goodstein, J. (1988) 'The political environments of organisation: an ecological view', *Research in Organisation Behaviour*, 10(1): 359–392.

Child, J. (1994) *Management in China during the Age of Reform*. Cambridge: Cambridge University Press.

Child, J. and Markoczy, L. (1993) 'Host-country managerial behaviour and learning in Chinese and Hungarian joint ventures', *Journal of Management Studies*, 30(4): 611–631.

Cox, A., Hannif, Z. and Rowley, C. (2014) 'Leadership styles and generational effects: examples of US companies in Vietnam', *International Journal of Human Resource Management*, 25(1): 1–22.

Davidson, W. (1980) 'The location of foreign direct investment activity: country characteristics and experience effects', *Journal of International Business Studies*, 11(2): 9–22.

Delery, J. (1998) 'Issues of fit in strategic HRM: implications for research', *Human Resource Management Review*, 8(3): 289–309.

Delery, J. and Doty, D. (1996) 'Modes of theorising in strategic HRM: tests of universalistic, contingency, and configurational performance predications', *Academy of Management Journal*, 39(4): 802–835.

Dowling, P.J. and Welch, D.E. (eds) (2004) *International Human Resource Management: Managing People in a Multinational Context*, 4th edn. London: Thomson.

Dyer, L. (1985) 'Strategic HRM and planning', in K.M. Rowland and G.R. Ferris (eds), *Research in Personnel and HRM*. Greenwich: JAI Press, pp. 1–30.

Easterby-Smith, M., Malina, D. and Lu, Y. (1995) 'How culture sensitive is HRM? A comparative analysis of practice in Chinese and UK companies', *International Journal of HRM*, 6(1): 31–59.

Evans, P. and Lorange, P. (1989) 'The two logics behind human resource management', in P. Evans, Y. Doz and A. Laurent (eds), *Human Resource Management in International Firms: Change, Globalisation and Innovation*. London: Macmillan, pp. 144–161.

Evans, P., Pucik, V. and Barsoux, J.L. (2002) *The Global Challenge: Frameworks for International Human Resource Management*. London: McGraw-Hill.

Filella, J. (1991) 'Is there a Latin model in the management of HR?', *Personnel Review*, 20(6): 15–24.

Florkowski, G.W. and Nath, R. (1993) 'MNC responses to the legal environment of international HRM', *International Journal of HRM*, 4(2): 305–324.

Gakovic, A. and Yardley, K. (2007) 'Global talent management at HSBC', *Organisation Development Journal*, 25(2): 201–205.

Galbraith, J.R. and Nathanson, D.A. (1978) *Strategy Implementation: The Role of Structure and Process*. St Paul, MN: West Publishing.

Gaugler, E. (1988) 'HRM: an international comparison', *Personnel*, 65(8): 24–30.

Ghemawat, P. (2005) 'Regional strategies for global leadership', *Harvard Business Review*, 83(12): 98–108.

Guest, D.E. (1991) 'Personnel management: the end of orthodoxy?', *British Journal of Industrial Relations*, 29(2): 149–175.

Guest, D.E. (1995) 'Human resource management, trade unions and industrial relations', in J. Storey (ed.), *Human Resource Management: A Critical Text*. London: Routledge, pp. 110–141.

Guest, D.E. (1997) 'HRM and performance: a review and research agenda', *International Journal of HRM*, 8(3): 263–276.

Gully, S.M., Philips, J.M. and Tarique, I. (2003) 'Collectivism and goal orientation as mediators of the effect of national identity on merit pay decisions', *International Journal of Human Resource Management*, 14(8): 1368–1390.

Hall, P.A. and Soskice, D. (2001) *Varieties of Capitalism: The Institutional Foundations of Comparative Advantage.* Oxford: Oxford University Press.

Heenan, D.A. and Perlmutter, H.V. (1990) *Multinational Organisation Development.* Reading, MA: Addison-Wesley Longman.

Hendry, C. and Pettigrew, A. (1990) 'HRM: An agenda for the 1990s', *International Journal of HRM*, 1(1): 17–43.

Hoffman, A. (1999) 'Institutional evolution and change: environmentalism and the US chemical industry', *Academy of Management Journal*, 42(4): 351–371.

Hofstede, G. (1984) *Culture's Consequences: International Differences in Work-Related Values* (abridged edn). London: Sage.

Hsu, Y.R. and Leat, M. (2000) 'A study of HRM and recruitment and selection policies and practices in Taiwan', *International Journal of HRM*, 11(2): 413–435.

Jackson, S.E. and Schuler, R.S. (1995) 'Understanding HRM in the context of organisation and their environment', *Annual Review of Psychology*, 46(1): 237–264.

Jackson, S.E., Schuler, R.S. and Rivero, J. (1989) 'Organisational characteristics as predictors of personnel practices', *Personnel Psychology*, 42(4): 727–786.

Jackson, T. (2004) 'HRM in developing countries', in A.W. Harzing and J.V. Ruysseveldt (eds), *International HRM*, 2nd edn. London: Sage, pp. 221–248.

Kerr, C., Dunlop, J., Harbison, F. and Myers, C. (1960) *Industrialism and Industrial Man.* London: Heinemann.

Lee, G.O.M. and Warner, M. (eds) (2007) *Unemployment in China.* London: RoutledgeCurzon.

Legge, K. (1995) *HRM: Rhetorics and Realities.* Chippenham: Macmillan Business.

Lockett, M. (1988) 'Culture and the problem of Chinese management', *Organisation Studies*, 9(4): 475–496.

MacDuffie, J.P. (1995) 'HR bundles and manufacturing performance: organisational logic and flexible production systems in the world auto industry', *Industrial and Labour Relations Review*, 48(2): 197–221.

Mayrhofer, W. and Brewster, C. (2005) 'European HRM: researching developments over time', *Management Revue*, 16(1): 36–62.

McGreal, I. (1995) *Great Thinkers of the Eastern World: The Major Thinkers and the Philosophical and Religious Classics of China, India, Japan, Korea and the World of Islam.* New York: Harper Collins.

Metcalfe, B.D. and Rees, C.J. (2005) 'Theorising advances in international HR development', *HR Development International*, 8(4): 449–465.

Meyer, J. and Rowan, B. (1977) 'Institutionalised organisation, formal structure as myth and ceremony', *American Journal of Sociology*, 83(2): 340–360.

Morgan, P.V. (1986) 'International human resource management: fact or fiction', *Personnel Administrator*, 31(9): 43–47.

Ngo, H.Y., Turban, D., Lau, C.M. and Lui, S.Y. (1998) 'Human resource practice and firm performance of multinational corporations: influences of country origin', *International Journal of HRM*, 9(4): 632–651.

Noronha, C. (2002) *The Theory of Culture-Specific Total Quality Management: Quality Management in Chinese Regions.* London: Palgrave; New York: St Martin's Press.

Paauwe, J. and Dewe, P. (1995) 'Human resource management in multinational corporations: theories and models', in A. Harzing and J. Ruysseveldt (eds), *International Human Resource Management.* London: Sage, pp. 75–98.

Peltonen, T. (2006) 'Critical theoretical perspectives on international human resource management', in G.K. Stahl and I. Björkman (eds), *Handbook of Research in International Human Resource Management.* Cheltenham: Edward Elgar, pp. 523–535.

Pfeffer, J. (1994) *Competitive Advantage through People: Unleashing the Power of the Work Force.* Boston: Harvard Business School Press.

Pieper, R. (ed.) (1990) *HRM: An International Comparison.* Berlin: Walter de Gruyter.

Plessis, A.J. (2010) 'International human resource management: an overview of its effect on managers in global organisations', *Interdisciplinary Journal of Contemporary Research in Business*, 2(4): 178–192.

Poole, M. (1990) 'Editorial: HRM in an international perspective', *International Journal of HRM*, 1(1): 1–15.

Poon, H.F. (2010) *Human Resources Management Changes in China: A Case Study of the Banking Industry.* Berlin: Lap Lambert Academic Publishing.

Poon, H.F. and Rowley, C. (2008) 'Company profile: East Asia', in C. Wankel (ed.), *Encyclopaedia of Business in Today's World.* Thousand Oaks, CA: Sage, p. 325.

Poutsma, E., Ligthart, P.E.M. and Veersma, U. (2006) 'The diffusion of calculative and collaborative HRM practices in European firms', *Industrial Relations*, 45(4): 513–546.

Priem, R.L., Love, L.G. and Shaffer, M. (2000) 'Industrialization and values evolution: the case of Hong Kong and Guangzhou, China', *Asia Pacific Journal of Management*, 17(3): 473–492.

Purcell, J. and Ahlstrand, B. (1994) *HRM in the Multi-divisional Company.* Oxford: Oxford University Press.

Qing, W. (2001) 'The challenges facing China: financial services industry?', in P. Nolan (ed.), *Changing the Chinese Business Revolution.* London: Palgrave, pp. 813–883.

Rodgers, R.A. and Wong, J. (1996) 'Human factors in the transfer of the "Japanese Best Practice" manufacturing system to Singapore', *International Journal of HRM*, 7(4): 455–488.

Rowley, C. and Abdul-Rahman, S. (eds) (2008) *The Changing Face of Management in South East Asia.* London: Routledge.

Rowley, C., Bae, J. and Chen, S.J. (2011) 'From a paternalistic model towards what? HRM trends in Korean and Taiwan', *Personnel Review*, 40(6): 700–722.

Rowley, C., Benson, J. and Warner, M. (2004) 'Towards an Asian model of HRM? A comparative analysis of China, Japan and South Korea', *International Journal of HRM*, 15(4/5): 917–933.

Rowley, C. and Paik, Y. (2009) *The Changing Face of Korean Management.* London: Routledge.

Rowley, C. and Poon, H.F. (2008) 'HRM best practices and transfers to the Asia Pacific region', in C. Wankel (ed.), *21st Century Management.* Thousand Oaks, CA: Sage, pp. 209–220.

Rowley, C. and Quang, T. (2009) *The Changing Face of Vietnamese Management.* London: Routledge.

Rowley, C., Truong, Q. and van der Heijden, B. (2010) 'Globalisation, competitiveness and HRM in a transitional economy', *International Journal of Business Studies*, 18(1): 75–100.

Rowley, C. and Ulrich, D. (2012a) 'Setting the scene for leadership in Asia', *Asia Pacific Business Review*, 18(4): 451–464.

Rowley, C. and Ulrich, D. (2012b) 'Lessons learned and insight derived from leadership in Asia', *Asia Pacific Business Review*, 18(4): 675–681.

Rowley, C. and Ulrich, D. (eds) (2013) *Leadership in the Asia Pacific: A Global Research Perspective.* London: Routledge.

Rowley, C. and Warner, M. (2005) *Globalisation and Competitiveness.* London: Taylor and Francis.

Rowley, C. and Warner, M. (2007a) *Globalising International HRM.* London: Routledge.

Rowley, C. and Warner, M. (2007b) 'Introduction: globalising IHRM', *International Journal of HRM*, 18(5): 703–716.

Rowley, C. and Yukongdi, V. (2009) *The Changing Face of Women Managers in Asia.* London: Routledge.

Schuler, R.S. (1992) 'Strategic HRM: linking the people with the strategic needs of the business', *Organisation Dynamics*, 21(1): 18–32.

Schuler, R.S. and Tarique, I. (2007) 'IHRM: a North American perspective, a thematic update and suggestions for future research', *International Journal of HRM*, 18(5): 717–744.

Schuler, R.S., Sowling, P. and De Cieri, H. (1993) 'An integrative framework of strategic international human resource management', *Journal of Management*, 19(2): 419–459.

Shen, J. (2005) 'Developing an integrative international human resource model: the contribution of Chinese multinational enterprises', *Asia Pacific Business Review*, 11(3): 369–388.

Smale, A. (2008) 'Foreign subsidiary perspectives on the mechanisms of global HRM integration', *Human Resource Management Journal*, 18(2): 135–153.

Sparrow, P.R. and Hiltrop, J.M. (1994) *European HRM in Transition*. London: Prentice Hall.

Stahl, G.K. and Björkman, I. (eds) (2006) *Handbook of Research in International Human Resource Management*. Cheltenham: Edward Elgar.

Storey, J. (ed.) (1995) *Human Resource Management: A Critical Text*. London: Routledge.

Taylor, F. (1911) *Scientific Management*. New York: Harper and Row.

Taylor, S., Beechler, S. and Napier, N. (1996) 'Towards an integrative model of strategic human resource management', *Academy of Management Review*, 21(4): 959–985.

Tempel, A. and Walgenbach, P. (2007) 'Global standardisation of organisational forms and management practices? What new institutionalism and the business-systems approach can learn from each other', *Journal of Management Studies*, 44(1): 1–24.

Tichy, N.M., Fombrun, C.J. and Devanna, M.A. (1982) 'Strategic HRM', *Sloan Management Review*, 23(2): 47–61.

Truong, Q. and Rowley, C. (2014) 'Vietnam: post-state capitalism', in M. Witt and G. Redding (eds), *Oxford Handbook of Asian Business Systems*. Oxford: Oxford University Press.

Tse, D.K., Pan, Y. and Au, K.Y. (1997) 'How MNCs choose entry modes and form alliances: the China experience', *Journal of International Business Studies*, 28(3): 779–805.

Valiukonyte, D. and Parkkonen, V. (2008) 'Conceptual framework for the analysis of business systems: national perspective', *Economics and Management*, 13(1): 729–738.

Walder, A.G. (1995) 'Local governments as industrial firms: an organisational analysis of China's transition economy', *American Journal of Sociology*, 101(2): 263–301.

Walsh, J. and Zhu, Y. (2007) 'Local complexities and global uncertainties: a study of foreign ownership and HRM in China', *International Journal of HRM*, 18(2): 249–267.

Walton, R.E. (1985) 'From control to commitment in the workplace', *Harvard Business Review*, 63(2): 77–84.

Warner, M. (1995) *The Management of HR in Chinese Industry*. London: Macmillan; New York: St Martin's Press.

Warner, M. (2003) 'China's HRM revisited: a step-wise path to convergence?', *Asia Pacific Business Review*, 19(4): 15–31.

Warner, M. (ed.) (2009a) *Human Resource Management with Chinese Characteristics: Facing the Challenges of Globalisation*. London and New York: Routledge.

Warner, M. (2009b) 'Making sense of HRM in China: setting the scene', *International Journal of Human Resource Management*, 20(11): 2169–2193.

Warner, M. (2012) 'Whither Chinese HRM? Paradigms, models and theories', *International Journal of Human Resource Management*, 23(19): 3943–3963.

Warner, M., Edwards, V., Polansky, G., Pucko, D. and Zhu, Y. (2005) *Management in Transitional Economies Central/Eastern Europe, Russia and China*. London: Taylor and Francis.

Watson, T. (1994) 'Recruitment and selection', in K. Sisson (ed.), *Personnel Management*. Oxford: Blackwell, pp. 185–252.

Wei, Q. and Rowley, C. (2011) 'International HRM', in C. Rowley and K. Jackson (eds), *Human Resource Management: The Key Concepts*. Abingdon, Oxon: Routledge, pp. 108–113.

Whitley, R. (1998) 'Internationalisation and varieties of capitalism: the limited effects of cross-national coordination of economic activities on the nature of business systems', *Review of International Political Economy*, 5 (3): 445–481.

Whitley, R. (1999) *Divergent Capitalisms: The Social Structuring and Change of Business Systems*. Oxford: University Press.

Wong, M. (1996) 'Shadow management in Japanese companies in Hong Kong', *Asia Pacific Journal of HR*, 34(1): 95–110.

Zhu, Y., Warner, M. and Rowley, C. (2007) 'HRM with "Asian" characteristics: a hybrid people-management system in East Asia', *International Journal of HRM*, 18(5): 745–768.

Part 2
International Assignments and Employment Practices

International Assignments

B. Sebastian Reiche and Anne-Wil Harzing

Contents

Learning objectives

After reading this chapter you will be able to:

- Understand and evaluate different staffing options that are available to MNCs
- Differentiate between the main motives for using international assignments in MNCs
- Identify different forms of international assignments and assess their distinct advantages and disadvantages
- Explain why selection, preparation and repatriation form an integral part of the international assignment process
- Critically evaluate the success of an international transfer, both from the perspective of the individual assignee and the company

Chapter outline

The chapter reviews the various staffing options in MNCs in general and then discusses different corporate motives for using international transfers as well as the different forms of international assignments available to MNCs. It also gives a detailed overview of the assignment process and presents a set of criteria for assessing assignment success.

1 Introduction

This chapter deals with several aspects of international assignments. First, section 2 reviews different staffing policies and looks in some detail at the factors influencing the choice between host country and parent country nationals. Subsequently, section 3 takes a strategic perspective on international transfers and looks at the underlying motives that MNCs have to transfer international assignees between MNC units. We review two of the motives for international transfers – control and coordination, and knowledge transfer – in detail. Section 4 then deals with alternatives to expatriation, including the use of inpatriate, short-term, self-initiated and virtual assignments. In section 5, we examine the international assignment process which consists of the pre-assignment phase, the actual assignment and repatriation. Here, we review recruitment and selection issues associated with international assignments, discussing both the prescriptive models found in the expatriate literature and the circumstances that seem to persist in practice. We also consider expatriate adjustment during the assignment and describe organizational support upon repatriation. The final section critically reflects on the concept of expatriate failure and outlines a multidimensional perspective on assignment success.

2 Staffing policies

In his seminal work, Perlmutter (1969) identified three different international orientations (ethnocentric, polycentric and geocentric) that have become the standard way to describe MNC staffing policies. MNCs following an ethnocentric staffing policy would appoint mostly parent country nationals to top positions at their subsidiaries, while MNCs following a polycentric staffing policy would prefer to appoint host country nationals. Firms with a geocentric staffing policy would simply appoint the best person, regardless of his/her nationality and that could include third country nationals, nationals of a country other than the MNC's home country and the country of the subsidiary (see Table 5.1). In a later publication, Heenan and Perlmutter (1979) defined a fourth approach, which they called regiocentric. In this approach, managers are transferred on a regional basis, such as Europe, and it often forms a mid-way station between a pure polycentric/ethnocentric approach and a truly geocentric approach. It is important to note that these staffing policies apply to key positions in MNC subsidiaries only. Some PCNs or TCNs might still be found at middle management, although MNCs normally appoint host country managers at this and lower levels.

Table 5.1   MNC staffing policies

Parent country national (PCN)	Nationality of employee is the same as that of the headquarters of the multinational firm	e.g. in a German headquartered MNC, a German employee working at its Chinese subsidiary
Host country national (HCN)	Nationality of employee is the same as that of the local subsidiary	e.g. in a German headquartered MNC, a Chinese employee working at its Chinese subsidiary
Third country national (TCN)	Nationality of employee is neither that of the headquarters nor the local subsidiary	e.g. in a German headquartered MNC, an Indian employee working at its Chinese subsidiary

More recent research has criticized the HQ-centric nature of these orientations. Indeed, irrespective of the specific approach chosen in a given MNC the staffing decisions are usually initiated centrally and then imposed on the foreign units by the HQ. In this regard, Novicevic and Harvey (2001) call for a pluralistic orientation in which subsidiaries are given more autonomy and flexibility in the staffing process. This pluralistic orientation would consist of multiple, diverse and possibly competing orientations of subsidiary staffing that operate independently within the MNC context and requires coordinating mechanisms such as the socialization of key MNC staff (see Box 5.1). Inpatriates (see section 4) may take on such an integrative role by serving as linking pins between the various subsidiaries and the HQ.

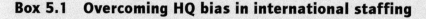

> ## Box 5.1   Overcoming HQ bias in international staffing
>
> Adidas, a premier global sporting goods company, is an example of how the HQ bias in international staffing can be overcome. Its corporate HQ – located in Herzogenaurach, a small town in the south of Germany – is merely one of many company units spread around the globe. Employees are transferred in all directions, with the HQ acting as a provider and recipient of international staff, just like every other unit. Further, each relocation is jointly managed through the central Human Resource department at HQ and the respective local HR department in the foreign subsidiary, providing comparability across assignments. According to HR managers at Adidas, this diversity in staffing provides employees with a broader understanding of the overall organization, offers career opportunities beyond the local context for parent country as well as foreign employees, and ultimately enables the company to better respond to local differences in tastes and preferences.
>
> *Source*: Reiche, 2010.

The term expatriation is often used to describe the process of international transfer of managers. Although the term expatriate could literally be taken to mean any employee who is working outside his or her home country, it is normally reserved for PCNs (and sometimes TCNs) working in foreign subsidiaries of the MNC for a pre-defined period, usually two to five years. Given the range of alternative forms of international transfers which we will discuss in section 4, it is common to use the generic term 'international assignee' to refer to any person who is relocated internationally.

In this section, we offer a more detailed discussion of the advantages and disadvantages of using PCNs, HCNs or TCNs as well as some recent statistics on the use of PCNs and HCNs in different countries and industries. We also present a conceptual model that summarizes the factors influencing the choice between PCNs and HCNs.

PCNs, HCNs or TCNs: (Dis)advantages and statistics

A review of the advantages and disadvantages of employing these different groups of employees will clarify the applicability of the different staffing policies identified above. Some of the most frequently mentioned advantages and disadvantages (Negandhi, 1987; Phatak, 1989; Dowling et al., 2008) are summarized in Table 5.2.

It will be clear that none of these options is without disadvantages. In the next section, we will discuss several factors that might influence the choice between these different types of manager, but first we will provide some statistics on the relative use of these groups. Given that staffing policies might have an important

Table 5.2   Advantages and disadvantages of using PCNs, HCNs or TCNs

	Advantages	Disadvantages
PCNs **Parent country nationals**	• familiarity with the home office's goals, objectives, policies and practices • technical and managerial competence • effective liaison and communication with home-office personnel • easier exercise of control over the subsidiary's operations	• difficulties in adapting to the foreign language and the socio-economic, political, cultural and legal environment • excessive cost of selecting, training and maintaining expatriate managers and their families abroad • the host country's insistence on localizing operations and on promoting local nationals in top positions at foreign subsidiaries • family adjustment problems, especially concerning the unemployed partners of managers
HCNs **Host country nationals**	• familiarity with the socio-economic, political and legal environment and with business practices in the host country • lower cost incurred in hiring them as compared to PCN and TCN • provides opportunities for advancement and promotion to local nationals and, consequently, increases their commitment and motivation • responds effectively to the host country's demands for localization of the subsidiary's operation	• difficulties in exercising effective control over the subsidiary's operation • communication difficulties in dealing with home-office personnel • lack of opportunities for the home country's nationals to gain international and cross-cultural experience
TCNs **Third country nationals**	• perhaps the best compromise between securing needed technical and managerial expertise and adapting to a foreign socio-economic and cultural environment • TCN are usually career international business managers • TCN are usually less expensive to maintain than PCN • TCN may be better informed about the host environment than PCN	• the host country's sensitivity with respect to nationals of specific countries • local nationals are impeded in their efforts to upgrade their own ranks and assume responsible positions in the multinational subsidiaries

impact on the functioning of the subsidiary, it is surprising that there is so little research on the relative use of PCNs, HCNs and TCNs. Initially, only two studies had been conducted which provide any details on this issue (Tung, 1982; Kopp, 1994). Kopp's results were limited to the use of PCNs in MNCs from various home countries only, and neither Tung nor Kopp discussed the use of PCNs in different industries. Moreover, both studies conceptualized Europe as one supposedly homogeneous group, both in terms of home and host country.

Another study (Harzing, 2001a) – based on archival data for 2,689 subsidiaries of nearly 250 different MNCs – provides us with detailed information on the relative use of PCNs for the managing director position in foreign subsidiaries. Overall, 40.8 per cent of the subsidiaries had a PCN as managing director, but as Table 5.3 shows, this percentage differed substantially by home country, host country cluster and industry. With regard to home countries, subsidiaries of Japanese MNCs are much more likely to have a PCN as managing director than subsidiaries of European MNCs. The exact percentage of PCNs in subsidiaries of European MNCs differed considerably across the various countries ranging from a low of 18.2 per cent for Denmark to a high of 48.1 per cent for Italy. At the subsidiary level, the highest percentage of PCNs can be found in Latin America, Africa, Asia and the Middle East, while expatriate presence is much lower in Canada and Western Europe and is particularly low in Scandinavia. In general, MNCs operating in the financial sector and the automobile industry show the highest percentage of PCNs as managing directors. A low expatriate presence is found in some service industries and in 'multi-domestic' industries such as food. As the sample size for some of the categories is relatively small, results for these categories should be treated with caution. It must be noted though that the overall sample size is much higher than that of either Tung's or Kopp's study. In a more recent study of 817 MNC subsidiaries located in nine countries/regions, Harzing et al. (2012) generally confirmed this structure of staffing patterns concerning home and host country. However, they also found that the overall proportion of PCNs in the managing director role has declined for nearly every home and host country studied and stands at around 60 per cent of the level that Harzing (2001a) reported earlier.

The results in Table 5.3 describe the percentage of PCNs in the managing director function only. Although much less information was available for the other job functions, the level of expatriate presence was generally found to be lower. Only 17.2 per cent of the subsidiary finance directors (N = 358) were PCNs, while this was the case for 10.1 per cent of the marketing directors (N = 218). The lowest percentage of PCNs, however, was found in the personnel director's function (2.2 per cent, N = 92). In general, MNCs tended to have more PCNs for the managing director function than for any of the other job functions. Again, more recent data have largely replicated these trends (Harzing et al., 2012). For both German and Italian MNCs, however, the percentage of PCNs for the financial director function comes close to the percentage of PCNs for the managing director function, while for British MNCs the financial director in subsidiaries is even more likely to be a PCN than is the managing director.

As less than 5 per cent of the positions in this study were occupied by TCNs we have not discussed this category in any detail. However, we can say that, similar to Tung's study, the highest percentage of TCNs in the sample can be found in African subsidiaries. Confirming the results of both Tung's and Kopp's studies, European MNCs tend to employ more TCNs than Japanese MNCs. This might be a reflection of the availability of near-nationals in European countries (e.g. Denmark-Sweden, Spain-Portugal). A more recent study of 136 multinationals based in Germany, the UK, Japan and the US replicated this latter finding and showed that the relative share of TCNs appears to have increased, with almost one in five foreigners occupying a managerial position in a subsidiary being TCNs (Tungli and Peiperl, 2009). Harzing et al. (2012) reported similar levels of TCN staffing.

Table 5.3 Sample size and percentage of PCN subsidiary managing directors in different HQ countries, subsidiary country clusters and industries

Country of origin of HQ	N	% of PCNs	Industry	N	% of PCNs
Denmark	88	18.2%	Business & management services	71	12.7%
UK	381	23.1%	Rubber & miscellaneous plastics	30	20.0%
Norway	49	24.5%	Stone, glass & clay products	72	23.6%
Switzerland	207	25.6%	Pharmaceutical	156	25.0%
France	247	30.0%	Food & related products	132	25.8%
Finland	200	30.0%	Advertising agencies	109	26.6%
Netherlands	196	32.7%	Electronic & electric equipment	160	30.6%
Sweden	389	34.2%	Industrial equipment	282	32.6%
Germany	279	40.9%	Instruments	70	32.9%
Italy	52	48.1%	Paper	101	33.7%
Japan	601	76.5%	Computers & office machines	128	34.4%
			Industrial Chemicals	175	37.7%
Total	2689	40.8%	Engineering services	41	39.0%

Subsidiary country cluster	N	% of PCNs	Insurance carriers & agents	139	39.6%
			Household appliances	84	40.5%
Scandinavia	164	14.6%	Metal products	83	42.2%
Western Europe	1351	33.3%	Printing & publishing	80	45.0%
Eastern Europe	81	39.5%	Oil & Gas	25	48.0%
Canada	94	41.5%	Non depository financial institutions	46	52.2%
Australia/New Zealand	135	41.5%	Telecommunications equipment	62	53.2%
Latin America	254	50.8%	Motor vehicles and parts	82	62.2%
Africa	53	58.5%	Banks & banking services	481	76.1%
Asia	515	60.2%	Security & commodity brokers	80	84.8%
Middle East	42	66.7%			
Total	2689	40.8%	Total	2689	40.8%

Harzing's (2001a) study also shows that a differentiated approach to subsidiary management, as advocated by many scholars in the field of international management (Bartlett and Ghoshal, 1989; Ghoshal and Nohria, 1993; Paterson and Brock, 2002), is important for staffing practices as well. Fewer than 10 per cent of the companies in this study had a uniform staffing policy (only HCNs or only PCNs). These companies were mostly Japanese MNCs in the financial sector, a sector that on average had a very high percentage of PCNs as managing directors. Other companies differentiated their approach according to host country and subsidiary characteristics. We will look into the factors that influence the choice between HCNs and PCNs in more detail in the next section.

Factors influencing the choice between HCNs and PCNs

The same study we referred to above (Harzing, 2001a) also provides some insight into the factors that influence the choice between HCNs and PCNs for the managing director position in foreign subsidiaries. Figure 5.1 summarizes the factors that had a

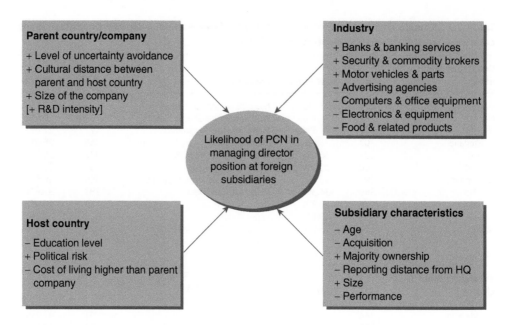

Figure 5.1   Factors influencing the choice between HCN and PCN

* (+) denotes a positive relationship. Example: + Size = The larger the organization the higher is the likelihood that a PCN holds the managing director position in its foreign subsidiaries.

significant impact on this choice. It is important to realize that this model was constructed based on multivariate statistical analysis (logistic regression). This means that although some of the factors might be intercorrelated, they all have a significant and independent impact on the choice between HCNs and PCNs.

With regard to parent country/company characteristics, MNCs from countries with a national culture that scores high on uncertainty avoidance (Hofstede, 1980, 2001) have a higher tendency to employ PCNs as managing directors for their subsidiaries. There is often scepticism in the parent country towards appointing foreigners as managers and a view that initiative arising from subordinates should be kept under HQ control. Managers are expected to be experts in their fields and generally are selected based on seniority (Hofstede, 1980, 2001). These characteristics usually point to a trusted PCN as the preferred alternative for senior positions in subsidiaries. Direct control of subsidiary operations will also be more important if the level of cultural distance or institutional distance (Gaur et al., 2007) between home and host country is high. In this case, HQ managers might not trust the information they receive from local managers. Additionally, HQ managers might fear that local managers are less committed to the company. However, Gong (2003a) found that the reliance on PCNs in cases of high cultural distance weakens over time, suggesting that MNCs' longer presence in a host country may facilitate the development of trusting relationships with HCNs leading to a reduced perceived need to deploy PCNs. Furthermore, communication between people from different cultural backgrounds can be very difficult (even if they speak the same language) and the opportunity for misunderstanding is usually high (Marschan-Piekkari et al., 1999). Therefore, HQ managers will prefer to have at least some home country managers in important positions to facilitate the information flow.

Larger MNCs have more PCNs as managing directors since they have more managerial resources and are more likely to have a formal management development programme in operation that involves the transfer of managers around the world. MNCs with a research intensive product are more likely to feel the need to transfer at least some of this knowledge to their subsidiaries and to train local managers (Hamill, 1989). Whereas Harzing (2001a) did not find support for this relationship, Harzing et al. (2012) showed that the proportion of PCNs in the R&D function was higher than any other function except for the managing director position.

Other research has highlighted the role of MNC competitive strategy for subsidiary staffing (Tarique et al., 2006). Whereas MNCs pursuing a global strategy are more likely to staff their subsidiaries with a focus on PCNs or HCNs/TCNs that have been socialized at the HQ, MNCs with a multidomestic strategy will concentrate on HCNs who have been socialized at the host country subsidiary. This influence is likely to be moderated by parent country cultural dimensions, the cultural similarity between parent and subsidiary country, and the managerial orientation in the HQ. For example, MNCs with a multidomestic strategy will more likely staff their culturally dissimilar subsidiaries with HCNs that have been socialized at the HQ. Similarly, MNCs with a global strategy and a polycentric managerial orientation will more likely staff their subsidiaries with HCNs that have been socialized at the HQ.

With regard to the influence of industry, only those with a significantly higher or lower level of PCNs as managing director are included in this model. A high percentage of PCNs as managing director is found in the financial services and motor vehicles and parts, while a low percentage of expatriates is found in the advertising industry, the computer and office equipment industry, the electronic and electric equipment industry, and the food industry. Some of the industry effects are easily explained. The control aspect will lead companies to employ a large percentage of PCNs in financial services, while the importance of knowledge of the local market will lead companies to employ a large percentage of HCNs in advertising and the food industry. The results for the other industries are less straightforward and would merit further investigation in a more controlled sample.

With regard to host country characteristics, MNCs are more likely to employ PCNs when the level of education in the host country is low, since in that case qualified local personnel will be scarce. Further, a high level of political risk in the host country is likely to make direct control through expatriates more important because the risks of loss of income or assets might be substantial. It also makes the speed and clarity of communication facilitated by the use of PCNs crucial (Boyacigiller, 1990). As we have seen above, one of the advantages of having HCNs in top management positions is that they are less expensive to employ than PCNs. This motive is more important when the cost of living in the host country is higher than in the home country. In this case, an expatriate will expect to get additional compensation to maintain his/her standard of living. By contrast, local managers have probably adjusted better to the high cost of living and would not require additional compensation.

Finally, there are several subsidiary characteristics that impact on the choice between HCNs and PCNs as managing director. Subsidiary age will be negatively related to the likelihood of using PCNs as managing directors. When a subsidiary has just been established, HQ will feel a higher need to ensure its operations are in accordance with HQ policies and will hence use trusted PCNs. Furthermore, MNCs might have difficulty in attracting high-calibre locals for employment in recently established subsidiaries. When subsidiaries become more established, local recruitment may be easier and some transfer of knowledge and training of local managers will already have been effected (Boyacigiller, 1990; Gong, 2003b). Hébert et al. (2005) even point to negative implications of using PCNs for an MNC's operational efficiency once the company has developed detailed host country expertise because PCNs entail substantial costs and resource commitments. The parent company's lack of knowledge of the local labour market and a lack of recruitment potential will also lead greenfield establishments to appoint PCNs to top management positions. By contrast, acquired subsidiaries often already have an established local managerial cadre. When a subsidiary is very important to HQ, there will be a preference for controlling the subsidiary through PCNs (Belderbos and Heijltjes, 2005). Large, majority-owned subsidiaries that report directly to the HQ or subsidiaries that possess resources necessary for the parent to execute its strategy successfully are more important to the HQ. Finally, control of the subsidiary will also be more important when a subsidiary is under-performing, and direct HQ intervention by means of a PCN is considered necessary.

3 Motives for international transfers

Now that we have established the advantages and disadvantages of using different groups of managers and have reviewed the factors influencing the choice between HCNs and PCNs, we will take a closer look at the motives that MNCs have to send their staff abroad. In this section, we will first discuss the classification by Edström and Galbraith (1977) and will show that the results of German studies largely confirm this classification. We will then review two of the motives for international transfers – control and coordination, and knowledge transfer – in more detail.

Why do companies assign employees abroad? Edström and Galbraith's typology

There are few theoretical concepts or forms of explanation regarding the motives for international transfers. At first sight, the study by Edström and Galbraith (1977) is the only one that theoretically explains why international transfer of managers occurs. They proposed three general company motives for making this type of transfer. The first was to fill positions, which concerns the transfer of technical and managerial knowledge. This motive is quite important for developing countries, where qualified local nationals might not be available, but specific knowledge transfer might be necessary to subsidiaries in developed countries as well. Expatriates can be seen as the key bearers of tacit knowledge. The second major motive is management development. The transfer gives the manager international experience and develops him/her for future important tasks in subsidiaries abroad or with the parent company. This kind of transfer would be carried out even if qualified host country nationals were available. For the third motive for international transfers, the final goal is not individual development but organization development. This motive consists of two elements: socialization of both expatriate and local managers into the corporate culture and the creation of a verbal information network that provides links between subsidiaries and HQ.

The classification of Edström and Galbraith is well accepted in the literature on international transfers. Virtually every publication that deals with this topic refers to Edström and Galbraith's landmark 1977 *Administrative Science Quarterly* article. There are also a substantial number of German studies, both conceptual and empirical, on this topic. The fact that they were initially published only in German seems to have limited their dissemination within the Anglophone research community. A summary of these studies and a comparison of their classifications to Edström and Galbraith's set of motives can be found in Table 5.4.

There seems to be a considerable amount of consensus on the principal functions of international transfers, well represented by the original classification of Edström and Galbraith. In many of the German studies, though, the focus is more on a direct type of expatriate control than on the informal type of control or coordination identified by Edström and Galbraith. At the same time, the ultimate goal is similar in both cases: making sure that the various organizational units strive towards common organizational goals. It is interesting to note, however, that although Edström and Galbraith termed their third motive 'organization development', their description of this organizational motive for international transfers focuses exclusively on control aspects. This is also the way in which this motive for international transfers has been interpreted in most of the English articles that refer to the Edström and Galbraith classification and the German studies. Pausenberger (1987), however, indicates that all three functions of international transfer can in fact lead to organization development defined as the increase of the company's potential to succeed and compete in the international market. Roessel (1988) advances a similar view when he discusses how the various functions of international transfers can lead to the further internationalization of the MNC, which would make it more effective in international markets. Maybe we should conclude that organization development is not a goal of international transfers as such, but is rather the result of knowledge transfer, management development and the

Table 5.4 Motives for international transfers according to various authors

Edström and Galbraith (1977)	Position Filling	Management Development	Organization Development/ Coordination and Control*
Pausenberger and Noelle (1977) [our translation]	• To ensure transfer of know-how • To compensate for a lack of local managers • Training and development of local managers	• To develop the expatriate's management capabilities • To develop managers' global awareness	• To ensure homogeneous practices in the company • To ensure a common reporting system in the company • Presence of different viewpoints in decision-making bodies
Welge (1980) [our translation]	• Position filling • Transfer of know-how	• International experience • Use management potential	• Coordination • Change management
Kenter (1985) [our translation]	• Lack of qualified local managers available • Transfer of know-how • Training of local managers	• Development of parent country nationals	• Control and coordination • Increase loyalty and trustworthiness of expatriates
Kumar and Steinmann (1986) [our translation]	• Transfer of know-how • The necessity to train German managers	• HQ wants Japanese managers to gain international experience	• To ensure coordination with HQ corporate policies and philosophies • To facilitate communication • Desired loyalty with HQ goals
Pausenberger (1987) [our translation]	• Transfer of know-how	• Management development	• To ensure a uniform company policy
Roessel (1988) [our translation]	• Transfer of management know-how • Lack of qualified local personnel	• Managerial development of expatriates and local managers	• Coordination, control and steering • Reciprocal information flows • Internationalization of the company as a whole
Groenewald and Sapozhnikov (1990) [our translation]	• Transfer of technological, administrative or sales know-how • Lack of qualified local personnel	• Management development • Better career opportunities for employees	• Steering and coordination
Kumar and Karlshaus (1992) [our translation]	• Transfer of know-how • Limited availability of local managers • The necessity to train foreign managers	• HQ wants German managers to gain international experience	• To ensure coordination and communication with HQ • Desired loyalty with HQ goals
Macharzina (1992) [our translation]	• Filling vacant positions	• Management development	• Coordination
Wolf (1994) [our translation]	• Filling vacant positions	• Personal or managerial development	• Coordination

* Coordination and control is an alternative term to Edström and Galbraith's organization development motive.

creation of a common organizational culture and an effective informal information network? It might then be more appropriate to call the third category coordination and control rather than organization development.

As Edström and Galbraith (1977) have argued, these three motives for international transfers are not mutually exclusive. The key point that companies should realize is the fact that expatriation is a strategic tool to achieve specific organizational goals and needs to be used as such. More recent research has highlighted the link between the reason for an international assignment and different dimensions of success (see Bolino, 2007). In this regard, Shay and Baack (2004) show that the management development motive positively relates to an assignee's personal change whereas the control motive is directly related to organizational change. Scholars have also highlighted the importance of offering a mix of different assignment forms to develop global leadership competencies within the MNC (Mendenhall et al., 2012). In section 6, we will look at assignment success in more detail.

Coordination through international assignees: of bears, bumble-bees and spiders

In this section we will take a closer look at one of the motives for international transfers: coordination and control, based on a study by Harzing (2001b). Data were analysed by correlating the level of expatriate presence with the coordination mechanisms in question (direct expatriate control, socialization/shared values and informal communication). The fact that there was a significantly positive relationship between expatriate presence and these three coordination mechanisms, while no such relationship was present for the other coordination mechanisms (e.g. bureaucratic control, output control) included in this study, independently confirms the importance of this function of expatriation.

As we have seen above, the coordination and control function of international transfers has three distinct elements. Expatriates are employed to provide personal/cultural control in both a direct and an indirect way. They can serve to replace or complement HQ centralization of decision making and direct surveillance of subsidiaries by HQ managers. This is the kind of control that is alluded to in many of the German studies discussed above. We call this the 'bear' role of expatriates. The bear is chosen as an analogy, because it reflects a level of dominance (and threat that might be perceived in the extreme case) associated with this type of expatriate control. Expatriates can also be used to realize control based on socialization and the creation of informal communication networks, which is the kind of control described by Edström and Galbraith and some of the German studies. The role of expatriates in socialization we refer to as 'bumble-bees'. Organizational bumble-bees fly 'from plant to plant' and create cross-pollination between the various off-shoots. Weaving an informal communication network is of course the role of expatriates as 'spiders'.

While expatriates seem to perform their roles as bears in any situation, an exploratory analysis showed that their roles as bumble-bees and spiders are more important in some situations than in others. They are more important in subsidiaries that were established more than 50 years ago than in younger subsidiaries, although the bumble-bee role is important in very young subsidiaries as well. Both the bumble-bee and the spider roles are particularly important in subsidiaries that show high levels of local responsiveness, and that are not at all or hardly dependent on the HQ for their sales and purchases. Finally, the bumble-bee and spider roles are more important in acquisitions than in greenfield subsidiaries. What these situations have in common is that they all represent contexts in which subsidiaries operate quite independently from HQ. Apparently, expatriate presence is most effective in facilitating informal control in subsidiaries that are otherwise relatively independent from the HQ, whereas in subsidiaries that are quite dependent on the HQ expatriate presence serves mostly to facilitate direct expatriate control. Since absolute expatriate presence is generally lower in subsidiaries that are relatively independent from the HQ (Harzing, 1999), we might also conclude that the 'marginal effectiveness' of expatriates in facilitating informal control decreases as expatriate presence increases. In other words: if there are no or only a few expatriates employed in a particular subsidiary, 'adding' expatriates might have a strong positive effect on shared values and informal communication, while the effect of adding another expatriate is much weaker in a subsidiary that already employs a large number of them.

International assignees as knowledge agents

Recently, research has increasingly highlighted the role of international assignees as carriers of knowledge between their home and host units. This is mainly due to MNCs' growing attempts to capitalize on business opportunities in developing and emerging economies. To offset their lack of experience in these culturally and institutionally more distant environments, MNCs face the challenge of accessing and applying local knowledge (Harvey et al., 2000). While the transfer of people is only one of many mechanisms to initiate knowledge flows in organizations, a large part of the knowledge transferred across MNC units is highly context-specific and tacit in nature (Riusala and Suutari, 2004). Contextual and tacit knowledge cannot be codified in written documents but requires the knowledge sender and recipient to interact directly in order to adapt the knowledge to the recipient's context and clarify the meaning.

Researchers have considered different directions in which assignees can transfer knowledge. One group of studies cover aspects of learning and knowledge creation from an individual point of view (e.g. Berthoin Antal, 2000; Hocking et al., 2007) and thus primarily focus on assignees as knowledge recipients. The knowledge assignees may acquire during their assignment is thought to help them in their future positions and includes:

- an understanding of the company's global organization and the corporate culture at the HQ
- factual knowledge about the assignment culture, and
- the acquisition of culture-specific repertoires.

Implicit to this perspective is the idea that assignees acquire knowledge at the host unit and then may apply it back at their home unit at a later stage. This type of knowledge transfer thus represents a knowledge outflow from the host unit. By contrast, a second group of studies concentrate on the knowledge that assignees share during their assignment to the host unit (e.g. Bonache and Brewster, 2001; Hébert et al., 2005), conceptualizing assignees as senders of knowledge. This type of knowledge transfer represents a knowledge inflow to the host unit. Relevant knowledge that assignees can share:

- helps to streamline cross-unit processes
- creates common corporate practices and routines, or
- increases the chances of subsidiary survival, for example, through the provision of local acquisition experience or product development know-how.

Scholars have also pointed out that the success of knowledge sharing through international transfers is not automatic but rather depends on social processes. Indeed, if we view individuals as carriers of knowledge we need to consider that this knowledge can only be shared through social interaction. In this regard, Reiche et al. (2009) argue that assignees need to establish social relationships, interpersonal trust and shared values with host-unit staff in order to share and acquire knowledge. In addition, assignees may act as boundary spanners that link the social networks of the home and host units. In doing so, assignees help to establish social interactions between MNC units and thus facilitate cross-unit knowledge exchange. Investigating the development of social relationships between people from different cultures and their effects on knowledge flows in MNCs has therefore become a key area of interest in current research on international assignments (Au and Fukuda, 2002; Reiche, 2012a).

4 Alternative forms of international assignments

We have seen that international transfers can fulfil a number of very important functions in MNCs. Unfortunately, there are increasing signs that barriers to mobility – especially the issue of dual-career couples (see Box 5.2) – are becoming more and more important, leading to a decline in the willingness to accept an assignment abroad (Harvey, 1998; Forster, 2000). In addition, sending out expatriates can be very costly. Increasingly, companies are therefore looking for alternatives to expatriation. In this section, we will discuss a range of other types of international assignments that include inpatriate, short-term, self-initiated and virtual transfers.

> ### Box 5.2   Managing dual-career considerations
>
> Dual-career issues are increasingly among the main reasons given for employees turning down an international assignment (Brookfield Global Relocation Services, 2011). How can companies address this challenge? The following activities may help multinationals to alleviate the pressures of dual careers (Evans et al., 2011):
>
> - Plan the assignment in terms of location, timing and duration based on the professional preferences and personal circumstances of the couple.
> - Approach the partner's employer and jointly prepare expatriation plans.
> - Provide career counselling and assistance in locating employment opportunities for partners abroad.
> - Subsidize educational programmes for partners while abroad.
> - Support entrepreneurial initiatives by partners.
> - Cooperate with other multinationals in finding jobs for partners.
> - Provide re-employment advice to partners after repatriation (see section 5).

Inpatriate assignments

One alternative to expatriation is inpatriation, which involves the transfer of subsidiary managers to the HQ for a specific period of time (Harvey et al., 2000). This would allow key subsidiary managers to get to know the workings of the parent company and build up informal communication networks. It also allows the HQ to inculcate the subsidiary managers into the corporate culture in a more direct way than would be possible by the transfer of expatriates. Inpatriation is also a useful option if tacit knowledge needs to be transferred from subsidiaries to the HQ and it has the added advantage of exposing parent company managers to an international perspective. It is to be expected that the use of inpatriates, especially in European and US multinationals, will increase in the future (see Figure 5.2). Indeed, recent studies showed that 46 per cent of subsidiaries employed staff that have been previously inpatriated to HQ and that about one in ten international staff occupied a managerial position at HQ (Tungli and Peiperl, 2009; Harzing et al., 2012).

At first sight, expatriate and inpatriate assignments only constitute alternative forms of establishing HQ–subsidiary linkages. Indeed, both groups of assignees may act as boundary spanners or may help to reduce existing information asymmetries between the HQ and its subsidiaries. However, despite their similarities, expatriates and inpatriates differ along several dimensions:

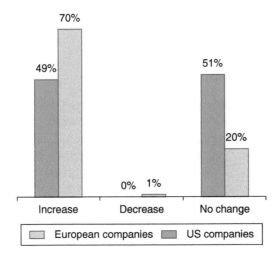

Figure 5.2   Expected future change in the inpatriate population

Source: Oddou et al. (2001)

- Status differences. Expatriates possess the status and influence related to their role as HQ representatives. Coming from the MNC's periphery, inpatriates are, on the contrary, unlikely to receive the same level of respect (Harvey et al., 2005; Reiche, 2006).
- Cultural adjustment challenges. Barnett and Toyne (1991) delineate increased adjustment challenges for inpatriates in comparison to expatriates. They argue that inpatriates not only need to adjust to the national culture (see section 5) but also need to be socialized into the MNC's HQ corporate culture. Indeed, learning the HQ corporate culture is considered an important motive for inpatriating foreign nationals. Expatriates, by contrast, often impose elements of the HQ corporate culture upon the subsidiary they are sent to.
- Differences in the underlying MNC staffing policies. The use of inpatriates also increases the cultural diversity and multicultural staff composition at the HQ, thereby fostering a geocentric approach to the allocation of human resources in MNCs. In particular, a higher share of employees with diverse cultural backgrounds will be collaborating directly as inpatriates are, for instance, temporarily integrated into the HQ's management teams. By contrast, the use of expatriates reflects an ethnocentric view towards international staffing and expatriates generally continue to coordinate with their own HQ management team.

Inpatriation seems to be an important addition to the company repertoire and can help to transfer knowledge, improve HQ–subsidiary relationships and develop managers. However, inpatriates have to cope with many of the same problems as expatriates, such as repatriation, and, as described above, in other cases even encounter additional problems such as increased adjustment pressures. It is therefore unlikely that they will ever completely replace expatriates.

Short-term assignments

Another alternative to expatriation that has received growing attention and helps MNCs to contain their costs are short-term assignments. The literature commonly refers to short-term assignments as postings between 1 and 12 months in length (Collings et al., 2007). In contrast to traditional expatriate or inpatriate assignments, the assigned manager is usually unaccompanied by his/her family, thereby avoiding the disruption of relocating entire families. Moreover, selection and preparation procedures (see section 5) for short-term assignments tend to be more informal and ad hoc. Short-term assignments are particularly useful when specific skills need to be transferred, for example in the scope of multinational project work, or when particular problem-solving needs arise. In addition to their increased cost effectiveness, short-term assignments also require less bureaucratic effort and can be executed in a more flexible and timely manner. At the same time, research has highlighted that short-term assignees may fail to develop effective relationships with local colleagues and customers while also facing increased risks of marital problems (Tahvanainen et al., 2005).

A related but even more temporary staffing option is the use of business trips that may last from a few days to several weeks. These transfers are also frequently referred to in the literature as international business travel or frequent flyer assignments (Welch et al., 2007), thereby characterizing work arrangements in which international travel forms an integral part. Frequent flyer trips are useful for conducting irregular specialized tasks such as annual budgeting meetings or for maintaining personal relationships with key colleagues and customers in the host country. Finally, companies make increased use of commuter and rotational assignments. Whereas the former refers to a work arrangement in which the individual commutes from his/her home unit to a foreign unit on a weekly or bi-weekly basis, the latter concerns alternations of intensive work postings abroad and prolonged periods of leave, as is common on oil rigs. Given the increased levels of stress associated with these assignment types, they are unlikely to be maintained over an extended period of time (Collings et al., 2007). Also, frequent international business travel and commuting have important tax implications that companies need to take into account (see Box 5.3).

Box 5.3   The case of 'accidental expatriates'

Given employees' more frequent international travel, companies are facing more complex tax compliance issues that are related to where a tax liability may arise. This is particularly relevant in the case of so called 'accidental expatriates' – employees that are based in one country but engage in extensive international business travel or commuting and may therefore trigger host country tax liabilities (Reiche, 2012b). These arrangements may lead to potential tax violations and/or unexpected tax liabilities because companies often do not include these employees in their formal expatriate programmes and hence do not monitor the relevant foreign tax regulations. Several tools can help companies to actively track the tax-related implications of international travel, including a company-wide calendar system, a security-card swipe system that registers employees' exit from and re-entry to their home base, or a comprehensive travel management programme that uses a single travel vendor and/or a single company credit card for all travel-related payments. Mobile Apps may also be used to trace international travel.

Self-initiated assignments

While the traditional view of international assignments has been to focus on the employing organization to initiate the transfer, a growing number of assignees make their own arrangements to find work abroad, facilitated by the introduction of free movement of labour in the European Union and other economic regions. In contrast to the aforementioned types of assignments, these so-called self-initiated assignees are employed on local work contracts. In their study of graduate engineers from Finland, Suutari and Brewster (2000) identified a series of distinct characteristics of self-initiated assignments compared to traditional expatriation. For example, self-initiated assignees tend to:

- be slightly younger, single and female
- work for organizations with a lower focus on international business activities, at lower hierarchical levels and on more temporary contracts than expatriates
- be motivated to move abroad due to an interest in internationalism and poor employment situations at home, and
- receive no repatriation promises and see their relocation as a more permanent move.

More recent research suggests that self-initiated assignees' motivations to relocate were relatively more driven by characteristics of the host country (e.g. host culture, host reputation) whereas company-backed assignees mainly focused on career-related motives (Doherty et al., 2011). By contrast, repatriation decisions of self-initiated assignees appear to be primarily driven by positive career prospects back home, expected lifestyle benefits, family encouragement, national identity or repatriation-related shocks such as current job satisfaction (Tharenou and Caulfield, 2010).

Overall, given the increased need for international and cross-culturally experienced personnel, self-initiated assignments serve as an important complementary staffing option for both domestic and international organizations.

Virtual assignments

Finally, companies have begun to make use of virtual assignments to address the competing needs for decentralization and global interrelation of work processes, in a more flexible way. A virtual assignment does not require the individual to physically relocate to a foreign organizational unit but rather distributes international responsibilities as managed from the individual's home base (Welch et al., 2003). The growth of virtual assignments has been facilitated by improvements in information technology over the last decade to the extent that whole teams now regularly collaborate and communicate via email, telephone and videoconferencing. Despite the many advantages of virtual assignments that often exceed those of short-term assignments, face-to-face communication remains crucial in many circumstances, thus limiting the use of virtual work arrangements.

Since expatriation fulfils many roles, these four alternatives are unlikely to completely replace expatriates. However, they are often a cheaper alternative to expatriation, especially in the case of virtual transfers, and it is much easier to involve a large number of managers through short-term postings or virtual assignments than it is through expatriation. Moreover, each alternative form of transfer may also serve distinct purposes that are directly related to the successful operation of the company, which is why they are resourcing methods that should form part of the repertoire of any MNC (see Box 5.4).

Box 5.4　Corporate policies for the use of different staffing forms

Brookfield Global Relocation Services is a US-based provider of relocation services and publishes an annual relocation trends survey. Based on a survey of 118 small, medium and large international companies headquartered in different regions worldwide for 2011, the Figure 5.3 below shows that multinational companies have established formal policies for the use of alternative assignment forms. While almost all companies had established policies for traditional long-term relocations (including both expatriation and inpatriation) a substantial share of companies have also formalized short-term transfers, permanent moves (i.e. an individual's international relocation that is followed by a localization of the employment contract in the host country) and business travel. This suggests that companies increasingly attempt to adapt their global staffing to their different strategic needs.

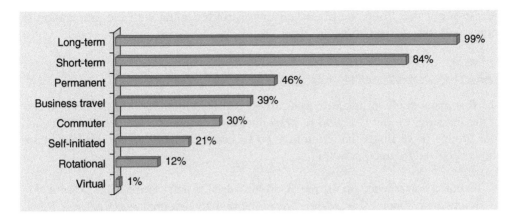

Figure 5.3   Brookfield Annual Relocation Trends Survey Findings (2011)

Source: Brookfield Global Relocation Services (2011)

5 The international assignment process

The international assignment process is commonly considered to encompass three distinct phases (see Figure 5.4): the pre-assignment stage (selection and preparation), the actual assignment and the post-assignment stage referred to as repatriation (Bonache et al., 2001).

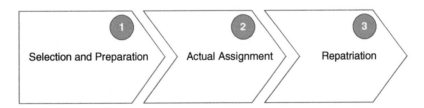

Figure 5.4   The international assignment cycle

The following sections will discuss these key elements in more detail. Although the literature has dealt with all three phases, the majority of studies have centred on cultural adjustment during the actual assignment (Harrison et al., 2004).

Selection and preparation

In this section, we will discuss two popular studies concerning the recruitment and selection of international assignees and then evaluate the situation that seems to persist in practice. Then, we briefly review research dealing with the preparation of individuals for an international transfer.

Selection criteria: prescriptions for good practice

The first major study in this area was carried out by Tung (1981). Based on a review of the literature on the selection of personnel for assignments abroad, she identified four groups of variables that contribute to success or failure on the job and hence should be used to guide selection:

- Technical competence on the job. As in the selection and placement of personnel in domestic operations, this factor is one of the primary determinants of success. It may be even more important for assignments abroad because the individual is located at some distance from the HQ, often the hub of technical expertise, and cannot consult as readily with his/her peers and superiors on matters related to the job.
- Personal traits or relational abilities. This refers to the ability of the individual to deal effectively with his/her superiors, peers, subordinates, business associates and clients. In assignments abroad, this variable greatly influences the probability of successful performance. This factor is not limited to simple knowledge of another culture. The crucial element is the ability to live and work with people whose value systems, beliefs, customs, manners and ways of conducting business may greatly differ from one's own.
- Ability to cope with environmental variables. In domestic operations the ability to identify and cope with environmental constraints, such as governments, unions, competitors and customers, is crucial to effective performance. This same requirement is no less valid in assignments abroad, but the political, legal and socio-economic structures which constitute the macro-environment in the host country may be very different from the systems with which the expatriate is familiar. This poses problems of adjustment. The expatriate has to understand these systems and operate within them. More broadly, researchers have highlighted the importance of boundary-spanning capabilities that enable global staff to connect functional, geographic and external boundaries to move ideas, information, decisions, talent and resources where they are most needed (Mendenhall et al., 2012).
- Family situation. This refers to the ability of the expatriate's family (the partner in particular) to adjust to living in a foreign environment. Researchers and practitioners are becoming increasingly cognizant of the importance of this factor to effective performance abroad. The situation often becomes even more complex if the partner (male or female) has had to give up a job or even a career to accompany his or her partner abroad (see Box 5.2).

A second important contribution is the study by Mendenhall and Oddou (1985). According to them, there is insufficient knowledge about the relevant dimensions in expatriate acculturation, leading to the use of inappropriate selection procedures. They distinguish four dimensions as components of the expatriate adjustment process:

- The self-orientation dimension: activities and attributes that serve to strengthen the expatriate's self-esteem, self-confidence and mental hygiene.
- The other's orientation dimension: activities and attributes that enhance the expatriate's ability to interact effectively with host nationals.
- The perceptual dimension: the ability to understand why foreigners behave the way they do, the ability to make correct attributions about the reasons or causes of host nationals' behaviour.
- The cultural toughness dimension: this dimension can modify the importance of the first three dimensions. In culturally tough countries (countries that are culturally very different from the home country), the first three dimensions become even more important than in culturally similar countries.

The expatriate selection process should focus explicitly on the strengths and weaknesses of the applicant on the above-mentioned dimensions. Moreover, the main corporate motive for sending a particular person abroad (see section 3) should form an integral part of the selection decision and be considered when defining selection criteria. If people are simply sent for the wrong reasons or the assignment objectives are not clearly defined or communicated, even the most sophisticated selection system may result in failure (Black and Gregersen, 1999). Job characteristics also play a role. For example, if a technical position that requires little customer contact is to be filled abroad, interpersonal skills may be a less relevant selection criterion than when relocating a marketing director.

Expatriate selection in practice

Recent studies have empirically confirmed that expatriate selection is a multi-faceted subject and that personality characteristics as well as interpersonal skills are very important (Spreitzer et al., 1997; Caligiuri, 2000). In practice, however, most companies still use technical competence and knowledge of company systems as selection criteria (Harris and Brewster, 1999a; Sparrow et al., 2004; Anderson, 2005). In fact, a recent global relocation trends survey revealed that only 18 per cent of the surveyed organizations had a formal candidate pool for international assignments and only 19 per cent used any candidate assessment tools at all (Brookfields Global Relocation Services, 2011). There are several reasons for this practice (see Bonache et al., 2001). First, it is difficult to identify and measure the relevant interpersonal and cross-cultural competences. Even in a domestic context there is still debate over the criteria that make good managers. Second, selection decisions are often made by line managers who circumvent selection criteria set out by the HR department, increasing the incoherence of the selection process. Third, there is also the self-interest of the selectors, who will try to minimize the personal risk involved in selecting a candidate who might fail on the job. Technical competence will almost always prevent immediate failure on the job.

Brewster (1991) notes that selection decisions for expatriate postings frequently rely on personal recommendations from either specialist personnel staff or line managers. The result is that the outcome of selection interviews is more or less pre-determined and negotiating the terms of the offer takes precedence over determining the suitability of the candidate. In their provocatively titled article, 'The coffee-machine system: how international selection really works', Harris and Brewster (1999a) develop this idea further and provide a typology of international manager selection systems based on the distinction between open and closed systems and formal and informal systems. The closed/informal system was most frequent among the organizations that Harris and Brewster studied. The researchers adopted the term 'the coffee-machine system', as a catchy summary for this type of selection system. The process starts with a senior line manager (usually male) who is joined by a colleague while waiting for his coffee at the coffee machine.

How's it going?

Oh, you know, overworked and underpaid.

Tell me about it. As well as all the usual stuff, Jimmy in Mumbai has just fallen ill and is being flown home. I've got no idea who we can get over there to pick up the pieces at such short notice. It's driving me crazy.

Have you met that Simon on the fifth floor? He's in the same line of work. Very bright and looks like going a long way. He was telling me that he and his wife had a great holiday in Goa a couple of years ago. He seems to like India. Could be worth a chat.

Hey thanks. I'll check him out.

No problem. They don't seem to be able to improve this coffee though, do they?

Excerpt from Harris and Brewster (1999a). Reprinted by permission of the publisher, Taylor and Francis Group, www.informaworld.com.

As Harris and Brewster indicate, the decision, that in effect has already been taken, is subsequently legitimized by organizational processes. The IHRM department will usually only become involved to deal with the financial aspects and practical arrangements related to the transfer. The disadvantages of this type of selection system are obvious. Candidates are not formally evaluated against relevant selection criteria, the pool of candidates is very much restricted and the organization takes a reactive rather than strategic approach to expatriation.

Preparation

In order to prepare individuals who have been selected for an international posting, and facilitate their adjustment to the foreign culture, diverse cross-cultural training programmes have been developed (Tung, 1981; Harris and Brewster, 1999b; Harvey and Miceli, 1999; see also Parkinson and Morley, 2006). The content and focus of these programmes are contingent upon factors such as:

- the individual's cultural background
- culture-specific features of the host country environment
- the individual's degree of contact with the host environment
- the assignment length
- the individual's family situation
- the individual's language skills.

The effectiveness of cross-cultural training has been examined by Deshpande and Viswesvaran (1992) who undertook a meta-analysis to demonstrate a positive effect of training on a number of assignment-related outcome variables. Others have argued that pre-departure training assists transferees in developing accurate expectations towards the assignment which enhances their effectiveness abroad (Black et al., 1991). More recently, Mendenhall and Stahl (2000) have called for additional training measures, specifically highlighting the importance of in-country, real time training, global mindset training and CD-ROM/internet-based training. However, research also suggests that a gap remains between individual training needs and the actual training offered by MNCs (Harris and Brewster, 1999b), with the provision of language courses and general information on the host country context often remaining the only available methods of training and induction. All too often, assignees are expected to take responsibility for their own training and preparation.

Expatriate adjustment during the assignment

Despite the undoubtedly positive nature of certain aspects of the international assignment experience, the exposure to a foreign culture will involve high levels of stress and uncertainty. It has been common to describe this phenomenon as 'culture shock' (Oberg, 1960). Accordingly, much research has centred on analysing the process of adjustment to a new environment during the assignment. Black et al. (1991) provided a comprehensive model of expatriate adjustment that integrates perspectives from theoretical and empirical work in both the domestic and international adjustment literature. They argue that expatriate adjustment includes two components: anticipatory adjustment and in-country adjustment. Anticipatory adjustment can have an important positive impact on in-country adjustment. It is positively influenced by cross-cultural training and previous international experience, although it is reasonable to expect that the latter will only result if the earlier experience abroad was a positive one. Both help to build up realistic expectations and the more accurate the expatriate's expectations, the lower the level of uncertainty, the fewer the surprises and the lower the level of culture shock. The MNC can help anticipatory adjustment by providing cross-cultural training and using comprehensive selection criteria.

The in-country adjustment part of their model, which is reproduced in Figure 5.5, was tested by Shaffer et al. (1999). Shaffer et al. introduced two moderating variables: previous assignments and language fluency. We have underlined the relationships that were confirmed in the empirical study in Figure 5.5. The model identifies three dimensions of adjustment: adjustment to work, adjustment to interacting with HCNs and general adjustment to the living conditions abroad. As expected, both role clarity (the extent to which what is expected from the assignee is clear and unambiguous) and role discretion (flexibility in the execution of the job) were positively related to work adjustment, while role clarity also positively related to general adjustment and role discretion positively related to interaction adjustment. Role conflict (conflicting signals about what is expected in the new work setting) and role novelty (the extent to which the current role is different from past roles) did not show the expected negative relationship to work adjustment, although role novelty was negatively related to general adjustment.

Support from co-workers and logistical support were positively related to interaction adjustment, although the expected impact of co-worker support on work adjustment and logistical support on general adjustment was not confirmed. Supervisor support did not have any significant influence on adjustment. Cultural novelty and spousal adjustment had a very strong impact on general adjustment and a weaker, yet still very significant, impact on interaction adjustment. Spousal adjustment did not influence work adjustment. The two self-efficacy variables seemed completely unrelated to adjustment, but both the number of previous assignments and language fluency have a significant positive direct effect on interaction adjustment.

As expected, both previous experience and language fluency had important moderating effects as well. Previous experience moderated the relationship between supervisor and co-worker support. For individuals on their first assignments, supervisor support was negatively related to all aspects of adjustments, while for more experienced assignees this relationship was reversed. The same was true for co-worker support: experienced assignees relied more on their support for their adjustment. Shaffer et al. conclude that experienced assignees have learned to rely more on host country management than on home country management. Language fluency moderated the relationship between role conflict and all three dimensions of adjustment, which was more strongly negative for those assignees fluent in the host country language. Shaffer et al. reason that the conflicting demands from host country management and home country management might go unnoticed for expatriates with fewer language skills. Shaffer et al. also found distinct differences between the PCNs, TCNs and inpatriates in the sample. Whereas role clarity and co-worker support influenced all three dimensions of adjustment for inpatriates, they only affected one adjustment

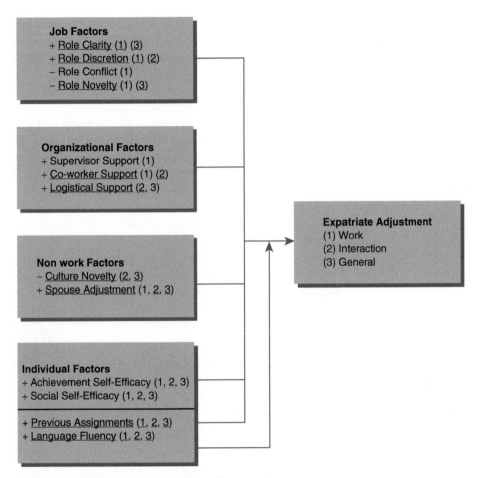

Figure 5.5 Determinants of expatriate adjustment*

* Numbers in parentheses indicate the corresponding dependent variables

Source: adapted from Black et al. (1991) and Shaffer et al. (1999)

dimension for the other two groups of assignees. Consequently, we can assume that the adjustment process involved in moving to a firm's HQ differs considerably from the process of relocating to or between subsidiaries.

Overall, Shaffer et al.'s results provide general confirmation of Black et al.'s conceptual model and clearly point to the importance of job design, organizational support systems, the inclusion of the spouse in any training and support programmes, and the importance of language fluency as a selection criterion. Extending these findings, Kraimer et al. (2001) found that assignees' perceptions of overall support provided by both the home and host unit will positively influence different dimensions of adjustment.

More recently, researchers have begun to examine the role of social networks that international assignees develop with local nationals and their positive effects on adjustment (Wang and Kanungo, 2004; Liu and Shaffer, 2005). In this regard, host unit employees are increasingly viewed as important socializing agents (Toh and DeNisi, 2007) or host country mentors (Mezias and Scandura, 2005) for assignees and therefore have to be explicitly considered in any meaningful assessment of expatriate adjustment.

In addition to expatriate adjustment, it is important for MNCs to develop and maintain adequate compensation packages for international assignees during the assignment. There are generally two approaches to international compensation (Dowling et al., 2008; see also Box 5.5): the going rate approach and the balance sheet approach. In the going rate approach, the base salary for international assignees is directly linked to the salary structure of the host country and thus driven by local market rates. In the case of low-pay countries, the base pay and benefits may then be supplemented by additional payments. By contrast, the main objective of the balance sheet approach is to equalize the purchasing power of the assignee compared to other employees at comparable position levels at home. The balance sheet approach also provides incentives to compensate for the cost of an international assignment and offset relevant differences between assignment locations.

Box 5.5   Design of compensation packages during relocation

Companies using the balance sheet approach need to regularly update compensation packages with new data on living costs. They also need to respond to unexpected events such as currency devaluation or a stock market crash, which may have substantial influences on prices and living costs. From that perspective, the going rate approach seems to be more cost-effective than the balance sheet approach. However, despite this advantage the balance sheet approach continues to be the most widely used method. According to Brookfield Global Relocation Services (2011), 62 per cent of respondents used a balance sheet approach to determine compensation for long-term assignments, while only 6 per cent used a going rate approach and 32 per cent used various combinations of the two approaches. This suggests that the attraction and motivation of potential candidates for international assignments remains clearly more important than cost saving.

Repatriation

Increased academic interest has also been placed on repatriation as the final phase of the assignment cycle. It has long been recognized that the return to one's home country after a prolonged stay abroad is subject to adjustment challenges similar to those of the initial transfer (Gullahorn and Gullahorn, 1963). However, despite the obvious importance of reintegration planning, this domain has only started to receive attention as an independent area of research and is still judged to lack coherence and systematic consideration in both academic and managerial contexts (Bolino, 2007; Lazarova and Cerdin, 2007). Given the trend towards using international transfers for knowledge transfer and management development purposes, the retention of repatriates is now even more crucial for MNCs to benefit from international staff transfers in the long run. Indeed, recent empirical research suggests that repatriates not only share the knowledge they acquired during their assignments upon return but also continue to access relevant knowledge from the host unit, facilitating ongoing cross-unit knowledge flows in the MNC (Reiche, 2012a). Against this background, it is surprising that academic studies continue to find assignees to be largely unsatisfied with MNCs' repatriation support and to perceive their positions upon repatriation to be inadequate, leading to repatriate turnover intentions (Tung, 1998; Stahl et al., 2002; see also Box 5.6), a phenomenon we will look at in more detail in section 6.

Box 5.6 Assignment in Saudi Arabia

[A senior engineer from a European electronics company] was sent to Saudi Arabia on a four-year assignment, at a cost to his employer of about $4 million. During those four years, he learnt fluent Arabic, gained new technical skills, and made friends with important businesspeople in the Saudi community. But upon returning home, the man was shocked to find himself frequently scolded that 'the way things were done in Saudi Arabia has nothing to do with the way we do things at headquarters'. Worse, he was kept waiting almost nine months for a permanent assignment which, when it came, gave him less authority than he had had abroad. Not surprisingly, the engineer left to join a direct competitor a few months later and ended up using the knowledge and skills he had acquired in Saudi Arabia against his former employer.

Source: Black and Gregersen, 1999: 60.

In one study, Lazarova and Caligiuri (2001) examined 11 repatriation support practices which were considered important by repatriates but were shown to be available in only 10–50 per cent of the MNCs under study. Among others, these practices included:

- pre-departure briefings on what to expect during repatriation
- career planning sessions
- an agreement outlining the type of position assignees will be offered upon repatriation

- mentoring programmes while on assignment
- reorientation programmes about the changes in the company
- repatriation training seminars on emotional responses following repatriation
- financial counselling and financial/tax assistance, and
- ongoing communication with the home office.

It is important to note here that repatriate turnover not only results in a loss of human capital investment for the MNC in general but also risks the possibility of losing this investment to the benefit of a direct competitor. Furthermore, repatriate turnover is likely to have negative implications for the willingness of repatriates' colleagues in the organization to accept an international transfer (Kamoche, 1997). To reduce the risk of repatriate turnover, MNCs should combine short-term oriented HR practices with longer-term resourcing methods such as integrating international assignments into individual career paths. However, this requires treating the actual transfer and repatriation not as isolated incidents but rather linking the assignment experience to the expatriate's overall career.

6 Dimensions of international assignment success

Considering the complex challenges that emerge within the scope of international transfers, the analysis of assignment success is of crucial value for organizations with a high share of international staff. Consequently, the investigation into factors that influence assignment success has been a major research focus in the field of international transfers (e.g. Clarke and Hammer, 1995; Harrison et al., 2004; Kraimer and Wayne, 2004). Past research has identified numerous operational measures. The most prominent operational measure of assignment success is the intention or motivation to remain in the job, i.e. to complete the assignment (Feldman and Thomas, 1992; Thomas, 1998). However, empirical evidence on the magnitude of expatriate premature returns is ambiguous. In this section, we will therefore critically evaluate the issue of expatriate failure and introduce a multi-dimensional categorization of assignment success.

Expatriate failure: Is it just a myth?

If there is one thing that most publications in the area of expatriate management – and in particular those dealing with either cross-cultural training or adjustment – have in common is that they all refer to the 'fact' that expatriate failure rates – measured as premature return of the expatriate – are very high, with commonly cited figures in the region of 16–50 per cent for developed countries. Harzing (1995, 2002) has argued that there is no empirical foundation for these claims and that the myth of high expatriate failure rates has been perpetuated by careless and inappropriate referencing. Harzing also argues that this myth may have had a negative impact on the effectiveness of expatriate management. When reading the academic and practitioner literature on expatriate management, practitioners cannot help but draw the false conclusion that expatriate premature return is one of the most important problems when sending employees abroad. This might lead companies to focus their attention and resources on avoiding assignees' premature return, while failing to notice or manage other issues that are, in fact, far more important for assuring the individuals' and the company's success. Forster and Johnsen (1996) suggest another practitioner reaction to the myth of high expatriate failure rates that might be equally detrimental to both expatriate and company success. They propose that this myth might well explain why the training and selection procedures of companies in their study diverge substantially from the ideal policies recommended in the literature. In reconciling the high expatriate failure rate figures with the actual practice in their company, each individual firm may believe that it is other firms who have a problem with high failure – not themselves. These companies would therefore see no reason to improve their training and selection policies and might lose out on the benefits of improved selection and training methods.

So should we conclude we can disregard expatriate failure? On the contrary! Further and more sophisticated research into expatriate failure is long overdue. Such research would first of all involve using a much broader definition of failure. The current definition used by the overwhelming majority of studies is the expatriate returning before his/her assignment contract expires. However, as Harzing and Christensen (2004) argue, in some circumstances a premature return might actually indicate a success – a job accomplished in less time than originally anticipated – while in others an expatriate that stays on, but is under-performing, might in fact do much more damage than one who returns early. And what about the assignee who returns home, but finds that his/her skills developed during the assignment are not really valued in the home company and is so frustrated that he/she leaves the company soon after returning? Any definition of expatriate failure should therefore include under-performance and failed repatriation. Companies should also acknowledge that the costs of expatriate failure might go well beyond a simple calculation of the assignee's salary, relocation costs and training costs. They might include indirect costs such as damage to customer relationships and contacts with host government officials and negative impact on the morale of local staff. Expatriate failure will also be very traumatic for the expatriate and his/her family and might impact on his/her future performance.

Multidimensional nature of assignment success

Given the evident problems arising from a narrow definition of expatriate failure, it is fruitful to view success as a multi-faceted construct. In developing a multidimensional categorization of success, we can differentiate between two key dimensions: the level at which assignment success is assessed and the time frame (Yan et al., 2002). First, a range of studies has demonstrated a relatively high willingness among repatriates to leave their current organization and look for employment opportunities elsewhere despite their generally positive assessment of the assignment, for example in terms of personal growth and new skill development (Tung, 1998; Stahl et al., 2002). A central problem in research on assignment success thus concerns the notion that a failure from the corporate perspective is not always a failure in terms of the individual assignee. Therefore, a meaningful assessment of assignment success must link both the individual and organizational perspectives. Second, the discussion in section 5 has highlighted the importance of long-term assignment outcomes. From the point of view of the individual assignee, career advancement in terms of attractive subsequent postings and continuous development opportunities play a crucial role. For the organization, learning is the most prominent aspect and refers to the transfer and application of acquired expertise within the firm. In this regard, Kamoche (1997) argues that any type of expatriate failure can be regarded as a waste of opportunities to learn and diffuse this newly acquired expertise within the organization. Building on the distinction between individual and organizational success criteria on the one hand and short-term and long-term assignment outcomes on the other, we can develop a more comprehensive categorization of assignment success criteria (see Table 5.5).

Table 5.5   Success criteria for international transfers

	Individual benefits	**Organizational benefits**
During the assignment (short-term)	• Task performance • Skill building, learning, growth • Adjustment • Job satisfaction	• Accomplishment of organizational tasks • Achievement of key organizational objectives (such as control and coordination, knowledge transfer)
After the assignment (long-term)	• Continued development • Attractive future assignments • Development of contacts with key people • Promotion • Enlargement of responsibility	• Retention of repatriated employee • Utilization of new expertise • Transfer of expertise • Encouragement of international mobility among colleagues • Willingness to accept future international transfers

Source: adapted from Yan et al. (2002)

However, it has to be acknowledged that a precise and applicable conceptualization of assignment success is still lacking in the corporate world (Thomas, 1998). In this vein, Gregersen et al. (1996) empirically demonstrate that systematic performance appraisal of international assignees in MNCs is far from being universally applied which may entail negative consequences for assignees' careers within the organization.

7 Summary and conclusions

This chapter has given an overview of various dimensions and issues related to international assignments. We provided an analysis of the different transfer policies, looked at the specific motives for international transfers, reviewed alternative forms of international transfers, examined the key elements of the assignment process and discussed dimensions of assignment success. We have seen that the group of what constitutes international assignees is in fact very diverse and includes different transfer directions, different assignment lengths and different levels at which the assignment is initiated. From this perspective, the various assignment forms provide MNCs with a detailed toolbox to address the challenges of globalization and tailor these staffing options to their individual needs. As a result, international assignments are increasingly becoming a strategic resource for MNCs to successfully compete internationally. The key challenge for MNCs will then be to link international assignments more directly to their organizational career paths to be able to capitalize upon the experiences and skills that assignees develop during their transfers in the long run. Changes in the way careers are perceived among the younger generations suggest that individuals are less willing to focus their professional lives on a single employer. Companies therefore have a lot to lose if they do not manage international assignments well from both individual and organizational perspectives.

Discussion questions

1. With the growth in modern communication technologies, such as email and video-conferencing, and the declining costs of international travel, expatriates will become an extinct species! Comment on this statement.
2. Imagine a European MNC having to staff one of its subsidiaries that acts as a regional HQ for the Asian market. Which staffing strategy would you choose? Explain why.
3. With regard to recruitment and selection, actual practice in MNCs seems to be quite different from recommendations for good practice. Why do you think this is the case?
4. Section 4 discusses alternative forms of international assignments. How will these types of assignees differ with regard to their role as knowledge agents between MNC units?
5. A successful international transfer from the perspective of the individual assignee does not necessarily imply success from the company's point of view. Find examples for this statement and discuss them.

CASE STUDY

Richard Debenham in Vienna – between Velvet Divorce and the Sydney Olympics

This case is an abridged version of IESE Business School Case DPO-121-E 'Richard Debenham in Vienna (A) – Between Velvet Divorce and the Sydney Olympics', prepared by B. Sebastian Reiche, Copyright © 2008, IESE.

It was a day in late November 1995 and Richard Debenham was sitting in the famous Café Sacher in Vienna's city centre reflecting on the offer he had received that morning. After six exciting years playing a major role in driving Softdrinks Australia's expansion into the Central and Eastern European market, he considered the opportunity to return to Sydney together with his family.

Company background

Softdrinks Australia, headquartered in Sydney, was the main Australian licensee of Softdrinks US, one of the leading soft drink brands worldwide. Starting as a British subsidiary in the tobacco industry, Softdrinks Australia had entered the Australian beverage industry in 1964. In the early 1980s, Ken Grant, Softdrinks Australia's managing director, was looking to further expand the existing franchise operations to become Australia's sole licensee. Softdrinks US initially was keen to prevent single franchisees from becoming too influential domestically and opposed this move. Instead, Softdrinks Australia was invited to expand the Australian franchise abroad. Incidentally, at this time local franchises in Graz and Vienna were for sale. Given Grant's personal attachments to Austria, Softdrinks Australia took advantage of the opportunity and acquired the two franchises in 1982. In the following years, Softdrinks Australia slowly expanded its operations throughout Austria.

The situation changed dramatically in 1989. With the fall of the Iron Curtain that had divided the whole of Europe, Softdrinks US suddenly found itself in an intense race with its major competitor to establish franchises in Central and Eastern Europe. Given that other Western European franchise owners seemed uninterested in expanding eastwards, Softdrinks Australia's office in Vienna and its newly acquired franchises in Austria were seen as the perfect base to actively drive the expansion into Central and Eastern Europe. Philip Cameron, Softdrinks Australia's new managing director, knew that it would be a dramatic international venture with an uncertain future but he also felt that his company's domestic success would give it the necessary resilience to shoulder the new challenge. Consequently, Cameron approached Werner Stegl, the local managing director in Vienna, to investigate the

Central and Eastern European markets and compile a business plan for expansion. However, Stegl didn't believe that an eastward expansion would provide any opportunity for the current operations and opposed the plans. Given the local resistance, Cameron convinced the Sydney executive board to overrule Stegl's decision and go ahead with his strategy.

The decision to relocate

Knowing that he needed people from the headquarters to be positioned in Vienna for pursuing his plans in Europe, Cameron approached Richard Debenham in December 1989. The two had maintained a close relationship for a long time and Cameron was confident that Richard would be the right person to drive the new business. Richard had been involved with Softdrinks Australia for 16 years and knew the operations part of the business very well.

When receiving the offer to move to Vienna, Richard was 44 years of age. He felt it was a good time for a change. However, he was also conscious about the many personal challenges involved in such a move. It was clear to him that he would only embark on this move together with his wife and his three children. Were there any potential disruptions to the children's education and lives? How would his wife enjoy the new life? Professionally, Richard was also concerned whether the transfer would be a positive move for his career. How would the transfer fit into his career path at Softdrinks Australia? He felt that if he accepted the transfer, he too would be following the company into an uncertain future.

Without much time on his hands, Richard decided to accept the relocation for a period of three years. He was certain that, being a Western city, Vienna would be a comfortable place for him and his family to base themselves compared to the more uncertain environment that would await them in Eastern Europe. In January 1990, Richard and his family relocated to Austria. Richard was accompanied by a colleague from the finance department and a newly recruited expert on Central and Eastern Europe.

Amidst the Velvet Divorce

The move to Vienna was quite rushed and although the company offered to pay for various relocation expenses, Richard and his family had to organize everything themselves. However, despite the many difficulties in their new surroundings, they adapted well. While Richard's wife was not allowed to work, she was able to get

(Continued)

(Continued)

involved with other spouses through their children's school and the children quickly built new friendships. Soon, Richard found that the real challenges he was facing occurred in his day-to-day professional life. The local staff in the Vienna office, having resisted the initial decision to expand Softdrinks Australia's operations eastwards, turned out to offer little support. At times, Richard even felt that local staff tried to complicate his already challenging assignments even further. For example, instead of being able to use office space at the local office, Richard had to find and lease separate premises upon arrival.

A significant issue also arose over the allocation of human resources. Given their relative proximity, Softdrinks Australia would have liked to transfer more Austrians to the different Eastern European countries to run the daily business there. With Prague being a three and a half hours commute by car from Vienna, it would have been a fairly undisruptive assignment without requiring complete relocation. However, local staff was disinclined to work there and so over time the company was forced to bring in more Australians.

Another difficulty that Richard faced when he started to negotiate acquisition agreements with local owners in Czechoslovakia was to find a suitable counterpart for negotiation. During the transition from a socialist to a free-enterprise system it was difficult for Richard and his colleagues to understand who owned the factory they wanted to purchase or establish a joint-venture agreement with. In addition, when Softdrinks Australia finally began its own production in Prague in 1992, the country's 'velvet divorce' – a term referring to the dissolution of Czechoslovakia – meant that Richard and his team needed to treat Slovakia as a separate country and hence search for a suitable production site.

Richard saw it as an important part of his role not only to serve as the local representative of the Sydney office in Europe but also to actively support the transition from a socialist to a free-enterprise system. In his many interactions with locals, he sensed a deep-seated central planning and command orientation and constantly struggled to change this mindset among his local colleagues.

The decision to prolong the stay

While Richard's transfer was initially intended to last only three years, in 1992 Softdrinks Australia was only at the beginning of a promising expansion path and was planning to further grow its ownership of local franchises. With the formal dissolution of Czechoslovakia and the completion of the separation of the Czech and Slovakian franchises on the horizon, Softdrinks Australia felt that it could now accelerate its expansion further eastwards. Without any clear prospect for a subsequent position in Sydney, Richard and his family decided to stay for a few more years in Vienna.

The following years saw a rapid expansion into other countries throughout Central and Eastern Europe, such as Slovenia, Ukraine, Belarus and Poland. In addition, driven by the early successes abroad the Sydney office also began to systematically explore different markets in Asia that were developing more rapidly and promised to offer substantial growth opportunities in geographically a less distant region from Australia.

Richard felt that he was able to build on his earlier experiences and his increasingly detailed understanding of the Eastern European cultures to further drive the company's expansion plans and operations. He was becoming more effective in negotiating with local parties and instilling a customer-oriented mindset among the various franchisees. At the same time, with every year that passed in Europe he sensed an increasing difficulty with making the return to living and working in Sydney. In the meantime, Cameron, who had initially offered the relocation to Richard, had left the company due to personal differences at the headquarters and Richard's contacts with his home office became less frequent. What was more significant, his two Australian colleagues who joined him in the beginning had both encountered difficulties in finding appropriate positions back at the headquarters, a disappointment which ultimately persuaded them both to quit Softdrinks Australia.

The offer

After six years of working in Europe, one morning in late November 1995 Richard received a call from headquarters. The Sydney office was looking for someone to manage the Sydney Olympic programme that was to be launched in January 1996. Softdrinks US had traditionally been an important sponsor of the Olympic Games and, with the next games to be staged Down Under, Softdrinks Australia was selected as one of the Team Millennium Olympic Partners. Aware of Richard's interest in returning to Australia, Sydney management offered him a position to manage this programme and gave him a week to decide whether or not to accept.

Hanging up the phone, Richard felt a strong sense of joy. He was about to call his wife to share the excellent news when he had second thoughts. He left the office and took a walk through the city centre until the cold November air forced him into one of the many Viennese café houses. He had always decided against pursuing an international career and knew that this would mean returning

(Continued)

(Continued)

to the domestic market he had worked in for the first 16 years of his career with Softdrinks Australia. However, he felt that he had invested considerable time and effort in building new skills that he was not sure he would be able to use back home. Wouldn't it be more sensible to stay in Europe, even if this might ultimately mean changing employer? Of course, his family had signalled a desire to return to Sydney but they also had become more hesitant to leave behind the rich social relationships they had developed in Vienna. Moreover, with many of his former colleagues having left the company, Richard felt more detached now from the Sydney office. How would he fit back into a company that had changed a lot during his absence? And what were his prospects after managing the Olympic programme? As he drank the last sip of his coffee, he realized the decision would be more difficult than he had initially thought.

Case study questions

1. Should Richard accept the offer to return to Sydney? Why/why not? What are the implications of his decision?
2. How would you evaluate the decision of Softdrinks Australia to expand to Europe?
3. Which skills has Richard developed during his assignment? How valuable are they?

Case study questions for further reflection

1. Imagine you are offered the opportunity to temporarily move overseas with your current employer. What are the main factors you need to consider for deciding whether to accept the transfer?
2. Imagine you are about to finish your studies and are looking for a job that provides the opportunity to work internationally. Would you work for Softdrinks Australia?

Further reading

- Harzing, A.W.K. (2001a) 'Who's in charge: an empirical study of executive staffing practices in foreign subsidiaries', *Human Resource Management*, 40(2): 139–158.
- Harzing, A.W.K. (2001b) 'Of bears, bumble-bees and spiders: the role of expatriates in controlling foreign subsidiaries', *Journal of World Business*, 36(4): 366–379.

The main conclusions of these two articles are summarized in this chapter, but the original articles provide much more detail on empirical studies dealing with staffing policies and the functions of international transfers.

- Collings, D.G., Scullion, H. and Morley, M.J. (2007) 'Changing patterns of global staffing in the multinational enterprise: challenges to the conventional expatriate assignment and emerging alternatives', *Journal of World Business*, 42(2): 198–213. This article provides a more detailed account of recent changes in the management of international assignments due to supply side issues, cost issues, demand side issues and career issues. It also reviews alternative forms of international assignments that have recently emerged and discusses the implications for the design of international HR policies and practices.

- Shaffer, M.A., Harrison, D.A. and Gilley, K.M. (1999) 'Dimensions, determinants and differences in the expatriate adjustment process', *Journal of International Business Studies*, 30(3): 557–581. This study provides the most comprehensive and up-to-date empirical test of the expatriate adjustment model by Black, Mendenhall and Oddou. It introduces two new variables in the model – international experience and language fluency – and shows that both variables have an important direct effect as well as a moderating effect on some of the other variables related to adjustment.

- Reiche, B.S., Harzing, A.-W. and Kraimer, M.L. (2009) 'The role of international assignees' social capital in creating inter-unit intellectual capital: a cross-level model', *Journal of International Business Studies*, 40(3): 509–526. This article offers a more complete picture of how international assignees initiate and contribute to knowledge flows in MNCs. It introduces two distinct roles that assignees possess as knowledge agents. First, assignees serve as knowledge brokers by linking their social networks at the home and the host unit, thereby generating access between previously unconnected knowledge resources. Second, assignees also act as knowledge transmitters, both by sharing their home unit knowledge with host unit staff and by transferring the knowledge they have acquired during the assignment to their home unit.

- Bonache, J. and Stirpe, L. (2012) 'Compensating global employees', in G.K. Stahl, I. Björkman and S. Morris (eds), *Handbook of Research in International Human Resource Management* (2nd edn). Cheltenham: Edward Elgar, pp. 162–182. This book chapter gives a good overview of issues related to the compensation of international assignees.

- Caligiuri, P.M. (2006) 'Performance measurement in a cross-national context', in W. Bennet, C.E. Lance and D.J. Woehr (eds), *Performance Measurement: Current Perspectives and Future Challenges*. Mahwah, NJ: Lawrence Erlbaum, pp. 227–243.

This book chapter discusses performance measurement strategies in MNCs and differentiates performance evaluation instruments with regard to different forms of international assignments.

- Black, J.S., Gregersen, H.B. and Mendenhall, M.E. (1992) *Global Assignments: Successfully Expatriating and Repatriating International Managers*. San Francisco: Jossey-Bass.
  This book is a good source of reference on issues related to the management of the various phases of the international assignment process, with a particular focus on the balancing of family concerns and the repatriation of assignees.

- Scullion, H. and Collings, D.G. (eds) (2006) *Global Staffing*. Milton Park: Routledge. This is an edited book that provides a wide range of topics on the strategic and operational aspects of staffing in MNCs, including international staff composition, international recruitment, talent management, cross-cultural management and the management of international assignments.

Internet resources

- www.brookfieldgrs.com. Brookfield Global Relocation Services is a US-based provider of relocation services and consulting that publishes an annual global relocation trends survey.
- www.dialogin.com. Delta Intercultural Academy is a knowledge community on culture and communication in international business that maintains online forums on different topic areas, advertises job postings, publishes online articles and book reviews, organizes e-conferences, etc.
- www.livingabroad.com. Living Abroad is an online provider of general information, country reports and tools for international assignees.
- www.relojournal.com. Relocation Journal is an online provider of news and information on global relocation that includes informative white papers, webinars, a newsletter and general relocation service information.
- www.expatexchange.com. Expatriate Exchange is an online community for meeting other expatriates, finding international jobs, getting expert advice on living abroad, international schools, taxes, relocation, etc.
- www.internations.org. InterNations is an online community for people living abroad that maintains very active city groups.
- http://blog.iese.edu/expatriatus. Expatriatus is a blog that addresses both individuals that have or are to experience international relocations and companies that actively manage international staff.

Self-assessment questions

Indicative answers to these questions can be found on the companion website at study.sagepub.com/harzing4e.

1. Why is it more appropriate to call Edström and Galbraith's third motive for using international transfers 'coordination and control' rather than 'organization development'?
2. What type of staff do MNCs with an ethnocentric staffing policy appoint to top management positions in their foreign subsidiaries?
3. Why are MNCs increasingly looking for alternative forms of international assignments?
4. What are the advantages and disadvantages of using short-term international assignments?
5. On what criteria should assignment success be evaluated?

References

Anderson, B.A. (2005) 'Expatriate selection: good management or good luck?', *International Journal of Human Resource Management*, 16(4): 567–583.

Au, K.Y. and Fukuda, J. (2002) 'Boundary spanning behaviors of expatriates', *Journal of World Business*, 37(4): 285–297.

Barnett, S.T. and Toyne, B. (1991) 'The socialization, acculturation, and career progression of headquartered foreign nationals', in S.B. Prasad (ed.), *Advances in International Comparative Management*, Vol. 6. Greenwich, CT: JAI Press, pp. 3–34.

Bartlett, C.A. and Ghoshal, S. (1989) *Managing Across Borders: The Transnational Solution*. Boston, MA: Harvard Business School Press.

Belderbos, R.A. and Heijltjes, M.G. (2005) 'The determinants of expatriate staffing by Japanese multinationals in Asia: control, learning, and vertical integration', *Journal of International Business Studies*, 36(3): 341–354.

Berthoin Antal, A. (2000) 'Types of knowledge gained by expatriate managers', *Journal of General Management*, 26(2): 32–51.

Black, J.S. and Gregersen, H.B. (1999) 'The right way to manage expats', *Harvard Business Review*, 77(2): 52–62.

Black, J.S., Mendenhall, M. and Oddou, G. (1991) 'Toward a comprehensive model of international adjustment: an integration of multiple theoretical perspectives', *Academy of Management Review*, 16(2): 291–317.

Bolino, M.C. (2007) 'Expatriate assignments and intra-organizational career success: implications for individuals and organizations', *Journal of International Business Studies*, 38(5): 819–835.

Bonache, J. and Brewster, C. (2001) 'Knowledge transfer and the management of expatriation', *Thunderbird International Business Review*, 43(1): 145–168.

Bonache, J., Brewster, C. and Suutari, V. (2001) 'Expatriation: a developing research agenda', *Thunderbird International Business Review*, 43(1): 3–20.

Boyacigiller, N. (1990) 'The role of expatriates in the management of interdependence, complexity and risk in multinational corporations', *Journal of International Business Studies*, 21(3): 357–381.

Brewster, C. (1991) *The Management of Expatriates*. London: Kogan Page.

Brookfield Global Relocation Services (2011) *Global Relocation Trends: 2011 Survey Report*. Toronto, Canada: Brookfield Global Relocation Services.

Caligiuri, P. (2000) 'Selecting expatriates for personality characteristics: a moderating effect of personality on the relationship between host national contact and cross-cultural adjustment', *Management International Review*, 40(1): 61–80.

Clarke, C. and Hammer, M.R. (1995) 'Predictors of Japanese and American managers job success, personal adjustment, and intercultural interaction effectiveness', *Management International Review*, 35(2): 153–170.

Collings, D.G., Scullion, H. and Morley, M.J. (2007) 'Changing patterns of global staffing in the multinational enterprise: challenges to the conventional expatriate assignment and emerging alternatives', *Journal of World Business*, 42(2): 198–213.

Deshpande, S.P. and Viswesvaran, C. (1992) 'Is cross-cultural training of expatriate managers effective? A meta-analysis', *International Journal of Intercultural Relations*, 16(3): 295–310.

Doherty, N., Dickmann, M. and Mills, T. (2011) 'Exploring the motives of company-backed and self-initiated expatriates', *International Journal of Human Resource Management*, 22(3): 595–611.

Dowling P.J., Festing, M. and Engle, A.D. (2008) *International Human Resource Management: Managing People in a Multinational Context*, 5th edn. London: Cengage Learning.

Edström, A. and Galbraith, J.R. (1977) 'Transfer of managers as a co-ordination and control strategy in multinational organizations', *Administrative Science Quarterly*, 22(2): 248–263.

Evans, P., Pucik, V. and Björkman, I. (2011) *The Global Challenge: International Human Resource Management*, 2nd edn. New York: McGraw-Hill Irwin.

Feldman, D.C. and Thomas, D.C. (1992) 'Career management issues facing expatriates', *Journal of International Business Studies*, 23(2): 271–293.

Forster, N. (2000) 'The myth of the international manager', *International Journal of Human Resource Management*, 11(1): 126–142.

Forster, N. and Johnsen, M. (1996) 'Expatriate management policies in UK companies new to the international scene', *International Journal of Human Resource Management*, 7(1): 177–205.

Gaur, A.S., Delios, A. and Singh, K. (2007) 'Institutional environments, staffing strategies, and subsidiary performance', *Journal of Management*, 33(4): 611–636.

Ghoshal, S. and Nohria, N. (1993) 'Horses for courses: organizational forms for multinational corporations', *Sloan Management Review*, 34(2): 23–35.

Gong, Y. (2003a) 'Subsidiary staffing in multinational enterprises: agency, resources, and performance', *Academy of Management Journal*, 46(6): 728–739.

Gong, Y. (2003b) 'Toward a dynamic process model of staffing composition and subsidiary outcomes in multinational enterprises', *Journal of Management*, 29(2): 259–280.

Gregersen, H.B., Hite, J.M. and Black, J.S. (1996) 'Expatriate performance appraisal in US multinational firms', *Journal of International Business Studies*, 27(4): 711–738.

Groenewald, H. and Sapozhnikov, A. (1990) 'Auslandentsendungen von Führungskräften: Vorgehenweisen internationaler Fluggesellschaften', *Die Unternehmung*, 44(1): 28–42.

Gullahorn, J.T. and Gullahorn, J.E. (1963) 'An extension of the U-curve hypothesis', *Journal of Social Issues*, 19(3): 33–47.

Hamill, J. (1989) 'Expatriate policies in British multinationals', *Journal of General Management*, 14(4): 18–33.

Harris, H. and Brewster, C. (1999a) 'The coffee-machine system: how international selection really works', *International Journal of Human Resource Management*, 10(3): 488–500.

Harris, H. and Brewster, C. (1999b) 'An integrative framework for pre-departure preparation', in C. Brewster and H. Harris (eds), *International HRM: Contemporary Issues in Europe*. London: Routledge, pp. 223–240.

Harrison, D.A., Shaffer, M.A. and Bhaskar-Shrinivas, P. (2004) 'Going places: roads more and less traveled in research on expatriate experiences', in J.J. Martocchio (ed.), *Research in Personnel and Human Resources Management*, Vol. 23. Oxford: Elsevier, pp. 199–247.

Harvey, M. (1998) 'Dual-career couples during international relocation: the trailing spouse', *International Journal of Human Resource Management*, 9(2): 309–331

Harvey, M. and Miceli, N. (1999) 'Exploring inpatriate manager issues: an exploratory empirical study', *International Journal of Intercultural Relations*, 23(3): 339–371.

Harvey, M., Novicevic, M.M., Buckley, M.R. and Fung, H. (2005) 'Reducing inpatriate managers' "liability of foreignness" by addressing stigmatization and stereotype threats', *Journal of World Business*, 40(3): 267–280.

Harvey, M., Novicevic, M.M. and Speier, C. (2000) 'Strategic global human resource management: the role of inpatriate managers', *Human Resource Management Review*, 10(2): 153–175.

Harzing, A.W.K. (1995) 'The persistent myth of high expatriate failure rates', *International Journal of Human Resource Management*, 6(2): 457–475.

Harzing, A.W.K (1999) 'MNC staffing policies for the CEO-position in foreign subsidiaries: the results of an innovative research method', in C. Brewster and H. Harris (eds), *International HRM: Contemporary Issues in Europe*. London: Routledge, pp. 67–88.

Harzing, A.W.K. (2001a) 'Who's in charge? An empirical study of executive staffing practices in foreign subsidiaries', *Human Resource Management*, 40(2): 139–158.

Harzing, A.W.K. (2001b) 'Of bears, bumble-bees and spiders: the role of expatriates in controlling foreign subsidiaries', *Journal of World Business*, 36(4): 366–379.

Harzing, A.W.K. (2002) 'Are our referencing errors undermining our scholarship and credibility? The case of expatriate failure rates', *Journal of Organizational Behavior*, 23(1): 127–148.

Harzing, A.W.K. and Christensen, C. (2004) 'Expatriate failure: time to abandon the concept?' *Career Development International*, 9(6–7): 616–626.

Harzing, A.-W., Pudelko, M. and Reiche, B.S. (2012) 'Changing patterns of international assignee staffing and their role in knowledge transfer'. Paper presented at the 10th EIASM Workshop on International Strategy and Cross-Cultural Management, Reykjavik, Iceland.

Hébert, L., Very, P. and Beamish, P.W. (2005) 'Expatriation as a bridge over troubled water: a knowledge-based perspective applied to cross-border acquisitions', *Organization Studies*, 26(10): 1455–1476.

Heenan, D.A. and Perlmutter, H.V. (1979) *Multinational Organization Development*. Reading, MA: Addison-Wesley.

Hocking, J.B., Brown, M.E. and Harzing, A.-W. (2007) 'Balancing global and local strategic contexts: expatriate knowledge transfer, applications and learning within a transnational organization', *Human Resource Management*, 46(4): 513–533.

Hofstede, G. (1980) *Culture's Consequences: International Differences in Work-related Values*. Beverly Hills, CA: Sage.

Hofstede, G. (2001) *Culture's Consequences: Comparing Values, Behaviors, Institutions, and Organizations Across Nations*, 2nd edn. Thousand Oaks, CA: Sage.

Kamoche, K. (1997) 'Knowledge creation and learning in international HRM', *International Journal of Human Resource Management*, 8(3): 213–225.

Kenter, M.E. (1985) *Die Steuerung ausländischer Tochtergesellschaften. Instrumente und Effizienz*. Frankfurt am Main: P. Lang.

Kopp, R. (1994) 'International human resource policies and practices in Japanese, European and United States multinationals', *Human Resource Management*, 33(4): 581–599.

Kraimer, M.L. and Wayne, S.J. (2004) 'An examination of perceived organizational support as a multidimensional construct in the context of an expatriate assignment', *Journal of Management*, 30(2): 209–237.

Kraimer, M.L., Wayne, S.J. and Jaworski, R.A. (2001) 'Sources of support and expatriate performance: the mediating role of expatriate adjustment', *Personnel Psychology*, 54(1): 71–99.

Kumar, B.N. and Karlshaus, M. (1992) 'Auslandseinsatz und Personalentwicklung. Ergebnisse einer empirischen Studie über den Beitrag der Auslandsentsendung', *Zeitschrift für Personalforschung*, 6(1): 59–74.

Kumar, B.N. and Steinmann, H. (1986) 'Japanische Führungskrafte zwischen ensandten und lokalen Führungskraften in Deutschland', *Zeitschrift für betriebswirtschaftliche Forschung*, 38(6): 493–516.

Lazarova, M. and Caligiuri, P. (2001) 'Retaining repatriates: the role of organizational support practices', *Journal of World Business*, 36(4): 389–401.

Lazarova, M.B. and Cerdin, J.-L. (2007) 'Revisiting repatriation concerns: Organizational support versus career and contextual influences', *Journal of International Business Studies*, 38(3): 404–429.

Liu, X. and Shaffer, M.A. (2005) 'An investigation of expatriate adjustment and performance: a social capital perspective', *International Journal of Cross Cultural Management*, 5(3): 235–254.

Macharzina, K. (1992) 'Internationaler Transfer von Führungskraften', *Zeitschrift für Personalforschung*, 6(3): 366–384.

Marschan-Piekkari, R., Welch, D. and Welch, L. (1999) 'In the shadow: the impact of language on structure, power and communication in the multinational', *International Business Review*, 8(4): 421–440.

Mendenhall, M. and Oddou, G. (1985) 'The dimensions of expatriate acculturation: a review', *Academy of Management Review*, 10(1): 39–47.

Mendenhall, M.E., Reiche, B.S., Bird, A. and Osland, J.S. (2012) 'Defining the "global" in global leadership', *Journal of World Business*, 47(4): 493–503.

Mendenhall, M.E. and Stahl, G.K. (2000) 'Expatriate training and development: where do we go from here?', *Human Resource Management*, 39(2–3): 251–265.

Mezias, J.M. and Scandura, T.A. (2005) 'A needs-driven approach to expatriate adjustment and career development: a multiple mentoring perspective', *Journal of International Business Studies*, 36(5): 519–538.

Negandhi, A.R. (1987) *International Management*. Newton, MA: Allyn and Bacon.

Novicevic, M.M. and Harvey, M.G. (2001) 'The emergence of the pluralism construct and the inpatriation process', *International Journal of Human Resource Management*, 12(3): 333–356.

Oberg, K. (1960) 'Cultural shock: adjustment to new cultural environments', *Practical Anthropology*, 7: 177–182.

Oddou, G., Gregersen, H.B., Black, J.S. and Derr, C.B. (2001) 'Building global leaders: strategy similarities and differences among European, U.S., and Japanese multinationals', in M.E. Mendenhall, T.M. Kühlmann and G.K. Stahl (eds), *Developing Global Business Leaders: Policies, Processes, and Innovations*. Westport, CT: Quorum Books, pp. 99–116.

Parkinson, E. and Morley, M. (2006) 'Cross cultural training', in H. Scullion and D.G. Collings (eds), *Global Staffing*. London: Routledge, pp. 117–138.

Paterson, S.L. and Brock, D.M. (2002) 'The development of subsidiary-management research: review and theoretical analysis', *International Business Review*, 11(2): 139–163.

Pausenberger, E. (1987) 'Unternehmens- und Personalentwicklung durch Entsendung', *Personalführung*, 20(11–12): 852–856.

Pausenberger, E. and Noelle, G.F. (1977) 'Entsendung von Führungskraften in ausländische Niederlassungen', *Zeitschrift für betriebswirtschaftliche Forschung*, 29(6): 346–366.

Perlmutter, H.V. (1969) 'The tortuous evolution of the multinational corporation', *Columbia Journal of World Business*, 4(1): 9–18.

Phatak, A.V. (1989) *International Management*. Boston, MA: PWS-Kent Publishing Company.

Reiche, B.S. (2006) 'The inpatriate experience in multinational corporations: an exploratory case study in Germany', *International Journal of Human Resource Management*, 17(9): 1572–1590.

Reiche, B.S. (2008) 'Richard Debehham in Vienna (A) – Between Velvet Divorce and the Sydney Olympics', IESE Business School Case DPO-121-E

Reiche, B.S. (2010) 'Welcoming the value that inpatriates bring', *IESE Insight*, 2(4): 38–45.

Reiche, B.S. (2012a) 'Knowledge benefits of social capital upon repatriation: a longitudinal study of international assignees', *Journal of Management Studies*, 49(6): 1052–1077.

Reiche, B.S. (2012b) 'Spotlight expatriate taxes: the case of "accidental expatriates"'. Online source: http://blog.iese.edu/expatriatus/2012/06/07/spotlight-expatriate-taxes-the-case-of-accidental-expatriates/#sthash.pJhUEpIh.dpbs (accessed 14 May 2014).

Reiche, B.S., Harzing, A.-W. and Kraimer, M.L. (2009) 'The role of international assignees' social capital in creating inter-unit intellectual capital: a cross-level model', *Journal of International Business Studies*, 40(3): 509–526.

Riusala, K. and Suutari, V. (2004) 'International knowledge transfers through expatriates', *Thunderbird International Business Review*, 46(6): 743–770.

Roessel, R.V. (1988) *Führungskräfte-Transfer in internationalen Unternehmungen*. Köln: Wirtschaftsverlag Bachem.

Shaffer, M.A., Harrison, D.A. and Gilley, K.M. (1999) 'Dimensions, determinants and differences in the expatriate adjustment process', *Journal of International Business Studies*, 30(3): 557–581.

Shay, J.P. and Baack, S.A. (2004) 'Expatriate assignment, adjustment and effectiveness: an empirical examination of the big picture', *Journal of International Business Studies*, 35(3): 216–232.

Sparrow, P., Brewster, C. and Harris, H. (2004) *Globalizing Human Resource Management*. London: Routledge.

Spreitzer, G.M., McCall, M.W. and Mahoney, J.D. (1997) 'Early identification of international executive potential', *Journal of Applied Psychology*, 82(1), 6–29.

Stahl, G.K., Miller, E.L. and Tung, R.L. (2002) 'Toward the boundaryless career: a closer look at the expatriate career concept and the perceived implications of an international assignment', *Journal of World Business*, 37(3): 216–227.

Suutari, V. and Brewster, C. (2000) 'Making their own way: international experience through self-initiated foreign assignments', *Journal of World Business*, 35(4): 417–436.

Tahvanainen, M., Worm, V. and Welch, D. (2005) 'Implications of short-term international assignments', *European Management Journal*, 23(6): 663–673.

Tarique, I., Schuler, R. and Gong, Y. (2006) 'A model of multinational enterprise subsidiary staffing composition', *International Journal of Human Resource Management*, 17(2): 207–224.

Tharenou, P. and Caulfield, N. (2010) 'Will I stay or will I go? Explaining repatriation by self-initiated expatriates', *Academy of Management Journal*, 53(5): 1009–1028.

Thomas, D.C. (1998) 'The expatriate experience: a critical review and synthesis', in J.L. Cheng and R.B. Peterson (eds), *Advances in International Comparative Management*, Vol. 12. Greenwich, CT: JAI Press, pp. 237–273.

Toh, S.M. and DeNisi, A.S. (2007) 'Host country nationals as socializing agents: a social identity approach', *Journal of Organizational Behavior*, 28(3): 281–301.

Tung, R.L. (1981) 'Selection and training of personnel for overseas assignments', *Columbia Journal of World Business*, 16(2): 68–78.

Tung, R.L. (1982) 'Selection and training procedures of U.S., European, and Japanese multinationals', *California Management Review*, 25(1): 57–71.

Tung, R.L. (1998) 'American expatriates abroad: from neophytes to cosmopolitans', *Journal of World Business*, 33(2): 125–144.

Tungli, Z. and Peiperl, M. (2009) 'Expatriate practices in German, Japanese, U.K., and U.S. multinational companies: a comparative survey of changes', *Human Resource Management*, 48(1): 153–171.

Wang, X. and Kanungo, R.N. (2004) 'Nationality, social network and psychological well-being: expatriates in China', *International Journal of Human Resource Management*, 15(4–5): 775–793.

Welch, D.E., Welch, L.S. and Worm, V. (2007) 'The international business traveller: a neglected but strategic human resource', *International Journal of Human Resource Management*, 18(2): 173–183.

Welch, D.E., Worm, V. and Fenwick, M. (2003) 'Are virtual assignments feasible?', *Management International Review*, 43(Special Issue 1): 95–114.

Welge, M.K. (1980) *Management in deutschen multinationalen Unternehmungen: Ergebnisse einer empirischen Untersuchung*. Stuttgart: Poeschel Verlag.

Wolf, J. (1994) *Internationales Personalmanagement: Kontext – Koordination – Erfolg*. Wiesbaden: Gabler, MIR Edition.

Yan, A., Zhu, G. and Hall, D.T. (2002) 'International assignments for career building: a model of agency relationships and psychological contracts', *Academy of Management Review*, 27(3): 373–391.

Multinational Companies and the Host Country Environment

Damian Grimshaw, Jill Rubery and Phil Almond

6

Contents

Learning objectives

After reading this chapter you will be able to:

- Appreciate some of the main features that distinguish host country business and employment environments
- Identify the key issues for multinational companies in developing their HRM policies and practices in different host country environments
- Critically assess the evidence for and against trends towards convergence of country employment systems
- Explain how HRM practices of pay, work organization and collective representation are shaped by host country factors

Chapter outline

This chapter explores the diversity of host country environments that MNCs must engage with when managing overseas subsidiaries, and analyses the extent to which these environments influence subsidiaries' HRM practices, particularly pay systems, work organization and collective representation. Evidence of trends towards cross-national convergence in employment arrangements is also explored.

1 Introduction

When multinational companies set up subsidiaries in foreign countries they are required not only to comply with legal regulations but also in practice need to take into account customary practices prevailing in the host environment, particularly if hiring local staff. MNCs need to understand the local labour market environment and identify the key attributes and expectations of their employees drawn from the host community. The outcome is shaped by both the MNC's internal environment (including the strategic importance of the subsidiary to the MNC and subsidiary managers' local sources of power) and the external environment shaped by the home and host country institutions (Kostova and Zaheer 1999). This chapter focuses on how the host country environment influences the diffusion of MNCs' preferred IHRM policies. We explore the variety of host environments that MNCs may encounter and identify conditions when it is important to adjust to host country economic conditions, institutional rules and social and cultural norms and expectations. This may vary according to the type of IHRM or local HRM policy and the group of staff under consideration.

While this chapter mainly discusses how host country environments influence MNCs, the influence also works in the other direction. Many governments have been willing to alter their country environments to attract inwards FDI, for example by de-regulating product and labour markets or having few requirements for protecting the environment such as pollution controls. Some developing countries have set up specific enclaves – export processing zones – where MNC subsidiaries are not subject to the normal regulations prevailing in the country. MNCs may affect the host country environment in more positive ways – through establishing higher standards of HR practices, within the subsidiaries and also possibly in local supplier organizations. This may increase pressure on domestic companies to compete with MNCs or may reduce their capability to compete if they cannot attract talented labour. While these effects may be more marked in developing economies, MNCs may also influence changes in more developed economies. They may actively lobby for changes to regulations and practices they find onerous or which restrict their access to markets. Furthermore, if MNCs opt out of national institutional arrangements such as national or sectoral level collective bargaining or training arrangements, they may weaken those institutions by also encouraging domestic employers to consider opting out. The overall message here is that MNCs are powerful organizational actors. While they may adjust their practices to meet host country environments, over time MNCs may also be influential in shaping those same environments (Geppert et al., 2006).

2 Varieties of host country environments

The vast majority of MNCs when setting up wholly owned subsidiaries or joint ventures in foreign environments will employ staff under an internal employment relationship. This is a relatively ubiquitous institutional arrangement in advanced countries, as well as in the formal sectors of developing countries. The internal employment contract is a social institution which is shaped both by legal (or contractual) conditions and by social arrangements including custom and practice. Countries vary in their legal traditions and arrangements (Botero et al., 2004; Deakin, 2009), as well as in their customs and social institutions. As a consequence, employment arrangements take on diverse forms in different societies. These differences arise in part because although employment is a means to produce goods and services its significance extends to a whole set of other institutional arrangements in society. The organization of employment is shaped not only by labour market regulations and industrial relations systems, but also by production systems, education and training arrangements and their associated career structures, social stratification and standards of living, welfare arrangements and household, family and gender systems. Below we identify some of the most important differences along these institutional and social dimensions and how they may impact on MNCs to provide an overview of the potential distinctions between host country environments. Chapter 7 by Martínez Lucio and MacKenzie provides a complementary analysis of the changing politics associated with forms of de-regulation and re-regulation.

International Assignments and Employment Practices

Labour market regulations

MNCs at a minimum need to follow legal labour market regulations. These may also be improved upon by collective bargaining and labour market standards in some countries are also legally enforceable. Legal regulation applies particularly to employment protection, minimum wages, working time and discrimination.

Employment protection is one area where there are wide differences between countries and which undoubtedly affects MNCs' practices. The United States is at one end of the spectrum with its renowned 'employment at will' system where employers can terminate an employee's contract without facing significant legal constraints and or requirements to state their reasons, give notice or make compensatory payments. In the Organisation for Economic Co-operation and Development's (OECD) employment

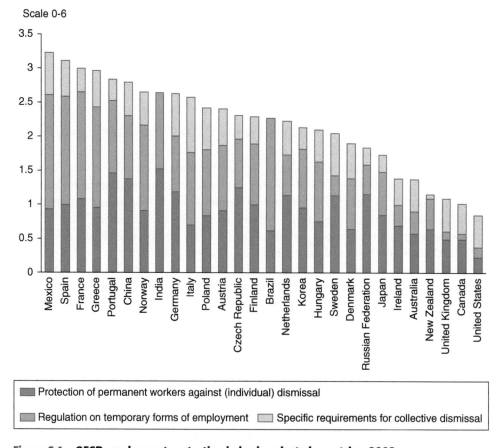

Figure 6.1   OECD employment protection index in selected countries, 2008

Notes: 2009 data for France and Portugal; see OECD notes for details of methodology and weights (available at www. oecd.org/employment/emp/42740190.pdf)

Source: OECD website – www.oecd.org/employment/emp/oecdindicatorsofemploymentprotection.htm

protection index (measuring 0 to 6 as protection increases), the United States scores less than 1 overall (and is especially weak in its protection against individual dismissals), compared to a score of 3 or more out of 6 in France, Spain and Mexico (see Figure 6.1). Japan scores below the average for this group of countries (1.7 out of 6) even though it has a tradition of providing 'jobs for life'. Custom and practice is more influential in shaping employment protection in Japan than actual legal provisions and lifelong employment contracts exist primarily in large firms among regular workers and are estimated to directly affect around one third of the country's total workforce, although the practice of lifetime employment arguably has wider influence in shaping what Ronald Dore calls a 'normative model' for society (see Keizer, 2010: 14–15). Wide variation is also found in country rules in relation to collective dismissals and temporary contracts, although regulation of the latter has been relaxed over recent years. Where legal regulations are bolstered by customary expectations of job security MNCs may have to respect these arrangements in order to attract high quality staff.

MNCs may also have to respect, where applicable, legal minimum wage regulations including higher minimum wages set through collective bargaining where these are extended to all relevant firms. Countries set the minimum wage at very different levels and have undergone contrasting trends in the last three decades (see Figure 6.2). These

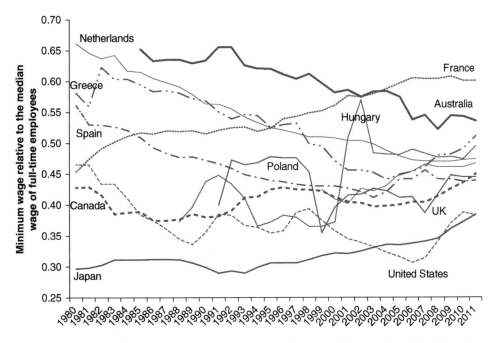

Figure 6.2   Trends in the level of minimum wages relative to median earnings for selected OECD countries, 1980–2011

Source: own compilation from OECD earnings database (full-time employees only), available at http://stats.oecd.org/

differences reflect complex interactions with competing government policy objectives, the character of collective bargaining and labour market conditions (Grimshaw, 2013). In many developing countries much employment is in the informal sector where the minimum wage is not applied although is likely to exert an influence as a benchmark against exploitative pay. MNC subsidiaries tend to be in the formal sector although they may subcontract to the informal sector where the gap in wages paid is large.

Legal working time regulations often set maximum working hours and minimum paid holiday entitlements. Collective bargaining agreements often include more detailed regulations on, for example, premium rates for overtime and weekend work. These regulations may affect MNCs' operating hours by changing cost structures. Again, there is wide cross-national variation. In France, national legislation has had a major impact on actual working time practices. In 1998 a standard 35-hour week was introduced, although the mandatory regulations were loosened following a change of government in 2002 (see Askenazy, 2013). This contrasts with the UK which in principle is bound by the maximum 48-hour week in the EU's working time directive, although UK employers are legally permitted to ask employees to voluntarily opt out from this provision. Regarding paid holidays, in the US and Japan employees have limited legal entitlements and often fail to take up their full entitlement due to work pressures. There is, however, a much stronger development of rights to paid holidays in Europe (Figure 6.3).

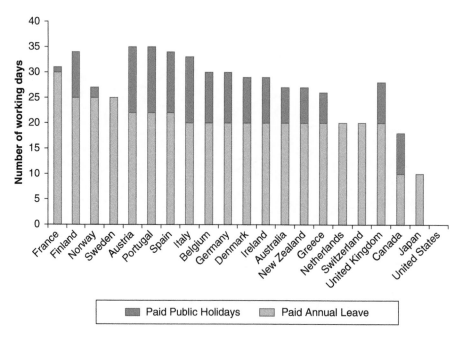

Figure 6.3   Paid annual leave and paid public holidays, OECD countries

Source: Ray and Schmitt (2007); data updated for the UK

Countries also vary in respect of their anti-discrimination laws. All members of the EU are bound by non-discrimination laws affecting not only discrimination by gender and ethnicity but also by age, sexuality and religion. In many countries MNCs may also have to give preference in hiring to local staff over non-citizens.

Industrial relations systems

Trade union membership and collective bargaining coverage constitute a second indicator of employment differences across countries (Figure 6.4). There is no simple correlation between trade union density and collective bargaining cover- age; for example trade union membership is low in France but collective bargain- ing coverage is high. In some countries the most common bargaining form is at national level covering multiple sectors (e.g. Norway), while in others it is either single sector bargaining (e.g. Germany, Denmark, Spain) or enterprise-level bar- gaining (Japan, the UK). National level bargaining is often associated with 'inclusive labour markets' where most employees enjoy similar forms of protection and wages are set at similar levels for all employers. Enterprise level bargaining is associated with more 'exclusive labour markets'; here, how much one is paid also

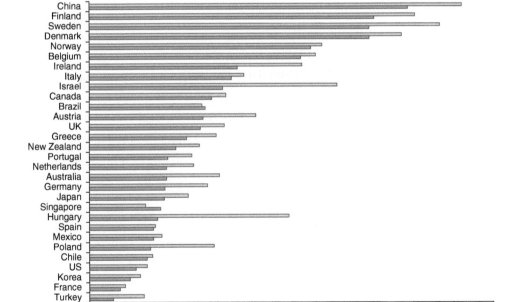

a. Change in trade union density, 1995–2010

□ 1995   ■ 2010

(Continued)

Figure 6.4   (Continued)

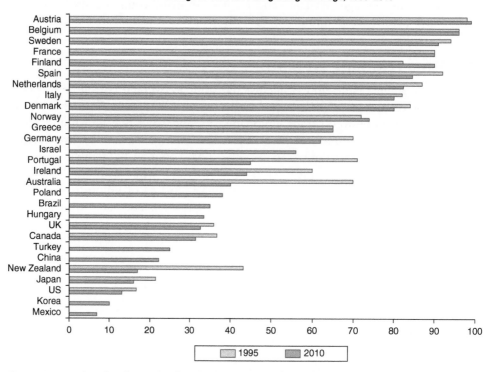

b. Change in collective bargaining coverage, 1995–2010

Figure 6.4   Union density and collective bargaining coverage

Note: start and end dates are not always 1995 and 2010 for all countries – see database for details.

Source: ICTWSS database (Visser, 2011) available at www.uva-aias.net/208

depends on where one is employed. Australia, for example, is a country which for most of the last century was dominated by national and state level bargaining, but after 1996 moved towards more enterprise level bargaining alongside the more inclusive bargaining forms.

National variations in legal arrangements for trade union recognition and collective bargaining coverage impact on MNCs, irrespective of MNCs' orientations towards recognizing unions or collective bargaining. In some countries, employers may be required to recognize trade unions where the workforce votes in favour of recognition. Further, in some countries collective agreements may bind all employers in the sector whether or not the individual employer is party to the negotiations. In others engagement in collective bargaining is more voluntary but where it is customary to follow collective agreements, not to do so may lead to poor employment relations or the MNC may find it has to pay higher wages to persuade the workforce that unions are not beneficial (Bennett and Kaufman, 2007).

Production systems and work organization

There are different ways to produce the same kinds of goods and services. The most known example is the distinction between Fordism and Toyotism in the production of automobiles. Fordism minimizes employee discretion to reduce the scope for human error while Toyotism harnesses human knowledge, particularly tacit knowledge, for the purpose of improving production processes (Appelbaum and Batt, 1994). These differences relate in part to the epochs when Ford and Toyota developed into major car producers but also to differences in the American and Japanese labour market systems. The low discretion system fits the US's short-term, less stable employment relationships while Toyotism's employee commitment model fits more with Japanese norms of lifelong employment.

More generally, countries may be associated with different approaches to work organization. Some adopt a 'production approach' focused on tasks to be done, while other countries adopt a 'training approach' focused on the capabilities of the job holder. Furthermore, each approach may be pursued through the design of systems that facilitate either high or low discretion (Marsden, 1999). The US is characterized as having a production approach based on a simple task-centred, low discretion work system (Mishel et al., 2005). Japan also follows a production approach but based on functions requiring high skill and discretion. Germany has a training-orientated system based on high skills and discretion; workers are assigned to functions, not individual tasks, according to their qualifications. These diverse ways of organizing work have implications for supervision. Where work is task-centred, managers are primarily coordinators and are not expected to have high technical competence; in contrast, function-centred systems rely on 'player managers', who supervise skilled workers and are themselves technically skilled.

The significance for MNCs lies in the expectations and competences of the staff hired from the local labour market. If an MNC with a task-oriented approach locates within a host country with a tradition of high discretion work organization, its employees may become dissatisfied if the MNC limits the scope of their influence on how work is to be undertaken (Muller, 1998; Geppert and Matten, 2006). Likewise, in host countries that typically organize work according to a low skills paradigm, an MNC may have difficulties in recruiting employees with sufficient skill and problem-solving abilities, or strong organizational commitment. Research has found that Japanese MNCs encountered such problems when they located in the UK and the US (Elger and Smith, 2005; Ferner et al., 2001).

Education, training and careers

Education and training systems provide the basis for developing the skills required by organizations and often shape individuals' career opportunities. All societies have hierarchical systems of education, but the gaps between, for example, elite and non-elite higher educational establishments are greater in some than others. Differences are also found in the status of particular degrees; for example, many more students study engineering in Germany than in the UK in part because engineering occupations hold higher status in Germany (Lee and Smith, 1992). Understanding the finer points of educational institutions and qualification systems will be of greater concern to MNCs in host countries where internal labour market systems are strong – that is, individuals pursue internal careers within a company rather than mobility across companies (Rubery and Grimshaw, 2003). In this context, MNCs may need to recruit staff direct from the education system, rather than already experienced staff since if job mobility is low it will tend to be more difficult to recruit individuals at mid-points in their careers.

The extent and value of workplace-based training also varies between societies. Where stable or quality employment is associated with workplace qualifications, MNCs may feel obliged to provide such training for their staff even if they might prefer to provide less intensive initial training. The outcome could be that similar occupations within the MNC may be staffed by people who in some host countries acquired skills primarily within the education systems but in others were primarily trained within the workplace. For example, employees in IT occupations in the UK are mainly graduates recruited from a wide range of subject areas, whereas in Germany apprenticeships have been expanded to meet this labour market need (Steedman et al., 2003).

In some countries MNCs may be required to participate in the host country's education and training system or be subject to training levies or other restrictions. Training levy systems are in operation, for example, in France and Singapore (Billet and Smith, 2005) and many countries set specific training and qualifications standards for professional and technical occupations to which MNCs have to conform or face difficulties in the local labour market.

Social stratification and living standards

Employment provides the main source of income for most adults and households. Employment rewards are thus a key factor in social stratification and income inequality. The size of wage differentials between occupational groups will often reflect differences that persist in countries' social hierarchies (see Figure 6.5 for illustrations of wide variations in the ratios of CEO to average worker pay). In some cases employment rewards may include benefits for household income needs, for example marriage or children allowances, or support for children's educational costs. Societies also vary in their arrangements to adjust wages to the cost of living. Institutionalized systems of wage adjustments that are independent of individual or group performance within the organization are more often found in host country environments where collective bargaining is extensive.

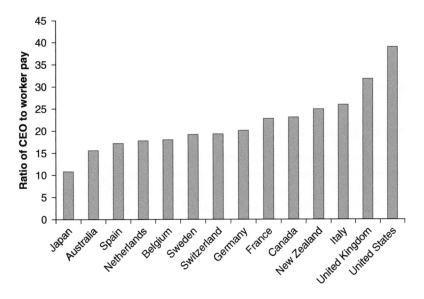

Figure 6.5   International comparison of CEO to worker pay

Source: Mishel et al. (2005)

Welfare systems

Welfare systems provide protection for employees during periods when they are not able to work. Even where welfare is primarily provided through universal, state financed schemes individual eligibility for benefits is often tied to employment history. Thus statutory unemployment benefits, paid maternity or parental leave, sick pay and pensions, often depend on length or continuity of employment and/or contributions to social protection made from wage income and/or by employers. In some countries there may be incentives for employers to utilize non-standard contracts to avoid social insurance costs. Contracts with the self-employed may be more costly in host countries where the self-employed have to pay high social protection insurance costs compared to countries where they are largely excluded from the state system. These exclusions may make it more difficult to find staff willing to work on non-standard contracts, perhaps thereby reinforcing standard full-time and continuous employment arrangements.

Where welfare provisions are limited, MNCs (and their subsidiaries) may fill the gap by providing, for example, company-based pension schemes or even health insurance. The US has primarily employer-based health insurance schemes, and the importance of access to this healthcare has a major impact on its labour market. Many women work full-time in the US despite the absence of state childcare support in part because part-timers can be legally excluded from health insurance benefits (Buchmueller and Valletta, 1999), while in the EU exclusion of part-timers is treated as indirect sex discrimination and thus illegal. Employer-based welfare policies tend to reduce worker mobility between employers if they risk loss of benefits. This introduces a form of rigidity into some apparently flexible labour markets – such as the UK and the US – that is not captured when only issues such as employment protection legislation are considered.

Household, family and gender systems

Despite the widespread trend of increases in women's employment, major variations between societies remain in women's employment rates and in provisions to facilitate reconciliation of wage work with family life (Anxo et al., 2007; see also Chapter 14 by Cooke). The growth of dual-earner households could be expected to encourage employers to take more account of their employees' household and family obligations in scheduling working time. However, even in societies where women stay at home, MNCs may be expected to organize working time taking into account expectations of shared family leisure time. Strong customary norms regarding working hours, limiting for example work on Fridays or Saturdays or Sundays and other religious and state holidays, may be even stronger in more traditional societies.

Differences in gender and family regimes affect arrangements at the workplace. In some societies it may not be regarded as appropriate for men and women to work in close proximity, while in others MNCs may need to be aware of strong societal norms and regulations promoting gender equality. There are also differences – and rapidly changing practices – with respect to employment patterns for women at the point of childbirth and afterwards. In some societies women may quit the labour market at childbirth, or indeed marriage, and may not have the right to return to work. This was still the case for occupations such as teaching in some Western countries during the 1950s–1960s. Increasingly, however, women are likely to return to employment after taking a period of leave. Length of leaves varies greatly (Moss and Korintus, 2008). In Central and Eastern European countries, women often take paid leave of three years but then return to full-time work, while in other European countries leave periods are shorter and many return to part-time work. In some societies there are also rights to return to full-time work later and in Sweden both mothers and fathers are able to reduce their hours of work while receiving some compensation for the lost hours. Chapter 14 by Fang Lee Cooke provides further analysis of the way gender equality legislation in different countries (especially equal opportunity and affirmative action laws) shapes women's employment position.

Summary

This section has outlined the potential differences in employment arrangements that MNCs are likely to encounter when establishing subsidiaries in different host country environments. The pivotal role that employment plays in the social and economic systems means that multiple institutions impinge upon employment arrangements and generate substantial variations. However, the increasing globalization of economies may be partially eroding differences, perhaps facilitating the diffusion of standard employment arrangements for MNCs across all their subsidiaries.

Box 6.7   Stop and reflect

The labour market position of workers with families varies significantly between countries. As an exercise in exploring these differences we suggest you visit the OECD family database website to compare your own country with two others from a choice of the United States, Italy, Sweden, France and Germany, since these five countries have varying public policies to assist working parents and display distinctive patterns of employment participation. In particular, we suggest you explore the following characteristics:

- employment profiles of men and women over the life-course
- employment patterns among families with children of varying age
- childcare support
- policies for child-birth related leave for mothers and fathers, and
- child poverty.

PDF reports and excel data can be found and easily downloaded at www.oecd.org/els/soc/oecdfamilydatabase.htm#TOOLS.

---

3 Sustainability of divergent employment arrangements

While all developed countries are part of the global capitalist economy, different models or brands of capitalism have been identified that are also associated with distinctive employment arrangements. Two schools of thought, the institutionalist and the culturalist, have dominated explanations for the development and persistence of these divergent employment forms (Rubery and Grimshaw, 2003).

Institutionalist and culturalist approaches

The institutionalist approach focuses on complementarities between institutions that give rise to 'varieties of capitalism' (VoC) and different 'worlds of welfare capitalism', popularized by Hall and Soskice (2001) and Esping-Andersen (1990), respectively. Countries are argued to cluster around two or three ideal types – liberal and coordinated market economies in the VoC approach and liberal, social democratic and conservative welfare systems in Esping-Andersen's approach. It is the complementarity or coherence of institutions that generates the development of distinctive models of capitalism, associated with particular forms of comparative advantage. So, for Hall and Soskice, the coordinated market economy is based on both stronger employment protection and stronger coordination among employers. Together, these arrangements encourage long-term investment planning, which further generates positive incentives for skill development, incremental innovation and stable economic growth. In the liberal market economy, labour markets are flexible and general education and short-term profit targets dominate. When combined these arrangements encourage market growth in fast-changing sectors, radical forms of innovation and high job mobility. The argument is that the more a country's institutional arrangements cohere around one of these ideal types, the greater is the likelihood that it will achieve superior economic performance and be sustainable when faced with external shocks.

Used as heuristic devices, ideal type models can assist our understanding and ability to organize the complex cross-country patterns of employment models. However, there is no reason to suppose that countries neatly form clusters around two or three ideal types. Also, as institutional arrangements and practices change there is a need to pay more attention to hybrid, changing forms (Whitley, 1999; Bosch et al., 2009).

The second approach to understanding country divergence draws on observations based on national cultural differences. Citizens of different countries are observed to differ in their approach, for example, to authority relations, decision making, gender relations, leadership behaviour and many other aspects of organizational life. In the most influential study Hofstede (1980, 2001) developed four abstract dimensions of a national culture – power distance, individualism, masculinity/femininity and uncertainty avoidance – to which a fifth, long-term orientation is often added. Comparing France with China, for example, France is said to be characterized by high power distance (that is, inequalities are accepted), high individualism (a preference for individual or private opinions), low masculinity (a high value associated with caring for others and quality of life), a very high uncertainty avoidance (including rules and planning to minimize risk) and a low long-term orientation (reflected in short-term company performance and limited orientation towards savings). China, on the other hand, is said to have a very high power distance, an extraordinarily low individualism, high masculinity, low uncertainty avoidance and a near maximum measure of long-term orientation.[1] Under a culturalist approach similar HRM policies in host country environments are expected to have different effects due to differences in cultural attitudes and social norms.

However, McSweeney (2002) and others have questioned the validity of the analytical devices and empirical evidence underpinning Hofstede's study. The data derive

---

[1]Sourced from the website, http://geert-hofstede.com/countries.html (accessed March 2013).

from a study of one company, IBM, so it is not clear whether the study is of IBM's employee culture or national cultures; only a narrow range of cultural variables are used to represent the dominant dimensions of a national culture; and no allowance is made for cultural values to be influenced by diverse and changing institutions (e.g. whether US accountants' attitudes may reflect the short-termism of the American finance system rather than US culture per se).

In practice the major challenge for both approaches is to determine whether pressures of globalization and new international governance are pushing all countries in a similar direction towards greater market orientation. These pressures include the long-standing trends towards free trade (governed through the WTO and the IMF) and fewer restrictions on FDI, but also more recent phenomena such as the massive expansion of financial markets, the increased power of institutional investors, and the pervasiveness of information and communication technologies. In addition, cultural ideas about lifestyle, gender relations and other norms are diffused worldwide far more rapidly in an age of fast-speed, broadband communications. Such pressures may be undermining the basis for varieties of capitalism by challenging those institutions associated with a coordinated market economy, for example, or a social democratic model welfare regime, leading to the emergence of a dominant US-type, market oriented model.

Towards convergence of country systems?

Many of these developments reduce the autonomy of nation states in the face of globalization. The massive increases in capital movements and offshore financial markets combine to diminish governments' capacity to pursue autonomous fiscal policy. Countries in the EU have had to prioritize inflation over growth objectives unlike the US Federal Reserve (Bush, 2003), and Eurozone countries under strong financial market pressures have been required by the EU and the IMF to reduce public expenditure and public debt. Pressures to de-regulate markets started with national utilities in the 1980s–1990s, services in the 2000s and labour markets in the 2000s. Policy has been increasingly oriented to promoting the internationalization of business while traditional protective barriers designed to manage a mixed domestic economy have been weakened.

For at least three decades the focus of policy-makers in many countries has been on fostering growth through free market reform rather than expansionary fiscal and industrial policies. Competition among national governments to attract FDI by, for example, reducing corporation tax has in turn restricted policy choices. The World Bank's 'Doing Business' website exemplifies this tendency (see Stop and Reflect Box 6.8 below). The implication of its international ranking of countries is that there is only one model of economic organization conducive to competitive success.

Against this background, several strands of empirical evidence do suggest that a process of convergence among developed countries is taking place. Policy reform suggests trends towards reduced or frozen public welfare expenditures and a lowering of welfare benefits. Many countries have switched investments from the specific, technical skills associated with vocational training to the 'symbolic analytical' skills acquired through higher education (Reich, 1992). For OECD countries, the share of first-time graduates from university level education increased from 20 per cent to 39 per cent between 1995 and 2010.[2]

National systems of wage-setting have also been changing. During the 1980s and 1990s collective bargaining often became more decentralized and unions lost strength in most countries. Countries as diverse as Sweden, Australia, the UK, Germany and Italy moved to greater intensity of local pay bargaining, workplace restructuring or concession bargaining in an overall context of weakened unions (Katz, 2004). In the 2000s the declining trend has continued (see Figure 6.4) in several countries with union density falling since 1995 by around a half in Turkey, Hungary, Poland and Israel, two fifths in Germany and Australia and one third in Singapore, the Netherlands, Austria and Ireland.

Yet much comparative research evidence reveals continued and distinctive national systems of employment, welfare and production. For example, during the economic crisis in Europe employment protection systems and short time work sharing arrangements had a major influence on the extent of job loss, with Germany, for example, managing to avoid any rise in unemployment thanks to various work sharing interventions (Bosch, 2011). Also, even when faced with international austerity pressures, governments still exercised choice over public expenditures and their policies towards public sector employment and public sector pay in part to offset exposed sectors of the economy (Vaughan-Whitehead, 2013). Moreover, governments still spend money in different ways; Scandinavian countries and continental European countries have remained true to the principles of their social democratic and conservative models, respectively. Glyn (2006: 115, Figure 5.5) found a clear divergence between liberal economies and Europe in a key indicator of welfare regimes – the ratio of unemployment benefits to average earnings.

Further, the common trend towards decentralized wage setting is characterized by specific country effects (Katz et al., 2004): local bargaining in the UK occurred at the expense of multi-employer agreements; in Germany, even though the influence of works councils has increased, the national and regional frameworks of sectoral agreements have remained substantially intact; and in Italy, social pacts agreed at a national level continue to provide framework agreements for local collective bargaining.

Consideration of employment protection regulation also reveals a nuanced pattern of change. OECD data on rules against individual dismissals for regular workers suggest that out of the 28 countries for which data are available for the period 1990–2008, eight saw an increase in strictness, 15 a decrease and five no significant change.[3] Moreover,

---

[2]Figures refer to graduation from what the OECD defines as 'type A' tertiary education and only include those countries for which both 1995 and 2010 data are available (see www.oecd.org/edu/highlights.pdf, accessed March 2013).

[3]Authors' computation based on OECD data available at www.oecd.org/employment/emp/oecdindicatorsofemploymentprotection.htm (accessed March 2013).

countries cannot be categorized along a simple one-dimensional continuum as they may combine institutional arrangements for both weak and strong forms of employment protection (Auer and Cazes, 2003). For example, the Danish model scores low on the OECD index of protection against layoffs (see Figure 6.1 above) but during the 1990s and much of the 2000s provided very strong income protection through generous unemployment benefits and high spending on active labour market policies (Madsen, 2003); policy reforms since the late 2000s have reduced the strength of this Danish so-called 'flexicurity' model but although some studies have questioned its resilience (Klindt and Halkjær, 2012), the model still retains very distinctive characteristics from a comparative perspective. Likewise there is a strongly distinctive Dutch model of flexicurity; this provides employers with considerable flexibility in the use of temporary agency workers but counterbalances these employer rights by key principles of security for the worker allowing for transitions from a temporary to permanent employment contract (Van Oorschot, 2004). These two divergent and distinctive models of 'flexicurity' suggest that the evidence in favour of convergence around one deregulated model of employment protection is weak.

Box 6.8 Stop and reflect

Controversy over the indicators used by the World Bank in its flagship 'Doing Business' reports provides a valuable insight into the ongoing tensions among policy-makers between, on the one hand, the one-size-fits-all approach to country business and employment models and, on the other hand, a recognition and appreciation that there are a variety of country trajectories. The World Bank ranks all countries in the world against several variables in an attempt to demonstrate the relative ease of doing business. Variables include 'getting credit', 'protecting investors', 'employing workers' and 'paying taxes'.

- As a brief exercise, compare your own country with that of one of the leading economies in the world (e.g. United States, Japan, Germany) and check how it compares against each of the key indicators. Don't miss the 'employing workers' indicator, which is listed as an additional topic (see www.doingbusiness.org/data).

Two indicators have proved to be controversial. The 'employing workers' variable appears to encourage an approach towards employment that maximizes flexibility

(Continued)

(Continued)

for employers and which fails to comply with core labour standards as specified by the International Labour Organization. Also, the 'paying taxes' variable is interpreted by some as calling for governments to reduce employers' contributions to tax and social security. For further insight, we recommend you read the brief 13-page consultation on these issues (available at: www.doingbusiness.org/data/explore-topics/employing-workers). Do you think it is possible to construct a composite, one-size-fits-all indicator for doing business in different countries around the world? To what extent does the doing business index encourage a 'race to the bottom' where the lowest standards are regarded as the best?

4 Understanding how MNCs act in diverse host country environments

In a context of diverse host country environments for doing business and organizing employment, much research investigates how MNCs implement and adapt their HRM practices in response to the 'receptiveness' or 'openness' of these local institutional environments. In reviewing this research we should note at the outset that whether a host country is 'open' or 'receptive' may matter less in the actual implementation of HR practices than the agency exercised by subsidiary managers and other employees in resisting, subverting or in complying with directions from head office (Morgan and Kristensen, 2006). MNCs are complex and powerful organizations, constituted by fragmented and often conflicting interests among subsidiary and head office managers, investors and employees. Kostova and Zaheer (1999) argue subsidiaries are engaged in a struggle for legitimacy in two institutional environments – the external (home and host country) and the internal (MNC). More detail on the internal political processes is described in Chapter 3.

The distinctiveness of each host country environment reflects not only structural factors – that is, types of markets, economic conditions and access to basic infrastructure and technologies – but also the complex web of institutional rules, cultural norms and traditions as described above. In some studies, the key research questions on HRM practices of MNCs relate to how 'open' or 'receptive' host country institutions are to novel practices introduced by MNCs (e.g. Ferner and Tempel, 2006). Other studies suggest it is the 'institutional distance' between home and host country that matters, defined using regulative, normative and cognitive dimensions drawn from the employment systems literature (e.g. Kostova and Roth, 2002). There is therefore

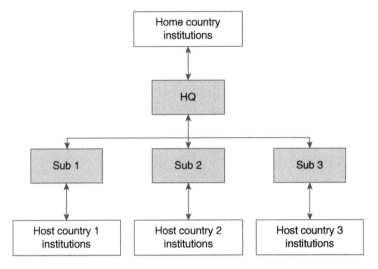

Figure 6.6   Organizational and institutional influences on multinational companies and their subsidiaries

Source: adapted from Geppert et al. (2006: 1454)

a strong connection between understanding the variety of country employment systems and identifying those factors that enable or hinder an MNC to transfer its HRM practices (Björkman and Lervik, 2007). The growing trend towards a 'high context' research approach on MNCs and their subsidiaries, as called for by Child (2000), is to be encouraged. Figure 6.6 above provides a representation of organizational and institutional characteristics influencing the MNC and its subsidiaries.

5 Host country effects on IHRM practices of MNC subsidiaries

The types of host country environmental conditions that potentially impinge upon key IHRM practices of MNC subsidiaries (Table 6.1) include socio-economic conditions (especially labour market conditions and the general economic climate for business), institutions (legal rules as well as formal and informal rules set by employers and unions) and norms (associated with cultural and social traditions and routines). These conditions vary by country and potentially constrain the MNC's capacity to harmonize IHRM practices across its global operations. Research suggests that some HRM practices are more sensitive to local environmental influence than others. In their widely cited study of HRM practices in 249 US subsidiaries of non-US MNCs, Rosenzweig and Nohria (1994) find that practices associated with executive bonus pay and participation in senior management decision making are very unlikely to be adapted to local

Table 6.1 Host country environment influences on HRM practices

HRM practices	Socio-economic influences	Institutional influences	Normative (social and cultural) influences
Recruitment	• Availability of suitably trained labour	• Legal requirement to recruit local labour • Equal opportunity laws • Restrictions on use of temporary agency workers	• Ethics regarding meritocratic/formal principles or informal customs based on personal recommendations • Tradition of offering a job-for-life
Pay	• Tightness of labour market • Inflation rate • Dispersion of wages	• Minimum wage system • Equal pay legislation	• Collective or individualized approach to rewarding effort • Norms of fair pay
Training and careers	• Education and training levels of available workers • Strength of occupational labour markets	• Legal requirements to train • System of vocational training	• Expectations of skill development as a career route
Work organization	• Gender division of labour	• Rules governing job classification and allocation • Regulation of working hours • Health and safety laws	• Attitudes towards teamwork • Norms of hierarchy
Job security	• Labour market conditions • Availability of temporary labour supply	• Legal rules on individual and collective dismissals	• Social perceptions of fairness
Collective representation	• Membership of trade unions • Coverage of collective bargaining agreements	• Role of employer associations and trade unions in economy and society • Use of legal mechanisms to extend collective agreements to non union firms • Union recognition requirements • Employee representation laws	• Attitudes towards trade unions • Tradition of employee democracy and representation in the workplace

Source: development of Table 8.2 in Rubery and Grimshaw (2003) based on Grønhaug and Nordhaug (1994)

conditions. In contrast, other HRM practices display relatively close similarity with local practices, especially working time, benefits and gender composition of the employees. In the following discussion, we review the evidence for a selection of HRM practices, pay practices, work organization and collective representation.

Pay practices

Researchers investigating subsidiaries of US MNCs operating in European countries have predicted there will be strong pressure to adopt a common pay policy across subsidiaries but detailed case studies (Almond et al., 2006: 126–128) reveal several examples of deviation reflecting local environmental influences. For example, Irish subsidiaries posted higher wage settlements than the company norm, reflecting the booming economic conditions at the time. They also negotiated a flexible benefits package to attract the mainly young and transient foreign workforce.

Several studies explore variations in implementing performance-related pay practices. Again drawing on data on US MNCs operating in Europe, Edwards et al. (2006: 78–79) report that the works council in one German subsidiary blocked managers' efforts to implement a company-wide policy of PRP by successfully arguing that PRP conflicted with group work traditions and used its legal powers to restrict it solely to senior managerial grades. Gooderham et al. (2006) also report significant country variation in implementation by US MNCs of individualized pay practices in subsidiaries. They found that individualized pay practices, bundled with performance appraisals and formal training evaluation, were most likely to be implemented in Australia, followed by the UK and Ireland and less likely in Germany, Denmark and Norway. Where subsidiaries were more strongly institutionally embedded in legal frameworks and industrial relations systems, they were more likely to be constrained in applying new management practices, particularly pay practices (Gooderham et al., 2006: 1496).

Work organization practices

Transfer of work organization practices has attracted considerable interest among practitioners and policy-makers as this could improve the learning and organizational capabilities of foreign-owned subsidiaries. During the 1990s, a key theme of research was the receptiveness of host country environments to the work organization practices of Japanese MNCs, which were widely assumed at that time to represent superior management techniques. One early study of ten Japanese subsidiaries in the US identified an interesting divergence of host country effects in shaping practices of job rotation and training (Beechler and Yang, 1993). Among the banking subsidiaries in New York there was a strong Americanization of all HRM practices, including hiring specialists, limited training and employment-at-will job security. By contrast, among the manufacturing subsidiaries based in Tennessee, Japanese practices were adopted with very limited adaptation to the host environment. Local socio-economic conditions assisted 'Japanization' among these plants as the slack labour market conditions led to low turnover rates.

National and regional differences in the availability of skilled workers and systems of vocational training that support continued investment in workers' skills play important roles in shaping the ability of MNCs to export a high skill/high productivity approach. Lam (1997) argued that the UK environment was insufficiently receptive to Japanese MNCs' novel practices due to the poor skill profile among the pool of available workers. Other studies identify significant host country variety in workers' skills among subsidiaries. For example, Woywode's (2002) study of MNC automobile companies' subsidiaries identified higher training qualifications among the German subsidiary's employees compared with the French counterpart (cited in Geppert and Williams, 2006). And Haipeter (2002) finds German workers enjoy higher levels of autonomy in teams compared to French workers in comparable subsidiaries with similar HRM practices.

Collective representation

Research on practices towards collective representation suggests that centralized head office control may be tempered by subsidiary pragmatism in response to local pressures. Colling et al. (2006) show that US multinationals practise what they refer to as 'double breasting' in their Irish and UK subsidiaries, characterized by union recognition in the older sites and non-recognition in the newer sites. This acceptance of collective channels of decision making at some sites has been explained by the generally weak environment for trade unions in Ireland and the UK that meant 'the consequences of conceding unionized relations were not as far-reaching' (Colling et al., 2006: 117–118). By contrast, US subsidiaries exhibited stronger resistance to collective channels where, as in Germany and Spain, they identified a real risk that such arrangements might delay decision making and restrict implementation of standardized practices.

Another study comparing coordinated and liberal market economies demonstrates that US MNCs are least likely to adapt subsidiaries' HRM policies to the host country environment in more coordinated economies (Fenton-O'Creevy et al., 2008), although where the subsidiary is strongly unionized the parent company is more likely to delegate control (Fenton-O'Creevy et al., 2008: 157, Table 7). Thus non-union subsidiaries in coordinated market economies show the weakest responsiveness to the local environment. These findings are consistent with Kostova and Roth's (2002) 'institutional distance' argument – as Fenton-O'Creevy et al. explain: 'US multinational companies clearly resist conceding HRM decision making to subsidiaries located in coordinated market economies. It is after all in coordinated market economies that there will be a particularly pronounced degree of inconsistency between institutional norms and the HRM concerns of US MNCs' (2008: 162).

So US subsidiaries may adopt strategies of resistance and avoidance: in Germany, managers have sometimes resisted collective bargaining by paying above agreed rates or by switching to another collective agreement with a less militant trade union (Colling et al., 2006: 109). Occasionally, unions make inroads in influencing MNCs and employment policies. In Italy, Pulignano (2006) describes how local unions at three US-owned subsidiaries successfully campaigned against the company's anti-union policy and gained a role for local unions in joint regulation of pay and working conditions, in line with the Italian institutional context of centrally regulated company bargaining but counter to the US MNC's policy of individualized employment relations. Likewise Meardi's (2006) comparative research on US and German MNCs in Central and Eastern European countries demonstrates numerous ways in which unions exercise formal and informal influence over subsidiaries' HRM practices. Examples include unions exercising veto power over the appointment of team leaders in a Polish subsidiary and local union adaptation of formalized employment relations in Slovenian subsidiaries.

6 Summary and conclusions

Although MNCs are frequently responsive to local host country environments, the degree and nature of responsiveness varies not only by MNCs' own characteristics (see Chapter 3), but also from practice to practice and country to country. It is difficult to measure precisely the degree of adaptation for two main reasons.

First, the host country environment is always changing, making it difficult to specify the goalposts. Moreover, the direction of change may in part reflect the powerful actions of MNCs; as Ferner and Tempel (2006: 21) put it, 'in the case of multinationals there is much evidence of the way in which they make the institutional weather'.

Second, it is difficult to disentangle what fraction of subsidiary actions are shaped by local institutions and conditions and what part results from what Morgan and Kristensen (2006) call 'micro-politics'. Our interpretation of some recent carefully conducted case studies of subsidiary practices is that the strength of institutions is not the only factor since organizational actors may be able to introduce change even in tightly regulated environments. In her comparative study of US subsidiaries in Italy and the UK, Pulignano argues, 'there is a space opened up by company specific organizational features of various groups of MNC actors to establish and pursue their group interests but this is mediated by the institutional effects of the host country environments' (2006: 513). More research is needed, therefore, that applies a combined organization-centred and comparative systems approach to the diffusion and adaptation of HRM practices in MNCs.

Discussion questions

1. For any two countries, compare and contrast the different features that shape the way employment is organized in each country. Is there evidence of convergence?
2. Why is it important to understand the character of a country's welfare system, including its family, household and gender system, for analysing IHRM practices?
3. Compare the relative merits of an institutionalist approach and a culturalist approach for assessing changing cross-country differences in employment.
4. Does the empirical evidence to date suggest an Americanization of HRM practices in European subsidiaries?

CASE STUDY

CMMCorp – HRM policies in a US MNC's European subsidiaries

CMMCorp is a US-owned engineering MNC. Its main European activities are in the manufacture and sale of engines and related products. Its major European operations are in the UK, France, Germany and Hungary. The company was historically family-owned and controlled, and generally allowed the managers of foreign subsidiaries a fairly large degree of autonomy in setting HRM policies. Consequently, there were substantial differences in policies in different European countries, particularly in the areas of industrial relations and pay and performance management, with practices broadly conforming to national norms in the engineering sector.

The founding family relinquished control of the corporation in the 1990s, and a new senior management team was put in place, largely recruited from outside the organization. A new emphasis was placed on shareholder value, performance management and subsidiary accountability. Within HRM, there was a new focus on more coherent, centrally driven industrial relations and performance management policies.

The American operations of CMM had long resisted independent union organization, but this had not been part of a strategic international HR philosophy. Now, though, foreign subsidiaries were expected to avoid trade union influence 'wherever possible', and subsidiary HR managers were monitored on their 'achievements' in union avoidance.

This posed difficulties for the European operations. Outside the Hungarian operations, which had been established relatively recently on a greenfield site and had always been non-union, there was substantial union influence in all the European facilities. The German operations had long based industrial relations management on the works council system, and German managers felt that challenging these arrangements risked reducing workforce cooperation. Under pressure from an expatriate manager assigned to Germany, the subsidiary left the metalworking sector collective agreement. This had little direct impact on pay and conditions, however, and most German managers saw the move as 'pointless symbolism'.

Union avoidance was not possible in France. Although few CMM employees were union members, the subsidiary was legally obliged to negotiate with representatives of the five nationally representative unions. There was a long history of overtly conflictual industrial relations in the main French plant, but no path available to a non-union model even if this were deemed desirable at the local level. As one senior French union official reflected, 'The managers here need no encouragement to be against unions, but they cannot just hope that we will disappear. They can never satisfy [corporate managers of CMM].'

The UK managers perhaps came under the most serious challenge here. This was because corporate managers could point to a number of successful large non-union establishments, often American-owned. The UK subsidiary had already derecognized unions for non-manual workers during the 1980s, at the height of Thatcherism, but stopped short of challenging the manual workforce over union recognition. Although the union was not particularly active in the workplace, high membership meant that under the current British industrial relations settlement, 'successful' derecognition would be highly unlikely. Most UK managers felt that union relations were 'simply not a big issue', and that it would be counter-productive to launch a frontal attack against a trade union which showed little militancy outside pay rounds, and had some value to the firm in dealing with discipline and related issues.

European managers were able largely to convince their American counterparts that strong challenges to the status quo with regard to industrial relations were either not possible or unwise. Like other large firms, though, where new workplaces have been established on greenfield sites, these have often been non-union.

The new performance management regime was a bigger challenge. Performance-related pay had long been present for managerial workers in all the European countries, but this was essentially treated by most workers as an annual bonus, with relatively little variation between 'high' and 'low' performers. The new corporate management team, however, had been inspired by the General Electric model of performance management. This uses a forced distribution, with each unit asked to identify pre-determined percentages of 'high' and 'low' performers. In CMM, the top

(Continued)

(Continued)

10 per cent, as well as being financially rewarded, would be seen as candidates for promotion, but the bottom 10 per cent would be seen as candidates for dismissal.

This caused problems in all the European operations. Although managers in all countries could 'find ways of getting rid of bad performers', formalizing a system in which a given percentage were to be seen as dismissal candidates was seen as unhelpful. As one British manager argued, 'I have twenty staff. How come two of them are automatically not up to the job, ready for the sack? This isn't football, I can't have people looking over their shoulder all the time.'

Several methods were used by European managers to resist this policy. Representations were made to corporate managers, both by individual subsidiary managers and through the European headquarters. For one international meeting of HR managers, British managers recruited an academic consultant to try to persuade their American counterparts of the potential effects on motivation and performance of the threat of dismissal under forced distributions.

These challenges were unsuccessful. Corporate HR were adamant that using a centralized system was cheaper, and allowed an easier identification of high potential candidates for entry into international management positions. 'What I don't get', argued the international HR director, 'is why you are so concerned with poor performers. I'm interested in good performers.'

The system is therefore in operation worldwide, although how closely it is followed in spirit is open to question. In Britain, for example, the typical practice, according to a senior HR manager, was to give poor performance rankings to those 'who were leaving anyway'. The system was also finessed by altering the definitions of 'units', to avoid situations where one manager has to choose 'poor performers' from among small groups.

In France, managers used the new system to identify candidates for redundancy. This led to a successful legal challenge, as it is not legitimate in French law to select candidates for redundancy on the grounds of competence. Although major corporations falling foul of employment law is not uncommon in France, this nevertheless led to unwelcome publicity for the company.

In Germany, the subsidiary was able to argue that the need to work with the works council meant that the immediate threat of dismissal for a poor position on a forced distribution was not practical. Instead, poorer performers are placed into 'developmental measures'. A more prominent problem in Germany was that the performance management system specified the pay gaps that should exist between different groups on the forced ranking. By German standards, these were very large. This not only upset nationally derived ideas about equity within organizations;

according to one manager, it also challenged ideas around collective performance within the German work ethic. The German subsidiary in fact has gradually moved away from the pay gaps indicated in the 'global' system on a unilateral basis.

Case study questions

1. From CMM's point of view, what arguments can be made in favour of standardized policies regarding union relations and performance management across the European subsidiaries? Do these outweigh the disadvantages?
2. In what ways, if any, would you expect HR policies in a greenfield site in the UK to be different from those of the rest of the UK subsidiary?
3. What would be the obstacles involved in creating a performance management system similar to the one outlined here in your own country?

Case study questions for further reflection

1. In what ways could an overseas company operating in the UK, France and Germany make use of the differences between these countries' employment systems, rather than seeing them as a barrier to having common policies?
2. What might be the advantages and disadvantages for CMM if it decided to give more control over its subsidiary HRM policies to American expatriate managers, rather than domestic subsidiary managers?

Further reading

- Freeman, R.B. (2002) 'The US economic model at Y2K: Lodestar for advanced capitalism?', in D. Coates (ed.), *Models of Capitalism: Debating Strengths and Weaknesses*. Cheltenham: Edward Elgar, pp. 150–163.
  Richard Freeman asks whether we ought to think of the world as following the logic of a 'single peak' economy or a 'multi-peak' economy. The answer clarifies the debate on convergence/divergence of employment systems.

- Katz, H.C., Lee, W. and Lee, J. (eds) (2004) *The New Structure of Labor Relations: Tripartism and Decentralisation*. Ithaca: Cornell University Press.
  An excellent collection of readings on changing industrial relations and collective bargaining. Each country chapter provides a detailed account of labour, management and government interactions.

- Esping-Andersen, G. (2002) *Why We Need a New Welfare State*. Oxford: Oxford University Press.
- Lewis, J. and Surender, R. (eds) (2004) *Welfare State Change: A Third Way?* Oxford: Oxford University Press.

Both books provide an overview of the diverse models of welfare state regimes in developed countries. Issues include the interactions with labour market policy, changing family and gender relations and policy approaches towards social cohesion.

- Grimshaw, D. (ed.) (2013) *Minimum Wages, Pay Equity and Comparative Industrial Relations*. London: Routledge.
- Vaughan-Whitehead, D. (ed.) (2009) *The Minimum Wage Revisited in the Enlarged EU*. Geneva: International Labour Organization.
- Auer, P. and Cazes, S. (eds) (2003) *Employment Stability in an Age of Flexibility*. Geneva: International Labour Organization.

  These edited collections provide useful detailed accounts of the diverse policies shaping minimum wages and employment protection. Minimum wage regulation has diverse effects on job growth and wage inequality contingent upon its level, the system of uprating and the surrounding industrial relations system. Policies of employment protection and social protection are shown to have diverse effects on employment stability and perceptions of job security.

- Rubery, J. and Grimshaw, D. (2003) *The Organisation of Employment: An International Perspective*. Basingstoke: Palgrave Macmillan. Chapter 5 'Skilling the labour force'.

  This chapter reviews the diverse characteristics of country systems of schooling, vocational training and higher education. It introduces the student to models of 'internal labour markets' and 'occupational labour markets' to understand country differences. It reviews the pressures for change and asks whether countries are equipped to sustain/develop a high-skill workforce.

- Rosenzweig, P.M. and Nohria, N. (1994) 'Influences on HRM practices in MNCs', *Journal of International Business Studies*, 25(2): 229–251.

  This valuable early test of the host country effect on HRM practices in MNC subsidiaries draws on data of 249 US subsidiaries from a range of countries. It explores the reasons why some HRM practices are more likely to be adapted to the local environment than others.

- Almond, P. and Ferner, A. (eds) (2006) *American Multinationals in Europe*. Oxford: Oxford University Press.

  This book explores on the one hand the US approach to employment relations and HRM and, on the other hand, the influence of different host country environments on its diffusion. Evidence of US MNCs operating in a mix of sectors (e.g. engineering, chemicals, IT services, logistics) illustrates the impact of host countries on selected HRM practices.

- Fenton-O'Creevy, M., Gooderham, P. and Nordhaug, O. (2008) 'HRM in US subsidiaries in Europe and Australia: centralisation or autonomy?', *Journal of International Business Studies*, 39: 151–166.

  This article makes a valuable contribution by applying an institutional typology of country employment systems to a test of diffusion of HRM practices among MNC subsidiaries.

Internet resources

- www.eurofound.europa.eu. Good, up-to-date reviews of country systems of industrial relations. Eurofound is a tripartite European Union agency, which provides knowledge to assist in the development of social and work-related policies.
- www.ilo.org. International developments in work and employment, labour market policy and labour standards.
- www.oecd.org. Detailed reports on employment trends in OECD economies, harmonized data.

Self-assessment questions

Indicative answers to these questions can be found on the companion website at study.sagepub.com/harzing4e.

1. Identify three types of legal regulation that shape the type of labour market in a host country environment and provide one example of country differences for each type.
2. What are the major pressures encouraging a convergence of country employment systems and what pieces of evidence suggest change has in practice been mixed in recent years?
3. Describe the employment characteristics associated with Hall and Soskice's two types of market capitalism.
4. What factors in host country environments have been found to constrain the diffusion of PRP and individualized payment practices in MNC subsidiaries?
5. What features of a host country environment can facilitate an MNC's attempt to diffuse a high skill, high value-added model of work organization?

References

Almond, P., Muller-Camen, M., Collings, D.G. and Quintanilla, J. (2006) 'Pay and performance', in P. Almond and A. Ferner (eds), *American Multinationals in Europe*. Oxford: Oxford University Press, pp. 119–145.

Anxo, D., Fagan, C., Cebrian, I. and Moreno, G. (2007) 'Patterns of labour market integration in Europe – a life course perspective on time policies', *Socio-Economic Review*, 5(2): 233–260.

Appelbaum, E. and Batt, R. (1994) *The New American Workplace*. Ithaca, NY: ILR Press, Cornell University Press.

Askenazy, P. (2013) 'Working time regulation in France, 1996 to 2012', *Cambridge Journal of Economics*, published online 4 February 2013, 37(2): 323–347. doi: 10.1093/cje/bes084.

Auer, P. and Cazes, S. (eds) (2003) *Employment Stability in an Age of Flexibility*. Geneva: International Labour Office.

Beechler, S. and Yang, J.Z. (1993) 'The transfer of Japanese-style management to American subsidiaries: contingencies, constraints, and competence', *Journal of International Business Studies*, 25(3): 467–491.

Bennett, J. and Kaufman, B. (2007) *What Do Unions Do? A Twenty-year Perspective*. Edison, NJ: Transaction Publishers.

Billet, S. and Smith, A. (2005) 'Enhancing enterprise expenditure on VET: policy goals and mechanisms', *Journal of Vocational Education and Training*, 57(1): 5–23.

Björkman, I. and Lervik, J.E. (2007) 'Transferring HRM practices within multinational companies', *Human Resource Management Journal*, 17(4): 320–335.

Bosch, G. (2011) 'The German labour market after the financial crisis', in D. Vaughan-Whitehead (ed.), *Work Inequalities in the Crisis: Evidence from Europe*. Cheltenham: Edward Elgar, pp. 243–276.

Bosch, G., Lehndorff, S. and Rubery, J. (2009) *European Employment Models in Flux: A Comparison of Institutional Change in Nine European Countries*. Basingstoke: Palgrave.

Botero, J., Djankov, S., La Porta, R., Lopez-de-Silanes, F. and Shleifer, A. (2004) 'The regulation of labor', *Quarterly Journal of Economics*, 119: 1339–1384.

Buchmueller, T. and Valletta, R. (1999) 'The effect of health insurance on married female labor supply', *The Journal of Human Resources*, 34(1): 42–70.

Bush, J. (2003) 'Outlook for Europe: the neoliberal stranglehold on growth', in A. Pettifor (ed.), *Real World Economic Outlook: The Legacy of Globalization, Debt and Deflation*. London: Palgrave, pp. 108–115.

Child, J. (2000) 'Theorizing about organization cross-nationally', *Advances in International Comparative Management*, 13: 27–75.

Colling, T., Gunnigle, P., Quintanilla, J. and Tempel, A. (2006) 'Collective representation and participation', in P. Almond and A. Ferner (eds), *American Multinationals in Europe*. Oxford: Oxford University Press, pp. 95–118.

Deakin, S. (2009) 'Legal origin, juridical form and industrialization in historical perspective: the case of the employment contract and the joint-stock company', *Socio-Economic Review*, 7(1): 35–65.

Edwards, T., Coller, X., Ortiz, L., Rees, C. and Wortmann, M. (2006) 'National industrial relations systems and cross-border restructuring: evidence from a merger in the pharmaceuticals sector', *European Journal of Industrial Relations*, 12(1): 69–87.

Elger, T. and Smith, C. (2005) *Assembling Work: Remaking Factory Regimes in Japanese Multinationals in Britain*. Oxford: Oxford University Press.

Esping-Andersen, G. (1990) *The Three Worlds of Welfare Capitalism*. Princeton, NJ: Princeton University Press.

Fenton-O'Creevy, M., Gooderham, P. and Nordhaug, O. (2008) 'Human resource management in US subsidiaries in Europe and Australia: centralisation or autonomy?', *Journal of International Business Studies*, 39: 151–166.

Ferner, A., Quintanilla, J. and Varul, M.Z. (2001) 'Country-of-origin effects, host country effects and the management of HR in multinationals: German companies in Britain and Spain', *Journal of World Business*, 36(1): 107–128.

Ferner, A. and Tempel, A. (2006) 'Multinationals and national business systems: a "power and institutions" perspective', in P. Almond and A. Ferner (eds), *American Multinationals in Europe: Managing Employment Relations Across National Borders*. Oxford: Oxford University Press, pp. 10–34.

Geppert, M. and Matten, D. (2006) 'Institutional influences on manufacturing organization in multinational corporations: the "cherrypicking" approach', *Organization Studies*, 27(4): 491–515.

Geppert, M., Matten, D. and Walgenbach, P. (2006) 'Transnational building and the multinational corporations: an emerging field of research', *Human Relations*, 59(11): 1451–1465.

Geppert, M. and Williams, K. (2006) 'Global, national and local practices in multinational corporations: towards a sociopolitical framework', *International Journal of HRM*, 17(1): 49–69.

Glyn, A. (2006) *Capitalism Unleashed: Finance, Globalization and Welfare*. Oxford: Oxford University Press.

Gooderham, P., Nordhaug, O. and Ringdal, K. (2006) 'National embeddedness and calculative human resource management in US subsidiaries in Europe and Australia', *Human Relations*, 59(11): 1491–1513.

Grimshaw, D. (ed.) (2013) *Minimum Wages, Pay Equity and Comparative Industrial Relations*. London: Routledge.

Haipeter, T. (2002) 'Banking and finance in France and Germany: new regulations of work and working time – a challenge – a challenge for the trade unions?', *Transfer: European Review of Labour and Research*, 8(3): 493–503.

Hall, P. and Soskice, D. (eds) (2001) *Varieties of Capitalism: the Institutional Foundations of Comparative Advantage*. Oxford: Oxford University Press.

Hofstede, G. (1980) *Culture's Consequences: International Differences in Work-related Values*. Beverly Hills, CA: Sage.

Hofstede, G. (2001) *Culture's Consequences*. Thousand Oaks, CA: Sage.

Katz, H. (2004) 'Introduction: the changing nature of labour, management and government interactions', in H.C. Katz et al. (eds), *The New Structure of Labor Relations: Tripartism and Decentralization*. Ithaca, NY: Cornell University Press, pp. 1–9.

Katz, H.C., Lee, W. and Lee, J. (eds) (2004) *The New Structure of Labor Relations: Tripartism and Decentralization*. Ithaca, NY: Cornell University Press.

Keizer, A.B. (2010) *Changes in Japanese Employment Practices: Beyond the Japanese Model*. London: Routledge.

Klindt, M.P. and Halkjær, J. (2012) 'Beyond flexicurity: gradual institutional change in Denmark's employment system in the 2000s', published in Spanish in *Sistema*, May (225–6): 33–74, and available from the authors at Aalborg University.

Kostova, T. and Roth, K. (2002) 'Adoption of an organizational practice by subsidiaries of multinational corporations: institutional and relational effects', *Academy of Management Journal*, 45(1): 215–233.

Kostova, T. and Zaheer, S. (1999) 'Organizational legitimacy under conditions of complexity: the case of the multinational enterprise', *Academy of Management Review*, 24(1): 64–81.

Lam, A. (1997) 'Embedded firms, embedded knowledge: problems of collaboration and knowledge transfer in global cooperative ventures', *Organization Studies*, 18(6): 973–996.

Lee, G. and Smith, C. (1992) *Engineers and Management: International Comparisons*. London: Taylor and Francis.

Madsen, P.K. (2003) 'Flexicurity through labour market policies and institutions in Denmark', in P. Auer and S. Cazes (eds), *Employment Stability in an Age of Flexibility*. Geneva: International Labour Office, pp. 59–105.

Marsden, D. (1999) *A Theory of Employment Systems*. Oxford: Oxford University Press.

McSweeney, B. (2002) 'Hofstede's model of national cultural differences and their consequences: a triumph of faith – a failure of analysis', *Human Relations*, 55(1): 89–118.

Meardi, G. (2006) 'Multinationals' heaven? Uncovering and understanding worker responses to multinational companies in post-communist Central Europe', *International Journal of HRM*, 17(8): 1366–1378.

Mishel, L., Bernstein, J. and Allegretto, S. (2005) *The State of Working America 2004/05*. Ithaca, NY: Economic Policy Institute and Cornell University Press.

Morgan, G. and Kristensen, G.H. (2006) 'The contested space of multinationals: Varieties of institutionalism, varieties of capitalism', *Human Relations*, 59(11): 1467–1490.

Moss, P. and Korintus, M. (2008) 'International review of leave policies and related research', *Employment Relations Research Series*, 100, London: Department for Business, Enterprise and Regulatory Reform.

Muller, M. (1998) 'Human resource and industrial relations practices of UK and US multinationals in Germany', *International Journal of HRM*, 9(4): 732–749.

Pulignano, V. (2006) 'The diffusion of employment practices of US-based multinationals in Europe', *British Journal of Industrial Relations*, 44(3): 497–518.

Ray, R. and Schmitt, J. (2007) 'No vacation nation USA – a comparison of leave and holiday in OECD countries', *European Economic and Employment Policy,* Brief No. 3 – 2007 ETUIREHS, Brussels.

Reich, R. (1992) *The Work of Nations: Preparing Ourselves for 21st Century Capitalism*. New York: Vintage.

Rosenzweig, P.M. and Nohria, N. (1994) 'Influences on HRM practices in multinational corporations', *Journal of International Business Studies*, 25(2): 229–251.

Rubery, J. and Grimshaw, D. (2003) *The Organisation of Employment: An International Perspective*. Basingstoke: Palgrave Macmillan.

Steedman, H., Wagner, K. and Foreman, J. (2003) 'The impact on firms of ICT skill-supply strategies: an Anglo-German comparison', London: Centre for Economic Performance, LSE.

Van Oorschot, W. (2004) 'Flexible work and flexicurity policies in the Netherlands: trends and experiences', *Transfer*, 10(2): 208–225.

Vaughan-Whitehead, D. (ed.) (2013) *Public Sector Shock: The Impact of Policy Retrenchment in Europe*. Cheltenham: Edward Elgar.

Visser, J. (2011) 'Data base on Institutional Characteristics of Trade Unions, Wage Setting, State Intervention and Social Pacts, 1960–2010 (ICTWSS)', AIAS University of Amsterdam.

Whitley, R. (1999) *Divergent Capitalisms: The Social Structuring and Change of Business Systems*. Oxford: Oxford University Press.

Woywode, M. (2002) 'Global management concepts and local adaptations: working groups in the French and German car manufacturing industry', *Organization Studies*, 23(4): 497–524.

Regulation and Multinational Corporations: The Changing Context of Global Employment Relations

Miguel Martínez Lucio and
Robert MacKenzie

Contents

Learning objectives

After reading this chapter you will be able to:

- Comprehend the complex and varied role of regulation
- Appreciate the competing narratives and approaches to regulation and de-regulation
- Understand the role of organizations and institutional bodies regarding regulation and the market
- Appreciate the current debate on re-regulation and how the control of business behaviour has re-emerged
- Critically discuss the different levels of re-regulation and their roles

Chapter outline

The chapter studies the ways that businesses are regulated and how this varies. The politics of IHRM and of industrial relations are an ongoing reality and raise important questions of power, control and democracy. The chapter studies the changing nature of the debate on regulation and the politics of regulation, raises questions about how we see the future role of regulation and examines how the concept of human rights is becoming increasingly prevalent in current discussions about IHRM.

1 Introduction

Strategic decision making within MNCs is constrained, and sometimes determined, by the implementation of laws and codes of practice and by pressure from political actors, including national governments, supranational institutions such as the EU and non-governmental organizations (NGOs) operating at various levels. Moreover, the economic environment and HRM attributes of any given national or regional context influences internal decision making on prevalent rates of pay, levels of skills and training, and the permissiveness of employment contracts, in terms of ease of termination. Managers in MNCs have to make strategic choices that are shaped by the nature of government intervention and the local economy, which include both the decision to pursue quality or cost-related advantages, and whether to invest or disinvest in any given national context.

However, it is easy to over-simplify what we mean by the political and economic dimensions of IHRM. This chapter will discuss how these concepts are related and explore a view of regulation which binds the role of political actors to the impact of the economic context. First, we examine how we should understand the concept of regulation and appraise why it is important for HRM/IHRM. This will help us to understand how political actors and institutions frame the behaviour of managers and attempt to influence the nature of HRM both nationally and internationally. We investigate how the role of regulation is not solely about government or the state but incorporates a range of players who shape the rules and processes influencing the firm and its decision making. To understand the political dimension of IHRM, we therefore must look beyond the national state and government to consider the various public, voluntary and private sector groups that may influence the shape of HRM in national and, increasingly, international contexts. Similarly, in terms of the economic dimension, there is a widening array of organizations shaping the economic context of IHRM, from fair trade organizations and social lobbies to transnational governmental institutions such as the World Trade Organization.

Second, the political and economic dimensions are not clearly separated entities, but have a symbiotic and mutually defining relationship. Political agendas are shaped by economic circumstances and perspectives, in turn economic relations are subject to the influence of policy and political pressure. This relationship is absent from much of the IHRM literature, where the conceptual separation of politics and economics has facilitated a downgrading of the notion of regulation. If we are to comprehend the role of these influential political and economic pressures then we need to be aware of the way different views of the role of regulation develop over time, in line with various political projects (Jessop, 2002). That is to say, there are dominant viewpoints within the political contexts of IHRM and HRM that change over time and which frame the way firms will react to economic factors such as wages and employment contracts.

The chapter will explain how politics and economics of IHRM has changed over time for IHRM. It briefly outlines the shift over the 1980s and 1990s away from a national and legally based view of regulation reflected in national governments' attempts to control MNCs, towards an agenda which gives priority to the de-regulation and removal of constraints on companies, especially MNCs. The ways that different actors were involved in propagating this change are discussed, for example the role of international consultancies, accountancy firms and think tanks. The new agenda represented not just a critique of the role of regulatory actors but a challenge to the idea of regulation itself, albeit often narrowly defined in terms of 'hard' legalistic intervention.

Yet the failure to win the argument for complete de-regulation left the door open to new forms of 'soft' regulation. Current modes of thinking favour some re-regulation of HRM practices within MNCs, through establishing codes of practice and ethical agendas in the light of a greater interest in worker rights and social responsibility. While ethical and social responsibility issues are discussed in this book (see Chapters 14 and 15), here we focus on the 'shift' in thinking towards a new form of soft regulation that has been developed by a new set of political actors and social movements. Throughout the chapter we will show how ideas and values that frame the economic and political context of IHRM are developed and often contested by a variety of actors and institutions.

2 What is regulation and why is the political context important?

When we speak of the political context of HRM and IHRM there is a tendency to think in terms of the legal framework within which companies engage in the labour market. For example, ensuring recruitment practices are consistent with equality and diversity legislation, and the ongoing administration of HRM conforms to any statutes for minimum wages, working time and health and safety. Likewise, when we think of the economic context of HRM we may be drawn to a vision of the quantitative aspects of the labour market in terms of wage rates or levels of skills and training. However, we argue that in order to understand the political and economic dimensions of IHRM it is important to think in terms of the economic purpose of the political process. The link between them is regulation, which is a vital concept if we are to understand the political and economic dimensions of HRM and IHRM.

The concept of regulation is perhaps best understood from the perspective of the purpose it serves. The purpose of regulation is to facilitate social and economic reproduction: that is to ensure a supply of 'orderly' and effective labour and a social environment supportive of economic development. The logic of reproduction is based on the establishment of order and regularity, in terms of establishing shared rules and sustaining consistent decision-making processes. Regulation provides a stable environment, which offers some predictability regarding the conduct of agents operating within that environment. Whereas the development of standard expectations regarding the behaviour of others provides the basis for social and economic interaction and reproduction (MacKenzie and Martínez Lucio, 2005), it does not imply that regulation is always effective in establishing a basis for economic activity (Jessop, 1990; Peck, 1996). Our understanding of regulation should go beyond viewing it as merely legal enactment in terms of passing and implementing laws relevant to work and employment (see Martínez Lucio and Mackenzie, 2004; MacKenzie and Martínez Lucio, 2005). In a survey of debates on the conceptualization of regulation, Baldwin et al. (1998) argue that three key strands of thought on regulation can be detected. The first views regulation in terms of 'targeted rules' 'accompanied by some mechanism, typically a public agency, for monitoring and promoting compliance' (Baldwin et al., 1998: 3). A second view is to be found in the area of political economy, which looks at the larger economic and political context beyond the firm, and conceptualizes regulation as being the state and its attempt to manage the economy. However, the third view adopts a broader perspective defining regulation to include 'all mechanisms of social control – including unintentional and non-state processes' (Baldwin et al., 1998: 4). This approach extends the discussion of regulation to include the panoply of institutions and processes that contribute to social and economic reproduction.

It has been long recognized that regulation involves a variety of actors such as state bodies, trade unions and management networks, to name some key examples

(Regini, 2000; Martínez Lucio and MacKenzie, 2004; MacKenzie and Martínez Lucio, 2005). Regulation also consists of a variety of levels and relations between them. The regulatory roles of organized labour (e.g. trade unions) and organized capital (e.g. employer organizations or networks), for instance, interrelate at various levels: from the macro-level peak organizations of national employer federations and trade unions organizations, to regional or sectoral level mechanisms and on to the level of company and workplace relations between management and trade unions, which may also include less institutionalized, informal practices. So trade unions and management interact at the level of the workplace and above, and through various mechanisms ranging from formal and informal workplace arrangements, through to centralized bargaining and corporatist structures, up to the national and even transnational level. These actors and their interrelations are central to national, and even supranational, systems of regulation.

The actual regulatory actors, and the roles they play in the regulation of social and economic relationships, vary according to the context. Regulation has formal and informal qualities, reflected in the increasing array of actors involved (Picciotto, 1999). Individuals and organizations may simultaneously operate within and be subject to a multiplicity of regulatory actors in terms of the state, employers, mechanisms of joint regulation, plus social agencies and institutions. In each case these regulatory actors provide a framework of relative stability, a space within which economic and social actors can act with reasonable confidence regarding the actions of others. Regulation therefore varies by context.

Although the European context is made up of a heterogeneous collection of historically distinctive national systems, on balance Europe is characterized by a tradition of state intervention, statutory protection of worker rights, plus levels of union membership and stronger traditions of joint regulation than would be experienced by managers operating in the US context (Brewster, 2004). While subject to reform over recent decades and further strained by the post-2008 economic crisis, the European context remains one in which regulation continues to assert constraints on managerial behaviour. Even the most individualized aspects of US inspired HRM practices have had to find accommodation with collective traditions in the European context. For example, individual payment systems were introduced in Germany in a way which 'harnessed' the regulatory influence of the traditional German industrial relations system through building them into collectively bargained agreements (Kurdlebusch, 2002).

The degree of institutionalization (the extent of stability and sustainability) of the key relationship between the three actors of the state, capital and labour also speaks to the regulatory traditions of the European context associated with corporatist concertation. Ranging from strongly institutionalized forms of dialogue between these three actors as seen in Austria or the Netherlands, to the tripartite agreements on specific aspects of employment – sometimes called social partnership agreements – in Spain and Ireland in the 1990s, most national industrial relations systems in Europe have experimented with some form of corporatist concertation, with governments drawing organized labour and organized capital into policy processes. Tripartite mechanisms of regulation – tripartite because they involve the three actors outlined above – have rarely been a feature of the US system, with organized capital and labour representing their sectional interests to government through lobbying rather than any formally institution-alized relationship. In the European context, however, the embedded traditions of tri-partism have been reproduced at the community level within the governance structures of the EU. 'Social dialogue' between the representatives of labour and capital at the community level of the EU became the celebrated answer to the policy impasse of the 1980s: although the extent of its impact is another matter. The facilitating legitimacy lent to the policy process by the involvement of organized labour (in the form of the European Trade Union Confederation) and organized capital (in the form of Business Europe) has seen their role institutionalized in the EU policy-making process.

The EU represents a unique supranational regulatory space, with institutional development and delegation of powers to the level of the community by its member states far exceeding other regional blocs of nations affiliated to trade agreements, such as NAFTA (the North American Free Trade Association) or ASEAN (Association of South East Asian Nations). As a regulatory entity the EU represents more than the sum of its parts, providing the opportunity for the first piece of transnational employment regulation in the form of the 1994 European Works Council Directive, which, as an attempt to regulate employee representation in multinationals in the EU, by its nature required a jurisdiction that spanned national boundaries.

Box 7.1   Stop and reflect

The European Union has developed rules and regulations on questions of health and safety at work for over 30 years. These are frameworks which must be imple-mented by national states such as Spain and Poland who are members of the European Union. This is an attempt to create a cohesive set of formal regulations that influence the environment within which workers are employed, covering for example the use of hazardous chemicals and personal protective materials. The European Union also has a European Agency for Safety and Health at work which collates data about such issues throughout the European Union and studies the impact of legislation. This is an example of regulating employment conditions. Reflect on the emergence of such interventions and identify how they can shape HRM strategies.

3 Why are there political agendas to de-regulate?

Historically, approaches to HRM have been nationally contextualized in terms of government regulatory influence, national cultures and political processes. Overall, from the mid-1940s until the late 1970s most European countries supported an interventionist role for the state, including spending more on social and economic infrastructure and, whether effective or otherwise, developing systems of regulation through legislation or other institutionalized means (Esping-Andersen, 2000). Taking this generalization into account, the precise nature and extent of regulation was still somewhat varied. The implementation of workers' rights on such issues as work place participation, from the right to information regarding employment issues to the right to be represented in decision-making processes, was not the same across these countries; nor was protection against discrimination on the basis of gender or ethnicity consistently upheld; similarly, investment in skills differed across national systems as did the permissiveness of protection against dismissal. Nonetheless, from the late 1970 and 1980s onwards these systems experienced common pressures for change, which heralded the steady emergence of the neo-liberal models of reform that downplayed the role of the joint regulation of work and employment through a dialogue between management and workers.

Regulatory bodies and agencies reflect particular political views and economic orientations, which influence their role and impact. Such framing occurs whether they are state agencies or voluntary and social organizations contributing to the system of regulation. For 30 years (mid-1940s onwards and up to the late 1970s) the dominant model of development and regulation in many advanced economies was based on the state as the central actor and major regulator. Macro-economic policy was based on Keynesian models of state intervention in the management of the economy, using demand management policies in an attempt to regulate the forces of demand and supply as an alternative to the laissez faire of the free market. In developed countries, Keynesian macro-economic policy included associated redistributive mechanisms such as the development of a welfare state to supports the poorer strata of society through social security payments and services (see Jessop, 2002: 55–79).The critique made was that extensive state intervention in the economy, the increasing rigidity of labour market regulations in terms of hiring and firing workers, and the steadily increasing power of trade unions created an untenable inflationary situation. While much of this critique is disputed, the belief in structured and nationally based systems of regulation as a central feature of economic and social progress became tarnished (see Jessop, 2002: 95–139). The new narrative that emerged portrayed the state as no longer being an effective 'caretaker' for social order and progress (Hall, 1988). Novel and innovative approaches were said to be needed to respond to the economic and social demands of a global order characterized more than previously by cost competition and new market choices (Alonso, 2006).

What began to emerge in the mid-to-late 1970s was a political view of regulation per se as being costly and prohibitive for the firm and for society in general (Friedman,

1968). The argument is relevant to HRM and IHRM because it underpins a series of narratives around strengthening management prerogative, or the right of management to manage without much external interference, and around making workers become more flexible in terms of their deployment in the firm or the cost to employers of their dismissal (see Martínez Lucio (2008) for a discussion). The basic contours of the argument are as follows. The state and regulation should play a less central role in economic management generally and in circumscribing the operations of the firm, including its HRM practices. Through the imperative of international competition, the 'market' will force organizations to be more efficient and dynamic. This will push firms either towards seeking cost-reduction strategies through forms of flexible employment and restructuring, or quality enhancing strategies through forms of work organization that capitalize on workers' skills and knowledge. These are also not mutually exclusive strategies and in both cases rely upon the assertion of management prerogative. The internationalized context in which these strategies are pursued means that the former may be controlled through coercive comparisons between national contexts, underpinned by the threat of 'capital flight' (Keenoy, 1990; Mueller and Purcell, 1992; Martínez Lucio and Weston, 1994), and the latter through the emulation of 'best practices' derived from different national systems, for example the adoption of quality circles and team working practices developed in Japan (Garrahan and Stewart, 1992; Pinnington and Hammersley, 1997). There are therefore economic and resource based advantages to be gained by employers from the new global market: from cheaper manufacturing labour costs in Malaysia or IT skills in India, to instilling global best practices in new start-up subsidiaries, internationalization offers a greater degree of choice for firms. There are also gains of a more indirect nature from this new marketized 'open' order in terms of greater opportunity to draw upon managerial experience and knowledge from different countries. The new ideational and ideological networks that emerge from the increasingly international nature of markets and economies (see Chapters 3 and 6) create an environment where national governments and politics are felt to be less important.

For some this marketization represents an Americanization of employment strategies (Guest, 1990; Brewster, 2004), where the role of regulation through the state and collective organization become secondary to management prerogative (Whitley et al., 2005). This model can be juxtaposed against a traditional European model where the state is more interventionist and collective worker rights are more influential in terms of HRM practices and decision making (Communal and Brewster, 2004). The reality is that the vision of the global environment is configured in terms of different perspectives (Lillie and Martínez Lucio, 2004), and within these general perspectives specific models such as the American model emerge (Boyacigiller and Adler, 1991). The political dimension of IHRM is linked, in rhetorical terms at least, to this policy oriented move away from state-led forms of regulation and towards the competitive advantage of new 'flexible' paradigms of work; competitive advantage that may come at considerable costs to workers.

Box 7.2   Stop and reflect

The World Bank is an inter-governmental body which intervenes in national states when they are in a precarious financial situation. The World Bank is, however, known to propagate a neo-liberal agenda by underpinning any financial support with demands for the privatization of state enterprises and the de-regulation of the labour market (e.g. lowering the cost to employers of dismissing workers). The conditions established by the World Bank are often seen to favour a neo-liberal view of employment relations. Can you think of examples of such interventions and assess the way in which they influence a specific approach to HRM?

4 What are the political and institutional drivers of de-regulation?

Regardless of the rhetoric of 'market-led' imperatives, the development of IHRM practices and the transmission of 'best practice' ultimately relies upon management and other actors actually implementing such practices. Therefore implementation is still essentially a political process – that is to say it is based on struggles between actors regarding the distribution of power. Competing views of a firm's management, based on divergent values pertaining to the market and the individual, exist within the same firm, not only between management and the representatives of labour but also between different cohorts of management. The process by which models of HRM/IHRM become predominant within firms is often not through some natural or inevitable evolutionary adaptation but actually emerges as the outcome of a variety of pressures. These pressures arise in the form of isomorphism, be it coercive, whereby companies are forced to comply due to strong sanctions, or mimetic, where companies copy practices because they are seen as successful or currently the 'best way' to work (DiMaggio and Powell, 1983). The implementation of IHRM practices is a political process that involves various actors' attempts to impose ideas and practices and is a conscious struggle between them over strategies and ideas.

In terms of HRM/IHRM developments associated with the Japanization debate in the UK, Stewart (1996) argues that the associated organizational and employment changes were the outcomes of political debates and struggles between unions, employers and even academics. The practices of teamworking and quality management were to a significant degree created not just by overseas MNCs in the early 1990s but also by consultancy firms such as Arthur Anderson. The large international consultancy and accountancy firms were in many ways MNCs in their own right, and were central to the propagation of these new ideas. Consultancies such as Price Waterhouse Coopers and McKinsey & Co among others developed consultancy and research into 'flexible systems of employment' based on temporary contracting or zero-hours contracts, which have influenced the development of HRM concepts in many national contexts. The contribution of other actors was also highly significant, such as the role of the right-wing pressure groups and think tanks. The Heritage Foundation was founded in the USA in 1973, and in the UK the Centre for Policy Studies was established in 1974 by right-wing politicians Keith Joseph and Margaret Thatcher for research and lobbying purposes. These political actors contributed much to the initial development of the reified notion of the 'market', and to the campaign for greater flexibility in the labour market, that were central to the opposition and undermining of state-led regulation (see Klein, 2007: 50–51). These views were echoed within management and business circles, as consultancy firms promoted more elaborate and 'scientific' models of management behaviour and organizational strategy. Their research-based status lent credibility to these models: albeit a scientific credibility that some would suggest has been prone to abuse by both consultants and management. The role of such political and private sector bodies has grown in significance in the past 20 years as a basis for networking and disseminating views on work and its organization in terms of HRM (Heller, 2002; Legge, 2002). At the more extreme end, anti-union and union-busting consultancies have become a common feature of such ideational networks.

Within this general framework of ideas and initiatives we also see the development and dissemination of expert knowledge through global university and business school networks. Expert knowledge is being sought in terms of the subject of work (the worker), the psychological framework of employment (motivation and commitment), the organizational context (owners, managers and employees), the social context (gender and ethnicity), the economic and labour market contexts (skills and HRM attributes), and the regulatory environment (legal constraints and rights).

The growth of the consultancies and business schools was due to a range of phenomena, including: new forms of competitive management, new forms of HRM, organizational factors in terms of a mushrooming management constituency, and institutional factors related to the restructuring and commodification of education (Gonzalez Rodriguez, 2014). Underpinning this has been the fact that the greater degree of management intervention in the administration of businesses (and the social and cultural spaces of organizations) has required initiatives specifically to address the inevitable cognitive gaps arising within management knowledge. This dimension has become central to the mapping of regulatory interventions and the attempts to realign them. These educational and research institutions have been paralleled and supported by more direct intervention from consultancy firms who research, motivate and legitimate organizational change (O'Shea and Madigan, 1997). This has provided the new regulatory actors, be they state agencies or particular consultancy firms, with knowledge resources, technical abilities and competences, and the degree of legitimacy necessary for influencing the terminology and practices of new forms of management strategy within HRM/IHRM. Yet these educational and knowledge-based spaces are changing and becoming the object of greater internal debate and challenge: the realities of what business schools 'do' can vary, especially in light of critical academic traditions within the teaching of HRM and Organizational Studies in many British business schools (Martínez Lucio, 2007). Increasingly, ethical issues, questions of equality and diversity, and CSR are beginning to move up the agenda, as are issues of employment and financial regulation – not least in the light of the economic downturn and problems of global finance since 2008–2009.

Even at the macro-level of the global political scene, ideas of harder management-led HRM are propagated, both directly and indirectly. The roles of the World Bank and the IMF, as transnational and inter-state publicly funded bodies, have been crucial in extending the idea of free markets, greater competition and the importance of continuous labour and organizational restructuring. The practices of these bodies vary but their role in using debt in developing countries as a vehicle for pushing through restructuring and supporting more managerially driven systems of control and performance management within work is key (Stiglitz, 2006: 211–244; Klein, 2007: 267–271). They link with the harder and more performance-driven aspects of HRM and help to legitimate and propagate the internal debates of governments or MNCs that promote harder and less involvement-based versions of HRM. Within the European Union, while there has been an historic agenda to develop a more social model of HRM – that is to say one that is based on common worker rights and a stronger sense of employer obligation – these have more recently been over-ridden by a strong pressure on governments to reduce public deficits due to the post-2008 economic crisis: this has led to the further restructuring of the state and the curtailing of social rights, including redundancy payments and welfare support (Fernández Rodríguez and Martínez Lucio, 2013). For some, the agenda for stabilizing the currency as the Eurozone was convulsed by successive national banking and finance crises, following the broader post-2008 economic downturn, demonstrated the ongoing zeal for de-regulation (Rubery, 2011). Hence transnational bodies of governance may move in various directions in terms of regulation and de-regulation, reflecting what might be called a transnational politics of regulation.

What we are arguing here is that the politics and economics of IHRM is as much about a variety of actors disseminating ideas and values, as it is about natural adaptation. Such approaches are forged through agency and political processes, and are not simply the natural or 'best' outcome in the light of the needs of the new global market. In the late 1970s the political project of the new right in the UK and USA defined views towards regulation for governments on both sides of the Atlantic. Successive governments elected from either side of the respective political divides did not demur, whether due to ideological commitment or political expediency. Indeed it was not until the international economic crisis emerged in 2008 that the recognized need for government intervention returned to the mainstream political narrative.

5 What are the problems with de-regulation and what is currently meant by re-regulation in a global context?

Due to their dynamic nature, the political landscapes of IHRM and the management of labour by MNCs have not stood still. The late 1990s began to see a change in the politics of labour management and a new set of actors emerge who were internationally intent on raising alternative approaches and issues. The cost of unfettered MNC development in terms of uneven and unfair labour standards, the increasing concern with the social condition of employment throughout the world, and the gradual increase in ethical issues placed on the agenda of business management (see Chapters 6, 14 and 15), meant that a new set of arguments and positions began to appear in the discussion of labour management.

Given the legitimacy and historical pre-eminence of the nation state, national governments and government bodies have been central political influences on the firm and its HRM strategies. Extending beyond the nation state there has been a long-standing tradition of international regulatory bodies: transnational governmental institutions which provide coordination between national governments. The International Labour Organization, for example, and its role in setting standards for work on behalf of the United Nations are discussed later in the chapter. These organizations took on increased importance during the new wave of internationalization in the 1980s and the growing concern with setting minimum benchmarks for treatment of workers. It is too soon to talk of a re-regulation of employment given the weak and uneven nature of transnational regulatory bodies, and the fact that the ideas underpinning them are not universally shared. The interaction of formal and informal regulatory processes around legal forms and codes of conduct is increasingly a part of modern business environments (Picciotto, 1999). The position of developing countries is also important as they are in many cases – although not all – competing and developing through lower labour costs, which brings a new set of tensions regarding the cost implications of employment regulation. Pressure from government organizations or even NGOs based in developed economies for increased regulation in developing economies is always at risk of accusations of double standards. Interference from developed countries in the chosen paths of development can be perceived as neo-colonialism: an indirect form of colonialism, which is based on economic and ideological influence over countries that are formally independent.

However, in our view, this brings a need to innovate in terms of regulation and to create new templates of regulation which allow for flexibility in the global arena, in keeping with the complex traditions of regulation noted above. If anything, it brings to the fore the need for innovation. There are three further dimensions, which we shall now discuss, that are important aspects of this partial return to regulation through a growing interest in re-regulation and the use of innovative forms of regulation.

Standardization and labour market knowledge

First, MNCs continue to develop and edge towards the potential of global systems of employment. At the same time migration continues to be a vital part of international labour markets and at virtually all skill and educational levels. This prompts the need to create structures and frameworks that assist in sharing and validating the content of work and the skills of workers. There are extensive government networks across countries throughout the world sharing information about qualifications, apprentice-ship systems, and new forms of skills development such as soft skills, which are creating common standards and templates.

These systems are complemented by international networks in specific sectors with a high level of inter-state activity. In the airlines industry, for example, there are various international regulatory bodies primarily focused on operational concerns that in addition cover work and employment related issues and standards when addressing health and safety. Here, international regulatory agencies collaborate to influence approaches in safety-related issues and assist in the pooling of knowledge and practice in IHRM. Many of these bodies have questionable regulatory efficacy as they have no form of effective sanction; nevertheless they form part of a tapestry of regulation which although 'soft' in orientation contributes to greater coordination on aspects of labour management and HRM/IHRM.

Box 7.3   Stop and reflect

There is an increasing number of organizations that are sponsored and run by gov-ernments to validate the qualifications of students travelling to study or work in different countries and to create common templates for learning. In the European Union there is increasing standardization of educational systems, especially at the higher and professional level. Employers are thus more able than they were in previ-ous decades to verify the authenticity of skills and qualifications when recruiting from the international pool of labour. As the world sees greater mobility and migra-tion of labour there is a need for employers and public organizations to ensure and validate the skills of workers. Reflect on your experiences – perhaps as someone who is mobile or migrating, or in terms of others you know in such a position – and assess the importance of these types of knowledge sharing for creating, generating and using higher skills at work.

Labour standards and codes of practice

Second, there is increasing interest in labour standards and the behaviour of employers from a range of bodies that are concerned with issues of malpractice, corruption and 'bad' employment practices. The International Labour Organization, the United Nations labour and work related department, was actually established as part of the UN's predecessor, the League of Nations, after the First World War (1919). The ILO historically outlined a basic body of labour codes and rights, which, while often ignored, were formally part of the system of inter-governmental relations. Over time it has established more explicit sets of conventions and rules, and a vast array of research and educational activities that map and outline 'good' practices in relation to employment issues. The ILO sets the benchmark against which firms and governments are measured in this area. Political sensitivities around issues such as child labour are directly informed by compliance to ILO standards. Furthermore, the ILO provides standards across the range of everyday employment issues which attract less media attention. Whether these standards are systematically developed or adhered to by member states is another issue. However, they constitute a part of the international dialogue on employment and HRM between governments, international employer bodies, and international trade union organizations.

The OECD is a body that has 34 members – mainly developed countries – which broadly share free market economies and liberal democratic political systems. This body has developed a range of economic and social agendas. In relation to MNCs it has produced a set of guidelines establishing a series of principles on the approach of member states to MNCs and the behaviour of MNCs themselves. They cover a range of areas related to employment issues, through to corruption and investment matters. Bodies such as the World Bank and the WTO have also begun to address the issue of labour standards and the basic rights of labour organizations. While such bodies are mainly focused on the economic and developmental aspects of their affiliate nations, they do increasingly address employment and work-related issues, although their prescriptions tend to reflect a particular neo-liberal orientation and vary in their social impact.

These international institutions provide a backdrop of minimum standards and benchmarks, which do on occasion influence the way that firms behave in relation to their workforce. How much and how often they have an influence depends on the industrial sector and its traditions of labour organization. However, the main point is that there exists an array of bodies addressing international issues and cross-national labour standards, which impact upon HRM and IHRM practices. They have not possessed a strong regulatory and sanctioning role in many cases, but that does not detract from the fact that there is a tapestry of international labour bodies and HR influencing agencies that challenge the recent vogue for seeing globalization as moving HRM matters beyond the remit or influence of government.

Moreover, these developments are not always 'soft' or voluntary but instead may have the potential for more systematic regulatory process based on the existence of interventionist mechanisms and sanctions to enforce standards. In some regions of the world, countries are beginning to form more permanent systems of supranational economic and social governance. The most developed manifestation of this is the EU – a political structure unifying 28 European nation states to varying degrees, with a range of social and employment related rules and laws (see Chapters 2 and 6). This has included systematic frameworks of HR related regulations on issues such as mass redundancy, health and safety, working hours and discrimination. The European Works Councils Directive provides legislation on worker participation in MNCs, and – as stated – represents the first supranational employment regulation within the EU. These are all developments that show the necessity of conceptualizing regulation within broader transnational frameworks.

The developing tapestry of supranational, transnational and inter-nation state based bodies is creating a framework of regulation affecting firms and their human resource practices. It is part of an evolving international dialogue on labour rights that has emerged since the end of the Second World War, and is underpinned by the Universal Declaration of Human Rights (see Cassese, 1992). There remains a great degree of cynicism regarding the development of such rights due to the highly variable responses of national governments and multinational employers. There is also a concern that the assertion of such rights favours the production regimes of developed countries and disadvantages developing countries where competitive advantage based on low labour costs has become common government strategy for economic development.

Another school of thought in the form of the 'boomerang theory' is more optimistic and argues that governments which ignore the increasing establishment of international rights systems may be shamed and compelled in the longer term to subscribe to them (Risse et al., 1999). Even if this is symbolic in the first instance, over time it establishes expectations within countries, arising from unions or political bodies, as well as pressures beyond from international consumer groups, other nation states (Norway, for example, has been highly active on such issues) and transnational interstate organizations such as the EU.

Box 7.4   Stop and reflect

There are a range of MNCs that sign International Framework Agreements at the highest level of their organizations and with a variety of worker representatives drawn from their operations in different countries. These are sets of voluntary rules which have managed to create frameworks covering representation and the conduct

(Continued)

(Continued)

of industrial relations within the different operating units of the firm across countries. These frameworks are seen as a way of creating an internal dialogue between the employer and the workforce and bring regulation into the heart of the firm. They try to instil the voluntary but systematic codes of conduct developed by such bodies as the ILO. In your view do these frameworks and agreements represent a viable way forward for the regulation of employment in MNCs? To what extent can such agreements be linked to broader ethical agendas within MNCs?

Ethics, values and context

Third, the developments described above dovetail with an increasing interest in social responsibility and ethics within HRM (Pinnington et al., 2007) – the growing belief that firms have to realize and act on the social impact of their actions and not just the economic effects. In relation to major issues such as child labour there exist emergent external pressures from NGOs such as OXFAM or War on Want. Movements such as Fairtrade, which campaigns for a decent wage for workers in the global agricultural sector, notably coffee, and in the textiles industry have provided a new reference point for ethically based regulation that is of growing importance, although there are views arguing that such initiatives could be more assertive and extensive.

The focus on social issues and the rights to participation at work in MNCs (Wills, 1998) has emerged as a renewed role for international trade union organizations such as the International Trade Union Congress (ITUC). While these bodies have less resources to access than do nation states (Smith et al., 1998), and indeed even compete with each other for scarce resources (Claude and Weston, 1992), they do form part of the global set of institutions that contribute to the tapestry of regulation shaping the political and economic context in which IHRM exists. They play a regulatory role in terms of diffusing expert knowledge, and informing and educating public agencies and nation states (Baehr, 1999). They also constitute a counterpoint to the private and market driven networks of consultancies and think tanks. These developments echo the interest in stakeholder theories of ethics and HRM, which espouse a more pluralist understanding of voice and the role of different actors (Greenwood and De Cieri, 2007): that is to say an approach which includes a range of stakeholder interests within the debate of HRM. What is more, a range of informal union and social activist networks have emerged, aimed at exchanging information on campaigns and coordinating across a range of disputes and mobilizations (Wills, 1998). The politics of such networks has given rise to broad coalitions combining trade unions with a diverse range of peace campaigners, environmentalist and anti-capitalist groups, into movements that are both innovative and increasingly entrenched (Thomas, 2007).

The internet has provided a forum for discussion and a conduit for the transmission of critiques of MNCs and the articulation of alternative, progressive perspectives on consumption. Consumer groups are utilizing this medium to bring pressure to bear on the activities of MNCs and the ethicality of their approach to issues such as employment and sustainable resourcing. Whereas there may be a more individualist and consumerist orientation to contemporary capitalism obsessed with the price and choice of goods (Alonso, 2006), a new politics of consumption is emerging that places social and employment rights on the agenda.

Box 7.5 Stop and reflect

The death of over a thousand textile workers in Bangladesh in 2013, when the building they worked in collapsed due to poor maintenance and an unauthorized design, raised the issue of how complex and non-transparent supply chains in the international textile sector could contribute to such poor working conditions. Workers are producing clothing for overseas transnational companies that do not directly employ them but who work through intermediaries and local firms. Various charities – some based in the UK – dealing with worker rights and poverty among other issues have been attempting to create a dialogue among MNCs regarding contracting with such firms. The initiative has sought to establish a series of agreements between these international firms based on increasing the level of inspection of workplaces and creating funds to support victims of poor health and safety standards. What do you think are the possibilities and challenges of developing such types of voluntary ethical agreements? In what ways could such agreements connect to other forms of regulation?

These three dimensions of transnational regulation are a vital part of the environment that MNCs inhabit. Indeed, they also encourage MNCs to internalize and develop regulatory roles themselves, as they increasingly need to ethically police their organizations and create sustainable and legitimate operations.

6 Summary and conclusions

The chapter has argued that the concept of regulation should be central to any discussion of the politics and economics of IHRM. Regulation involves various levels and actors, and in any given context these will vary. There has also been a shift in the way regulation is viewed and who is involved in it. Where once stood the apparatus of the state and direct forms of intervention, there is now an even more complex scenario. While there has been a move towards more neo-liberal economies where the remit of regulation is limited, this is only part of the story. First, such a shift towards a marketized and more individualistic perspective is itself the political product of a range of policy related actors and knowledge networks – such as think tanks, consultancy firms and business schools – which can be prone to shifting economic and political contingencies, as witnessed in the clamour for regulatory responses to the economic crisis that emerged since 2008. Second, sustaining the hegemony of marketized perspectives has always been a contested process and there is again increasing concern with the need to rebuild regulation and create a more effective platform for regulating international employment issues. That this has emerged is indisputable – whether or not it will be as influential as are the more established and traditional forms of regulation remains to be seen.

Increasingly, we need to appreciate that the politics of IHRM involves a variety of factors influencing the way that people are managed. The illusion that the emergence of market-oriented HRM would deliver a new world of autonomous managerial decision making has been shown to be questionable and surpassed by processes of re-regulation. There are competing views on how firms should conduct their HR strategies and in the case of MNCs this has now become a question at the centre of a range of policy and social debates (see Klein, 2007). The once dominant view of the reassertion of the prerogative of management, as a new and invigorated actor that can assimilate many of the requirements of regulation and actually regulate in relation to the internal context of the firm, is highly problematic and contested. This is the key challenge for IHRM: as MNCs seek to develop their own geocentric forms of governance (see Chapters 4, 5 and 13), which are influenced by neither national systems of origin nor the contexts they operate in, it is becoming clear that there is an urgent need for new forms of global regulation. MNCs can create their own idiosyncratic HRM systems that are hybrids of what went before but there are limits to the extent to which they can create systems that respond to internal business and operational requirements and minimize external regulatory influences.

Pressures remain in terms of national governments, transnational public bodies, transnational organizations, social movements, consumer organizations, and transnational trade union structures and networks. This new environment is about setting standards and creating alternative visions of how people should be managed: therefore, it presents a whole new challenge to the political dimension of IHRM. This political dimension will be a global struggle of ideas about the way capitalism should be regulated, involving clusters of nation states, national systems and international bodies and networks (supranational regulatory spaces such as the European Union among others). Regulation, far from disappearing, has become a significant and ever more complex reality. It would be too easy to dismiss this tapestry of often soft regulation – which consists of transnational ILO-type or voluntary codes of practice as well as the impact of pressure groups – for not being sufficiently coordinated, or backed by a meaningful sanction apparatus, to provide an international equivalent to the regulatory role historically played by nation states.

So while the current economic context will mean that the roles of regulation and the capacity of regulators will be refined, it would be unwise to assume that the kinds of regulation we discuss in this chapter in relation to employment relations and management at the transnational level will be easily marginalized. The imperative for regulation will remain. The social and political consequences of the post-2008 economic crisis will continue to shape any discussion of regulation for some time, and will demand ever more strategic and innovative forms of state response (Rubery, 2011). It could be argued that the current context puts greater pressure on soft regulation to develop in a more effective manner.

Discussion questions

1. What are the main political ideologies driving the debates on regulation and de-regulation?
2. What is the purpose of regulation and why does it matter who leads and governs projects of regulation?
3. What are the main features of re-regulation and what kinds of pressures are MNCs experiencing in relation to these features?
4. How sustainable are new forms of regulation and state intervention within a global context?

CASE STUDY

A motor company in England

Bartlett Motor Cars produces some of the most expensive and luxurious cars in the world, and has been long established as a much sought after brand. The workforce was relatively more skilled than the typical industrial car worker,

(Continued)

(Continued)

due to the craft-based expertise that went into production. During the 1960s and 1970s it was known for having a traditional industrial relations approach and strong workplace representation. The company was firmly locked into the national tradition of industrial relations which consisted of workplace discussions on operational matters between worker representatives and line management, along with a formal, collective agreements and sets of procedures between trade unions and management for the company as a whole. However, the management culture was uncertain about extending a strong system of participation in terms of strategic issues to the workforce, and the lines of communication were limited to dealing with issues and problems as they arose. There were also changes in the product market at the quality end of the car industry, with intensified competition and new entrant rivals.

While this segment of the car market remained relatively robust over time, the changing industrial relations context of the 1980s brought with it a set of tensions and problems. The Conservative government passed legislation which restricted the role of trade unions and limited their political activity (in theory, although not always in practice). The increasing competition from German high value motor cars, and the move towards new more speed-oriented models, meant that British high status, luxury cars faced new competitive challenges to their sales and position in the market. Restructuring became common but the practices of industrial relations remained adversarial and initiatives to develop new individual HR systems of control and communication challenged the legitimacy and role of unions. There appeared to be a tension between the more collective and standardized system of national industrial relations, with its informal workplace features, and the new pressure for Japanese and American style HRM practices as adopted, to some extent, by the firm's management. In many respects it appeared that the local system of regulation through informal and formal processes would be undermined by more market-based and individually oriented approaches.

Case study questions

1. What were traditional forms of labour relations like?
2. How was the national system of regulation put under pressure by global developments in the market and management practices within the workplace?
3. What do you imagine are the trade unions' long-term prospects?

CASE STUDY

A European company with subsidiary businesses in the UK and elsewhere

Note: The interviews for the case studies were conducted in 2007–2009 by Miguel Martinez Lucio.

Bartlett Motor Cars, the luxury car company referred to in the previous case study, was bought by a leading European car manufacturer which we will call People Motors. It became part of a transnational corporation with operations in many parts of the world. Local management was supported in terms of the development of new systems of workplace organization and operations; although the nature of the car manufactured in the UK was of such a high value-added nature that the local management was able to convince their transnational headquarters of the different challenges facing the local operator. Suddenly, local management in Bartlett Motors found themselves a small player in a much larger pool of senior and international managers, regardless of the strength of their local brand worldwide. They were exposed to new systems of international management control and performance management systems.

At the same time the presence of a European Works Council and a Global Works Council meant that local trade unionists began to have access to a higher tier of negotiation and consultation. This provided them with information that local management did not always obtain. What is more, with the concern with ecological and ethical pressures, a series of projects were developed worldwide which involved key individuals from the UK factory. Trade unionists began to engage explicitly with the agenda of CSR. The consequence of these developments was that there arose a new, albeit soft, system of regulation and consultation, which provided information and networks to local trade unionists. This was part of the new attempt to set common benchmarks and socially oriented standards of employment.

In some cases members of these councils were used as mediators and 'consultants of sorts' to deal with problems in People Motors production plants in Africa and Latin America. These trade unionists therefore became new players within the firm, linking up with external organizations including the ILO, international union bodies and international social organizations. Through these networks they lobbied for more regulation and negotiation within the wider structures of the MNC. The trade union representatives found themselves travelling throughout Europe, and the world, attending meetings and lobbying. The trade unionists referenced the increasing presence of international frameworks, corporate social responsibility

(Continued)

(Continued)

declarations, codified labour standards and even the greater interest in ecological and sustainability issues within their repertoire of actions and narratives.

Roles within the workplace at Bartlett Motor Cars began to change as trade unionists began to engage with such international networks. Trade union representatives faced increased pressure from competing claims on their time and resources in terms of balancing their traditional workplace responsibilities with their new international roles. By their nature such international networks could appear to be somewhat remote from daily experiences of the workplace, which created an additional source of tension for trade union representatives in terms of balancing their roles. This was countered by consciously sustaining a strong dialogue with the range of activists and members within the plant's union structures, and actively encouraging their involvement in these broader processes. The concern was that over the longer term such international developments would require greater resources and time if they were not to evolve at the expense of day-to-day local union activity. What is more the company began contemplating – and in part enacting – switching production of aspects of the local firm to Eastern European contexts, which can bring tensions between different national interests. Hence supra national forms of regulation and representation can be undermined by a company's mobilization of national interest and the manner in which the 'common interest' of the firm can be defined in specific and problematic ways. New forms of soft transnational regulation and representation still face challenges in terms of decision making and strategy making in core MNCs, and the role of dominant interests within them.

Case study questions

1. Are the new forms of activity by trade unionists soft or hard regulation? Why do you reach this conclusion?
2. What do these new forms of activities and regulation tell us about the political context of MNCs?
3. Is there a risk that such developments may become a form of control over local management (strengthening the role of transnational headquarters)? Explain your answer.
4. Is there a risk that trade unionists may be caught in roles that disconnect them from more traditional roles in terms of worker representation? Explain your answer.
5. What kinds of work and personal pressures do such new roles bring to individuals involved? What can be done about this issue?
6. What kind of training and preparation is required to sustain and develop effective forms of dialogue and engagement between unions, workers and managers at various levels within these new types of international forums?

Further reading

- Freeman, M. (2002) *Human Rights*. Cambridge: Polity.
  This is a good introduction to the concept of human rights. It covers a range of areas that are essential for the study of international human rights issues. This is becoming a key feature of the CSR agenda and students will find no better guide for exploring the competing meanings and the significance of this concept.

- Picciotto, S. and Mayne, R. (eds) (1999) *Regulating International Business: Beyond Liberalisation*. Basingstoke: Macmillan and Oxfam.
  The book explores the way the regulation of international business has developed. It offers a set of very detailed chapters on different dimensions of regulation and how they function. It is seen as one of the first real attempts to engage with a broader set of approaches to regulation.

- Pinnington, A.H., Mackin, R.E. and Campbell, T. (2007) 'Introduction' in A.H. Pinnington, R.E. Macklin and T. Campbell (eds), *Human Resource Management: Ethics and Employment*. Oxford: Oxford University Press.
  The edited collection is a very informative outline of the different concerns and issues associated with the ethics of HRM. The introduction to this text is a very good starting point for those wishing to develop their understanding of this increasingly important topic.

- Stiglitz, J. (2006) *Making Globalization Work*. London: Penguin.
  This book is written by the Nobel Prize winner Joseph Stiglitz. Students will find this to be an important read, which suggests how the new global order needs to be regulated and made to work for social as well as economic reasons. The book was written prior to the financial crisis of 2008 but it serves to help understand how regulation is a key feature of the debate regarding international economic relations.

- Whitley, R., Morgan, E. and Moen, E. (2005) *Changing Capitalisms? Internationalization, Institutional Change and Systems of Economic Organization*. Oxford: Oxford University Press.
  No discussion of capitalism can proceed without understanding the basic differences in the models of capitalism and the way they are regulated. The book is useful for explaining how capitalism varies and how institutional change is shaped through the system of economic organization.

- Claude, R.P. and Weston, B.H. (1992) 'International human rights: overviews', in R.P. Claude and B.H. Weston (eds), *Human Rights in the World Community: Issues and Action*, 2nd edn. Philadelphia: University of Pennsylvania Press.
  This is a brief and succinct overview of the way international human rights have developed and explores the meaning of its different dimensions. The concept of rights is becoming part of the teaching of business and management – yet we need to be clearer how this concept evolves and how it varies.

- Greenwood, M. and De Cieri, H. (2007) 'Stakeholder theory and the ethicality of human resource management', in A.H. Pinnington, R.E. Macklin and T. Campbell (eds), *Human Resource Management: Ethics and Employment*. Oxford: Oxford University Press.

  The chapter points to the importance of democratic participation within the firm and the importance of a stakeholder approach. It is part of a set of positions which argue that the question of ethics necessitates a more open view of organizations.

- Giddens, A. and Hutton, W. (2000) 'Anthony Giddens and Will Hutton in conversation', in W. Hutton and A. Giddens (eds), *Global Capitalism*. New York: New York Press.

  Put two visionaries on a park bench to talk about capitalism and this is what emerges. This is a vivid insight into the views of two significant commentators on what has been happening in the past 20 years.

- MacKenzie, R. and Martínez Lucio, M. (2005) 'The realities of regulatory change: beyond the fetish of deregulation', *Sociology*, 39(3): 499–517.

  If we are to talk about regulation then we cannot simply think in terms of it as legal systems. Regulation is a broad process involving many players and processes. The employment relation is regulated in a variety of ways, and this article points to how this can be understood, and how the politics of regulation is itself a matter for discussion.

- Wills, J. (1998) 'Taking on the Cosmocorps: experiments in transnational labor organization', *Economic Geography*, 74: 111–130.

  One of the first pieces to systematically discuss the way organized labour is developing in international terms and as part of a broader alternative in global capitalism. It provides the student with a discussion of how unions and workers are active and essential to a global social order and locates this within an effective historical analysis.

- Wills, J. (2000) 'Great expectations: three years in the life of a European Works Council', *European Journal of Industrial Relations*, 6(1): 85–107.

  The article is a detailed case study of the life of a European Works Council. It is a seminal study which critiques such developments and highlights how they are constrained and limited within the context of industrial relations structures. It is a good case of why such structures need a broader more independent union approach to internationalism. It contrasts and compliments the next reading.

- Whittall, M., Knudsen, H. and Huijgen, F. (2009) 'European Works Councils: identity and the role of information and communication technology', *European Journal of Industrial Relations*, 15(2): 167–185.

This is a series of case studies on European Works Councils which argues that with regards to any formal system of transnational representation and union activity within firms we must account for the important way in which information and communication technology impacts on and moulds developments. The current context of the internet has added a strong dimension of support in terms of how trade unionists manage to coordinate activity across national boundaries within MNCs.

- Thomas, N.H. (2007) 'Global capitalism, the anti-globalisation movement and the third world', *Capital and Class*, 92 (Summer): 45–80.
  This article is a good introduction to debates about alternatives to the neo-liberal global order. It is a strong stand for a more mobilization-based response to the problems of contemporary capitalism. The analysis is forthright and marks the kind of literature that is becoming more common due to the negative consequences of global capitalism and the behaviour of MNCs.

- Martínez Lucio, M. (2010) 'Dimensions of internationalism and the politics of the labour movement: understanding the political and organisational aspects of labour networking and co-ordination', *Employee Relations*, 32(6): 538–556.
  The article is concerned with labour internationalism and debates about how it is developing. It argues that trade union coordination at an international level is framed by competing projects, national/regional traditions and sector based factors. In effect, there are different internationalisms and a politics of internationalism.

Internet resources

- www.oecd.org/home. The OECD has plenty of material on MNCs and you can search for the OECD's voluntary codes of conduct which are a basic outline for the governance of MNCs within an ethical context.
- www.ilo.org/global/lang--en/index.htm. As the labour department of the ILO this is a significant organization. The website has many national and international reports and research papers. It also has a series of outlines and codes on MNCs and their behaviour.
- www.ituc-csi.org. The International Trades Union Congress is the organization that represents most national unions at an international level. It has many resources and links. It will show how unions approach the issues at hand and are responding to greater internationalization and the need for new forms of regulation.
- www.labourstart.org. Labour Start is an important and independent source of information about union activity supported by trade unionists. It provides insight into developments around national and international labour related agendas. There are many campaigns around MNCs reported here.

Self-assessment questions

Indicative answers to these questions can be found on the companion website at study.sagepub.com/harzing4e.

1. Given the growth of MNCs what are the possibilities of effectively regulating them?
2. What are the chances of global forms of governance and regulation in terms of employment related issues developing in the coming years?
3. Do NGOs such as War on Want in the UK have a role to play in the regulation of employment?
4. Do voluntary codes of conduct have a realistic chance of influencing IHRM or should a stronger form of regulation develop?
5. How would you design into the learning curricula within business schools and universities greater sensitivity concerning international employment regulation and rights, and the role of broader social organizations?

References

Alonso, L. (2006) 'Fordism and the genesis of the post-Fordist society: assessing the post-Fordist paradigm', in L.E. Alonso and M. Martínez Lucio (eds), *Employment Relations in a Changing Society*. London: Palgrave, pp. 18–31.

Baehr, P.R. (1999) *Human Rights: Universality in Practice*. Basingstoke: Macmillan.

Baldwin, R., Scott, C. and Hood, C. (1998) 'Introduction', in R. Baldwin, C. Scott and C. Hood (eds), *A Reader on Regulation*. Oxford: Oxford University Press, pp. 1–55.

Boyacigiller, N.A. and Adler, N.J. (1991) 'The parochial dinosaur: organizational science in a global context', *Academy of Management Review*, 16(2): 262–290.

Brewster, C. (2004) 'European perspectives on human resource management', *Human Resource Management Review*, 14(4): 365–382.

Cassese, D. (1992) 'The General Assembly: historical perspective 1945–1989', in P. Ashton, *The United Nations and Human Rights: A Critical Appraisal*. New York: Cambridge University Press, pp. 25–54.

Claude, R.P. and Weston, B.H. (1992) 'International human rights: overviews', in R.P. Claude and B.H. Weston (eds), *Human Rights in the World Community: Issues and Action*, 2nd edn. Philadelphia: University of Pennsylvania Press, 1–14.

Communal, C. and Brewster, C. (2004) 'HRM in Europe', in A.-W. Harzing and J. Van Ruysseveldt (eds), *International Human Resource Management*. London: Sage, pp. 167–194.

DiMaggio, P.J. and Powell, W. (1983) '"The iron cage revisited": institutional isomorphism and collective rationality in organizational fields', *American Sociological Review*, 48: 147–160.

Esping-Andersen, G. (2000) 'Who is harmed by labour market de-regulation', in G. Esping-Andersen and M. Regini (eds), *Why Deregulate Labour Markets*. Oxford: Oxford University Press, pp. 66–98.

Fernández Rodríguez, C.J. and Martínez Lucio, M. (2013) 'Narratives, myths and prejudice in understanding employment systems: the case of rigidities, dismissals and flexibility in Spain', *Economic and Industrial Democracy*, 34(2): 313–336.

Friedman, M. (1968) 'The role of monetary policy', *American Economic Review*, March: 1–17.

Garrahan, P. and Stewart, P. (1992) *The Nissan Enigma*. London: Mansell.

Gonzalez Rodriguez, C.J. (2014) 'The learning environment and politics of globalisation: consultants and business schools between standardization and rhetoric', in M. Martínez Lucio (ed.), *IHRM: An Employment Relations Perspective*. London: Sage, pp. 181–200.

Greenwood, M. and De Cieri, H. (2007) 'Stakeholder theory and the ethicality of human resource management', in A.H. Pinnington, R.E. Macklin and T. Campbell (eds), *Human Resource Management: Ethics and Employment*. Oxford: Oxford University Press, pp. 119–136.

Guest, D. (1990) 'Human resource management and the American dream', *Journal of Management Studies*, 27(4): 377–397.

Hall, S. (1988) *The Hard Road to Renewal*. London: Verso.

Heller, F. (2002) 'What next? More critique of consultants, gurus and managers', in T. Clark and R. Fincham (eds), *Critical Consulting: New Perspectives on the Management Advice Industry*. Oxford: Blackwell, pp. 206–271.

Jessop, B. (1990) *State Theory*. Oxford: Polity.

Jessop, B. (2002) *The Future of the Capitalist State*. Cambridge: Polity.

Keenoy, T. (1990) 'HRM: a case of wolf in sheep's clothing', *International Journal of Human Resource Management*, 11(5): 4–10.

Klein, N. (2007) *The Shock Doctrine*. London: Penguin.

Kurdlebusch, A. (2002) 'Multinationals and the rise of variable pay in Germany', *European Journal of Industrial Relations*, 8(3): 325–349.

Legge, K. (2002) 'On knowledge, business consultants and the selling of total quality management', in T. Clark and R. Fincham (eds), *Critical Consulting: New Perspectives on the Management Advice Industry*. Oxford: Blackwell, pp. 74–92.

Lillie, N. and Martínez Lucio, M. (2004) Varieties of unionism: strategies for union revitalization in a globalizing economy', in C. Frege and J. Kelly (eds), *Labour Movement Revitalization in Comparative Perspective*. Oxford: Oxford University Press, pp. 159–180.

MacKenzie, R. and Martínez Lucio, M. (2005) 'The realities of regulatory change: Beyond the fetish of deregulation', *Sociology*, 39(3): 499–517.

Martínez Lucio, M. (2007) '¿Neoliberalismo y neoconservadurismo interrumpido? El porqué de la existencia de una tradición crítica en las escuelas de dirección de empresas británicas', in C. Fernandez (ed.), *Estudios Sociales de la Organización: El Giro PostModerno*. Madrid: Siglo VeintiUno, pp. 235–268.

Martínez Lucio, M. (2008) 'The organization of human resource strategies: narratives and power in understanding labour management in a context of change', in Stewart Clegg (ed.), *Oxford Handbook of Organisational Behaviour*. Oxford: Oxford University Press, pp. 323–339.

Martínez Lucio, M. and MacKenzie, R. (2004) 'Unstable boundaries? Evaluating the "new regulation" within employment relations', *Economy and Society*, 33(1): 77–97.

Martínez Lucio, M. and Weston, S. (1994) 'New management practices in a multinational corporation: the restructuring of worker representation and rights?', *Industrial Relations Journal*, 25(2): 110–121.

Mueller, F. and Purcell, J. (1992) 'The Europeanization of manufacturing and the decentralization of bargaining: multinational', *International Journal of Human Resource Management*, 3(2): 15–34.

O'Shea, J. and Madigan, C. (1997) *Dangerous Company: The Consulting Powerhouses and Businesses They Save and Ruin*. New York: Times Business.

Peck, J. (1996) *Workplace: The Social Regulation of Labour Markets*. New York: Guilford Press.

Picciotto, S. (1999) 'Introduction: what rules for the world economy', in S. Picciotto and R. Mayne (eds), *Regulating International Business: Beyond Liberalisation*. Basingstoke: Macmillan and Oxfam, pp. 1–28.

Pinnington, A.H. and Hammersley, G.C. (1997) 'Quality circles under the new deal at Land Rover', *Employee Relations*, 19(5): 415–429.

Pinnington, A.H., Macklin, R.E. and Campbell, T. (2007) 'Introduction', in A.H. Pinnington, R.E. Macklin and T. Campbell (eds), *Human Resource Management: Ethics and Employment*. Oxford: Oxford University Press, pp. 1–22.

Regini, M. (2000) 'The dilemmas of labour market regulation', in G. Esping-Andersen and M. Regini (eds), *Why De-regulate Labour Markets*. Oxford: Oxford University Press, pp. 11–29.

Risse, T., Ropp, S.C. and Sikkink, K. (eds) (1999) *The Power of Human Rights: International Norms and Domestic Change*. Cambridge: Cambridge University Press.

Rubery, J. (2011) 'Reconstruction amid deconstruction: or why we need more of the social in European social models', *Work, Employment and Society*, 25(4): 658–674.

Smith, J., Pagnuncco, T. and Lopez, G.A. (1998) 'Globalising human rights: the work of transnational human rights NGOs in the 1990s', *Human Rights Quarterly*, 20(2): 379–412.

Stewart, P. (1996) *Beyond Japanese Management*. London: Taylor and Francis.

Stiglitz, J. (2006) *Making Globalization Work*. London: Penguin.

Thomas, N.H. (2007) 'Global capitalism, the anti-globalisation movement and the Third World', *Capital and Class*, 92 (Summer): 45–80.

Whitley, R., Morgan E. and Moen, E. (2005) *Changing Capitalisms? Internationalisation, Institutional Change and Systems of Economic Organization*. Oxford: Oxford University Press.

Wills, J. (1998) 'Taking on the Cosmocorps: experiments in transnational labor organization', *Economic Geography*, 74: 111–130.

Human Resource Management in Cross-Border Mergers and Acquisitions

Vladimir Pucik, Ingmar Björkman, Paul Evans and Günter K. Stahl

Contents

Learning objectives

After reading this chapter you will be able to:

- Understand the impact of cultural differences on M&A performance
- Master the logic behind different approaches to cross-border post-merger integration

- Identify which cultural and people issues are particularly critical to the success or failure of mergers and acquisitions
- See the importance of HRM in executing international M&A strategies

Chapter outline

The chapter reviews prior research dealing with integration processes in cross-border M&As and then considers the meaning and strategic logic of cultural integration. Major HRM challenges occurring at different stages of the M&A are discussed and conclusions made on the implications for research and practice.

1 Introduction

Mergers and acquisitions have become an increasingly popular strategy for achieving corporate growth and diversification, and there has been a dramatic growth in M&As in the global marketplace during the last two decades. During this period the global profile of M&As has changed. One significant shift is that the proportion of cross-border M&As increased from less than 30 per cent in 2000 to nearly a half of the total value of M&As worldwide a decade later.

The ultimate driver of cross-border M&A activity is the increase in global competition and the corresponding erosion of national boundaries. Companies have followed their customers as they respond to the pressures of obtaining scale in a rapidly consolidating global economy. In combination with other trends, such as increased corporate restructuring, reduced trade barriers, easier access to global pools of capital, and access to new markets and specialized resources, globalization has spurred an unprecedented surge in cross-border M&As (Finkelstein, 1999; Shimizu et al., 2004; Stahl and Javidan, 2009). Even if M&A fever subsides whenever the global economy cools off – such as after the dot.com boom ended in 2000 and during the global financial crisis of 2008 – more M&A deals can be expected in the long run. Another important change in the worldwide profile is that more M&As (about a fifth of the total value) are now carried out within Asia and by Asian firms (Evans et al., 2011). Again, this trend is expected to continue.

Extensive research has been conducted on the performance of M&As. Much of the early research was conducted by consulting firms and investment banks but there is now also a large and rapidly growing body of academic research on the topic. Several early non-academic studies suggested that only a minority of the deals achieved the promised financial results (Zweig, 1995; A.T. Kearney, 1999; KPMG, 1999). Subsequent academic research (King et al., 2004; Moeller and Schlingemann, 2005; Dobbs et al., 2006) and consulting reports are more positive – for example, it was reported that 31 per cent of deals created value while 26 per cent reduced value (KPMG, 2006). In other words, some M&As are successful, some have little effect on the performance of the acquiring firm, and some are disasters for the buyer, and specifically its owners. The sellers virtually always emerge as winners as the buyer typically pays a significant premium for the target. When the buyer does overpay, no amount of post-merger integration skill can bring back the value lost when the deal was signed. However, many companies, such as Cisco and GE in the US, AXA or Unilever in Europe, Mexican CEMEX, or Teva in Israel – the world's largest generic drug company – have become very experienced and effective in managing M&As. For every troubled mega-deal that attracts publicity, there will be many small acquisitions that are substantially more successful.

M&A failures are often due to problems of integrating the different cultures and workforces of the combined firms (Cartwright and Cooper, 1996; Schweiger and Lippert, 2005; Marks and Mirvis, 2010; Stahl and Sitkin, 2010). Problems are often exacerbated when M&As occur between companies based in different countries. Cross-border M&As involve unique challenges as countries have different legal systems and regulatory requirements, accounting standards, employment systems, and so on (Child et al., 2001; Aguilera and Dencker, 2004; Shimizu et al., 2004). In addition to obstacles created by differences in the broader institutional environment, cultural differences in management styles and business norms as well as the often unanticipated challenges of communicating across long distances, can undermine the success of M&As that otherwise have a sound strategic and financial fit – along with problems arising from different communication styles, and, in some instances, cultural chauvinism and xenophobia (Olie, 1990; Vaara, 2003; Goulet and Schweiger, 2006).

For example, the poor performance of DaimlerChrysler, one of the most talked-about cross-border mergers in the recent past, is often attributed to a culture clash that resulted in major integration problems (Vlasic and Stertz, 2000; Epstein, 2004; Kühlmann and Dowling, 2005). Differences between Daimler and Chrysler in management philosophy, compensation systems and decision-making processes caused friction between members of senior management, while lower level employees fought over issues such as dress code, working hours and smoking on the job. Language also became an issue. While most managers on the Daimler side could speak some English, not all were able to do so with the ease and accuracy that is needed for effective working relationships. And among the Chrysler managers and employees, few had any knowledge of German. Cases like these highlight the need for sharper insights into the cultural aspects of international M&As. Considering that after a separation from Daimler and acquisition by Fiat, the 'new' Chrysler is reporting record profits, we need better answers to questions such as how much of the tension and conflict that emerged in the Daimler–Chrysler merger was due to cultural differences and how much was caused by poor execution of post-merger integration and in particular the neglect of its people-related dimensions.

This chapter begins with a review of prior research dealing with integration processes in cross-border M&As, examining the potentially critical role that cultural differences play in the M&A process. The second part of the chapter focuses on how the meaning of cultural integration depends on the strategic logic behind the merger or acquisition. The third part discusses the key HRM challenges at different stages of the M&A process. The chapter concludes with a discussion of the implications for M&A research and practice.

2 Cultural differences and cross-border M&A performance

It has often been argued that cross-border M&As may be less successful than domestic transactions, largely due to the greater 'cultural distance' (Jemison and Sitkin, 1986), 'cultural misfit' (Weber et al., 1996), 'management style dissimilarity' (Larsson and Finkelstein, 1999) or 'acquisition cultural risk' (David and Singh, 1994) involved in cross-border deals. This logic suggests that achieving organizational fit, mutual understanding and value creation in cross-border M&As is a particularly arduous task due to the problem of 'double-layered acculturation' (Barkema et al., 1996). In addition, at both national and organizational levels, similarities in norms and values facilitate the development of trust (Williams, 2001; Stahl and Sitkin, 2010), which has been shown to be an important factor in post-acquisition success (Björkman et al., 2007).

However, empirical evidence suggests that the fear of cultural differences may be exaggerated. Contrary to the 'cultural distance' hypothesis, much of the subsequent research shows that cross-border M&As are not less successful than domestic transactions (for reviews, see Schoenberg, 2000; Schweiger and Goulet, 2000; Teerikangas and Very, 2006; Stahl and Voigt, 2008). In fact, there is some evidence that the success rate of cross-border deals may even be higher (Bleeke et al., 1993; KPMG, 1999; Larsson and Finkelstein, 1999; Bertrand and Zitouna, 2008; Chakrabarti et al., 2009). One source of evidence comes from studies that examined the impact of cultural distance on M&A performance. While some studies found that cultural differences had a negative effect on M&A performance (e.g. Datta, 1991; Chatterjee et al., 1992; Weber, 1996), others found a positive effect (e.g. Very et al., 1996; Larsson and Risberg, 1998; Morosini et al., 1998).

A number of reasons have been suggested for these contradictory findings. One explanation is that there tend to be greater complementarities between the parties in international acquisitions (Morosini et al., 1998; Vermeulen and Barkema, 2001; Björkman et al., 2007). Cross-border acquirers often buy companies in related industries – familiar businesses to which they can add value and, conversely, from which they can gain value. For instance, the acquisition of a foreign competitor can give the buyer access to local markets as well as to new products, technologies and local market knowledge. The target may benefit from similar resources and competences from the buyer, while the increased scale and international experience of the combined organization are additional benefits of such mergers. Synergistic benefits most often arise when the level of cultural distance is moderate so that, on the one hand, there will be sufficient differences to create room for mutual learning and synergy realization; but on the other hand, the differences are not so high that cognitive and normative gaps between the merging organizations hamper transferring complementary capabilities and skills (Björkman et al., 2007).

Also, companies that acquire internationally often have prior M&A experience, learning from their mistakes and implementing processes that enable them to execute cross-border deals more and more effectively (Pucik and Evans, 2004). Higher cultural distance can also help members of merging organizations become psychologically prepared for the upcoming changes and challenges. Weber et al. (1996: 1223) note that individuals tend to make several 'anticipatory adjustments' to their behaviour since they 'expect differences and the changes related to those differences, and therefore are less likely to resist them'. This effect is also corroborated by the so-called psychic distance paradox, according to which the perceived similarity between psychically close countries may hide unexpected and unforeseen barriers to successful M&A (O'Grady and Lane, 1996). Related to the previous point, it may be that the more overt cross-cultural dimensions of such deals lead buyers to pay more attention to the softer, less tangible, but critical human resource aspects of M&A management (Morosini et al., 1998; Björkman et al., 2007).

Larsson and Risberg (1998) found higher degrees of acculturation (defined as the development of jointly shared meanings that foster cooperation between the merging firms), lower levels of employee resistance and a higher realization of synergy in cross-border M&As in comparison to domestic deals. Acculturation and synergy were particularly high in cross-border acquisitions that were characterized by strong differences in organizational culture – culture clash – a finding that directly contradicts the cultural distance hypothesis. They argue that, in contrast to domestic M&As, where organizational culture differences tend to be neglected, the presence of more obvious national cultural differences may increase the awareness of the significance of such cultural factors in the integration process. They conclude that 'cross-border M&A may not only be "cursed" with additional culture clashes but also be "blessed" with a higher propensity for culturally aware selection and integration management' (Larsson and Risberg, 1998: 40).

Other authors have offered additional explanations for why cultural differences in M&As, under some circumstances, can be an asset rather than a liability. Morosini and colleagues (1998), in a study of cross-border acquisitions, found that national cultural distance enhanced post-acquisition performance by providing access to the target's and/or the acquirer's diverse set of routines and repertoires embedded in national culture. In a study of acculturative stress in European cross-border M&As, Very and colleagues (1996) found that cultural differences elicited perceptions of attraction rather than stress, depending on the nationalities of the buying and acquiring firms. Consistent with the findings of Morosini and colleagues (1998) and of Larsson and Risberg (1998), they concluded that the cultural problems associated with integrating acquisitions may be amplified in domestic rather than cross-national settings: 'Acculturative stress is a complex phenomenon, sometimes influenced by cultural differences, but not necessarily in the expected direction' (Very et al., 1996: 103). Finally, Dikova and Sahib (2013) explain the positive stock reactions to acquisitions in culturally distant countries by acquirers with extensive international experience in terms of their learning about how to recognize and deal with cultural issues.

Beyond cultural difference

In summary, there is evidence that cross-border M&As, under some circumstances at least, can be more successful than domestic deals, and that the inherent cultural differences can be as much of an asset as a liability. Indeed, results from a recent study of 800 cross-border acquisitions suggest that these may perform better in the long run if the acquirer and the target come from countries that are culturally more disparate (Chakrabarti et al., 2009), reinforcing the conclusion that the cultural distance hypothesis provides too simplified a view of the cultural processes involved in international M&As.

Consistent with a 'process perspective' on acquisitions (Jemison and Sitkin, 1986; Haspeslagh and Jemison, 1991), research suggests that M&A outcomes depend heavily on the strategic logic behind the merger as well as the management of the integration process (Evans et al., 2011). Whether cultural differences have a positive or negative impact on M&A performance is likely to depend on the nature and extent of the cultural differences, the interventions chosen to manage these differences and the integration approach that is adopted. Here, the research on the impact of culture in cross-border M&As offers two important conclusions.

First, it is important to distinguish between different levels of culture. For example, in a related acquisition that may need a high degree of business integration, cultural differences can create tensions that make integration more difficult. However, these differences are more likely to be due to differences in organizational than national culture (Stahl and Voigt, 2008). In a recent acquisition of a French-owned global business by an American firm, what mattered for the integration in China to be successful was not the difference between the Americans and the French, but between the 'Beijing' and 'Shanghai' cultures of the two local affiliates to be merged. Also, organization cultures differ widely within countries – not all American firms are like GE, not all German firms are like Daimler. Second, the nature of the deal matters (Chakrabarti et al., 2009). Cultural differences were found to be positively associated with post-acquisition performance in M&As that required lower integration, probably due to increased opportunities for mutual learning (Stahl and Voigt, 2008).

In today's global business environment, where strategic imperatives drive many potential M&A deals forward, companies no longer have the luxury of avoiding potential deals on the grounds of cultural issues. The proper response to cultural differences between buyer and target is not to avoid deals where there is a risk of culture clash but to manage and mitigate the risks. This requires disaggregating imprecisely defined cultural issues into discrete, manageable elements. Most of these are connected to the management of people. In this context, Evans and colleagues (2011) observed that cross-border M&As promote some convergence in HRM policies and practices towards accepted 'best practice', such as performance-related compensation and team-based work organization.

Successful acquirers are not afraid of cultural differences – they learn how to manage them. When Lincoln Electric – a company well-known for its unique culture resulting from a combination of financial incentives with strict performance management and job security – first attempted to expand abroad through acquisitions, it failed. According to the company's CEO at that time, a lack of understanding of how local norms and values may inhibit implementation of Lincoln's management approach was one of the main obstacles (Hastings, 1999). However, two decades later, cross-border acquisitions have become an integral part of Lincoln's aggressive global strategy, as the company mastered the task of adapting its core management practices to local social and institutional environments (Siegel and Zepp Larson, 2009).

3 What does integration mean?

In a merger or acquisition, the concept of 'integration' has different meanings depending on the strategic logic behind the merger in question. Most companies use the term 'integration' to describe the post-merger activities designed to bind the two companies. But what happens in many integration processes is actually assimilation, a process that is fundamentally different from 'true' integration – indeed, the vast majority of so-called mergers are in fact acquisitions.

The logic of assimilation is simple: make the acquired company just like the purchaser. However, companies are sensitive to public perceptions and do not want to be seen as a foreign bully, and so they are often hesitant to proclaim their objective of assimilating the acquired firm, fearing that it may compromise the deal. This frequently creates confusion and mistrust that makes the assimilation process more difficult. In contrast, GE Capital, the financial services arm of General Electric offers blunt advice to the management of firms that it acquires around the world: 'If you do not want to change, don't put yourself for sale.' GE makes it clear to the acquired company that it now has to play by GE's rules, and provides a framework for guiding the process of integration and formation of new relationships.

In the case of true integration, the emphasis is on capturing hidden synergies by sharing and leveraging capabilities. Sometimes companies may decide to establish a new identity as with Novartis, which was formed through the merger of Ciba-Geigy and Sandoz in 1996 to create a global life sciences giant. Both approaches to M&A implementation have their merits. The choice between assimilation and true integration depends on the strategic intent behind the acquisition and the desired cultural characteristics of the new organization. Choosing an approach that does not match with the strategy or the desired cultural outcomes can significantly reduce the value created by the acquisition.

Christensen and his colleagues argue that the integration strategy should be determined by the purpose of the acquisition. If the objective is to improve the current business model's effectiveness, the resources of the acquired company should be absorbed into the acquirer. In contrast, if the company is bought for its business model, then it is better to keep the model intact, by operating it separately (Christensen et al., 2011). For example, although GE's preference for a quick and full integration is well known, when GE Medical acquired one of their local low-cost competitors in China, a decentralized, local approach allowed the acquired company to preserve its capability to compete in the local market, but also to enter new product segments in the developed world (Immelt et al., 2009).

A complementary way of formulating the acquisition logic, as shown in Figure 8.1, is to focus on the cultural 'end-state' and the path to reach this (Mirvis and Marks, 1994). What kind of culture is desired for the new entity, and how much change will be required within both acquiring and acquired companies in order to achieve the goal? When no cultural change is desired in the acquired company, then it can be considered as a preservation acquisition. When a large amount of change in the acquired company

Absorption Acquired company conforms to acquirer – cultural assimilation		**Transformation** Both companies find new ways of operating – cultural transformation
	Best of Both Additive from both sides – Cultural integration	
Preservation Acquired company retains its independence – cultural autonomy		**Reverse Merger** Unusual case of acquired company dictating terms – cultural assimilation

Degree of Change in Acquired Company — High / Low

Degree of Change in Acquiring Company — Low / High

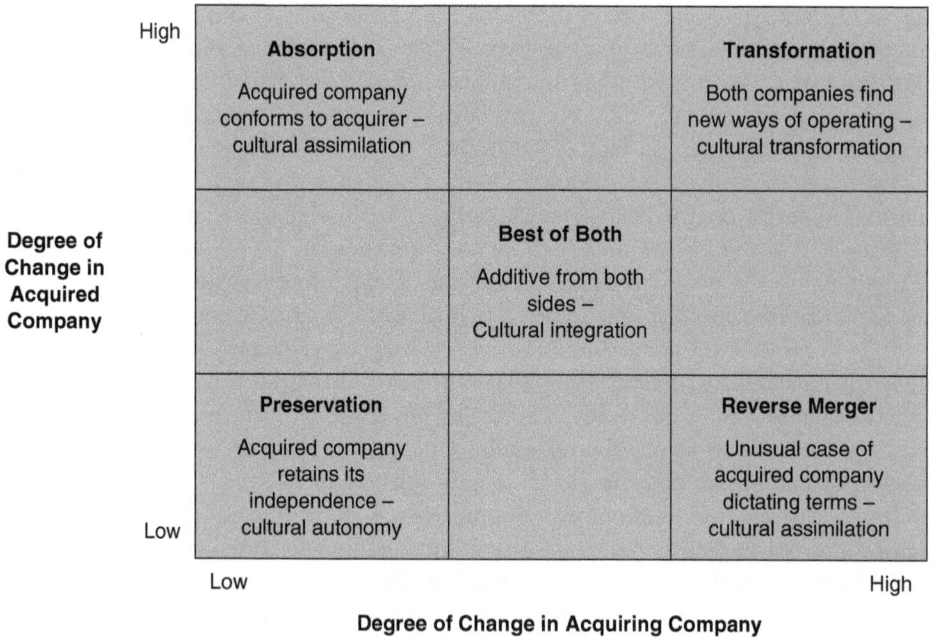

Figure 8.1   Strategies for post-merger outcomes

Source: reprinted with kind permission from the authors (Mirvis and Marks, 1994)

is expected but with relatively little change for the acquirer, then absorption is the most likely path. When major cultural change is expected in both entities then the result is a cultural transformation, while the selective combination of the most appealing features of the two cultures is often described as a 'best of both' acquisition. In rare cases, the culture of the acquirer is blended into that of the acquired firm in a reverse merger.

Preservation acquisitions

When a deal is announced, the official press release often contains a statement that the acquired company will preserve its independence and cultural autonomy. This often occurs not only in cross-border deals when explicit 'outsider' control may be resented, but also when one of the rationales behind the merger is to secure talented management or other soft skills (such as speed of product development) and to retain them; or when conformance to the rules and systems of the acquiring company could be detrimental to the acquired company's competitive advantage, as in the GE Medical case above.

The 'preservation' approach is also often favoured by companies from emerging countries acquiring firms in the developed markets who possess superior product capabilities or valuable brands, such as when Tata Motors bought Jaguar Land Rover – then a loss making subsidiary of Ford. Tata ownership provided much needed capital and strategic stability, allowing Jaguar to complete a successful turnaround.

The key to success here is to protect the boundary of the new subsidiary from unwarranted and disruptive intrusions from the parent, though this can be hard to ensure. However, even with the best of intentions, there is a danger of creeping assimilation – while the buyer allows the new unit to work in its own way, there is encouragement to develop systems and processes that match those of the parent organization. Due to operational pressures, most stand-alone acquisitions do not last (Killing, 2003). When Air France acquired KLM, the two companies agreed to maintain separate brands and identities for eight years, but now, while KLM may appear independent to the outside world, some functions at least are being integrated into a common corporate centre organization (Bouchikhi and Kimberly, 2012).

Absorption acquisitions

This kind of acquisition is fairly straightforward, and it is probably most common when there are differences in size and sophistication between the two partners involved in the deal. The acquired company conforms to the acquirer's way of working and the focus is on full cultural assimilation. Such deals are particularly common when the acquired company is performing poorly, or when the market conditions force consolidation. The majority of the synergies may be related to cost cutting, most likely on the side of the acquired company, although some may come from improvements in systems and processes introduced by the acquiring firm. The key to success is to choose the target well and move fast so as to reduce uncertainty and capture the available synergies.

The logic of absorption is simple. However, terms like absorption or assimilation carry a pejorative meaning in the minds of many; and assimilation may at times be an ugly process. Many companies for reasons mentioned earlier do not explicitly declare their absorption objective in order not to compromise the deal. But when the assimilation is what is actually intended – and strategically desirable – this 'double-speak' creates confusion, mistrust and makes the process more difficult. As mentioned earlier, the well-known fiasco of the Daimler–Chrysler integration is perhaps the most striking and expensive example.

Not pushing for absorption can destroy value. When Japan's Bridgestone purchased US-based Firestone, it refrained from making significant changes in the acquired organization, even though the acquisition was losing money and the company was essentially bankrupt – not considered worthy of purchase except by the management of the Japanese company who adopted a long-term 20 year horizon on the acquisition. Bridgestone did not want to be seen as a foreign intruder taking over a venerable national institution. In reality, many local middle managers were looking forward to the takeover, expecting that their new owners would tackle both the unions and the entrenched old-style of top management – so when nothing happened, they left in droves. Faced with growing losses, Tokyo finally moved in several years later to 'clean up the mess'. But it was too late: Firestone was by then too thin on local talent, drifting for years from crisis to crisis at a heavy cost to the parent company.

When managed well, absorption can be of benefit to the employees of the acquired firm. This is especially true when these employees are afraid of losing their jobs and see the new owner as helping them to remain competitive; or when they are unhappy with the management style of the old leaders and see the acquiring company as having a more progressive culture; or there again when employees see other positive outcomes associated with the acquisition (such as better pay and benefits, better career or more prestige). Cisco, for example, is well known for buying smaller companies to gain access to their technology and R&D talent, assimilating them into the Cisco culture. During the post-acquisition process of assimilation, it strives to retain most of the employees, including top management. Here, the emphasis is on finding targets that will match Cisco's way of managing the business, thus increasing the likelihood of cultural compatibility.

Sometimes, assimilation is a gradual process. When companies such as Bosch or ABB first entered China two decades ago, the only path forward was through joint ventures with local firms. As the legal environment changed, most of them were converted into 100 per cent owned affiliates, but by the time the conversion occurred, the employees were already fully familiar with the culture and work practices of their Western parent – and could also see the full benefits of being a part of an international firm.

Reverse mergers

This is the mirror opposite of assimilation, although it does not happen that frequently. In a reverse merger, the organization that makes the purchase usually hopes to gain capabilities from the acquired company. Recently, more and more Chinese firms have attempted to buy companies in Europe in order to acquire capabilities to move the whole company towards higher value-added products, or to achieve an 'instant' global reach. Because of its relative size, Geely's acquisition of Volvo is probably the best-known example. Sometimes the acquired company is even made into a business unit that then absorbs the parallel unit from the acquiring firm. When Nokia, for instance, bought a high-tech firm in California for its R&D knowledge, it gave the new unit global responsibilities, which meant that part of the business in Finland now reports to California.

Sometimes, the reverse merger is unintended. A few years ago, a French metal products company acquired its smaller British competitor. Today, to the surprise of many, the management style and systems of the new company resemble the culture of the acquired firm. What happened? When the two companies merged, it was easier for everyone to adopt the explicit and transparent systems of the British firm, more suitable for cross-border business, than to emulate the ambiguous and subtle rules embedded in the French organization. If the practices of the company that has been acquired are more clear and transparent, it is quite possible that they will prevail.

Best of both

This intriguing option is meant to be the 'best of both' worlds and is often described as a 'merger of equals'. This holds out the promise of no pain since in theory it adopts best practices from both sides and integrates them. There are, however, very few examples of such mergers that have succeeded since it is very difficult to undertake. The strength of a culture comes from the internal consistency of the practices, which may evaporate when the best parts from different organizations are put together (see Chapter 4).

Another danger in the 'best of both' situation is that the integration process may become too political and time consuming. Who decides what is 'best'? When the Swedish bank Nordbanken and the Finnish bank Merita were combined in a 'merger of equals' in the late 1990s, the Finnish employees coined and used the phrase 'Best practices are West practices' – 'West' meaning 'Swedish', as Sweden is located west of Finland (Vaara et al., 2003).

The process of decision making can be excessively complex, plagued by inconsistencies. If both companies declare that the merger is to be one of equals, does that mean that top management is split 50/50, even if the real split is 80/20 in terms of competences? The controversy surrounding the Daimler–Chrysler merger is a visible example of this dilemma. Without strong mutual respect for the knowledge and skills of each company, the 'best of both' strategy cannot work.

The key to success is the fairness of the process. The test of the 'best of both' approach may be the ability to retain the people who do not get the top jobs. Having similar cultures helps to keep everyone together. The AstraZeneca and Exxon/Mobil mergers have proceeded relatively smoothly because the similarities were more pronounced than the differences. The new groups have been relatively successful at identifying the best practices from each side, as well as having a balance of top management from the two firms.

Whether the final outcome is a 'balance' of both is also determined by the direction the merged company decides to take. When Brahma from Brazil and Interbrew from Belgium merged to create InBev (now called AB Inbev, and the world's largest brewer after a hostile 'absorption' acquisition of Anheuser-Busch), the 'best of both' was the guiding principle. However, Brahma had superior capabilities in managing a globally integrated business, while the multi-local cultural heritage of Interbrew did not fit the new strategy. Consequently, the top management team that finally emerged consisted of 11 executives who came from Brahma (including the CEO), and only two who came from Interbrew (as well as several newcomers).

Transformation

In contrast with 'best of both' acquisitions that take the existing cultures as they are, both companies in a transformation merger are hoping to use the merger to break sharply with the past. Merger or acquisition can be the catalyst for trying to do things differently, for reinventing oneself. This can focus on the way in which the company is run, what business it is in, or both. When Novartis was created by the merger of two Swiss-based pharmaceutical firms, the proposed management style for the new company reflected the desired transformation: 'We will listen more than Sandoz, but decide more than Ciba.'

For a long time, the creation of ABB through the merger of Asea and Brown Boveri, was considered an archetype of transformational merger, with its successes and failures (Barham and Heimer, 1998). More recently, the merger of the two pharmaceutical companies Astra and Zeneca into AstraZeneca could be described as a case of transformation through M&A (Killing, 2004), as was Lenovo's acquisition of IBM's money-losing PC business – remaking the combined company into a global leader (Stahl and Koester, 2013).

This kind of merger is complex and difficult to implement. It requires a full commitment to strong leadership at the top to avoid getting trapped in endless debates while the ongoing business suffers. In Lenovo's case, several senior Chinese executives, including the CEO, relocated to the US in order to understand better the culture of the acquired business. The company language is now English as half of the top executive team (now located back in Beijing) are former IBM managers or recruited outside of China.

Speed is essential, with top management in the merging companies using the time period immediately after the merger announcement to carry out major changes. Like the 'best of both' strategy, the transformation strategy has a better chance of success if key people from both parties are excited by the vision of the merger leading to a new leading company with superior capabilities (Killing, 2003).

Finally, another complicating factor in international acquisitions is that there will often be parts of the organization where a particular approach to the merger makes sense and others where it does not. There are few M&As that fit neatly into the assimilation, integration or other categories. For some countries or regions, or for some parts of the business, a full assimilation may be the best approach; in other parts of the firm, a reverse merger might be a more appropriate strategy.

4 Managing cross-border integration: the HRM implications

There is no shortage of evidence that attention to people and to cultural issues is one of the most critical elements in achieving the cross-border acquisition strategy. In an early McKinsey study of international M&A, the four top ranked factors identified by responding firms as contributing to acquisition success all related to people: retention of key talent (identified by 76 per cent of responding firms), effective communication (71 per cent), executive retention (67 per cent) and cultural integration (51 per cent) (Kay and Shelton, 2000). According to a subsequent consulting report, published nearly a decade later, the problems remained the same. Differences in organizational culture (50 per cent) and people integration (35 per cent) were top of the list of M&A challenges – in fact, four of the six top issues were people related (Torborg et al., 2008).

In fact, it is hard to find an acquisition where people issues do not matter (Schmidt, 2002). In particular, when the objective of the acquisition is to establish a new geographic presence, then managing people, communication and cross-cultural issues are top of the list of priorities. When the aim is to acquire new technology or to buy market share or competencies, retaining key technical employees or account managers is the principal challenge. When the objective of the deal is consolidation, dealing effectively with redundancies at all levels is the dominant concern.

Based on these observations, it may seem natural that the HR function should play a significant role in all phases of the acquisition. The acquisition process is typically divided into stages – the initial planning stage, including due diligence; the closing of the deal; and the post-merger integration stage. Yet while human resource management issues tend to receive attention during the last – implementation – phase, the overall influence that HR has during the whole acquisition process is patchy, even though many of the problems of merger integration stem from failure to consider these issues early on. In addition, many companies have neither the resources nor the know-how to give this HR area the priority it deserves (KPMG, 1999: 15).

As suggested earlier, one of the reasons why cross-border mergers may be successful, despite their complexity, is that the people, cultural and integration challenges are more obvious, leading management to pay close attention to them at all stages in the acquisition process. We focus here on those cultural and people issues that seem to be particularly critical to the success or failure of mergers and acquisitions (see Evans et al. (2011) for an extended discussion of the issues in this section):

- assessing culture
- undertaking a human capital audit and selecting the management team
- effective communication
- retaining talent
- creating the new culture
- managing the transition.

Assessing culture in the due diligence phase

The purpose of cultural assessment is to evaluate factors that may influence the organizational fit, to understand the future cultural dynamics as the two organizations merge, and to prepare a plan for how the cultural issues should be addressed if the deal goes forward. Before a valid cultural integration strategy can be developed on the part of the acquiring company, or between the two merger partners, differences and similarities of the cultures of both companies must be well understood. This crucial step is often neglected, sometimes even ignored, in most M&A planning processes.

Metaphorically, cultural understanding has often been likened to an iceberg (Schein, 1987; Black et al., 1999). The tip of the iceberg, visible to the observer, does not reflect the way in which it is connected to a much larger mass beneath the ocean's surface. Similarly, the external manifestations of cultural dynamics – artefacts and behaviours – do not fully reflect the dynamics behind the scenes that create and sustain them. One common mistake that is often made in the cultural due diligence process is that measures used to delineate the culture are superficial in nature (such as the number of levels in the organizational structure, the type of employee benefit programmes, level of detail in policy manuals) and do not adequately plumb its depths (Mendenhall et al., 2001).

Before moving ahead on any deal, GE routinely conducts a behavioural and cultural assessment of the takeover target, focusing on possible business and cultural barriers to a successful integration, such as possible resistance to GE management style (Marks and Mirvis, 2010). Evans and colleagues (2011) suggest that cultural due diligence teams must focus their efforts on data collection to extract the 'deep knowledge' of the culture. Cultural due diligence teams need to ask questions and find answers to questions such as:

- What are their core beliefs about what it takes to win?
- What drives their business strategy? Tradition or innovation?
- Is the company short-term or long-term in its outlook and execution of initiatives?

- How much risk is the company used to accepting?
- Is the company results-oriented or process-oriented?
- How is power distributed throughout the company?
- How are decisions made: consultation, consensus or authority?
- How is information managed and shared?

Questions of this nature require the due diligence team to probe into the normative structure, core values and assumptions, and the core philosophy of the company itself in order to understand the company from a holistic cultural perspective. In addition, the culture of a company does not exist in a vacuum. It is usually embedded in a specific industry and it reflects as well the regional and national culture (Schneider et al., 2003). The cultural due diligence team must assess not only the company itself but also the context in which the company exists, with its different cultural strands.

Finally, the due diligence team must not only pay attention to the target's or potential partner's culture, but to its own culture as well. Cultural assessment is not just a question of assessing the other company's culture; it is also a matter both of having a clear culture oneself and understanding it. The criteria used in cultural assessment of the target will to a great extent reflect the cultural attributes of the buyer. The 'know thyself' adage applies equally well to companies as it does to people.

Undertaking a human capital audit and selecting the management team

There are two dimensions to the human capital audit (Pucik and Evans, 2004). One dimension is preventive, focused on liabilities such as pension plan obligations, outstanding grievances and employee litigation. It also includes comparing the compensation policies, benefits and labour contracts of both firms. The other dimension is focused on talent identification, and in the long run it is probably more critical to the success of the acquisition. A number of facets on this are important – ensuring that the target company has the talent necessary to execute the acquisition strategy, identifying which individuals are critical to sustaining the value of the deal, and assessing any potential weaknesses in the management cadre. It is also important to understand the motivation and incentive structure, and to highlight any differences that may impact retention. Finally, understanding the structure of the organization means not just reporting lines but clarifying who is who.

Here are some examples of questions to consider (Chaudhuri and Tabrizi, 1999; Pucik and Evans, 2004):

- What kind of employees creates most value for the organization?
- What unique skills do the employees have?
- How does the target's talent compare to the quality of our own?
- What is the background of the management team?

- What are the reporting relationships?
- What will happen if some of the management team leave?
- What is the compensation philosophy?
- How much pay is at risk at various levels of the firm?

Getting access to talent data may take some effort, and many companies ignore the talent question in the early stages of the M&A process. They do not take the time to define the skills that are critical to the success of the deal, relying instead on financial performance data as a proxy. Early assessment helps to pinpoint the potential risk factors so the acquiring company can develop strategies to address them as early as possible. In the case of Chinese electronics giant TCL, it acquired a struggling French competitor Thompson in 2004, only to close it three years later. One of the main factors of the failure was a lack of awareness about the challenges the company would face to integrate Thompson's people. As a consequence, TCL was caught unprepared when culture clashes erupted soon after the acquisition (Williamson and Raman, 2011).

Without early assessment, companies may acquire targets with weaker than expected skills or talent that has a high likelihood of departure. The consequence will be delays after the merger announcement in deciding on the structure and management team in the acquired company, which fuels post-merger anxiety and confusion, often prompting the most valuable contributors to exit. At the same time, the audit may also uncover significant weaknesses that may call for recruiting replacement candidates (external local hires or expatriates) to be ready to commence work immediately after closing the deal and speed up decisions about who should stay and who should leave (Harding and Rouse, 2007).

Effective communication

Communication is always a vital part of any process of change, but it is critical in cross-border acquisitions where cultural differences may intensify tensions that stem from misunderstanding and distance. For example, the intention of top managers in an acquired company to stay rather than leave following an acquisition is associated with their positive perceptions of the merger announcement (Krug and Hegerty, 2001). Furthermore, in the design of the communication process there are two additional objectives that are particularly important in any acquisition. On the one hand, communication is intended to alleviate the anxiety and stress that accompany every acquisition, and on the other hand it provides feedback to top management about the progress of the integration process and any potential roadblocks.

Many M&As are shrouded in secrecy during their pre-merger phases, and the ensuing public announcement often triggers shock and anxiety in the workforce and local communities. Rumours of possible layoffs, reassignments and changes can drain employees' energy and productivity. Whereas the employees in the acquiring or dominant partner feel a sense of superiority, victory and power; conversely, feelings of fear, betrayal and anger are relatively common among employees in the acquired or less dominant company especially when the acquirer is a foreign rival.

In the first hundred days of a merger, Mirvis and Marks (1994) argue that certain actions must be taken in order to counter this 'merger syndrome' in employees. First, everyone should appreciate that it is a normal and human response to experience a wide variety of emotions regarding the merger or acquisition. Employees should be helped in developing the necessary coping skills to deal with stress created during major organizational change. Second, information must be honest and transparent. When Daimler's CEO announced the joining of two companies' names to form DaimlerChrysler using the 'merger of equals' metaphor without really meaning it, it raised unrealistic expectation that the acquired firm will retain its autonomy and identity (Bouchikhi and Kimberly, 2012). Unmet expectations then produced cynicism, resistance and poor morale. The merger syndrome with its stress and anxiety is exacerbated when executives guard and delay decisions announcing them often abruptly and only 'as needed'. This fuels an emerging distrust of management's motives, ethics and decision-making effectiveness on the part of employees (Stahl and Sitkin, 2005). Information can be shared in a wide variety of forums: lunch gatherings, company intranets, emails and so forth.

Third, senior management must communicate a positive vision throughout the company, pointing to a new and better future. Combined with symbolic acts that show positive regard for all employees, messages to create a positive image of the new company as it moves ahead are a critical aspect of initial post-merger management. Finally, it is important to involve people at all levels from both companies. Forming cross-border teams to share knowledge, pushing for direct contact to break down stereotypes, and extensive training workshops were some of the initiatives introduced by Carlos Ghosn when attempting to integrate the cultures of Nissan and Renault (Donnelly et al., 2005) in order to dissipate the destructive power of ethnocentric 'us versus them' factions (Stahl and Brannen, 2013).

Retaining talent

Many acquired businesses lose key employees soon after the acquisition, and this is a major contributing factor to the failure of acquisitions. Research evidence from US acquisitions indicates that the probability of executives leaving increases significantly when their firm is acquired by a foreign multinational (Krug and Hegerty, 1997). When insufficient attention is paid to retaining talent, and especially if staff cuts are expected, employees will leave. Head-hunters inevitably move in, and the best will exit first since they have other choices. Given this context, it is not surprising that when Lenovo acquired IBM's PC division, the board of Lenovo's controlling shareholder allowed the company to proceed with the deal if, and only if, it could retain IBM's senior executives to manage the merged enterprise (Harding and Rouse, 2007). But the talent that

Lenovo wanted was not limited to senior executives. When the deal closed, the company offered a job to every IBM employee worldwide, with no obligation to relocate or accept a pay-cut.

Retention of talent is particularly important for firms, such as Lenovo, where the value of the deal lies in the acquisition of intangible assets – the knowledge and skills of the people inside the acquired firm. This is the situation for many such deals in the high technology sector where companies use acquisitions to plug holes in their R&D portfolio or to rapidly build new capabilities (Chaudhuri and Tabrizi, 1999).

This means knowing exactly who the talented people are and why they are essential to the new organization, including identification of valuable employees from the lower levels of the acquired firm. Obtaining this information as part of the human capital audit may not be a simple task; indeed one of the biggest obstacles in international acquisitions is the difference in performance measures and standards. Even if standards are comparable, many companies are not aware of where their talent is; in one study only 16 per cent of surveyed executives believed that their employers could identify their high performers (Michaels et al., 2001). Furthermore, local managers may be protective of their people and therefore be unwilling to provide information about poor performers.

Effective and open communication is the foundation for retaining talent. While financial incentives are also important (stock options, retention bonuses or other incentives given to employees who stay through the integration or until completion of a specific merger-related project), they cannot substitute for a one-on-one relationship with executives from the acquiring firm. Senior management involvement is critical to successful retention. High potential employees in most companies are used to receiving attention from senior management. Without the same treatment from the acquiring company, they question their future and will be more likely to depart. Distance may be an obstacle to be overcome, but it cannot be used as an excuse. When BP acquired Arco, another international oil major, it quickly organized Key Talent Workshops – two-day events to network senior BP executives with Arco's high-potential employees.

Talent retention efforts should not stop after the completion of the first hundred days of integration. Junior employees may find the initial impact of the acquisition to be quite positive, offering them opportunities for responsibility and higher pay (especially when their seniors leave en masse). Even so, many of them will depart later if they do not become integrated into the leadership development of the new parent company (Krug and Hegerty, 2001).

Creating the new culture

Strong and committed leadership is the foundation for successful integration – and for successful change management. Lack of clear vision and the leadership style of top management have consistently topped lists of factors explaining why acquisitions failed to deliver their expected value. Three capabilities are seen as fundamental to the effectiveness of the top leadership: a credible new vision, a sense of urgency and effective communication (Sitkin and Pablo, 2005; Fubini et al., 2006). In a study of M&As in Japan, respondents indicated again and again that creating a sense of urgency around implementing the vision as well as maintaining momentum in driving change are the keys to success (Pucik, 2008).

The role of top management is especially important in large-scale mergers because creation of a new common culture is difficult unless there is some explicit leadership philosophy with values and norms that guide practice and behaviour. To create the new culture of ABB after the cross-border merger of Asea and Brown Boveri in the late 1980s (one of the first large cross-border mergers in Europe), the CEO Percy Barnevik spent three months with the new senior management team defining a policy bible to guide the intended new organization. This was a manual of 'soft' principles such as speed in decision making ('better to be quick and roughly right than slow and completely right') and for conflict management ('you can only kick a conflict upstairs once for arbitration'), as well as 'hard' practices such as the Abacus measurement system that would apply across all units of the newly merged enterprise.

Companies with strong and successful cultures usually impose their culture onto the acquired company. Corporations that grow rapidly through cross-border acquisitions, such as GE, Haier (the leading Chinese appliance maker) or the European consumer goods company Reckitt Benkiser, typically perceive their success as originating from their own culture and the practices based on it. Therefore GE will impart to the acquired company GE's meaning of a performance commitment which is anchored to stretch goals, its underlying business planning process and the way it goes about managing people.

However, as illustrated by Evans and colleagues (2011), acquiring a 'culture' may be part of the reason behind an acquisition. A case in point is the takeover of an Anglo-Saxon competitor by a French multinational that is the global leader in its industry. Top management in the French corporation had known for some time that their own culture had to change, but it was unable to do so organically. The most attractive feature of acquiring its competitor was not the expanded market share but the opportunity to accelerate change in its own company. Senior management recognized that the whole integration process would have to be managed with this aim in mind.

In the process of culture building or cultural assimilation after an acquisition, values and norms have to be translated into behaviours. One model of change implementation argues that it is a four-step process (Beer et al., 1990). It commences with establishing the new roles and responsibilities after the restructuring, ensuring that skilled champions of the desired culture are in place to drive the culture change process. The second step is coaching and training, helping people to develop the desired competences and behaviours. Then, the third step is being prepared and focusing on recruitment, succession planning and rewards. People who are not responding well to the coaching will be replaced, and those who respond ably may be given broader responsibilities. The fourth and final step in the implementation and culture change process is the fine-tuning and formalization of the new system into a coherent, consistent and transparent whole.

The quality of coaching is particularly important for the effectiveness of culture change. Take AXA as an example, a French company that grew in a relatively short time through acquisitions from being a local player in the French insurance industry to become a top global financial services institution. Just as BP, Cisco and GE all do, AXA made no pretence that its acquisitions were mergers, moving quickly to AXA-ise the cultures of the firms it acquired. Managers from companies brought into AXA commented that one of the most helpful tools for them to assimilate quickly into the company was its 360° feedback process. The AXA values were encoded in this appraisal instrument, and to accelerate the process of cultural integration, all managers and professionals in the acquired company participated in feedback workshops. It helped to make the desired culture and values more concrete, identify personal needs for improvement and provide coaching implemented in the AXA way.

Managing the transition

As all acquisitions require some degree of integration (even preservation deals generally require the integration of financial reporting systems), it is important to tailor integration to the purpose of the acquisition and the characteristics of the companies involved. The integration process requires an engaged leadership and often a dedicated integration manager working with a transition team. In most cases, moving with speed is an advantage. A critical part of the process is focusing on those areas where the acquisition can create new value, while maintaining the ongoing business.

Integration manager and transition team

Post-merger integration is always a delicate and complicated process. Who should be responsible for making it happen? After closing, the due diligence team with its deep knowledge of the acquired company disbands or goes on to another deal. Meanwhile, the new management team is not yet fully in place. To avoid the vacuum, companies are increasingly turning to dedicated integration managers supported by transition teams (Marks and Mirvis, 2010). The role of the integration manager is to guide the integration process, making sure that timelines are followed and that key decisions are taken according to the agreed schedule. The first task is to spell out the logic of the new business model and translate this into operational targets. This is important in international acquisitions where 'big picture' statements from the corporate centre may not mean much in a different national and business context. Integration managers should also champion norms and behaviours consistent with new standards, communicate key messages across the new organization and identify new value-adding opportunities (Ashkenas and Francis, 2000; Ashkenas et al., 1998).

An important aspect of the job is helping the acquired company to understand how the new owner operates and what it can offer in terms of capabilities. The integration manager can help the new company take advantage of the owner's existing capabilities and resources, facilitate social connections and assist with essential but intangible aspects such as interpreting a new language and way of doing things. Acquired companies typically do not know how things work in the corporation that now owns them. Moreover the integration manager can likewise help the parent to understand the acquired business and what it can contribute.

A major source of frustration in many deals is not so much what the parent wants the newly acquired unit to do, but what it wants to know. Therefore, another role for the integration manager is that of an information 'gatekeeper' between the two sides, protecting the acquired business from the eager embrace of an owner who unintentionally could undermine what makes the business work. When Nokia acquires small high-tech venture companies, one of the rules is that all requests for information from the parent go to the integration manager. He or she will decide if and how the unit should comply with the request.

In most acquisitions, the integration manager is supported by integration teams and task forces. These teams should have a clear mandate, with targets and accountability for a specific area where integration is required. Since many of these teams are expected to start work on the first day after the acquisition is completed, the identification of potential members should ideally be an outcome of the pre-acquisition due diligence process. HR professionals are often key members of the team because many of the team's activities will have implications for human resource policies and practices.

Who else should be appointed to the transition team? It may be attractive to leverage functional and business unit managers by adding this transition project role to their responsibilities. However, the mixing of line responsibility with transition task-force roles often means that neither is done well. Customers do not like to wait until the transition team reaches agreement. On the other hand, integration teams should be staffed by people with leadership qualities and not by low priority managers or by laggards in the race for line business jobs – they simply will not have the credibility to get the job done successfully. So probably the best staffing approach is to appoint 'up-and-coming' managers, leaving the daily business under the original leadership until the new organization can be created.

Transition teams are most effective when members come from both the acquired and acquiring companies. By facilitating personnel exchange, the transition team can help to develop a better understanding of each other's capabilities. People who are suited for a transition team usually have a mix of functional and interpersonal competencies (including cross-cultural skills), backed up by strong analytical skills. Having an ability to accept responsibility without full authority and being effective in mobilizing resources across organizational boundaries are two competencies that are especially important, and consequently such roles are good development opportunities for those with high potential.

The effective transition team serves as a role model for how the new organization should act. It disseminates the shared vision and makes sure that practices are appropriately aligned with the vision. However, too many task forces and teams will slow things down, creating coordination problems, conflict and confusion. The projects should focus on the integration tasks with high potential savings at low risk, leaving those with greater risk or lower benefits until later. In the process of transition, prioritization is critical.

Moving with speed

Evans and colleagues (2011) observe that most companies with experience in acquisitions recommend rapid implementation of the integration. Creeping changes, uncertainty and anxiety that last for months are debilitating and immediately start to drain value from an acquisition (Ashkenas et al., 1998). While this may seem counterintuitive to some, a problem jeopardizing the success of many acquisitions has been a tendency to restructure too slowly. Even when such delays are motivated by the best of intentions, spending time and resources on giving people time to adjust by not upsetting the old culture, competitors will seize the opportunity to take away the business. Such procrastination and indecision fails to make use of the window of opportunity that occurs for a short period of time immediately after acquisition when the organization is in effect 'unfrozen' – employees expect change and are thus more open to new ways of doing things (Stahl, 2006). As one AstraZeneca executive noted: 'A merger is like an erupting volcano. Everything turns to lava, and lava is fluid. You can mould it and shape it and turn it into new things, but eventually it solidifies. In the period when the lava is molten you have an incredible opportunity to do things differently – take advantage of that situation' (Killing, 2004: 43).

Sometimes, foreign acquirers' fear of cultural backlash slows down the process. At one foreign-owned financial company in Japan, the implementation of several elements of performance-based global HR policies was suspended for two years to give employees a chance to adapt. In retrospect, the company's Japanese CEO thinks this may have been overcautious. 'I think perhaps the grace period could have been a bit shorter. Some people got too comfortable for their own good. I think I may have been a bit too lenient because foreign companies are always criticized for being too harsh, for being vultures' (Pucik, 2008).

The issue of speed is embedded within different contexts (institutional environment, socio-economic context, competitive dynamics, within organization rhythms) and considerations of time itself (Angwin and Savill, 1997; Angwin, 2004, 2007). To give one example, in different national institutional contexts, regulations may determine specific time periods within which actions have to be framed (Morgan, 2007). These frames will affect how HRM takes place and in cross-border transactions may give rise to significant variation in M&A outcome. In other parts of the M&A process, acquiring companies may have much more discretion about determining their own timeframes and the speed at which change may take place, but these will be affected by socio-cultural contexts. The desired speed of change may also be influenced by norms in the business or regional culture of the acquiring firm. A survey of European acquisitions of US high-tech firms in the Silicon Valley reported that speed in integration was one of the key drivers of successful post-merger integration – but also one of the most problematic (Inkpen et al., 2000). The understanding of what is 'quick' or 'fast' among most of the European acquirers (usually large, established companies with entrenched routines and procedures) was very different from the norms of the Valley. This created confusion, frustration and ultimately the loss of market opportunities.

Research indeed shows differences in the speed of the integration process according to the national origins of the acquiring firm. Japanese and Northern European acquirers tend to move cautiously, conscious of potential cultural conflicts (Child et al., 2001). This works well if the approach involves preserving the culture and autonomy of the acquired organization, but it may exacerbate the stress of the transition when expected decisions are not forthcoming, making subsequent changes more difficult to implement.

The other aspect of speed is a focus on delivering quick, visible wins, such as new sales through a joint effort, or improvements based on shared practices. It is important to take time to celebrate each success and to communicate the accomplishments to the whole organization (Kouzes and Posner, 1987; Kotter, 1996). A quick win can motivate target employees because it offers tangible proof that the merger or acquisition was a step in the right direction, and shows that their efforts are appreciated.

Yet speed also has some unintended consequences. Bad decisions made under pressure can be avoided if time is spent on a judicious review of the issues. Conversely, good decisions meet resistance when no time is taken to explain the new business logic. Again, the optimal speed depends on the strategic intent of the acquisition and the desired end-state for the culture of the new organization (Homburg and Bucerius, 2006).

An absorption strategy generally requires more urgency than a 'best of both' approach. When the objective of the acquisition is to acquire knowledge and intellectual capital, the pace of change must be particularly carefully calibrated to minimize the risk of alienating talent. Also, it has been argued that successful cross-border acquirers from emerging economies whose aim is to obtain competencies, technology and knowledge essential to their global strategies – such as India's largest aluminium producer Hindalco acquiring companies abroad that would offset its own lack of technical and organizational capabilities – do not see quick integration as a priority (Kumar, 2009).

In project management terms, the speed can be increased only to the degree to which a comprehensive integration plan has been formulated in the pre-merger phase. Indeed, 'speed kills' if decisions are taken without being guided by a carefully crafted plan. Alternatively, a slow pace due to the lack of a credible plan also has a negative impact, as it reinforces the impression in the minds of many subordinates that the executives do not know what they are doing, that no progress is being made, and that the entire merger or acquisition was a folly to begin with. If the post-merger phase is to be successful, then good preparation during the pre-merger/acquisition phase is essential.

5 Summary and conclusions

In mergers and acquisitions special emphasis is often focused on the strategic and financial goals of the transaction while the psychological, social and cultural implications do not receive sufficient attention (see Chapter 2). The purpose of this chapter has been to delineate the dynamics of people issues and cultural processes inherent to M&As, and to discuss their implications for management and in particular HRM.

What happens before a deal is signed is important. A well thought-out strategy and thorough due diligence are essential to success, as well as a negotiation team that does not succumb to escalation of commitment during the negotiation process that might lead to paying too much for the acquisition. However, even deals which are well structured and negotiated have to cope with the complexities of merging organizations across boundaries; inevitably the capacity to add value in the merged company depends mostly on what happens after the deal is done (Pucik and Evans, 2004). Not surprisingly, high returns are attained by organizations that execute post-merger integration well (A.T. Kearney, 1999). With this in mind, the research evidence discussed in this chapter indicates that when managed adequately, cultural differences inherent to cross-border M&As actually can be an asset rather than a liability. Cultural differences should not be confused therefore with ineffective communication and poor cross-cultural management (see Chapter 1).

The approach to the HRM challenges in a particular merger or acquisition depends on the strategic logic behind the deal and the integration approach that is adopted. Each of the integration approaches discussed in this chapter has different people and managerial implications. For example, in absorption acquisitions, one of the key managerial challenges is to ease the transition from separate to joint operations and to allay the fears of target firm employees through clear communication; whereas preservation acquisitions require arm's length status and a willingness on the part of managers to learn from the acquired firm. In general, attention to cultural and people issues is most critical to M&As that require a high degree of integration (Haspeslagh and Jemison, 1991; Stahl and Sitkin, 2010).

Although most M&A failures are linked to problems in post-merger integration, our discussion of the key HRM challenges suggests that cultural and people issues have to be considered at an early stage in the M&A process – as early as the phase of evaluation and selection of a suitable target as well as in planning the post-merger or post-acquisition integration. In the due diligence process, the assessment of the organization structure, corporate culture and HR system in the company to be acquired is just as important as are the financial analysis and strategic fit considerations. Essential preconditions for the long-term success of the M&A are undertaking a human capital audit to ensure that the target company has the talent to execute the M&A strategy; identifying which individuals are important to sustain the value of the deal; and assessing any potential weaknesses in the management cadre.

No matter how well the M&A has been prepared, one can neither anticipate nor avoid all problems in the integration phase. In this chapter, we have identified various paths to follow to manage more effectively the challenges of post-merger integration. Most of the key management tasks are in the domain of HRM, such as open and timely communication, choosing the right management team, retaining key executives and leadership talent, facilitating the cultural integration process and managing the transition process. The research evidence shows that effective responses to these HRM challenges can go a long way towards reducing dysfunctional culture clashes in cross-border M&As, and consequently increase the chances of successful integration.

The cultural and HRM implications of M&As discussed in this chapter also provide a rich field for further research. Although the psychological, social and cultural issues involved in integrating merging or acquired firms have received considerable research attention in recent years (for reviews see Schweiger and Goulet, 2000; Stahl and Sitkin, 2005; Evans et al., 2011), several important issues related to the post-merger integration process have been left unexplored. For example, few systematic attempts have been made to examine, either conceptually or empirically, the role that processes related to trust building, employee sense making and leadership may play in the M&A process. Other aspects of the post-combination integration process, such as the consequences of cultural fit or misfit, have received more research attention, but the empirical findings are mixed. Clearly, our current understanding of the socio-cultural dynamics in cross-border M&A is still limited.

One reason – and challenge – is that research in this complex area needs to be interdisciplinary or broad in its disciplinary orientation – linking strategic, cross-cultural and HRM perspectives. Each of these perspectives has something to contribute, but none can contribute significantly independently of the others (see Chapter 2). For example, as has been discussed earlier in this chapter, frameworks that focus exclusively on the cultural issues involved in integrating merging or acquired firms, such as the 'cultural distance' hypothesis, cannot explain why some cross-border M&As succeed and others fail. Whether cultural differences have a positive or negative impact on M&A performance will likely depend on a variety of factors, including the nature of the cultural differences, the interventions chosen to manage these differences and the strategic intent behind the M&A. Interdisciplinary research is needed to find out how these dimensions interactively influence M&A performance and to provide fresh insights into the socio-cultural processes and HRM issues involved in cross-border M&A.

Discussion questions

1. What are the various post-merger/post-acquisition strategies that one can pursue and what are the factors to consider in determining the appropriate strategy? And what are the corresponding HRM implications?
2. What are the cultural and people issues that HR should focus on to ensure the success of a merger or an acquisition?
3. What is the role of the integration manager and the transition team? What professional and personal qualities should these incumbents possess?

CASE STUDY

CEMEX

This case draws mainly on Marchand, D. and Leger, K. (2008) 'Cemex Way to profitable growth: leveraging post-merger integration and best-practice innovation' (Case study no. IMD-3-1884). Lausanne: IMD. Copyright © 2008 by IMD, Lausanne, Switzerland. Not to be used or reproduced without prior written permission directly from IMD.

In September 2004, only a few months after defining its new global governance model and deciding to implement one global operating system, the Mexican building materials company CEMEX announced its intention of acquiring the UK-based Ready Mix Concrete (RMC) group for US$5.8 billion. With this acquisition CEMEX aimed to consolidate its position as one of the top three global players in the industry.

CEMEX was established in 1906 in Monterrey, Mexico. The current CEO, Lorenzo Zambrano, is the grandson of the company's founder and was appointed to his position in 1985 after working his way up through the organization over 18 years. At that time, the company had five plants and 6,500 employees. Zambrano refused to diversify into other businesses, the route favoured by many other Latin American industrialists. Instead he focused on the cement and building materials business he knew well and built up his company through a series of carefully considered and implemented acquisitions, first in Mexico and then from 1992 in Spain, Latin America, the Philippines and the US.

Top management quickly realized that the newly acquired companies were guided by different operating practices, structures and cultures than CEMEX. Most had been run quite ineffectively and CEMEX saw an opportunity to create value by implementing new processes and instilling new management behaviour. The backbone of this strategy was a global operating platform, labelled the CEMEX Way.

The aim of the CEMEX Way was to unify global operations, promote sharing of best practices, streamline and improve the value chain all the way down to the final customers, and allow rapid and simultaneous deployment of strategic initiatives. With the CEMEX Way in place, the company could move fast and confidently with the post-merger integration, largely because its own systems and practices were well developed and explicit.

To enable faster and smoother acquisitions, CEMEX put in place a systematic post-merger integration (PMI) process to promote best practices and learn from previous experiences. Overlapping teams of managers and functional specialists from different countries were sent to each newly acquired company so that knowledge and best practices would be passed on to the team responsible for each new acquisition.

The typical PMI had four stages. An initial integration and planning stage, during which pre-assessment teams were sent to the newly acquired company to analyse the situation and plan next steps, which was then followed by three execution phases. In phase one, also called 'the 100-day plan', transition teams worked to identify further synergies through a gap analysis covering all business activities. Phase two focused on implementation, with the expectation that the CEMEX Way would be fully operational by the end of this stage. Phase three was to return to business as usual – at a higher level of operational efficiency.

The RMC acquisition was bigger, covered more countries (22), and included more diverse cultures and languages than anything CEMEX had encountered previously. The PMI office divided the work between functional teams, like 'cement operations' and 'back-office'; each of these teams was replicated on a country by country basis. In total, 600 people from within CEMEX and over 400 RMC managers were involved in the RMC PMI. The HR integration was by far the most complex part of the process and CEMEX spent more than six months defining and building a framework that took staffing and country differences into consideration. At the kick-off of the execution phase Zambrano addressed RMC managers and executives:

> You will quickly discover that CEMEX time seems to have fewer minutes in every hour and more hours in every day. We are highly disciplined and dedicated to consistent, high level performance. We believe in continuous innovation. ... our goal – and our track record – is to out-perform our competitors year in and year out.

(Continued)

(Continued)

The absorption of RMC did not result in large-scale firings and layoffs. In fact, 80 per cent of identified synergies were realized by changes in its processes, repositioning of business operations, and implementation of common management platforms. The results were impressive. Under its old owners, a large cement plant in Rugby, England often ran at only 70 per cent capacity. Two months after the takeover and the implementation of CEMEX Way it was increased to running at 93 per cent.

In October 2006, CEMEX announced an unsolicited offer to purchase Sydney-based Rinker group, with operations in Australia and the US. The target company was known to be very well managed. This acquisition was an opportunity to blend the best parts of CEMEX and Rinker to improve overall profitability, rather than to improve operating efficiency, the motive for previous acquisitions. The Rinker deal was sealed at the beginning of 2007. Instead of scrapping what Rinker had, the plan was to start with a thorough evaluation, identify the best of both parties, and determine which parts of Rinker's operating system should be incorporated in the CEMEX Way – an obvious example was a waste burning initiative common to most Rinker plants.

CEMEX's integration of Rinker could be considered a 'best of both' approach, as Rinker's production processes were very advanced in a number of technological areas and geographies. It would be to CEMEX's advantage to leverage this capability within the whole firm. However, without strong mutual respect for the knowledge and skills of each company, this kind of strategy will not work.

By December 2007, CEMEX had operations on four continents and in more than 50 countries – 85 cement plants, 2,365 ready-mix concrete facilities and 564 aggregates quarries. The only gaps in its global presence were China and India. CEMEX reported net sales of $21.7 billion and a net income of $2.6 billion. The company was also one of the world's leading traders of cement, as it maintained its own shipping fleet and trading relationships with customers in close to 100 nations.

Yet, by early 2009, because of the financial and economic crisis, the company global expansion was put on hold. A question which has to be asked is did the company's ability to grow through acquisitions lead it to underestimate the economic risks involved?

Case study questions

1. Assess and discuss the extent that CEMEX may be in difficulty in 2009.
2. What do you think CEMEX should do in 2010 in relation to the four following HRM and operational issues: (a) multi-skilling, (b) cost reduction, (c) talent management and retention, and (d) process improvement?

3. What should CEMEX do regarding its global business operations and in relation to future expansion into China and India?

Case study questions for further reflection

1. What during different stages of CEMEX's company history were the key success factors behind its growth and development through merger and acquisition?
2. What constitutes best practice in post-merger integration?

Further reading

Journal articles

- Ashkenas, A., DeMonaco, L. and Francis, S. (1998) 'Making the deal real: how GE Capital integrates acquisitions', *Harvard Business Review* (January–February): 165–178.

  This well-known article takes the reader through the GE approach to post-merger integration. It subdivides the process into four key stages and explains each. These stages are: (1) pre-acquisition (due diligence, negotiation and announcement, close); (2) foundation building (launch, acquisition integration workout, strategy formulation); (3) rapid integration (implementation, course assessment and adjustment); and (4) assimilation (long-term plan evaluation and adjustment, capitalizing on success).

- Bower, J. (2001) 'Not all M&As are alike – and that matters', *Harvard Business Review* (March): 93–101.

  Joseph Bower begins his article by relating the collective wisdom on M&As. Acquirers usually pay too much; friendly deals done using stock often perform well; CEOs fall in love with deals and don't walk away when they should; integration is hard but a few companies do it well consistently. He then explains in depth the frequency, strengths and weaknesses of five reasons for M&As: (1) to deal with overcapacity through consolidation in mature industries; (2) to roll-up competitors in geographically fragmented industries; (3) to extend into new products or markets; (4) to substitute for R&D; and (5) to exploit eroding industry boundaries by inventing an industry.

- Aguilera, R.V. and Dencker, J.C. (2004) 'The role of human resource management in cross-border mergers and acquisitions', *International Journal of Human Resource Management*, December, 15(8): 1355–1370.

  This *IJHRM* article considers how cross-border mergers and acquisitions have become the dominant mode of growth for firms seeking competitive advantage in the global business economy. The authors examine contingencies in national contexts that influence outcomes in the merger process. The empirical evidence is discussed to highlight HRM roles in terms of resources, processes and values that reflect the influence of both strategic fit and national context in the integration stage of cross-border M&A.

- Williamson, P.J. and Raman, A.P. (2011) 'How China reset its global acquisition agenda', *Harvard Business Review*, 89(4): 109–114.

  China's economic progress has been so dazzling that people often forget that China Inc. has seen its share of failures too. This article looks at the first cross-border acquisitions that Chinese companies made. Many of those high-profile deals – including TCL's acquisition of France's Thomson, SAIC's takeover of South Korea's Ssangyong Motor Company, and the D'Long Group's purchase of America's Murray, Inc. – ended badly. As a result, many Chinese companies quietly changed course, altering the kinds of targets they pursued and their rationale for M&A. Chinese acquirers have learned to steer clear of deals that involve costly turn-arounds or tricky integration. Instead of buying brands, sales networks and goodwill, they now look for hard assets, like mineral deposits and oil reserves, or state-of-the-art technology and R&D. And where they once tried to buy market share abroad, today they focus on acquisitions that will help them strengthen their share in China.

Books

- Child, J., Faulkner, D. and Pitkethly, R. (2001) *The Management of International Acquisitions*. Oxford: Oxford University Press.

  Excellent summary of the M&A issues, targeted both for academics and managers, based on research on acquisition by foreign companies in the UK. Three areas explored in detail are a review of key management challenges, which post-acquisition practices lead to better performance, and whether national management style can survive an international acquisition.

- Fubini, D., Price C. and Zollo, M. (2006) *Mergers: Leadership, Performance and Corporate Health*. New York: Palgrave Macmillan.

  The book was written by a team of academics and McKinsey consultants based on survey data generated from company clients. It covers a wide range of M&A issues from M&A strategy and due diligence to various approaches to managing integration and the role of the senior leadership team in this process.

- Haspeslagh, P.C. and Jemison, D.B. (1991) *Managing Acquisitions: Creating Value through Corporate Renewal*. New York: The Free Press.

Written for academics as well as executives, this now classic text introduces a well-known model of the post-acquisition integration process. Although the primary focus is on the business aspects of determining M&A value drivers, the book is highly relevant to those interested in the human resource management aspects of M&A. Perhaps the most influential book on M&A management.

- Marks, M.L. and Mirvis, P.H. (2010) *Joining Forces: Making One Plus One Equal Three in Mergers, Acquisitions, and Alliances*. San Francisco: Jossey-Bass.
  Popular and useful book on human resource management aspects of M&A. Targeted more towards practitioners than academics (both authors have extensive consulting experience), this book contains numerous mini-cases and best practice examples.

- Stahl, G.K. and Mendenhall, M.E. (2005) *Mergers and Acquisitions: Managing Culture and Human Resources*. Stanford: Stanford University Press.
  This edited book provides a comprehensive research-based, yet practitioner-oriented, overview of a range of cultural and human resources issues in M&A. While the chapters are written by academics from Europe, North America, Asia and Australia, experienced corporate executives comment on each chapter.

- Weber, Y. (2012) *Handbook of Research on Mergers and Acquisitions*. Cheltenham: Edward Elgar.
  For the last four decades, researchers in various disciplines have been trying to explain the enduring paradox of the growing activity and volume of M&A versus the high failure rate of M&A. This handbook will stimulate scholars to focus on new research directions. It presents research that incorporates multi-disciplinary, multi-level, multi-stage and cross-cultural models and analyses, and also focuses on such issues as knowledge transfer, due diligence, performance measures, communication, trust, grief, integration approaches, individual values, change management and consulting.

Internet resources

A quick internet search for merger and acquisition yields nearly 2 million hits – considerably more information than most people will find helpful, especially when they are facing complex M&A transactions.

For general reference

- http://en.wikipedia.org/wiki/Mergers_and_acquisitions. Wikipedia is a convenient reference site to look up definitions of principal terms, including historical overview and links for further reading.

For library of articles on M&A issues

- www.deloitte.com/view/en_US/us/Services/consulting/hot-topics/mergers-acquisitions/article/acb2d1800c0fb110VgnVCM100000ba42f00aRCRD.htm. The Deloitte Merger & Acquisition Library features a wide range of articles, points of view, discussion papers, research and industry reports. Topics drill deep into tough business issues, global strategies, investment and acquisition patterns, industry trends, management issues, private and public sector concerns, practical resources and more.
- www.imaa-institute.org/en/index.php. Institute of Mergers, Acquisitions and Alliances (IMAA) is based in Switzerland and provides information on the use and benefits of mergers, acquisitions and strategic alliances. Among other services, it collects, maintains and provides specialized resources and information with respect to various aspects of M&A focusing on specific sectors and countries.

For M&A trends and list of deals

- www.reuters.com/finance/deals/mergers. This Reuters website is the product of a merger with Thompson Financials, and is a great source for comprehensive and up-to-date information about latest M&As. It also includes feature articles and insights on key trends and issues and analysis of M&As by industry and regions.
- http://money.cnn.com/data/markets. CNN Money provides a listing of the most recent deals indicating the names of targets and acquirers, and the dollar value of the deal with a link to a report on each deal. See also a related Top 25 Deals year-to-date list, arranged by the dollar value of the deal.
- www.mergers.net/index.php?id=deal_of_the_month. M&A International provides an informative section on 'Deal of the month'.

Self-assessment questions

Indicative answers to these questions can be found on the companion website at study.sagepub.com/harzing4e.

1. Why is it that the role of cultural difference in influencing the success or failure of an M&A may be exaggerated?
2. A useful way of conceptualizing M&As is to consider their desired end-state. What are the five end-states according to Marks and Mirvis (1998)? Briefly define each one.
3. What are the top ranked factors contributing to acquisition success according to well-known surveys and reports?

4. What do Evans and colleagues (2011) propose are the cultural and people issues in cross-border M&As?
5. Specify some of the questions that a cultural due diligence team should ask in order to understand the 'deep knowledge' of the culture.

References

Aguilera, R.V. and Dencker, J. (2004) 'The role of human resource management in cross-border mergers and acquisitions', *International Journal of Human Resource Management*, 15: 1357–1372.

Angwin, D.N. (2004) 'Speed in M&A integration: the first 100 days', *European Management Journal*, 22(4): 418–430.

Angwin, D.N. (2007) *Mergers and Acquisitions*. Oxford: Blackwell.

Angwin, D.N. and Savill, B. (1997) 'Strategic perspectives on European cross-border acquisitions: a view from top European executives', *European Management Journal*, 15: 423–435.

Ashkenas, R.N., DeMonaco, L.J. and Francis, S.C. (1998) 'Making the deal real: how GE Capital integrates acquisitions', *Harvard Business Review* (January–February): 165–178.

Ashkenas, R.N. and Francis, S.C. (2000) 'Integration managers: special leaders for special times', *Harvard Business Review* (November–December): 108–116.

A.T. Kearney (1999) *Corporate Marriage: Blight or Bliss – A Monograph on Post-Merger Integration*. Chicago: A.T. Kearney.

Barham, K. and Heimer, C. (1998) *ABB: The Dancing Giant*. London: Financial Times Management.

Barkema, H.G., Bell, J.H. and Pennings, J.M. (1996) 'Foreign entry, cultural barriers, and learning', *Strategic Management Journal*, 17: 151–166.

Beer, M., Eisenstat, R. and Spector, B. (1990) *The Critical Path to Corporate Renewal*. Boston, MA: Harvard Business School Press.

Bertrand, O. and Zitouna, H. (2008) 'Domestic versus cross-border acquisitions: which impact on the target firms' performance?', *Applied Economics*, 40(17): 2221–2238.

Björkman, I., Stahl, G.K. and Vaara, E. (2007) 'Cultural differences and capability transfer in cross-border acquisitions: the mediating roles of capability complementarity, absorptive capacity, and social integration', *Journal of International Business Studies*, 38(4): 658–672.

Black, J.S., Gregersen, H.B., Mendenhall, M.E. and Stroh, L.K. (1999) *Globalizing People through International Assignments*. New York: Addison-Wesley Longman.

Bleeke, J., Ernst, D., Isono, J. and Weinberg, D.D. (1993) 'Succeeding at cross-border mergers and acquisitions', in J. Bleeke and D. Ernst (eds), *Collaborating to Compete: Using Strategic Alliances and Acquisitions in the Global Marketplace*. New York: John Wiley, pp. 79–90.

Bouchikhi, H. and Kimberly, J. (2012) 'Making mergers work', *MIT Sloan Management Review*, 54(1): 63–70.

Cartwright, S. and Cooper, C.L. (1996) *Managing Mergers, Acquisitions, and Strategic Alliances: Integrating People and Cultures*, 2nd edn. Oxford: Butterworth and Heinemann.

Chakrabarti, R., Gupta-Mukherjee, S. and Jayaraman, N. (2009) 'Mars–Venus marriages: culture and cross-border M&A', *Journal of International Business Studies*, 40(2): 216–235.

Chatterjee, S., Lubatkin, M.H., Schweiger, D.M. and Weber, Y. (1992) 'Cultural differences and shareholder value in related mergers: linking equity and human capital', *Strategic Management Journal*, 13: 319–334.

Chaudhuri, S. and Tabrizi, B. (1999) 'Capturing the real value in high-tech acquisitions', *Harvard Business Review* (September–October): 123–130.

Child, J., Faulkner, D. and Pitkethly, R. (2001) *The Management of International Acquisitions*. Oxford: Oxford University Press.

Christensen, C.M., Alton, R., Rising, C. and Waldeck, M. (2011) 'The new M&A playbook', *Harvard Business Review* (March): 44–57.

Datta, D.K. (1991) 'Organizational fit and acquisition performance: effects of post-acquisition integration', *Strategic Management Journal*, 12: 281–297.

David, K. and Singh, H. (1994) 'Sources of acquisition cultural risk', in G. von Krogh, A. Sinatra and H. Singh (eds), *The Management of Corporate Acquisitions: International Perspectives*. Macmillan: Houndmills, pp. 251–292.

Dikova, D. and Sahib, P.R. (2013) 'Is cultural distance a bane or a boon for cross-border acquisition performance?', *Journal of World Business*, 48: 77–86.

Dobbs, R., Goedhart, M. and Suonio, H. (2006) 'Are companies getting better at M&A?', *McKinsey Quarterly* (December), www.mckinseyquarterly.com (online only).

Donnelly, T., Morris, D. and Donnelly, T. (2005) 'Renault–Nissan: a marriage of necessity', *European Business Review*, 17(5): 428–440.

Epstein, M.J. (2004) 'The drivers of success in post-merger integration', *Organizational Dynamics*, 33(2): 174–189.

Evans, P., Pucik, V. and Björkman, I. (2011) *The Global Challenge: Frameworks for International Human Resource Management*, 2nd edn. New York: McGraw-Hill.

Finkelstein, S. (1999) *Safe Ways to Cross the Merger Minefield: Mastering Global Business*. London: Financial Times Pitman Publishing.

Fubini, D., Price C. and Zollo, M. (2006) *Mergers: Leadership, Performance and Corporate Health*. New York: Palgrave Macmillan.

Goulet, P.K. and Schweiger, D.M. (2006) 'Managing culture and human resources in mergers and acquisitions', in G.K. Stahl and I. Björkman (eds), *Handbook of Research in International Human Resource Management*. Cheltenham: Edward Elgar, pp. 405–429.

Harding, D. and Rouse, T. (2007) 'Human due diligence', *Harvard Business Review* (April): 124–131.

Haspeslagh, P. and Jemison, D.B. (1991) *Managing Acquisitions: Creating Value Through Corporate Renewal*. New York: The Free Press.

Hastings, D.F. (1999) 'Lincoln Electric's harsh lessons from international expansion', *Harvard Business Review* (May–June): 162–178.

Homburg, C. and Bucerius, M. (2006) 'Is speed of integration really a success factor of mergers and acquisitions? An analysis of the role of internal and external relatedness', *Strategic Management Journal*, 27(4): 347–367.

Immelt, J.R., Govindarajan, V. and Trimble C. (2009) 'How GE is disrupting itself', *Harvard Business Review* (September): 56–65.

Inkpen, A., Sundaram, A.K. and Rockwood, K. (2000) 'Cross-border acquisitions of U.S. technology assets', *California Management Review*, 42: 50–71.

Jemison, D.B. and Sitkin, S.B. (1986) 'Corporate acquisitions: a process perspective', *Academy of Management Review*, 11: 145–163.

Kay, I.T. and Shelton, M. (2000) 'The people problems in mergers', *McKinsey Quarterly*, 4: 29–37.

Killing, P. (2003) 'Improving acquisition integration: be clear on what you intend, and avoid "best of both" deals', *Perspectives for Managers*, 97. Lausanne: IMD.

Killing, P. (2004) 'Merger of equals: the case of AstraZeneca', in P. Morosini and U. Steger (eds), *Managing Complex Mergers: Real World Lessons in Implementing Successful Cross-cultural Mergers and Acquisitions*. London: Financial Times Prentice Hall, pp. 93–115.

King, D.R., Dalton, D.R., Daily, C.M. and Covin, J.G. (2004) 'Meta-analyses of post-acquisition performance: indications of unidentified moderators', *Strategic Management Journal*, 25(2): 187–200.

Kotter, J.P. (1996) *Leading Change*. Boston: Harvard Business School Press.

Kouzes, J.M. and Posner, B.Z. (1987) *The Leadership Challenge: How to Get Extraordinary Things Done in Organizations*. San Francisco: Jossey-Bass.

KPMG (1999) *Mergers and Acquisitions: A Global Research Report – Unlocking Shareholder Value*. New York: KPMG.

KPMG (2006) *The Morning After: Driving for Post Deal Success*. London: KPMG.

Krug, J. and Hegerty, W.H. (1997) 'Postacquisition turnover among U.S. top management teams: an analysis of the effect of foreign versus domestic acquisition of U.S. targets', *Strategic Management Journal*, 18: 667–675.

Krug, J. and Hegerty, W.H. (2001) 'Predicting who stays and leaves after an acquisition: a study of top managers in multinational firms', *Strategic Management Journal*, 22(2): 185–196.

Kühlmann, T. and Dowling, P.J. (2005) 'DaimlerChrysler: a case study of a cross-border merger', in G.K. Stahl and M.E. Mendenhall (eds), *Mergers and Acquisitions: Managing Culture and Human Resources*. Stanford, CA: Stanford University Press, pp. 351–363.

Kumar, N. (2009) 'How emerging giants are rewriting the rules of M&A', *Harvard Business Review* (May): 115–121.

Larsson, R. and Finkelstein, S. (1999) 'Integrating strategic, organizational, and human resource perspectives on mergers and acquisitions: a case survey of synergy realization', *Organization Science*, 10: 1–26.

Larsson, R. and Risberg, A. (1998) 'Cultural awareness and national versus corporate barriers to acculturation', in M.C. Gertsen, A.-M. Søderberg and J.E. Torp (eds), *Cultural Dimensions of International Mergers and Acquisitions*. Berlin: De Gruyter, pp. 39–56.

Marks, M.L. and Mirvis, P.H. (2010) *Joining Forces: Making One Plus One Equal Three in Mergers, Acquisitions, and Alliances*. San Francisco: Jossey-Bass.

Mendenhall, M., Caligiuri, P. and Tarique, I. (2001) 'Assessing and managing culture in mergers and acquisitions', presentation at the Conference on Managing Culture and Human Resources in Mergers and Acquisitions, Thurnau, Germany, 21 October.

Michaels, E.H., Handfield-Jones, H. and Axelrod, B. (2001) *The War for Talent*. Boston, MA: Harvard Business School Press.

Mirvis, P.H. and Marks, M.L. (1994) *Managing the Merger: Making it Work*. Upper Saddle River, NJ: Prentice Hall.

Moeller, S.B. and Schlingemann, F.P. (2005) 'Global diversification and bidder gains: a comparison between cross-border and domestic acquisitions', *Journal of Banking & Finance*, 29: 533–564.

Morgan, G. (2007) 'M&A as power', in D. Angwin (ed.), *Mergers and Acquisitions*. Oxford: Blackwell, pp. 116–152.

Morosini, P., Shane, S. and Singh, H. (1998) 'National cultural distance and cross-border acquisition performance', *Journal of International Business Studies*, 29: 137–158.

O'Grady, S. and Lane, H.W. (1996) 'The psychic distance paradox', *Journal of International Business Studies*, 27(2): 309–333.

Olie, R. (1990) 'Culture and integration problems in international mergers and acquisitions', *European Management Journal*, 8: 206–215.

Pucik, V. (2008) 'Post-merger integration process in Japanese M&A: the voices from the front-line', in C.L. Cooper and S. Finkelstein (eds), *Advances in Mergers and Acquisitions*, Vol. 7. Bingley, UK: JAI Press, pp. 71–92.

Pucik, V. and Evans, P. (2004) 'The human factor in mergers and acquisitions', in P. Morosini and U. Steger (eds), *Managing Complex Mergers*. London: Financial Times Prentice Hall, pp. 161–187.

Schein, E.H. (1987) *Organizational Culture and Leadership*. San Francisco: Jossey-Bass.

Schmidt, J.A. (ed.) (2002) *Making Mergers Work: The Strategic Importance of People*. Alexandria, VA: Towers Perrin and SHRM Foundation.

Schneider, S.C., Stahl, G.K. and Barsoux, J. (2003) *Managing Across Cultures*, 2nd edn. London: FT-Prentice Hall.

Schoenberg, R. (2000) 'The influence of cultural compatibility within cross-border acquisitions: a review', *Advances in Mergers and Acquisitions*, 1: 43–59.

Schweiger, D.M. and Goulet, P.K. (2000) 'Integrating mergers and acquisitions: an international research review', *Advances in Mergers and Acquisitions*, 1: 61–91.

Schweiger, D.M. and Lippert, R.L. (2005) 'Integration: the critical link in M&A value creation', in G.K. Stahl and M.E. Mendenhall (eds), *Mergers and Acquisitions: Managing Culture and Human Resources*. Stanford, CA: Stanford University Press, pp. 17–45.

Shimizu, K., Hitt, M.A., Vaidyanath, D. and Pisano, V. (2004) 'Theoretical foundations of cross-border mergers and acquisitions: a review of current research and recommendations for the future', *Journal of International Management*, 10(3): 307–353.

Siegel, J.I. and Zepp Larson, B. (2009) 'Labor market institutions and global strategic adaptation: evidence from Lincoln Electric', *Management Science*, 55 (7): 1527–1546.

Sitkin, S.B. and Pablo, A.L. (2005) 'The neglected importance of leadership in M&As', in G.K. Stahl and M.E. Mendenhall (eds), *Mergers and Acquisitions: Managing Culture and Human Resources*. Stanford, CA: Stanford University Press, pp. 208–223.

Stahl, G.K. (2006) 'Synergy springs from cultural revolution', *Financial Times*, 6 October.

Stahl, G.K. and Brannen, M.Y. (2013) 'Building cross-cultural leadership competence: an interview with Carlos Ghosn', *Academy of Management Learning and Education*, Advance online publication, 29 May, doi: 10.5465/amle.2012.0246.

Stahl, G.K. and Javidan, M. (2009) 'Comparative and cross-cultural perspectives on cross-border mergers and acquisitions', in R.S. Bhagat and R.M. Steers (eds), *Handbook of Culture, Organisation, and Work*. Cambridge, UK: Cambridge University Press, pp. 118–147.

Stahl, G.K. and Koester, K. (2013) 'Lenovo-IBM: bridging cultures, languages, and time zones integration challenges'. WU Case Series, 5. WU Vienna University of Economics and Business, Vienna.

Stahl, G.K. and Sitkin, S.B. (2005) 'Trust in mergers and acquisitions', in G.K. Stahl and M.E. Mendenhall (eds), *Mergers and Acquisitions: Managing Culture and Human Resources*. Stanford, CA: Stanford University Press, pp. 82–102.

Stahl, G.K. and Sitkin, S.B. (2010) 'Trust dynamics in acquisitions: the role of relationship history, interfirm distance, and acquirer's integration approach', *Advances in Mergers and Acquisitions*, 9: 51–82.

Stahl, G.K. and Voigt, A. (2008) 'Do cultural differences matter in mergers and acquisitions? A tentative model and examination', *Organisation Science*, 19(1): 160–176.

Teerikangas, S. and Very, P. (2006) 'The culture-performance relationship in M&A: from yes/no to how', *British Journal of Management*, 17(1): 31–48.

Torborg, K.B., Bundy, B. and Jones, C.M. (2008) *M&A Beyond Borders: Opportunities and Risks*. New York: Marsh, Mercer, Kroll (in cooperation with the Economic Intelligence Unit, The Economist), http://graphics.eiu.com/upload/eb/marsh_cross_border_report.pdf (accessed 26 May 2014).

Vaara, E. (2003) 'Post-acquisition integration as sense making: glimpses of ambiguity, confusion, hypocrisy, and politicization', *Journal of Management Studies*, 40(4): 859–894.

Vaara, E., Tienari, J. and Björkman, I. (2003) 'Global capitalism meets national spirit', *Journal of Management Inquiry*, 12(4): 377–393.

Vermeulen, G.A.M. and Barkema, H.G. (2001) 'Learning through acquisitions', *Academy of Management Journal*, 44(3): 457–476.

Very, P., Lubatkin, M. and Calori, R. (1996) 'A cross-national assessment of acculturative stress in recent European mergers', *International Studies of Management & Organization*, 26: 59–86.

Vlasic, B. and Stertz, B. (2000) *How Daimler-Benz drove off with Chrysler*. New York: Morrow.

Weber, Y. (1996) 'Corporate cultural fit and performance in mergers and acquisitions', *Human Relations*, 49: 1181–1202.

Weber, Y., Shenkar, O. and Raveh, A. (1996) 'National and corporate fit in mergers & acquisitions: an exploratory study', *Management Science*, 4(8): 1215–1227.

Williams, M. (2001) 'In whom we trust: group membership as an affective context for trust development', *Academy of Management Review*, 26(3): 377–396.

Williamson, P.J. and Raman, A.P. (2011) 'How China reset its global acquisition agenda', *Harvard Business Review*, 89(4): 109–114.

Zweig, P. (1995) 'The case against mergers', *Businessweek*, 29 October, www.businessweek.com/stories/1995-10-29/the-case-against-mergers (accessed 26 May 2014).

Part 3

IHRM Policies and Practices

Part 3
HRM Policies and Practices

Managing Knowledge in Multinational Firms

9

Ingmar Björkman, Paul Evans, Vladimir Pucik, and Dana Minbaeva

Contents

Learning objectives

After reading this chapter you will be able to:

- Explain the importance of knowledge sharing for the competitiveness of the multinational enterprise
- Distinguish the range of mechanisms that multinationals have at their disposal to enhance knowledge sharing
- Discuss how multinationals can access and retain external knowledge
- Understand the dualities involved in exploring existing knowledge and exploiting new areas

Chapter outline

In this chapter we discuss knowledge sharing in multinationals, arguing that it is facilitated by cross-unit social capital, organizational values of collaboration and sharing, and global mindsets. We also examine structural mechanisms and a range of HR practices that enhance knowledge sharing. We then assess how multinational corporations can access and retain external knowledge. In the final section we discuss the dualities involved in exploring existing knowledge and exploiting new knowledge.

1 Introduction

The argument was made two decades ago, in the early days of scholarly and practitioner interest in knowledge management, that a primary rationale for the existence of multinational firms is their ability to transfer knowledge more effectively and efficiently than through market mechanisms (Kogut and Zander, 1992, 1993). The competitive advantage of a multinational corporation stems in part from its ability to replicate operating routines that have proved to be effective elsewhere in the corporation, and in part from its ability to access and recombine new knowledge from different parts of the world into innovations. This is a perspective on multinational organizations that today seems very significant. Certainly, the way in which the multinational firm manages knowledge is important for its competitiveness.

In this chapter we will lead the reader through the challenges of how to manage knowledge in the multinational enterprise. After first having defined different types of knowledge and elements of knowledge transfer in the multinational corporation, we discuss knowledge sharing across geographically dispersed units. We argue that within multinationals, knowledge sharing is facilitated by cross-unit social capital, organizational values of collaboration and sharing, and global mindsets among employees, among other factors. We also discuss structural mechanisms and a range of human resource management practices that enhance knowledge sharing.

We then assess how multinationals can access and retain external knowledge from different parts of the world. Knowledge acquisition requires investment in external scanning on a global scale; the development of partnerships with customers, research labs and other organizations; and an ability to use the open market to identify complementary knowledge and interesting ideas. Again, people management and social capital play an important role in this endeavour.

In the final section we discuss the dualities involved in both exploring existing knowledge and exploiting new knowledge. Throughout the chapter the focus is on HRM aspects of how to manage knowledge in multinationals.

2 Different types of knowledge

To understand different types of knowledge, it is helpful first to establish what we mean by the term 'knowledge'. Knowledge can be distinguished from information, which is a statement of facts such as numerical data about the size of a geographical market or the number of employees in a corporation. Knowledge can be defined as justified true belief (Nonaka, 1994). In this chapter we will focus on knowledge as the (justified true) beliefs that organizational members hold about what constitutes effective organizational actions and practices. However, we will also discuss the organizational practices that knowledge is both embedded in and reflects (Kostova, 1999).

In discussions of knowledge in organizations, a distinction between explicit and tacit knowledge was first advanced by Polanyi (1967) and developed by Nonaka (1994; Nonaka and Takeuchi, 1995). Both types of knowledge are important to multinational firms. Explicit or codified knowledge is knowledge that individuals and organizations know that they have – objective, formal, systematic, incorporated in texts and manuals, and relatively easy to pass on to others at a low marginal cost. Virtually all knowledge stored in IT-based databases and systems is explicit. In contrast, tacit knowledge is personal, context specific, and hard or perhaps even impossible to formalize and communicate. Individuals may not even be conscious of the tacit knowledge they possess. Tacit knowledge often underlies complex skills and is fundamental to the intuitive feel acquired through years of experience.

In the past, the success of internationalization was typically dependent on the ability of the firm to transfer the superior tacit knowledge residing in the home country organization to its overseas affiliates. When multinational firms established new units abroad, this knowledge allowed them to compete successfully against national enterprises that enjoyed the advantage of superior local knowledge. Expatriates played key roles in the transfer of tacit knowledge from headquarters to foreign subsidiaries. In spite of technological advances over the last few decades, the transfer of personnel and person-to-person interaction are still the main ways in which tacit knowledge can be shared across boundaries.

The development and sharing of these two types of knowledge should be managed in different ways. Codified knowledge can be shared through databases, manuals and blueprints, often known as collections. Tacit knowledge sharing requires connections or networks. The development of information technology has had a big impact on the ability to store and transfer codified or explicit knowledge. While written manuals and blueprints have always been important in the transfer of knowledge across units, the development of advanced IT-based systems fuelled interest in knowledge management during the 1990s. For example, the consultancy firm Accenture made big investments in the development of a global knowledge management system consisting of several thousand databases. The system is managed and promoted by 500 knowledge managers around the globe. Consultants are expected to enter knowledge about their projects into the system, where other members of the organization can access it. One study reported that it was common for an Accenture consultant to tap into more than ten different databases daily (Paik and Choi, 2005). However, most organizational members are notoriously bad at entering useful knowledge into databases, and not all tacit knowledge can be made explicit. And even though some knowledge is codified, there is usually a need to combine it with the sharing of tacit knowledge through interactions between people from different parts of the multinational (Noorderhaven and Harzing, 2009).

Another important issue is the value of knowledge. Some knowledge is unique to the enterprise, and this should be managed differently from knowledge that is generic and freely available to all competitors. Knowledge also varies according to its strategic importance for the enterprise. Lepak and Snell (1999) developed a framework that emphasizes the need for a differentiated approach to knowledge management and HRM depending on the strategic value and firm specificity of the knowledge. Core knowledge is both unique to the firm and high in strategic value, such as Wal-Mart's expertise in logistics and inventory control, or Toyota's manufacturing capabilities. It is crucial to retain and develop such knowledge within the corporation, which implies a focus on retaining and developing the talent of people in whom this core know-how resides. Compulsory knowledge is of high strategic importance but is generally available. It is akin to the notion of 'table stakes' in card games, essential for an opportunity to compete but offering no distinctive competitive advantage. Consequently it is more likely to be managed through close attention to performance management. Idiosyncratic knowledge refers to know-how that is unique to the firm but does not have clear strategic value at the present time, though it may represent the core knowledge of the future. The risks with idiosyncratic knowledge may be managed best through partnerships such as R&D alliances. Ancillary knowledge, which is low on both strategic value and uniqueness, may be outsourced or automated. Different types of knowledge thus imply different strategies in the employment relationship that can create HR challenges when employees in the same firm expect to be managed in comparable ways.

Finally, two basic categories of knowledge processes can be identified, one concerned with exploiting existing knowledge and the other concerned with generating (or exploring) new knowledge (March, 1991). In this context, we highlight the issues concerning knowledge sharing, which refers to the process of exchange of existing knowledge among individuals, teams and units. And as organizations and their units learn and thus generate new knowledge through their individual members, we will also examine how units can generate new knowledge either through deliberate efforts at learning or as a by-product of activities that may have other objectives (Chakravarthy et al., 2003).

The capability of the firm to develop, retain and exploit core knowledge through internal sharing across geographically dispersed units is an important source of competitiveness. In today's world of sophisticated worldwide markets and increasingly competent affiliates, the focus has increasingly shifted from a focus on the home country organization (transferring knowledge and new products from the parent organization abroad) to the ability to generate and transfer knowledge from local units to the parent and other parts of the corporation. The ability of the firm to access and recombine new knowledge from different parts of the world into innovations has become important, leading MNCs to become more concerned with the exploration of new knowledge as well as the exploitation of existing know-how from the home country.

3 Factors influencing knowledge sharing

MNCs have the potential to access knowledge across a variety of different geographic, cultural, institutional and social contexts (see Chapter 2). Units located in different environments are likely to develop different types of knowledge. For the multinational, the diversity of knowledge residing throughout the organization can be a great asset if it can be shared effectively across these boundaries to improve existing capabilities, while combining local knowledge from different environments may also lead to innovation, further enhancing the company's competitive edge.

Knowledge sharing, however, is not easy and is often a complex task. Knowledge is 'sticky' in the sense that there are costs associated with sharing (Szulanski, 1996), creating particular difficulties if it is tacit ambiguous knowledge (Simonin, 1999; van Wijk et al., 2008). To overcome the challenges involved in inter-unit knowledge sharing, firms will need to pay attention to a range of technological, organizational and people-related issues. Our focus here is on HRM aspects of knowledge sharing but we also address a number of organizational issues.

Consider the following example from a firm with which one of the authors has been working. This multinational corporation has six factories around the world, manufacturing almost identical products using the same equipment, the same tools and roughly the same work processes. The yields of the subsidiaries varied from 77 to 98 per cent but they neither knew the productivity of the other units nor shared information about the production process. The obvious question to ask in this situation is how to make sure that the units share knowledge with each other, improving the productivity of the laggards and perhaps also that of the top performers. Based on research by Argote et al. (2003) and Minbaeva (2007), we suggest that the following determinants of internal MNC knowledge transfer and sharing should be analysed when attempting to answer this question:

- the ability and willingness of the sending unit or source to share knowledge (disseminative capacity)
- the ability and willingness of the receiving unit to absorb knowledge (absorptive capacity), and
- the characteristics of the relationship between the sending and receiving units.

Sender unit's ability and willingness

The term disseminative capacity refers to the ability and willingness of organizational members to share knowledge (Minbaeva and Michailova, 2004). For sharing explicit knowledge, this pedagogical ability is partly evidenced by the source unit's proficiency in codifying knowledge in manuals, reports and physical systems that are available to other parts of the corporation, though sharing tacit knowledge is more difficult. It almost always requires skill in interpersonal and often face-to-face interaction. Good language and communication skills and an understanding of cross-cultural factors are some of the ingredients of the pedagogical ability needed to share knowledge across borders. One of the many paradoxes that we meet in the knowledge management arena is that much of the most valuable knowledge, typically firm specific and tacit in nature, is hard to share and transfer.

For knowledge sharing to take place, the source of the knowledge must be willing to share it (Szulanski, 1996). In the example presented at the beginning of this section, the manufacturing units were unwilling to share information about their productivity with others, and they saw no interest in teaching others how to improve their operations. The strong competition that existed between plants helps to explain their attitudes. These units were competing for resources, even for survival, since the headquarters executives were reviewing critically the structure of the company's international network of manufacturing units. Why then help others to learn something that is a key advantage for one's own unit? The subsidiary managers were mostly evaluated only on their own unit's performance, which reinforced the inward-looking atmosphere of the firm.

Social status and reputation play important roles in shaping the context for knowledge sharing. People gain status when they are perceived as knowledgeable, and sharing knowledge with others is a good way for them to enhance their reputation. People who are given credit for having shared knowledge are more likely to do so again in the future (Cross and Prusak, 2003). This mechanism operates both at the inter-unit level (does the other unit acknowledge the knowledge source?) and the corporate level (does top management recognize those who share knowledge?). Knowledge sharing requires strong social networks within the multinational organization where reputations are built and where people learn not only what are the useful sources of knowledge but also who is willing to engage in joint problem solving.

Norms of reciprocity are also important. Units and individuals are more willing to invest in sharing their knowledge with others if they trust them to reciprocate these favours in the future. Teaching others requires considerable effort, and in the absence of strong social relationships between the parties, the decision to engage in knowledge sharing is usually based on some instrumental calculation of whether or not it is worth the time and money (Cross and Prusak, 2003). A higher level of trust is therefore associated with more knowledge sharing, as is the existence of a strong organizational culture where knowledge sharing is an important shared value.

Receiver unit's ability and willingness

The term absorptive capacity (Cohen and Levinthal, 1990) is commonly used in the scholarly literature to describe the ability of the receiving unit to evaluate, assimilate and exploit new knowledge from outside the organization (see Zahra and Georg (2002), and Lane et al. (2006) for discussions of the concept of absorptive capacity). A meta-analysis of 75 studies revealed a significant relationship ($r = 0.19$) between receiver absorptive capacity and knowledge transfer (van Wijk et al., 2008). Naturally, a subsidiary may have a higher level of absorptive capacity in some areas than in others. Since knowledge changes when it is introduced into or absorbed by a new context, the ability to absorb new know-how requires a certain knowledge base and experience with its transfer.

However, although the unit's general absorptive capacity undoubtedly is important, much of the knowledge transfer that occurs within multinational firms takes place in dyadic relationships between two units. Therefore, in many instances it makes more sense to examine absorptive capacity at the level of two units interacting and sharing knowledge. The term relative absorptive capacity (Lane and Lubatkin, 1998) has been coined to refer to the unit-specific ability to absorb knowledge from another party. While it would seem natural for units with similar levels of relative absorptive capacity to seek each other out, there are knowledge management paradoxes associated with relative absorptive capacity. When two units are similar, it is much easier for them to understand and absorb knowledge from the other. But on the other hand, similar units usually have less to learn from each other. In other words, the more their knowledge overlaps, the less there is to be gained from investment in knowledge sharing.

Furthermore, those involved must speak a common language well enough to share tacit knowledge. Fluency in a common language has also been found to be positively associated with inter-unit trust and shared cognition (Barner-Rasmussen and Björkman, 2006), which in turn are important drivers of knowledge sharing. While multinationals from many different countries have adopted English as their corporate language, this has not eliminated the language-related problems in knowledge sharing among geographically dispersed units. A Swedish multinational provides an illustration. Headquarters managers noticed that there was a lack of sharing between the German subsidiary and its Scandinavian sister units. On investigation, it turned out that the general manager of the German subsidiary was not a confident English speaker and therefore did not participate in the informal discussions with his Scandinavian peers that were intended to lead to exchange of know-how. The appointment of an English-speaking deputy to the German subsidiary solved this problem (Monteiro et al., 2008).

Absorptive capacity is more than just the ability of a unit to recognize the value of new information, to assimilate and apply it to commercial ends (Zahra and George, 2002; Lane et al., 2006). It also includes the capacity to unlearn, to challenge existing ways of doing things. Generally speaking, the more satisfied people are with current practices and results, the less willing they are to seek out and absorb new knowledge. And even if people realize that they are facing a problem that needs to be tackled, inward-looking units with strong internal social networks may not actively search for relevant knowledge held by other parts of the multinational.

Lack of motivation to learn from other units, even within the same enterprise, is well documented. There is a natural psychological tendency to inflate the perceived quality of one's own knowledge while deflating that of others. The not-invented-here (NIH) syndrome has been described in a number of case studies, and it can be particularly strong if a unit is financially successful and has a long proud history. One of the major challenges facing many multinationals is the unwillingness of units in mature markets to learn from subsidiaries in emerging economies as the flow of knowledge was historically one-way.

Also, for the receiving unit the value of the knowledge held by another unit is rarely clear. When the source unit is perceived as knowledgeable, others will be more interested in learning from it (Szulanski, 1996). In the absence of reliable information about the quality of other units' knowledge, people tend to rely more on the knowledge residing in well performing subsidiaries and those located in the most advanced markets, discounting the potential value of low performers; the term 'halo effect' is used to describe this tendency (Gupta et al., 2008). There is also an understandable tendency to prefer to learn from similar units, those that follow a similar strategy and share common organizational characteristics (Darr and Kurtzberg, 2000). Moreover, it is not only the potential usefulness of the knowledge that is difficult to assess; the effort and costs associated with accessing and assimilating this knowledge into the receiver units are also unclear. Therefore, the likely return on investment associated with knowledge acquisition and sharing is difficult to estimate (Cross and Prusak, 2003).

In our view, too much emphasis has been placed on the push of knowledge transfer and sharing, and too little on the pull from the receiving unit (see Szulanski, 1996). As the old saying goes, you can lead a horse to water but you cannot make it drink – unless it wants to. We therefore recommend that multinationals focus more on stimulating units to seek and adopt knowledge and practices from other parts of the corporation.

Characteristics of the relationship between the sending and receiving units

Internal MNC knowledge transfer is possible only when close relationships are established between senders and receivers. Relationships provide communication bridges, possibilities for dialogue across organizational hierarchy, conditions for team learning, and systems to capture and share learning within the organization (Levitt and March, 1988; Senge, 1990; Argyris and Schon, 1996).

There are several empirical studies on internal MNC knowledge transfer that support these ideas. Szulanski (1996: 31–32) claimed that since 'intrafirm exchanges of knowledge are embedded in an organizational context … a transfer of knowledge, especially when the knowledge transferred has a tacit component, may require numerous individual exchanges'. Bresman et al. (1999) showed that interpersonal communication, such as visits and meetings, were significant facilitators of international knowledge transfer. Gupta and Govindarajan (2000) considered not only the existence of communication channels but also the richness of communication links, captured as informality, openness and density of communication. Hansen (1999) concluded that the absence of direct relations and extensive communication among people from different departments inhibits knowledge transfer, while strong inter-unit relations facilitate it. In his work on knowledge networks, he also explored why some business units are able to benefit from knowledge in other parts of the company while others are not. He found that units that were more involved in their respective knowledge networks were able to acquire more knowledge from other divisions in the network (Hansen, 2002).

These and other research findings provide powerful support for the prediction that the existence and richness of lateral inter-unit integration mechanisms (channels linking a subsidiary to the rest of an MNC) are positively associated with the transfer of knowledge.

4 How to stimulate knowledge sharing

The three determinants of knowledge sharing within MNCs identified above (disseminative capacity, absorptive capacity and relationships between units) can be affected directly and indirectly by organizational mechanisms and HRM practices. Specifically, MNCs can make knowledge sharing effective, efficient and fast by:

- disseminating information about superior performance and knowledge
- employing HRM practices that influence the ability and motivation of employees to absorb knowledge
- selecting expatriates with knowledge sharing in mind
- designing appropriate structural mechanisms
- building a conducive social architecture.

Disseminating information about superior performance and knowledge

One of the most basic reasons for not using knowledge from other parts of the multinational is that people are unaware that it exists. For instance, several units may encounter similar problems in the manufacturing process but be unaware that one has already found a viable solution. An often-heard expression illustrates this common problem: 'If we only knew what we know'. In fact, much of the interest in knowledge management in large corporations focuses on the challenge of locating potentially valuable knowledge.

As we pointed out earlier, units perceived by others to be highly capable are more likely to be sought out as sources of knowledge (Monteiro et al., 2008). However, the evaluation of a subsidiary's capabilities is relatively subjective. Studies have revealed that there are only modest correlations between how managers from headquarters and those from foreign subsidiaries view the capabilities of overseas units (Denrell et al., 2004). Therefore, it is important to identify superior practices by measuring relevant dimensions of unit performance. By making performance data widely available – turning the multinational into a fishbowl where strong performance is showcased – the units can themselves uncover examples of unique and valuable knowledge. For instance, Alfa Laval Agri from Sweden held quarterly meetings for all its subsidiary managers where they were required to present performance data along multiple dimensions. This approach helped to reduce the bias and ambiguity present in internal assessments of capabilities, and stimulated knowledge sharing among the units (Monteiro et al., 2008).

Employing HRM practices that influence the ability and motivation of employees to absorb and share knowledge

Previous research shows that successful implementation of traditional HR practices can enhance a unit's absorptive capacity (Minbaeva et al., 2003), for example by recruiting people with required skills and knowledge. Investments in the training and development of employees can also contribute, as training enhances the quality of human capital needed to achieve the knowledge goals of an organization (Minbaeva et al., 2003; Zárraga and Bonache, 2003; Beugelsdijk, 2008). Performance management systems provide employees with feedback on their performance and competencies, and give them direction for enhancing their competencies to meet the organization's knowledge needs (Minbaeva, 2007; Lopez-Cabrales et al., 2009; Simonin and Özsomer, 2009). Indeed, an integral part of most performance management systems is the establishment of objectives and targets for self-development and employee training (see Chapter 10).

Organizations can also rely on job design, promotion and performance-based compensation. The design of jobs to ensure that they contain certain motivational factors such as autonomy, task identity and feedback stimulates different aspects of the motivation for knowledge sharing (e.g. Cabrera et al., 2006; Foss, 2009). Rewarding knowledge-sharing behaviour with bonuses and acknowledging contributions to the work of others boosts the motivation of employees to share their know-how (e.g. Minbaeva et al., 2003; Cabrera et al., 2006; Lopez-Cabrales et al., 2009). If knowledge sharing has career implications, this sends strong signals about the kind of behaviour that is valued and rewarded in the corporation.

In addition, the incorporation of rewards for knowledge sharing in performance-based compensation reduces uncertainty with regard to issues surrounding goal prioritization (Minbaeva et al., 2003; Cabrera et al., 2006; Lopez-Cabrales et al., 2009). But it should be noted that compensation strategies can lead to significant obstacles to knowledge sharing (Bock et al., 2005; Minbaeva, 2007). When individuals perceive that they are rewarded individually for their performance and expertise, sharing knowledge with others may naturally be seen as contrary to their interest. That is, when pecuniary rewards are introduced, an incentive for the individual to withhold knowledge for future gains is also added. Furthermore, as Osterloh and Frey (2000) suggest, intrinsic motivation is more effective than the motivation of extrinsic rewards when tacit knowledge is involved. Also, multiple-task problems arise when combined with the problem of 'free riding' in teams, which can arise whenever individuals see that they can rely on others to do the work and are unlikely to be held accountable for their comparatively lower contribution. So, in certain circumstances, the use of rewards may be counter-productive. This implies that we cannot simply pay for knowledge-sharing behaviour: such collaborative behaviour must above all be encouraged and facilitated (Bock et al., 2005: 89).

At Schlumberger, GE and many other firms, knowledge sharing is part of the formal performance reviews for managers and engineers. Most Schlumberger field engineers have objectives relating to best practices, lessons learned and other aspects of knowledge sharing (Åbø et al., 2001). Not surprisingly, an incentive system that encourages collaboration and knowledge sharing is more likely to produce these outcomes than a performance evaluation system where the hoarding of knowledge and internal competition are tolerated or even encouraged (Björkman et al., 2004; Gupta et al., 2008). The logic of systems in place at many multinationals is that managers and executives should be motivated to contribute to company performance at least one level above the unit for which they are responsible. A foreign subsidiary manager may receive a bonus based on the regional or even global performance of the division or the corporation as a whole. This can encourage knowledge sharing and wider collaboration between organizational units.

Conversely, tying incentives to the performance of a subsidiary relative to its sister companies will create a disincentive to share information and knowledge. A retail company where the heads of neighbouring areas were married to each other constitutes an amusing example of the perverse effects that such reward systems may have. The general managers – husband and wife – failed to share knowledge with each other because their bonuses were tied to the relative performance of the two units!

Selecting expatriates with knowledge sharing in mind

Cross-border transfers of personnel is one of the most important levers of knowledge sharing that multinationals have at their disposal. Typically, the transfer and assimilation of complex tacit knowledge into a new context requires the physical relocation of someone with experience – in the past usually an expatriate from headquarters, today the source can be anywhere in the world. The motives for why multinationals choose to deploy expatriates have been extensively discussed in the literature, and they are also discussed elsewhere in this book (see Chapter 5). The close interactions of experienced expatriates with employees in their local units offer many opportunities for sharing tacit knowledge (Lazarova and Tarique, 2005). Inpatriates may be expected to play similar knowledge-sharing roles during assignments at headquarters and on their return to foreign units. Short-term personal interactions during visits, international conferences and meetings, and corporate training sessions may fulfil the same function but they are likely to be most successful for knowledge that is explicit and/or relatively narrow in scope (Bonache and Zárraga-Oberty, 2008).

More recently, some researchers have focused on knowledge accumulated through expatriate, inpatriate or repatriate assignments, and how the transfer of that knowledge contributes to the firm's objectives (Lazarova and Tarique, 2005; Hocking et al., 2007; Reiche, 2012). Hocking et al. (2007) studied how expatriates contribute to the strategic objectives of multinationals in the domains of global efficiency, local responsiveness and worldwide learning. They find that the impact of expatriate knowledge results from frequent knowledge access as well as communication with corporate headquarters and other units of the firm, while expatriates derive experiential learning from frequent access to local knowledge that is subsequently adapted to the global corporate context. Reiche (2012) finds that the boundary spanning competence of inpatriates is positively related to their individual efforts to transfer knowledge and their perception of how willing headquarters is to learn from abroad (its absorptive capacity).

In spite of the importance of international assignments for knowledge sharing, expatriation has its limitations. Consider the example of Toyota. Over the last three decades the company's global strategy has been to gain market share by adding new manufacturing capacity in all its major markets (Takeuchi et al., 2008). To ensure Toyota's reputation for quality and performance, the company taught local employees in every new location the Toyota Way – its production and management philosophy of continuous improvement. This essentially tacit knowledge was transferred through extensive use of expatriates. However, as effective as Toyota was in deploying expatriates to diffuse tacit knowledge, it simply did not have enough of them to support the company's rapid global expansion (Watanabe, 2007). The company had to become even better and faster in building its operating capabilities abroad. In order to speed up the learning process and to reinforce the knowledge transfer mechanism, Toyota created a Global Production Center in Toyota City. Its goal was to accelerate the development of local employees with deep knowledge of the Toyota production system (TPS) so the company would not have to rely solely on its experienced – and increasingly expensive – expatriates.

When selecting people for international assignments, some of the general characteristics that one looks for in expatriates are relevant here:

- professional and technical competence
- relationship and communication abilities
- cultural sensitivity and flexibility.

Appropriate professional and technical competence is a prerequisite for most international assignments. The person must have the relevant training and experience not only to teach and coach others but also to learn him/herself on the job. Relationship and communication abilities help the expatriate build close interpersonal contacts that improve collaboration and facilitate knowledge transfer to the local unit, also giving the person access to local knowledge. Cultural sensitivity and flexibility improves the ability to adapt knowledge to the different local context. Expatriates who are non-evaluative when interpreting the behaviour of local employees are more likely to be effective in sharing and acquiring knowledge.

Pre-departure training as well as training, coaching and mentoring during the assignment abroad can assist the expatriate in the knowledge-sharing role. More important, however, may be the objectives that are set for expatriates within the performance management system. If transfer of knowledge or organizational practices to the local unit is defined as a key performance indicator (KPI) for the expatriate, it provides a clear motivation to focus on achieving this target. An explicit localization strategy for which the expatriate is held responsible may also further enhance the transfer of knowledge.

Structural mechanisms

Various lateral structural mechanisms are used in part or even primarily to stimulate knowledge sharing. For instance, product development committees with members representing different geographic units and functional areas (e.g. R&D, manufacturing and marketing) are established with the aim of tapping into the different perspectives and pools of experience that the members bring to the committee. Temporary international task forces can serve the same purpose. Multinationals may also appoint individuals with the specific task of liaising between units, for example within a specific functional area.

The Knowledge Management Programme (KMP) at the world's largest steel manufacturer ArcelorMittal (formed in 2006 through Mittal Steel's acquisition of Arcelor) illustrates how multinationals may create horizontal teams or committees to enhance inter-unit knowledge sharing. Mittal Steel developed the programme during the 1990s when it expanded into Eastern Europe. KMP continues to play an important role in the new ArcelorMittal group, where the KMP process helps build peer networks and facilitates the integration process. Mittal Steel chose 25 activities, including manufacturing, finance, maintenance, purchasing, legal work and information technology, for their programme. Each of these had groups of approximately 20 members from different plants. They would meet regularly to benchmark the activities undertaken in the different units and to discuss common problems. For specific problems, the groups used conference calls and smaller specialized ad hoc meetings. The diversity of the groups was viewed as a particular strength – according to Mittal Steel's chief operating officer: 'These countries have some very good technology. The Poles, for instance, have always been good in coke-making, and we have recently had a Romanian manager who was very helpful in sorting out a blast furnace problem in Chicago' (ICFAI, 2005).

Working in project or so called 'split egg' roles (Evans et al., 2011) where managers and professionals have vertical and horizontal responsibilities, is at the heart of BP's focus on global knowledge management in its oil exploration and production business (Hansen and von Oetinger, 2001). Peer groups of business unit heads meet regularly. They are given joint responsibility for capital allocation and for setting unit performance goals, complemented by a host of cross-unit networks on shared areas of interest. These 'top of the egg' knowledge-sharing activities take up to 20 per cent of the manager's time. 'The model here is an open market of ideas', says one business unit head. 'People develop a sense of where the real expertise lies. Rather than having to deal with the bureaucracy of going through the centre, you can just cut across to somebody in Stavanger or Aberdeen or Houston and say, "I need some help. Can you give me a couple of hours?" And that is expected and encouraged' (Hansen and von Oetinger, 2001: 111).

The knowledge management groups at ArcelorMittal and BP have many of the features associated with open communities of practice. These communities are characterized by some form of collaboration around a common set of interests. They differ from project teams and committees in that the participants' roles are not defined by the firm. Although the focus of these communities is on internal company issues, they may also broker relationships with outside experts. Communities of practice cannot and should not be fully controlled by the firm, building instead on voluntary participation, although support and guidance is essential (Wenger and Snyder, 2000; Probst and Borzillo, 2008). BT Global even provides a corporate version of Facebook, allowing people to mix professional and private networking, so that staff can tap into the experience of others around the world.

Research on communities of practice offers some guidelines on how to make them successful. First, it is important to have clear, shared objectives and a leader tasked with making sure that knowledge and best practices are shared and developed further. Second, the quality of interactions can be reinforced with workshops, training, exchange of staff and an appropriate reward structure, with part-time coordination funded by the corporate budget. A study of unsuccessful communities of practice revealed that they lacked a core group of members; there was little one-to-one interaction between members; members did not identify with the community; participants had a strong belief in their own competence; and the issues discussed were not illustrated concretely enough for others to understand and visualize them (Probst and Borzillo, 2008).

ArcelorMittal refrained from appointing a 'best plant' for others to emulate, believing that all units had something to teach others. Some multinationals have appointed geographically dispersed centres of excellence that, among other things, are in charge of knowledge sharing. Such centres can for instance be formed in various locations around a small group of individuals recognized for their leading edge, strategically valuable knowledge. These centres of excellence are mandated to make their knowledge available throughout the global firm and enhance it so that it remains at the cutting edge. Three types of centre have been identified in global service firms: charismatic (formed around an individual), focused (a small group of experts in a single location) and virtual (a larger group of specialists in multiple locations, linked by a database and proprietary tools). The charismatic and focused centres are well equipped to handle tacit knowledge, while the focused and virtual centres can process more firm-specific knowledge than a single individual (Moore and Birkinshaw, 1998). In contrast to parent-driven knowledge development, these centres tend to rely more on informal networks, often acting as a hub for knowledge-sharing activities.

Social capital, social norms and global mindsets

The social relationship between the source and the receiver is another strong determinant of knowledge sharing within multinationals (Hansen et al., 2005). Taken as a whole, these relationships constitute the social capital of the firm. They comprise an intangible resource – a form of capital in the same way that human skills represent human capital – since the firm derives benefits from the connections and interpersonal relationships of people within the organization and outside it.

According to Nahapiet and Ghoshal (1998), social capital comprises three interrelated dimensions: the relational, the cognitive and the structural. Tsai and Ghoshal (1998) empirically examined the relationships between these three dimensions and found that all dimensions had significant effects – both direct and indirect – on intra-organizational resource exchange. In line with this, Inkpen and Tsang argue that 'access to new sources of knowledge is one of the most important direct benefits of social capital' (2005: 146) and conclude that assets that reside in networks of relationships affect the conditions necessary for knowledge transfer, encouraging cooperative behaviour. Social capital increases the organization's ability to acquire and transfer new knowledge (Gooderham et al., 2011). All three dimensions of social capital – structural, relational and cognitive – are important.

The structural dimension of social capital refers to the pattern of relationships between people and units in the multinational. Unless there is a connection of some kind between two units or individuals, it is virtually impossible to share tacit knowledge. Moreover, two units that have a history of interaction are more likely to be aware of potentially useful knowledge residing in the other unit. Through relationships people may also gain important and fortuitous insights even when they are not searching for ideas on immediate problems. As indicated earlier, a large number of studies have confirmed that the degree of inter-unit communication is positively associated with knowledge sharing and innovation (Nahapiet and Ghoshal, 1998).

The cognitive dimension reflects the extent to which two parties are capable of sharing their understanding. A shared language and specialized vocabulary facilitate the interaction between organizational units and greatly enhance their ability to learn from each other. It has been suggested that the construction and recounting of shared narratives – collective stories and myths – in a community can aid the sharing of tacit knowledge. The use of metaphors may fulfil the same purpose.

Trust is at the core of the relational dimension of social capital. When two parties trust each other, they are more likely to share knowledge, in part because they are confident that the other party will reciprocate tomorrow for help they receive today. Units or individuals that are perceived as trustworthy are likely to be sought out by others to share their know-how and experience. Therefore, the reputation of an organizational unit, team or individual will influence whether or not others initiate processes of knowledge sharing with them. Trust was found to be the strongest predictor of inter-unit knowledge transfer in a recent meta-analysis of research on knowledge transfer (van Wijk et al., 2008).

Social networks naturally emerge in all social settings, although corporations can work with the explicit aim of strengthening social capital across units. The establishment of committees, projects and centres of excellence leads to the emergence and development of social relationships among the participants. A range of HR practices have the growth of social capital as one of their aims – from corporate training programmes with participants from different parts of the corporation to regional induction programmes for new recruits to transfers of personnel. However, it is also important to build a context that makes it more likely that people from different units around the world will engage in collaborative efforts. Therefore, two other aspects of the social architecture of the multinational – social norms and global mindset – are also crucial for knowledge sharing.

Social norms should support knowledge sharing. Appropriate behaviours will be encouraged if hoarding knowledge is seen as violating the company's values and if those who transfer know-how to other units are presented as heroes. In such firms, knowledge is more likely to be viewed as a corporate resource to be exploited throughout the organization (Gupta et al., 2008).

Wider knowledge sharing can be expected in organizations where employees are encouraged to identify areas where improvements are necessary, and in firms where nobody fears that saying something negative about their own unit or organization will be detrimental to their career (Currie and Kerrin, 2003). During one stage in GE's globalization, the company set up a series of workshops where executives shared their 'global battlefield' experiences – with an explicit focus on where and why they failed. The message was loud and clear. It is OK to try something new and fail, but you had better learn from the experience and make sure that others do not repeat your mistake.

Knowledge sharing is also influenced by peoples' state of mind, and the term global mindset has recently gained prominence in the international management and HRM literatures. There are two different and complementary perspectives on global mindset, both relevant to knowledge management. One is rooted in a psychological focus on the development of managers in multinational firms, while the other comes from scholars and practitioners with a strategic viewpoint on the transnational enterprise. The first views global mindset as the ability to accept and work with cultural diversity, reflected in research that tries to map the skill or competency sets associated with management of diversity. Cultural self-awareness, openness to and understanding of other cultures are the core elements of the psychological or, as some scholars prefer to label it, the cultural perspective on global mindset (Levy et al., 2007). This dimension of global mindset is concerned with why some persons are better in sharing – and especially receiving – knowledge across cultures. For instance, a paint technician with a global mindset in a car plant in China would seek knowledge from colleagues in the US or India.

The second complementary perspective on global mindset focuses on a way of thinking (or cognition) that reflects conflicting strategic orientations; it can therefore be labelled a strategic perspective. Since most multinational firms face strategic contradictions (the determining feature of the transnational enterprise), scholars have emphasized the need for 'balanced perspectives', arguing that a critical determinant of success in multinationals lies in the cognitive orientations of senior managers – their ability to cope with complexity embedded in the business (Levy et al., 2007). Knowledge embedded in diverse roles and dispersed operations is easier to harness when managers understand the need for multiple strategic capabilities, and view problems and opportunities from both local and global perspectives.

The task for the multinational firm is not to build a sophisticated structure, but to create a matrix in managers' minds (Bartlett and Ghoshal, 1989). International mobility and project work, international training programmes, performance objectives that go beyond their own local unit, and top managers who 'walk the talk' are some of the ways in which multinationals can build global mindsets (Evans et al., 2011).

5 Gaining access to external knowledge

Historically, firms paid little attention to ways in which they might get access to new external knowledge through their international operations. Today, put simply, innovations are more likely to come from the field than from the headquarters. Academics and practitioners agree that the successful multinational corporations are increasingly those that are better at exploiting the possibilities offered by their worldwide networks to gain access to new knowledge and ideas from foreign locations. These opportunities can then be shared and combined with knowledge residing in the parent company with the aim of producing new innovations. This was the objective of the Connect + Develop model championed by Procter & Gamble (P&G), the aim of which was to find external ideas that could be further developed within the corporation, often in collaboration with external partners (Huston and Sakkab, 2006; Lafley and Charan, 2008). Many other firms are now trying to emulate P&G's model. In this section we discuss different strategies for gaining access to external knowledge as well as how to ensure that valuable knowledge is retained.

Turning new knowledge that has been acquired from outside the corporation into a commercially viable innovation involves capabilities in assimilating and recombining that new knowledge. So the acquisition of new knowledge also requires internal knowledge sharing, as discussed earlier. The levers that multinationals have at their disposal to enhance cross-border knowledge sharing are also relevant for external knowledge acquisition. Indeed the meta-analysis conducted by van Wijk and colleagues (2008) found that both external and internal knowledge sharing/transfers were largely influenced by the same mechanisms. However, firms may use additional approaches to access knowledge from the outside: scanning or tapping into the local knowledge base, partnering or merging with other firms, and what might be called playing the virtual market. Each of these has its own set of HRM implications.

Scanning global learning opportunities

Scanning involves gaining access to external knowledge from what people read, hear or experience at first hand. Important observations and innovative ideas can emerge from anywhere in the multinational. Although new insights typically come as a by-product of ongoing operations, specific investments in scanning may also enhance the external acquisition of new knowledge especially when innovation and development are encouraged in the organization.

The establishment of a 'listening post' is a fairly inexpensive way to begin. P&G appointed 70 technology entrepreneurs to work in the company's regional hubs to scan their environments for ideas that might be useful for the corporation worldwide. The Taiwanese PC-manufacturer Acer established a small design shop in the US, through which it acquired skills in ergonomic design that were fed back to the parent organization (Doz et al., 2001). Ericsson, the Swedish telecommunications firm, created 'cyberlabs' in New York and Palo Alto (next to Stanford University in Silicon Valley) whose task was to monitor developments in these markets and to build relationships with local companies (Birkinshaw, 2004).

While listening posts can be a useful way to access codified knowledge and facilitate the firm's identification of potential partners, they are less effective when the objective is to acquire tacit knowledge. Small units and individual scanners may lack the necessary influence to get the attention of corporate headquarters for new ideas. Many multinationals therefore establish fully fledged units in business centres at the forefront of the development of their respective industries, such as Silicon Valley (high technology), North Italy (fashion) and the City of London (financial services) (Inkpen and Tsang, 2005). These districts contain networks of producers, advanced users, supporting industries, universities and research labs, and have fluid labour markets with highly competent individuals. Scanning in centres like these takes place through formal collaboration among organizations, formalized networks like trade associations and professional organizations, and more informal social networks.

From an HRM perspective, there are pros and cons associated with establishing a unit in locations such as Silicon Valley. On the one hand, there is an ample supply of people with relevant experience and the opportunity for social contacts can be invaluable. However, at the same time there is often fierce competition for talent, escalating salaries and the attendant risk of losing people to competitors. The winners are firms that are better than others at retaining their star performers, the losers tend to be those firms that suffer from high rates of attrition. Tight social networks not only help a firm tap into external knowledge but also serve as a conduit for its proprietary knowledge. Research has shown that firms that try to constrain their employees, in terms of what they are allowed to talk about with others, are likely to lose. They tend to get a bad reputation, which impairs their ability to hire the best people (Fleming and Marx, 2006).

Accessing and assimilating complex tacit knowledge requires considerable investment in time and resources. Shiseido from Japan learnt this when establishing itself in France to learn about designing, manufacturing and selling scent. After attempting an unsuccessful joint venture with a French company, it formed a wholly owned subsidiary, Beauté Prestige International, to develop and produce fragrances. It also established a high-end beauty parlour in Paris and bought two functioning beauty salons. After a prolonged process, Shiseido learnt to let host country people with long-term industry experience take charge of its operations in France. In the end, Shiseido succeeded in acquiring capabilities in product development, manufacturing and marketing that the company was able to transfer back to Japan, through close observation and interaction between Japanese expatriates and French employees (Doz et al., 2001).

A crucial HRM issue when establishing a unit abroad is the company's ability to attract competent personnel at competitive costs. Experienced multinationals like Nokia always carry out in-depth HR analyses before they set up new units. Questions they typically ask include: Do the local universities produce engineering graduates with the required competence level for an R&D centre? Will the influx of other corporations to hotspots like Bangalore or Beijing lead to salary escalation that undermines current cost advantages?

Partnering or merging

A significant proportion of knowledge acquisition comes about through partnering, that is, deep relationships with other organizations. Partners include suppliers, distributers, competitors and research organizations. Some alliances and joint ventures with partner organizations are established with the explicit objective of co-creating new knowledge; but much knowledge acquisition takes place in partnerships where the focus is on ongoing manufacturing or distribution of products. P&G quickly realized the potential of the 50,000 R&D staff in their 15 top suppliers. Several measures were taken to increase the number of joint R&D projects with suppliers, including the development of a secure IT platform used to communicate technology briefs with them (descriptions of what P&G is looking for), as well as face-to-face meetings to improve relationships and strengthen the understanding of the other's capabilities. The effect was a clear increase in the number of jointly staffed projects (Huston and Sakkab, 2006).

One of the challenges in learning alliances and joint ventures is that they may involve firms with competing interests, where parties strive to learn from each other to improve their individual position (Pucik, 1988). The Nummi joint venture formed between Toyota and GM in California more than two decades ago is a classic example. GM's aim was to learn about lean manufacturing from Toyota, whereas the Japanese firm wanted to learn about the US market and gain experience in establishing and operating a local production unit. Most observers agree that Toyota was the more successful of the two in this 'race to learn', and it has been argued that to a large extent this was because its HRM strategy and learning objectives were fully aligned (Tapscott and Williams, 2007).

The use of outsourcing has become widespread in virtually all industries. However, while most attention has been given to the outsourcing of support activities, like accounting and customer service, to India, companies also use contractors for more advanced activities. For instance, over the last few years, original equipment manufacturers in the mobile phone industry have invested in building their own product development capabilities, which they offer to companies like Nokia and Motorola. The development of a new mobile phone can be a highly complex process, involving an OEM, a specialized R&D company and several units from the mobile phone company. There are significant challenges in developing appropriate structures for such projects and considerable attention must be paid to developing the social relationships needed for the collaboration to run smoothly. A major challenge for firms is to capture the individual learning of the key people involved in such partnerships, translating it into organizational know-how that can be conveyed to others.

Mergers and acquisitions are the ultimate form of partnering. Not all M&As focus on knowledge acquisition, but a key objective in cross-border M&As is usually the acquisition and retention of local knowledge. The mechanisms for encouraging knowledge sharing that were discussed earlier in this chapter (such as creating social capital and social norms, developing structural mechanisms, and specifying supportive performance management and incentive systems) are relevant also in M&As.

Playing the virtual market

In the last decade we have seen a tremendous increase in the variety of mechanisms used to access company-external knowledge. One of the effects of the digital revolution described by Friedman (2005) in *The World Is Flat* is the use of new technologies to link individuals and organizations in all parts of the world. For example, firms can post a specification of what they are looking for on the internet, together with information about the reward that will be given to anyone who comes up with a solution. In 1999, the CEO of a troubled Canadian goldmine (an intensely secretive industry) decided to post all the geological data about the mine on the web, offering half a million dollars in prize money to virtual inspectors. The resulting ideas and gold discoveries catapulted Goldcorp from a $100 million underperformer into a $9 billion juggernaut that is one of the most innovative and profitable mining firms in the industry today. Companies can also issue more general calls for research projects. In 2008, HP's open innovation office announced a call for research proposals. It received more than 450 submissions from 200 universities in 22 countries. Forty-one of those proposals were funded (Jaruzelski and Dehoff, 2008).

P&G has paid considerable attention to the question of how best to use the 'market' for knowledge acquisition. Together with other large corporations, P&G has helped create firms specializing in connecting companies with technology problems with other companies, universities, labs and individuals who may be able to offer solutions. These market brokers can help write technology briefs and facilitate the interaction between the corporation with the problem and the organization or individual with the potential solution. Market brokers often have a relatively well-specified scope of activities. P&G works with NineSigma which connects companies and organizations, InnoCentive which brokers solutions to more narrowly defined technical problems, and with YourEncore, a business that connects retired scientists and engineers with client corporations (Huston and Sakkab, 2006).

The challenges involved in the use of virtual cross-border teams and international alliances are amplified when playing the virtual market. The professional competences and interpersonal skills of the people managing these relationships are particularly important – they must be able to develop trust-based relationships swiftly with new partners. They also need to reach a shared understanding of performance expectations and decide how they will work together to achieve their objectives. Aligning the reward structure is critical. Without incentives, knowledge will not flow in. But with too many incentives, some talented individuals may decide that playing the market is more rewarding than staying with the firm – which brings us to the problem of retention.

6 Knowledge retention

While codified knowledge can be physically stored in databases and reports, tacit knowledge resides in people. When individuals with unique and valuable knowledge walk out of the door, the company might be losing part of its competitive advantage. What can the firm do to dissuade core tacit knowledge from making that exit?

There are three basic knowledge retention strategies. The first, which we have already discussed, is to stimulate knowledge sharing among individuals and units, so that the company is less dependent on a small number of people. An obvious illustration of this is when people with unique knowledge are approaching retirement, though with increasing turnover of professional employees in most countries and corporations, knowledge sharing has to be encouraged on a continuous basis.

A second strategy is to try to reduce employee turnover, reducing in turn the leaking of proprietary knowledge to competitors. This means, among others, trying to make sure that employees believe that they have good development opportunities in the firm and paying attention to the individual interests of the person (for a more extensive discussion see Evans et al., 2011). However, knowledge retention should also be a factor when considering involuntary turnover, during periods of recession, or when companies are considering relocating operations.

When the price of oil reached its nadir in the late 1990s, many energy firms responded by curtailing exploration activities and laying off experienced staff. Less than five years later, when prices moved in the opposite direction, they had to buy back the same skills from outside at a much higher cost. In some cases they even had to forgo major opportunities as they simply did not have a sufficiently experienced workforce to manage the projects.

The third strategy is to invest in making tacit knowledge explicit. The Japanese knowledge management scholar Ikujiro Nonaka (1994) calls this 'externalization'. He suggests that metaphors can help individuals to explain tacit concepts that are otherwise difficult to articulate by conveying intuitive images that people can understand. The explicit knowledge can then be codified and saved in databases and the like, where they can be accessed after the people with the embedded knowledge have left the firm. For this strategy to work, the firm must be clear about the type of knowledge that is accorded high value and how it will be made accessible.

The example of how to manage repatriates illustrates all three strategies. Multinationals typically pay too little attention to how the organization can benefit from the knowledge that repatriates have gained abroad. Many returnees are dissatisfied with the career opportunities they are offered and begin looking for jobs elsewhere. Numerous studies and anecdotes have shown that a large percentage of international assignees resign shortly after returning home. Successful retention management is therefore part of a successful approach to repatriate knowledge sharing. The receiving organization must make sure that repatriates have opportunities to share their knowledge by appointing them to positions where they can work with others on issues related to their experience, and by assigning them to relevant projects and committees (Oddou et al., 2009). In some situations, reports and presentations can be appropriate tools for capturing and sharing insights gained during overseas assignments (Lazarova and Tarique, 2005).

7 From the management of knowledge to innovation

So far we have discussed knowledge transfer within the multinational and acquisition of new knowledge from outside the company. Both activities are crucial for nurturing innovation in the multinational. The fact is that big, complex global organizations have difficulty with innovation. As Kanter (1989) notes, it is like teaching elephants how to dance. The biggest problem may not be that multinationals do not know how to be innovative – it is that the properties needed to be innovative are different from those needed to be successful in exploiting what they are doing well today. This is just one of the many paradoxes in the domain of global knowledge management.

Effective knowledge management is important both to exploit existing capabilities on a global scale and to explore new ideas that can be developed into new product and service offerings. While both exploration and exploitation are needed, finding a balance between the two is challenging (March, 1991). Companies easily fall into the trap of focusing too much on one at the expense of the other, one of the many dualities that multinationals are facing (see Evans et al., 2011). We have considered other dualities in this chapter – balancing network and structural modes of organization, and inside versus outside orientations to gain access to new knowledge.

Let us take two other paradoxes that we have not yet explicitly mentioned – the transfer paradox and the evaluation paradox. The transfer paradox argues that the most valuable knowledge – complex and contextual tacit knowledge – is also the most sticky. It is expensive and difficult to transfer within the multinational, requiring linking mechanisms that build on face-to-face relationships. The evaluation paradox holds that this same tacit know-how is also the most difficult and expensive to evaluate and assess. Organizing for innovation means managing the tensions that underlie such dualities.

The management of knowledge and innovation on a global scale is clearly a challenge, with numerous HRM implications, although nothing that confers sustainable competitive advantage comes easily. Performance management systems and compensation schemes have to encourage both exploration and exploitation. Multinationals need to recruit and select employees bearing in mind the acquisition of valuable external knowledge, but they also need to socialize new employees to make sure that this knowledge is shared across units. And a key decision-making criterion for staffing decisions should increasingly be the innovative ability of the firm. Multinationals that handle such HRM issues well can achieve a competitive advantage that will be difficult for their competitors to match.

8 Summary and conclusions

In this chapter we have reviewed knowledge management in multinational firms and conclude that HRM is central to firms' knowledge sharing and strategic capabilities. The achievement of sustainable competitive advantage will depend substantially on the ability of the firm to explore new and exploit existing knowledge.

In the second section we distinguished explicit and tacit knowledge noting that these different types of knowledge are typically shared through different mechanisms. Knowledge varies according to its strategic significance and may therefore be subdivided into core, compulsory, idiosyncratic and ancillary knowledge. Then, in the third section, we considered the different factors that influence knowledge sharing between units including the ability and willingness of senders to disseminate, the motivation and ability of receivers to absorb, and the relationship between sender and recipient. It is clear that the richness of links between units of a multinational organization strongly influences knowledge transfer.

We reviewed in the fourth section various ways of stimulating knowledge sharing and considered information on performance, HR practices, expatriation, structural mechanisms, social architecture (social capital and global mindset), performance management and supportive incentive systems. Ways of exploiting and sharing knowledge were discussed such as showcasing performance data in review meetings, product development committees and international task forces, knowledge management programmes, communities of practice, centres of excellence (charismatic, focused and virtual), and informal networks. We emphasized the importance of HR practices. At all levels in the organization (corporate, unit, group and individual) the performance management and incentive systems will influence employees' motivation and commitment to knowledge sharing, and job design plays a role. In firms such as Schlumberger and GE, knowledge sharing is part of managers' and engineers' formal performance reviews. In relation to expatriation and inpatriation, we noted the wide range of competences required if the expatriate is to be successful. We then discussed key factors that characterize units engaging in effective knowledge sharing. The research on these units reveals that they have relatively high levels of inter-unit trust and collaborate through deploying their social capital (structural, relational and cognitive). Social norms across these units encourage knowledge sharing and promote a global mindset involving coping productively with cultural diversity and showing balanced perspectives on the strategic interests of the firm.

The fifth section explored how knowledge can be acquired from outside the firm, and we noted that access to internal and external knowledge is often influenced by similar mechanisms. However, firms can develop specific initiatives to identify and appropriate external knowledge. This requires a culture of open boundaries and activities to scan the environment. It may also lead to structural reorientation such as when Cisco decided to divide its corporate headquarters into two locations (Silicon

Valley and Bangalore). Partnering, M&A and virtual surveys/competitions are three major ways used by companies to capture and utilize external knowledge.

In addition to identifying and capitalizing on new knowledge, companies continuously face the threat of losing valuable knowledge and skills and so many ensure a number of strategic and HRM initiatives to promote the appropriate level of employee retention. As the final section demonstrates, as well as retaining valuable knowledge and expertise, companies must retain their competence in innovation, which means dealing with complexity and its many contradictions and uncertainties as illustrated by the transfer and evaluation paradoxes.

Discussion questions

1. With so much information available through the internet and so much data stored in company-internal databases, social interaction will gradually become less important for knowledge sharing. Comment on this statement.
2. For a foreign subsidiary that controls unique and valuable knowledge, it does not make much sense to share such knowledge with other units of the corporation because it will lose an important source of power. Discuss arguments for and against this statement.
3. What advice would you give a multinational corporation that plans to change its global performance and incentive system in order to increase knowledge sharing across its international units?
4. Discuss the pros and cons of different approaches to retaining knowledge in the corporation.

CASE STUDY

Spurring innovation through global knowledge management at Procter & Gamble

Procter & Gamble was founded in Cincinnati in 1837. Initially, the company produced soap and candles, but the firm eventually diversified into a range of consumer goods. An important reason behind P&G's growth and success in the

(Continued)

(Continued)

decades after the Second World War was its ability to create innovations, like the industry's first cavity-prevention toothpaste Crest, the heavy-duty synthetic detergent Tide, and the two-in-one shampoo product Pert Plus.

P&G had established its first overseas marketing and manufacturing unit through an acquisition in the UK in 1930, and it proceeded to expand abroad rapidly after 1946. The company originally based its R&D activities in the US, but since the mid-1980s, P&G established a worldwide R&D network, with research hubs in the US, Europe, Japan and Latin America (see www.pg.com/tranlations/ history_pdf/english_history.pdf). However, while the company continued to develop innovative new products in the 1990s, by 2000 profits were lacklustre, the stock was underperforming (*New York Times*, 2008), and P&G was facing decreasing returns on its investments in R&D (Huston and Sakkab, 2006). In fact, from all of its new product introductions, only a minority were returning their development costs (*New York Times*, 2008).

At the beginning of this century, the US operations were still dominant, with the flow of knowledge and innovations mostly flowing from the centre to its foreign subsidiaries. P&G had some positive experiences of leveraging knowledge from foreign subsidiaries (see Bartlett, 2003) and also with acquiring new products from outside the firm. The problem was that such successes occurred all too infrequently. While the company knew that many of its best innovations came when combining ideas from different parts of the corporation, the inflow of knowledge from the overseas units was limited as was lateral knowledge transfer among the foreign subsidiaries. The foreign units were fairly autonomous and had limited experience in sharing knowledge across borders. For instance, it took P&G five years after the successful launch of the Pampers diapers in Germany to introduce the product in France, allowing Colgate-Palmolive to enter the market with a similar product that gained a dominant market share (Hansen and Birkinshaw, 2007).

While P&G had some positive experiences acquiring new products from outside the firm, these innovations and their connections were too infrequent. Consequently, in 2000, the new CEO, A.G. Lafley, set out to change radically how the company went about innovation. He set a challenging strategic goal that 50 per cent of new products should stem from ideas acquired from outside the company. Lafley believed that this would require a change in the company's attitude, overcoming resistance to innovation and a 'not invented here' syndrome and moving it to an enthusiasm for ideas and products 'proudly found elsewhere'. Reflecting on this need for fundamental change, Lafley further observed: 'And we needed to change how we defined, and perceived, our R&D organization – from 7,500 people inside to 7,500 plus 1.5 million outside, with a permeable boundary between them' (Huston and Sakkab, 2006: 61).

Clearly, enhancing how P&G captured and shared knowledge across borders would not be an easy undertaking. The functional barriers between R&D, marketing research, manufacturing and other siloed functions would have to be eliminated, as well as reducing those between the different business units. There was also a need to improve the linkage between problem identification, external knowledge acquisition, internal knowledge sharing across units and global exploitation of innovations (in terms of products but also in terms of internal ways of working).

The new model that P&G developed was called 'Connect + Develop' (Lafley and Charan, 2008). The goal was to tap into knowledge and ideas outside the company, from small and medium-sized companies, university labs, individual researchers, its business partners and even from its competitors. An additional aim was to improve the sharing of knowledge and ideas within the company. P&G appointed 70 senior technology entrepreneurs to work in six regional Connect + Develop hubs, focusing on finding products and technologies that were specialties within their regions. P&G established 21 global communities of practice – networks of experts working in the different business areas (*Businessweek*, 2004). The company also helped to create several firms that operated open networks, typically web-based, connecting scientists, companies, universities and government labs (Huston and Sakkab, 2006).

A number of additional organizational changes were also implemented. The country organizations lost much of their previous independence. New regional organizations were introduced – for instance, a new European regional headquarters was established in Geneva, mostly staffed by expatriates from different parts of Europe. While P&G had always used expatriation as a management development tool, the new structure led to increased interaction and knowledge sharing among people with diverse experiences and networks in different parts of the corporation. The co-location of the different business unit management teams also led to stronger connections and relationships across the units. Finally, P&G established regional service centres responsible for a range of functional activities.

The Connect + Develop model has led to significant changes in how P&G approaches its innovation projects. A striking case in point was the development of a new Pringle potato chip printed with words and pictures. Somebody had come up with the idea in a brainstorming session but it was not clear how it could be done technically. In the past, P&G would have launched an internal R&D project, but for the printed Pringle it developed a technology brief that was communicated

(Continued)

(Continued)

throughout the corporation and its external networks (when a new opportunity is spotted, such briefs are developed and circulated throughout the corporation). This led to the identification of a small bakery in Bologna, run by a university professor who had invented a method for printing on food products that could be adapted to fit the purpose. The new product, Pringles Prints, was launched in 2004. In less than a year and at a fraction of what it otherwise would have cost, P&G had developed a double digit growth business. P&G's innovation success rate (the percentage of new products that return the investments made on them) has more than doubled since 2000. The number of new products originating from outside the firm has risen to 35 per cent, while R&D spending has been reduced from 4.5 per cent of sales in the late 1990s to 2.8 per cent in 2007 (see www.strategy-business.com/press/freearticle/08304).

Case study questions

1. Evaluate P&G's approach to managing knowledge and innovation.
2. What are the barriers that a multinational organization has to overcome so as to harness the potential of a Connect + Develop model? What are the implications for HR?

Case study question for further reflection

1. What are the lessons of P&G's success in enhancing innovation through global knowledge management, and how does this apply to another organization that you know well – perhaps in a different industry?

Further reading

- Van Wijk, R., Jansen, J.J.P. and Lyles, M.A. (2008) 'Inter- and intra-organisational knowledge transfer: a meta-analytic review and assessment of its antecedents and consequences', *Journal of Management Studies*, 45: 830–853.
  Recent meta-analysis of factors associated with knowledge sharing.

- Kamoche, K. (1997) 'Knowledge creation and learning in international HRM', *The International Journal of Human Resource Management*, 8(3): 213–225.
  As this chapter has argued, the issues of knowledge creation and learning are central to successful knowledge management. This article examines how IHRM specifically can contribute to improving the performance and achievements of international assignments.

- Doz, Y., Santos J. and Williamson, P. (2001) *From Global to Metanational: How Companies Win in the Knowledge Economy*. Boston, MA: Harvard Business School Press.
  Doz, Santos and Williamson's highly influential book discusses the 'metanational' corporation that excels in managing knowledge and innovation on a global scale.

- Furuya, N., Stevens, M.J., Bird, A., Oddou, G. and Mendenhall, M. (2009) 'Managing the learning and transfer of global management competence: antecedents and outcomes of Japanese repatriation effectiveness', *Journal of International Business Studies*, 40: 200–215.
  Furuya et al. (2009) provide a comprehensive analysis of factors affecting individual learning during expatriate assignments and the application of their competences in new assignments following repatriation.

- Easterby-Smith, M. and Lyles, M.A. (eds) (2003) *The Blackwell Handbook of Organisational Learning and Knowledge Management*. Malden, MA: Blackwell.
  Excellent overview of a range of issues related to management of knowledge and organizational learning.

- Evans, P., Pucik, V. and Björkman, I. (2011) *The Global Challenge: International Human Resource Management*, 2nd edn. New York: McGraw-Hill.
  Takes a general management perspective on people management issues in the multinational, including the role of HRM for the management of knowledge and innovation.

Internet resources

- http://info.emeraldinsight.com/products/journals/journals.htm?PHPSESSID=u6odf e9017skkoegsq42cakua7&id=jkm. The *Journal of Knowledge Management* is a peer-reviewed publication dedicated to the exchange of the latest academic research and practical information on all aspects of managing knowledge in organizations.
- www.cio.com/article/40343/Knowledge_Management_Definition_and _Solutions. CIO magazine and its portfolio of properties offer technology and business leaders articles on information technology trends and a keen understanding of IT's role in achieving business goals.
- www.bing.com/images/search?q=Knowledge+Management&form=QB&qs=n#. Knowledge Management is a bing website offering access to many images relating to the topic of knowledge management. Very useful content materials, for example, to illustrate PowerPoint presentations on the topic.
- http://web.worldbank.org/WBSITE/EXTERNAL/WBI/WBIPROGRAMS/KFDLP/0,, contentMDK:20934415~menuPK:2882148~pagePK:64156158~piPK:64152884~the

SitePK:461198,00.html. World Bank Institute's Knowledge Management Initiative aims to enhance the capacity of development-oriented organizations in the client countries to achieve greater impact through the application of knowledge management tools and practices.

Self-assessment questions

Indicative answers to these questions can be found on the companion website at study.sagepub.com/harzing4e.

1. List three ways of assessing the capacity of an organization to stimulate knowledge sharing.
2. Define tacit and explicit knowledge. In what ways are they different and also how are they the same?
3. List nine ways of gaining access to external knowledge (discussed in section 5 of this chapter).
4. What aspects of the knowledge management groups and centres of excellence at ArcelorMittal and the unit heads networks and meetings at BP are associated with typical features of open communities of practice?
5. Give two examples of 'listening posts' established to scan the environment and diffuse innovation from one geographical location to other parts of the company.

References

Åbø, E., Chipperfield, L., Mottershead, C., Old, J., Prieto, R., Stemke, J. and Smith, R.G. (2001) 'Managing knowledge management', *Oilfield Review*, 13(1): 66–83.

Argote, L., McEvily, B. and Reagans, R. (2003) 'Managing knowledge in organizations: an integrative framework and review of emerging themes', *Management Science*, 49(4): 571–582.

Argyris, G. and Schön, D. (1996) *Organizational Learning II: Theory, Method and Practice.* Reading, MA: Addison-Wesley

Barner-Rasmussen, W. and Björkman, I. (2006) 'Language fluency, socialization and inter-unit relationships in Chinese and Finnish subsidiaries', *Management and Organization Review*, 3(1): 105–128.

Bartlett, C.A. (2003) *P & G Japan. The SK-II Globalization Project (case 303003).* Boston: Harvard Business School.

Bartlett, C.A. and Ghoshal, S. (1989) *Managing Across Borders: The Transnational Solution.* Boston, MA: Harvard Business School Press.

Beugelsdijk, S. (2008) 'Strategic human resource practices and product innovation', *Organization Studies*, 29(06): 821–847.

Birkinshaw, J. (2004) 'External sourcing of knowledge in the international firm', in H. Lane, M.J. Maznevski, M.E. Mendenhall and J. McNett (eds), *Handbook of Global Management.* Oxford: Blackwell, pp. 289–300.

Björkman, I., Barner-Rasmussen, W. and Li, L. (2004) 'Managing knowledge transfer in MNCs: the impact of headquarter control mechanisms', *Journal of International Business Studies*, 35(5): 443–455.

Bock, G.W., Zmud, R.W., Kim, Y.G. and Lee, J.N. (2005) 'Behavioral intention formation in knowledge sharing: examining the roles of extrinsic motivators, social-psychological forces, and organizational climate', *MIS Quarterly*, 29(1): 87–111.

Bonache, J. and Zárraga-Oberty, C. (2008) 'Determinants of the success of international assignees as knowledge tranferors: a theoretical framework', *International Journal of Human Resource Management*, 19(1): 1–18.

Bresman, H., Birkinshaw, J. and Nobel, R. (1999) 'Knowledge transfer in international acquisitions', *Journal of International Business Studies*, 30(3): 439–462.

Businessweek (2004) 'Online extra: at P&G, it's "360-Degree Innovation"', 10 October, www.businessweek.com/stories/2004-10-10/online-extra-at-p-and-g-its-360-degree-innovation (accessed 26 May 2014).

Cabrera, A., Collins, W.C. and Salgado, J.F. (2006) 'Determinants of individual engagement in knowledge sharing', *International Journal of Human Resource Management*, 17(2): 245–264.

Chakravarthy, B., McEvily, S., Doz, Y. and Rau, D. (2003) 'Knowledge management and competitive advantage', in M. Lyles and M. Easterby-Smith (eds), *Handbook of Organizational Learning and Knowledge Management*. Oxford: Blackwell, pp. 305–323.

Cohen, W.M. and Levinthal, D.A. (1990) 'Absorptive capacity: a new perspective on learning and innovation', *Administrative Science Quarterly*, 35(1): 128–152.

Cross, R. and Prusak, L. (2003) 'The political economy of knowledge markets in organizations', in M. Lyles and M. Easterby-Smith (eds), *Handbook of Organisational Learning*. Oxford: Blackwell, pp. 454–472.

Currie, G. and Kerrin, M. (2003) 'Human resource management and knowledge management: enhancing knowledge sharing in a pharmaceutical company', *International Journal of Human Resource Management*, 14(6): 1027–1045.

Darr, E.D. and Kurtzberg, T.R. (2000) 'An investigation of partner similarity dimensions on knowledge transfer', *Organizational Behavior and Human Decision Processes*, 82(1): 28–44.

Denrell, J., Arvidsson, N. and Zander, U. (2004) 'Managing knowledge in the dark: an empirical study of the reliability of capability evaluation', *Management Science*, 50(11): 1491–1503.

Doz, Y., Santos, J. and Williamson, P. (2001) *From Global to Metanational: How Companies Win in the Knowledge Economy*. Boston, MA: Harvard Business School Press.

Evans, P., Pucik, V. and Björkman, I. (2011) *The Global Challenge: International Human Resource Management*, 2nd edn. New York: McGraw-Hill.

Fleming, M. and Marx, M. (2006) 'Managing creativity in small worlds', *California Management Review*, 48(4): 6–27.

Foss, N. (2009) 'Alternative research strategies in the knowledge movement: from macro bias to micro-foundations and multi-level explanation', *European Management Review*, 6(1): 16–28.

Friedman, T.L. (2005) *The World Is Flat: A Brief History of the Twenty-first Century*. New York: Farrar, Straus and Giroux.

Gooderham, P., Minbaeva, D. and Pedersen, T. (2011) 'Governance mechanisms for the promotion of social capital for knowledge transfer in multinational corporations', *Journal of Management Studies*, 48(1): 123–150.

Gupta, A.K. and Govindarajan, V. (2000) 'Knowledge flows within multinational corporations', *Strategic Management Journal*, 21(4): 473–496.

Gupta, A.K., Govindarajan, V. and Wang, H. (2008) *The Quest for Global Dominance*. San Francisco: Jossey-Bass.

Hansen, M.T. (1999) 'The search-transfer problem: the role of weak ties in sharing knowledge across organization subunits', *Administrative Science Quarterly*, 44(1): 82–111.

Hansen, M.T. (2002) 'Knowledge networks: explaining effective knowledge sharing in multiunit companies', *Organization Science*, 13(3) (May–June): 232–248.

Hansen, M.T. and Birkinshaw, J. (2007) 'The innovation value chain', *Harvard Business Review*, 85(6): 121–130.

Hansen, M.T., Mors, M.L. and Løvås, B. (2005) 'Knowledge sharing in organizations: multiple networks, multiple phases', *Academy of Management Journal*, 48(5): 776–793.

Hansen, M.T. and von Oetinger, B. (2001) 'Introducing T-shaped managers: knowledge management's next generation', *Harvard Business Review* (March): 107–116.

Hocking, J.B., Brown, M. and Harzing, A.W. (2007) 'Balancing global and local strategic contexts: expatriate knowledge transfer, applications, and learning within a transnational organization', *Human Resource Management*, 46(4): 513–533.

Huston, L. and Sakkab, N. (2006) 'Connect and develop: inside Procter & Gamble's new model for innovation', *Harvard Business Review*, 84(3): 58–66.

ICFAI (2005) *Mittal Steel's Knowledge Management Strategy*, ICFAI Case Study, no. 305-543-1.

Inkpen, A.C. and Tsang, E.W.K. (2005) 'Social capital, networks, and knowledge transfer', *The Academy of Management Review*, 30(1): 146–165.

Jaruzelski, B. and Dehoff, K. (2008) *Beyond Borders: The Global Innovation 1000*, www.strategyand.pwc.com/global/home/what-we-think/reports-white-papers/article-display/beyond-borders-global-innovation-1000 (accessed 15 May 2014).

Kanter, R.M. (1989) *When Giants Learn to Dance: Mastering the Challenge of Strategy, Management, and Careers in the 1990s*. New York: Simon and Schuster.

Kogut, B. and Zander, U. (1992) 'Knowledge of the firm, combinative capabilities, and the replication of technology', *Organization Science*, 3(3): 383–397.

Kogut, B. and Zander, U. (1993) 'Knowledge of the firm and the evolutionary theory of the multinational corporation', *Journal of International Business Studies*, 24(4): 625–645.

Kostova, T. (1999) 'Transnational transfer of strategic organisational practices: a contextual perspective', *Academy of Management Review*, 24(2): 308–324.

Lafley, A.G. and Charan, R. (2008) *The Game Changer*. New York: Crown Business.

Lane, P.J., Koka, B.R. and Pathak, S. (2006) 'The reification of absorptive capacity: a critical review and rejuvenation of the construct', *Academy of Management Review*, 31(4): 833–863.

Lane, P.J. and Lubatkin, M. (1998) 'Relative absorptive capacity and interorganizational learning', *Strategic Management Journal*, 19(5): 461–477.

Lazarova, M. and Tarique, I. (2005) 'Knowledge transfer upon repatriation', *Journal of World Business*, 40(4): 361–373.

Lepak, D.P. and S.A. Snell (1999) 'The human resource architecture: toward a theory of human capital allocation and development', *Academy of Management Review*, 24(1): 31–48.

Levitt, B. and March, J.G. (1988) 'Organizational learning', *Annual Review of Sociology*, 14: 319–340.

Levy, O., Beechler, S., Taylor, S. and Boyacigiller, N.A. (2007) 'What we talk about when we talk about "global mindset": managerial cognition in multinational corporations', *Journal of International Business Studies*, 38(2): 231–258.

Lopez-Cabrales, A., Pérez-Luño, A. and Cabrera, R.V. (2009) 'Knowledge as a mediator between HRM practices and innovative activity', *Human Resource Management*, 48(4): 485–503.

March, J.G. (1991) 'Exploration and exploitation in organisational learning', *Organization Science*, 2(1): 71–87.

Minbaeva, D. (2007) 'Knowledge transfer in multinational corporations', *Management International Review*, 47(4): 567–593.

Minbaeva, D. (2013) 'Strategic HRM in building micro-foundations of organizational knowledge-based performance', *Human Resource Management Review*, 23(4): 378–390.

Minbaeva, D. and Michailova, S. (2004) 'Knowledge transfer and expatriation practices in MNCs: the role of disseminative capacity', *Employee Relations*, 26(6): 663–679.

Minbaeva, D., Pedersen, T., Björkman, I., Fey, C. and Park, H. (2003) 'MNC knowledge transfer, subsidiary absorptive capacity and knowledge transfer', *Journal of International Business Studies*, 34(6): 586–599.

Monteiro, L.F., Arvidsson, L. and Birkinshaw, J. (2008) 'Knowledge flows within multinational corporations: explaining subsidiary isolation and its performance implications', *Organizational Science*, 19(1): 90–107.

Moore, K. and Birkinshaw, J. (1998) 'Managing knowledge in global service firms: centers of excellence', *Academy of Management Executive*, 12(4): 81–92.

Nahapiet, J. and Ghoshal, S. (1998) 'Social capital, intellectual capital, and the organisational advantage', *Academy of Management Review*, 23(2): 242–266.

New York Times (2008) 'Changing the game with innovation', 24 May.

Nonaka, I. (1994) 'A dynamic theory of organisational knowledge creation', *Organization Science*, 5(1): 14–37.

Nonaka, I. and Takeuchi, H. (1995) *The Knowledge-creating Company: How Japanese Companies Create the Dynamics of Innovation*. Oxford: Oxford University Press.

Noorderhaven, N.G. and Harzing, A.W.K. (2009) 'Factors influencing knowledge flows within MNCs', *Journal of International Business Studies*, 40(5): 719–741.

Oddou, G., Osland, J.S. and Blakeney, R.N. (2009) 'Repatriating knowledge: variables influencing the "transfer" process', *Journal of International Business Studies*, 40(2): 181–199.

Osterloh, M. and Frey, B.S. (2000) 'Motivation, knowledge transfer, and organizational forms', *Organization Science*, 11(5): 538–550.

Paik, Y. and Choi, D.Y. (2005) 'The shortcomings of a global knowledge management system: the case of Accenture', *Academy of Management Executive*, 19(2): 81–84.

Polanyi, M. (1967) *The Tacit Dimension*. Garden City, NY: Doubleday.

Probst, G. and Borzillo, S. (2008) 'Why communities of practice succeed and why they fail', *European Management Journal*, 26(3): 335–347.

Pucik, V. (1988) 'Strategic alliances, organizational learning, and competitive advantage: the HRM agenda', *Human Resource Management*, 27: 77–93.

Reiche, S. (2012) 'Knowledge benefits of social capital upon repatriation: a longitudinal study of international assignees', *Journal of Management Studies*, 49(6): 1052–1077.

Senge, P. (1990) *The Fifth Discipline: The Art and Practice of the Learning Organization*. New York: Doubleday.

Simonin, B.L. (1999) 'Ambiguity and process of knowledge transfer in strategic alliances', *Strategic Management Journal*, 20(7): 596–623.

Simonin, B.L. and Özsomer, A. (2009) 'Knowledge processes and learning outcomes in MNC's: an empirical investigation of the role of HRM practices in foreign subsidiaries', *Human Resource Management*, 48(4): 505–530.

Szulanski, G. (1996) 'Exploring internal stickiness: impediments to the transfer of best practice within the firm', *Strategic Management Journal*, 17(1): 27–43.

Takeuchi, H., Osono, E. and Shimizu, N. (2008) 'The contradictions that drive Toyota's success', *Harvard Business Review* (June): 96–104.

Tapscott, D. and Williams, A.D. (2007) *Wikinomics: How Mass Collaboration Changes Everything*. New York: Penguin.

Tsai, W. and Ghoshal, S. (1998) 'Social capital and value creation: the role of intrafirm networks', *Academy of Management Journal*, 41: 464–476.

Van Wijk, R., Jansen, J. and Lyles, M.A. (2008) 'Inter- and intra-organizational knowledge transfer: a meta-analytic review and assessment of its antecedents and consequences', *Journal of Management Studies*, 45(4): 830–853.

Watanabe, K. (2007) 'Lessons from Toyota's long drive', *Harvard Business Review* (July–August): 74–83.

Wenger, E.C. and Snyder, W.M. (2000) 'Communities of practice: the organizational frontier', *Harvard Business Review*, 78 (January): 139–145.

Zahra, S.A. and George, G. (2002) 'Absorptive capacity: a review, reconceptualization, and extension', *Academy of Management Review*, 27(2): 185–203.

Zárraga, C. and Bonache, J. (2003) 'Assessing the team environment for knowledge sharing: an empirical analysis', *International Journal of Human Resource Management*, 14: 1227–1245.

Training and Development: Developing Global Leaders and Expatriates

10

Ashly H. Pinnington, Yaw A. Debrah and
Christopher J. Rees

Contents

Learning objectives

After reading this chapter you will be able to:

- Outline potential benefits and challenges of training and development (T&D) in global and local contexts
- Identify different forms of training delivery, the activities of Assessment and Development Centres, and reasons for MNC investments in T&D and human resource development (HRD)
- Explain the term global leader with reference to (a) the main tasks that global leaders undertake, and (b) the competencies global leaders need to practise in order to be effective
- Discuss the nature of development programmes for global leaders with reference to the objectives, content and limitations of these programmes
- Critically evaluate the main objectives and effectiveness of cross-cultural skills training for expatriates
- Identify and discuss a range of emerging issues relating to the design, content and delivery of cross-cultural skills training for expatriates

Chapter outline

The chapter presents an overview of the potential of training and development and then examines, in more detail, the development of global leaders and expatriates. First we introduce and review the current situation for training and development. Then, the competencies and tasks associated with global leaders' work, and global leadership development programmes are discussed. Finally, we consider issues surrounding cross-cultural training for expatriates.

1 Introduction

In this chapter we will consider the global challenges facing T&D, and the development of global leaders and expatriates in both international and domestic organizations. International here is defined as covering MNCs, joint ventures and other organizations such as international non-governmental organizations (Chang, 2005) including those whose activities may be mainly domestically based, but still are operating within the global environment. The first part of the chapter will focus on T&D and subsequent sections attend to the development of global leaders and expatriates.

2 Training and development in the global environment

Definition

There is good reason to assume that the forces of globalization will continue to create new needs in international and domestic organizations. Demographic changes in labour markets, competitive trends in business markets, developments in MNCs and many other factors in the global environment will stimulate demand for T&D. Training can be defined as 'the systematic approach to affecting individuals' knowledge, skills, and attitudes in order to improve individual, team, and organizational effectiveness' (Aguinis and Kraiger, 2009: 452). T&D can have benefits at many levels of analysis, including individuals, groups, organizations and societies. Development can be defined as 'systematic efforts affecting individuals' knowledge or skills for purposes of personal growth or future jobs and/or roles' (Aguinis and Kraiger, 2009: 452). In T&D, it is common therefore for 'training' activities to be focused on making relatively short-to-medium-term specific performance gains, whereas 'development' tends to be more general in its strategic intent to develop individual, group and organizational capabilities which are important for competitive performance in the future.

Benefits and limitations

The purpose behind many T&D objectives is to develop skills and competences and to improve the performance of individuals, groups and organizations. T&D activities can be categorized into two types, 'generic training' for skill development and 'company-specific training' which is job or company focused, such as induction and specialist on-the-job training. Numerous organizations outsource substantial parts of their generic T&D, often for cost and quality reasons. It may simply be more cost effective to contract an external training provider as well as not be feasible to employ trainers who can sustain the required level of quality. For these and other reasons, T&D is therefore one of the most widely outsourced HRM activities in Europe (Galanaki, 2008).

Despite the advantages of HRM outsourcing, other organizations choose to retain in-house some areas of T&D. Many MNCs and other international organizations still have extensive in-house training departments or teams of trainers. Case studies of local and foreign MNCs operating in India have identified companies with substantial capital outlay on in-house T&D. For example, an MNC in the IT industry based in India with an international network of 54 development centres and more than 95,000 employees has over 80 trained instructors providing 380,000 days of training each year. Among other training programmes, cross-cultural, technological and leadership training is provided by this company (Jain et al., 2012).

From the perspectives of HRM and IHRM, there are many reasons for individuals and organizations to engage in T&D activities. T&D is important for preparation of employees for future career roles. For example, nurses who progress into line management will require systematic training and career development to perform well in these management roles (Townsend et al., 2012). Individuals can reap higher rewards and career benefits from improving their skills. T&D can improve individual and team job performance (e.g. task execution, tacit skills, innovation and communication). T&D is also known to have the capacity to increase employees' well-being, motivation and sense of belonging. For example, T&D has been found to influence job satisfaction, self-efficacy, empowerment and trust. T&D can lead to higher organizational performance outcomes (e.g. efficient operations, effective ways of working, improved sales and profitability). It can also have positive outcomes for the organization's culture and stakeholders through increasing customer satisfaction and consumer brand reputation. Overall, T&D activities can improve nations' human capital and economic growth (see Aguinis and Kraiger (2009) for a review).

Some researchers have produced empirical evidence that T&D leads to high organizational performance and even competitive advantage. For example, an empirical study of training policy in the hotel industry in Spain identified T&D and human capital development as a source of differentiation and competitive advantage (Ubeda-Garcia et al., 2013). Many more research investigations have found evidence of T&D leading to improvements in HR performance. Positive employee attitudes sometimes lead to improved organizational performance. Another study in Spain on financial institutions with international operations found that the higher the average number of training hours delivered for employees the greater was their knowledge and commitment to their employing organizations (Vidal-Salazar et al., 2012). Another study conducted in Canada found that the higher the percentage of employees receiving T&D the more the surveyed organizations perceived training to be beneficial (Ng and Dastmalchian, 2011).

There is generally more abundant evidence for T&D having a positive impact on employee attitudes and this is an important step towards improving organizational performance, although the links between the two are often uncertain. As has been discussed in other chapters, it is often difficult to assess the actual contribution of HRM practices such as T&D to organizational performance. A large number of research studies on HRM and performance continue to find evidence though for a significant relationship between HRM practices and performance. For example, a study of the steel industry in Taiwan concluded that six HRM practices (including T&D) are associated with firms' performance and strategies of cost reduction, quality enhancement and innovation (Lee et al., 2010). However, other studies have failed to find a direct link between T&D and firm performance (e.g. Cunha et al., 2003; Nikandrou et al., 2008).

It is frequently mentioned that employers worry that T&D provision can actually increase their organizations' employee turnover. Especially in organizations and industries that have high employee turnover, there is good reason to be concerned about this potential outcome. Koster et al. (2011), however, actually found the reverse effect in a study of 2,833 Dutch pharmacy assistants. By implementing T&D for improving employees' generic and occupational skills these pharmacies enhanced the pharmacy assistants' organizational commitment. It may have increased their value on the external labour market but in general they chose to stay with their respective employers. This relationship was moderated by job satisfaction, demonstrating that the employees have to be reasonably satisfied in their jobs for T&D to have a positive impact on organizational commitment.

Regarding the benefits of T&D, Nikandrou et al. (2008) developed and tested a model of T&D and performance among 14 EU member states. Their purpose was to investigate whether there is a direct and significant relationship between T&D and firm performance, and also, whether it is affected by national and organizational factors. The results were interesting in that they failed to find a direct link between T&D and performance. These researchers concluded that their results show the importance of national culture for the training process, such as the national culture characteristic of performance orientation and institutional support (percentage of GDP spent on education). They recommended that MNCs operating in country contexts where education levels are high, and where the performance orientation is also high, should emphasize systematic T&D through use of comprehensive training needs analysis and systematic training design, implementation and evaluation. These results show the importance for MNCs of attending to differences in host country contexts and deciding how national and organizational factors prompt adaptations in T&D.

Forms of training delivery

There is a wide variety of approaches to T&D available for organizations. Some of the most popular forms of training delivery identified in a study in Greece, for example, included: on-the-job training, mentoring, apprenticeship, simulation, web-based learning, instructor-led classroom training, programmed self-instruction, case studies/role playing, systematic job rotations and transfers (Chatzimouratidis et al., 2012). Employers and training specialists will encounter diverse training needs, different organizational contexts and varied resource constraints. Often, this will mean that they have to make different implementation decisions on the extent of training provision and choice of delivery modes.

It is important we note that comparative international studies of T&D have found significant differences between countries. There are in fact few instances of universal T&D practices (Drost et al., 2002). Similarities in T&D are more commonplace in regional clusters of countries since T&D is strongly influenced by institutional and cultural values (see Chapter 2). An exception to country differences is that some industry-specific trends will lead to similar T&D approaches both locally and globally within an industry.

Box 10.1 Stop and reflect

Alternative forms of training delivery

There are alternative established methods of delivering T&D and individual preferences for these learning methods can differ. There is no one right way of training, and various approaches to T&D can be effective in different environments. In the research study on T&D in Greece by Chatzimouratidis et al. (2012) mentoring and simulation were found to be most effective in comparative terms for total training cost, employee motivation and training duration. Web-based learning was generally considered the lowest cost with high ease of delivery, but on-the-job training was often found to be beneficial for increasing employee motivation.

The 2013 Kelly Global Workforce Index, an annual survey of around 122,000 people across the world, found different results for popularity of various training methods. On-the-job training was most highly rated as employees' preferred method of skill development and mentoring the lowest rated out of the following methods:

1. On-the-job experience   70%
2. Continued education/training   58%
3. Professional certification   31%
4. Seminars/webinars   26%
5. Special/stretch/rotational assignments   19%
6. Structured mentoring   19%

Source: www.kellyocg.com/Knowledge/Kelly_Global_Workforce_Index/Career_Development_and_Upskilling (accessed 27 May 2014). Reprinted with permission of Kelly Services, Inc.

Practical task

• Briefly describe three training objectives for improving: (a) individual employee performance, (b) the effectiveness of a team of employees, and (c) overall organizational performance. Then:

  o For each training objective, specify two options for training methods and delivery.
  o Assess each training option for its likely effectiveness for the following parameters: Ease of use? Speed of training materials development? Overall cost of delivery? Learner choice? Employee motivation?

Question for further reflection

• How much variety could there be in organizational provision of different forms of T&D?

Assessment and Development Centres

Systematic T&D is an important part of the work of Assessment Centres which were pioneered by AT&T over 50 years ago and are now popular in organizations in many countries throughout the world. Assessment Centres are used for a variety of recruitment, selection and development activities and although generally concentrated on the organization's internal labour market they are also frequently used for assessment and recruitment of people from the external labour market. Assessment Centres or Assessment and Development Centres usually have two primary tasks: selection and development. Selection activities often concentrate on selection among external applicants and on internal candidates for promotion. Development activities include diagnosis of learning needs, developmental planning and training.

A study of 144 organizations in 18 different countries found that some organizations concentrate on selection goals and others attend more to development (Thornton and Krause, 2009). This research compared a range of Assessment Centre characteristics:

• job analysis techniques
• job dimensions (requirements)
• observer pools
• methods of assessor training
• exercises and psychometric testing procedures
• information provided to participants, and areas of evaluation of the programme by participants.

Due to cost considerations, many domestic and international organizations still do not have Assessment Centres. There is a need for establishing more Assessment Centre activities in the future. For example, considered from the perspective of labour market demographics, in recent years, in the Middle East (and many other regions across the world) a growing number of women have been entering the labour market (Afiouni et al., 2014). Assessment Centres can improve their employment circumstances by more effective provision of induction to the workplace, increasing their skills for career development, giving more opportunities for promotion and supporting their long-term retainment in the workforce. These

Assessment Centre outcomes are all important T&D and HRD objectives for women, their organizations, local labour markets and the national economies where they work.

Reasons for MNC investment in T&D

MNCs often meet skill gaps and training needs across their global subsidiaries. While, according to the ILO *World of Work Report* (2013) over 200 million people are formally unemployed, employers still face recruitment shortages in many areas and cannot find the right people with the required work experience and skills. For example, MNCs operating in Africa often face problems arising from shortages of skilled individuals and therefore have to find more cost effective and productive ways of developing local talent (Kamoche et al., 2012).

MNCs frequently encounter new as well as enduring training needs arising from their global scope and reach. Li et al. (2008) found in a survey of non-Chinese MNCs operating in China that the greater their global extent the higher the number of training programmes these MNCs delivered. Another study by Holtbrügge and Mohr (2011) on the subsidiaries of German MNCs found that the higher the inter-dependencies of overseas subsidiaries for inputs, then the higher the intensity of cross-cultural training provided to subsidiary managers. So, the global context of MNCs and their local subsidiaries can stimulate more use of T&D in response to identified opportunities and problems.

MNCs routinely have to make investments in their subsidiaries and major business operations. Such investments in T&D have been identified in many different host countries, for example, a study of large MNCs in Brunei Darussalam found HR directors in these organizations placed higher importance than did domestic organizations on the HRM practices of recruitment and selection, training and internal career opportunities (Mohamed et al., 2013). Through T&D, MNCs can invest in human capital where one key strategic objective is to gain a return on their HR investment and achieve the corporate strategy. T&D can assist MNCs by increasing employees' capacity to meet global standards and adjust to the practices of the corporation and demands of its local markets.

Some country and industry contexts are highly favourable to organizations making T&D investments. For example, education and T&D are highly valued by many employees in Singapore (Reiche, 2009). Career and project management of employees in the IT industry requires organizational strengths in the HRM areas of recruitment and T&D. For example, T&D in information services companies in Taiwan was found helpful and relevant for planning, acquiring, developing and utilizing competences (Shih et al., 2009). In summary, skill gaps, skill requirements of subsidiaries and employee expectations are three major reasons for MNCs to invest in T&D.

Box 10.2   Stop and reflect

Training priorities

The priorities for T&D change over time and often will differ between individuals, groups, organizations and countries. Drost et al. (2002) conducted a comparison of T&D practices across countries, comparing Australia, Canada, Indonesia, Japan, Korea, Latin America, Mexico, PRC, Taiwan and the US. They asked survey respondents to rate the following T&D practices for the extent that these are: (a) a priority now and, (b) how far they should be a priority in the future.

	Employee Group 1.		Employee Group 2.		Employee Group 3.	
	T&D Objective:		T&D Objective:		T&D Objective:	
	PRIORITY: (a) Now? (1–5)	(b) Future? (1–5)	PRIORITY: (a) Now? (1–5)	(b) Future? (1–5)	PRIORITY: (a) Now? (1–5)	(b) Future? (1–5)
T&D PRACTICES						
1. As a reward for employees	......	......	......	......	......	......
2. Improve technical abilities	......	......	......	......	......	......
3. Improve interpersonal abilities	......	......	......	......	......	......
4. Remedy poor performance	......	......	......	......	......	......
5. Prepare for future job	......	......	......	......	......	......
6. Build teamwork	......	......	......	......	......	......
7. Orientation to work	......	......	......	......	......	......

(Continued)

(Continued)

8. Help understand   ....
    business

9. Provide skills to   ....
    do different jobs

10. Teach employees   ....
    about values

Practical task

*   Select three different groups of employees and identify one important training objective for each. Then, for each employee group training objective, rate each of the above items twice on a scale of 1–5 (where 1 = low and 5 = high) giving a rating for the extent that it is: (a) a priority now, and a rating for the amount it is likely to be (b) a priority in the future.

Question for further reflection

*   How far is it feasible for T&D objectives and activities to remain the same over a five year period?

T&D and HRD: exploitative and exploratory activities

'Exploitative' strategic and operational activities most commonly advance the organization by using formal and centralized systems whereas 'exploratory' activities are characterized by more informal systems of connectedness and coordination. T&D and HRD initiatives that are exploitative will tend to be typified by a relatively high degree of formalization and centralization, while their exploratory initiatives will often be more informal.

There are different definitions of T&D and hence its relationship to HRD is understood in a variety of ways. When examining common usage of the two terms, it is noticeable that their meaning is often overlapping where T&D and HRD are frequently used to refer to the same learning activities. T&D can be connected with other support areas of organizations such as quality management, performance improvement, project management, as well as specific areas of HRD (Tomé, 2011) such as organization development, career management and educational activities and collaboration (e.g. internships, graduate recruitment). In this chapter, T&D and HRD are considered primarily as HRM and IHRM activities supporting the capacity of organizations to operate successfully in the global environment.

Petranek (2004) has argued that successful global HRD is based on cooperation, collaboration, communication and culture. Global T&D is similar to Petranek's definition of global HRD in so far as it similarly involves people cooperating and working jointly towards the same goals, collaborating on projects within a common framework of group practices, communicating with each other sending and receiving information, and sustaining the organization culture's customs, norms and institutions.

For strategic reasons, T&D often has to be understood in relationship to other areas of HRM, in particular, it has important links with recruitment. T&D and recruitment are related to each other since both areas aim to build the stock of knowledge and are concerned with human capital development in organizations (Kamoche and Mueller, 1998; Kamoche et al., 2011). A common purpose of recruitment and T&D is to build human capital by identifying who is available on the internal and external labour markets, assessing their specific competences and evaluating their effectiveness (Hansen and Alewell, 2013). Often, the actual implementation of T&D will vary in large organizations such as MNCs. Some of the differences relate to inconsistencies in training provision across the organization. Resources for training often differ across subsidiaries and even when the corporate HQ resource allocation is similar, different local priorities and local management attitudes to training needs leads to variable T&D provision.

T&D has also been found to be influenced along with other HRM practices by the strategic purpose, organization culture and environment (Kang et al., 2007). MNC activities which are entrepreneurial and exploratory will tend to be characterized by less formalized HRM practices, and often are suitable for HRD interventions. Whereas those MNC activities categorized as cooperative and exploitative often become more formalized (Gupta et al., 2006) and are particularly suited to planned T&D. Formal approaches to T&D are intended to encourage broader skill development across employees. Broad skill development is typical of organizations that require interdependent working practices and are based on standardization of sets of skills within groups. Therefore, the extent of formalized T&D will partly be a function of the amount the MNC follows cooperative, exploitative strategies.

There is even some evidence of T&D varying consistently across exploratory and exploitative activities of managers. Medcof and Song (2013) analysed the exploratory (extra-departmental) and cooperative (inter-departmental) activities of managers in organizations in China. They found that T&D, along with other HRM practices, was more informal in the managers' exploratory work activities outside their department and more formalized inside where activities tended to be primarily cooperative ones.

Systematic T&D is important wherever there are major needs to change or raise workplace skills. Empirical research conducted in 30 UK international firms by Scullion and Starkey (2000) identified an emerging corporate HR focus on senior management development, succession planning and developing a cadre of international managers. They argue that this demonstrates more evidence of interest in the learning organization, which holds formal and informal methods of learning in high esteem, and includes proactive attitudes towards T&D. We choose in this chapter to concentrate on global leadership and expatriates since they are both characteristic of the global business environment and prompt discussion about the role of T&D and HRD.

It is worthwhile keeping in perspective the fact that T&D for new job roles is only one of many different HRM activities that are important to the management of careers in organizations. The large range of practices in career management separate to formal T&D provision for promotion into new job roles is made apparent in a recent study of HR directors from 306 companies in Belgium by De Vos and Dries (2013: 1831) who list a large number of examples of formalized career management practices:

> Career planning workshops, Formal mentoring, Succession planning, Coaching, Prescribed career paths, Internal announcement of vacancies, Individual career counseling by internal or external career counselors, Training outside current function, Talent reviews, Job rotation, Development centers to assess potential, Self-assessment instruments, Personal development plan, Information about career development and Formal career conversations between supervisor and employee.

The above list of practices in career management exemplifies the way that, in addition to its relationship with HRD, T&D is part of a large range of available IHRM and management practices in MNCs and other international organizations.

Box 10.3   Stop and reflect

Developing managers

As was mentioned above in the first paragraph of section 2, 'Development' tends to be more general in its strategic intent to develop individual, group and organizational capabilities which are important for competitive performance in the future. This exercise gives an opportunity to reflect on T&D activities in management development. The Management Development Council (2010: 17) defined Management Development (MD) as, 'Any form of training, formal or informal, accredited or non-accredited, which enhances the ability of managers to provide direction, facilitate change, use resources, work with people, achieve results, or manage self and personal skills'.

In a study of management development by UK MNCs the perceived performance outcomes for their subsidiaries in the Czech Republic, Hungary and

Poland included:

- quality of products/services
- development of new products/services (innovation)
- efficiency of factors of production (average, labour and capital)
- customer/client satisfaction and retention (average)
- overall perceived subsidiary performance exceeded forecasts/expectations.

Source: Sheehan, 2012: 2498, Figure 1: Model of Management Development (MD) and perceived subsidiary performance outcomes.

Practical task

- For an organization of your choice, select two performance outcomes from the list above. Write a brief three-year management development plan with outcomes to be delivered during the 24 months training at the end of years 1 and 2, and 12 months after the training at the end of year 3. Ensure that you include the following in your plan:

  o desired management development performance outcomes (years 1, 2 and 3)
  o learning objectives for the participating managers
  o selected forms of T&D delivery for management development
  o a plan describing the implementation of the training over the 24 months.

Question for further reflection

- To what extent should management development initiatives by an organization be compulsory?

Interest in the HRD practices of international organizations is manifested in an emerging body of literature on the subject of international or global HRD (see Wang and McLean, 2007). Global HRD, in contrast to comparative HRD and national HRD, is a broad term that concerns processes that address the formulation and practice of HRD systems, practices and policies at the organizational and societal level (Metcalfe and Rees, 2005: 455). It can incorporate comparative analyses of HRD approaches across nations and also addresses how societies develop national HRD policies (see Figure 10.1).

Global HRD involves the development of transnational HRD interventions and is seen as especially important in policy areas of global management development (Metcalfe and

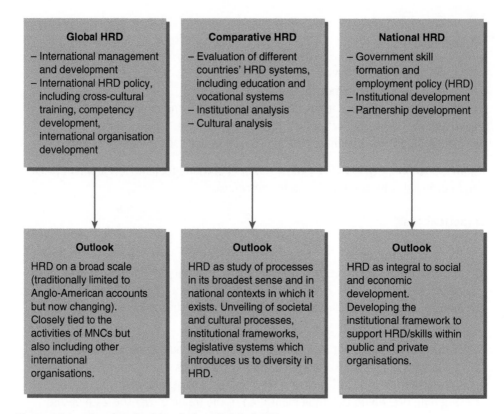

Figure 10.1   Mapping the boundaries of global HRD

Source: abridged from Metcalfe and Rees (2005)

Rees, 2005: 456) and in knowledge sharing and learning communities (OECD, 2000; Iles and Yolles, 2003). Global HRD is directly concerned with issues ranging from how governments and international organizations develop global HRD systems, to the development of global leaders via activities such as cross-cultural training, cultural reorientation, foreign language and relocation services (see Figure 10.1). In the following sections of this chapter, we seek to explore the notion of a global leader, the competencies required by global leaders, and global leadership development programmes.

3 Global leaders

International organizations need globally competent leaders to achieve success (Adler and Bartholomew, 1992; Caligiuri and DeSanto, 2001). In this respect, the development of global leaders is seen as a source of competitive advantage for organizations (Csoka and Hackett, 1998; Black et al., 1999). The gradual shift towards global leadership development is beginning to generate more interest in the study of HRD practices of international organizations (Thomas et al., 2005). For example, Thomas and Inkson (2004) highlight the urgent need for effective global leaders as an emerging issue for global firms and HRD is increasingly being recognized as a major determinant of the success or failure of global leaders (Deresky, 2008). Gregersen et al.'s (1998) study revealed, however, the lack of an adequate number of globally competent executives. Almost all of the companies that participated in the study indicated that they required more global managers with high quality global leadership capabilities. This reflects a shortage of global leaders in international firms and the need for focused HRD strategies to tackle the problem.

Defining the term global leader

In recent years, considerable effort has gone into developing our understanding of what constitutes a 'global leader', and there is no consensus on its exact definition (Jokinen, 2005: 201) within the extensive literature on leadership, management and competence.

Spreitzer et al. (1997) define global leaders as executives who are in jobs with duties and responsibilities which encompass some international scope, and must operate effectively and competently in an ever-changing, complex and ambiguous global business environment (McCall, 1998). Global leaders are seen as people who must be capable of extending business into foreign markets, initiating and developing global strategies, and managing and motivating geographically dispersed and diverse teams (McCall et al., 1988; Bartlett and Ghoshal, 1992).

Caligiuri and Tarique (2009: 1) offer a helpfully succinct definition of the term global leader. Citing Suutari (2002) and Bartlett and Ghoshal (1992), they state that global leaders are: 'high level professionals such as executives, vice presidents, directors, and managers who are in jobs with some global leadership activities such as global integration responsibilities'. It can be seen that this approach to defining global leadership places a heavy emphasis on the organizational seniority of global leaders as well as on the types of leadership activities in which they engage.

The definitions cited above provide some insight into the nature of global leadership. In order, however, to address a series of issues surrounding the identification and development of global leaders, there are two key questions that researchers have considered over recent years: (a) what are the main tasks that global leaders undertake? and (b) what competencies do global leaders need to practise in order to be effective?

The tasks associated with global leadership

Definitions of global leaders such as those cited above tend to employ general phrases such as 'initiating and developing global strategies', 'motivating geographically dispersed and diverse teams' and 'global integration responsibilities'. These phrases provide a valuable flavour of the activities and tasks associated with the role of global leaders, however, some researchers have sought to isolate in more depth the generic tasks carried out by global leaders, with a view to influencing the design of global leadership development activities and programmes. For example, in one such study involving focus group meetings and surveys of leaders from European and North American firms, Caligiuri (2004, 2006), identified ten tasks or activities that are common among, and unique to, those occupying global leadership positions (see Table 10.1).

Given the radical change environments in which global leaders operate, it is difficult to outline a more detailed typical job description for global leaders than that presented in Table 10.1. This reflects a more general trend in HRM theory and practice that has seen a move away from traditional HRM selection activities which sought to construct precisely written task-based job descriptions to select and subsequently develop employees (Rees and Doran, 2001). In rapidly changing environments, it is more realistic to identify the behaviours associated with effective performance as opposed to detailing the day-to-day tasks associated with a role, as these tasks are likely to change on a relatively frequent basis. In fact, inspection of the literature on global leaders reveals the relative lack of attention that has been given to defining the precise tasks associated with global leadership. The field has increasingly focused upon identifying the behaviourally linked competencies that are associated with effective global leadership, as opposed to attempting to construct comprehensive task-based job descriptions for global leadership positions within organizations.

Table 10.1   Tasks and activities associated with global leadership

Global Leadership	Global Leadership Activities
	• Work with colleagues from different countries
	• Interact with external clients from different countries
	• Interact with internal clients from different countries
	• May need to speak in a language other than their mother tongue at work
	• Supervise employees who are of different nationalities
	• Develop a strategic business plan on a worldwide basis for their unit
	• Manage a budget on a worldwide basis for their unit
	• Negotiate in other countries with people from other countries
	• Manage foreign suppliers or vendors
	• Manage risk on a worldwide basis for their unit

Source: derived from Caligiuri (2006)

The competencies of global leaders

Before examining emerging themes on the competencies of global leaders, it is worthwhile considering the nature of a competency. In his seminal work entitled *The Competent Manager*, Boyatzis (1982: 21) defines a competency as: 'an underlying characteristic of a person … that could be a motive, trait, skill, aspect of one's self-image, … or a body of knowledge that he or she uses'. Woodruffe (1993: 29) defines a competency more directly in relation to behaviours and task performance as 'the set of behaviour patterns that the incumbent needs to bring to a position in order to perform its tasks and functions with competence'. Both of these definitions emphasize in common that there are a set of personal characteristics that a position holder needs to demonstrate in order to perform effectively. Such personal characteristics, which are likely to involve specific skills, knowledge and personality variables, will vary according to the demands of a position. Thus, while there may be a set of common (or generic) competencies that are required for all mainstream management and leadership positions, the performance of specific management and leadership roles are likely to require distinctive competencies.

According to Gregersen et al. (1998) global leaders exhibit character, embrace duality and demonstrate savvy. The character aspect involves ability to attain an emotional connection with people from various backgrounds while at the same time maintaining an uncompromising degree of personal integrity. In addition, global leaders seem to embrace duality in the management of uncertainty. This involves competences in acting at the appropriate time, balancing tensions and understanding change and continuity in various countries and regions. Global leaders also exhibit savvy in both business and organizational matters. They demonstrate a great deal of understanding of the competitive business environment and identify and take advantage of opportunities in the market. They are familiar with the firm's SWOT, its competitive position and are capable of capitalizing on the organization's capabilities to capture market opportunities. A strength underlying global leaders' acquisition of such skills is inquisitiveness. This often means that global leaders possess a spirit of adventure and desire to see and experience new things. In essence, they possess adventuresome characteristics, such as curiosity and open-mindedness (Gregersen et al., 1998).

Kedia and Mukherji (1999) argue that global leaders need to acquire knowledge not just in areas such as cross-cultural management, socio-political and economic effectiveness, but also mastery of technology. The global mindset extends beyond knowledge of ICT to include the management information system and the impact of technology on the global operations of the organization. Skills in global leadership represent the ability to put knowledge into action. These include acculturation and leadership skills for leading and motivating a diverse workforce. They note in addition that the current competitive global environment requires managers to be flexible and responsive.

In addition, organizations increasingly rely on global management teams to manage their global operations and, as a result, global leaders need to possess a range of competencies to enable them to be effective actors in global management teams (Gupta and Govindarajan, 2002). These teams aim to share resources and manage the transnational including the transfer of knowledge (Deresky, 2008). Deresky defines global management teams as collections of managers in or from several countries who must rely on group collaboration if each member is to experience optimum success and goal achievement. She cites companies as diverse as Whirlpool International and Timberland UK, and Honeywell Bull (HBI). Global management teams are often multicultural and operate from different countries. They include virtual teams, whose geographically dispersed members interact and coordinate their work through computer mediated communication (CMC) technologies. These technologies, such as desktop videoconferencing systems, internet and intranets, and group support systems are linked together across time, space and organizational boundaries (Hertel et al., 2005; Deresky, 2008) and make it possible for global leaders to make more effective use of their talents irrespective of location (Dowling and Welch, 2004; Collings et al., 2007). Clearly, there are some serious challenges associated with leading and participating in global teamwork, not least problems relating to geographical dispersion, cultural differences, language and communication difficulties associated with electronic media such as email, telephone and videoconferencing (Hertel et al., 2005; Maznevski et al., 2006; Deresky, 2008).

It is apparent from the above discussion that many distinctive competencies potentially may be associated with effective global leadership. In one review of the field, Mendenhall and Osland (2002) identified 53 competencies associated with the construct of global leadership, a finding, however, which is 'hardly a helpful boon to those assigned to develop corporate global management development programmes' (Mendenhall, 2006: 423). Consequently, some of the research work in this field mirrors approaches in occupational psychology which seek to reduce numerous overlapping personality traits into fewer and more coherent personality dimensions. A number of typologies of global leadership competencies have been constructed and four such examples are summarized in Table 10.2.

The frameworks summarized in Table 10.2 reveal the extent to which intrapersonal and interpersonal attributes (perhaps as opposed to highly developed technical skills in areas such as ICT, law and finance) are central to effective global leadership. Nevertheless, in discussing distinctive competency clusters, Brownell (2006: 320) argues that competency requirements for global leaders are heavily influenced by contingent features of the task, organization and environment in any given context. For example, she proposes that in situations of high task complexity, it is likely that there will be a contingent priority need for the global leader to display highly developed decision-making competencies such as decisiveness and sound judgement. Similarly, in situations where there is a weak organizational culture, there is likely to be a contingent priority need for the global leader to display positive outlook competencies such as vision, passion and optimism. When discussing cross-cultural competence, Johnson et al. (2006: 537) also acknowledge the effects of external factors such as the physical,

Table 10.2   Competency typologies of global leaders

<table>
<tr><td colspan="1" align="center">Brownell (2006)</td></tr>
</table>

- **Intercultural:** cultural sensitivity, cultural intelligence, global mindset.

- **Social:** emotional intelligence, empathy, self-control.

- **Creativity/resourcefulness:** breakthrough-thinking, innovativeness, synergistic orientation.

- **Self-knowledge:** self-efficacy, self-reflective.

- **Positive outlook:** vision, passion, optimism.

- **Responsiveness**: flexible, agile, opportunistic.

- **Decision-making:** decisive, sound judgement, intuitive.

<table>
<tr><td align="center">Connor (2000)</td></tr>
</table>

- **Business savvy:** global leaders are results driven and they achieve outstanding business results. They have a broader view of the business and the world, and an extensive knowledge of the business. They adapt well to new situations, new cultures and new bosses.

- **Knowledge of how to use their personal influence:** global leaders know how to tap into and leverage corporate resources including formal and informal networks. They know how to use teams and how to work well with others. They have strong influencing skills. Their communication skills are excellent.

- **Global perspective:** global leaders understand the global marketplace. They have a high degree of cultural sensitivity. When they move to a new country they make a serious effort to fit in, respect the culture and learn the language.

- **Strong character:** global leaders talk about vision, purpose and values with clarity. They can be counted on to do what is right and to resist something they oppose. They understand there are changing employee expectations, they inspire trust, and they value and respect the differences each person brings to the workplace. Global leaders meet commitments, act consistent with their words and are interested in the well-being of others.

- **Knowledge of how to motivate others:** global leaders understand that employees want direction from above and want opportunities for growth and development. They have vision and communicate a clear sense of direction. They are role models. They are comfortable with conflict and know how to deal constructively with conflict among their people.

- **Act like entrepreneurs:** global leaders understand that international competition is challenging companies to act faster and smarter. They put greater emphasis on new product development, standardization of business processes and speed to the market. They are creative and encourage others to be innovators. They take risks and have become skilled at overcoming obstacles. They have a sense of urgency. They are self-starters committed to their work.

<table>
<tr><td align="center">Jokinen (2005)</td></tr>
</table>

- **Core global leadership competencies:** self awareness, engagement in personal transformation, and inquisitiveness.

- **Desired mental characteristics of global leaders**: optimism, self-regulation, social judgement skills, empathy, motivation to work in an international environment, cognitive skills, acceptance of complexity and its contradictions.

- **Behavioural level global leadership competencies:** social skills, network management skills and knowledge.

(Continued)

Table 10.2   (Continued)

Mendenhall and Osland (2002)

- **Relationship**: close personal relationships, cross-cultural communication skills, 'emotionally connect' ability, inspire/motivate others, conflict management, negotiation expertise, empowering others, managing cross-cultural ethical issues, social literacy and cultural literacy.

- **Traits/dispositions:** curiosity, inquisitiveness, continual learner, accountability, integrity, courage, commitment, hardness, maturity, results-orientation and personal literacy.

- **Business expertise:** global business savvy, global organizational savvy, business acumen, total organizational astuteness, stakeholder orientation and results-orientation.

- **Cognition:** environmental sense-making, global mindset, thinking agility, improvisation, pattern recognition, cognitive complexity, cosmopolitanism, managing uncertainty, local vs. global paradoxes and behavioural flexibility.

- **Organizing expertise:** team building, community building, organizational networking, creating learning systems, strong operational codes, global networking, strong customer orientation and business literacy.

- **Visioning:** articulating a tangible vision and strategy, envisioning, entrepreneurial spirit, catalyst for cultural change, change agency, catalyst for strategic change, empowering and inspiring.

Source: derived and abridged from Connor (2000), Mendenhall and Osland (2002), Jokinen (2005), Brownell (2006) and Mendenhall (2006)

economic, political and legal environments which moderate and affect the performance of individuals who are working in international business settings. They state that even a culturally competent individual might not be successful in, for example, a company 'that manufactures products that are unsuited to the local market and/or is located in a country that is experiencing a deep economic recession'.

4 The development of global leaders

Research evidence indicates that successful international organizations are often those that equip their global leaders with global perspectives (Stroh and Caligiuri, 1998a, 1998b). Here the research focuses on the links between the development of leaders and the bottom line performance of their organizations. For instance, Stroh and Caligiuri's (1998a, 1998b) research found that the most successful international organizations are those that support their leaders with HRD practices that provide opportunities to develop a global orientation and, in effect, global leadership skills. This study also reveals that developing leadership cross-cultural competence was identified as among the top five organization-wide practices influencing their effectiveness. They conclude from the results that there is a positive relationship between an organization's bottom line financial success and its ability to successfully develop leadership competencies. This implies that for an organization to sustain its competitiveness, it must continually develop its leaders and prepare them for future challenges in its business environment (Adler and Bartholomew, 1992).

Caligiuri and DeSanto (2001) assert that there are two assumptions underpinning the development of global leadership programmes. The first assumption is that global competence can be defined in terms of developmental dimensions and the second assumption is that once defined these dimensions are amenable to development through global experience. These assumptions manifest themselves in the design of training programmes for global leaders, which are clear evidence that international organizations are increasingly making use of global (as opposed to domestic) leadership development programmes to groom future leaders (for example, see Box 10.4).

Box 10.4 Stop and reflect

An example of a development programme for global leaders

Automatic Data Processing, Inc. (NASDAQ: ADP), with nearly $9 billion in revenues and over 585,000 clients, is one of the world's largest providers of business outsourcing solutions. ADP's Global Leadership Development Programme (GLDP) is designed to provide high potential individuals with a combination of stretch assignments, development, coaching and mentoring. Upon successful completion of the programme, participants will be positioned to assume a domestic or international leadership role in one of ADP's growing business units.

The GLDP is centred on three key elements: (a) challenging rotational assignments, (b) leadership support and (c) hands on coaching and development.

- Challenging rotational assignments: delegates receive opportunities to rotate across different functions, geographies, business units and various business situations (e.g. start-up, realignment, sustaining success and turnaround).
- Leadership support: delegates are provided with leadership support designed to help them to navigate successfully through the programme. This consists of support from senior management, the host manager, an assigned talent manager and a mentor.
- Hands on coaching and development: delegates are assigned a talent manager who provides coaching that focuses on strengths and leadership potential.

Source: www.adp.com/careers/global-leadership-development-programme.aspx (accessed 23 March 2009).

Many global leadership development programmes have been designed to offer individuals the opportunity to work in different countries (Rhinesmith, 1996; Thaler-Carter, 2000; Suutari, 2002). Developing global leaders, however, does not have to focus only on training or preparing employees for overseas assignments (Neary and O'Grady, 2000). As was noted earlier, Stroh and Caligiuri (1998a) assert that the development of global leadership skills should not be limited to expatriates from the home country. Rather it should include both host country and third country nationals and a proactive implementation of 'inpatriation' where host country talents work at corporate head office as well as in other subsidiaries around the world.

What, however, are the precise objectives of global leadership development programmes? Following their analysis of the global leadership training programme delivered by TRW Inc., Neary and O'Grady (2000: 190–191) offer some insights into the design, delivery and, importantly, the objectives of global leadership development programmes:

- Global leadership programmes are not designed to develop leaders from scratch but rather to enhance the skills of existing outstanding leaders to help to make them outstanding global leaders as well.
- Global leadership programmes should encourage leaders to be sensitive to their own assumptions and the assumptions of those around them. Global leaders may not be familiar with the cultural assumptions of the people with whom they are working, so they need to develop the ability to (a) adapt multiple leadership styles, and (b) to adapt to an unfamiliar environment.
- Global leadership programmes should help global leaders to exploit diversity by helping them to understand that a wide range of heritages and experiences also supplies a larger pool of business solutions.
- Global leadership programmes should help delegates to tolerate and address ambiguity in order to adapt appropriately. There is an increased necessity for global leaders to move effectively between cultures and countries and this requires greater flexibility in terms of style.

It is evident that training and development objectives of this nature are likely to be achieved using a variety of different techniques. Suutari (2002) suggests that specific techniques used for the development of global leaders may, as noted above, include international assignments, but they may also include techniques such as short-term development assignments, international training and development, international meetings and forums, participation in international or global teams, the application of action learning and international travel.

The limitations of global leadership development programmes

Perhaps the most contentious aspect of the literature on the development of global leaders/managers is the issue of whether all managers can be trained and developed to acquire global perspectives. On this issue, Caligiuri (2006) maintains that managers differentially benefit from participation in intercultural training or development exercises, depending on their individual aptitude, knowledge, skills, abilities and other personality characteristics. The assumption here is that organizations should be selective in terms of who they offer opportunities for development as global leaders. In particular, it is argued that although certain personality characteristics are needed for global leadership they cannot be developed through global assignments, that is, some KSAOs (knowledge, skills, abilities and other characteristics such as personality dimensions of openness and flexibility) are relatively immutable. Consequently, global leadership programmes may not be able to achieve their objectives if they depend on global assignments to shape the aspects of global competence and capability that are influenced by personality (Caligiuri and DeSanto, 2001). On the issue of knowledge development, Caligiuri and DeSanto's findings are consistent with that of the extant literature (Adler, 1981; Napier and Peterson, 1991; Black, 1992; Baughn, 1995; Osland, 1995; Adler, 1997) in the sense that it can be developed through global assignments.

Caligiuri and DeSanto (2001) in their attempt to determine the competencies required by global managers defined global competence in terms of KSAOs. Their study revealed that while the knowledge dimensions can be developed through global assignments, personality characteristics are highly resistant to change. In view of the difficulties involved in changing personality characteristics, Gregersen et al. (1998) also conclude that not everyone has the ability to acquire the competencies that are needed to become a global leader. Hence, they suggest that organizations should be selective in their provision of developmental opportunities.

If not everybody can be trained to become a global leader then it follows that training opportunities should only be provided to those whom it is perceived can benefit from such training. This is consistent with Caligiuri's (2006) view that the requisite immutable attributes must be present before training and development interventions can improve or equip individuals with global leadership skills. Where these attributes are not present it may be more effective for organizations to buy-in such people rather than attempt to develop employees who do not have the prerequisite attributes. Nevertheless, even those managers with the right attributes or required immutable attributes still need development. Gregerson et al. (1998) recommend strategies along the lines of: (a) travel, (b) teams, (c) training and (d) transfer to develop global leaders. Similarly, Caligiuri (2006) has identified some HRD strategies for global leaders based on knowledge, skills, abilities and personality characteristics, their relative immutability and suitable developmental interventions. These HRD strategies incorporate: 'didactic learning opportunities' (such as cross-cultural communication training and training in conflict resolution techniques); 'experimental interventions' (such as cultural immersion programmes and attending global meetings); and 'intensive experience' (such as international assignments and salient non-work cultural experience).

5 Expatriate development

Cross-cultural training and development for expatriates

Cross-cultural training is vital if organizations are to avoid high levels of expatriate failure rates (premature returns). Cross-cultural training facilitates the expatriate's cross-cultural adjustment in the host country and hence minimizes problems of adjustment (Brislin, 1981; Tung, 1981; Mendenhall and Oddou, 1985; Black and Mendenhall, 1990; Kealey and Protheroe, 1996). In particular, it helps employees to become effective in their jobs within the host country as quickly as possible (McFarlin and Sweeney, 2006) because it provides coping techniques relevant to living and working in a specific foreign environment (Earley, 1987). Cross-cultural training has been formally defined as: 'the educative processes used to improve intercultural learning via the development of the cognitive, affective and behavioral competencies needed for successful interactions in diverse cultures' (Littrell et al., 2006: 356). In essence, cross-cultural training fosters appropriate transitions, adjustment and general adaptability skills (Sappinen, 1993; Forster and Johnsen, 1996).

Cross-cultural training may be integrated with a career management system or delivered in an ad hoc manner. Assessment and Development Centres often have routine responsibilities for cross-cultural training. Different methods of cross-cultural training continue to be advocated and one common approach is based on the idea of cultural intelligence (CQ). This approach is different from training specifically in cultural value differences and concentrates more on our capabilities to adjust to others (Earley and Peterson, 2004). The idea behind CQ is people vary as to the degree that they are conscious of cultural knowledge (metacognitive), the amount that they are motivated to engage in different cultures (motivation) and the extent that they are sensitive and flexible in their behaviour (behaviour). It is also assumed that these differences can be measured (e.g. McNab et al., 2012). Dependent on individual differences and the cross-cultural contexts, groups of employees can be trained in ways that increase their self-efficacy and effectiveness in cross-cultural settings.

Recently, more sophisticated psychometric test measures have been developed to assess motivation for cross-cultural working such as in international assignments. These tests assessing motivation for working with people from different cultures (e.g. Kupka et al., 2009) are based on measuring individual differences in personality dimensions such as anxiety, trust and self-efficacy. While our focus here is on expatriates, Adler and Bartholomew (1992) highlight that, for organizations operating worldwide, cross-cultural skills actually are essential throughout the organization, not just for those few employees leaving for expatriate assignments. They further contend that both 'expatriates' and 'inpatriates' should become well versed in cultural adaptation skills as well as specific local knowledge, but these are not the only skills managers should possess. In global organizations all managers need broader international, cross-cultural and diversity skills, and a global mindset; what has been referred to by

Caligiuri and DeSanto (2001) as a form of 'cosmopolitanism'. Similarly, Adler and Bartholomew (1992) state that while organizational and career development programmes should be components of foreign assignments, such HRD opportunities should not be limited to expatriates. Rather international organizations should send 'transpatriates' all over the world to equip them with global perspectives, orientation, mindsets and awareness as well as cross-cultural skills appropriate for a cadre of globally sophisticated managers. This approach, then, downplays the distinction between expatriation and inpatriation and uses international assignments to encourage and enhance both individual and organizational leadership throughout the organization. Furthermore, it serves a dual purpose of fulfilling technical and managerial needs as well as providing developmental experiences for potential leaders (Stroh and Caligiuri, 1998a).

In their review of research on expatriate preparation, Littrell et al. (2006: 338), drawing upon Cushner and Brislin (1997), identify the following as key objectives for cross-cultural training in personal adjustment, work adjustment and interactions with host nationals:

- *Learning to learn* – this objective draws attention to the fact that no training is likely to prepare the expatriate for every eventuality that will be encountered in the new culture. Hence, cross-cultural training needs to assist the expatriate to learn how to acquire information about another culture.
- *Making isomorphic attributions* – isomorphic attributions occur when the expatriate makes the same judgements and decisions regarding behaviour as do host nationals. Thus, a key objective of cross-cultural training is to help equip the expatriate to recognize, understand and act upon cultural nuances surrounding behaviours in another culture.
- *Overcoming difficulties* that undermine effectiveness while in another culture.
- *Developing positive relationships* – this relates particularly to expatriate relationships with host nationals.
- *Accomplishing work-related tasks* – for example, the expatriate may require certain technical skills that relate specifically to work in another culture.
- *Coping with stressors* – this objective is recognition of the fact that expatriate work is often associated with a range of task and family pressures that can lead to stress.

The effectiveness of cross-cultural training and development for expatriates

The literature is replete with statistics and comparisons between organizations that offer expatriate training with those that do not. Brewster and Pickard (1994) present an excellent review of the findings of some of these studies. They mention that the early literature was mainly based on expatriates from the USA and was also somewhat anecdotal and prescriptive in nature. The general conclusion from the research was that little preparation takes place before the expatriate departs for an international assignment. In the 1970s, studies of US MNCs revealed that only two-thirds provided any training and less than a quarter provided formal orientation training (Baker and Ivancevich, 1971; Rahim, 1983; Brewster and Pickard, 1994). The picture did not differ much during the 1980s since only 25 per cent of the largest US multinationals provided extensive pre-departure orientation training programmes to their expatriates (Baliga and Baker, 1985).

In a survey of MNCs in Europe, USA and Japan, Tung (1982) found that whereas only 32 per cent of the US firms provided training, 69 per cent and 57 per cent of European and Japanese firms respectively provided training for their expatriates (Brewster and Pickard, 1994; Forster and Johnsen, 1996). Thus, the research evidence indicates that in the 1970s and 1980s European firms delivered more formal training for their expatriates than did the US firms (Brewster, 1988). In the 1990s, however, the European firms appear to have reduced their training activities. Survey evidence indicates that only 13 per cent of European firms provided some form of cross-cultural training to their expatriates although a further 47 per cent provided briefings for culturally 'challenging' international assignments (Dowling et al., 2008).

It is not clear from the literature whether MNCs' reluctance to offer cross-cultural training for their expatriates is due to a lack of access to such training programmes or sheer misgivings about the value and necessity of such training for expatriate managers or perhaps both. There is some evidence from the literature to support either interpretation. Osman-Gani (2000) states that the main reason for the lack of provision of cross-cultural training appears to be the assumption that 'good management is good worldwide'. Senior managers and CEOs supposedly hold two views on this issue. The first is related to the transferability of management skills. The assumption here is that if a manager with general management skills is effective in his/her own country and culture then that person will inevitably be effective in any other country or culture. In other words, the location of the international assignment is immaterial to the effectiveness of the manager. Consequently, no preparation would be required for an expatriate before taking up an international assignment. Drawing from research on the transferability of management practices and in particular the experiences of expatriate managers in Asia, Osman-Gani (2000) debunks this view.

The second view relates to lingering doubts about the value of training for international assignments. Essentially, it asserts that good management skills are important but they do not in themselves guarantee the future effectiveness of managers on international assignments (Osman-Gani, 2000). There is ample evidence from the literature to refute this second viewpoint. For example, Earley (1987) argues that cross-cultural training facilitates an individual's ability to cope and work in a foreign environment. Similarly, evidence from the extant literature leads us to conclude that by virtue of their lack of international experience and cultural skills in foreign societies, these managers will almost inevitably be deficient in some cross-cultural knowledge and skills that they need to perform their duties efficiently (Black and Mendenhall, 1989; Barratt, 1995).

Nevertheless, it is apparent that many international organizations do acknowledge and appreciate the usefulness of training programmes for expatriates and in recent years have supported it. Dowling et al. (2008) attributes this development partly to the increasing provision of internal and external training programmes that are available to MNCs. Evidence from the Global Relocation Trends Survey Reports (conducted by GMAB Global Relocations together with the US National Foreign Trade Council and the SHRM Global Forum) indicates that 64 per cent and 62 per cent of companies offered or made available cross-cultural training in 2002 and 2004 respectively. Despite this development, 76 per cent and 74 per cent of the firms surveyed made cross-cultural training optional in 2002 and 2004 respectively. This suggests that perhaps there are expatriates working for international organizations who still do not receive any cross-cultural training before embarking on international assignments (Dowling et al., 2008).

In spite of some lingering doubts, there is substantial evidence on the positive outcomes of cross-cultural training. In fact, many studies have assessed the effectiveness of cross-cultural training and shown the numerous benefits that expatriates derive from cross-cultural training (Selmer et al., 1998; Eschbach et al., 2001; Morris and Robie, 2001). Tung (1982), Earley (1987), Black and Mendenhall (1990), Deshpande and Viswesvaran (1992) and Harrison (1994) all report that cross-cultural training has a strong and positive impact on cross-cultural skills development, adaptation, adjustability and job performance. In addition to improving performance in international organizations, cultural training facilitates the transition and adjustment of expatriates and their families (Cavusgil et al., 1992). Harrison (1994) reports that a number of companies (for example, Fortune 500 firms such as Motorola Inc., Dupont, and IBM and MNCs including BP, Johnson Wax, Shell Oil) now routinely provide cross-cultural training to their expatriates. These programmes are designed to make the managers 'trans-culturally competent' (Callahan, 1989) and intended to reduce expatriate failure rates (Caudron, 1991) and to maximize organizations' competitive advantage.

Harrison (1994) contends that cross-cultural training helps to develop a more cosmopolitan outlook and gives managers a deeper understanding and appreciation of cross-cultural situations. It can also help employees to learn about the culture, its values and norms as well as appropriate and acceptable behaviours in the society and how that affects the performance of duties in organizations (Black and Mendenhall, 1990; Kealey and Protheroe, 1996). Furthermore, it helps expatriates to minimize the effects of cultural shock, by developing coping methods to deal with new and unforeseen or unpredictable events in the culture and to reduce conflict arising from new, unexpected and unfamiliar encounters (Earley, 1987; Harrison, 1994). Cross-cultural preparation and training also facilitates the international assignment and expatriate adaptation by helping them to form realistic expectations about living and working in a foreign country (Black and Mendenhall, 1990).

6 Summary and conclusions

In recent years, the changing global environment has led to an increasing interest in the potential benefits of T&D for MNCs and domestic organizations. This chapter has considered general trends in global T&D and then concentrated on international HRD related to the need for organizations to employ competent global leaders and expatriates.

T&D can deliver individuals and organizations numerous benefits in performance improvement over the short, medium and long term. T&D objectives should be assessed for how they should be delivered as in-house activities and through outsourced provision. Many forms of training delivery are available and the different options should be considered and evaluated. T&D is not exclusive to specialist training organizations and departments because it occurs through a wide range of HRM and IHRM policies and practices, including Assessment and Development Centres and a wide range of HRD interventions such as organization development initiatives and individual career management practices. T&D and HRD should be considered for their roles and contribution to 'exploitative' and 'exploratory' strategies of organizations.

While various definitions of the term global leader have been offered, it is concluded that global leaders are executives who operate at a very senior level within international organizations and who engage in activities such as developing global strategies, integrating global activities and leading diverse teams. These leadership capabilities are essential for organizational learning and the management of change. Such leadership skills and competencies are also important for domestic organizations competing with international businesses, working in international joint ventures and collaborating locally with NGOs. Inevitably, then, global leadership is central to the growth and sustainability of domestic organizations as they find they are operating in an increasingly global competitive environment.

Literature on the subject of the effectiveness of global leaders places a relatively strong emphasis on the competencies of global leaders as opposed to seeking to describe in detail the precise tasks that they undertake. These competencies are developed through global leadership development programmes which include activities such as international assignments, participation in global teams and cross-cultural sensitivity training. There is some debate in the literature, however, about the extent to which all managers can be trained and developed to acquire global leadership perspectives.

In the later sections of this chapter, the discussion was broadened to consider not just the development of global leaders but the development of expatriates in general. There is evidence to suggest that some international organizations neglect this training perhaps due to the untested premise that managerial effectiveness is cross-culturally transferable almost regardless of training. It is clear though that many international organizations do appreciate the benefits of global T&D, for example, by providing intensive cross-cultural training for expatriates which is focused upon cross-cultural learning and adjustment.

Discussion questions

1. You work as the HRM director for an international organization based in Germany. The marketing director needs to recruit someone to manage the section of her department which is responsible for advertising the organization's products in Germany. She tells you that her idea is to advertise in top international publications for a 'global leader' to ensure that a candidate of the highest quality is appointed. You discuss this idea with her and it soon becomes clear that the two of you have a difference of opinion about the meaning of global leadership. As a result, you agree to send her a summary of your understanding of the term global leader. What will you include in your summary of this term?

2. You are the HRM director employed in a European manufacturing organization with its headquarters in London. The board of directors has decided to open two subsidiaries in Belgium and France. In order to inform the search for a global leader who will oversee this growth and expansion strategy and subsequently direct the subsidiaries in Belgium and France, the board of directors has asked you to advise them on the competencies that the global leader will need to possess to undertake the role successfully. What competencies do you think are essential for this executive role?

3. In the past, the MNC you work for has filled overseas positions by identifying effective leaders in the home country and then encouraging/pressurizing them to complete overseas assignments lasting approximately 18 months. As the HRM director, you have some concerns about this policy and suspect that it may not be working very well. What information would you seek, and from whom, in order to evaluate this approach to HRM planning?

4. The international organization for which you work employs approximately 180 expatriates based in Africa, Asia and Europe. As a cost-cutting exercise, the organization is considering setting up virtual global teams using ICT. What do you think will be the main communication issues associated with this initiative?

5. What would you regard to be the essential features of a cross-cultural training and development programme intended for a group of 20 male and female expatriates from England (United Kingdom) who will be taking up international assignments in the hotel sector in the Middle East?

Closing the Gulf – preparing US executives for assignments in Mexico

Background information

On a summer's day in 2008, Charles Ramoz-Ramírez was chairing a meeting of the six most senior employees of the HR consultancy he established almost five years ago. His decision to establish the consultancy was an extremely difficult one for him, as he held a senior, well-paid and secure position as an HR executive within an MNC based in New York. This HR position within the MNC involved training and developing professional executive staff such as engineers and project managers to undertake overseas assignments mainly in Spanish speaking countries in South America.

At this meeting with his senior staff, Charles reminded them about the history of the consultancy for which they now work. He reminded them that there were two main reasons which underpinned his decision to leave the employment of the MNC and set up the consultancy business. First, he found himself being invited to deliver, on an increasingly frequent basis, specialized training sessions on expatriate programmes organized by independent training organizations and even other MNCs. He concluded from the frequency of these requests that there was a scarcity of HR professionals who possessed genuine expertise in preparing US executives for assignments in Mexico. Second, he did not agree with his HR director's view of expatriate training which was very much a case of 'send them and see'. That is, his HR director did not doubt that pre-departure training for expatriates was helpful but she did not see it as a critical success factor. Charles's view was that pre-departure training of expatriates was not just helpful; he saw it as a prerequisite for any overseas assignment no matter what its duration. His belief in the value of pre-departure training thus became a key operating principle of the CRR Expatriate Development consultancy organization which he formed on the day he left the employment of the MNC. In essence, Charles established a consultancy which aimed to design and deliver in-house pre-departure training programmes for employees of US MNCs who would be taking up assignments in Spanish-speaking countries in South America.

The approach by the MNC: problems with employees' pre-departure training

After reminding his senior staff of how the consultancy came into being, Charles explained to them that a recent event had served to convince him that the emphasis he placed on the training of expatriates was fully justified. Charles informed them that he had recently been approached by the current HR director of the MNC which had previously employed him. (The previous HR director for whom Charles worked had retired approximately two years ago.) The current HR director told Charles that, over the last 12 months, the senior management of the MNC had become increasingly concerned about the general failure of its expatriate workforce to adjust to life in Mexico. As a result, the HR department had commissioned an independent training needs analysis. Part of this analysis was based on responses from 40 engineers who had returned home in the last two years from assignments in Mexico. Charles proceeded to inform his staff about the findings of this analysis which were supplied to him by the HR director of the MNC.

The independent analysis provided a fascinating insight into the pre-departure training that the 40 employees had received. Notably, only 25 of them had received any formal pre-departure training at all. Subsequent investigations revealed no obvious explanation as to why the remaining 15 staff had received no formal training. Further, when the MNC's training records were examined, they showed that the duration of the training received by the 25 staff varied tremendously (see Table 10.3).

Table 10.3   Length of pre-departure training received by the 25 employees

	1 to 5 days	6 to 10 days	11 to 15 days	More than 15 days
Number of employees	6	3	11	5

Again, organizational records offered no obvious explanation as to why these 25 employees received training which varied so much in terms of duration.

The training needs analysis document proceeded to report further information about the nature of the pre-departure training received by the group of 25 employees. The 25 employees experienced various pre-departure training methods such as lectures and tutorials including basic language classes, access to online material about Mexico, and cultural awareness workshops delivered by an outside training agency. Prior to their assignments, four of the 25 employees were offered the opportunity to undertake seven day field visits to Mexico. These visits enabled them to meet colleagues already based in Mexico and to visit organizations and places in Mexico that were linked to their assignments. The variation in the pre-departure training received by the 25 employees made it difficult to evaluate the employees' views about the effectiveness of the pre-departure training they had received. Some

(Continued)

(Continued)

anecdotal evidence presented in the analysis did, however, indicate that seven employees who accessed online training material found it to be of little value in terms of cultural preparation for their assignments.

Finally, with an eye on future training, the 40 employees who had returned from assignments in Mexico were asked to identify the two biggest challenges that they had faced when working in Mexico. A summary of their responses to this question is presented in Table 10.4.

Table 10.4   The 'two biggest challenges' faced by the employees (N = 40) during their assignments in Mexico

'Biggest Challenge'	Number of employees citing this challenge*
Communication problems with local workers	28
Technical issues relating to their work	15
Travelling within Mexico	10
Health and diet issues	10
Accommodation issues	6
Loneliness/boredom	4
Safety including crime	3
Pressure from family in USA	2
Other challenges cited by only one employee	2

*Total number of responses is 80, that is, two responses per employee

The implications of the analysis

At this point of the meeting, Charles revealed to his team that, on reading the fairly scathing independent report on pre-departure training, the board of directors of the MNC reached the conclusion that training for employees undertaking assignments in Mexico was a priority issue. The members of the board decided that they wanted to bring in an external consultancy with real expertise in this area. It was opportune that the independent investigation into current training arrangements had unearthed a number of documents in which Charles, during the time he was employed by the MNC, had expressed his concern with the training that employees were receiving to prepare them for their overseas assignments. It was quickly established that Charles had left the MNC in order to open a consultancy specializing in this very issue.

Charles then informed his colleagues: 'The HR director of the MNC is commissioning CRR Expatriate Development to design and facilitate a ten-day long pre-departure programme for 30 engineers and project managers who will be taking up medium-term (that is, six months to one year) assignments in Mexico over the next year. Using the information we already have from the independent analysis, I want us to put together an initial draft of what this training programme should look like.'

Case study questions

1. Assume that you are a member of the senior team of CRR Expatriate Development. On the basis on the case study material and also your wider knowledge of the subject area, highlight what you think should be included in the content of the new ten-day pre-departure programme for the 30 engineers and project managers.
2. Having drawn up your list of the essential elements of this programme, (a) explain why you think that each element is necessary, and (b) state how much programme time you would devote to each element.
3. Assuming that you were permitted access to the 40 employees who have already completed their assignments in Mexico, state what further information you would seek from them to help you to design the ten-day pre-departure programme.

Case study questions for further reflection

1. Highlight what further information you would seek about (a) the 30 engineers and project managers, and (b) their forthcoming assignments in Mexico, before finalizing the design and content of the pre-departure programme.
2. Explain how you would seek to augment the content of a programme, such as the one you are proposing, with ongoing cultural training during an expatriate's assignment.

Further reading

- Kamoche, K., Chizema, A., Mellahi, K. and Newenham-Kahindi, A. (2012) 'New directions in the management of human resources in Africa', *International Journal of Human Resource Management*, 23(14): 2825–2834.
  The articles in this special issue identify important new developments in theory and practice of HRM in Africa, and open up avenues for further debate in the areas of career development, knowledge appropriation, mergers and acquisitions, the role of HR professionals, the informal sector and the most effective ways to engage foreign investors.

- Brownell, J. (2006) 'Meeting the competency needs of global leaders: a partnership approach', *Human Resource Management*, 45(3): 309–336.
  This article is likely to be of interest to readers who want to examine, in more detail, the design of development programmes for global leaders. In one section, the article specifically examines the complementary role that HR professionals can play in identifying and developing leadership talent by focusing upon issues such as graduate admissions processes, curriculum content, out-of-class leadership experiences, guest speakers, research partnerships and performance management.

- Littrell, L.N., Salas, E., Hess, K.P., Paley, M. and Riedel, S. (2006) 'Expatriate preparation: a critical analysis of 25 years of cross-cultural training research', *Human Resource Development Review*, 5(3): 355–388.
  In reviewing an extensive body of research literature on cross-cultural training, this article is likely to be of real interest to readers who are seeking to establish how the field has developed over the last 25 years. It offers helpful summaries of key studies and explores various theoretical frameworks which have been proposed by researchers investigating the subject of cross-cultural training.

- Mohamed, A.F., Singh, S., Irani, Z. and Darwish, T.K. (2013) 'An analysis of recruitment, training and retention practices in domestic and multinational enterprises in the country of Brunei Darussalam', *International Journal of Human Resource Management*, 24(10): 2054–2081.
  This article presents an interesting empirical analysis of ways that IHRM practices of multinational enterprises can differ from the HRM practices of domestic organizations, which are likely to reflect more closely the local country institutional and cultural context. Analysis of the literature led the researchers to predict MNEs will be more stringent in their recruitment and training and rigorous with promotion practices. These hypothesized differences were largely supported.

- Mendenhall, M.E., Osland, J.S., Bird, A., Oddou, G.R. and Maznevski, M.L. (2008) *Global Leadership: Research Practice and Development*. London and New York: Routledge.
  This textbook offers an excellent review of a wide range of literature on the subject of global leadership. Subjects that are covered include: assessing global leadership competencies, leading global teams and global leadership development.

Internet resources

- www.outpostexpat.nl. Outpost Expatriate Network is an excellent example of an MNC website that is designed to provide practical help and personal advice for the organization's expatriates and their families. The site emanates from the Global Expatriate Policy Department within the Central Human Resource function of Shell Global.

- www.aafsw.com. The Associates of the American Foreign Service Worldwide is a non-profit organization that has been representing Foreign Service spouses, employees and retirees since 1960 and provides practical information for the expatriate. The website provides an interesting insight into the wide range of work and personal issues that are associated with expatriate living such as thrift shopping, voting rights and giving birth abroad. The scope of the website draws attention to the need for organizations to provide thorough cross-cultural training and development for expatriates.
- www.global-dynamics.com/services/expatriate.htm; www.global-integration.com; and www.mercer.com/expatmanagement. Organizations such as these offering training and development programmes for global leaders and expatriates provide relevant information about the types and content of training and development programmes designed for expatriates.
- www.telegraph.co.uk/expat; www.guardianabroad.co.uk/expat. Newspaper websites such as Expat Weekly Telegraph and Guardian Abroad Global Community provide in-depth information about expatriate issues from various perspectives including blogs from those actually working abroad.

Self-assessment questions

Indicative answers to these questions can be found on the companion website at study.sagepub.com/harzing4e.

1. State three major reasons for MNCs to invest in T&D.
2. What are the main arguments for focusing on how global leaders undertake their work as opposed to what work they actually do?
3. Using Neary and O'Grady's (2000) work, how would you summarize the goals of global leadership development programmes?
4. There is evidence to indicate that cross-cultural training is vital in order for expatriates to perform effectively. There is also evidence that some MNCs are reluctant to offer cross-cultural training. What are some of the arguments used to support this reluctance?
5. What are the major issues that need to be considered when designing training programmes to improve expatriates' cross-cultural skills?

References

Adler, N.J. (1981) 'Re-entry: managing cross-cultural transitions', *Group and Organisational Studies*, 6 (3): 341–356.

Adler, N.J. (1997) *International Dimensions of Organisational Behaviour*, 3rd edn. Cincinnati, OH: South-Western College.

Adler, N.J and Bartholomew, S. (1992) 'Managing global competent people', *Academy of Management Executive*, 6 (3): 52–65.

Afiouni, F., Rüel, H. and Schuler, R. (2014) 'Introduction: HRM in the Middle East: toward a greater understanding', *International Journal of Human Resource Management*, 25(2): 133–143.

Aguinis, H. and Kraiger, K. (2009) 'Benefits of training and development for individuals and teams, organizations, and society', *Annual Review of Psychology*, 60: 451–474.

Baker, J.C. and Ivancevich, J.M. (1971) 'The assignment of American executives abroad: systematic, haphazard, or chaotic?', *California Management Review*, 13: 39–44.

Baliga, C. and Baker, J. (1985) 'Multinational corporate policies for expatriate managers: selection, training, evaluation', *SAM Advanced Management Journal*, 50(4): 31–38.

Barratt, A. (1995) 'Training and development of expatriates and home country nationals', in O. Shenkar (ed.), *Global Perspectives of Human Resource Management*. Englewood Cliffs, NJ: Prentice Hall, pp. 132–146.

Bartlett, C.A. and Ghoshal, S. (1992) 'What is a global manager?', *Harvard Business Review* (September–October): 124–132.

Baughn, C. (1995) 'Personal and organisational factors associated with effective repatriation', in J. Selmer (ed.), *Expatriate Management: New Ideas for International Business*. Westport, CT: Quoram Books, pp. 215–230.

Black, J.S. (1992) 'Coming home: the relationship of expatriate expectations with repatriation adjustment and job performance', *Human Relations*, 45(2): 172–192.

Black, J.S., Gregerson, H.B., Mendenhall, M.E. and Stroh, L.K. (1999) *Globalizing People Through International Assignments*. New York: Addison-Wesley/Longman.

Black, J.S. and Mendenhall, M. (1989) 'A practical but theory-based framework for selecting cross-cultural training methods', *Human Resource Management*, 28(4): 511–539.

Black, J.S. and Mendenhall, M. (1990) 'Cross-cultural training effectiveness: a review and theoretical framework for future research', *Academy of Management Review*, 15: 113–126.

Boyatzis, R. (1982) *The Competent Manager*. New York: Wiley.

Brewster, C. (1988) *The Management of Expatriates*. Human Resource Centre Monographs Series No. 2. Bedford, UK: Cranfield Institute of Technology.

Brewster, C. and Pickard, J. (1994) 'Evaluating expatriate training', *International Studies of Management and Organisation*, 24(3): 18–35.

Brislin, R. (1981) *Cross-Cultural Encounters*. New York: Pergamon.

Brownell, J. (2006) 'Meeting the competency needs of global leaders: a partnership approach', *Human Resource Management*, 45(3): 309–336.

Caligiuri, P.M (2004) 'Global leadership development through expatriate assignments and other international experiences', paper presented at the Academy of Management New Orleans Symposium on Expatriate Management: New Directions and Pertinent Issues.

Caligiuri, P.M. (2006) 'Developing global leaders', *Human Resource Management Review*, 16: 219–228.

Caligiuri, P.M. and DeSanto, V. (2001) 'Global competence: what is it, and can it be developed through global assignments?', *Human Resource Planning Journal*, 24(3): 27–38.

Caligiuri, P. and Tarique, I. (2009) 'Predicting effectiveness in global leadership activities', *Journal of World Business*, 44(3): 336–346.

Callahan, M. (1989), 'Preparing the new global manager', *Training and Development Journal*, March: 29–32.

Caudron, S. (1991) 'Training ensures overseas success', *Personnel Journal*, December: 27–30.

Cavusgil, T., Yavas, U. and Bykowicz, S. (1992) 'Preparing executives for overseas assignments', *Management Decision*, 30(1): 54–58.

Chang, W. (2005) 'Expatriate training in international nongovernmental organisations: a model for research', *Human Resource Development Review*, 4(4): 440–461.

Chatzimouratidis, A., Theotokas, I. and Lagoudis, I.N. (2012) 'Decision support systems for human resource training and development', *International Journal of Human Resource Management*, 23(4): 662–693.

Collings, D.G., Scullion, H. and Morley, M.J. (2007) 'Changing patterns of global staffing in the multinational enterprises: challenges to the conventional expatriate assignment and emerging alternatives', *Journal of World Business*, 42: 198–213.

Connor, J. (2000) 'Developing the global leaders of tomorrow', *Human Resource Management*, 39(2/3): 147–157.

Csoka, L. and Hackett, B. (1998) *Transforming the HR function for Global Business Success*. New York: Conference Board (Report No. 1209-98-RR).

Cunha, R., Cunha, M., Morgado, A. and Brewster, C. (2003) 'Market forces, strategic management, HRM practices and organizational performance: a model based in a European sample', *Management Research*, 1(1): 79–91.

Cushner, K. and Brislin, R. (1997) 'Key concepts in the field of cross-cultural training: an introduction', in K. Cushner and R.W. Brislin (eds), *Improving Intercultural Interactions: Modules for Cross-Cultural Training Programs*, Vol. 2. Thousand Oaks, CA: Sage, pp. 1–17.

Deresky, H. (2008) *International Management: Managing Across Borders and Cultures*. Upper Saddle River, NJ: Pearson Prentice-Hall.

Deshpande, S.P. and Viswesvaran, C. (1992) 'Is cross-cultural training of expatriate managers effective: a meta analysis', *International Journal of Intercultural Relations*, 16: 295–310.

De Vos, A., Dries, N. (2013) 'Applying a talent management lens to career management: the role of human capital composition and continuity', *International Journal of Human Resource Management*, 24(9): 1816–1831.

Dowling, P.J., Festing, M. and Engle, A.D (2008) *International Human Resource Management: Managing People in a Multinational Context*. London: Cengage/South-Western.

Dowling, P.J. and Welch, D.E. (2004) *International Human Resource Management: Managing People in a Global Context*, 4th edn. London: Thomson Learning.

Drost, E.A., Frayne, C.A., Lowe, K.B. and Geringer, J.M. (2002) 'Benchmarking training and development practices: a multi-country comparative analysis', *Human Resource Management*, 41(1): 67–86.

Earley, P.C. (1987) 'International training for managers: a comparison of documentary and interpersonal methods', *Academy of Management Journal*, 30(4): 19–35.

Earley, P.C. and Peterson, R.S. (2004) 'The elusive cultural chameleon: cultural intelligence as a new approach to intercultural training for the global manager', *Academy of Management Learning and Education*, 3(1): 100–115.

Eschbach, D.M., Parker, G.E. and Stoebert, P.A (2001) 'American repatriate employees' retrospective assessments of the effects of cross-cultural training on their adaption to international assignments', *International Journal of Human Resource Management*, 12: 270–287.

Forster, N. and Johnsen, M. (1996) 'Expatriate management policies in UK companies new to the international scene', *International Journal of Human Resource Management*, 7(1): 177–205.

Galanaki, E. (2008) 'A decision model for outsourcing training functions: distinguishing between generic and firm-job-specific training content', *International Journal of Human Resource Management*, 19(12): 2332–2351.

Gregersen, H.B., Morrison, A. and Black, J.S. (1998) 'Developing leaders for the global frontier', *Sloan Management Review*, 40: 21–32.

Gupta, A.K. and Govindarajan, V. (2002) 'Cultivating a global mindset', *Academic of Management Executive*, 16: 116–126.

Gupta, A.K., Smith, K.G. and Shalley, C.E. (2006) 'The interplay between exploration and exploitation', *Academy of Management Journal*, 49(4): 693–706.

Hansen, N.K. and Alewell, D. (2013) 'Employment systems as governance mechanisms of human capital and capability development', *International Journal of Human Resource Management*, 24(11): 2131–2153.

Harrison, J.K. (1994) 'Developing successful expatriate managers: a framework for the structural design and strategic alignment of cross-cultural training programmes', *Human Resource Planning*, 17(3): 17–35.

Hertel, E., Geister, S. and Konradt, U. (2005) 'Managing virtual teams: a review of current empirical research', *Human Resource Management Review*, 15: 69–95.

Holtbrügge, D. and Mohr, A.T. (2011) 'Subsidiary interdependencies and international human resource management practices in German MNCs: a resource-based view', *Management International Review*, 51: 93–115.

Iles, P. and Yolles, M. (2003) 'International HRD alliances in viable knowledge migration and development: the Czech Academic Link project', *Human Resource Development International*, 6(3): 301–324.

International Labour Organization (ILO) (2013) *World of Work Report 2013*. Geneva: ILO, International Institute for Labour Studies.

Jain, H., Mathew, M. and Bedi, A. (2012) 'HRM innovations by Indian and foreign MNCs operating in India: a survey of HR professionals', *International Journal of Human Resource Management*, 23(5): 1006–1018.

Johnson, J.P., Lenartowicz, T. and Apud, S. (2006) 'Cross-cultural competence in international business: toward a definition and a model', *Journal of International Business Studies*, 37: 525–543.

Jokinen, T. (2005) 'Global leadership competencies: a review and discussion', *Journal of European Industrial Training*, 29(3): 199–216.

Kamoche, K., Chizema, A., Mellahi, K. and Newenham-Kahindi, A. (2012) 'New directions in the management of human resources in Africa', *International Journal of Human Resource Management*, 23(14): 2825–2834.

Kamoche, K. and Mueller, F. (1998) 'Human resource management and the appropriation-learning perspective', *Human Relations*, 51(8): 1033–1060.

Kamoche, K., Pang, M. and Wong, A.L.Y. (2011) 'Career development and knowledge appropriation: A genealogical critique', *Organization Studies*, 32(12): 1665–1679.

Kang, S.-C., Morris, S.S. and Snell, S.A. (2007) 'Relational archetypes, organizational learning, and value creation: extending the human resource architecture', *Academy of Management Review*, 32(1): 236–256.

Kealey, D. and Protheroe, D. (1996) 'The effectiveness of cross cultural training for expatriates: an assessment of the literature on the issue', *International Journal of Intercultural Relations*, 20: 141–165.

Kedia, B.L. and Mukherji, A. (1999) 'Global managers: developing mindset for global competitiveness', *Journal of World Business*, 34(3): 230–242.

Koster, F., De Grip, A. and Fouarge, D. (2011) 'Does perceived support in employee development affect personnel turnover?', *International Journal of Human Resource Management*, 22(11): 2403–2418.

Kupka, B., Everett, A.M., Atkins, S.G., Mertesacker, M., Graf, A., Brookshill, L., Dodd, C. and Bolten, J. (2009) 'The intercultural communication motivation scale: an instrument to assess motivational training needs of candidates for international assignments', *Human Resource Management*, 48(5): 717–744.

Lee, F.-H., Lee, T.-Z. and Wua, W.-Y. (2010) 'The relationship between human resource management practices, business strategy and firm performance: evidence from steel industry in Taiwan', *International Journal of Human Resource Management*, 21(9): 1351–1372.

Li, J., Qian, G., Liao, S. and Chu, C.W.L. (2008) 'Human resource management and the globalness of firms: an empirical study in China', *International Journal of Human Resource Management*, 19(5): 828–839.

Littrell, L.N., Salas, E., Hess, K.P., Paley, M. and Riedel, S. (2006) 'Expatriate, preparation: a critical analysis of 25 years of cross-cultural training research', *Human Resource Development Review*, 5(3): 355–388.

Management Development Council (2010) *Management Development in Ireland: The Report of the Management Development Council*. Dublin: Management Development Council.

Maznevski, M.L., Canney-Davison, S. and Karsten, J. (2006) 'Global virtual team dynamics and effectiveness', in K.G. Stahl and I. Björkman (eds), *Handbook of Research in International Human Resource Management*. Cheltenham: Edward Elgar, pp. 364–384.

McCall, M.W. (1998) *High Fliers: Developing the Next Generation of Leaders*. Boston, MA: Harvard Business School Press.

McCall, M.W., Lombardo, M. and Morrison, A. (1988) *The Lessons of Experience*. Boston, MA: Lexington Books.

McFarlin, D.B. and Sweeney, P.D. (2006) *International Management: Strategic Opportunities and Cultural Challenges*. New York: Houghton, Mifflin.

McNab, B., Brislin, R. and Worthley, R. (2012) 'Experiential cultural intelligence development: context and individual attributes', *International Journal of Human Resource Management*, 23(7): 1320–1341.

Medcof, J.W. and Song, L.J. (2013) 'Exploration, exploitation and human resource management practices in cooperative and entrepreneurial HR configurations', *International Journal of Human Resource Management*, 24(15): 2911–2926.

Mendenhall, M. (2006) 'The elusive, yet critical challenge of developing global leaders', *European Management Journal*, 26(6): 422–429.

Mendenhall, M. and Oddou, G. (1985) 'The dimension of expatriate acculturation: a review', *Academy of Management Review*, 10: 39–47.

Mendenhall, M. and Osland, J.S. (2002) 'An overview of the extant global leadership research', Symposium Presentation, Academy of International Business, Puerto Rico, June.

Metcalfe, B.D. and Rees, C.J. (2005) 'Theorizing advances in international human resource development', *Human Resource Development International*, 8(4): 449–465.

Mohamed, A.F., Singh, S., Irani, Z. and Darwish, T.K. (2013) 'An analysis of recruitment, training and retention practices in domestic and multinational enterprises in the country of Brunei Darussalam', *International Journal of Human Resource Management*, 24(10): 2054–2081.

Morris, M.A. and Robie, C. (2001) 'A meta-analysis of the effects of cross-cultural training on expatriate performance and adjustment', *International Journal of Training and Development*, 5: 112–125.

Napier, N. and Peterson, R. (1991) 'Expatriate re-entry: what do expatriates have to say', *Human Resource Planning*, 14(1): 19–28.

Neary, D.B. and O'Grady, D.A. (2000) 'The role of training and developing global leaders: a case study at TRW Inc.', *Human Resource Management*, 39(2/3): 185–193.

Ng, I. and Dastmalchian, A. (2011) 'Perceived training benefits and training bundles: a Canadian study', *International Journal of Human Resource Management*, 22(4): 829–842.

Nikandrou, I., Apospori, E., Panayotopoulou, L., Stavrou, E.T. and Papalexandris, N. (2008) 'Training and firm performance in Europe: the impact of national and organizational characteristics', *International Journal of Human Resource Management*, 19(11): 2057–2078.

OECD (2000) *Knowledge Management in Learning Society*. Paris: OECD.

Osland, I. (1995) *The Advantages of Living Abroad: Hero Takes from the Global Frontier*. San Francisco, CA: Jossey Bass, Inc.

Osman-Gani, A. (2000) 'Developing expatriates for the Asia-Pacific region: a comparative analysis of multinational enterprise managers from five countries across three continents', *Human Resource Development Quarterly*, 11(3): 213–235.

Petranek, G.F. (2004) 'Global human resource development: the four C approach', *Human Resource Development Quarterly*, 15(2): 249–252.

Rahim, A. (1983). 'A model for developing key expatriate executives', *Personnel Journal*, 62: 312–317.

Rees, C.J. and Doran, E. (2001) 'Employee selection in a TQM context: taking a hard look at a soft issue', *Total Quality Management*, 12(7/8): 855–860.

Reiche, B.S. (2009) 'To quit or not to quit: organizational determinants of voluntary turnover in MNC subsidiaries in Singapore', *International Journal of Human Resource Management*, 20(6): 1362–1380.

Rhinesmith, S. (1996) *A Manager's Guide to Globalization*, 2nd edn. New York: McGraw-Hill.

Sappinen, J. (1993) 'Expatriate adjustment on foreign assignment', *European Business Review*, 93 (5): 3–11.

Scullion, H. and Starkey, K. (2000) 'In search of the changing role of the corporate human resource function in the international firm', *International Journal of Human Resource Management*, 11(6): 1061–1081.

Selmer, J., Torbiorn, I. and de Leon, T. (1998) 'Sequential cross cultural training for expatriate business managers: predeparture and post-arrival', *International Journal of Human Resource Management*, 9: 831–840.

Sheehan, M. (2012) 'Investing in management development in turbulent times and perceived organisational performance: a study of UK MNCs and their subsidiaries', *International Journal of Human Resource Management*, 23(12): 2491–2513.

Shih, Y.-W., Wu, Y.-L., Wang, Y.-S. and Wang, Y.-M. (2009) 'Competence maps for the information service industry', *International Journal of Human Resource Management*, 20(7): 1618–1633.

Spreitzer, G.M., McCall, M.W. and Mahoney, J.D. (1997) 'Early identification of international executive potential', *Journal of Applied Psychology*, 82(1): 6–29.

Stroh, L.K. and Caligiuri, P.M. (1998a) 'Increasing global competitiveness through effective people management', *Journal of World Business*, 33(1): 1–16.

Stroh, L.K. and Caligiuri, P.M. (1998b) 'Strategic human resource: a new source of competitive advantage in the global arena', *International Journal of Human Resource Management*, 9(1): 1–17.

Suutari, V. (2002) 'Global leader development: an emerging research agenda', *Career Development International*, 7(4): 218–233.

Thaler-Carter, R.E. (2000) 'Whither global leaders', *HR Magazine*, 45(5): 83–88.

Thomas, D.C. and Inkson, K. (2004) *Cultural Intelligence: People Skills for Global Business*. San Francisco, CA: Berrett.

Thomas, D.C., Lazarova, M.B. and Inkson, K (2005) 'Global careers: new phenomenon or new perspectives?', *Journal of World Business*, 40: 340–347.

Thornton, G.C. and Krause, D.E. (2009) 'Selection versus development assessment centers: an international survey of design, execution, and evaluation', *International Journal of Human Resource Management*, 20(2): 478–498

Tomé, E. (2011) 'Human resource development in the knowledge based and services driven economy: An introduction', *Journal of European Industrial Training*, 35(6): 524–539.

Townsend, K., Wilkinson, A., Bamber, G. and Allan, C. (2012) 'Accidental, unprepared, and unsupported: clinical nurses becoming managers', *International Journal of Human Resource Management*, 23(1): 204–220.

Tung, R. (1981) 'Selecting and training for overseas assignment', *Columbia Journal of World Business*, 16: 68–78.

Tung, R. (1982) 'Selection of training procedures of U.S. and Japanese multi-nationals', *California Management Review*, 25(1): 57–81.

Ubeda-Garcia, M., Marco-Lajara, B., Sabater-Sempere, V. and Garcia-Lillo, F. (2013) 'Training policy and organizational performance in the Spanish hotel industry', *International Journal of Human Resource Management*, 24(15): 2851–2875.

Vidal-Salazar, M.D., Hurtado-Torres, N.E. and Matias-Reche, F. (2012) 'Training as a generator of employee capabilities', *International Journal of Human Resource Management*, 23(13): 2680–2697.

Wang, X. and McLean, G.N. (2007) 'The dilemma of defining international human resource development', *Human Resource Development Review*, 6(1): 96–108.

Woodruffe, C. (1993) 'What is meant by a competency?', *Leadership and Organisation Development Journal*, 14: 29–36.

Global and Local Resourcing

11

Chris Rowley, Alan Nankervis and Malcolm Warner

Contents

Learning objectives

After reading this chapter you will be able to:

- Understand and evaluate the HR competencies approach
- Rationalize and illustrate the political economy and strategic choice approaches
- Identify the key external factors that determine change in recruitment and retention
- Differentiate between the key characteristics of capitalist market economies and socialist market economies in Asia
- Critically evaluate the reasons for economic reform and adoption of HR policies and practices in Asia

Chapter outline

This chapter discusses recent changes to labour market policy and regulations and assesses their impact on HRM policies and practices in Asia, in particular in the area of employee-resourcing, i.e. recruitment, selection and retention. Four significant Asian economies are used as examples to represent the range of different economic systems, namely Japan and Taiwan as two 'capitalist' models, and China and Vietnam as two 'socialist' models.

1 Introduction

This chapter identifies recent changes in labour market policy and regulations and assesses their impact on enterprises' HRM policies and practices in Asia, in particular in the area of employee-resourcing (see Rowley and Harry, 2011; Warner, 2013a). Four significant Asian economies are used as examples, namely Japan and Taiwan representing 'capitalist' market economies, on the one hand, and China and Vietnam, representing 'socialist' market economies on the other (for other Asian examples, see Rowley and Benson, 2004; Chatterjee and Nankervis, 2007; Rowley and Abdul-Rahman, 2008; Nankervis et al., 2012; Warner, 2014; Rowley and Warner, 2014).

There are many interesting global resourcing developments and impacts that could be included, such as the roles of corporate social responsibility, race and gender, but space precludes these. Rather, the chapter commences with an overview of literature related to the HR competency approach in the areas of 'recruiting and retaining competencies'. Then it examines the interaction between external changes in political, economic and labour market policy, and enterprises' strategic adaptation and adjustment of HR policies and practices. We review these systems respectively in Japan, Taiwan, China and Vietnam, focusing on their impact on employee-resourcing. The final section illustrates the policy implications for government policy-makers, regulators and management in Asia, and also considers its significance elsewhere for achieving an appropriate degree of 'fit' between external changes and the strategic adaptation and internal adjustment of HR policies and practices.

> ## Box 11.1   Stop and reflect
>
> Divide into small groups (of two to four students). Find another group. Choose one of the positions each and debate your findings.
>
> Position 1: Following a universalism perspective, the forces of globalization and best practice will make all employee-resourcing policies and practices increasingly similar across the world.
>
> Position 2: Following a divergence perspective, the forces of national, regional and local cultures will mean that employee-resourcing policies and practices become more dissimilar and distinct across the world.

2 Review of HR competencies approach

Increasing competition in global markets has encouraged management to pay greater attention to improving 'employee competencies'. After the 1997 Asian financial crisis, most Asian economies introduced a 'competency model' incorporating the main activities for HRM (see Bae and Rowley, 2004; Chatterjee and Nankervis, 2007). The conceptualization of competencies has undergone quite a dramatic change. In the past, the notion of competencies was used only in the areas of vocational training and education. The concept has gradually become embedded in the field of HRM with a broader domain beyond the narrow view of basic work capabilities such as 'following rules and procedure and performing limited and routine tasks'. Indeed, competencies have also spread to encompass areas such as leadership (on Asia, see Rowley and Ulrich, 2012a, 2012b, 2013).

No matter what models and perspectives are used, employee-resourcing policies and practices are an integral component of HRM. In fact, resourcing not only seeks to attract, obtain and retain the human resources that the organization needs to achieve its strategic goals, but also aims to have a significant impact on the composition of the workforce; the ultimate 'fit' with the organization's needs and culture, and long-term employment stability (Beer et al., 1984). This chapter examines resourcing in Asia and adopts two elements of the model of four HR competencies constructed by Bae and Rowley (2004) (see Box 11.2), namely 'recruiting competencies' and 'retaining competencies'. The first element, 'recruiting competencies', consists of recruitment and selection activities. The third one, 'retaining competencies', includes two activities, namely training/development and job design.

> ## Box 11.2 Theoretical perspectives of HR competencies
>
> - Recruiting competencies – consists of recruitment and selection activities.
> - Reinforcing competencies – encompasses evaluation and rewards.
> - Retaining competencies – includes two activities, namely job design, training and development.
> - Replacing competencies – through employment flexibility and outplacement.
>
> *Source*: Bae and Rowley, 2004.

These competencies are incorporated under the broad categories of 'capability builder', 'change champion' and 'HR innovator and integrator' in a large global study and associated global HR competency model developed by the University of Michigan in conjunction with the RBL Group consultancy firm (Ulrich et al., 2013). Their model suggests that HR professionals in any context require both recruiting and retaining competencies for the successful attraction and retention of scarce talent in increasingly dynamic and competitive local and global labour markets.

Our competency model (Bae and Rowley, 2004) is selected for two reasons. First, the model emerged from empirical research aimed at capturing the changes in HRM activities conducted among Asian economies (see Rowley and Benson, 2004). Second, it groups HRM activities in a systematic way that enables a more integrated analysis. Further, in line with the central theme of this chapter, namely recruitment and retention, these two elements of competency are addressed in detail.

3 External labour market changes and internal strategic choice

In the past two decades research has focused on the specific circumstances of individual countries and their impact on HR practices at the enterprise level. Two major approaches dominate the debate about the factors that influence HR in different political, social and economic environments – the political economy (external factors) and the strategic choice (internal factors) approaches (Warner, 2000; Martin and Bamber, 2005; Bamber et al., 2011) (see Box 11.3).

Box 11.3   Theoretical perspectives of external and internal factors

- External factors – the political economy approach illustrates the integration of a system of production, the role of government, the broader social and economic environment under globalization, labour market regulations and employment relations institutions, and its impact on enterprises' development.
- Internal factors – the strategic choice approach identifies key elements of internal factors for business success and focuses on choice in terms of organizations' business strategies and their links with HR practice.

Source: Martin and Bamber, 2005: 377–386.

In considering the influence of external factors, the political economy approach illustrates the integration of a 'system of production, the role of government, the broader social and economic environment under globalization, labour market regulations and employment relations institutions and their impact on enterprises' development' (Martin and Bamber, 2005: 381). The international political economy has changed dramatically during the last few decades and HR systems have adjusted accordingly. In general, there are three main trends: the intensification of international competition, widespread de-regulation across industrialized countries, and the collapse of Soviet communism that boosted the confidence of neo-liberal ideologues (Martin and Bamber, 2005; Bamber et al., 2011). Murray et al. (2000) claim that this approach involves analysing the interaction between interest groups and institutions. This interaction influences the manner in which nations integrate with the international political economy and ultimately determines the impact of globalization in each country and region, with their HR systems being influenced accordingly (Van Ruysseveldt, 1995; Chatterjee and Nankervis, 2007).

In relation to internal factors, the strategic choice approach identifies key elements for business success and since the 1980s has been part of the vocabulary for many comparative studies (see Chapter 2) of HR practices (Martin and Bamber, 2005; Chatterjee and Nankervis, 2007). Its major area of concern is organizations' business strategies and their relationship to HR practices (Boxall and Purcell, 2003; Martin and Bamber, 2005; Nankervis et al., 2012; Ulrich et al., 2013). This approach emphasizes the role of management initiatives (Kochan et al., 1986) and the integration of HR practices with business strategies (Guest, 1987; Storey and Sisson, 1993; Ulrich et al., 2013). It favours increased management autonomy, rejection of collective bargaining and a reduced union role in employment relations (Beer et al., 1984; Dowling and Welch, 2004; Bamber et al., 2011). In the next section we apply these theoretical perspectives to HR transformation and to debates on the factors influencing adoption of HR practices.

Box 11.4   Stop and reflect

In the small groups, debate:

1. The advantages and disadvantages of the external versus internal approaches to HRM.
2. Their relevance in Western and Asian contexts.

We chose four Asian economies to represent both developed and developing nations in terms of their economic and labour market policies and consequently their impact on HR practices at the firm level.

4 Capitalist market economies: Japan and Taiwan

It is useful to group Japan and Taiwan together – given that each is an island economy, although their populations are different in size and origins, and that they share some philosophical and religious traditions. Historically, Japan colonized Taiwan over the first half of the twentieth century and both of them were dominated by a feudalist system and have since transformed to state-led capitalism and industrialization, and more recently developed into more open capitalist market economies. Hence, similarities as well as differences can be found.

Japan

Japan is the leading developed capitalist economy in East Asia with many unique management characteristics (see Warner, 2013a). Its HRM has been identified as the 'Japanese style of people management' due to the mix of its Confucian legacy with a modern welfare corporatist system (Benson and Debroux, 2004). By facing the challenges of globalization and regional competition, the Japanese HRM system has undergone a process of transformation that has become known as a Japanese model with a more individualistic focus (Benson and Debroux, 2004). However, this emerging model is inherently unstable and contradictory (Benson, 2005) and the following section will address those changes in relation to the central theme of this chapter.

Two major aspects of the transformation in Japan are first the changes in labour market policy and its impact on HR practices at firm level and second the changes in employee-resourcing and HRM. The key elements of government labour market policy are related to the changing realities of the economy and labour market. For most of the 1990s and 2000s, the Japanese economy fluctuated between periods of recession and extremely low rates of economic growth. This long-term economic instability has had a negative impact on employment with relatively high rates of unemployment. The adverse economic situation has created pressure on the labour market and this situation continues at the time of writing. The key elements of labour market policy have been implemented by the government with the aims of reducing unemployment and the cost of employment, improving labour productivity and managing the problems associated with an ageing workforce. Specific policies have been introduced with the purpose of providing incentives for firms to employ more people, particularly younger age groups, and support labour flexibility and if possible not dismiss employees. At the same time, the government has provided more funding for training and development, pension and unemployment benefits, while extending the retirement age to retain relatively older employees within the workforce.

During the first half of the 1990s, the ratio of openings to applicants remained quite high for professional and technical occupations. Large companies that formerly had recruited many high school graduates started to reduce the amount of employment, in addition, many companies reduced the size of their workforce by transferring manufacturing abroad and resorting to new employment policies that relied on atypical work contracts and arrangements. After the 1997 Asian financial crisis, poor economic conditions coupled with an acceleration of the restructuring process brought about a fall in the demand for labour and reduced recruitment of young graduates and high school leavers. Following the redundancies of mid-career employees during the recession and business closures, other companies started to recruit some of these more experienced mid-career employees who had been sacked during the downturn.

The late 1990s economic downturn forced Japanese companies to adopt a more flexible employment arrangement – by dividing the workforce into three categories:

1. a core group with long-term employment
2. a contractor group of specialists with mid-term employment
3. a peripheral group undertaking simple and routine tasks with short-term employment. (Benson and Debroux, 2004)

Each of these groups exhibited a pattern of distinct recruitment, remuneration, welfare, training and promotion schemes.

The second area, namely HR retention, covers two elements: job design, and training and development. In order to develop a system that realized 'talent-value' as well as retained capable people within the organization, most companies have had to reassess their HR retention policies. In fact, the current generation of Japanese employees has developed a new set of work-values, and beliefs that flexible, ability-based and performance-oriented job design, evaluation, incentives and promotion will benefit their careers (see Chapters 12 and 13). Consequently, there has been a gradual shift away from traditional seniority-based ranking, promotion and incentive systems towards meritocratic values and approaches.

As for training and development, the influence of both external and internal factors – such as global competition, technological changes and innovation, and domestic and regional economic downturns – has increased pressure on both the government and industries to pay more attention to human resource development. Both national and prefectural governments in Japan have had to allocate more funds for establishing public HRD facilities throughout the country, targeting unemployed people and graduate students and assisting them to gain new jobs and acquire new skills. As for industry, there has been an uneven distribution of job-based training opportunities in terms of size and sector. Generally speaking, large companies provide more training opportunities than do small- and medium-size companies. For instance, companies with 1,000 or more employees are reported to have had a 99 per cent rate of implementation of job-related training programmes, in contrast to 66 per cent of companies with less than 99 employees.

In addition, although formal and informal on-the-job training (OJT) has been the norm in Japan, off-the-job training (Off-JT) in special skills and knowledge has not been widely adopted by employers. So, whereas the Japanese economy evolved towards a more knowledge-based focus during the late 1990s and early to mid-2000s, HRD policy and its implementation still lag far behind. In fact, there are multiple challenges still facing the government and industry that require not only training in basic knowledge and skills, but also other programmes, such as improving special work-related skills, responses to technology changes, improvements in business and economic literacy, handling market competition and globalization, and developing specific competencies within the workforce.

Taiwan

Since the 1960s, Taiwan has experienced many complex political and economic developments. On the political front, the pressure for democratization became overwhelming during the late 1980s and early 1990s. Over the last three decades, the political system has become more complex and government policy has moved towards a more pro-labour orientation following the process of democratization (Rowley and Harry, 2011; Zhu and Warner, 2013b). The government has also expanded the range of worker benefits through the creation of a social welfare system. Some of the laws that have been established, for instance the rules on unemployment benefits, were a direct response to the effects of the 1997 Asian financial crisis.

In Taiwan, different stages of development in the economy have been accompanied by specific patterns of management. Economic development since the 1960s can be divided into three stages: the 'export' expansion period between 1961 and 1980, the 'technology-intensive industries' expansion period from 1981 to 1997 before the Asian financial crisis (Zhu and Warner, 2004) and the 'hi-tech' era of the 2000s (see Zhu and Warner, 2013b).

In the labour market, important changes have also taken place (Rowley et al., 2011). In the 1980s, after three decades of rapid industrial expansion, the supply of land and labour both became scarce leading to rapid increases in labour costs and land prices. As a consequence, many labour-intensive industries relocated from Taiwan to low-cost countries, especially in South East Asia and mainland China. Government policy also shifted from developing labour-intensive industries to encouraging the development of technology-intensive and service industries in order to maintain the momentum of economic development.

Taiwan's economy experienced economic slowdown during both the 1997 and 2008 financial crises. These changes in the economy and labour market, the challenges of the crises and, more broadly, global economic competition, have produced different HRM responses from Taiwanese enterprises.

HRM policies have changed from the early years of an export expansion related policy to the more recent technology-intensive industry policy. During the export expansion period, recruiting blue-collar workers relied heavily on informal channels of recruitment by employee referral and via company networks. For the recruitment of white-collar workers, such as managers and public servants, formal channels and recruitment procedures were used. In fact, colleges' and universities' graduate recruitment was one of the major sources of applicants for filling those positions. Due to long-term contracts and conditions of employment combined with seniority-based systems of employment, there was little extensive mid-career recruitment in the labour market during this period.

The HR retention policies of organizations were based on long-term employment and seniority-based systems of job design, training provision and employee promotion. With the traditional culture of avoiding conflict between management and employees, most employees would be promoted along the grades of their job titles only if their annual performance was classified as 'above average'. However, company-sponsored training was not popular during this period and apprenticeships were not common in Taiwan. In practice, skilled workers more often received formal OJT than did semi-skilled and unskilled workers (Zhu and Warner, 2004). Also, foreign-owned enterprises (FOEs) offered more OJT programmes than did local companies.

During the technology-intensive industries' period of expansion, the industrial system became more complex and formal, and government policy shifted towards a more pro-labour orientation. The development of the labour market and growing demand for a more skilled workforce led to more formal recruitment and selection procedures in the public and private sectors, as well as performance-based compensation, job design and promotion with less emphasis on seniority (Hsu and Leat, 2000). However, internal recruitment methods such as 'promotion-from-within', 'transfers' and 'job rotation' are still commonly used by the majority of Taiwanese enterprises. External recruitment methods are mainly used to obtain candidates with specialist knowledge, technical or managerial skills for appointments to middle and senior posts (Hsu and Leat, 2000). In terms of selection practices, 'knowledge or skill tests' and formal interviews are most frequently used, whereas 'psychometric tests' and 'assessment centres' are less common (Hsu and Leat, 2000).

Training and development became a key element of HRM policy and practice for upgrading skills in the more technology-intensive industries. Given the trends towards developing learning organizations and the shift towards the knowledge economy, many Taiwanese enterprises adopted organizational learning strategies by (a) focusing on the diffusion of individual learning with team learning and organizational learning, and (b) using the knowledge management system to create an opportunity for individuals, teams and the organization to learn (Lien et al., 2007: 219).

In practice, after the 2008 global financial crisis the Taiwanese government and industry community have been collaborating to invest more in training and development, while also reducing salary levels and encouraging employees to take unpaid leave in order to avoid creating more unemployment (see Zhu and Warner, 2013b). Therefore, in Taiwan new HRM retention policies became one way of reducing unemployment and maintaining social stability.

5 Socialist market economies: China and Vietnam

The People's Republic of China (PRC) and the Socialist Republic of Vietnam (SRV) represent a different kind of political and economic system. Both countries have been transformed from centrally planned socialist systems to more market oriented economies, while still retaining some 'socialist characteristics'. Economic reforms and an open door policy have led to significant changes in these socialist market economies. The emergence of new interest groups, the inflow of foreign capital and the diversity of ownership of enterprises, combined with a large mobile population with many people migrating from the countryside to the cities, have accentuated conflicts of interest and require a more relevant labour market policy at the macro-level and HRM strategies at the micro-level to cope with these challenges.

China

After the 'Liberation' in 1949, China established its 'socialist' industrial and labour relations system, particularly during the 1950s. However, in the 1960s Mao Zedong tried to undermine what he had originally thought was the correct path to take when he partially emulated Soviet practices. After ten years of Cultural Revolution (1966–1976) the level of enterprise performance was weak and unlikely to improve greatly under a system in which the workers were not strongly motivated. In order to catch up,

China began to encourage Western technological (and managerial) transfer by way of the new 'Open Door' policy and looked eastwards, especially to the Japanese pattern of economic development and management as a possible route for modernization (Warner, 2014).

The main reforms of labour market policy in general, and HRM policy and practice in particular, reflect strategies of marketization set within the overall national economic development policy. The major changes include the following (see Zhu and Warner, 2004; Rowley and Cooke, 2009; Warner, 2009, 2010, 2011, 2012, 2013a, 2014):

- New policies mainly centred on the reform of wages, employment, welfare and management.
- Reforms seen as breaking the 'three irons' ('iron rice-bowl', 'iron wages', 'iron position'), and establishing three new systems (labour contract system, floating wage system and a cadre or manager engagement system) with the purpose of increasing labour flexibility and competition.
- Under Deng Xiaoping's new reformist ideology, policy aimed to assert the principle of 'distribution according to work' and link individuals' performance, skills and position with their income in order to increase their motivation for greater production.
- New types of wage systems, such as the 'piece (-work) wage system', 'bonus system' and later the 'structural wage system', 'floating wage system' and 'post plus skills wage system'.
- Allowing variations in rewards based on productivity was part of this reform. Moreover, labour was to be encouraged to move from less productive firms to more efficient ones.
- Immobility of labour has been a feature of the old system dominated by state-owned enterprises, where there was over-manning and zero turn-over of workers.

Establishment of a new labour market was therefore high on the reformers' agenda. However, improvements in labour mobility did not take place overnight. Even by the end of the 1990s, the level of job mobility was still relatively low, although rising in the non-state sector such as in domestic private enterprises (DPEs), joint ventures and FOEs.

In terms of employment in the early 1980s, many young graduates from school could no longer obtain the guaranteed employment opportunity their parents had enjoyed in the past and in fact became temporarily unemployed. The practice of job inheritance ('dingti'), with posts passing from parents to offspring, was gradually phased out. In addition, many young people who came back to the cities after several years of settlement in the countryside and obtaining their education from peasants ('cha dui') could not find jobs. However, this situation was described by the officials as waiting to be employed ('daiye') but not as unemployment ('shiye') (Zhu and Warner, 2004; Warner, 2011). It could not be admitted openly that a socialist society might have 'unemployment', which was formerly associated with capitalism.

The meaning of the term 'daiyie' was even expanded to include the workers who were laid off from factories throughout the late 1980s and early 1990s (Warner, 2011). Since the mid-1990s, unemployment has been used to refer to people who have not been employed for several years and unemployment benefit is now available for some of them (Warner, 2011). In fact, the level of unemployment has grown steadily as the reforms have deepened and downsizing has taken place (Warner, 2011); many young workers have been forced into precarious forms of 'self-employment' such as street-hawkers. Since the 2008 global financial crisis and subsequent economic turbulence, this kind of unemployment has increased and become worse, in particular among college and university graduates, as well as migrant workers ('nongmingong').

Since 2000, the term HRM has become more prominent in Sino-foreign joint ventures and FOEs, particularly the larger ones (see Warner, 2011). However, even in these types of firm, management often seems to be comparatively inward-looking, with a focus on issues like wages, welfare and promotion, as found in conventional personnel management, rather than strategic activities like long-term organizational and employee development normally associated with HRM.

Research based on Special Economic Zones (SEZs) (see Warner, 2005) shows that the market-oriented economy reforms have had a profound impact on organizational changes and HRM practices. The pressure towards being competitive and flexible has created a diverse pattern of HRM in relation to companies' organizational cultures based on their specific histories and values. The case studies reveal substantial competition in the HR arena for recruiting and retaining skilled and capable employees. Better work organization has led to higher productivity and competitiveness, and helped to manage the workforce, achieve higher employee commitment, and realize individuals' values and aspirations within the organization. Improved teamwork, quality management (e.g. quality circles), and adopting new technology have enabled these Chinese companies to achieve their business goals.

A number of factors influence the ways enterprises recruit employees (Cooke, 2005). First, there was the gradual withdrawal of the government from direct intervention in the state sector and direct recruitment of people from the external labour market. Second, there was labour market segmentation – with a shortage of skilled labour and oversupply of unskilled/semi-skilled labour that forced enterprises to adopt a more sophisticated recruitment strategy to compete for talent from more diverse sources including expatriates and overseas Chinese graduate-returnees (see Zhu and Warner, 2013a). Third, the common recruitment methods for the low-paid and low-skilled jobs was mainly through family, friends and village networks, in contrast to the more formal, skilled or white-collar jobs with more formal labour market advertising, recruitment and selection procedures (for HRM in small enterprises see Rowley and Li, 2006, 2008).

Since the late 1990s, when further reform of the SOEs was implemented, retraining of redundant workers in this sector became one of the main training activities in China to increase their employability. Other areas of management and HRM policy and practice such as pay (see Wei and Rowley, 2009) have also been changing (Rowley and Cooke, 2009).

In the last decade, Chinese enterprises have been facing a major shortage of skilled and experienced technical and professional talent, caused on the one hand by the growing labour demand of both low-tech manufacturing and high-tech industries, and on the other by the inability of vocational and higher education systems to meet demand (Cooke, 2009, 2012). These circumstances have been exacerbated by a significant 'brain drain' of Chinese graduates to the United States and Europe. In response to these challenges, the government, local private and foreign firms have adopted innovative approaches to attract suitable employees (see Zhu and Warner, 2013a). As examples, the Chinese government launched its 'Thousand Talents Plan' in late 2008 in order to recruit high skilled professionals and managers from its diaspora, especially for employment in key innovation projects, high-tech science parks and the top banking institutions (Cooke, 2012: 29); and is currently reviewing the pedagogy, curricula and linkages between vocational and higher education systems in order to produce 'job-ready' graduates (Nankervis et al., 2012). Local private employers are reported to be continuing to rely on employee referral recruitment methods for both cost and cultural reasons (Cooke, 2012: 29), together with offering an array of intrinsic and extrinsic rewards (e.g. good wages, ongoing training, career paths and supportive work climates). Chinese companies such as Sany Heavy Industries (construction), Nensoft and Alibaba (IT), and Mindray (medical diagnostic devices) use their reputational advantages to attract high value employees (Yeung and Tao, 2013), together with career development programmes including regional learning networks, internships for university students and systematic methods of job rotation. At the lower level, franchises such as Haidilao Hotpot Restaurants (see Box 11.5) rely on their unique service cultures.

Box 11.5   Examples from practice 1: Hotshots in hotpots

Haidilao Hotpot Restaurants (HDL) has provoked considerable interest and growing patronage throughout China, as a result of its reputation for specialist cuisine and excellent customer service. HDL began operations in 1994, but now employs more than 10,000 chefs, waiters and cleaning staff across China, with impressive profits of over US$240 million. HDL's business success is not attributed primarily to its cuisine, which is both Chinese and Western, but rather to its remarkable customer service and value proposition. It uses local social media such as Weibo to great advantage, attracting mainly young people but also their parents and friends. HDL provides its customers with free internet access, snacks, drinks, hot towels, complimentary nail and shoe polishing services. It also sends free faxes, provides childcare and waives bills for unsatisfied customers. All of these add-on services distinguish HDL from its local restaurant competitors, and represent a new level of service quality in a country which has not generally been perceived as a high performer in this area. Thus, HDL can be seen as a pioneering service provider, appealing to the new Chinese middle classes, who have significantly higher expectations than did previous generations.

In support of its business strategy, HDL encourages its employees to exercise some autonomy and empowers them to meet or exceed customer needs. It chooses to primarily recruit lowly educated staff from poor rural backgrounds for chef, waiting and cleaning roles, despite the availability of graduates from hospitality schools. Most new employees are recruited through referrals and recommendations from existing employees. This staffing practice is partly based on labour costs, but also on the company's belief that less privileged employees are more likely to commit themselves to an employer demonstrating concern for employees through traditional methods of paternalistic management, support and teamwork. HDL also recognizes that staff satisfaction is key to excellent customer service, and consequently business success, and that this aspect is all the more important in the absence of substantive career opportunities. Thus, HDL's CEO (Zhang Yong) emphasizes strong commitment to the relationship between employee and customer satisfaction. To maintain high levels of employee satisfaction, the company offers air-conditioned staff apartments, children's educational allowances and parental support, among other benefits. HDL's business strategy can be considered as a blend of traditional and modern approaches, as its competitive edge is predicated on superior customer service which reflects the management and HRM practices often used in Western countries, but its recruitment and retention processes reflect older cultural values, including paternalism and broad social responsibility imperatives.

Source: adapted from Yeung and Tao, 2013: 95.

Foreign-owned companies in China, including Microsoft, Atlas Copco and HP have imported and adapted their more comprehensive talent attraction and retention systems, combining sophisticated promotion campaigns with integrated learning and development programmes that are complemented with impressive incentives and benefits (Nankervis et al., 2012: 90–91). The following case illustrates the approach taken by an Indian-owned global company to recruit and retain high quality Chinese employees (see Box 11.6).

Box 11.6   Example from practice 2: Tata Consulting in China

The Tata Group is one of the largest conglomerates in India, and has developed a formidable global presence in the last two decades. Currently there are ten Tata companies operating in China – Tata Steel, Jaguar Land Rover, Tata AutoComp Systems, Tata Communications, Tata Consultancy Services, Tata Refractories, Tata Global Beverages, Tata International, Tata Projects and TKM Global Logistics – and the group plans to further expand its activities in the future. Its businesses yielded more than US$3.7 billion in 2011, with Jaguar Land Rover and Tata Steel generating the most profits.

In partnership with Microsoft and the Chinese government, Tata Consultancy Services (TCS) aims to use its global IT capability to increase business opportunities in order to become the largest IT company in the country. It was the first Indian IT wholly owned foreign enterprise in China, and China is an integral part of TCS's Global Network Delivery Model, which includes large delivery centres in India, Latin America, North America and Europe. TCS currently has five global delivery centres in China (Beijing, Hangzhou, Tianjin, Shanghai and Shenzhen). In 2005, TCS was invited by the Chinese government to form a joint venture to create a large-scale global off-shoring base in China. The joint venture, supported by the National Development and Reforms Commission (NDRC), leverages the strengths of the different partners in technology, software development and consulting, including the best-of-class processes and practices of TCS. The company holds 75.64 per cent in the joint venture while the rest is held by local partners.

The CEO of TCS China is a foreign-educated and experienced Chinese manager, Qiqi Dong. The company employs more than 1,500 associates, most of whom are locals (home country nationals), and its recruitment preference is to hire talented engineers and IT professionals from surrounding regions and universities. This can be a difficult task, even though Chinese universities supply large numbers of engineering graduates annually, as many of them are inexperienced with only limited exposure to global business practices.

Staffing issues and challenges

Apart from the difficulties associated with attracting sufficient numbers of qualified and experienced engineers in a highly competitive internal labour market, there are also cultural issues for Chinese employees working for an Indian multinational corporation. With respect to the former, competitive salaries and benefits, career opportunities, generous benefits, and close personal relationships between employees and their managers, are provided in order to reduce employee turnover and to engender loyalty to the company. Ongoing development opportunities are also essential to complement TCS employees' technical skills with interpersonal competencies such as capabilities in client consultation and negotiation.

While China and India have cultural commonalities, there are also differences with respect to religious traditions, managerial styles and the problematic history between the two countries. The Tata Group is renowned for its strong cultural values, and its inherent commitment to corporate social responsibility. These characteristics need to be constantly reinforced by the company in its Chinese operations, together with an appreciation of the cultural protocols involved in dealing with clients from its diverse Asian nations. TCS in China was considered among the 100 'Best Human Resource Management Companies' listed by China's premier job site, 51 Jobs, and has won the 'Best Performance Review Management' award.

Source: adapted from Tata, 2011: 64–65.

Vietnam

Economic reform in Vietnam likewise aims to replace direct government administration at the enterprise level with government management of the economy and enterprise autonomy oriented to a market economy (Rowley and Quang, 2009; Collins et al., 2011; Collins et al., 2013; Warner, 2014). Major tasks of reform have included the rationalization of SOEs into joint stock companies (JSCs) and the introduction and expansion of private enterprises, which extends to DPEs and FOEs (Warner, 2013b). Key priorities of the 'doi moi' reforms (1988–1991) included reducing the role of the state bureaucracy, liberalizing the economic system and establishing a comprehensive legal framework for employment relations (Collins, 2009; Collins et al., 2013). Among the reform's initiatives, changing HRM is one of the critical points at which economic imperatives spill over into social and political considerations.

The pre-reform system

Under the pre-reform Vietnamese system, SOEs were integrated into a system of mandatory state planning. Enterprise inputs, including labour, were assigned by government plans. Enterprises did not necessarily acquire labour with the right set of skills and were invariably over-staffed because the labour administration recruited and selected employees for individual firms (Collins et al., 2011). In addition, enterprises had few methods available to motivate or discipline employees. The rewards system had only an indirect relation to enterprise efficiency and individual labour effort. It was based on a narrowly defined egalitarianism, as well as the tendency to reward labour on the grounds of seniority and contribution to the Party, as well as to the war effort in the past.

Personnel management was a rigid function confined to areas such as allocating jobs and managing personnel files. Due to the absence of labour markets, pre-reform personnel management was inward-looking and concentrated on issues such as distribution of wages, provision of welfare, and routine promotion of workers and cadres from lower ranks to higher ranks according to the regulations.

Reform of the HR system

In the early stages of 'doi moi', reform of the SOEs was intensified owing to the loss of financial assistance from the former Soviet Union (Truong et al., 2010; Collins et al., 2013). In order to create a more flexible HR system, the government relinquished its control over the recruitment and employment of workers. Therefore, individual firms gained more autonomy to decide on the number of workers hired, the terms of employment and release of employees.

The pace of transforming life-time employment into a new contract-employment system has been relatively slow and the dominant change has been the fixed-term contract of employment that was initially introduced in 1987. Since the late 1990s, there have been further changes, with three types of contracts covering different types of employees: first, the unlimited-term contract for employees who joined the work unit before the introduction of the new system; second, the fixed-term contract with a duration of one to three years for employees who joined the work unit after the introduction of the new system; and third, the temporary contract with a duration of less than one year for casual workers or seasonal workers. However, due to the economic difficulties in a large number of SOEs, many so-called 'permanent employees' who are on unlimited-term contracts have been retrenched through further restructuring of SOEs in recent years (Collins et al., 2011). Therefore, the term 'unlimited-term contract' nowadays has lost much of its meaning.

Generally speaking, staffing activities in local enterprises are considered to be not as effective as they are in FOEs (Thang and Quang, 2005; Quang et al., 2008; Collins et al., 2011; Zhu and Verstraeten, 2013; Cox et al., 2014). FOEs tend to extend their search efforts in recruitment and to apply a rigorous selection process to acquire the most appropriate candidates for the job. A recent study by Zhu and Verstraeten (2013), for example, found that FOEs, joint venture firms and local private companies are generally using more sophisticated recruitment and selection techniques (formal interviews, resumé reviews, selection tests) than their SOE counterparts, although all types of organizations also employ 'try-outs' and network-based sourcing. This may be the result of SOEs having an excessive number of workers due to historical factors, and consequently being preoccupied with reducing the burden rather than engaging actively in recruitment and selection of new personnel. It is also likely due to traditional legacies and relative inexperience with HRM techniques of employee-resourcing. As for the JSCs and DPEs, their business started more recently and business growth has enabled them to rely on employing more capable people.

For many years, Vietnam has been seen as a place with cheap labour as a source of competitive advantage. However, its relatively lower skills and productivity can raise alarm bells for foreign companies when they assess its opportunities and threats as a country for potential investment. As a result, many people in government and the business community appreciate the importance of upgrading the workforce's skills through training and development. The Vietnamese Labour Code (2002) provided some stimulus for greater on-the-job training, in order to overcome the employee skills deficiencies revealed within national vocational and higher education systems (Cox and Warner, 2013), and recent government reviews of the Vocational Training Law imply that these underlying problems may soon be concertedly addressed. Full-scale training activities were initiated within the FOE group due to a common perception that technical and managerial skills among employees were insufficient. In recent years, some JSCs and DPEs have become more keen to invest in employees through training, in addition, DPEs have continued to seek to recruit experienced employees for their organizations' needs (Thang and Quang, 2005; Collins et al., 2011; Collins et al., 2013). Under increasing competition, local companies have begun to experiment with innovative measures of acquiring high-quality management expertise. Other areas of management in Vietnam have also been changing (Rowley and Quang, 2009). Some enterprises have tried to hire foreigners, even as CEOs, for the top jobs that are currently in short demand (Quang et al., 2008).

The following example (Box 11.7) illustrates the ways in which a FOE has adapted its recruiting and retention approach to its Vietnamese subsidiary.

Box 11.7   Example from practice 3: The Wong Shin Company

The Wong Shin Company is a wholly Taiwanese-owned garment manufacturing firm which has been operating in Vietnam for the last eight years. Located in the Mekong Delta, it produces up-market clothing for several well-known global brands, using state of the art technology. It claims to adhere to strong quality and safety standards and has developed effective relationships with both provincial and national governments through its careful selection of party cadres and partnership with the plant union. In line with usual business traditions, the general manager is Taiwanese (parent company national) as are the deputy general manager, the financial and production managers. All other managers and workers were locally recruited, most from the Mekong Delta district. It is intended to gradually replace the financial and operations managers with Vietnamese staff over time, if suitable candidates can be sourced, and they will be provided with considerable training

(Continued)

(Continued)

and development activities complemented by a 'shadowing' career development stage with the present occupants of those positions. Communication between the company managers and local workers takes several forms, including regular work team meetings, overall company social occasions, management–union forums and employee suggestion boxes. Given the nature of the local workforce, however, most communication tends to be mainly top-down.

HRM approach and issues

Although organizational structures are essentially hierarchical, in conformance with Taiwanese traditions, the general manager is keen to devolve some production quality responsibilities to work teams and to allow line managers a degree of autonomy in areas such as work scheduling, performance criteria and employee recognition programmes. There is also a new emphasis on workers' health and safety, including mental health issues. Since its establishment, the Wong Shin Company has experienced difficulty in attracting workers, partly because of its rural location, and partly because the manufacturing jobs are only semi-skilled and historically were poorly paid. Most high school graduates in the Mekong Delta prefer to seek better paid jobs in Ho Chi Minh City or Hanoi.

In their efforts to recruit more effectively, apart from the communication and health and safety initiatives mentioned earlier, the company has developed a series of new rewards and incentives. These include above-minimum wages and benefits schemes, comprehensive job rotation systems coupled with OJT and occasional off-JT activities, together with management development programmes designed to enhance managers' team leadership and coaching competencies. These actions, combined with closer associations between the company and local government agencies for promotion and potential employee attraction, have yielded considerable benefits.

Box 11.8   Stop and reflect

Undertake research in the mass media of investment into Asia from the West and from Asia into the West and factory openings. What are the implications of this for employee-resourcing?

6 Summary and conclusions

This chapter has provided an overview of key elements related to employee-resourcing in terms of recruitment and retention. Through theoretical and practical insights derived from four Asian economies, namely, Japan, Taiwan, China and Vietnam, we have endeavoured to develop knowledge and understanding of the key factors determining the outcomes of HR policies and practices. Regarding the factors that influence enterprises to adopt specific HR practices, the findings in the research literature indicate that government policy on economic reform has had a fundamental influence on these changes (see Warner, 2013a).

Under the reform agenda, management at enterprise level adapted their decisions and practices to meet the more competitive external challenges. The subsequent strategic change, including the internal adjustment of HR practices, has maintained a clear purpose which is to improve the efficiency and level of productivity of these businesses.

The study has several implications for both HRM theory and practice when facing the challenges of globalization, greater market competition and enhanced economic reform and transition.

First, the development of 'people management' is a process of policy integration involving a number of factors, including political-economic changes and enterprise management reform. In fact, a combination of the political economy approach and strategic choice approach can be used to analyse the phenomenon of people management reform in the context of economic transition and globalization, and these two approaches can be applied in ways that are inclusive rather than exclusive areas of policy and practice.

Second, the implications for policy-makers are also significant. The government's purposes in economic reform in general and people management reform in particular are two-fold: on the one hand, economic reform might lead to the improvement of economic growth and living standards; on the other hand, if people benefit from the reform then they may more strongly support economic reform policy and, in return, social stability can be maintained and the government sustains its 'legitimacy' to rule society.

Third, the implications for enterprise management are also clear. Under the current process of globalization and market competition, now accompanied by global financial crises and economic uncertainty, individual enterprises have to find ways to survive and prosper. Adequate HR policies and practices are a crucial part of business survival strategies. 'Downsizing' and 'retrenchment' could well be the dominant dimension for HR policy when enterprises experience an economic downturn. However, a balanced approach is necessary – not only with the focus on the short-term outcome – but also vis-à-vis the long-term sustainability of enterprises. Recruitment and retention are important – given that finding, recruiting and selecting the right people with adequate skills may reduce costs and improve efficiency. Moreover, job design and training and development can be crucial for the successful achievement of business outcomes, particularly given the continuing demand for high quality work outcomes and better skills and knowledge.

Discussion questions

1. With the increasing economic uncertainty and problems of the 2008 global financial crisis, enterprises should focus their HR policy solely on downsizing and retrenchment, rather than other activities such as recruitment and retention. Comment on this statement.
2. How do we identify the key factors influencing enterprises' adoption or adjustment of specific HR policies and practices?
3. Recruitment and selection practices in these four Asian economies seem to be different. What are the reasons for these differences?
4. What is the purpose of enterprises adopting more advanced training and development policies and practices?
5. What is the role of the government in labour market development at the macro-level and in reforming HR policy and practices at the enterprise level?

CASE STUDY

ITOCHU – A Japanese firm in the era of retrenchment and reform

The Japanese economy has been experiencing severe problems since the early 1990s, when its long-term national economic recession began to emerge. Enterprises have been under tremendous pressure since then to restructure their organizations and reform their people management systems. As one of the leading Japanese MNCs, ITOCHU may be seen as a leader in this era of Japanese reform and has adopted many new ways of people management into the company's routine HR practices. The areas of recruitment and retention, for instance, have been crucial aspects for developing innovative management practices and ensuring business survival. The following case is used as an example, showing what changes have been made in adopting new methods, systems and techniques of people management and in organizational restructuring.

Company background

The history of ITOCHU Corporation dates back to 1858 when the founder Chubei Itoch commenced linen-trading operations. Since then, ITOCHU has evolved and grown into a 'sogo shosha' (general trading company), engaging in domestic trading, import/export and overseas trading of various products, such as textiles, machinery, information and communications-related products, metals, products related to oil and other energy sources, general merchandise, chemicals, and provisions and food. In addition, ITOCHU has made multi-faceted investments in insurance, finance, construction, real estate trading and ware-housing, as well as operations and businesses incidental or related to those fields (www.itochu.co.jp/). The total number of employees at the Tokyo headquarters was reduced from over 5,000 people in the early 2000s to the current level of 4,222 (excluding local employees working at overseas branches, offices and other subsidiaries), with a more robust organizational structure (see Figure 11.1) and an extensive global network (see Figure 11.2). The combined sales of Mitsubishi, Mitsui, ITOCHU, Sumitomo, Marubeni and Nissho Iwai, Japan's top six 'sogo sosha', have for some years been nearly equivalent to the combined GDP of all of the countries in South America, and our case example is the third largest of these companies.

Under a former mid-term management plan 'Frontier-2006', ITOCHU obtained its objective of becoming a highly profitable corporate group achieving over ¥100 billion in consolidated net income in a steady and sustainable manner. ITOCHU then moved forward with the implementation of its new mid-term management plan, 'Frontier+ 2008', under which the management hope to adopt an even more aggressive management policy striving to enhance corporate value on the world stage, in order to become a global enterprise that is 'highly attractive to all stakeholders'.

As the President and CEO, Eizo Kobayashi pointed out:

> In the fiscal year ended March 2008, the Company posted consolidated net income of ¥218.6 billion – achieving record earnings for the fourth consecutive year. Without a doubt natural resource price hikes contributed to that favourable performance, but in addition, our growth strategies are steadily bearing fruit … Our medium-term management plan, Frontier+ 2008 – Enhancing Corporate Value on the World Stage, will be ending in the fiscal year ending March 2009. We will be stepping up the pace of aggressive corporate management – based on measures for maintaining a global perspective, creating new initiatives, and enhancing human resources – to dramatically increase earnings.

(Continued)

(Continued)

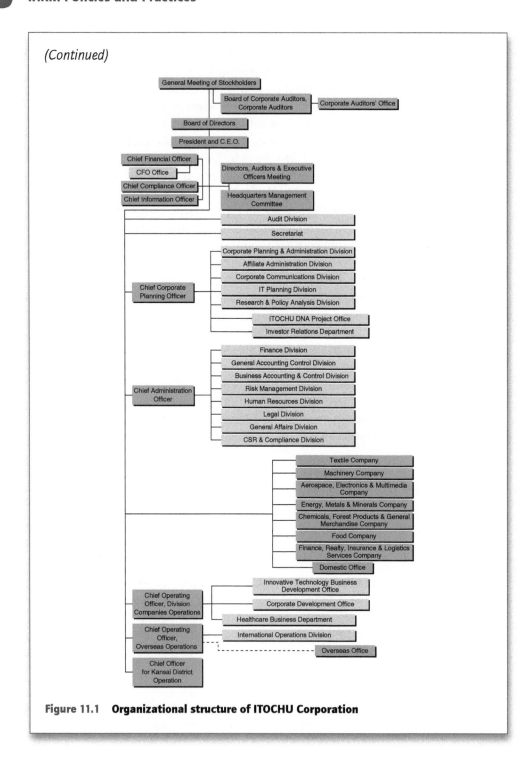

Figure 11.1   Organizational structure of ITOCHU Corporation

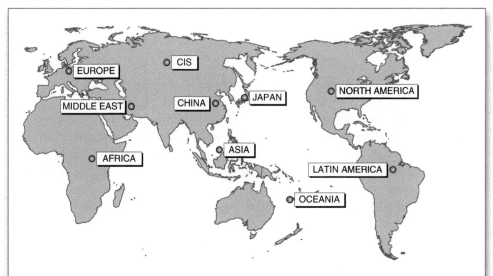

Figure 11.2   ITOCHU: global network

Recruitment

Change in the HRM area of employee-resourcing and in particular recruitment is widespread. Generally speaking, two types of recruitment belong to the traditional system, namely: (a) high school and vocational school graduate recruitment, and (b) college and university graduate recruitment. In recent years, new types of recruitment have emerged as part of HR policies to deal with unemployment, the ageing population and organizations' needs for special skills and experiences under circumstances of global competition and economic recession. These new types of recruitment are: (c) mid-career professional recruitment, (d) late-career (semi-retiree) recruitment, and (e) foreign professional recruitment for special positions.

In recent years, government policy set out to promote greater mobility of employees. Two important schemes have been introduced, namely the 'shukko' scheme (external mobility) and the 'haken' scheme (internal mobility). This step has had its impacts on companies such as ITOCHU. Use of the schemes has gradually reduced the number of employees at the headquarters level. A number of people have been relocated into subsidiaries and more capable and experienced people have been recruited externally through the mid-career professional recruitment system.

(Continued)

(Continued)

HR retention

In recent years, HR retention policies have been re-designed through job allocation/design and training and development. In ITOCHU, each department was in charge of job allocation and line managers made decisions on tasks and employees' responsibility. The more recent focus has been on specialization rather than job rotation and multi-tasking. Each department had HR personnel who had facilitating roles to support the line managers with implementing issues related to HRM. The HR department at the top level of the company was only in charge of HR planning and other general issues, and not responsible for detailed job allocation.

In addition, in order to attract capable young people to join the organization and promote long-term commitment, ITOCHU changed its job ranking system from nine grades into six grades. The company also made it possible for young talented people to be placed on a fast track for early promotion. The new systems of job design and promotion were based on performance assessment rather than seniority. Furthermore, training and development become the key area of HRM policy and practice for developing people's skills and in return motivating higher commitment to the organization. The most common practices include orientation training, formal and informal OJT and Off-JT. In ITOCHU, orientation training and formal OJT were compulsory with the former lasting three weeks and the latter lasting a year. Informal OJT was encouraged through team-based discussion and peer assistance. Specialist and managerial training programmes normally took Off-JT forms that enabled the core technicians and managerial staff to enrol in professional training centres or institutions. Overseas training was also common and the company sent 30–40 young people to the US for three to four months' training every year.

Discussion

The change in the macro-economic environment, in particular the global financial crisis of 2008, has been an important influence on the kind of HRM changes adopted in Japanese companies. As a leading MNC in Japan, ITOCHU has adopted some new practices alongside preserving conventional good practices. The case shows that substantial changes can occur in the areas of recruitment, job allocation, labour mobility as well as training and development. We see an increasing combination of East and West concepts of people management being adopted in such leading MNCs. In fact, the management philosophy has been adjusted to consider the 'traditional' dimensions of the well-being of stakeholders and company, as well as the new dimensions of market competition and foreign influence. This finding once again is consistent with our previous research on hybrid HRM systems – with a sense of balance between improving short-term efficiency, flexibility and competitiveness under the influence of globalization and market-driven economy on the one hand, and maintaining a long-term humanist management philosophy with an Asian emphasis on harmony, care and equality, and a community orientation, on the other. This pattern seems to be a logical outcome of the ongoing management transition in general in East Asia.

Sources: Company websites, reports and interviews.

Case study questions

1. What are the key changes in the area of employee-resourcing at ITOCHU during the recent economic restructuring?
2. How would you evaluate the effectiveness of the new HR retention policy at ITOCHU?
3. What are the driving forces for ITOCHU to adopt these changes?

Case study questions for further reflection

1. Imagine you are the HR manager at ITOCHU. What would be your proposed HR strategy to maintain the balance between traditional management philosophy and current market-oriented management practices?
2. Imagine you are the HR manager at ITOCHU. How do you introduce and develop the strategic role in the current HR management system?

Further reading

- Rowley, C. and Benson, J. (2002) 'Convergence and divergence in Asian HRM', *California Management Review*, 44(2): 90–109.
  This article provides an overview on similarity and difference of HR policy and practices among Asian countries.

- Rowley, C. and Warner, M. (2004) 'The Asian financial crisis: the impact on human resource management', *International Studies of Management and Organization*, 34(1): 3–9.
  This article illustrates the impact of the Asian financial crisis on changes in HRM in Asia. It is useful for considering the current HR strategies used to cope with the economic crisis.

- Warner, M. (2000) 'Introduction: The Asia-Pacific HRM model revisited', *International Journal of Human Resource Management*, 11(1): 171–182.

This article highlights many of the key elements related to HRM practices in the Asia-Pacific region.

- Collins, N., Nankervis, A. and Sitalaksmi, S. (2011) 'Labour–management relations in transitional economies: convergence or divergence in Vietnam & Indonesia', *Asia Pacific Business Review*, 17(3): 316–327.
This article compares and contrasts the development of labour–management relationships in two emerging economies.

- Bae, J. and Rowley, C. (2004) 'Changes and continuities in South Korean HRM', in C. Rowley and J. Benson (eds), *The Management of Human Resources in the Asia Pacific Region: Convergence Reconsidered*. London: Frank Cass, pp. 76–105.
This chapter explains the concepts of HR competencies and employs the competency-based approach to analyse the company cases in South Korea.

- Beer, M., Spector, B., Lawrence, R., Quinn, M.D. and Walton, E. (1984) *Managing Human Assets*. New York: Free Press.
This book analyses strategic HR policy and emphasizes the significance of its 'fit' with individual, organizational and societal needs and culture, and its importance for achieving long-term employment stability.

- Benson, J. (2005) 'Unemployment in Japan: globalization, restructuring and social change', in J. Benson and Y. Zhu (eds), *Unemployment in Asia*. London and New York: Routledge, pp. 39–57.
This chapter examines the background and factors influencing economic restructuring, changes to government labour market policies, and the unemployment problem in Japan.

- Boxall, P. and Purcell, L. (2003) *Strategy and Human Resource Management*. Basingstoke: Palgrave.
This book provides a comprehensive review of strategic HRM, its policies and practices.

- Storey, J. and Sisson, K. (1993) *Managing Human Resources and Industrial Relations*. Milton Keynes: Open University Press.
This book illustrates the relations between HRM and IR under the influence of globalization and industrial restructuring.

- Warner, M. (ed.) (2013) *Managing Across Diverse Cultures in East Asia*. London and New York: Routledge.
This edited book updates the current state of management and HRM in East Asia.

- Warner, M. (2014) *Understanding Chinese Management: Past, Present and Future*. London and New York: Routledge.
A recently published overview of Chinese management, including HRM.

Internet resources

- www.apmforum.com/emerald/human-resource-asia.html. Asia Pacific Management Forum is an archive of weekly themed reviews of free research articles on Asian business management.
- www.apj.sage pub.com/cgi/content. An online provider of research results for comparative HRM research in the Asia-Pacific region offering information on change and diversity of HRM in Asia.
- www.hrmguide.net. An online provider of links with issues on HRM in Asia.
- www.themanager.org/Knowledgebase/HR. An online provider of useful information on employee retention.
- human resources.about.com/od/training. An online provider of employees' training and development for organizations.

Self-assessment questions

Indicative answers to these questions can be found on the companion website at study.sagepub.com/harzing4e.

1. Why is it more important to adopt the HR competencies approach in HR policy formation?
2. What are the key external and internal factors influencing HR policy?
3. What are the labour market pressures in Japan forcing companies to adopt a more flexible HR policy?
4. What are the interrelationships between economic development stages and HR recruitment policy in Taiwan?
5. What are the key factors that influence HR policy under the economic reform in China?

References

Bae, J. and Rowley, C. (2004) 'Changes and continuities in South Korean HRM', in C. Rowley and J. Benson (eds), *The Management of Human Resources in the Asia Pacific Region: Convergence Reconsidered*. London: Frank Cass, pp. 76–105.

Bamber, G., Lansbury, R. and Wailes, N. (eds) (2011) *International and Comparative Employment Relations: Globalization and Change*, 5th edn. Sydney: Allen & Unwin.

Beer, M., Spector, B., Lawrence, R., Quinn, M.D. and Walton, E. (1984) *Managing Human Assets*. New York: Free Press.

Benson, J. (2005) 'Unemployment in Japan: globalization, restructuring and social change', in J. Benson and Y. Zhu (eds), *Unemployment in Asia*. London and New York: Routledge, pp. 39–75.

Benson, J. and Debroux, P. (2004) 'Flexible labour-markets and individualized employment: the beginnings of a new Japanese HRM system?', in C. Rowley and J. Benson (eds), *The Management of Human Resources in the Asia Pacific Region: Convergence Reconsidered*. London: Frank Cass, pp. 55–75.

Boxall, P. and Purcell, L. (2003) *Strategy and Human Resource Management*. Basingstoke: Palgrave.

Chatterjee, S.R. and Nankervis, A. (2007) *Asian Management in Transition: Emerging Themes*. London: Palgrave Macmillan.

Collins, N. (2009) *Economic Reform and Employment Relations in Vietnam*. London: Routledge.

Collins, N., Nankervis, A., Sitalaksmi, S. and Warner, M. (2011) 'Labour-management relations in transitional economies: convergence or divergence in Vietnam and Indonesia?', *Asia Pacific Business Review*, 17(3): 316–327.

Collins, N., Sitalaksmi, S. and Lansbury, R. (2013) 'Transforming employment relations in Vietnam and Indonesia', *Asia Pacific Journal of Human Resources* (Special Issue: HRM in Vietnam), 51(2): 131–150.

Cooke, F.L. (2005) *HRM, Work and Employment in China*. London and New York: Routledge.

Cooke, F.L. (2009) 'A decade of transformation of HRM in China: a review of literature and suggestions for future studies', *Asia Pacific Journal of Human Resources*, 47(1): 6–40.

Cooke, F.L. (2012) *HRM in China: New Trends and Practices*. London: Routledge.

Cox, A., Hannif, Z. and Rowley, C. (2014) 'Leadership styles and generational effects: the case of US companies in Vietnam', *International Journal of Human Resource Management*, 25(1): 1–22.

Cox, A. and Warner, M. (2013) 'Whither "training and development" in Vietnam?: learning from United States and Japanese MNCs' practice', *Asia Pacific Journal of Human Resources* (Special Issue: HRM in Vietnam), 51(2): 175–192.

Dowling, P.J. and Welch, D.E. (eds) (2004) *International Human Resource Management: Managing People in a Multinational Context*, 4th edn. London: Thomson.

Guest, D.E. (1987) 'Human resource management and industrial relations', *Journal of Management Studies*, 24(5): 503–521.

Hsu, Y. and Leat, M. (2000) 'A study of HRM and recruitment and selection policies and practices in Taiwan', *International Journal of Human Resource Management*, 11(2): 413–435.

Kochan, T.A., Katz, H.C. and McKersie, R.B. (1986) *The Transformation of American Industrial Relations*. New York: Basic Books.

Lien, B., Hung, R. and McLean, G. (2007) 'Organizational learning as an organization development intervention in six high-technology firms in Taiwan: an exploratory case study', *Human Resource Development Quarterly*, 18 (1): 211–228.

Martin, R. and Bamber, J. (2005) 'International differences in employment relations: what are the relative merits of explanation in terms of strategic choice or political economy?', in *Reworking Work: AIRAANZ 05*, Vol. I. (refereed papers), Proceedings of the 19th Conference of the Association of Industrial Relations Academics of Australia and New Zealand, ed. Marian Baird, Rae Cooper and Mark Westcott, http://airaanz.econ.usyd.edu.au/papers/Refereed%20papers.pdf (accessed 26 May 2014).

Murray, G., Levesque, C. and Vallee, G. (2000) 'The re-regulation of labour in a global context: conceptual vignettes from Canada', *Journal of Industrial Relations*, 42(2): 234–257.

Nankervis, A., Cooke, F.L., Chatterjee, S.R. and Warner, M. (2012) *New Models of HRM in China and India*. London and New York: Routledge.

Quang, T., Thang, L.C. and Rowley, C. (2008) 'The changing face of human resource management in Vietnam', in C. Rowley and S. Abdul-Rahman (eds), *The Changing Face of Management in South East Asia*. London: Routledge, pp. 186–220.

Rowley, C. and Abdul-Rahman, S. (eds) (2008) *The Changing Face of Management in South East Asia*. London: Routledge.

Rowley, C., Bae, J. and Chen, S.J. (2011) 'A paternalistic model towards what? HRM trends in Korea and Taiwan', *Personnel Review*, 40(6): 700–722.

Rowley, C. and Benson, J. (eds) (2004) *The Management of Human Resources in the Asia Pacific Region: Convergence Reconsidered*. London: Routledge.

Rowley, C. and Cooke, F. (eds) (2009) *The Changing Face of Management in China*. London: Routledge.

Rowley, C. and Harry, W. (2011) *Managing People Globally: An Asian Perspective*. Oxford: Chandos.

Rowley, C. and Li, X. (2006) 'Chinese SMEs: development and HRM', in E. Mrudula and P. Raju (eds), *China: Trading Empire of the New Century*. India: ACFAI Press, pp. 108–119.

Rowley, C. and Li, X. (2008) 'The development of Chinese SMEs and HRM', *Asia Pacific Journal of Human Resources*, 46(3): 353–379.

Rowley, C. and Quang, T. (eds) (2009) *The Changing Face of Management in Vietnam*. London: Routledge.

Rowley, C. and Ulrich, D. (2012a) 'Setting the scene for leadership in Asia', *Asia Pacific Business Review*, 18(4): 451–464.

Rowley, C. and Ulrich, D. (2012b) 'Lessons learned and insights derived from leadership in Asia', *Asia Pacific Business Review*, 18(4): 675–681.

Rowley, C. and Ulrich, D. (2013) (eds) *Leadership in Asia*. London: Routledge.

Rowley, C. and Warner, M. (2014) (eds) *Demystifying Chinese Management*. London and New York: Routledge.

Storey, J. and Sisson, K. (1993) *Managing Human Resources and Industrial Relations*. Milton Keynes: Open University Press.

Tata (2011) 'Right-shoring innovation', *Tata Review*, May: 64–65.

Thang, L.C. and Quang, T. (2005) 'Antecedents and consequences of dimensions of human resource management and practices in Vietnam', *International Journal of Human Resource Management*, 16(10): 1830–1846.

Truong, Q., Van der Heijden, B. and Rowley, C. (2010) 'Globalization, competitiveness and HRM in a transitional economy: the case of Vietnam', *International Journal of Business Studies*, 18(1): 75–100.

Ulrich, D., Brockbank, W., Younger, J. and Ulrich M. (eds) (2013) *Global HR Competencies: Mastering Competitive Value from the Outside In*. New York: McGraw-Hill.

Van Ruysseveldt, J. (1995) 'Growing cross-national diversity or diversity tout court? an introduction to comparative industrial and employment relations', in J. Van Ruysseveldt, R. Huiskamp and J. Van Hoof (eds), *Comparative Industrial and Employment Relations*. London: Sage, pp.1–15.

Warner, M. (2000) 'Introduction: the Asia-Pacific HRM model revisited', *International Journal of Human Resource Management*, 11(1): 171–182.

Warner, M. (ed.) (2005) *Human Resource Management in China Revisited*. London: Routledge.

Warner, M. (ed.) (2009) *Human Resource Management 'with Chinese Characteristics'*. London and New York: Routledge.

Warner, M. (2010) *'Making Sense' of HRM in China: Economy, Enterprises and Workers*. London and New York: Routledge.

Warner, M. (ed.) (2011) *In Search of Confucian HRM in Greater China: Theory and Practice*. London and New York: Routledge.

Warner, M. (2012) 'Whither Chinese HRM? Paradigms, models and theories', *International Journal of Human Resource Management*, 23: 3943–3963.

Warner, M. (ed.) (2013a) *Managing Across Diverse Cultures in East Asia*. London and New York: Routledge.

Warner, M. (2013b) 'Comparing human resource management in China and Vietnam: an overview', *Human Systems Management*, 32(4): 217–229.

Warner, M. (2014) *Understanding Chinese Management: Past, Present and Future*. London and New York: Routledge.

Wei, Q. and Rowley, C. (2009) 'Changing patterns of rewards in Asia: a literature review', *Asia Pacific Business Review*, 15(4): 489–506.

Yeung, A. and Tao, W. (2013) 'China', in D. Ulrich, W. Brockbank, J. Younger and M. Ulrich (eds), *Global HR Competencies: Mastering Competitive Value from the Outside In*. New York: McGraw-Hill, pp. 91–92.

Zhu, Y. and Verstraeten, M. (2013) 'HRM practices with Vietnamese characteristics: a study of managers' responses', *Asia Pacific Journal of Human Resources* (Special Issue: HRM in Vietnam), 51(2): 152–174.

Zhu, Y. and Warner, M. (2004) 'HRM in East Asia', in A.W. Harzing and J.V. Ruysseveldt (eds) *International Human Resource Management*, 2nd edn. London: Sage, pp. 195–220.

Zhu, Y. and Warner, M. (2013a) 'Workforce development in China', in J. Benson, H. Gospel Y. and Zhu (eds), *Workforce Development and Skill Formation in Asia*. London and New York: Routledge, pp. 142–158.

Zhu, Y. and Warner, M. (2013b) 'Workforce development in Taiwan', in J. Benson, H. Gospel and Y. Zhu (eds), *Workforce Development and Skill Formation in Asia*. London and New York: Routledge, pp. 158–177.

Global Performance Management

12

Arup Varma and Pawan S. Budhwar

Contents

Learning objectives

After reading this chapter you will be able to:

- Identify the key components of an effective performance management system (PMS)
- Explain why PMSs developed for domestic employees are not automatically usable at international locations
- Explain the role that a nation's culture plays in the effective execution of PMSs
- Compare and contrast PMSs in some leading world economies
- Design a comprehensive and effective PMS for an MNC

Chapter outline

This chapter discusses the key issues related to performance management systems, with a special emphasis on performance evaluation. It also discusses the factors affecting PMSs, especially in global organizations, and presents the key features of PMSs in six leading economies.

1 Introduction

This chapter discusses performance management systems in a global context, by identifying the key components of such systems. We consider the key factors that can impact on organizational objectives of ensuring that managerial decisions are both consistent with corporate strategy and meet local contexts and needs. Next, we discuss the role that a nation's culture can play in the effective execution of PMSs, followed by a description of PMSs in a few leading economies (e.g. China, India, Japan, South Korea, the UK and USA). Then, we examine the unique nature and requirements of expatriate evaluation. Throughout the chapter, we present relevant research on PMSs, with special emphasis on multinational companies. Finally, we end the chapter with an explanation of the reasons why organizations need to develop unique systems for each country and its cultural context (MNCs), rather than simply implementing systems in the host country that were initially developed for the home country.

2 Key components of PMSs

From a broad theoretical perspective, PMSs are designed to help organizations gain the best out of their employees, by enabling individual employees to perform at optimal levels. However, as we will see, the execution of such systems is not easy, and thus performance management practices frequently do not achieve their goals, with the result that both employees and their supervisors are often dissatisfied with the system. Indeed, as Deming (1982) argued, performance appraisals often have the opposite of their intended effect. In other words, if the system is not used properly, evaluations can lead to frustration, anger and lowered levels of motivation, rather than encouraging employees to perform better! The process of performance appraisal:

> nourishes short-term performance, annihilates long-term planning, builds fear, demolishes teamwork, nourishes rivalry and politics … It leaves people bitter, crushed, bruised, battered, desolate, despondent, dejected, feeling inferior, some even depressed, unfit for work for weeks after receipt of rating, unable to comprehend why they are inferior. It is unfair as it ascribes to the people in a group differences that may be caused totally by the system they work in. (Deming, 1982: 102)

It should be clarified that while performance appraisals form a major part of PMSs, and the terms are often used interchangeably, effective performance management comprises several other activities, including (a) setting goals/objectives, (b) providing feedback, and (c) motivating employees. We explain these activities in this chapter.

In terms of practice, performance evaluations traditionally have two main functions: they are used first, for administrative decisions such as promotions, merit raises, etc., and second, for developmental purposes such as coaching and feedback (Murphy and Cleveland, 1995). Thus, organizations typically require an individual's direct supervisor to evaluate the subordinate's performance once a year, and determine his/her ratings. These ratings form the basis for individual pay awards based on merit and may also be used to allocate bonuses. While most organizations have some form of PMS in place, managers and employees often treat the process more as an administrative burden, than a developmental tool. Indeed, the developmental role of such systems can provide managers with an effective mechanism to monitor and improve employee performance levels, through continuous feedback and discussion. However, most managers are reluctant to give performance based feedback to employees, as these discussions can often become uncomfortable and lead to participants being defensive.

In order for PMSs to be effective, several key issues need to be addressed, and organizations have to ensure that critical components of such systems are in place.

Goal-setting

First, it is critical that the supervisor sets individual employees' goals for the coming year, through discussions with subordinates, keeping in mind the organization's business strategy, and ensuring alignment of these goals with the department or business unit's objectives. Goals help employees to understand what is expected of them, and assists them in planning and prioritizing their work accordingly. It is well documented that individuals who have goals work better and are more productive than those who are not given goals, and must rely on their understanding of the job, and their title, to work on a day-to-day basis (Locke, 1968). Further, in order for goal-setting to be effective and for the individual to be able to use the goals in accomplishing his/her work, these goals should be:

- specific
- measurable
- attainable
- relevant and realistic
- timely.

Feedback

In order for an individual to know how he/she is doing on the job, it is critical that supervisors provide regular feedback to employees (see Murphy and Cleveland, 1995). However, the feedback process is complicated and is often avoided by both managers and employees, especially in cases where the manager is required to give constructive or negative feedback. Timely feedback can help employees correct performance deficiencies and prevent errors from increasing. Thus, it is clear that, in spite of some evidence of reluctance, it is very important that managers provide feedback on a consistent basis and deliver it in a spirit of constructive counselling. As such, organizations need to create a culture where feedback is readily accepted by all people concerned, and is seen as a critical part of the performance management process. In cases where managers deliver inadequate feedback, HRM departments may need to institute policies that mandate feedback-giving for managers, perhaps by requiring documentation of their feedback meetings.

Performance evaluation process guidelines

In order for annual evaluations to proceed smoothly and serve their critical purpose, it is essential that organizations establish comprehensive processes, that are clearly spelled out in organizational handbooks or operating manuals. Further, all employees should be made familiar with the form and content of the performance evaluation system in place in their organization, so that they know what to expect, when to expect it and how to go about achieving a fair and timely evaluation of employees' performance. The evaluations guidelines should clearly spell out the key features of the process, including:

- How the evaluation will be conducted (i.e. employee input, types of forms to be used, etc.).
- Who will conduct the evaluation (i.e. immediate supervisor, divisional head, corporate office, etc.).

- When the evaluation will be conducted (i.e. annually, bi-annually, etc.).
- What is to be evaluated (traits, behaviours, outcomes).
- The potential rewards/penalties for the ratings received by the individual (i.e. merit raises, bonuses, promotions, terminations, etc.).

Table 12.1   PMS tips for organizations

1. Decide, design and publicize the evaluation process
2. Clearly set the timing
3. Inform employees of the judgement criteria
4. Clarify individual roles in the PMS
5. Ensure clear and obvious links between performance and ratings, and ratings and outcomes

Each of these five steps is critical to the proper and fair execution of the appraisal process, and thus worthy of further discussion.

How will the evaluation be conducted?

The process for conducting the evaluation should be explained clearly, with information on managers' and employees' responsibilities, dates and venues, and specific steps. The essence of this recommendation is that the performance appraisal (and feedback) process should not be a surprise. The employee should be well aware of their role – so, for example, if they are expected to complete a self-evaluation, they can start well in advance of the scheduled meeting date, and not have to rush through the process. In addition, being aware of the process and the schedule can allow the employee to be prepared for explaining any deviation in performance, and support their arguments with facts and figures.

Who will conduct the evaluation?

This is an integral part of the process, and needs to be clearly articulated. From the perspective of fairness, it is important that the employees know who is ultimately responsible for evaluating their performance, as this would help the employees to organize their efforts, as well as seek guidance and coaching from the supervisor. Too often, we hear complaints from individuals about having 'ten different bosses', all claiming that their tasks should be treated as a priority. In the case of expatriates, this issue has added significance, as very often expatriates may report to someone at the location of their day-to-day operational activities and concurrently report to someone at headquarters, on their strategic objectives. While organizational or departmental objectives sometimes make it necessary for an individual to work and report to several managers, such demanding situations can create confusion for individuals, thus result-ing in lowered performance and motivation, unless the reporting relationship(s) are clearly laid out.

When will the evaluation be conducted?

While most traditional PMSs rely on the annual evaluation, there are numerous different models practised by organizations, including: (a) quarterly evaluations, (b) bi-annual evaluations, (c) evaluations at the end of a project, (d) evaluations conducted when the manager has time, or (e) no formal evaluations. Indeed, even the annual evaluation has different versions in practice, with some organizations evaluating all employees on or around a particular date, every year, while others conduct staggered evaluations, with individual employees evaluated yearly on the anniversary of their date of joining the organization. Whichever method is followed, it is important that the employees be well aware of the timing. This will help them to prepare for the evaluation and collect rel-evant performance information for discussions. Too often, managers rely on conducting the evaluation when they find some time available. This ad hoc scheduling does not allow the employee to be mentally prepared for the evaluation; it often comes as a surprise, and does not support the seriousness and significance of the process.

Box 12.1   Stop and reflect

Scheduling the evaluation meeting

In one organization that I consulted with, almost every manager complained that they did not have time for performance appraisal 'stuff'. When I asked them how they actually went about scheduling the meetings, the most common response was 'I do it whenever I have time', while some even admitted asking their subordinates to come in on weekends to take care of 'this HR stuff!' Sadly, this situation is not unique to this organization. The performance appraisal literature is replete with studies confirming that most supervisors find the whole performance appraisal and PMS process to be a burden. Not surprisingly, this apathy is not lost on the subor-dinates. When I spoke to subordinates in the organization, the common refrain was 'this organization does not take the process seriously'.

The problem here is that the perceptions of employees play a critical role in the success of any HR system. If employees believe that the organization does not really care about the system, they are likely to believe that the organization does not care about them. Thus, it is critical that supervisors take the whole process seriously, especially since the outcomes of the performance evaluation meeting directly affect the subordinates.

In addition to training supervisors in the performance appraisal process, another way to get supervisors to take the process seriously is to make it a part of their own goals and evaluations.

Source: Varma et al., 2008.

What will be evaluated?

The performance appraisal literature has continued to debate the merits of evaluating traits, behaviours and outcomes for several decades, without arriving at a definite conclusion (see DeNisi, 1996). Those in favour of evaluating traits argue that if an individual has the right traits, performance will automatically follow. As an example, if we believe an employee has high levels of sincerity and conscientiousness, he or she is likely to perform well. Those that are in favour of evaluating behaviours argue that possessing certain desirable traits does not automatically guarantee acceptable or optimal levels of performance. Thus, an individual may be very sincere and loyal, but may consistently produce sub-standard work, though it might be completed well before the deadline. In addition, some have argued that evaluating personality traits like sincerity is akin to passing judgement on an individual, and that it is preferable to restrict judgements to an employee's work. The third option is often popular with managers who are primarily, if not solely, driven to achieve revenue targets – thus the exclusive emphasis on outcomes and results. The danger of the third option is that employees may be driven to cheat, as they are aware that they will only be evaluated on their results, and not how they achieved them. Further, this option does not allow managers to use the high performers' behaviours to develop new employees, as the primary information available is all about outcomes. In addition, there are numerous jobs where results are not immediately available, and thus behaviours, and sometimes traits, are what can be evaluated. For example, for over 20 years now, thousands of researchers around the world have been working on finding a cure for AIDS. While a cure hasn't been found yet, this does not necessarily imply that the individuals have not performed at acceptable levels, or even exceeded expectations. So, the question is, what should be evaluated – just traits, just behaviours, or just outcomes, or all three? This decision will depend on the organization's culture, its objectives and management philosophy. In addition, the national culture will also have an impact, since many countries emphasize traits over behaviours and/or results. What is important is that companies decide what will be evaluated, and share this information with their employees.

Potential consequences of evaluation

One of the reasons why employees often dislike PMSs, and more specifically their evaluations, is that they do not see any connection between their performance and the rewards obtained. In order for employees to take the process of evaluation and feedback seriously, it is critical that they can see a logical and causal relationship between the PMS and the outcomes. So, if an employee is evaluated as having exceeded performance expectations, they should receive rewards that are commensurate with that level of performance. As reinforcement theory (Skinner, 1953) suggests, desired levels of performance will be repeated if the outcomes are seen as positive, while neutral or negative outcomes increase the likelihood that the behaviour is not repeated.

Another way that this phenomenon often operates is when the ratings themselves do not reflect the actual performance level(s). This is most often seen in organizations that have implemented a forced distribution of ratings, whereby no more than a certain percentage (e.g. 10 per cent) of a manager's direct reports (or a department's workforce) can be rated as having exceeded expectations, and roughly the same percentage (i.e. 10 per cent) must be rated as having performed below expectations. In theory, this seems like a great system, as it will motivate everyone to work harder, since (a) they know that positions in the top category are limited, and (b) they presumably will want to avoid being assessed as falling within the low category. In addition, this system enables the organization to identify its top performers and concentrate efforts on retaining them, and might replace the bottom 10 per cent with better performers or new recruits.

In practice, this does not work out so well. Imagine that a manager objectively evaluates their staff, and finds that 30 per cent have performed in an outstanding fashion and thus have exceeded expectation. In the spirit of behavioural reinforcement theory, they must rate them accordingly, and recommend commensurate merit-based rewards. However, the forced distribution permits them to rate as outstanding only one third of this high performing group – the others will be told to continue to work hard and hope they get into the top 10 per cent the following year. Not only does this lead to a system-led distortion of ratings, the individuals who are not rated according to their performance have an incentive to work less hard the next year, as they will lose confidence in the validity of the PMS.

Training

For efficient and effective conduct of the performance management process, it is critical that organizations train all managers who are responsible for supervising individuals. The training should familiarize managers with (a) the performance management process implemented in the organization, (b) the objectives and philosophy behind the process, and (c) the tools used in the process (i.e. rating forms and scales, etc.). In addition, training can help managers learn how to avoid potential biases and errors, such as halo and recency effects. Where relevant, organizations should also provide training for employees, so that they can have a more participative role in the performance management process, rather than be treated as passive recipients. Thus, for example, if the organization provides employees the opportunity for self-evaluation, they should be trained in how to complete the form objectively, using relevant performance data. In addition, performance management training can be very helpful in preparing both managers and employees for a meaningful and productive exchange during feedback meetings.

3 Factors affecting PMSs

While the above guidelines apply to all organizations, it should be noted that performance management does not occur in a vacuum, and that there are numerous factors that can affect the success or failure, no matter how well-intentioned or well-designed the PMS. In their recently published comprehensive model of the appraisal process, Murphy and DeNisi (2008) have identified several key factors that can directly or indirectly affect the performance management process in any organization. The authors group these factors under five categories:

1. Distal factors (e.g. national or cultural norms, technology)
2. Proximal factors (e.g. purpose of appraisal and organizational norms)
3. Judgement factors (e.g. time pressures and availability of standards)
4. Intervening factors (supervisor–subordinate relationships and rater motivation), and
5. Distortion factors (e.g. consequences of appraisal and reward systems).

We draw upon the authors' model to emphasize five critical issues (one from each of the authors' five factor-groups) that, in our opinion, need to be addressed by HR managers, in order to design and execute successful PMS, *especially* in global organizations.

Table 12.2   Key factors affecting PMSs

1. Technology
2. Purpose
3. Performance standards
4. Supervisor–subordinate relationships
5. Reward systems

Technology

The technological advances made over the last three decades have had a clear impact on human resource systems in organizations. In many cases, technology has made the work of HRM departments easier and faster. So, for example, HR professionals no longer need to search through numerous employee files to identify how many employees have college degrees or a specific skill that the organization needs. Human Resource Information Systems (HRIS) are commercially available that enable the HR professional to access in a few seconds such information from the company's databases. Needless to say, technology has also made inroads into PMSs, with several software applications available to track, monitor, record and rate employees' performance, often on an ongoing basis. In addition, global organizations can now receive almost instant information on individual performance, through computer-monitoring, and provide necessary feedback in a timely manner, thus avoiding the traditional problems of time delay in communication between locations. However, caution needs to be exercised in the use of technology for performance management systems and processes. First, no amount of sophistication in technology can replace the value of face-to-face interaction between an employee and his or her manager. Next, managers should be careful not to become overly reliant on computer-generated data for making judgements, and must ensure the individual is given opportunity to explain any variance in performance. Finally, the quality and reach of technology varies substantially between nations and across regions, so managers should ensure that employees throughout the organization are able to access and use computer-based systems with sufficient ease.

Purpose of appraisal

The purpose of the appraisal can have significant impact on the conduct and acceptance of the appraisal system and results. Thus, if the appraisal is designed for administrative purposes, such as performance evaluation and pay increases, the individual's immediate supervisor is most likely going to be responsible for evaluating the employee and determining merit awards. Further, the purpose of the appraisal is also likely to impact on the manager's use of data, and may influence their motivation to be objective in conducting the evaluation. Thus, if the manager is interested in getting one of his/her subordinates promoted or awarded a substantial merit increase, it is possible that they could distort the data and its interpretation in order to justify their recommendations. In addition, managers are likely to rely heavily on performance data available and collected by themselves. On the other hand, if the purpose of the appraisal is to provide developmental feedback to subordinates, managers are more likely to try and supplement their evaluation with information from the employee's peers, and subordinates, clients and customers, where relevant. In 360 degree appraisal, the manager has the benefit of multiple sources and raters and thus access to more data, which increases capacity for making more objective assessment and judgements, in preparing evaluation feedback for the employee. Finally, in countries where the appraisal might be seen as a mere formality, and where the manager might be motivated more by the need to 'take care' of their team members (Varma et al., 2005b) than provide objective evaluations, the whole process may lose its original purpose.

Box 12.2 Stop and reflect

Evaluations and national culture

Multinational corporations often struggle with creating performance management and evaluation systems that are consistent across all locations, yet address local context and culture. Given the continuing globalization, it is not surprising that MNCs are now emerging from nations on almost every continent, making it even more critical that organizations address contextual and cultural issues. Often, it is difficult to implement home country systems in other locations, due to differences in cultural practices and nuances. For example, in their study, Varma et al. (2005a) reported that 'the ratings of low performers were consistently inflated by raters with positive interpersonal affect towards them, in the Indian sample, but not in the US sample'. Clearly, this is an issue that needs to be addressed by (a) US-based organizations operating in India, (b) India-based organizations operating in the US, and (c) third-country-based organizations operating in India and the US. Since paternalism is deeply rooted in the Indian culture, it is not surprising that supervisors might sometimes inflate the ratings of their poorly performing subordinates. In addition to being unfair, this affects the very subordinates who are rated higher than their performance deserved, because they are less likely to be concerned with improving their performance, since they may start to believe that the ratings they received were deserved.

Each nation has its own cultural peculiarities, and organizations need to try and minimize the impact of these on the performance appraisal process, while still being respectful of the culture.

Source: Varma et al., 2005a.

Performance standards

In addition to setting objectives, it is essential that performance standards be established and shared with the employee at the beginning of the performance period.

Once performance standards are established (i.e. acceptable versus unacceptable performance etc.) and shared with the employee, subsequent evaluations of the candidate can then be measured against these standards (see also, Bobko and Colella, 1994). Thus, an employee will know from the outset how work performance will be judged at the conclusion of the period under review. So, for example, let us say it is established that a rating of 5 on the dimension 'quality of customer service' (on a 5-point scale, with 5 being the highest possible level of performance and 1 being the lowest level) can only be obtained by individuals who have zero customer complaints during the evaluation period. An individual who has even a single case of a customer complaint should know that the best rating they can achieve on this dimension is a 4. Providing clear standards reduces unpleasant surprises and makes it easier for employees to keep track of how they are performing, by periodically measuring their achievements against the established standards. In addition, this practice can motivate employees to be more proactive and seek out feedback, so they know more about the dimensions on which they should improve their performance.

Box 12.3   Stop and reflect

The importance of communicating performance standards

In another organization I worked with, managers had the habit of telling their subordinates to simply 'do their best'. When I asked them why they used this approach, instead of providing the employees specific expectations and standards, most of them responded that this approach would motivate the employees and not put any undue pressure on them. When I inquired how the performance appraisal conversations went, almost all managers reported that 'every employee seems to believe that he/she is outstanding!'

It is not difficult to see the cause and effect relationship between these two situations. If an employee is simply asked to do their best, then no matter what they produce, it has to be accepted as their best, which should logically earn them a rating of 5 (on a 1 to 5-point scale, with 5 being best). After all, they did their best! Instead, organizations need to provide clear expectations and standards, so employees know beforehand how they will be judged, and can work towards achieving the rating(s) they desire. Further, providing clear standards also helps employees keep track of their performance throughout the period, and if they discover that they are not meeting the standards, they can seek out relevant feedback and necessary coaching.

> To use a sports analogy, before a basket-ball game begins, the 2-point and 3-point lines are clearly demarcated, and all other rules are clearly spelled out. If players were simply told to 'do their best', most of them would be very confused, though the spectators might have a lot of fun!
>
> *Source*: Varma et al., 2008.

Supervisor–subordinate relationships

The leader–member exchange theory (Graen and Cashman, 1975) posits that most individuals in managerial roles do not treat all of their subordinates in the same way. Instead, consciously or sub-consciously, managers create in-groups and out-groups among those who report to them. A manager's relationships with individuals in their in-group are characterized by higher quality interactions and more attention and support, as compared to relationships with subordinates in the out-group. Further, research consistently has shown that individuals in a manager's in-group receive significantly higher performance ratings than those in the out-groups, even when they have performed at the same level (Varma and Stroh, 2001). It is worth noting too that while the initial research on leader–member exchange was conducted in the United States, empirical trials of this theory in other countries such as China, India and Japan have also reported the same pattern of results (Wakabayashi et al., 1988; Varma et al., 2005b). Thus, it is critical that managers receive training in PMS that includes information on (a) the potential for them to create in-groups and out-groups, (b) advice on how to avoid creating preferential groups, and (c) specific means of ensuring that evaluations are based on objective performance data and are not biased by their relationships with their subordinates.

Reward systems

In relation to reward systems, Murphy and DeNisi (2008) have argued that organizations often punish managers for producing accurate ratings and reward them for distorting them. Specifically, in organizations that practise forced distribution of ratings, managers are required to assign a fixed percentage of their team members into set categories. So, for example, a manager might be required to place a minimum of 10 per cent of their direct reports as having performed at 'unacceptable' levels, and no more than 10 per cent at levels 'exceeding expectations', with the remaining 80 per cent being rated as having performed at 'acceptable' levels. Clearly, it is very rare that

the performance of individuals on any manager's team will follow the exact propor-
tions mandated by a pre-established system of forced distribution. For example, one
manager may have a situation where half their team has achieved outstandingly,
exceeding performance expectations. However, if they were to rate all of them at the
highest level, the HR department will most likely return the set of ratings to the manager, and request them to 'fit' the individuals into the required pattern of distribution.
Clearly, in such situations the manager is required to distort the assessment by presenting inaccurate ratings. If the managers refuse to adjust the ratings to fit the distribution,
they might even be reprimanded for not following the organization's policies. Clearly,
such reward/punishments systems will lead many managers to distort their ratings – in
other words, providing ratings that 'do not reflect the judgement made about the subordinate's performance'.

We propose that there are ways that reward systems can be motivating in ways that
persuade managers to take the performance management process seriously (thus, an
intervening factor, in Murphy and DeNisi's typology). It is well known that most managers consider the performance management process a 'necessary evil', and many
believe that the system is kept alive by HRM departments to justify their existence. In
general, managers will look to the organization's senior management team to get a
sense of how they view performance management, and the importance they attach to
the process and its outcomes. While organizational handbooks and policy manuals
may detail how the PMS works, and the manager's role in executing it, managers are
unlikely to take it seriously unless there are associated rewards and/or punishments.
Thus, if an organization wants its managers to treat the process as an integral part of
their roles, it should allocate a certain percentage of the manager's own evaluation to
considering how well they conduct the PMS with their team members. Here, organizations could track (a) whether goals and objectives were provided to each subordinate
at the beginning of the year, (b) how often managers meet with their team members
to provide feedback, (c) whether appraisals are given on time, and (d) the extent that
the administrative decisions recommended by the manager reflect the subordinate's
actual performance. Ironically, in many organizations, the manager's evaluation is
based primarily on their achievement of revenue or budget targets and capacity to
generate profits and make savings. Unless managers are formally evaluated for how
they conduct the performance management of their subordinates, they will continue
to treat PMS more or less as an additional burden.

4 Culture and PMSs

Following the publication of Hofstede's (1980) classic treatise on cultural comparisons
of various nations, management scholars have paid close attention to the impact of
national culture on organizations. While Hofstede's methods have subsequently been
criticized (all his data were collected from employees of one organization – IBM),

there is no denying the fact that he alerted both scholars and practitioners to the critical role of culture, especially in international organizations.

Specifically, Hofstede proposed (See Chapter 1, Table 1.2) five dimensions of culture:

1. Power distance – the degree to which people accept status and authority differences between themselves and their supervisors.
2. Individualism versus collectivism –the degree to which people find their identity, or define themselves, as unique individuals, versus seeking group identity.
3. Masculinity/femininity – where masculine cultures are defined by assertiveness, competitiveness, success, etc., and feminine cultures are known for being relationship-oriented and valuing quality of life issues.
4. Uncertainty avoidance – the degree to which people seek structure versus their willingness to accept unstructured situations.
5. Long-term versus short-term orientation – which deals with whether the culture emphasizes long-term commitments and respect for tradition, while short-term orientation emphasizes the now and here, and change is more readily acceptable.

Drawing upon Hofstede's typology, it is easy to see how a nation's culture might impact on practices related to PMSs. For example, the United States scores 40 on power distance, meaning low acceptance of status and hierarchy differences, while India scores a rather high 77 when measured against the world average of 56.5. Thus, in this instance, individuals are more likely to accept, often without argument, downward supervisor feedback in India, than they are in the United States. So, a company that operates in both nations will have to adapt its PMS practices and feedback mechanism, as managers are less likely to be willing to receive upward feedback in India. Similarly, in a country like China, that is known for collectivistic values, people prefer group-based, rather than individual-focused training (Earley, 1994) and may respond better to group-based, rather than individual-focused feedback (van de Vliert et al., 2004).

Culture can also influence how supervisors evaluate their subordinates. For example, Varma et al. (2005a) reported that managers in India gave significantly higher ratings to employees that they liked, awarding substantially beyond the amount warranted by their performance. Such behaviour is often motivated by culturally accepted practices, such as the need to protect and support members of one's in-group, even though their performance may not warrant the high ratings awarded. In a similar vein, Law et al. (2000) reported that managers in China are likely to go out of their way to help those subordinates with whom they share high quality relationships.

Clearly, the culture of a nation can have a significant impact on how performance is viewed, managed and evaluated. Thus, organizations would do well to take this into account when designing their PMSs for different cultures. A word of caution is appropriate here, culture is not a static concept and it keeps changing, with the rate of change dependent on a number of factors. For example, the recent economic growth of China is creating a group of individuals who are slowly moving away from collectivistic values – this shift is often identified among those working for MNCs. Thus, organizations need to attend to the shifts in culture, as they attempt to adjust and adapt their HR systems – and, clearly, these systems need to be audited on a continuous basis, to ensure that they accurately reflect the times.

5 PMSs in six leading economies: China, India, Japan, South Korea, UK, USA

In this section, we present some of the key features of PMSs in some of the world's leading economies, specifically China, India, Japan, South Korea, the UK and USA. We recognize that this is a short and incomplete list – however, our purpose here is to demonstrate some of the major differences in how PMSs operate in these countries, and thus emphasize the general importance of creating systems that serve corporate objectives while at the same time ensuring they remain consistent with local realities.

PMS in China

The first two countries included in this section are known to be culturally similar, yet have evolved very differently in terms of history and governance over the last five or six decades. Both China and India are relatively collectivist nations, with an emphasis on relationship-building in the workplace. Interestingly, PMSs have existed in both these countries for much longer than one might expect. As Cooke (2008) notes, a Chinese version of assessment and performance appraisal has been practised in China for a very long time. The key features of current PMS practice in China are as follows:

1. Since the late 1980s there has been widespread implementation of PMSs, both in the private and the public sectors.
2. PMSs in China continue to be strongly influenced by the culture, including respect for age and seniority, and the emphasis on harmony and *face*.
3. The collectivist nature of society means that group-based evaluations and feedback are often preferred to individual evaluations and feedback.
4. However, there is still a strong emphasis on traits and behaviours, and less on outcomes, as opposed to PMSs in the USA.
5. PMSs are often seen as an administrative formality.
6. The validity and reliability of these systems often suffer from high levels of subjectivity in the evaluations exercised by managers.

PMS in India

PMSs have existed in India for a long time. Indeed, the public sector has used confidential evaluations of civil servants and other government employees for over a century.

Several private sector organizations (e.g. Tata Steel) have also had formal evaluations in place for a similar length of time. However, the PMSs keep evolving with socio-economic and cultural changes, and the key features of current PMSs include:

1. The recent advent of numerous MNCs into Indian business has caused many domestic firms to review their PMSs, and many report revising and upgrading existing systems.
2. There is a clear shift in the workplace, from traditional collectivist values to more of an individualist orientation.
3. Individual employees often expect and appreciate immediate and short-term rewards.
4. The paternalistic nature of the culture continues to influence PMSs, as many blue-collar employees rely on their supervisors to 'take care of them'. As we discussed above, this can often lead to inflated ratings being awarded by managers.
5. On the other hand, white-collar professionals, especially those working in technology-related jobs, pride themselves in having the skills to manage their careers.
6. One of the significant challenges faced by organizations in designing PMSs for their Indian operations is the significant diversity of the Indian workforce, which comprises individuals who belong to numerous different ethnicities and religions, and speak a variety of different languages.

PMS in Japan

For many decades, Japanese organizations focused on long-term employment, and thus emphasized employee learning. As a result, their appraisal practices included measures of employee competence and skills/ability development. However, the last two decades have involved a marked shift in several organizational practices, mainly as a result of the changing global economic scene, which has seen Brazil, Russia, India and China emerge as economic leaders. Not surprisingly, HR practices in Japanese organizations have also undergone some major changes, especially in relation to performance appraisal, presenting several challenges to HRM professionals. The key features of current HR practices in Japan include:

1. The emphasis in performance appraisal has shifted from employee skills to individual performance.
2. The traditional role played by seniority in determining promotions is being replaced by an evaluation of merit and competence, evaluated in conjunction with actual performance.
3. As a result of these changes, life-time employment is now less the norm in corporations – most firms hire mid-career employees from other organizations, including competitors, something that was unthinkable just a few decades ago.
4. Individual differentiation of performance is much more prevalent now, leading to the need for appropriate systems and processes.

5. Outsourcing of jobs is also becoming a commonly accepted practice, once again leading to the need for new systems, policies and practices.
6. Overall, the shift from predominantly long-term to more short-term employment relationships has resulted in a strong focus on procedural justice, and while many organizations have begun to respond to this concern, much more needs to be done to address fairness in procedures such as hiring, promotion, evaluations and terminations, etc. As Pichler et al. (2013) reported, perceptions of procedural justice play a significant role in the acceptance of performance appraisal.

PMS in South Korea

In order to understand PMSs in South Korea, it is important to understand the influence of Confucian values on Korean society and culture, as it impacts on the workplace and performance appraisal. Among other features, this impact is seen in the respect for hierarchy, and the wide acceptance of collectivism and paternalism. Not surprisingly, appraisal systems were developed with these values in mind, as it was believed that rewarding or recognizing employees based on their individual performance would be detrimental to the sense of community and camaraderie, and would ultimately have a negative impact on organizational culture and productivity. Furthermore, similar to past practice in Japan, seniority played a major role in determining promotions.

However, the change in the global economic scene as well as the Asian financial crisis of 1997 have led to substantial change, and the current HR environment in South Korea is very different, as reflected in HR practices and, more specifically, in performance appraisal policies and procedures. The key features of the current performance appraisal practices are listed below.

1. A majority of corporations in South Korea have now adopted merit-based pay and reward systems, which require differentiation of individual performance, and this marks a clear shift from past practices.
2. While performance appraisal systems continue to be used primarily for administrative decisions, the feedback and developmental role of performance appraisal is increasingly being emphasized.
3. Employees of South Korean organizations are very sensitive to performance appraisal outcomes, especially since the introduction of merit-based systems, though the overall nature of Korean culture, where harmony is emphasized, prevents them from openly challenging the outcomes.
4. Some organizations have tried to introduce the forced-distribution system in ratings, in order to prevent leniency in performance ratings. However, once again, the forced-distribution system has been shown to result in high levels of dissatisfaction, as well as forcing employees to compete rather than collaborate, something that continues to be a critical part of the Korean culture.

PMS in the UK

PMSs in the United Kingdom have a long history, and most UK organizations use some form of PMS. As Sparrow (2008) notes, PMSs in the UK could be classified as being 'mature', with the ability to adapt to changes in the UK's socio-economic, political and legal frameworks.

The key features of PMS in the UK are:

1. There is significantly more emphasis on the developmental aspect of performance management, as compared to the US.
2. There is an ongoing emphasis on cost effectiveness.
3. A recent emphasis on 'talent management' requires PMSs to be able to identify and reward 'high talent' employees.
4. There is a new emphasis on total rewards management, which has led to the development of PMSs that assess and reward individual performance, in terms of both monetary and non-monetary rewards.
5. There is, however, an ongoing need to address issues such as work–life balance, rater bias, and diversity.

PMS in the USA

In their comprehensive summary of PMSs in the USA, Pulakos et al. (2008) argue that the history of the USA and its fundamentally individualistic culture have had a significant impact on the workplace and performance management practices. Thus, individual performance, accountability and performance-linked rewards form an integral part of the performance management process. As the authors argue, it is difficult to identify a single PMS as being the American system, given that almost every type and size of business exists in the USA. However, there are some clear themes that emerge from a review of PMSs in the USA:

1. PMSs are primarily used for administrative purposes, such as awarding merit raises, and informing promotion decisions, with the use of PMS for developmental purposes remaining rather limited.
2. There is a very strong focus on results – thus, performing the desired behaviours or demonstrating the right traits will not suffice.
3. The legal system is very well attuned to organizational issues and there are numerous reported instances of individual legal challenges to performance-related decisions.
4. There is an ongoing emphasis on the use of technology in PMSs, thus facilitating the easy access and sharing of performance information.
5. Acceptance of, and trust in, PMSs continues to be rather low, and both managers and employees report dissatisfaction with the process and its outcomes.

6 PMS for expatriates

Expatriate assignments play a critical role in MNCs, and thus it is imperative that organizations find ways to ensure they have high rates of success. Expatriate PMSs can provide critical measures of the success of an organization's strategic objectives, as well as be an important means of evaluating the expatriate's actual on-the-job performance. However, as Tung and Varma (2008) have noted, it seems that expatriate performance evaluations are based primarily on systems developed for domestic purposes, both in US and non-US MNCs. Clearly, this is an issue that warrants attention both from MNC executives and scholars, as performance issues are context-driven and should be evaluated accordingly (Murphy and Cleveland, 1995). In addition, it is important that MNCs clearly define the parameters of expatriate performance (Shaffer et al., 2006). Hitherto, several different criteria have been used to measure expatriate effectiveness, although these are not consistent across organizations (Shaffer et al., 2006). Finally, as Yan et al. (2002) argue, the expatriate's own goals should also form an integral part of the evaluation system.

In addition to designing appraisal systems based on the expatriate's specific job objectives, expatriate PMSs should incorporate the unique environmental factors related to the host country, such as laws, technology (Shen, 2005) and cultural norms (Tahvanainen, 2000). Another issue that needs to be addressed is the issue of host country national categorization. Several scholars (see, for example, Toh and DeNisi, 2007) have argued that expatriates often have to rely on HCNs for information that can help them on their assignments. However, as Toh et al. (2004) argue, HCNs are likely to share information only with those expatriates whom they accept into their in-groups, due to perceived shared values or other similarities. Indeed, HCN categorization of expatriates can be based on a whole range of factors, such as collectivism, and ethnocentrism (Zeira, 1979), etc. Recent empirical investigations of HCN categorization have reported that this phenomenon operates in numerous countries, and thus clearly is worthy of further attention. For example, Varma et al. (2006) examined HCN attitudes towards expatriates in India and the United States. These authors found that Indian HCNs (both male and female) would prefer to work with female expatriates from the US, rather than male expatriates. In another study, Varma et al. (2012), found that Chinese HCNs categorized expatriates from both the US and India into in-groups and out-groups, based on their personal levels of collectivism and 'guanxi'. Finally, Varma et al. (2011) report similar results from their investigation in the United Kingdom. Clearly, the conditions on the ground in the host country are likely to be different according to the location of the expatriate's assignment, and will have a significant impact on the expatriate's ability to do his or her job. Further, since the goals of expatriate assignments vary between locations, it is clear that expatriate evaluation mechanisms should incorporate the context or unique circumstances of the expatriate's assignment. After all, performance management is the medium through which the organization can assess the expatriate's performance, and thus gauge the success of the organization's strategic objectives (Dowling and Schuler, 1990).

Box 12.4 Stop and reflect

Expatriate evaluations and host country national reactions

In their study of HCN willingness to offer support to expatriates in China, Varma et al. (2012: 762) reported that 'HCN perceptions of values similarity (with expatriates), *and the levels of HCN* dogmatism, and ethnocentrism are related to their willingness to provide role information and social support to expatriates.' Several other studies by Varma and colleagues have confirmed that HCNs in most nations base their decision to offer support to expatriates depending on whether they categorize the expatriate as a member of their in-group or out-group. In other words, those expatriates who are categorized as in-group are more likely to receive required support from HCNs, while those who are categorized as out-group are not likely to receive required support. Since almost all expatriates need role information and social support to succeed on their assignments, those who do not receive such support from HCNs are unlikely to have the same level of success on their assignments, as those expatriates who do receive such support.

However, expatriate evaluations rarely make allowances for such factors, which happen to be beyond the control of the expatriate, in any case. After all, the expatriate may be included in the in-group or cast into the out-group for any of a whole host of factors – for example, the HCNs' own ethnocentrism, dogmatism, collectivism, or the expatriate's appearance, race, national origin, etc. If organizations are to derive optimum performance levels from all expatriates, they must address HCN related issues through training and other interventions, while also making allowances for such factors in the performance evaluation itself. At the very least, organizations need to be aware of the existence of such factors.

Source: Varma et al., 2012.

7 Summary and conclusions

In this chapter, we have discussed PMSs in a global context, and tried to emphasize the unique nature of such systems. We started by outlining the core components of PMSs, followed by an examination of the key factors that can impact on such systems. We included the all-important issue of national culture, especially as it relates to people-related systems. We also provided an overview and comparison of PMSs in six leading economies (China, Japan, India, South Korea, the UK and USA), and have identified some of the principal differences occurring between PMSs implemented in these country cultures. This was followed by an assessment of the unique nature and requirements of expatriate evaluations. Throughout the chapter, we have presented relevant research on PMSs, with special emphasis on MNCs. We concluded our discussion by emphasizing the main reasons why organizations need to develop unique systems for each country in which they operate, rather than simply transferring systems developed for the home country environment.

As Tung and Varma (2008) have argued, globalization is here to stay, and will continue to grow for the foreseeable future. Further, as Peretz and Fried (2012) reported, the culture of a nation has a significant impact on performance appraisal practices. This makes the role of the MNC critical in the economic and socio-political well-being of nations around the world. While organizations may be able to adapt home-based financial and technical systems to the new location, people-related systems do not lend themselves so easily to cross-national transfer, as they are often the most context-driven of all organizational systems. Specifically, the subject of performance management presents unique challenges, as it is heavily impacted by local issues, such as national culture and practices – yet, PMS is the primary process through which organizations set goals, assign and evaluate work, and measure successful implementation of business strategy. While all organizations face similar challenges, the strategies adopted to address them will often depend on the organization's home country and host countries. In other words, the differences in culture, laws, technology or simply past practices make it very difficult to directly apply systems from one setting, to another.

We concentrated on MNCs in this chapter, as these organizations are the ones most affected by the issues. For organizations that operate solely in a domestic region, the issues are different and much more localized. Setting aside the necessity of competing on PMSs, they have the luxury of deciding whether to develop their own systems, adopt foreign-developed systems or even have no system at all. As long as their practices conform to local legal and social requirements, they are not 'burdened' by the necessity to adapt or adopt other systems. Due to their global reach and diversity, MNCs need to operate according to a different set of principles and rules.

At first sight, it may seem that the transfer of PMSs across countries is relatively easy, since the majority of MNCs originated in the US, and the majority of MNCs from other nations seem to have adopted versions of PMSs similar to those initially developed in the US. Thus, one might suggest that all MNCs have to do is to take their existing systems and adapt slightly to account for cultural differences. However, this is an overly simplistic view. First, it is reasonable to assume that as economies like China and India grow and become leaders, some influential individuals and groups in these nations will demand more 'local' systems that address HQ country relevant issues such as collectivism, deference to seniority and issues of face. At the same time, employees of MNCs in these and other similar nations will also demand that they be treated consistent with their counterparts in Western nations, in terms of rewards, evaluation and promotion practices. Coordinating and satisfying this set of conflicting demands placed on organizations and their HRM departments will require balancing multiple demands. These systems cannot be developed and left alone to run themselves, they have to be maintained and improved to ensure that they remain current and appropriate. This is not to say that MNCs have solely emerged from the West or the US in particular, but there is no denying that such MNCs have dominated global business systems for more than 50 years. Indeed, there is a new generation of MNCs emerging on the global business scene – demonstrated by major corporate mergers and acquisitions such as the purchase of IBM's personal computer division by China's Lenovo, and India's Tata group acquiring Jaguar and Land Rover. This trend of new MNCs arising from countries around the world is adding a new and somewhat complex dimension to the development and implementation of appropriate systems for managing people.

We hope we have been able to make it clear why PMSs should be adopted following critical evaluation and after making appropriate modifications. We have argued that, in addition to ensuring that organizations have proper PMSs in place, it is critical that the PMS be relevant to the environment – especially in the case of global organizations. As Goderis of Underwriters Laboratories Inc. asserts, the emphasis on having a sophisticated system should not override the practical need to have a system that is appropriate to the location (see Box 12.5), and emphasizes the main purpose of PMSs – which is to encourage optimal levels of performance.

Box 12.5   Stop and reflect

Global PMS design

As someone directly involved in global PMS design and implementation for over a decade, I have seen everything – from manager and employee apathy, to engagement, tears, frustration, disbelief, and yes performance excellence too. As our organization and culture has evolved, we have modified our PMS to align with, and support business changes while balancing the needs and concerns of our employees. Over the years, our PMS has evolved, along with the business – today we have a simple, single globally consistent approach, anchored by a strong set of global behavioral competencies, supported by a robust and flexible HRIS tool. Of course, we

(Continued)

(Continued)

will make changes again – if anyone could design the perfect PMS, history would be made and we would all be wealthy ... but human beings, even more so than MNEs, are complex entities, and never perfect, so my recommendation to HR professionals in MNEs is not to spend their time trying to come up with a perfect global PMS – instead, what we need is simplicity, with a 'glocal' (globally consistent and locally appropriate) flavor, in an effort to continually motivate the best employee performance possible. Therein lie our challenge, and our future.

Josh Goderis, CCP, PHR Director, Global Talent Management Underwriters Laboratories Inc.

Indeed, it is critical that HR practitioners everywhere critically evaluate the PMS before adopting it – systems developed in the US, or elsewhere, may not be automatically appropriate for implementation in other locations. Most HRM systems and practices are context-specific, and performance-related systems may be even more so, since performance may not be defined the same way in different locations and organizations. Practitioners therefore must judge the suitability of the systems, adapting and modifying them, as necessary. As has been discussed above, feedback systems designed for a low power distance culture like the US will likely fail in high power distance cultures like China, Japan and India, unless the systems are modified to reflect local realities.

As more and more organizations around the world begin to introduce and implement PMSs, it is important that HR professionals do not uncritically import a system simply because it has worked somewhere else. Such an adoption strategy is likely to be counter-productive, as it will fail to deliver the desired results, and may even end up negatively impacting on performance. If creating a home-grown system is not practical, and one must import the PMS from headquarters, the key is to select the best elements of the system and customize it so that it suits local needs.

As DeNisi et al. (2008) noted, 'Visitors to India will find that McDonalds doesn't sell hamburgers but sells vegetable burgers. This "Indianization" of the hamburger seems to be exactly the approach we need in the area of performance management. As countries develop more sophisticated systems they should learn from other countries, but also make sure that, where needed, they modify existing programmes to fit with local "tastes".'

Discussion questions

1. In order to achieve their goals of maximizing individual potential and helping each individual reach their optimal level of performance, organizations must go beyond performance appraisals and implement all the components of PMSs. Discuss.
2. Why is it important that organizations clearly specify the performance appraisal process (i.e. who will conduct the evaluations, when will it be conducted, what will be measured, etc.)? What impact does the lack of a clear process have on employees?
3. In section 4, we discuss the impact that culture can have on PMSs. How can culture impact how performance is viewed in different cultures? Using the six countries we cover in section 5, discuss how performance might be interpreted differently by supervisors and subordinates in each of these cultures.
4. As we discuss above, performance management systems for expatriates need to be specifically designed and implemented keeping in mind the unique context and ground realities of the location where the expatriate is based. Talk to some individuals who have been on expatriate assignments, and discuss what kinds of factors organizations might need to address in setting up PMSs for expatriates.

CASE STUDY

V-Pharmel Performance Management

Overview

V-Pharmel is an integrated consumer products company, producing a wide range of quality, affordable household products, with a mission to provide a better life for citizens of the world. It has been ranked on numerous lists among the top 100 'preferred employers'. The company has manufacturing facilities in 14 countries, and its products are sold in over 90 countries around the world. The excerpt below, from the company's website, is intended to demonstrate its management philosophy.

> V-Pharmel is committed to values-based leadership, and the ethical treatment of all its constituencies. In keeping with our philosophy, we will uphold the highest ethical integrity in all business transactions, and practise the following values in all our transactions, both inside and outside the company:

(Continued)

(Continued)

1. Honesty and integrity in all our dealings – with co-workers, customers, clients, and all others.

2. Respect for each other's individuality, and diversity in all its forms.

3. Being a responsible corporate social citizen.

4. Maintaining a profit-orientation, without compromising our values.

Attachment 1

V-Pharmel

Document 07PMS

Management Trainee Evaluation Form

(To be completed every 6 months for the first 2 years)

Name of Trainee _____

Date of Joining _____

Division _____

Supervisor Name _____

To the rater: Please use the following scale to evaluate the Management Trainee

1 = Poor; 2 = Below Average; 3 = Average; 4 = Above Average; 5 = Outstanding

Initiative	1	2	3	4	5
Attendance	1	2	3	4	5
Timeliness	1	2	3	4	5
Written Communication	1	2	3	4	5
Verbal Communication	1	2	3	4	5

Signature of HR Head _____

Signature of Management Trainee _____

Date _____

Note: This form is to be placed in trainee's file after completion, and becomes a part of his/her permanent record.

The case of the management trainee

Background

V-Pharmel has a comprehensive management trainee (MT) scheme, whereby they hire MTs from the top-ranked business schools in the US, and put them through a two-year training programme, after which the trainee is assigned to a functional area, and assigned the title of Specialist.

In August 2007, they hired five MTs for the marketing department – four from schools in the US, and one from Singapore. This was the first time they had hired internationally for the MT scheme, and AJ was the only 'foreigner' in the marketing department. The MTs had similar backgrounds, in that they had Bachelor's degrees in the arts, and had specialized in marketing in their graduate studies. However, AJ, the MT from Singapore, was the only one in the group who had worked in consumer products sales for four years, in between his Bachelor's and Master's. The other four had gone straight from undergraduate to graduate studies. Because of AJ's experience, he was assigned to work directly with Scott, head of marketing, while the other four were assigned to heads of product development teams within the marketing department. The MT scheme was supervised by Jim, head of HR.

AJ's evaluation experience

According to AJ, Scott was very polite and respectful towards him, and often told him that the first year of an MT's career should be spent learning the ropes and getting to know people. However, Scott rarely gave him any work of substance, and whenever AJ stopped by to speak with Scott, he was asked to meet later because Scott was 'busy'. AJ remarked that, very often, when he passed by, he could hear Scott chatting with other colleagues about movies or dinners.

Sometime in March 2008, six months into the probationary period for the MTs, the five supervisors met with Jim, to discuss the progress of the MTs. Each supervisor spoke briefly about the MT assigned to them, and then filled out the appraisal form, and submitted it to Jim. Normally, the MTs were not invited to this meeting. Instead, Jim met with them individually, and gave them a letter he had written, based on the supervisor's comments. After the conclusion of the March meeting, one of the supervisors, Susan, stopped by AJ's cubicle, and informed him that Scott had given him a very negative report at the meeting, and that he should expect a 'tough' meeting with Jim, with the high probability that his contract might be terminated.

(Continued)

(Continued)

AJ approached Jim, and wanted to talk about what 'he had heard' (since he did not want to reveal Susan's name). Jim told him there was 'nothing to worry about', and that he would meet with him (and the other MTs) in a few days. Over the next week, Jim met with the MTs individually, and gave them feedback about their performance to the current date. AJ was scheduled to be the last one to meet with Jim. AJ checked with the other MTs about their meetings, and they all reported being very pleased with their reports, having received all 4s and 5s on their forms. On Friday at 4 p.m., AJ met with Jim in his office, and Jim presented him a 2-page letter, detailing Scott's evaluation of AJ's performance. While AJ was prepared for a somewhat negative report, based on Susan's confidential warning, he was shocked to see that he had been rated 1 on all 5 categories (see sample form below).

AJ tried to explain to Jim that he had never been given any indication of problems with his performance, and that Scott was always very pleasant to him, and kept telling him that he needed to 'get his feet wet' during the first year, as later on, he would be swamped with work. Jim told AJ not to worry about the report – that he was confident that subsequent reports would be much better. Over the weekend, AJ kept wondering what had gone wrong, and why he had received such a big shock. He had always been to work on time, often stayed late reading company manuals and reports, and since Scott barely gave him any work to do, he had spent a lot of time speaking to other managers taking copious notes to learn about the company. Yet, he had been evaluated so poorly, that he began to wonder if he had chosen the wrong company – indeed, he wondered if he had chosen the wrong profession.

AJ kept looking at the letter written and signed by Jim, whom he considered as a friend, yet the contents were not friendly by any stretch of imagination. As he pored over the form one more time, he started to get upset and angry, not knowing what to do next. All other MTs had received good ratings, and he did not believe they were too different from him – either in career background (he was the one with real work experience!), or in the way they had worked over the last six months. As he looked over the form one more time, he suddenly realized that he had never written anything for Scott, so it made no sense that Scott had rated him on that category. On Monday, he approached Jim with this information, but Jim told him to just forget about it, since no one else would see the file, and in any case, Jim said 'I think very highly of you'.

Over the next three months, AJ kept approaching Jim, with the same issue, but each time Jim told him not to worry. During these meetings, AJ also realized that even though Jim would not budge on the Scott issue, he did indeed respect AJ, and they were becoming quite friendly and collegial. Also, during these three months, Scott stopped talking to AJ completely, and gave him no work at all.

Ultimately, AJ decided he had no option left, but to quit the company and move back to Singapore. When AJ approached Jim to share his decision, Jim expressed surprise, but accepted AJ's resignation, and wished him all the best 'in his future endeavours'.

Case study questions

1. Please critique the MT performance evaluation process at V-Pharmel. What could have been done differently?
2. What, in your opinion, was the purpose of the supervisors meeting as a team to evaluate all of the MTs?
3. In your opinion, what role did AJ and Scott's backgrounds play in this case?
4. How would you rate the form used to evaluate the MTs?
5. Please critique the role played in this scenario by all the major players – i.e. AJ, Scott, Phil, and even Susan.
6. To what extent did the managers at V-Pharmel practise the company's stated values? If they had truly internalized those values, would AJ's experience have been different? How? Why?

Further reading

- DeNisi, A.S. (1996) *Cognitive Processes in Performance Appraisal: A Research Agenda with Implications for Practice*. London: Routledge.
  This research-oriented book provides a comprehensive overview of the cognitive processes involved in the performance appraisal process, including (a) information-processing models, (b) information storage, (c) recall, (d) managerial judgements, and (e) issues with memory-based judgements.

- Murphy, K.R. and Cleveland, J.N. (1995) *Understanding Performance Appraisal: Social, Organizational, and Goal-based Perspectives*. Thousand Oaks, CA: Sage.
  This book provides a comprehensive overview of the performance appraisal process, summarizing and critiquing relevant research. In addition, the authors discuss the impact of (a) social norms, (b) organizational objectives, and (c) linking individual performance goals to strategic objectives.

- Varma, A., Budhwar, P.S. and DeNisi, A. (eds) (2008) *Performance Management Systems: A Global Perspective*. Global HRM Series, London: Routledge.

This edited volume presents an international perspective on the study of PMSs. The initial chapters discuss some critical issues relating to PMSs, such as motivation and rewards. The book also presents a comprehensive model of PMSs, which is used by the various authors to describe PMSs in 11 different countries, including France, Germany, Mexico and Turkey.

Internet resources

- www.shrm.org. This is the website of the Society for Human Resource Management, the world's largest organization of human resource professionals. The site provides information and articles on all aspects of human resource management. Membership is required for access to all the sections, though students will find lots of information on the main page.
- www.performance-appraisal.com. This website provides a complete online guide for performance appraisals, including access to several tools and online forms, etc.
- www.geert-hofstede.com. This website is designed to provide information on national and organizational culture. Students can compare country scores on the various dimensions, and even take a survey to determine their own scores.

Self-assessment questions

Indicative answers to these questions can be found on the companion website at study.sagepub.com/harzing4e.

1. How can organizations ensure that supervisors take the performance management process seriously, instead of just going through the motions?
2. How can the quality of an individual's relationship with his/her subordinate impact individual performance?
3. How can national culture impact performance management systems?
4. Discuss the key issues that organizations should address when designing PMSs for expatriates.

References

Bobko, P. and Colella, A. (1994) 'Employee reactions to performance standards: a review and research propositions', *Personnel Psychology*, 47(1): 1–29.

Cooke, F.L. (2008) 'Performance management in China', in A. Varma, P.S. Budhwar and A.S. DeNisi (eds), *Performance Management Systems: A Global Perspective*, Global HRM Series. London: Routledge, pp. 193–209.

Deming, W.E. (1982) *Out of the Crisis*. Cambridge: Cambridge University Press.

DeNisi, A.S. (1996) *Cognitive Processes in Performance Appraisal: A Research Agenda with Implications for Practice*. London: Routledge.

DeNisi, A.S., Varma, A. and Budhwar, P.S. (2008) 'Performance management around the globe: what have we learned?', in A. Varma, P.S. Budhwar and A.S. DeNisi (eds), *Performance Management Systems: A Global Perspective*, Global HRM Series. London: Routledge, pp. 254–262.

Dowling, P.J. and Schuler, R.S. (1990) *International Dimensions of Human Resources Management*. Boston, MA: PWS Kent.

Earley, P.C. (1994) 'The individual and collective self: an assessment of self-efficacy and training across cultures', *Administrative Science Quarterly*, 39: 89–117.

Graen, G. and Cashman, J. (1975) 'A role-making model of leadership in formal organizations: a developmental approach', in J.G. Hunt and L.L. Larson (eds), *Leadership Frontiers*. Kent, OH: Kent State University Press, pp. 143–165.

Hofstede, G.H. (1980) *Culture's Consequences: International Differences in Work-related Values*. Beverly Hills, CA: Sage.

Law, K.S., Wong, C.S., Wang, D. and Wang, L. (2000) 'Effect of supervisor–subordinate guanxi on supervisory decisions in China: an empirical investigation', *International Journal of Human Resource Management*, 11(4): 751–765.

Locke, E.A. (1968) 'Toward a theory of task performance and incentives', *Organizational Behavior and Human Performance*, 3: 157–189.

Murphy, K.R. and Cleveland, J.N. (1995) *Understanding Performance Appraisal: Social, Organizational, and Goal-based Perspectives*. Thousand Oaks, CA: Sage.

Murphy, K.R. and DeNisi, A.S. (2008) 'A model of the appraisal process', in A. Varma, P.S. Budhwar and A.S. DeNisi (eds), *Performance Management Systems: A Global Perspective*, Global HRM Series. London: Routledge, pp 81–95.

Peretz, H. and Fried, Y. (2012) 'National cultures, performance appraisal practices, and organizational absenteeism and turnover: a study across 21 countries', *Journal of Applied Psychology*, 97(2): 448–459.

Pichler, S., Varma, A., Michel, J., Budhwar, P. and Levy, P. (2013) 'The role of procedural justice climate in reactions to performance appraisals', paper presented at the Academy of Management Meetings, Orlando, FL.

Pulakos, E.D., Mueller-Hanson, R.A. and O'Leary, R.S. (2008) 'Performance management in the United States', in A. Varma, P.S. Budhwar and A.S. DeNisi (eds), *Performance Management Systems: A Global Perspective*, Global HRM Series. London: Routledge, pp. 97–114.

Shaffer, M.A., Harrison, D.A, Gregersen, H., Black, J.S. and Ferzandi, L.A. (2006) 'You can take it with you: individual differences and expatriate effectiveness', *Journal of Applied Psychology*, 91(1): 109–125

Sharma, T., Budhwar, P.S. and Varma, A. (2008) 'Performance management in India', in A. Varma, P.S. Budhwar and A.S. DeNisi (eds), *Performance Management Systems: A Global Perspective*, Global HRM Series. London: Routledge, pp. 180–192.

Shen, J. (2005) 'Effective international performance appraisals: easily said, hard to do', *Compensation & Benefits Review*, 37(4): 70–79.

Skinner, B.F. (1953) *Science and Human Behavior*. New York: Macmillan.

Sparrow, P. (2008) 'Performance management in the U.K.', in A. Varma, P.S. Budhwar and A.S. DeNisi (eds), *Performance Management Systems: A Global Perspective*, Global HRM Series. London: Routledge, pp. 131–146.

Tahvanainen, M. (2000) 'Expatriate performance management: the case of Nokia Telecommunications', *Human Resource Management*, 37: 267–275.

Toh, S.M. and DeNisi, A.S. (2007) 'Host country nationals as socializing agents: a social identity approach', *Journal of Organizational Behavior*, 28: 281–301.

Toh, S.M., Varma, A. and DeNisi, A.S. (2004) 'Host country national helping on the adjustment of expatriates', paper presented at the conference of the Society for Industrial/Organizational Psychology, Chicago, IL.

Tung, R.L. and Varma, A. (2008) 'Expatriate selection and evaluation', in P.B. Smith, M.F. Peterson and D.C. Thomas (eds), *Handbook of Cross-Cultural Management Research*. London: Sage, pp. 367–378.

Van de Vliert, E., Shi, K., Sanders, K., Wang, Y. and Huang, X. (2004) 'Chinese and Dutch interpretations of supervisory feedback', *Journal of Cross-Cultural Psychology*, 35: 417–435.

Varma, A., Budhwar, P.S. and DeNisi, A. (eds) (2008) *Performance Management Systems: A Global Perspective*, Global HRM Series. London: Routledge.

Varma, A., Pichler, S. and Budhwar, P.S. (2011) 'The relationship between expatriate job level and host country national categorization: an investigation in the United Kingdom', *International Journal of Human Resource Management*, 22(1): 103–120.

Varma, A., Pichler, S., Budhwar, P.S. and Kupferer, S. (2012) 'Expatriate – local interactions: An investigation in China', *Journal of Managerial Psychology*, 27(7): 753–768.

Varma, A., Pichler, S. and Srinivas, E.S. (2005a) 'The role of interpersonal affect in performance appraisal: evidence from two samples – U.S. and India', *International Journal of Human Resource Management*, 16: 2029–2044.

Varma, A., Srinivas, E.S. and Stroh, L.K. (2005b) 'A comparative study of the impact of leader member exchange relationships in U.S. and Indian samples', *Cross-Cultural Management: An International Journal*, 12(1): 84–95.

Varma, A. and Stroh, L.K. (2001) 'The impact of same-sex LMX dyads on performance evaluations', *Human Resource Management*, 40: 309–320.

Varma, A., Toh, S.M. and Budhwar, P.S. (2006) 'A new perspective on the female expatriate experience: the role of host country national categorization', *Journal of World Business*, 41: 112–120.

Wakabayashi, M., Graen, G., Graen, M. and Graen, M. (1988) 'Japanese management progress: mobility into middle management', *Journal of Applied Psychology*, 73: 217–227.

Yan, A., Zhu, G. and Hall, D.T. (2002) 'International assignments for career building: a model of agency relationships and psychological contracts', *Academy of Management Review*, 27: 373–391.

Zeira, Y. (1979) 'Ethnocentrism in host-country organizations', *Business Horizons*, 22(3): 66–75.

Total Rewards in the International Context

K. Galen Kroeck and Mary Ann Von Glinow

Contents

Learning objectives

After reading this chapter you will be able to:

- Understand complexities due to *cultural differences regarding incentives* and *performance metrics* faced by international human resource managers
- Identify some international total rewards objectives for multinational companies to compensate expatriates and host country nationals
- Understand some of the issues involved in setting up compensation systems in other countries
- Explain the going rate and balance sheet approaches to international compensation and their advantages/disadvantages
- Understand some of the cultural shifts around the globe and how they affect compensation

Chapter outline

International compensation has received substantial attention in recent years due to the increasingly compelling effects of globalization. This chapter examines some complex issues faced by IHR managers in designing international total rewards systems by providing comprehensive examples of rewards policies and practices for expatriates as well as design of pay systems for subsidiaries in host countries. First, we discuss the intricacies that arise when MNCs design total rewards systems for an international assignment (IA) versus a typical headquarters assignment. We briefly highlight traditional and newer forms of IAs since rewards are often a function of the type of IA (i.e. three year versus six week versus commuter/virtual assignment). Second, we outline key components of an international total rewards programme, namely, base salaries, hardship premiums, allowances and benefits. Third, we discuss the going rate and balance sheet approaches to total rewards, followed by a discussion of their advantages and disadvantages. Fourth, we examine best practices in international total rewards systems. For practical reasons, we present current international cost-of-living data which are useful for IHR managers who face problems associated with limited information/statistics on cross-country comparisons. We also review the specific problems that IHR managers face when compensating third country nationals relative to those of host country nationals. Finally, we close our discussion by elaborating on recent international trends in global total rewards.

1 Recap: differentiating between PCNs, TCNs and HCNs

We primarily rely on use of the term expatriate to describe employees working internationally, although MNCs may assign either PCNs or TCNs to work on foreign assignments (Moshe and Sama, 2000).

PCNs are employees hired by the MNC at the headquarters location and assigned to a foreign location for a period usually lasting two to five years. MNCs following an *ethnocentric approach* (i.e. appreciation for the cultural values and business practices in the MNC's home country) have a predisposition to reject employees from other countries. Thus, in the context of rewards, MNCs with an ethnocentric policy may prefer PCNs because they have a high degree of familiarity with the MNC's national compensation and benefits practices. However, the cost associated with maintaining these employees and their families abroad can be excessive.

TCNs are foreign nationals hired by the MNC to work in any of their foreign locations with the exception of the TCN's own home country. For example, an Australian citizen working in the UK for a US-based MNC is a third country national. MNCs with a *geocentric approach* (i.e. an appreciation for the cultural values and business practices in the MNC's home country and in the foreign location) believe that nationality does not matter when selecting the best people for an overseas assignment. MNCs with a geocentric staffing policy believe that they will choose the best people for the job, regardless of their home country. However, MNCs with a geocentric policy may prefer TCNs because they have a high degree of familiarity with various types of compensation and benefits practices. TCNs typically work in areas usually less expensive to maintain than PCNs. TCNs may work in various international business settings for their MNC throughout their careers. However, they may experience perceptions of inequality as they move between foreign locations.

HCNs are employees hired by the MNC at a foreign location. MNCs with a *polycentric approach* (i.e. an appreciation for the cultural values and business practices in the foreign location) believe that local foreign nationals are the best people to manage their foreign subsidiary. Thus, MNCs with a polycentric policy may prefer HCNs because they have a high degree of familiarity with the compensation and benefits practices in the foreign location, unlike PCNs.

2 Introduction: the current state of total rewards

International compensation has quickly moved beyond the limited domain of expatriate pay. Worldwide total rewards now more commonly refers to a mechanism through which IHR managers can perform a number of critical activities including: (a) combining MNC's local and global data in order to develop appropriate compensation packages for a global workforce, (b) using centralized or decentralized rewards systems to maintain financial control over compensation and benefits programmes that span multiple geographic locations, and (c) linking global financial outcomes with geographically dispersed costs.

Among the many complexities that are often associated with growing international total rewards programmes include use of outsourcing and offshoring activities in order to further corporate interests. Certainly, international total rewards programmes are of strategic value to most MNCs due to interest in establishing operations in desirable emerging markets such as China, India, Pakistan, Mexico and Brazil. A second complexity often associated with using international total rewards programmes includes the increasing attractiveness of foreign assignments to employees. International opportunities are generally appealing to employees since they can often improve their financial situation and increase their upward career mobility. There are many benefits that accrue to both employees and their organizations of international total rewards programmes, although employees and MNCs face some difficulties. For instance, MNCs are confronted with balancing incentive, benefit and pension programmes through both centralized and decentralized systems and controls resulting in the need to manage employees across multiple geographic locations. MNC's must also deal with repatriation whenever employees transition from an international assignment to a home country domestic assignment.

Whenever the international assignment is to an emerging market, where institutions and legal structures are not fully developed, this becomes exceptionally challenging to the MNC. Total rewards in countries such as China are exacerbated by a lack of an abundant workforce that is highly talented. Accordingly, MNCs may end up paying HCNs a heftier salary than their counterparts, say in Indonesia or Malaysia. This is in stark contrast to countries like India, where talent is more abundant for high-end positions; however, it is the lower level ones that Indian workers eschew nowadays, much more than in the past. Thus, any total rewards programme needs to consider the country of destination for the international assignee, and realize that total compensation may differ significantly across geographic locations. Emerging markets present perhaps the greatest challenge, since everything shifts frequently (i.e. exchange rates, country risk factors, etc.).

3 Complexities faced by IHR managers

Vast cultural differences

The endurance of institutional characteristics provides a host country with a foundation for cultural stability. These characteristics often impact on a multitude of economic issues including employee compensation. Tang and Koveos (2008) found a curvilinear relationship between GDP per capita and the cultural dimensions of individualism, long-term orientation and power distance (for more information, see http://geert-hofstede.com/countries.html). In other words, economic and compensation changes may affect the values of the people of a particular nation. Cultural traditions such as language, religion and ethnic homogeneity tend to be more stable institutions but other cultural dimensions like uncertainty avoidance may be impacted by economic conditions. To the extent that changes in cultural values change over time has implications for compensation, recruitment and retention of effective employees. We do know that cultural values change (albeit very slowly) over time and over generations. It has frequently been observed that the millennials (those born in the 1990s and beyond) have a much more 'individualistic' orientation, even in collectivist societies like Korea, Japan and China, than did their parents who were born in the 'baby boom' era (1946–1964). China, with its 'one child policy' for example, has created a generation of 'little emperors' who, when they grow up (now in their late twenties, early thirties), are spoiled and tend more towards a 'me orientation'. The net result is that they shift jobs regularly for minor increases in pay and compensation. This adds to China's talent acquisition problem, and the implications are clear for MNCs doing business in China: a 'me generation' concentrates more on material rewards and the MNC must factor that in to any total rewards programme. High turnover among the best and brightest will occur unless the pay and remuneration meets their expectations.

Steers et al. (2010) extensively discuss how culture affects work and motivation. They note that there are cultural drivers that create both opportunities and constraints on efforts by managers and MNCs to motivate employees through various incentive systems. They contrast societies like the US with societies that generally tend to be more collectivist with high power distance orientation (e.g. most of Latin America), noting that individualistic societies have preferences for performance-based compensation, whereas a more culturally compatible approach to motivation in a collectivistic, high power distance society would show preferences for seniority or group-based compensation. We raise this because as countries shift more towards individualism with the accumulation of national wealth, employee behaviours, work motivation and performance will each be influenced by factors such as the availability of valued rewards and incentives, legal or contractual obligations, mutual trust, personal and situational differences. Those impacts may result in a lack of employee buy-in, commitment to the MNC, resistance to intra-group competition and poor work attitudes. As a general observation, emerging market countries where MNCs operate with increasing frequency, with significant talent shortages (i.e. China, Brazil) are increasingly demanding pay equity across the board (from PCNs, to HCNs to even TCNs). This clearly has implications for IHR professionals in charge of any total rewards programme. However, those that study culture and its impact on pay and motivation are quick to note that even though we have advanced our understanding of the generalizability of content theories of motivation, we still know relatively little about what affects work motivation in different nations, how national culture shapes work motivation and what national characteristics lead to variation in work motivation (Xu, 2008).

Turning now to executive talent, the impact of culture is even more difficult to assess. Modern motivation theory has its roots in the West, where motivating factors are linked to the 'self'. How the 'self' is defined can vary substantially from nation to nation, and the same type of work can have different meanings and be valued differently across nations. Although the ratios of top wage earners to bottom wage earners varies widely (800:1 in the US versus 40:1 in Japan), we do see some commonalities on the compensation horizon, even in emerging markets.

Southam and Sapp (2010), for example, were concerned with global competition for top executive talent. Examining why Canadian executives make 50 per cent less than US executives, they found Canadian cross-listed firms had to keep pace with their US counterparts while non-cross-listed firms did not. One question they posed asked whether compensation was allied with the power of the CEO over the board. While many CEOs in the US are able to set their own and other executives' compensation, they are primarily reined in by the 'outrage constraint' that limits their package to what relevant outsiders may become incensed by and publically express outrage (Krugman, 2002). Apparently the 'outrage sensitivity level' for Canadians is a lower dollar figure than in the US, which may explain many of the differences in compensation for CEOs around the world.

Buck et al. (2008) explained executive pay in China as a function of the outrage constraint. They discuss how China is attempting to avoid illegitimate equity-based rewards that have been shown to exist in some countries such as Germany (Sanders and Tuschke, 2007). According to these authors, Chinese policy-makers have achieved institutional changes that converge on Western practices with regard to executive pay being consistent with market forces.

One area of executive compensation likely to gain importance with globalization concerns ethical values found in Islamic business law. Martin and Hunt-Ahmed (2011) illuminate issues surrounding Shari'a compliance in executive compensation. They note that in the global competition for executive talent, values across the globe should be considered since Islamic law governs all financial and business transactions in Islamic countries and this directly impacts executive stock options offered. Specifically, the nature of what stock options are tied to determines whether they are acceptable in a package that has Shari'a compliance. Where this becomes challenging for IHR professionals managing total rewards across geographic locations, is when those who practise Shari'a try to implement these practices in non-Islamic countries such as France and the Netherlands, which can lead to enormous cultural complexities.

Balancing performance metrics

A second complexity faced by IHR managers placing employees in foreign assignments is the balancing of performance metrics. Traditionally, HR managers focused on developing performance metrics that maximize outcomes in a domestic environment. Recently, however, there is greater focus on understanding the influence of employee differences in cultural orientations and their preferences for particular HRM practices and policies (Aycan et al., 2007). IHR managers now must understand how the barriers they encounter when operating in non-domestic contexts influence their domestic HRM practices (Leat and El-Kot, 2007). Despite the complexities that IHR managers face, they must manage the highly complex nuances between their MNC entities and expatriates in order to meet the objectives of both organizations and individuals.

Varying compensation laws in different countries

Compensation laws are highly unique to each country. Some countries have required salary supplements with guaranteed payments beyond salary and not tied to performance such as allowances for meals, transportation or holidays. There are countries in Latin America that require additional pay such as a 13-month bonus, holiday bonus or profit-sharing. In Brazil and Argentina 13-month salary (an additional month of pay annually) is required by law. Brazilian companies also are required by law to pay a vacation bonus. In Mexico and Puerto Rico, holiday bonuses are likewise required by law. Profit sharing is mandatory in Mexico. Reimbursements for public transportation or a car allowance are common in Brazil, Chile and Colombia but not in the United States or Canada. A per diem for lunch is mandated in Venezuela.

In the EU, some countries, including Spain, Portugal and Italy, require non-salary compensation. In these three countries, most companies grant a thirteenth or fourteenth month of salary to employees. Belgium, France and Norway require a transportation allowance. Providing company cars is common in Belgium and Ireland, but not in the US, Canada or Latin America. In Asia, countries including India, Indonesia and the Philippines require salary supplements. In Singapore and Taiwan, a requirement of a thirteenth or fourteenth month of salary is common, while in China and Malaysia salary supplements also exist but are not customary. Transportation (sometimes automobile) allowances and meal allowances are conventional throughout Asia.

All members of the EU provide the right of employees to have at least 20 days paid leave annually, with some countries having a legal requirement of 25, 30 or more days. Australia and New Zealand mandate 20 paid leave days, while Canada and Japan provide ten days of paid vacation. The US is the only developed economy in the world that does not guarantee any paid leave or mandate holidays for workers. All wealthy countries in the rest of the world offer 5–13 paid public holidays per year.

It is evident that compensation laws differ extensively from country to country. Laws about minimum wages, overtime, separation, legal holidays and paid leave including maternity, vacation, illness and other types of accrued leave can be extremely different. French workers are eligible for vacation if employed in a firm any time of the year if they have a minimum of one month of actual work. In Greece, paid holiday is available to an employee with one year of continuous service in the same company. A parent can qualify for maternity allowance, after working 200 hours in the past two years. Part-time Irish employees can take 14 weeks maternity leave after 13 weeks of employment. Many countries protect their citizens from wage abuse by setting minimum wages for all host country nationals. For example, in the UAE, there is a £12,000 minimum contrasting with the Philippines where minimum wages are set depending on industry (slightly below $9/day); all require cost-of-living adjustments.

Across the EU, 12 million, or 9 per cent, of full-time employees typically work more than 48 hours per week, the maximum number of working hours before overtime is statutorily required. Overtime work is classified as either overtime that an employee agrees to work or overtime the company requires. About half of EU countries have the same rules but in the others, major differences among classifications are found. Ukraine and Tajikistan have the most restrictive overtime rules where employees cannot agree to work overtime unless there are exceptional circumstances. Other countries like Estonia, Georgia and Romania also require employee or union representative consent. Kazakhstan and Azerbaijan, however, have no limits on overtime.

In other countries, overtime rules may be set based not on weekly, but other time frames like daily, monthly or yearly. Poland and Slovakia set overtime as that which exceeds 400 hours per year while in Hungary, overtime is granted after 200 hours per year or 300 hours by collective bargaining. Other CIS states set limits such as a maximum of 120 overtime hours or per cent of hours worked, like 25 per cent in the Czech Republic and Slovakia up to 100 per cent in Latvia. Other countries, like Slovenia and Montenegro, determine overtime rules by collective agreements.

In EU countries, the maximum number of weekly overtime hours varies widely from two in Spain to 15 in the Netherlands. The required compensation premium for overtime hours differs across countries as well ranging from 25 per cent premium (France, Germany and Greece) to 50 per cent premium (Austria, Portugal and Denmark) up to 100 per cent in Finland for overtime work after the first two hours and 100 per cent in Belgium on holidays or weekends. (Source: Kuddo, 2009.)

Mandatory salary increases

Multinational organizations attempt to manage global employment costs, but this goal is often challenged by mandated salary increases in different countries. In North America, most countries including the US and Canada do not require employers to give salary increases. In South America, many countries mandate regular salary adjustments. Brazilian unions dictate mandatory salary increases and in Colombia salary increases are required for all employees earning a minimum wage. In the US, unions may negotiate provisions for salary increases in the labour contract but it is not required by the government.

Similarly, salary increases often are provided in collective labour agreements throughout Europe. Although salary increases are not mandated in Germany, Finland or Sweden, they are common in collective bargaining contracts. Turkey and Denmark require regular pay increases in unionized companies. In Greece, automatic increases were mandated after every three years of service, but the policy has been suspended by the Troica representing financial lenders to the country. Other European countries, including the United Kingdom and Poland, do not have mandated salary increases. Most Asian countries, including Thailand, Japan, Indonesia and India do not have mandatory salary increases. Malaysia, however, requires regular pay increases for unionized workers.

The challenge of managing the costs of a global workforce is dependent upon reconciling the company's reward strategy with many government regulations or local practices. When a company's reward strategy is at odds with host country practices, the MNC must think through how to position itself in the local market. Adapting to host country practices is what differentiates an MNC employer making it more attractive for securing the best local talent. (Source: http://shrm.org.)

4 International total rewards objectives for the MNC

Ensuring that total rewards policies are consistent with business strategies

One objective of MNCs is to ensure that IHRM compensation and benefits policies are consistent with business strategies. Many MNCs pursue a low-cost strategy and thereby create offshore facilities in countries (e.g. India, China, Mexico, etc.) where labour is less expensive than in the United States. As an example, US technology MNCs are attracted by low labour costs and high quality technical and professional employees working in India. MNCs also want to capitalize on the absence of labour unions by creating facilities in emerging markets. With union membership in many emerging nations declining, MNCs are attracted to those areas because they provide MNCs with critical information about restrictions on planned compensation and benefit programme modifications as well as potential liabilities (Fealy and Kompare, 2003). MNCs that pursue a differentiation strategy by offering unique products and/or services may create opportunities in countries by ensuring that their IHRM policies, programmes and practices are consistent with product attributes and brand names as well as the needs of local consumers. As an example, US MNCs are attracted by innovative and creative employees working in Finland, Ireland, Sweden and Switzerland due to their ability to develop new products. MNCs are also attracted to those areas because employees working there provide MNCs with ideas about how to create novel total reward systems that effectively motivate and reward employee success.

Developing total rewards policies that maximize recruiting and retention efforts

A second objective of MNCs when developing their international total rewards system is to ensure that compensation and benefits policies maximize recruitment and retention efforts. Most MNCs want to ensure that they assign the right people to international operations. Thus, when assigning employees to work in foreign nations, MNCs want employees who are sensitive to cultural norms (i.e. dress, standards of behaviour, consumption of alcohol). Furthermore, IHR managers also want to make sure that employees are open to non-traditional ways of approaching work-related problems. By guaranteeing that there is little employee turnover arising from cultural insensitivity and lack of openness, MNCs can address the needs of expatriates and take advantage of opportunities while doing business in foreign locations (cf. Birdseye and Hill, 1995).

When hiring within countries, the assumption is that what works in the home country may or may not apply. A much deeper appreciation of the values in the host country should become part of standard practice in design of compensation factors. Recruitment advertisements should be capable of attracting the 'right type' of employee and screening out those who are unlikely to be successful. The description of compensation in such ads should consider culture carefully if they are to have the desired impact. An example of cultural influences in recruitment was demonstrated in Mexico by García et al. (2010) who showed that detailed descriptions of benefits increased top applicants' pursuit of vacancies much more so than ads that offered generically described benefits, which tended to attract less desirable applicants.

Searching for talent in a global economy

Ancillary to the Towers Watson (2012) *Global Workforce Study*, the Global Talent 2021 project found that HR executives anticipate high future demand for *digital skills* – such as working on virtual teams and comfort with social media; *agile thinking* – the ability to deal with complexity, ambiguity and plan for multiple scenarios; *interpersonal skills* – teaming and collaborating; and *global operating ability* – including managing the diversity of people by cultural sensitivity in global markets. Preparing for this reality will require firms to cope with a realignment of the supply and demand for talent around the world, including ageing populations and low birth rates in developed economies, and vastly improving educational opportunities in developing economies. According to Global Talent 2021 (Towers Watson, 2012), 54 per cent of the world's college graduates come from Brazil, China, India, Indonesia, Mexico, Russia and Turkey, compared with 46 per cent from France, Germany, the UK, US and other industrialized countries that have traditionally been the source of highly skilled talent. This shift may require rethinking traditional Western styles and working arrangements that sometimes will not be appropriate for these cultures. Emerging economies like Brazil, India and Indonesia must balance becoming a source of talent for other countries while keeping talent at home to continue investing in education and development of the next generations of their young populations.

Developing cost-effective global total rewards policies

A third objective of MNCs when developing international total rewards is to ensure that compensation and benefits policies are cost effective. MNCs must ensure that employees receive incentives or premiums for foreign service, reimbursements for reasonable costs (e.g. relocation assistance or education reimbursement), and tax equalization when discrepancies exist.

Creating global total rewards policies that result in fair processes and outcomes

Another objective of organizations when developing international total rewards is to ensure that compensation and benefits policies result in fair processes and outcomes (cf. Chen et al., 2002). Most MNCs design programmes so that employees are treated with procedural fairness with regard to their overseas assignment, namely, 'the ability to voice one's views and arguments during a procedure' and 'the ability to influence the actual outcome itself' (Colquitt, 1999: 388). The consequences of fair processes are that employees are likely to have higher levels of job satisfaction and performance while on their overseas assignment and are likely to remain upon repatriation (cf. Colquitt et al., 2001).

Box 13.1   Stop and reflect

Dannon acquires ONA subdivision

Omnium Nord Africain (ONA) is the largest company in Africa, headquartered in Casablanca, Morocco, with divisions in energy, IT, agriculture, mining, telecommunications and real estate. Founded in 1919 as the Compagnie Générale de Transport et de Tourisme (CGTT) it became ONA in 1934. At that time, Morocco was a French Protectorate (until 1956) and access to Moroccan mines was coveted. In the late 1970s, ONA became nationalized and today it is owned by the Royal Family. King Mohammed VI wants the company to be the major regional force with ambitions for social development central to its mission. Many agreements still exist with French companies such as the one between its dairy products division, Centrale Laitière, and Danone (better known as Dannon outside of France). This contract required substantial cooperative production, marketing and sales activities between the two companies.

Some mandated restrictions on compensation exist in Morocco including: $9.60 per day in the industrialized sector and $6.30 per day for agricultural sector

(Continued)

(Continued)

minimum pay, time off for national and religious holidays and a working day and a half for each month of service vacation per year. The Caisse Nationale de Sécurité Sociale of Morocco now is encouraging companies to provide social security coverage for the many 'gray market' or off-book employees working in the country. Nevertheless, a tradition of weak HR practices and governmental regulation afflicts employment there. For example, highly autocratic Centrale Laitière gave bonuses to managers by dropping off an envelope or box of cash with no explanation for how it tied to performance. The company would buy cars or provide housing assistance for some managers with no explanation or policy, creating a sense of inequity and perceptions of corruption.

As of 2006, virtually no formal performance appraisal existed in the company. Compensation was well below market rates and there were no clear benefits offered. The most highly trained employees began leaving for jobs at better managed MNCs like Coca-Cola, Unilever and P&G operating in Morocco. In 2008, the company started to make compensation practices more transparent and get salaries to market rate using survey data from 'the salary explorer' research. The company began to urge more participative management practices, but this modern style was unfamiliar to both managers and employees.

In March 2013, ONA sold its dairy division, Centrale Laitière, to Danone of France. Danone had numerous marketing and R&D expatriates working in Morocco (primarily to ensure a high level of product freshness and non-contamination), but now needed to fortify its presence there with an assembly of managers and functional workers.

Danone is listed by L'Institut Great Place to Work®. Recently, sales in emerging markets became over half of their total sales. The firm uses what they call 'proximity management' to promote their CODE (Committed, Open, Doer, Empowerment). The company has strong prohibitions regarding use of child labour and discrimination, focusing on the values of diversity, freedom in collective bargaining, safety and employment of the disabled. Since 2008, the top 1000 executives receive variable remuneration based on three components. One third is based on how well the executive achieves societal goals by meeting targets related to protecting the environment and impacting social development by training and promoting employees to carry out these objectives. Another third is based on how well they meet specific management goals set for each manager and the final third is tied directly to how well the total company meets its global economic and financial targets for sales, margins and cash flow. They attract talent worldwide through benchmarked salaries with comparable companies. Danone has profit sharing and financial remuneration that encourages commitment to the company. While salary is locally benchmarked, they encourage international mobility of their employees and cover moving expenses.

Danone uses midyear and annual performance appraisal to define clear objectives. Danone provides extensive social protection (e.g. medical coverage and pensions) in accordance with local standards. Benefits vary by branch and from country to country. However, the Danone takeover of Centrale Laitière may require more than just opening a subsidiary in a new country.

Questions for discussion

1. To attract top host nationals and compete with the other MNCs in Morocco, how can Danone overcome the image of Centrale Laitière in Morocco as having low pay, undefined benefits, no clear pay-for-performance plan and use of whimsical perks?
2. How would you establish the company values through the compensation system offered locally in Morocco? Does Danone have exposure of their good name if they are not able to quickly turn the subsidiary into a 'great place to work' in Morocco?
3. What would you include in the package offered to the PCN Danone expatriates that must now be sent to Morocco? Would it differ from the package offered to those who have worked there for years?
4. How are the values of a company directly linked to its compensation practices, particularly regarding perceptions of companies operating in host countries?

5 Newer forms of international assignments

Commuter and virtual IAs

The length of an international assignment can vary drastically depending on the nature of the job and the proximity of the foreign assignment to the home country. Assignments that are expected to last for less than six weeks are known as commuter assignments. When expatriates are expected to travel back-and-forth during their short stay, these assignments are often treated like business travel. If this is the case, then MNCs will determine foreign living costs for short-term assignees (e.g. per-diem restaurant meals, local transportation, hotels, etc.) and then reimburse employees for their expenses as they would if they were travelling domestically.

The US State Department (www.state.gov) publishes a monthly schedule of foreign per-diem rates for nearly 1,100 foreign locations. Their table includes not only a per-diem rate for civilians travelling in foreign areas but also breaks down their rate by lodging, meals and incidentals. Similarly, the Australian Taxation Office (www.ato.gov.au) publishes a schedule of daily travel allowance expenses that vary according to salary levels and destinations. The Treasury Board of Canada Secretariat National Joint Council (www.tbs-sct.gc.ca) publishes a schedule of per-diem rates that includes meals and incidentals for individuals travelling abroad. Indeed, most countries publish allowable per-diem rates, which helps IHR managers make accurate travel allowances (for an extensive review of the IA literature, see Meyskens et al. (2009)). In some cases, the 'commuting' is done from home, as in a virtual assignment. The virtual IA is gaining in popularity and may significantly reduce costs. Employees on virtual IAs are occasionally referred to as 'armchair' travellers, since the individual does not leave his/her armchair in order to meet the demands of the virtual assignment. Short term virtual IAs are gaining popularity whenever quick technical decisions need to be made on any given assignment or consulting project.

6 Key components of global total rewards programmes

Base salary

Base pay is the building block of employees' compensation package both domestically and internationally, and it takes on new meaning when employees are working abroad. In a domestic setting, the term 'base salary' refers to the amount of pay (e.g. hourly pay or salary) that employees earn on a regular basis for performing their jobs. In turn, the base pay serves as a benchmark for other forms of discretionary compensation that employees may receive such as merit pay, bonuses and incentives. In contrast, for employees working abroad, base salary may be either the comparable pay that they would receive for performing the same job in their home country or the amount of pay that they would receive for performing the job in the host country. Adjustments are then made to expatriates' base salary for accepting a foreign assignment and stark discrepancies can occur in an employee's compensation package depending on whether the base pay is linked to the home or host country.

Levels of base pay vary depending on the MNC's headquarters location. The compensation mix for managerial employees working for MNCs headquartered in countries such as Australia, New Zealand, Austria, Finland and France is comprised of over 80 per cent base pay. By comparison, the compensation mix for managerial employees working for MNCs headquartered in India is less than 40 per cent base pay (Mercer Annual Total Remuneration Survey, 2014). Base salaries may also differ substantially between management and professional occupational categories of expatriates working for MNCs within the same country. Base pay for professional employees working for Italian MNCs exceeds 80 per cent while base pay for management employees is less than 70 per cent (Mercer Annual Total Remuneration Survey, 2014).

Foreign service inducements: foreign service premiums, mobility premiums, hardship premiums and danger pay

There are four types of foreign service inducements, each with a different goal. The first type, a foreign service premium, is given to expatriates to encourage them to accept assignments in other countries for more than one year. Service premiums vary depending on base pay, and typically range between 10 per cent and 30 per cent of base salary, disbursed incrementally as a reminder to employees of the reward they are receiving for the assignment. Short-term premiums differ among MNCs depending on where the MNC is headquartered. Nearly all MNCs headquartered in Brazil provide short-term premiums ranging between 8 per cent and 50 per cent of base pay for expatriates working at the professional and above levels.

Second, mobility premiums are lump-sum cash bonuses paid to employees for their willingness to move between two foreign posts. Twenty-six per cent of US MNCs pay mobility premiums to expatriates assigned to both short- and long-term assignments (Culpepper Compensation and Benefits Survey, 2008). In addition to mobility premiums, 25 per cent of US MNCs also provide expatriates with field allowances in order to cover the additional costs that they incur simply by travelling and working in numerous locations (Culpepper Compensation and Benefits Survey, 2008).

Third, hardship premiums are lump-sum cash bonuses paid to expatriates for adversities they may face. The US government pays hardship premiums to employees assigned to locations where living conditions are tough or unhealthy and/or physical hardships are excessive. Depending on the total hardship rating (based on a standard evaluation of environmental conditions), employees are paid differentials of 5 per cent to 35 per cent of base salary.

The fourth type of foreign service inducement is given to expatriates to compensate them for working in situations where they are exposed to either hazards or danger. Imminent danger pay is provided to members of the US uniformed services who work in foreign areas where there is a threat of physical harm due to civil disobedience, terrorism or wartime conditions. Depending on the level of danger exposure, employees are paid differentials of 5 per cent to 35 per cent of base salary, like hardship premiums discussed above. Currently, US uniformed service personnel are eligible to receive a $225 per month premium. In comparison to the premiums given to US uniformed and federal employees, only 21 per cent of private US MNCs provide hardship or danger pay premiums (Culpepper Compensation and Benefits Survey, 2008).

Cost-of-living allowance (COLA)

The most widely used discretionary allowance, COLA, is given to compensate expatriates for differences in expenditures between the home country and foreign country. COLAs are currently offered to expatriates by nearly 80 per cent of US MNCs. A city is considered high cost if the cost of living exceeds 108 per cent of the national average of non-housing costs and when local taxes are excessively high. Typically, employees are only eligible to receive COLAs when they are assigned to an area where the cost of living is higher than it would be in the city where their organization is headquartered in the United States. COLA rates are typically a percentage of base salary.

Goods and services allowance

Goods and service allowances are given to expatriates to compensate for differentials in the price of merchandise (e.g. grocery, devices, etc.) or activities (e.g. lessons, repair work, etc.). Illustrated in Table 13.1, the US Department of State publishes quarterly 'Indexes of Living Costs Abroad'. Their index compares costs of goods and services in Washington, DC, to similar goods and services in foreign locations. Table 13.1 contains six columns of pertinent information. The survey date column represents when the US Department of State received cost data. The exchange rate column represents a country's foreign currency units traded in exchange for US $1. The local relative column is a comparison of goods and service prices between the foreign country and Washington, DC. The local index column is a comparison of goods and services prices between the foreign country and Washington, DC, with price ratios weighted by the pattern of expenditures in the foreign country. The local index is most appropriate for US MNCs to establish cost-of-living allowances for US-based employees working abroad (www.state.gov).

Table 13.1   Index of Living Costs Abroad (Washington, DC = 100), January 2012

| Country and City | Survey Date | Exchange Rate | | Local Index | US Government Index |
		Foreign Unit	Number Per US$		
Australia: Canberra	07/29/2010	Austrian Dollar	1.17	135	130
Brazil: Rio de Janeiro	12/29/2009	Real	1.71	156	142
Canada: Toronto	01/18/2011	Canadian Dollar	0.97	157	148
China: Beijing	05/17/2010	Yuan	6.83	138	125
Cuba: Havana	04/30/2010	Chavitos	0.9260	146	128
Denmark: Copenhagen	03/30/2009	Kronor	5.62	190	160
Egypt: Cairo	03/13/2006	Egyptian Pound	5.73	96	83

Country and City	Survey Date	Exchange Rate		Local Index	US Government Index
		Foreign Unit	**Number Per US$**		
El Salvador: San Salvador	03/07/2011	U.S. Dollar	1.00	127	110
France: Paris	10/11/2009	Euro	0.68	201	176
Germany: Munich	01/10/2010	Euro	0.68	174	149
Greece: Athens	12/14/2010	Euro	0.67	158	140
Haiti: Port-au-Prince	12/13/2010	Gourde	38.5	150	127
Hong Kong: Hong Kong	04/26/2011	HK Dollar	7.78	151	137
India: New Delhi	12/01/2010	Indian Rupee	44.1	129	116
Israel: Tel Aviv	06/08/2010	Shekel	3.85	146	128
Italy: Milan	03/31/2011	Euro	0.70	181	158
Jamaica: Kingston	01/21/2011	Jamaican Dollar	85.8	123	115
Japan: Tokyo City	05/12/2011	Yen	80	213	173
Korea: Seoul	02/16/2010	Won	1110	140	112
Mexico: Mexico City, DF	03/06/2009	Mexican Peso	14.3	99	93
New Zealand: Wellington	09/27/2010	NZ Dollar	1.25	159	144
Nigeria: Lagos	03/09/2009	Naira	148	152	127
Norway: Oslo	01/26/2009	Kronor (Norway)	6.96	176	155
Pakistan: Islamabad	12/10/2004	Pakistani Rupee	59.5	102	98
Philippines: Manila	05/04/2010	Philippines Peso	44.5	108	104
Poland: Warsaw	09/17/2009	New Zloty	2.91	130	121
Russia: Moscow	05/08/2011	Ruble (Russia)	27.7	206	166
Saudi Arabia: Riyadh	04/09/2010	Saudi Riyal	3.75	122	114
Singapore: Singapore	03/16/2011	Singapore Dollar	1.24	152	136
S. Africa: Johannesburg	09/30/2010	Rand	7.11	143	133
Spain: Madrid	04/11/2010	Euro	0.72	160	146
Sweden: Stockholm	05/13/2010	Kronor (Sweden)	7.26	185	169
Switzerland: Geneva	11/15/2010	Swiss Franc	0.99	217	185
Thailand: Bangkok	02/26/2008	Baht	32.6	126	114
Turkey: Istanbul	04/11/2011	New Lira	1.78	135	117
United Kingdom: London	03/27/2011	Pound Sterling	0.5976	178	158
Venezuela: Caracas	09/23/2010	Bolivar Fuerte	2.60	180	152
Vietnam: Hanoi	05/05/2008	Viet man Dông	16613	113	109

Source: US Department of State (2012). The Department of State Indexes of Living Costs Abroad. Washington, DC: US Government Printing Office (online). Available: www.state.gov

Exchange rate protection programmes

Thirty-nine per cent of US MNCs offer expatriates exchange rate protection programmes (Culpepper Salary Budget and Compensation Planning Survey, 2013). These increasingly popular programmes are due to the volatility of the US dollar against other currencies. It is important to note that a company can gain or lose from exchange rates, depending on when the contract was signed. Compensation can be complicated for outsourced or offshore employment due to changes in exchange rates in contract renegotiation.

Housing and utilities allowance

Sixty-two per cent of US MNCs provide housing and utilities allowances to expatriates to compensate for differentials in the cost of lodging, electricity, gas, fuel, water, garages, furniture, taxes and insurance premiums required by local law in the foreign country. Housing allowances are designed so that employees will be able to maintain their home country living standards. These costs may be fixed or variable and are paid on an incremental basis. Fifty-two per cent of MNCs headquartered in the US also provide free housing (Mercer Annual Total Remuneration Survey, 2014).

Home leave allowance

Home leave allowances cover employees' expenses for making return trips to their home country. This paid time-off assists employees with maintaining both family and business ties so that they will have fewer adjustment problems during the repatriation process. Most MNCs restrict home leave allowances to trips home; however, some firms also give expatriates the opportunity for foreign travel.

Rest, relaxation and rehabilitation leave and allowance

Many expatriates who work in designated hardship or danger areas receive rest, relaxation and rehabilitation leave and allowance benefits. These allowances represents paid time off given beyond vacation time because progressive employers understand that expatriates may need a break from unpleasant and/or dangerous working conditions to re-energize. For instance, service members and US Defense Department civilians on 12-month orders in countries with dangerous working conditions are entitled to a recuperation leave programme that allows up to 15 days, excluding travel time, to visit family or friends in the United States or Europe (Banusiewicz, 2003).

Education allowance for expatriate's children

Sixty-eight per cent of US MNCs extend education allowances to expatriates to cover schooling costs associated with placing their children in private schools designed for English speaking students. Since the cost of tuition in foreign countries is often much more expensive than tuition for private schools in the US, expatriates are reimbursed rather than given a percentage of their base salary.

Relocation allowance

Relocation allowances are given to expatriates for costs associated with moving. One category of relocation expenses includes actual moving transportation charges, shipping, storage and packaging charges associated with moving household goods to the foreign location. A second category includes reimbursement for temporary living costs while looking for permanent housing. Many organizations also reimburse expatriates for temporary housing prior to departure to the foreign post when the expatriate's house has been rented or sold. Furthermore, many MNCs also reimburse the purchase of household appliances in the foreign location since many expatriates may have left those items behind. A third category includes reimbursement for travel to the foreign post for employees and their families. These reimbursements typically cover costs associated with relocating automobiles to the foreign post, or the purchase of a new vehicle. Ninety-two per cent of US MNCs offer relocation allowances (Culpepper Salary Budget and Compensation Planning Survey, 2013).

Spouse/family allowance

Increasingly, many organizations provide spousal assistance to help defray the income lost by a spouse as a result of relocating abroad. Some MNCs may also provide marriage allowances to blue-collar workers while working abroad in countries such as Turkey (Mercer Annual Total Remuneration Survey, 2014).

Benefits

International benefits programmes often present complexities above-and-beyond those associated with international compensation. Pension plans and saving and investment plans are difficult to manage between countries due to variations in national rules and regulations. There is also very little portability of retirement plans and health insurance programmes. Furthermore, required benefits arising from national labour or employment legislation such as workers' compensation plans have no applicability in foreign environments. Social security programmes and medical leave exist in many countries, however, those programmes are not simple replications of schemes in the home country. Accordingly, MNCs must address important questions when designing foreign benefits programmes such as: (a) Considering tax deductions, should an expatriate's home country benefit programmes be maintained? (b) Should the firm enrol expatriates in the host country benefits programme? (c) Should expatriates be given home country or host country social security benefits? The tax implications will be considered later in this chapter.

Benefit levels vary extensively depending on the MNC's headquarters location. Generally, benefits comprise less than 20 per cent of expatriates' compensation mix. However, the compensation mix for professional employees working for MNCs headquartered in Venezuela is comprised of over 40 per cent benefits. By comparison, the compensation mix for professional employees working for MNCs headquartered in Finland is comprised of only 2–3 per cent benefits (Mercer Annual Total Remuneration Survey, 2014). Benefits may also differ substantially between management- and professional-level expatriates working for MNCs within the same country. As previously mentioned, benefits for professional-level employees working for MNCs headquartered in Venezuela exceed 40 per cent; however, the benefits for management-level employees working for MNCs headquartered in Venezuela is only 23–24 per cent (Mercer Annual Total Remuneration Survey, 2014).

Protection programmes

In the US, the Social Security Act of 1935, the Family Medical Leave Act of 1993, and state worker's compensation programmes direct MNCs to provide expatriates and their families with standard benefits. Despite their foreign assignments, if expatriates are US citizens they are able to continue to participate in the US Social Security Programs (retirement, survivor and disability insurance; supplemental security income; and Medicare) as long as they are eligible. US Treasury Department regulations do not allow payments to eligible US Citizens residing in Cuba or North Korea.

Paid time off

Similar to employees working domestically, expatriates are eligible to receive time off for annual vacations, holidays and emergency leave. Expatriates typically do not receive extended periods of annual vacation relative to their domestic counterparts. However, US MNCs must comply with foreign laws regarding the amount of time that employees are given for vacation. Thus, as shown in Table 13.2, in many European countries (e.g. Austria, Denmark, France and Spain) where employees receive as many as 30-days minimum annual leave by law, US expatriates are also required to receive the same minimum number of annual vacation days even though the US has no legal minimum annual vacation days. Many countries also have laws governing vacation bonuses. For instance, MNCs headquartered in Brazil are required to pay a vacation bonus equivalent to one-third of the expatriate's monthly wage at the time of vacation. Expatriates receive paid time off for local and national holidays that are observed in their geographic work assignment. Also US expatriates are given time off for nationally

Table 13.2 Vacation and holiday days

Country	Minimum paid vacation days	Paid public holidays	Total
Brazil	30	11	41
Lithuania	28	13	41
Finland	30	10	40
France	30	10	40
Russia	28	12	40
Austria	25	13	38
Greece	25	12	37
Japan	20	16	36
Spain	22	14	36
Sweden	25	11	36
United Kingdom	28	8	36
Norway	25	10	35
Portugal	22	13	35
Denmark	25	9	34
South Korea	19	15	34
South Africa	21	12	33
Czech Republic	20	12	32
Italy	20	11	31
New Zealand	20	11	31
Belgium	20	10	30
Germany	20	10	30
Romania	21	9	30
Ireland	20	9	29
Switzerland	20	9	29
Australia	20	8	28
India	12	16	28
Netherlands	20	8	28
Taiwan	15	13	28
Hong Kong	14	12	26
Singapore	14	11	25
United States*	15	10	25
China	10	11	21

Source: CNN at www.cnn.com/2011/WORLD/asiapcf/07/29/country.comparisons.vacation/index.html

*The US has no minimum number of annual vacation days required by law.

observed US holidays. Expatriates may also receive time off for family emergencies such as those involving critical illnesses and/or deaths of family members. When these events occur, MNCs provide expatriates with either paid time off emergency leave or an unpaid leave of absence.

Pension contributions

The US Employee Retirement Income Security Act of 1974 (ERISA) protects the integrity of pensions for expatriates. Despite their foreign assignments, US expatriates are allowed to continue to participate in their company's pension plan as long as they are eligible.

Other benefits

Increasingly US MNCs offer additional perquisites to expatriates to accommodate them during their overseas assignments including: (a) making contributions to savings and investments plans and equity portions of mortgage payments, and (b) paying insurance premiums, alimony, child support, student loans and car subsidies particularly in hardship and danger situations. In some countries, such as Brazil, Norway and Israel, MNCs are mandated by the government to provide transportation allowances. Company cars are also common perquisites in Brazil (Mercer Annual Total Remuneration Survey, 2014). Other perquisites such as allowances for meals, clothing, club memberships, domestic help, medical, telecommunications and security are provided on a case-by-case basis.

Vast benefit differences across the globe

Martocchio and Pandey (2008) described high variability worldwide in paid time off and protection benefits. Paid time off in Japan, for example, allows for ten days after six months of consecutive service, and one additional day for each year thereafter up to a maximum of 20 days. An interesting difference is that menstruation leave is available to females when they find attendance at work difficult. In the UK, workers are entitled to four weeks paid annual leave, including public holidays and employees are entitled to 28 weeks of statutory sick pay in any three-year period. In the UK, free medical services for residents are provided by hospitals, doctors and dentists under contract with the National Health Service. The Netherlands provides national medical coverage for workers earning less than $60,000 a year. Those who make more must have private insurance, paid either by the individual or by the company. Germany has over 20 diversified Health Care Benefits Organizations (known as HMOs) to serve the population. China has a unified medical insurance system in which employers contribute 6 per cent of the payroll while employees contribute 2 per cent of salary. In

Mexico, medical services are mandated for patients through the Mexican Social Security Institute. Clearly, as indicated in just these three countries, vast differences exist in healthcare and paid leave benefits. Far more paid leave is available in some countries like Spain and employer healthcare costs are considerably higher in some countries like the US. The Towers Watson (2012) *Global Workforce Study* surveyed workers across 29 countries and found that 65 per cent of the 32,000 full-time workers studied were not highly engaged in their jobs. Other key findings from the survey included:

- stress and anxiety about the future are common
- security is taking precedence over almost everything
- attracting employees is almost entirely about security
- retaining employees has more to do with the quality of the work experience overall.

Uncertainty about retirement prospects has led to growing desire among employees worldwide for greater security in their reward package. Fuelled by financial crises and market volatility, it appears that employees have come to value the attributes of something equivalent to a defined benefit plan. At the same time, many organizations are switching to risk amelioration strategies that meet their long-term pension obligations. The answer to the dilemma is to give employees a sense of long-term security through account-based approaches that will be solely or largely under employees' direct control.

7 Approaches to international compensation

The going-rate approach

The going-rate approach is based upon typical market values found in the foreign country. To establish the expatriates' base salary and benefits, MNCs gather compensation information from local sources in the foreign environment to determine the best method of benchmarking. Typically, the MNC supplements both pay and benefits if the foreign location is considered a low pay country.

One simple but clever method of determining pay adjustments for expatriate assignments is the 'Big Mac Adjustment'. Basically the cost of a McDonald's Big Mac sandwich is used as an adjusting factor around the world; it serves as a common measure of cost-of-living differentials, corrects for fluctuations unavailable in last year's reports and is incredibly accessible. Table 13.3 shows current values of the Big Mac Factor.

Advantages and disadvantages

An advantage of MNCs using the going-rate approach is that it is easy to understand. It is also commonly used because of the perceived equality that exists between

Table 13.3   Big Mac Index, 2014

Country	Big Mac Prices in Dollars	Under/Over valuation against the dollar, %
United States	4.2	0
Argentina	4.64	10
Australia	4.94	18
Brazil	5.68	35
Britain	3.82	−9
Canada	4.63	10
Chile	4.05	−3
China	2.44	−42
Colombia	4.54	8
Costa Rica	4.02	−4
Czech Republic	3.45	−18
Denmark	5.37	28
Egypt	2.57	−39
Euro Area	4.43	6
Hong Kong	2.12	−49
Hungary	2.63	−37
India	1.62	−61
Indonesia	2.46	−41
Israel	4.13	−2
Japan	4.16	−1
Latvia	3.00	−29
Lithuania	2.87	−32
Malaysia	2.34	−44
Mexico	2.70	−36
New Zealand	4.05	−4
Norway	6.79	62
Pakistan	2.89	−31
Peru	3.71	−12
Philippines	2.68	−36
Poland	2.58	−38
Russia	2.55	−39
Saudi Arabia	2.67	−36
Singapore	3.75	−11
South Africa	2.45	−42
South Korea	3.19	−24
Sri Lanka	2.55	−39

Country	Big Mac Prices in Dollars	Under/Over valuation against the dollar, %
Sweden	5.91	41
Switzerland	6.81	62
Taiwan	2.5	−40
Thailand	2.46	−41
Turkey	3.54	−16
United Arab Emirates	3.27	−22
Ukraine	2.11	−50
Uruguay	4.63	10

Source: The Big Mac Index (2014)

expatriates and local nationals. One disadvantage has to do with variations that may exist in compensation when an expatriate moves between assignments in different countries. Expatriates' pay can fluctuate considerably due to disparities in pay between low- to high-pay countries. Such variations can also occur when an expatriate moves between assignments within a country.

Balance sheet approach

The home country-based balance sheet approach is the most common and widely used approach and is based upon typical market values found in the home country. It ensures that expatriates are able to preserve the standard of living that they experience in their home country and prevents them from experiencing important losses due to their foreign assignment. Once baseline pay and benefits are established, adjustments are then made to balance additional expenses that expatriates face in the foreign country. The home country-based balance sheet approach is designed to cover four categories of expenses that are met by MNCs and expatriates in locations where costs exceed equivalent costs in the parent country. First, MNCs share costs associated with goods and services, namely expenditures associated with food, personal care, clothing, household furnishings, recreation, transportation and medical care in the foreign location. Second, MNCs share costs associated with housing in the foreign location. Third, MNCs share costs associated with income taxes in both the expatriates' home and host country. Fourth, MNCs provide what are known as reserves to expatriates in the form of investments, savings and/or pension contributions, payments for benefits, education expenses and taxes.

Advantages and disadvantages

There are four advantages to MNCs of using the home country-based balance sheet approach. First, it creates perceptions of equity regarding foreign assignments for employees faced with choosing among locations. Second, it creates perceptions of equity between parent country nationals since those working at or near headquarters and those on foreign assignments are compensated equally. Third, this approach facilitates re-entry for expatriates. Repatriation is less arduous because employees' standard of living during their foreign assignment is not compromised under the home country-based balance sheet approach. Fourth, this system of pay and benefits is easy to communicate to employees.

While there are advantages to the home country-based balance sheet approach, it also has disadvantages. Specifically, the home country-based balance sheet approach may create feelings of disparity if expatriates discover that local nationals receive significantly more pay for performing the same job. For instance, in the Hong Kong regional office of a US MNC, a US-based expatriate and a Beijing third country national performing the same job duties may have huge disparities in salary. Home country-based balance sheets may create problems when intellectual property issues or discovery of new processes through R&D are involved (Trommetter, 2010). One Motorola employee in Beijing saved the company millions of dollars through his ideas but was well aware that his compensation was less than one quarter of his US counterpart. Lastly, the home country-based balance sheet approach may present MNCs with difficulties in helping expatriates cover goods and services, namely those regarding tax deductions and pension contributions.

8 Repatriation issues

Perhaps the biggest obstacle that expatriates face is readjusting to work once their overseas assignment has ended. Even when MNCs expend an enormous amount of effort to meet the compensation and benefits needs of expatriates on assignment, they must also apply the same amount of energy to ensure that expatriates' concerns are met once they return to their home country. Foremost, the expatriate needs to have a job to come home to. As companies are often unprepared to keep 'lines' open while the expatriate is away, there must be some equivalent position for the expatriate once he or she returns, particularly after a long-term assignment abroad. It is surprising how many MNCs do not plan the repatriation process. Typically, the MNC and the expatriate should start planning at least six months prior to re-entry, and IHR needs to monitor this closely, in terms of utilizing knowledge gained by the expatriate. Accordingly, IHR managers must ensure that repatriates are satisfied with their base salaries when they return. Specifically, upon return, repatriates might develop negative attitudes towards their MNC if they compare their work inputs and resulting outputs to the work inputs and resulting outputs of co-workers.

9 International trends in global total rewards

Global convergence of values

As the number of workers employed in countries other than their own increases, and as MNC management practices become more globally dispersed, there will be an inevitable blending of cultural values. There is clear evidence that management practices and employee values may be converging across the globe (Ohmae, 1990; Sparrow and Hiltrop, 1995). The potent pull of 'competitive isomorphism' compels firms to utilize best practices of other firms operating in this globally competitive environment (Fenton-O'Creevy et al., 2008). Theoretically, convergent management practices can be transported across the planet.

There appears to be increasing agreement among employees in different countries about the criteria that *should be* used to determine rewards. Individual performance, skills and job responsibility consistently rank as highly important. However, there are non-cultural factors that create reward preference variability from country to country. For example, preference for job security, common in Canada and Finland, may be the result of situational factors, such as massive layoffs, downsizing and increased use of technology to replace labour in these countries' banking industries as well as general recessions or psychological effects of an economic crisis. Preference for performance rewards and criteria may also be due to non-culture related influences, such as the nature of the company (profit-oriented, competitive) or its goals (efficiency, productivity). Beyond culture, numerous other potential forces may impact reward preferences. Short-term rewards – cash bonuses or commission-based pay – generally maximize performance objectives for about a year. Long-term rewards – stock options or a long-term incremented salary – are intended to target specified strategic goals and provide employees with incentives showing how their work benefits the company in the long term.

Revising the total rewards mindset

Nazir et al. (2012) questioned the 'total rewards' concept as merely representing a renaming of traditional compensation/benefit packages. They explain that expatriate and host nationals working in China, for example, are offered what amounts to traditional packages that do not have any extras unless the firm uses a mix of both localized and traditional home country cafeteria style compensation options. Considerations for matters such as educational allowances, childcare, domestic help, transportation and housing costs, and non-financial rewards are highly localized and often are not considered in designing compensation packages. Expatriates in some countries like Haiti, Mexico or Iraq may require special security measures where protection costs can easily exceed $50K per year.

WorldatWork (2010) issued a report that identifies five elements of rewards to attract, motivate and retain talented employees:

- Compensation – salary, premium or on-call pay, incentives like commission and bonus, team incentives, stock and profit sharing
- Benefits – healthcare, insurance, retirement, pay for time not worked
- Work–life – flexible arrangements, leave allowances, wellness services, community involvement opportunities, dependent care services, financial planning services, perks like expense accounts, culture-change initiatives
- Performance recognition – development opportunities, recognition, goal setting sessions
- Career opportunities – learning and training, education funding, coaching and mentoring, advancement opportunities
- Other – relocation assistance, prestige of firm, travel allowances to visit family.

What is missing from this list is perhaps one of the most important rewards that any job can offer: enjoyment of the work itself. Opportunities to accomplish things, impact the firm or society, learn from and collaborate with experienced co-workers, have autonomy to make a change in how things are done, the chance to develop and use one's skill-set, and the power to create or fulfil one's personal vision are arguably the most important characteristics of any job, yet they are not included in the list described above as total rewards elements. These opportunities clearly attract, motivate and retain talented employees. It could be expected that characteristics of the work itself are the most important ones for expatriates and host country nationals, particularly as part of the compensation package for jobs in emerging markets.

When executives in the parent country make decisions about compensation packages without regard for those factors, they have made the first great mistake among many to follow. They would likely be better off to allow the expatriate to live in the host country for a while, gaining localized knowledge, before finalizing the compensation options. The new concept of total rewards should take into account many local parameters in the host country, as well as non-financial rewards, with options far beyond what traditional packages have included.

10 Summary and conclusions

We have explored the complex area of rewards for designing pay systems, which in MNCs must encompass the circumstances of expatriates from diverse countries as well as employees in all of the different host country subsidiaries. We have argued for a comprehensive approach which acknowledges the diversity of economic and cultural contexts, and attends to both the design and implementation of total rewards policies.

In conclusion, these global and local incentives are central to IHRM in MNCs. Total rewards systems have the potential to motivate employees so that they will sustain high levels of performance and achieve their organizations' strategic goals.

Recommendations for total rewards practice

1. Develop a deep understanding of how the combination of culture, geographical distance, time zones, pricing, legal systems and language produces complex challenges for compensation management.
2. Recognize that employees in different cultures are motivated by different rewards.
3. Create packages that have options with both company-wide and localized compensation/benefits for host country nationals.
4. Recognize that implementing a global incentive programme includes characteristics such as consistency, compatible programme messaging, accurate translation across languages, a common centralized administrative platform, ready access to information about rewards and careful global analysis.
5. Success in emerging markets requires motivated employees as well as performance-driven strategies to strengthen customer loyalty and grow new business: costs of the programme should always balance the costs and potential benefits of expatriates, outsourcing, offshoring or other types of new market entry.
6. Pay scales and benefits need to be benchmarked: both regional and local labour market data must be compiled regularly.
7. Focus on the attributes of non-financial rewards as having equal or greater importance than financial elements of the package in attracting, motivating and retaining highly talented employees. Major changes are occurring worldwide in how and where to find, attract and retain talented employees.

Discussion questions

1. How do cultural differences affect compensation of expatriates, HCNs or TCNs when employees are hired in host countries? What are the most important things to consider in creating a compensation package for workers abroad?
2. Imagine an Australian MNC having to staff one of its subsidiaries in India. What staffing approach would you chose? What factors would you consider in designing a compensation plan?
3. Stark discrepancies can occur in an employees' compensation package depending on whether employees' base pay is linked to their home or host country. How can MNCs ensure that these differences are justifiable?

CASE STUDY

Zurich Santander Insurance America

Banco Santander Grupo is a Spanish firm with worldwide operations. Santander currently has 102 million customers worldwide in ten primary markets. Five of these primary markets are in the emerging economies of Brazil, Mexico, Chile, Argentina and Poland accounting for 54 per cent of Santander profits. The remaining 46 per cent of profits are generated in five industrialized countries: Spain, the UK, Portugal, Germany and the US. While its UK offices continue to be highly profitable, operations in Spain have not been so lucrative primarily due to problematic real estate investments. Headlines are common about shareholder revolts, bailouts or customer complaints. Santander UK is investing in major projects to reshape its reward programmes. Elliot Rees-Davies, head of reward at Santander, stated: 'Santander is trying to make a name for itself. So our focus is around culture and becoming the best bank to work for, the best bank for our customers and the best bank for our shareholders. That is the strategy we are building.' Reward and benefits are key to establishing the organization's culture and values. The reward team has therefore had to consider some fundamental questions. Tim Robertson, senior reward manager, says: 'The biggest challenge has been to define what being the best bank means. It is a very easy phrase to throw around, but the challenge for us, as it comes back to the reward strategy, is what does that mean and what does that look like?'

Santander launched two major reward projects, both of which were different from previous strategies. One was intended to bring a fundamental cultural change for both employees and managers, through implementing a simplified pay and job families structure. The bank's acquisitions had created 45 different job families and 1,200 pay ranges. The new plan was to reduce this to just 12 job families. Robertson explained the intent as geared to reposition how employees fit within the organization down to a very simple and clear approach, so any employee in any part of the organization could see how they fit.

The plan consisted of:

1. *Identify career paths*: intended to make it easy to identify potential career paths and to manage talent better. Managers would have a major decision authority in identifying where employees fit in terms of job role and pay level. The new pay requires managers to re-think the distribution of their employees in simpler salary ranges, and discuss alternative career directions and options. The reward

    team would work with managers to provide guidance and challenge them on their decisions.

2. *HR portal launch*: Santander's other new reward initiative was the launch of an HR portal as part of a new HR communication system. The portal, provided by Grass Roots, included a flexible benefits scheme to bring the bank's benefits package into line with those of competitors.

Stephen Gambles, senior reward manager, says: 'We see many of them have fairly established flexible benefits schemes. When we have a stated ambition of being the best bank to work for, we need to at least match them as a starting point. We are not kidding ourselves that this is the end of the road and that we've done everything we need to do. "This is getting us to the starting line" is a phrase we have used quite regularly.'

Having set out to implement flex, the project evolved quickly, says Gambles: 'We took it away from just being about flexible benefits and we started talking about our employee value proposition.'

The portal would include all parts of HR, from career development and performance management to reward, benefits and employee health and well-being. It was branded with its global employer brand, Santander Is You, and content is divided across four sections: Welcoming You, Developing You, Supporting You and Rewarding You. Rees-Davies says: 'We have tried to put ourselves in the shoes of the employee and are trying to make things as easy and accessible as possible.'

The flex scheme is a significant shift from Santander's previous benefits, a traditional-style package that offered employees little choice. Through flex, staff can access almost three times the previous number of benefits, which Santander funded by levelling their coverage of existing benefits and by salary sacrifice arrangements. 'We are not going down the classic route of providing a separate flex pot funding because we match the market on a total compensation basis, so we have kind of already accounted for it', says Gambles.

HR portal launch

The HR portal was launched in phases, but in quick succession to maintain momentum. Employee feedback post-launch would also help to shape the scheme. Gambles adds: 'I expect there to be extremes [of responses]. There will be some people who absolutely hate it because it really challenges their perspective and their view of

(Continued)

(Continued)

how things are done here. There will also be some people who love it. My hope is that category B outranks category A.' Santander's reward team is already looking to the future. For example, Rees-Davies says: 'We are trying to get into a space where we proactively manage talent, proactively look at people's careers and then look at them themselves, so we get those talent moves for the sake of the business and the sake of the individual.' But, ultimately, ensuring the bank's reward strategy supports employee performance is key.

Benefits offered under new plan

Pension

Defined contribution scheme with service-related contributions. In the first year of employment, if an employee contributes 8 per cent, the organization will contribute a maximum of 10 per cent. Employer contributions increase by 0.5 per cent with each year's service to a maximum of 12.5 per cent after five years.

Healthcare

Private medical insurance available through flex.
Dental cover available through flex.
Health cash plan available through flex.
Health assessments.

Group risk benefits

Life assurance available through flex.
Critical illness insurance available through flex.

Share schemes

Three- and five-year sharesave schemes.
Share incentive plan (Sip) offering partnership shares.

Holiday

Entitlement based on employee grades.
Maximum of 30 days available for senior managers or directors.
Staff can buy or sell up to five days a year.

Voluntary benefits

Bikes for work.

Childcare vouchers.

Home computers.

Employee discounts.

Charity lottery.

Payroll-giving scheme.

Santander UK delivered a strong performance in 2012, and they decided to commensurately reward employees. Their clever discounted bicycles for employees to ride to work programme and the automobile allowances programme won awards for innovative benefits ideas. Happy employees contributed to their progress on goals to improve customer service.

Merger with Zurich Financial Services Group

To offset some of its losses and costs, Santander sold off the majority of its Latin American insurance operations to the second largest European insurance company, Zurich Financial Services Group. On 22 February 2011 they announced that Zurich plans to buy a majority stake in the insurance operations of Banco Santander in Latin America for $1.67 billion.

Under the executed memorandum of understanding, Santander's insurance operations became part of a newly established holding company, Zurich Santander Insurance America, based in Madrid. Zurich owns 51 per cent of the new entity, while Santander owns the remaining 49 per cent with a 25-year strategic distribution agreement with Santander. Zurich expects the deal will make it the #4 insurer in Latin America by giving it access to insurance operations in Brazil, Mexico, Chile, Argentina and Uruguay.

Zurich Financial Services Group is a financial services provider offering primarily general corporate, life and property-and-casualty insurance. Founded in 1872, Zurich's global corporate unit focuses on risk management for large international and domestic clients with operations focused in Latin America, Asia/Pacific, China, South Africa and other emerging markets. The North America commercial division provides services including personal auto, homeowners, life and small-business insurance. Now it is shifting to opportunities in emerging markets and untapped niches in Europe and the US. Zurich Insurance sees rapidly expanding economies in Asia

(Continued)

(Continued)

and Latin America as potential growth areas. Among BRIC emerging markets, Brazil has one of the largest developing economies in the world, and with over 200 million people, has the fifth largest population on earth. As these countries get richer and more people make enough money to afford cars, big-ticket household items and even luxury goods, demand for insurance to protect this wealth is also rising.

Zurich Insurance has a reputation of being dull. For an insurance company, however, that's not a bad reputation. The company operates by a policy of 'what gets measured, gets done', by setting specific numerical targets for all managers and asking for monthly progress reports to make sure the company's strategy is being implemented. Martin Senn, a 55-year-old Swiss, took the reins at the beginning of 2010 with a disciplined approach to growth through acquisitions. Mr Senn explained that landing a deal is one thing, executing it another. Many deals have failed because management proved unable to integrate two different corporate cultures. When Western companies attempt to grow in emerging markets they often operate in societies with very different values. 'The cultural aspect is the most difficult one to get good judgement on, and it often can be a deal-breaker', he says. Once the deal has been signed, it is important to integrate the acquired company quickly and local staff must be involved from the beginning. For Zurich, which has been present in Latin America for more than 50 years, finding local expertise is usually not a big problem, he says. Mr Senn concedes that the integration of Santander's insurance operations has presented a particular challenge, because they span several countries, each with its own accounting standards and regulations.

While emerging markets are important for future growth, so too are established markets. Mr Senn points out, 'The balance is very important'. To attract recent graduates, they try to attract people to their training programmes including education subsidies, chance to work in a dynamic, challenging environment, and rewards for creativity, initiative and contributions. Their rather stolid package is based on large insurance discounts for employees to buy policies issued by the company.

Case study questions

1. Do you think that the new HR portal at Santander will be seen as attractive to prospective talent (HCNs and TCNs) in all areas where the company operates?
2. Do you anticipate any problems in the new company, Zurich Santander Insurance America, with joining two cultures with a very different approach to employee rewards and talent attraction?

3. Will the new company have difficulties in that it is being managed by Zurich employees yet headquartered in Spain? How should the differences in how compensation and benefits are viewed by the two companies be managed?
4. How might the merger change the perspective of those employees coming over from Santander? How about the ones coming over from Zurich?
5. Should the new company design its own compensation and benefits system or fall in line with one of the two merged firms? Should compensation be equal across the different cultures in all the Latin American countries? What special considerations should be given for compensation in Brazil?

Sources: www.globalsurance.com/blog/date/2011/02 and www.employeebenefits. co.uk/resource-centre/case-studies/santander-reshapes-reward-in-quest-to-be-the-best/100385.article.

Further reading

- Warneke, D. and Schneider, M. (2011) 'Expatriate compensation packages: what do employees prefer?' *Cross Cultural Management: An International Journal*, 18(2): 236–256.
  This article examines the connection between international strategy and strategic design of expatriates' salaries.

- Lowe, K.B., Milliman, J., De Cieri, H. and Dowling, P.J. (2002) 'International compensation practices: a ten-country comparative analysis', *Human Resource Management*, 41(1): 45–66.
  This article focuses on how local employees in ten countries perceived disparity between how compensation is and how it should be in their home country.

- Herod, R. (2009) *Expatriate Compensation: The Balance Sheet Approach*, Global HR Management Series. Alexandria: Society for Human Resource Management (SHRM).
  This book discusses the most important issues involved in developing a total rewards system for international expatriates, with an emphasis on the differences in the cost of goods and services, housing and income taxes in international assignments. The book examines the compensation challenges faced by businesses expanding globally by describing the basic components of expatriate compensation and providing examples of strategies.

- Meyskens, M., Von Glinow, M.A., Werther, W. and Clarke, L. (2009) 'The paradox of international talent: alternative forms of international assignments', *International Journal of Human Resource Management*, 20(6): 1439–1450.

This article examines the different forms of international assignments, and how sourcing talent is often contingent on the length of assignment abroad.

- Paik, Y., Parboteeah, K.P. and Shim, W. (2007) 'The relationship between perceived compensation, organizational commitment and job satisfaction: the case of Mexican workers in the Korean Maquiladoras', *International Journal of Human Resource Management*, 18(10): 1768–1781.

  This article uses equity theory to examine the effects of perception gaps in compensation between host country nationals and expatriates on organizational commitment and its impact on job satisfaction and job performance.

- Tornikoski, C. (2011) 'Fostering expatriate affective commitment: a total reward perspective', *Cross Cultural Management: An International Journal*, 18(2): 214–235.

  This article examines the sources of company loyalty relative to issues of taxation, availability of information about local cost levels, standard of living, currency rate risks, social security and pension issues, and spouse-related issues among expatriates.

- Wentland, D.M. (2003) 'A new practical guide for determining expatriate compensation: the comprehensive model', *Compensation & Benefits Review*, 35(3): 45–50.

  This article discusses a model of expatriate compensation that incorporates and combines an expatriate selection process with a detailed foreign assignment evaluation and then links that situational analysis with a specific compensation package. The article also describes the recommended compensation approaches for each situational analysis.

Internet resources

- www.worldsalaries.org. International Average Salary Income Database is an online provider of an international comparison of average salary for various professions and an international comparison of average personal income and expenditure.
- http://data.worldbank.org/indicator/SI.POV.GINI. The World Bank's Gini index measures the extent to which the distribution of income or consumption expenditure among individuals or households within an economy deviates from a perfectly equal distribution.
- www.state.gov. The US Department of State is a United States federal department that publishes average costs of subsistence expenses outside of the United States.
- www.numbeo.com/cost-of-living. Numbeo is the world's largest database of user contributed data about cities and countries worldwide. Numbeo provides current and timely information on world living conditions including cost of living, housing indicators, health care, traffic, crime and pollution.
- www.tbs-sct.gc.ca. The Treasury Board of Canada Secretariat National Joint Council is a cabinet committee of the Queen's Privy Council of Canada that publishes a

schedule of per-diem rates that includes meals and incidentals for individuals travelling abroad.

- www.ssa.gov. Social Security Administration is an independent agency of the United States federal government that administers a social insurance programme consisting of retirement, disability and survivors' benefits, which US expatriates should contact in order to avoid penalties, avoid the loss of future benefits, and to report changes in family status when working on foreign assignments.
- www.ato.gov.au. The Australian Taxation Office publishes a schedule of daily travel allowance expenses that vary according to salary levels and destinations.
- www.glassdoor.com/index.htm. Glassdoor is a web site that gives inside data on salaries and companies, and comments from employees. Search jobs from over 20,000 job sites, newspapers and company career pages.

Self-assessment questions

Indicative answers to these questions can be found on the companion website at study.sagepub.com/harzing4e.

1. How does an MNC pursuing differentiation business strategy ensure that its HRM compensation and benefits policies are consistent?
2. How might MNCs ensure that their total rewards policies maximize recruiting and retention efforts?
3. Why is it important for MNCs to develop compensation and benefits policies that result in fair processes and outcomes?
4. What are the complexities of international benefits programmes above-and-beyond those associated with international compensation?
5. How does employees' domestic base pay differ from employees' international base pay?

References

Aycan, Z., Al-Hamadi, A.B., Davis, A. and Budhwar, P. (2007) 'Cultural orientations and preferences for HRM policies and practices: the case of Oman', *International Journal of Human Resource Management*, 18: 11–32.

Banusiewicz, J.D. (2003) 'R&R leave program begins for service members, civilians in Operation Iraqi Freedom', American Forces Press Service, Washington, 24 September, www.defense.gov/news/newsarticle.aspx?id=28432 (accessed 15 May 2014).

The Big Mac Index (2014) http://bigmacindex.org (accessed 15 May 2014).

Birdseye, M.G. and Hill, J.S. (1995) 'Individual, organizational/work and environmental influences on expatriate turnover tendencies: an empirical study', *Journal of International Business Studies*, 26: 787–813.

Buck, T., Liu, X. and Skovoroda, R. (2008) 'Top executive pay and firm performance in China', *Journal of International Business Studies*, 39: 833–850.

Chen, C., Choi, J. and Chi, S.-C. (2002) 'Making justice sense of local-expatriate compensation disparity: mitigation by local referents, ideological explanations, and interpersonal sensitivity in china-foreign joint ventures', *Academy of Management Journal*, 45: 807–817.

Colquitt, J.A. (1999) 'On the dimensionality of organizational justice: a construct validation of a measure', *Journal of Applied Psychology*, 86: 386–400.

Colquitt, J.A., Conlon, D.E., Wesson, M.J., Porter, C. and Ng, K.Y. (2001) 'Justice at the millennium: a meta-analytic review of 25 years of organizational justice research', *Journal of Applied Psychology*, 86: 425–445.

Culpepper Compensation and Benefits Survey (2008) www.culpepper.com/Surveys/Compensation (accessed 16 June 2014).

Culpepper Salary Budget and Compensation Planning Survey (2013) www.culpepper.com/Surveys/SalaryBudget (accessed 16 June 2014).

Fealy, L. and Kompare, D. (2003) 'Forging new territory – people challenges of emerging markets', *Journal of Business Strategy*, 24: 9–13.

Fenton-O'Creevy, M., Gooderham, P. and Nordhaug, O. (2008) 'Human resource management in US subsidiaries in Europe and Australia: centralisation or autonomy', *Journal of International Business Studies*, 39(1): 151.

García, M.F., Posthuma, R.A. and Quiñones, M. (2010) 'How benefit information and demographics influence employee recruiting in Mexico', *Journal of Business and Psychology*, 25(3): 523–531.

Krugman, P. (2002) 'The outrage constraint', *New York Times*, 23 August.

Kuddo, A. (2009) 'Labor Laws in Eastern European and Central Asian Countries: Minimum Norms and Practices', SP Discussion Paper No. 0920, Social Protection & Labor, The World Bank. Available at: http://siteresources.worldbank.org/SOCIALPROTECTION/Resources/SP-Discussion-papers/Labor-Market-DP/0920.pdf (accessed 26 May 2014).

Leat, M. and El-Kot, G. (2007) 'HRM practices in Egypt: the influence of national context', *International Journal of Human Resource Management*, 18: 147–158.

Martin, W.M. and Hunt-Ahmed, K. (2011) 'Executive compensation: the role of Shari'a compliance', *International Journal of Islamic and Middle Eastern Finance and Management*, 4(3): 196–210.

Martocchio, J.J. and Pandey, N. (2008) 'Employee benefits around the world', in L.R. Gomez-Mejia and S. Werner (eds), *Global Compensation: Foundations and Perspectives*. London: Routledge, pp. 179–191.

Mercer Annual Total Remuneration Survey (2014) Mercer TRS Database, www.imercer.com/content/total-remuneration-survey.aspx (accessed 26 May 2014).

Meyskens, M., Von Glinow, M.A., Werther, W. and Clarke, L. (2009) 'The paradox of international talent: alternative forms of international assignments', *International Journal of Human Resource Management*, 20(6): 1439–1450.

Moshe, B. and Sama, L.M. (2000) 'Ethical dilemmas in MNCs' international staffing policies a conceptual framework', *Journal of Business Ethics*, 25: 221–235.

Nazir, T., Shah, S.F.H. and Zaman, K. (2012) 'Literature review on total rewards: an international perspective', *African Journal of Business Management*, 6(8): 3046–3058.

Ohmae, K. (1990) *The Borderless World: Power and Strategy in the Interlinked Economy*. New York: Harper Business.

Sanders, W.G. and Tuschke, A. (2007) 'The adoption of institutionally contested organizational practice: the emerges of stock option pay in Germany', *Academy of Management Journal*, 50(1): 33–56.

Southam, C. and Sapp, S. (2010) 'Compensation across executive labor markets: what can we learn from cross-listed firms?', *Journal of International Business Studies*, 41: 70–87.

Sparrow, P. and Hiltrop, J.M. (1995) *European Human Resource Management in Transition*. London: Prentice-Hall.

Steers, R.M., Sanchez-Runde, C.J. and Nardon, L. (2010) *Management Across Cultures: Challenges and Strategies*. New York: Cambridge University Press.

Tang, L. and Koveos, P. (2008) 'A framework to update Hofstede's cultural value indices: economic dynamics and institutional stability', *Journal of International Business Studies*, 39(6): 1045–1063.

Towers Watson (2012) *Global Workforce Study*, www.towerswatson.com/Insights/IC-Types/Survey-Research-Results/2012/07/2012-Towers-Watson-Global-Workforce-Study (accessed 15 May 2014).

Trommetter, M. (2010) 'Flexibility in the implementation of intellectual property rights in agricultural biotechnology', *European Journal of Law and Economics*, 30(3): 223–245.

WorldatWork (2010) *The Relative Influence of Total Rewards Elements on Attraction, Motivation and Retention*, www.worldatwork.org/waw/adimLink?id=37008 (accessed 15 May 2014).

Xu, H. (2008) 'Motivation and job satisfaction across nations: how much do we really know?', in P.B. Smith, M.F. Peterson and D. Thomas (eds), *The Handbook of Cross-cultural Management Research*. Thousand Oaks, CA: Sage, pp. 77–94.

Equal Opportunity and Diversity Management in the Global Context

Fang Lee Cooke

Contents

Learning objectives

After reading this chapter you will be able to:

- Understand the concepts of equal opportunity, diversity management and work–life balance
- Understand sources of discrimination and disadvantage in workplaces
- Critically evaluate the gaps between the aspirations of equal opportunity and diversity management and actual practices in workplaces
- Appreciate the global challenges to multinational corporations in developing and implementing equality and diversity management strategies

Chapter outline

This chapter provides an overview of the emergence of the concepts of equal opportunity, work–life balance (WLB) and diversity management. It describes how these concepts gain popularity as part of strategic human resource management in firms seeking competitive advantage. It critically analyses how different societal contexts may influence the way these notions are sensitized. It discusses how issues related to equality, diversity and work–life balance are dealt with in workplaces.

1 Introduction

Equal opportunity (EO) and diversity management (DM) have emerged as two important issues for academic research and corporate practice in the field of employment and human resource management. While differences exist in the foci and arguments of these two notions, a shared concern is the need to create a level playing field in an inclusive workplace so that employees with different backgrounds and attributes can exert their work efforts and seek self-development. This chapter provides an overview of the international context in which the ideas of equal opportunity, diversity management and work–life balance have emerged and been debated by some as part of strategic HRM and a potential source of competitive advantage. Different societal contexts may influence the way these ideas are understood and managed in workplaces. Informed by primary and secondary empirical data, the chapter presents examples from different countries to demonstrate the complexity of these issues and challenges that multinational corporations may encounter. The chapter also examines the extent to which firms have shifted from an EO (compliance) approach to a value-added (business case) approach to DM.

The chapter begins with a discussion of issues related to EO in employment legislation and policy at the national level, and employers' strategy and practices at the organizational level. This is followed by a section that provides an overview of the origin of, and growing interest in, DM in people management. We examine tensions and dilemmas that MNCs may face in managing a diverse workforce in their global operations. The third section of the chapter presents different perspectives and critiques on the current state of WLB research and practice. WLB is a topic that is closely related to, and often addressed as part of, DM. It is important to note that, although not widely recognized, EO and DM are an integral part of the corporate social responsibility in the form of ethical employment and HRM practices. Readers are therefore encouraged to read this chapter in conjunction with Chapter 15, in which we will discuss other key issues related to HRM and CSR, particularly employment ethics and international labour standards.

2 Equal opportunities

Labour laws and government policy intervention

The term 'equal opportunities' is associated with employment equity legislation related to discrimination arising from characteristics such as gender, age, ethnicity, religion, physical ability and sexual orientation. The elimination of inequality necessitates state intervention through legislation and affirmative action (AA) policies to provide at least a basic level of protection in principle. Many governments have issued EO legislation during the last 30 years, although what the term 'equal opportunities' means, and who are included in the category for protection, differs across countries. The introduction of EO legislation has often been accompanied by the introduction of AA programmes encouraged by the state. However, the focus of and pressure for establishing EO legislation and policy interventions are not the same across nations and their introduction is often a response to the changing political, socio-economic, labour market and employment relations environment (e.g. Casey et al., 2011; Özbilgin et al., 2012; Tomlinson, 2011).

For example, Casey et al.'s (2011: 627) comparative study of Norway and New Zealand on their respective approach to state intervention on gender equality showed that the Norwegian government adopted a 'no nonsense, no-delay approach in enacting legislation to gain gender equality', whereas the New Zealand government took a softer approach that persistently favours 'voluntarism and normative equality persuasion'. To some extent, these different approaches reflect the nuances of the political traditions of the two nations that share much in common (also see below for examples of other countries).

Where international bodies, such as donors and non-governmental organizations, are involved in EO policies and actions in nation states, such efforts may be undermined due to a lack of local legitimacy. For example, Özbilgin et al.'s (2012) country case study of Turkey and Pakistan on gender equality employment policy interventions found that transposing equal employment opportunities (EEO) initiatives from Western countries to Muslim majority countries (MMCs) and across MMCs is fraught with difficulties if they ignore due consideration of institutional and cultural conditions, organizational processes and individual choices in each country. Özbilgin et al.'s (2012: 364) study concluded that 'employment practices are gendered in different ways across national borders', and that an 'essentialist and deterministic' approach to gender, work and cross-national transfer of good practices does not work. This is because 'discourses of gender equality and the macro-national and cultural approaches towards women's status and roles' in societies are distinctive, despite similar patterns of gender disadvantages (Özbilgin et al., 2012: 364).

As mentioned above, gender equality constitutes a significant part of EO legislation, AA programmes and public debates. Unfortunately, despite the increasing provisions of anti-discrimination legislation and espoused commitment from organizations to equality, gender inequality in various stages of the employment process remains a salient feature in the labour market in most countries, and is more pronounced in some than in others (e.g. Yukongdi and Benson, 2006; Davidson and Burke, 2011; Tomlinson, 2011; Drolet and Mumford, 2012).

Numerous factors and reasons can contribute to the failure or only partial success of legislative and policy interventions. Some national legal systems are impeded by the complexity and multiplicity of employment-related laws, directive regulations and administrative policies issued at different administrative levels. For example, Forstenlechner et al.'s (2012) case study of a finance company in the UAE about the success and failure of imposing a quotas system to improve demographic diversity of the workforce and employment equity found several main reasons that have led to the normative failure of the quota system. These include competing ideologies and priorities, as well as the lack of coordination and integration at various levels. Other national legal systems lack clear enforcement channels and support through which workers can seek to secure compliance with the law. In some cases, governments' determination to advance social equality is compromised by competing demands from their economic agendas.

Table 14.1 provides an overview of gender equality laws and other administrative mechanisms adopted by the governments of four Asian countries – Japan, the Republic of Korea (hereafter Korea), China and India – and their limited effects.

In Japan, it was reported that despite the establishment of the Equal Employment Opportunity Law (EEOL) in 1986, the country had a much lower proportion of women managers in government organizations than it had in its corporations in the early 1990s (Steinhoff and Tanaka, 1993). The introduction of EEOL was controversial among the legislator, employers and the state from the outset and 'produced few gains in employment opportunities for women' (Gelb, 2000: 385). There is a widespread consensus among scholars in Japan that the government passed EEOL more as a response to international pressure than as an acknowledgement of changing social values in Japan (Gelb, 2000). EEOL has been criticized for its 'over-reliance on voluntary compliance' with 'little government enforcement power', although it is recognized that 'it has led to renewed efforts at litigation, increased consciousness and activism among women, and amendments to the law, passed in 1997' (Gelb, 2000: 385). More than two decades after the introduction of EEOL, women's managerial career paths with domestic employers 'remain blocked by traditional and institutional practices' in Japan (Bozkurt, 2012: 225).

In Korea, the Gender-Equal Employment Act of 1987 'stipulates that employers can be imprisoned for up to two years if they pay different wages for work of equal value in the same business; but few, if any, employers have actually gone to jail' (van der Meulen Rodgers, 1998: 746). By condoning employers' discriminative practices, the state is actually 'perpetuating gender norms and stereotypes that disadvantage women' (Seguino, 2000: 34). To-date, few of the top Korean firms have women in their senior executive team (Kim, 2005), and with the exception of the catering and hotel industry, over half of the Korean industries do not have any female managers (Cho and Kwon, 2010).

For both Japan and Korea, affirmative action programmes have been adopted only in the 2000s on a voluntary basis with little enforcement power. Private sector employers have autonomy to decide whether they wish to adopt the AA programme or not, and evidence suggests that there is little incentive for them to do so (Benson et al., 2007).

In China, state intervention as part of its socialist campaign of gender equality during its state planned economy period (1949–1978) had led to significant advances in pay and social equity for female workers. As a result, China has achieved possibly greater gender equality than industrial capitalist societies (Stockman et al., 1995). This is in spite of persistent inequalities in recruitment and promotion, particularly in government organizations. However, the achievement of gender equality has been eroded by ensuing efforts towards marketization and integration with the global economy, partly as a result of the loosening control of the state on business affairs (Cooke and Xiao, 2014).

Similarly, although the Constitution of India 'allows affirmative action through reservations in education and employment' (Venkata Ratnam and Chandra, 1996: 85), the enforcement of the constitutional rights of Indian women is uneven due to 'the lack of a uniform civil code in India' (Ghosh and Roy, 1997: 904). Nevertheless, the Indian courts have been considered to be playing an important role in defending women's rights 'in a context where government, employers and unions largely remained either indifferent and unconcerned, or reluctant and ineffective in addressing the issues of gender equality' (Venkata Ratnam and Jain, 2002: 281). This is in spite of the criticism that the Indian courts suffer from a number of weaknesses including alleged corruption.

According to the Human Development Report 2007/8 from the United Nations Development Program (UNDP), Japan, Korea and China were ranked No. 54, 64 and 57 respectively out of 177 countries ranked in the UNDP Gender Empowerment Measure (UNDP, 2009).

Table 14.1 Labour and EO laws in China, India, Japan and Korea

Country	Labour and equal opportunities laws	Purpose	Impact
China	Constitution (1954, latest version 2004) Labour Insurance Regulations of the People's Republic of China (1953) Announcement on Female Workers' Production Leave by the State Council (1955) Female Employees Labour Protection Regulations (1988) Regulations of Prohibited Types of Occupational Posts for Female Employees (1990) Law on the Protection of Women's Rights and Interests (1992, amended 2005) Labour Law (1995) Employment Promotion Law (2008)	To ensure equal rights in employment between men and women To protect married women from being discriminated due to their maternity status	Ineffective enforcement, little, if any, punishment to non-compliant employers
India	Constitution (1950) The Employees State Insurance Act (1948) The Factories Act (1948) The Maternity Benefits Act (1961) Equal Remuneration Act (1976)	To guarantee women's equal rights	Ineffective enforcement due to lack of uniform civil code Complex and restrictive laws deter employers from creating jobs in the formal sector
Japan	Constitution (1946) Equal Employment Opportunity Law (1986, amended in 1997 to take effect in 1999)	To ensure equal rights in employment between men and women	Controversial introduction Over-reliance on voluntary compliance with little government enforcement power Limited impact on increasing women's employment but has led to increased awareness of gender inequality among women
Korea	Equal Employment Opportunity Act (1988, amended in 1989) Guidelines to Eliminate Sexual Discrimination in Employment (1991) Labour Standards Law (1998)	To guarantee equality between men and women in employment To protect women's job security on their marital status, pregnancy, and childbirth To allow employers to lay off workers	Ineffective enforcement Informalization of employment with declined employment terms and conditions

Legislation that is intended to provide an enhanced level of equality may actually prove to be counter-productive, especially when effective enforcement remains problematic. For example, India's labour regulations are considered to be 'among the most restrictive and complex in the world' and 'have constrained the growth of the formal manufacturing sector where these laws have their widest application' (World Bank, 2006: 3). This discourages employers from creating employment with a better job quality in the formal sector and forces millions to continue to be trapped in poor quality jobs in the informal sector. Banning women from night shifts in India has also led to a reduced scope of employment for women, 'even though there is great potential for employment in information technology-related areas involving tele-work in call centres, where round-the-clock work is the norm' (Venkata Ratnam and Jain, 2002: 279). Mandatory maternity leave and the requirement of breast-feeding breaks and crèches at workplaces where the majority of workers are women are often perceived by employers as liabilities and discourage them from employing women (Venkata Ratnam and Jain, 2002).

The effective implementation of employment equity legislation may yield positive psychological and employment outcomes to those who were previously disadvantaged. For example, in South Africa, the Constitution of South Africa (1996) and the Employment Equity Act (1998) were introduced, through AA at workplace level, to promote the constitutional right of equality, eliminate unfair discrimination in employment and achieve a diverse workforce broadly representative of its people. These regulations are said to have led to positive outcomes for some employees. However, this positive effect may simultaneously be accompanied by a higher level of turnover or intention to quit of incumbents as a result of their improved labour market position (e.g. Wöcke and Sutherland, 2008). Therefore, where employers' efforts to build workforce relationships are undermined by labour market conditions, as is the case where employment laws are not effectively enforced, employers may have less incentive to observe regulations and adopt EO policies that develop the psychological contract with employees.

Employer strategy and discrimination

As we can see from the above discussion, employers play an important role in influencing the level of gender (in)equality. Where firms are facing shortages of labour and talent, they may introduce a proactive HR policy to attract and retain women workers. Where the labour market is slack and the pressure of business competition is heightened, employers often adopt a labour cost reduction strategy and women tend to be more vulnerable than men. For example, in Korea, a large proportion of Korean (married) women have inferior employment status mainly due to discrimination based on their marital status (Kang and Rowley, 2005). Women are more likely to be laid off by their employer than men because of the enduring cultural norm and (mis)perception that women are less productive than men (Patterson et al., 2013). In Japan, new opportunities created for women by the EO laws in the late 1980s and early 1990s became eroded when Japan's economic growth 'bubble' burst after 1992 (Gelb, 2000). It was 'the marginal nature of Japanese women's employment' used as a deliberate strategy by employers that reinforced the core employment system privileging men 'during a period of heightened international competition, reduced growth rate, a rapidly aging workforce and the inflexible hiring and firing system' (Kucera, 1998: 28). Similarly, women workers in China had been selected disproportionately and laid off or forced into early retirement during the radical downsizing that took place in the state sector during the mid-1990s and early 2000s (Cooke, 2010).

Employers in Japan and Korea are reported to exert pressure, albeit now more implicitly following the introduction of EO laws in the late 1980s, persuading women to resign when they get married and become pregnant. Age limits are also used in recruitment and selection to screen out women (Gelb, 2000). Although the 'marriage bar' is far less common in China, employers in private and foreign-funded factories are known to impose an age limit on female workers. In some ways, if the marriage bar for Japanese and Korean women aims primarily at protecting men's jobs and earnings, then age discrimination in China is intended to increase labour productivity (Cooke, 2010).

In addition to gender and race, age is another main source of labour market discrimination. However, by comparison, age discrimination has received far less research, policy and corporate attention than gender and race (e.g. Billett et al., 2011; Fuertes et al., 2013). In spite of population ageing in many developed and some developing economies and the growing pressure of staff shortage and recruitment difficulties, older workers, commonly defined as those aged 45 or above, often encounter institutionalized discrimination in selection for training and development, promotion and displacement (e.g. Li et al., 2011; Cooke, 2012; Kunze et al., 2013; Lazazzara et al., 2013). Drawing on experience from Australia, Billet et al. (2011: 1248) argued that research and policy focusing on age discrimination needs to de-emphasize 'the term "older workers" and reconsider how human resource management and government policies, as well as practices by workers themselves, might pursue longer and more productive working lives for employees aged over 45'. It is important to note that age discrimination is not restricted to older workers, but also applies to young workers with little work experience and less human capital. For example, specifying the age limit and minimum years of prior work experience is a widespread practice in recruitment advertisements in China (Cooke, 2012).

While earlier studies on age discrimination tackle the issue mainly from a legal compliance and equality perspective, a number of academic studies have now emerged that explore the links between the age diversity of the workforce and firm performance which may be mitigated by a number of contextual factors (also see the next section on DM more generally). In other words, they examine the issue from a resource-based view and strategic perspective to identify what organizational interventions may be possible to improve productivity. For example, Kunze et al.'s (2013: 434) study of 147 firms in Germany found that top managers, especially their stereotypes with regard to older workers, are a significant contextual factor that explains 'if age diversity is inciting social-categorization processes that lead to higher levels of a perceived negative age-discrimination climate'. Kunze et al. (2013: 433) also found that in organizations which carry out diversity-related HR efforts, age diversity does not appear to 'relate to heightened levels of age discrimination climate and reduced levels of performance'. Backes-Gellner and Veen's (2013) study of age diversity and firm productivity in Germany revealed that the benefit of age diversity outweighs the cost of managing age diversity only in firms with innovative tasks, but not in work environments with highly standardized routines. This is because the latter have limited opportunities to apply new knowledge gained by the workers through interactions with colleagues in other age groups. Similarly, Li et al.'s (2011) study in the Chinese context showed that a firm's level of market diversification influences the relationship between age diversity and firm performance. Their study further revealed that there is a significant relationship and positive effect between age diversity and firm profitability for firms from Western societies but not for firms from East Asian societies.

Box 14.1   Stop and reflect

Retaining the workforce by changing their age profile?

A call centre company in India that provides outsourcing services to its corporate clients in the UK and US is confronted with staff turnover problems. The company employs over 1000 staff, most of whom are young university graduates aged between 22 and 28. According to the HR manager of the call centre, these young workers want to change their jobs every one to two years in order to gain promotion and experience working in different environments before they settle. What is the prospect of advising the company to improve staff retention by changing its workforce age profile? Think of a plan and discuss. Can the same idea be transferred to other countries if the same challenge occurs?

3 Diversity management

Diversity management as a strategic HRM initiative

Since the 1990s, a complementary, or what some would call a competing, concept to EO has emerged in the HRM literature – diversity management. The concept of managing diversity has its origin in the US and emerged as an HR intervention in the mid-1980s. It is primarily a response to the demographic changes (e.g. more immigrants and women) in the workplace as well as the customer base (Agocs and Burr, 1996). It is also a response to the corporate discontent with AA approaches imposed by the US government. Organizations are searching for an alternative to broaden the perceived narrow scope of AA legislation that focuses primarily on recruitment. DM is seen as a way to address retention, integration and career development issues (Agocs and Burr, 1996). The growing demands from the ethnic minority, women, older, disabled, gay and lesbian groups for equal rights and the consequent human rights legislation in the 1990s and 2000s give further impetus to the need for recognizing, accepting and valuing individual differences at workplaces and in society more generally (Mor Barak, 2005).

The concept of DM began to be advanced in countries outside of North America during the late 1990s. For example, Süß and Kleiner (2007) observed a sharp increase in the use of the concept of DM in Germany since the late 1990s. In the UK, the concept of managing diversity has undoubtedly become more influential since the mid/late 1990s in part due to the demographic change of the workforce, but more so because DM is seen as a more comprehensive and sophisticated approach to EO management that adds value to business. The Chartered Institute of Personnel and Development (CIPD), defines diversity as 'valuing everyone as an individual – valuing people as employees, customers and clients' (CIPD, 2006: 2).

It is suggested that the objectives of DM is for organizations to increase awareness of cultural differences, develop the ability to recognize, accept and value diversity, minimize patterns of inequality experienced by those not in the mainstream, and modify organizational culture and leadership practices (Cox, 1993; Soni, 2000). DM is regarded as a better approach than EO because it adopts an inclusive approach that 'focuses on valuing people as unique individuals rather than on group-related issues covered by legislation' (CIPD, 2007: 6). More recent DM literature advocates an inclusive approach to managing diversity that goes beyond organizational and national boundaries (e.g. Mor Barak, 2005).

Box 14.2   Stop and reflect

What is an inclusive workplace?

According to Mor Barak (2005: 8), an inclusive workplace model includes the following features:

- values and utilizes individual and intergroup differences within its workforce
- cooperates with, and contributes to, its surrounding community

(Continued)

(Continued)

- alleviates the needs of disadvantaged groups in its wider environment
- collaborates with individuals, groups and organizations across national and cultural boundaries.

Imagine you are the HR director of a German-owned automotive manufacturing firm with subsidiaries and joint ventures in 57 countries in Europe, North and South America, Asia and Africa. How would the above features help you formulate a corporate inclusive strategy that will be meaningful to the local subsidiaries?

The transition from a focus on EO to managing diversity signals a move away from an emphasis on procedural justice to a utilitarian approach that views DM as a means to an end which should be managed strategically. In other words, it is a shift away from a negative perspective emphasizing disadvantaged and discriminated staff to a positive and liberal perspective of celebrating and valuing the differences among all employees and utilizing them in a creative way to benefit both the organization and individuals (Maxwell et al., 2001). This has been advocated as being a strategic approach to HRM informed by the resource-based view (Richard et al., 2013). At the policy level, Özbilgin and Tatli (2011: 1247) have also observed that there is a discernible trend where key actors in the EO and DM field are turning away from 'regulation- and collectivism-oriented approaches'; instead, 'voluntaristic and individualistic discourses' are increasingly adopted and 'dominate the public debates on workplace equality and diversity' (also see Kramar, 2012).

Foster and Harris (2005) identified a number of key differences between managing EO and DM (see Table 14.2).

Table 14.2   Key differences between managing EO and managing diversity

Equal opportunities	Managing diversity
Addresses inequality through rights	Promotes diversity for organizational benefits
Neutralizes individual differences	Recognizes individual differences
Treats people the same	Treats people differently
A narrow view of difference	An inclusive view of difference
A focus on HR processes	Concerns all functions of the organization
Promote assimilation	Promote variety
An emphasis on procedures and regulation	An emphasis on organizational objectives

Source: Foster and Harris (2005: 124)

However, the distinction between EO and DM may be far less clear in practice than the above table implies (Foster and Harris, 2005). Organizations may find it awkward to promote EO policies that tend to emphasize sameness and underplay differences on the one hand, and promote diversity that aims to address individual differences on the other. Conceptual ambiguity and confused organizational practices may create indifference to EO and DM initiatives, resulting in managers and employees believing that the latter is simply the former given a different name (Foster and Harris, 2005; Özbilgin and Tatli, 2011).

According to the CIPD's (2007) survey of 285 DM managers/officers in a wide range of organizations based in the UK, only 17 per cent of survey respondents believed that the business case was the most important driver stimulating their organization to adopt DM initiatives. There was a general feeling of lack of senior management support among respondents and very few of the organizations participating in the survey undertook activities to mainstream diversity. Not surprisingly, there is 'little evidence of organizations mainstreaming diversity into operational practices such as marketing, product development and customer services – which is where significant gains could be made in improving business performance' (CIPD, 2007: 8). In fact, despite the active promotion by Western HR consulting firms and HR associations of the moral and strategic importance of DM, legal compliance remains the top reason for organizations implementing DM initiatives (CIPD, 2007).

A large-scale survey of global Fortune 500 companies and other global organizations revealed similar attitudes – while all respondent firms agreed on the importance of global diversity, 'only 50 per cent of firms surveyed reported considering global stakeholders when determining their diversity strategies, only 39 per cent provide extensive multicultural training for all employees, and only 27 per cent routinely evaluate progress towards diversity goals' (Dunavant and Heiss, 2005, cited in Nishii and Özbilgin, 2007: 1883).

In Australia, Kramar (2012) observed that there is no common approach to DM and that, in spite of the rhetoric of the business case in the private sector, legal compliance appears to be the main motive for DM. Kramar (2012) further noted that gender equality has been the main focus of DM and that there is a decline of actions in both the public and private sector that promote changes to embrace the diversity discourse.

Diversity management and organizational performance

In ways analogous to the arguments made for CSR, advocates of DM believe that there are three important reasons for managing diversity (e.g. Agocs and Burr, 1996; CIPD, 2006; Cox and Blake, 1991):

- *Effective people management* – DM creates an open, inclusive workplace culture where everyone feels valued, which then helps to recruit, retain and motivate good people. Diversity can create teams that are more innovative and flexible which may increase their productivity and ultimately organizational performance. DM helps to promote awareness of individual difference and empathy for those who are different, and encourages attitude change.

- *Market competition* – A diverse workforce can help the organization to understand diverse customer needs, open up new market opportunities, improve market share and broaden its customer base.
- *Corporate reputation* – Adopting an effective DM policy enables organizations to demonstrate their commitment to CSR through engagement with local communities.

Existing studies have provided evidence to support the assumption that strategic DM can lead to enhanced HR outcomes. For example, Ng and Burke's (2005) survey study of 113 MBA job seekers showed that women and ethnic minorities considered DM to be important when accepting job offers. In addition, 'high achievers and new immigrants rated organizations with diversity management as more attractive as potential employers' (Ng and Burke, 2005: 1195). Scott et al.'s (2011) review of DM practices of best companies suggests that organizations that emphasize inclusion and integrate DM into all of their policies and practices may benefit more than companies that deal with DM as a stand-alone practice. Similarly, Houkamau and Boxall's (2011: 440) survey study of 500 New Zealand workers' perceptions of, and responses to, DM activities found a 'widespread use of family-friendly employment practices and a general perception of a good climate for diversity'. The study also found that employees who reported a higher level of family-friendly and proactive EO practices appeared to show a high level of trust and commitment to their organization, as well as enjoying a higher level of job satisfaction.

According to the CIPD (2007: 12), there is a wide range of measures that organizations may use to monitor the impact of DM. These include:

- employee attitude surveys
- number of complaints and grievances
- labour turnover
- employee performance appraisals
- absenteeism
- ability to recruit
- number of tribunal cases
- impact assessment
- level of customer satisfaction
- employee commitment surveys
- business performance
- balanced scorecard
- diversification of customer base
- improvements to problem solving and decision making
- psychological contract issues.

We cannot assume that a positive relationship invariably holds between diversity and productivity improvement (also see the previous section on age diversity). Academic studies on diversity–performance relationships have so far yielded non-conclusive results. While some researchers argue that diversity leads to better group and ultimately organizational performance (e.g. Cox et al., 1991), others contend that diversity leads to a negative organizational performance outcome in part due to intra- and inter-group conflicts and communication deadlock derived from differences (e.g. Tsui et al., 1992; Lau and Murnighan, 1998). Moreover, there can be tensions between a collective approach to managing diverse employee groups and a more individualized approach focusing on individual needs and abilities which may actually increase, rather than decrease, inequalities (e.g. Agocs and Burr, 1996; Liff, 1996). Jones et al. (2013: 55) observed that the existing literature on diversity training has yielded 'little evidence of their overall effectiveness'. They argued that diversity training informed by an ethical perspective, instead of the business case approach, may be more effective because the ethical perspective aligns the values of the organization and the employees and sends a signal to the employees that 'the organization cares about their well-being' (Jones et al., 2013: 55)

Other studies have revealed that the benefits of DM rhetoric can be overstated (e.g. Williams and O'Reilly, 1998; Wise and Tsehirhart, 2000), that DM initiatives may actually undermine efforts in EO programmes (e.g. Subeliani and Tsogas, 2005), and that DM might be adopted as a new disguise to mask exploitation (Taylor et al., 1997). Affirmative actions associated with DM are also found to meet disapproval from the workforce as those recruited or promoted under AA are perceived to be less competent or qualified, thus violating the principle of merit (Ng and Burke, 2005). Studies by Kochan et al. (2003) revealed that participation in a diversity education programme does not foster a positive relationship between racial and gender diversity and performance. Richard et al. (2004) offered a reconciling 'third way' perspective which suggests that contextual factors (e.g. entrepreneurial orientation) play an important moderating role for diversity to enhance organizational performance.

Kochan et al. (2003: 17) further observed that practitioners paid little attention to analysing their organizational environment for managing diversity and that few companies 'are equipped to assess the impact of their diversity efforts on their performance'. Kochan et al. (2003) questioned whether the business case rhetoric of managing diversity has run its course. Nevertheless, they contended that while we may be sceptical about the positive impact of DM on organizational performance, diversity is a labour market imperative as well as a societal value and expectation. Therefore, 'managers should do their best to translate diversity into positive organizational, group and individual outcomes' (Kochan et al., 2003: 18).

It is apparent that DM is a poorly understood, increasingly slippery and controversial concept that is used 'in an all-embracing fashion to include not just the social categories of AA such as race and sex but a wide range of personal characteristics'

(Ferner et al., 2005: 309). Consequently, the concept and moral soundness of DM remains a contentious issue (see Lorbiecki and Jack (2000) for an overview of the conceptual premises and critique of DM; also see van Dijk et al. (2012) for a conceptual debate on the virtue ethics perspective versus business case perspective of DM). In addition, the utility of this concept originating from the US for other societal contexts has been questioned by many researchers (e.g. Agocs and Burr, 1996; Ferner et al., 2005; Healy and Oikelome, 2007; Nishii and Özbilgin, 2007). Similarly, Jonsen et al. (2011) argue that existing knowledge of DM has been dominated by US-centric research studies and that future research should look beyond North America and include more diversity themes and forms of intervention specific to societal contexts. In the next section, we examine the tensions and dynamics of societal patterns of diversity in different countries.

Diversity management in the global context

A number of country-specific studies have revealed unique societal contexts in which diversity issues are embedded (see Tatli and Özbilgin (2012) for a discussion of conceptual approaches to researching DM that emphasize intersectionality and multi-level analysis). For example, Jones et al.'s (2000) study showed that the language used to describe diversity and the perception of diversity issues in New Zealand are markedly different from those manifested in the dominant discourse of DM imbued with US cultural assumptions. In African countries, politics assumes supreme importance in DM and ethnicity dominates 'most national debates on diversity' as the central issue (Healy and Oikelome, 2007: 1923). This is because some disadvantaged ethnic groups historically have been oppressed and there are now increasing calls for radical remedial action to address racial grievances. By contrast, ethnic groups in Japan and Korea are relatively homogenous and as a result, gender, women's marital status and their related employment status are key sources of workforce diversity (Cooke, 2010).

In the US and UK, workforce diversity may include: gender, race, ethnicity, religion, age, disability, immigration status, social class, political association, marital status, parental status, sexual orientation, ex-offenders, and so on. Many of these differences are accepted by Western societies, protected by law and acknowledged in company policies. However, some of these characteristics may not be acceptable socially or legally in oriental countries like China and India (Cooke and Saini, 2012). Furthermore, significant differences may exist even within oriental countries. For example, caste, ethnicity, religion and gender are the main sources of diversity in India, whereas age, gender, disability and place of origin (e.g. rural versus urban) are the main causes of social inequality in China. India is the largest democratic country in the world, albeit a fragile one compared to some, where the talk of empowerment to the socially disadvantaged groups is often used as a powerful weapon to connect political parties with their constituencies. By contrast, China is a socialist regime with centralized control by the communist party. Elimination of social inequality is intended to be achieved by introducing government policies and regulations through a top-down interventionist approach (Cooke and Saini, 2012). Cooke and Saini's (2012) comparative study of DM in China and India revealed that as a strategic HRM concept, DM featured little in management discussions and presentations, particularly in China where the concept was largely unheard of. In addition, management's indifferent attitude to DM may well be linked to the low level of bargaining power possessed by the disadvantaged groups in these countries.

In many less developed countries, employment insecurity is relatively high and the provision of social security benefits is extended to few. Large groups of poor people are fighting for the very right to a basic living through low paid employment with long working hours and poor conditions. The fact that they are treated unfairly is much less of a concern for some and inequality in the workplace and in society generally is often accepted, internalized and unchallenged due to historically deep-rooted discrimination and the evident absence of remedial prospects.

It is perhaps not surprising then that studies on DM in MNCs have found that attempts to roll out US domestic diversity programmes globally often fail to achieve their objectives and/or meet with strong resistance in the host country operations (e.g. Ferner et al., 2005; Nishii and Özbilgin, 2007). This is mainly because these US-specific programmes fail to reflect the specific demographic profile and the legal, historical, political and cultural contexts of equality in the host countries. Many US-owned MNCs studied in fact made little attempt to adapt their US-designed diversity programmes to capture local characteristics (Nishii and Özbilgin, 2007). As a result, MNCs may encounter 'regulatory, normative and cognitive challenges' when designing and implementing their global DM initiatives (Sippola and Smale, 2007: 1895). While the philosophy of diversity might be acceptable globally within the corporation, a more multi-domestic approach to implementing diversity programmes has been found to be necessary, as was revealed in Sippola and Smale's (2007) study.

Company-based case studies of DM in various countries have further revealed the distance between reality and the inspiration projected in DM rhetoric. For instance, Dameron and Joffre's (2007: 2053) study of the integration team created to manage the post-merger integration of France Telecom Mobile and Orange UK found that the co-existence of the French and English cultures was 'never seen as an opportunity, a differentiation and a source of creativity'. Rather, 'cultural diversity was always experienced by the members of the integration team as a difficulty to overcome' (Dameron and Joffre, 2007: 2053). Subeliani and Tsogas's (2005) study of managing diversity in a large bank in the Netherlands showed that the diversity initiative was designed and implemented in large cities where a large ethnic market existed from which the bank could benefit. Employees with immigrant backgrounds were mostly recruited for lower positions, where they could be visible to customers, but promotion for them was very difficult, if not impossible. They were trapped at the lower end of the organizational hierarchy, with little freedom to express their cultural and religious views. In this case of DM programme adoption, it is clear that business motives took precedence over moral concerns.

4 Work–life balance: practices and discourses

Since the mid-1990s, work–life conflict (WLC) has become a major issue in different parts of the world for different reasons. In Western economies, work–life issues emerged primarily as a result of demographic changes (e.g. declining labour force and an ageing population) and work intensification due to globalized competitive pressure. In particular, the participation of women with childcare/elderly care responsibility in part-time and increasingly full-time employment has been a major focus of the WLC debates and policy orientation (e.g. Fleetwood, 2007; Greenhaus, 2008; Gregory and Milner, 2009; Özbilgin et al., 2012). Many governments are made aware of the gap between the growing presence of WLC and the deficiency of institutional supports and cultural change to reduce the negative impacts. As Pocock (2005: 202) pointed out, 'the political case for work–life balance is increasingly evident in industrialized countries that are more and more dependent upon the paid work contributions of women and workers with dependants'.

Policy initiatives have been promoted by various governments to address the issue of WLC, often as part of the EO and DM programmes, in order to enhance the well-being of those in employment and their families. Organizations, particularly those in the public sector and large MNCs, have also introduced a range of HR practices, such as flexible work arrangements, partly in response to these policy initiatives (e.g. Brough et al., 2008; Burgess and Connell, 2008; Abendroth and den Dulk, 2011). It is argued that organizations play a central role in providing quality jobs that will not only raise the standard of material life of the employees and their families, but also the intrinsic rewards and psychological well-being of the workforce (Burgess and Connell, 2008).

Existing studies on work–life balance point to the fact that the adoption of WLB initiatives does have a positive impact. For instance, Abendroth and den Dulk's (2011) survey study of 7,867 service-sector workers in eight European countries found that organizational support for employee WLB satisfaction has a direct and moderating effect, and that emotional support and instrumental support at the workplace have a complementary relationship. Similarly, Avgar et al.'s (2011) study of WLB practices and organizational support in 172 hospitals in the UK and their direct and indirect effects on three key stakeholders found that the greater use of WLB practices enhances outcomes for hospitals, their employees and the patients they serve. In addition, the effective adoption of WLB practices is often associated with the adoption of good HR practices. For example, Wang and Verma's (2012) analysis of the Workplace and Employee Survey of 3,943 workplaces in Canada revealed that firms with a product leadership business strategy are more likely to have WLB programmes in place than those with a cost leadership strategy. In addition, firms that adopt WLB programmes also adopt high performance work practices such as investment in training, employee involvement, and so forth.

Despite the strong political, social and economic case for WLB legislative intervention and policy/HR initiatives, a common finding of the growing body of empirical studies conducted in different societal contexts is that WLB policies and practices in general have been less than effective, for various reasons (e.g. Pas et al., 2011; Xiao and Cooke, 2012; Chou and Cheung, 2013).

Fundamental differences also exist between the Western and Eastern countries in their political ideologies, demographic and labour market characteristics, work–family values and the resultant positions held by the government and employers towards WLC. Typically, a *laissez faire* approach has been adopted in the East with no or little government policy. The existence of WLB practices relies largely on employers' discretion, and the ability of individuals to demand the placement of work–life policy and practice in the workplace. For example, according to Chou and Cheung (2013: 9), in Hong Kong family-friendly policy as part of employment policy is predominantly voluntary and implemented in only a few private sector organizations. Despite much policy effort to promote family-friendly work and family values, the government adopts 'a minimalist market-based employer approach' in which employers are given freedom to design and implement their family-friendly measures based on the needs of the employees and the feasibility and affordability of the firm. As a result, few employers have a family-friendly policy in place. Where WLB initiatives exist in workplaces, they convey strong characteristics of Eastern societal values. For instance, Chandra's (2012) study comparing Eastern and Western perspectives on WLB revealed that American MNCs focus on flexible working practices, whereas Indian companies focus on employee welfare programmes such as cultural, recreational, health and educational programmes (also see Xiao and Cooke (2012) for practices in China). In addition, sources of WLC are very different between those employed in sweatshop and informal employment and the professional/managerial categories – the former need to work long hours for a living wage, the latter to gain promotion and remain in the elite middle class. Therefore WLB initiatives may not be well received by employees (Xiao and Cooke, 2012).

Academically, the WLB discourse and associated flexibility practices that have emerged from the European and North American politico-socio-economic contexts have attracted much critique (e.g. Abendroth and den Dulk, 2011; Özbilgin et al., 2012). For example, based on a critical review of the work–life literature through the lens of diversity, Tatli and Özbilgin (2012: 187) pointed out that work–life studies should go beyond the narrow analytical framework of domestic and economic life to incorporate a wide range of demands 'placed on an individual's temporal, spatial, and relational commitments in the domestic and non-domestic spheres'. They cogently argued that issues related to life, diversity and power need to be addressed by taking into account 'the intersectionality of social and historical factors in their relational complexity in order to reveal the dynamics of power, disadvantage and privilege as they relate to the work–life interface' (Tatli and Özbilgin, 2012: 191).

Özbilgin et al.'s (2012) argument is echoed by Pocock et al. (2012: 391), who critiqued that the literature on work–life and work–family is mostly 'under-conceptualized', focuses primarily on professional and managerial workers, and largely neglects the wider 'terrain of work, family and community'. Pocock et al. (2012: 391) argue:

> It is vital to unpack the 'black box' of 'work' in a multi-layered way, to give appropriate weight to various sources of power, and to avoid an individualistic approach to the reconciliation of work, home and community life by locating analysis in a larger social and political context.

Drawing on Bronfenbrenner's (1979) and Voydanoff's (2007) theses, Pocock et al. (2012: 405) propose a 'socio-ecological systems' model of work, home and community that is attentive to four key concepts: 'power, time, space and life stage'. According to Pocock et al. (2012), these concepts are crucial to improve our understanding of work, family and community outcomes, because they open up a broader macro-system within which to examine how work, home and community exist, and interact with and impact on each other.

Box 14.3   Stop and reflect

Breaking the boundaries of work, home and community

Pocock et al.'s (2012) analytical framework that examines issues related to work, home and community and their interactions through the lens of power, time, space and life stage carries profound analytical power. An implicit assumption of this model, however, is that work, home and community of an individual worker, albeit now examined in a broader terrain, are situated in relatively stable locales. This may not always be the case for workers whose working site changes frequently, such as consultants and auditors. Not only may these professional workers' working site change daily or weekly due to the need to perform tasks on the client's site, but also their rest place after work may be transient if the client's site is far away from home. For example, a management consultant working for a global firm based in Europe may have to travel weekly to a different country in the continent to provide services. This exposes the consultant to different work environments and living cultures to which he/she has to adapt. It may also create a sense of isolation and displacement from the community due to frequent changes in dwelling as a result of living in hotels and rental accommodation (also see Xiao and Cooke (2012) on the implications of external auditing work for female auditors in China). What can the firm do to alleviate the potential negative impacts on their employees who are required to make short trips frequently?

5 Summary and conclusions

This chapter has provided an overview of the conceptual debates concerning EO, DM and WLB as key issues in HRM. We have examined legislation and policy initiatives of nation states in various parts of the world to highlight the diverse societal contexts within which these terms are to be understood and employment practices are shaped. By comparison, gender and ethnicity have featured more prominently than other forms of discrimination in academic research and practical publications. The compound effect of gender, race, age or other demographic characteristics may be more pronounced, as some studies have shown. In tracing the origin and the growing research and policy attention on issues related to EO, DM and WLB, we can see a discernible trend that the argument has been steadily shifting from an emphasis on legal compliance and moral obligation towards a business case discourse that emphasizes the benefits of EO, DM and WLB on organizational performance. This may be a dangerous shift, as discrimination of various forms and disguise still widely exist, especially where law enforcement capacity is low and the labour market is slack. While a key concern of employers is to maintain productivity and competitiveness, this goal needs to be achieved with employment ethics and corporate social responsibility in mind. It is to these issues that we will turn in the next chapter.

Discussion questions

1. It is argued that there is tension between implementing EO legislation that is informed by the notion of 'sameness treatment' and adopting DM programmes that focus on individual and group characteristics. How do you think this tension can be reconciled?
2. A US-owned software development MNC has been facing serious talent retention problems in its subsidiary in India. The MNC has a successful DM programme in its US operations and is intending to adopt a similar programme in its Indian operations in an attempt to improve talent recruitment and retention. Do you think this idea will work? If so, how would you design and implement the initiative in order to make it effective?
3. In an international practitioners' conference of HRM, a Chinese HR manager said to you: 'work–life balance initiative is originated in the West and it does not suit the Chinese culture that values diligence, self-sacrifice, life-long learning and self-improvement'. How would you reconcile this view?

CASE STUDY

Managing diversity in a Chinese-owned multinational IT firm

Company background

Established in 1988 in Beijing, Lenovo Group Limited (formerly known as 'Legend Group Limited') is the largest IT enterprise in China. Lenovo employs some 25,000 staff in all its operations in nearly 70 countries, but with the majority of employees working in China. In 1984, with an initial capital of RMB 200,000 funded by the Chinese Academy of Sciences, a government-funded institution, 11 researchers formed the parent company of Lenovo. It was the first company to introduce the concept of the home computer in China. Lenovo's main business activities are in the sale and manufacturing of desktop computers, notebook computers, mobile handsets, servers and printers. Lenovo is a stock-listed company, with the Chinese government holding over a quarter of its shares.

In April 2003, the group adopted a new logo and the English brand name 'Lenovo', replacing the original English brand name 'Legend' in order to appeal to the international market. The English company name was also officially changed to 'Lenovo Group Limited' a year later. In December 2004, Lenovo spent US$1.25 billion to acquire IBM's PC business. This was the largest cross-border acquisition in China's IT industry (*China Business*, 13 December 2004). The acquisition process was completed in May 2005. The marriage of IBM and Lenovo created one of the world's largest PC powerhouses. IBM possessed strong competitive advantage in the higher end of the customer market in its distribution channel, high quality customer resources, which complemented that of Lenovo. The two companies have maintained a long-term cooperative strategy since the acquisition, with Lenovo having access to some of IBM's key resources, such as technology, sales force, PartnerWorld, Global Finance and IBM Credit.

The continuing expansion and globalization of Lenovo has brought a number of challenges to its HRM function, including the alignment of corporate HR strategy and DM after the acquisition of IBM's PC business. Below are some of the issues that illustrate the challenges.

Managing foreign employees in China

Lenovo's growing global presence in the IT sector has in recent years attracted an increasing number of non-Chinese citizens who wish to work in its operations in China. This is in part because they want to spend time in China to gain wider work experience and a deeper understanding of the country. These foreign citizens are employed by Lenovo under the same employment conditions as those offered to Chinese citizens. Free working meals and company-subsidized accommodation are some of the benefits that Lenovo offers its employees. These are traditional and typical workplace welfare provisions of Chinese firms. Under the housing scheme, newly recruited single employees are provided dormitory accommodation. Since housing is expensive in Beijing, this often takes the form of one bedroom shared by a few employees of the same gender. This arrangement is normal and acceptable to Chinese employees – Chinese students also share their dormitories in schools and universities, and in sweatshop manufacturing plants the situation is far worse where ten or more rural migrant workers are crowded in a room with poor facilities. However, foreign employees, though only very small in number compared with the Chinese employees, find it difficult to get used to this idea because of the lack of privacy. Lenovo (China) has no special policy to accommodate their needs. Different management style is another source of cultural shock to foreign employees. According to an HR manager, foreign employees all emphasize their cultural shock when they come to China. However, Lenovo (China) has not developed a formal policy to manage these cultural shocks. This has led to the turnover of a few of the foreign employees and the company has made no effort to retain them.

Managing Chinese graduate returnees from overseas

Since the early 2000s, an increasing number of Chinese who went abroad for their higher education have been returning to China to seek employment and career development. The majority of Chinese overseas graduate returnees (known as *haigui* in China) are keen to work for multinational firms, and are often the favourite candidates. Lenovo is among the top employers of choice for which *haiguis* want to work. These repatriated Western educated and trained graduates bring with them different life styles, perspectives and (often unrealistic) expectations that may depart from Chinese norms. Some of them are said to be complacent and consider themselves superior to other graduate employees who have not been abroad for education or training. They expect high salaries up front, fast promotion, flexibility and autonomy in their work. Turnover is common among *haiguis* when expectations are unmet or better offers are available elsewhere. How to recruit and manage overseas graduate returnees effectively is an important issue for MNCs operating in China. Companies are now reportedly more cautious in recruiting and managing these returnees because they are seen as 'demanding' employees who are difficult

(Continued)

(Continued)

to retain. Lenovo shares some of these issues. Although turnover has not been a major problem, how to harmonize the relationship between *haiguis* and home-grown graduate employees is sometimes a challenge for line managers.

Gender equalities

Prior to Lenovo's acquisition of the IBM PC business unit, Lenovo had more women at the senior management level. The proportion of women in senior management has actually declined since the acquisition because it is now part of a bigger international operation. Two main reasons are attributed to this change. One is that there is a lower proportion of women at senior management level in the acquired business unit of IBM than in the Chinese operation. Another reason is that Lenovo has been through successive rounds of senior management restructuring after the acquisition, partly to do with the post-acquisition integration and partly to do with the poaching of senior managers among IT firms in China. Cultural clashes triggered by the post-acquisition integration have led to the departure of a number of senior managers. When new managers are recruited, they tend to bring their own people and HR initiatives with them, which will later be displaced by their successors when those managers depart. As an HR director observed, 'It is organizational politics, rather than equal opportunities, that we consider in the recruitment of senior managers. You need to be competent as well as well connected to get the senior management's job, and men tend to be better connected than women in the IT sector in general.'

Developing a global diversity management strategy

According to informants from Lenovo (China), diversity is not a key issue in the workforce in China. Therefore, it is not a priority of the company. The major task is post-acquisition integration to align the organizational cultures and become a truly international company. Nevertheless, Lenovo (China) does emphasize the need for employees to respect other employees' rights and privacy. Aggressive or discriminatory behaviours are forbidden, even as jokes. These expectations are written in the business conduct guidelines for employees. However, Lenovo (China) does not have any specific equal opportunities or diversity management programmes to enforce these clauses. The acquired business unit of IBM has good HR practices, for example, WLB and DM. These have not yet been transferred to the Chinese operation due to staff shortages. There was a corporate initiative (stimulated from the US side) about grouping women at international level together to have a global forum to discuss diversity issues in 2006. Unfortunately, budget constraints meant that the plan was set to one side.

The HR directors from Lenovo (US) are well aware of the challenge they face in transferring their US-developed diversity management programme to other branches across different countries and cultures. The US HR team are the people who are familiar with the concept and responsible for promoting its global diffusion, and they are approaching the task with extreme caution. This is in part, as they admitted, due to their unfamiliarity with the local environments in different parts of the world, although they are planning to visit Lenovo (China) for the first time. How to accommodate the diversity of the global workforce and leverage it to enhance the performance of the firm on the one hand, and how to develop a strong corporate culture that all employees will identify with on the other hand is their main HR concern, and a solution has yet to be found.

According to all managerial informants, the corporate priority is talent management. A new scheme called 'Mobility Plan' has been implemented at the international level. The purpose of the plan is to give managers an opportunity to work overseas to gain international experience to be able to lead at a global level. It is not aimed at Chinese managers in principle, but in reality has mainly involved sending Chinese managers to the US for development.

Source: compiled by the author based on information obtained from: Lenovo company website: www.lenovo.com (accessed 14 December 2008); *China Business*, 13 December 2004; and interviews by the author with HR directors, senior managers and employees of Lenovo in China and US in 2007.

Case study questions

1. What are the key issues of diversity management in this case study and how are they manifested?
2. How would you design a global cross-cultural management policy for Lenovo, taking into account its increasingly diverse workforce?
3. Chinese firms generally suffer from a poor image of low product quality, poor CSR and HRM; how would you help Lenovo to attract non-Chinese talent to work for the Company in its global operations, particularly outside China?

Further reading

- Foster, C. and Harris, L. (2005) 'From equal opportunities to diversity management', in J. Leopold, L. Harris and T. Watson (eds), *The Strategic Managing of Human Resources*. Essex: Pearson Education Ltd, pp. 116–139.
  This chapter highlights tensions and issues that can arise for employers, managers and employees in the development and application of EO and DM policies. It contains several insightful mini-case studies as examples to illustrate organizational dilemmas.

- Tatli, A. and Özbilgin, M. (2012) 'An emic approach to intersectional study of diversity at work: a Bourdieuan framing', *International Journal of Management Reviews*, 14(2): 180–200.
  This article provides a comprehensive review of the DM literature and critiques its predominantly etic nature. The authors propose an emic approach to researching diversity at work, which helps identify emergent and situated categories of diversity as embedded in a specific time and place. Drawing on Bourdieu's theory of capitals, they explain that relations and processes of power manifest themselves in the struggle for and accumulation of different forms of capitals. An emphasis on intersectionality is central to the authors' argument and they offer a five-step research guide.

- Abendroth, A. and den Dulk, L. (2011) 'Support for the work–life balance in Europe: the impact of state, workplace and family support on work–life balance satisfaction', *Work Employment & Society*, 25(2): 234–256.
  This article studies the relevance of different types of support for satisfaction with work–life balance, using Esping-Andersen's welfare regime typology as a benchmark. It focuses particularly on the relevance of state, instrumental and emotional workplace and family support based on a survey of 7,867 service-sector workers in eight European countries. The study examines the impact of the different support sources and found that emotional support and instrumental support in the workplace have a complementary relationship.

Internet resources

- www.shrm.org. The Society for Human Resource Management (SHRM) is the world's largest professional association devoted to HRM. Its webpages contain up-to-date research reports, case studies, professional advice and latest publications on a wide range of topics in HRM, including EO, DM, WLB and CSR.
- www.undp.org/content/undp/en/home/ourwork/womenempowerment/overview. html. The United Nations Development Programmes (UNDP) coordinates global and national efforts to integrate gender equality and women's empowerment into poverty reduction, democratic governance, crisis prevention and recovery, and environment and sustainable development. The website contains statistical information on gender

progress in nation states as well as gender development initiatives, programmes and stories.

Self-assessment questions

Indicative answers to these questions can be found on the companion website at study.sagepub.com/harzing4e.

1. What issues may arise if Lenovo (China) started to provide single-occupancy housing arrangements for its foreign employees to accommodate their needs for privacy while continuing to provide shared dormitories for its Chinese employees?
2. Which of the issues of diversity management in Lenovo are concerned with individual diversity and which are the collective-oriented diversity issues?
3. If you are a project manager of Lenovo and have to manage two groups of graduate employees, *haiguis* and home-grown graduates, and some of the former are being demanding and causing friction in the project team, how are you going to manage this situation?
4. Is the pattern of organizational politics displayed in the power struggle at the senior management level in Lenovo in which women are likely to be displaced or disadvantaged unique to Lenovo?
5. How would you advise the HR team of Lenovo (US) to develop a global diversity management programme for talent management?

References

Abendroth, A. and den Dulk, L. (2011) 'Support for the work–life balance in Europe: the impact of state, workplace and family support on work–life balance satisfaction', *Work, Employment and Society*, 25(2): 234–256.

Agocs, C. and Burr, C. (1996) 'Employment equity, affirmative action and managing diversity: assessing the differences', *International Journal of Manpower*, 17(4/5): 30–45.

Avgar, A., Givan, R. and Liu, M.W. (2011) 'A balancing act: work–life balance and multiple stakeholder outcomes in hospitals', *British Journal of Industrial Relations*, 49(4): 717–741.

Backes-Gellner, U. and Veen, S. (2013) 'Positive effects of ageing and age diversity in innovative companies – large-scale empirical evidence on company productivity', *Human Resource Management Journal*, 23(3): 279–295.

Benson, J., Yuasa, M. and Debroux, P. (2007) 'The prospect for gender diversity in Japanese employment', *International Journal of Human Resource Management*, 18(5): 890–907.

Billett, S., Dymock, D., Johnson, G. and Martin, G. (2011) 'Overcoming the paradox of employers' views about older workers', *International Journal of Human Resource Management*, 22(6): 1248–1261.

Bozkurt, Ö. (2012) 'Foreign employers as relief routes: women, multinational corporations and managerial careers in Japan', *Gender, Work and Organization*, 19(3): 225–253.

Bronfenbrenner, U. (1979) *The Ecology of Human Development*. Cambridge, MA: Harvard University Press.

Brough, P., Holt, J., Bauld, R., Biggs, A. and Ryan, C. (2008) 'The ability of work–life balance policies to influence key social/organizational issues', *Asia Pacific Journal of Human Resources*, 46(3): 261–274.

Burgess, J. and Connell, J. (2008) 'Introduction to special issue: HRM and job quality: an overview', *International Journal of Human Resource Management*, 19(3): 407–418.

Casey, C., Skibnes, R. and Pringle, J. (2011) 'Gender equality and corporate governance: policy strategies in Norway and New Zealand', *Gender, Work and Organization*, 18(6): 613–630.

Chandra, V. (2012) 'Work–life balance: eastern and western perspectives', *International Journal of Human Resource Management*, 23(5): 1040–1056.

Cho, J. and Kwon, T. (2010) 'Affirmative action and corporate compliance in South Korea', *Feminist Economics*, 16(2): 111–139.

Chou, K.L. and Cheung, K. (2013) 'Family-friendly policies in the workplace and their effect on work–life conflicts in Hong Kong', *International Journal of Human Resource Management*, DOI:10.1080/09585192.2013.781529.

CIPD (Chartered Institute of Personnel and Development) (2006) *Diversity: An Overview*, CIPD factsheet, www.cipd.co.uk/hr-topics/diversity-equality.aspx (accessed 20 August 2007).

CIPD (Chartered Institute of Personnel and Development) (2007) *Diversity in Business: A Focus for Progress*. London: Chartered Institute of Personnel and Development.

Cooke, F.L. (2010) 'Women's participation in employment in Asia: a comparative analysis of China, India, Japan and South Korea', *International Journal of Human Resource Management*, 21(10–12): 2249–2270.

Cooke, F.L. (2012) *Human Resource Management in China: New Trends and Practices*. London: Routledge.

Cooke, F.L. and Saini, D. (2012) 'Managing diversity in Chinese and Indian firms: a qualitative study', *Journal of Chinese Human Resource Management*, 3(1): 16–32.

Cooke, F.L. and Xiao, Y.C. (2014) 'Gender roles and organizational HR practices: the case of women's careers in accountancy and consultancy firms in China', *Human Resource Management* 53(1): 23–44.

Cox, T. (1993) *Cultural Diversity in Organizations: Theory, Research and Practice*. San Francisco: Barrett-Koehler Publishers.

Cox, T. and Blake, S. (1991) 'Managing cultural diversity: implications for organizational competitiveness', *Academy of Management Executive*, 5(3): 45–56.

Cox, T., Lobel, S. and McLeod, P. (1991) 'Effects of ethnic group cultural differences on cooperative and competitive behaviour on a group task', *Academy of Management Journal*, 34(4): 827–847.

Dameron, S. and Joffre, O. (2007) 'The good and the bad: the impact of diversity management on co-operative relationships', *International Journal of Human Resource Management*, 18(11): 2037–2056.

Davidson, M. and Burke, R. (eds) (2011) *Women in Management Worldwide: Progress and Prospects*, 2nd edn. Oxford: Ashgate Publishing.

Drolet, M. and Mumford, K. (2012) 'The gender pay gap for private-sector employees in Canada and Britain', *British Journal of Industrial Relations*, 50(3): 529–553.

Dunavant, B.M. and Heiss, B. (2005) *Global Diversity 2005*. Washington, DC: Diversity Best Practices.

Ferner, A., Almond, P. and Colling, T. (2005) 'Institutional theory and the cross-national transfer of employment policy: the case of "workforce diversity" in US multinationals', *Journal of International Business Studies*, 36(3): 304–321.

Fleetwood, S. (2007) 'Re-thinking work–life balance: Editor's introduction', *International Journal of Human Resource Management,* 18(3): 351–359.

Forstenlechner, I., Lettice, F. and Özbilgin, M. (2012) 'Questioning quotas: applying a relational framework for diversity management practices in the United Arab Emirates', *Human Resource Management Journal*, 22(3): 299–315.

Foster, C. and Harris, L. (2005) 'From equal opportunities to diversity management', in J. Leopold, L. Harris and T. Watson (eds), *The Strategic Managing of Human Resources*. Essex: Pearson Education Ltd, pp. 116–139.

Fuertes, V., Egdell, V. and McQuaid, R. (2013) 'Extending working lives: age management in SMEs', *Employee Relations*, 35(3): 272–293.

Gelb, J. (2000) 'The equal employment opportunity law: a decade of change for Japanese women', *Law and Policy*, 22(3–4): 365–407.

Ghosh, R. and Roy, K. (1997) 'The changing status of women in India: impact of urbanization and development', *International Journal of Social Economics*, 24(7/8/9): 902–917.

Greenhaus, J.H. (2008) 'Innovations in the study of the work–family interface: introduction to the special section', *Journal of Occupational and Organizational Psychology*, 81: 343–348.

Gregory, A. and Milner, S. (2009) 'Editorial: work–life balance: a matter of choice?', *Gender, Work and Organization*, 16(1): 1–13.

Healy, G. and Oikelome, F. (2007) 'A global link between national diversity policies? The case of the migration of Nigerian physicians to the UK and USA', *International Journal of Human Resource Management*, 18(11): 1917–1933.

Houkamau, C. and Boxall, P. (2011) 'The incidence and impacts of diversity management: a survey of New Zealand employees', *Asia Pacific Journal of Human Resources*, 49(4): 440–460.

Jones, D., Pringle, J. and Shepherd, D. (2000) '"Managing diversity" meets Aotearoa/New Zealand', *Personnel Review*, 29(3): 364–380.

Jones, K., King, E., Nelson, J., Geller, D. and Bowes-Sperry, L. (2013) 'Beyond the business case: an ethical perspective of diversity training', *Human Resource Management*, 52(1): 55–74.

Jonsen, K., Maznevski, M. and Schneider, S. (2011) 'Diversity and its not so diverse literature: an international perspective', *International Journal of Cross Cultural Management*, 11(1): 35–62.

Kang, H.R. and Rowley, C. (2005) 'Women in management in South Korea: advancement or retrenchment?', *Asia Pacific Business Review*, 11(2): 213–231.

Kim, Y. (2005) 'Issues and observations: for women leaders in Korea, gains but miles to go', *Leadership in Action*, 25(5): 20–22.

Kochan, T., Bezrukova, K., Ely, R., Jackson, S., Joshi, A., Jehn, K., Leonard, J., Levine, D. and Thomas, D. (2003) 'The effects of diversity on business performance: report of the diversity research network', *Human Resource Management*, 42(1): 3–21.

Kramar, R. (2012) 'Diversity management in Australia: a mosaic of concepts, practice and rhetoric', *Asia Pacific Journal of Human Resources*, 50(2): 245–261.

Kucera, D. (1998) 'Foreign trade and men and women's employment and earnings in Germany, and Japan', *Centre for Economic Policy Analysis Working Paper 9*, www.newschool.edu/cepa (accessed 16 March 2007).

Kunze, F., Boehm, S. and Bruch, H. (2013) 'Organizational performance consequences of age diversity: inspecting the role of diversity-friendly HR policies and top managers' negative age stereotypes', *Journal of Management Studies*, 50(3): 413–442.

Lau, D. and Murnighan, J. (1998) 'Demographic diversity and faultlines: the compositional dynamics of organizational groups', *Academy of Management Review*, 23(2): 325–340.

Lazazzara, A., Karpinska, K. and Henkens, K. (2013) 'What factors influence training opportunities for older workers? Three factorial surveys exploring the attitudes of HR professionals', *International Journal of Human Resource Management*, 24(11): 2154–2172.

Li, J., Chu, C., Lam, K. and Liao, S. (2011) 'Age diversity and firm performance in an emerging economy: implications for cross-cultural human resource management', *Human Resource Management*, 50(2): 247–270.

Liff, S. (1996) 'Two routes to managing diversity: individual differences or social group characteristics', *Employee Relations*, 19(1): 11–26.

Lorbiecki, A. and Jack, G. (2000) 'Critical turns in the evolution of diversity management', *British Journal of Management*, Special Issue, 11(3): S17–31.

Maxwell, G., Blair, S. and McDougall, M. (2001) 'Edging towards managing diversity in practice', *Employees Relations*, 23(5): 468–482.

Mor Barak, M. (2005) *Managing Diversity: Towards a Globally Inclusive Workplace*. Thousand Oaks, CA: Sage.

Ng, E. and Burke, R. (2005) 'Person-organization fit and the war for talent: does diversity management make a difference?', *International Journal of Human Resource Management*, 16(7): 1195–1210.

Nishii, L. and Özbilgin, F. (2007) 'Global diversity management: towards a conceptual framework', *International Journal of Human Resource Management*, 18(11): 1883–1894.

Özbilgin, M., Syed, J., Ali, F. and Torunoglu, D. (2012) 'International transfer of policies and practices of gender equality in employment to and among Muslim majority countries', *Gender, Work and Organization*, 19(4): 345–369.

Özbilgin, M. and Tatli, A. (2011) 'Mapping out the field of equality and diversity: rise of individualism and voluntarism', *Human Relations*, 64(9): 1229–1253.

Pas, B., Peters, P., Doorewaard, H., Eisinga, R. and Lagro-Janssen, T. (2011) 'Feminisation of the medical profession: a strategic HRM dilemma? The effects of family-friendly HR practices on female doctors' contracted working hours', *Human Resource Management Journal*, 21(3): 285–302.

Patterson, L., Bae, S. and Lim, J.Y. (2013) 'Gender equality in Korean firms: recent evidence from HR practitioners', *Asia Pacific Journal of Human Resources*, 51(3): 364–381.

Pocock, B. (2005) 'Work–life "balance" in Australia: limited progress, dim prospects', *Asia Pacific Journal of Human Resources*, 43(2): 198–209.

Pocock, B., Williams, P. and Skinner, N. (2012) 'Conceptualizing work, family and community: a socio-ecological systems model, taking account of power, time, space and life stage', *British Journal of Industrial Relations*, 50(3): 391–411.

Richard, O.C., Barnett, T., Dwyer, S. and Chadwick, K. (2004) 'Cultural diversity in management, firm performance, and the moderating role of entrepreneurial orientation dimensions', *Academy of Management Journal*, 47(2): 255–266.

Richard, O., Roh, H. and Pieper, J. (2013) 'The link between diversity and equality management practice bundles and racial diversity in the managerial ranks: does firm size matter?', *Human Resource Management*, 52(2): 215–242.

Scott, K., Heathcote, J. and Gruman, J. (2011) 'The diverse organization: finding gold at the end of the rainbow', *Human Resource Management*, 50(6): 735–755.

Seguino, S. (2000) 'Accounting for gender in Asian economic growth', *Feminist Economics*, 6(3): 27–58.

Sippola, A. and Smale, A. (2007) 'The global integration of diversity management: a longitudinal case study', *International Journal of Human Resource Management*, 18(11): 1895–1916.

Soni, V. (2000) 'A twenty-first-century reception for diversity in public sector: a case study', *Public Administration Review*, 60(5): 395–408.

Steinhoff, P. and Tanaka, K. (1993) 'Women managers in Japan', *International Studies of Management and Organizations*, 23(2): 25–48.

Stockman, N., Bonney, N., Sheng, X.W. (1995) *Women's Work in East and West: The Dual Burden of Employment and Family Life*. London: UCL Press Ltd.

Süß, S. and Kleiner, M. (2007) 'Diversity management in Germany: dissemination and design of the concept', *International Journal of Human Resource Management*, 18(11): 1934–1953.

Subeliani, D. and Tsogas, G. (2005) 'Managing diversity in the Netherlands: a case study of Rabobank', *International Journal of Human Resource Management*, 16(5): 831–885.

Tatli, A. and Özbilgin, M. (2012) 'An emic approach to intersectional study of diversity at work: a Bourdieuan framing', *International Journal of Management Reviews*, 14(2): 180–200.

Taylor, P., Powell, D. and Wrench, J. (1997) *The Evaluation of Anti-Discrimination Training Activities in the United Kingdom*. Geneva: International Labour Office.

Tomlinson, J. (2011) 'Gender equality and the state: a review of objectives, policies and progress in the European Union', *International Journal of Human Resource Management*, 22(18): 3755–3774.

Tsui, A., Egan, T. and O'Reilly, C. (1992) 'Being different: relational demography and organizational attachment', *Administrative Science Quarterly*, 37(4): 549–579.

UNDP (United Nations Development Program) (2009) 'Gender empowerment measure', in *Human Development Report 2007/8*. http://hdr.undp.org/en/media/HDR_20072008_GEM.pdf (accessed 16 April 2013).

Van der Meulen Rodgers, Y. (1998) 'A reversal of fortune for Korean women: explaining the 1983 upward turn in relative earnings', *Economic Development and Cultural Change*, 46(4): 727–748.

Van Dijk, H., van Engen, M. and Paauwe, J. (2012) 'Reframing the business case for diversity: a values and virtues perspective', *Journal of Business Ethics*, 111: 73–84.

Venkata Ratnam, C. and Chandra, V. (1996) 'Source of diversity and the challenge before human resource management in India', *International Journal of Manpower*, 17(4/5): 76–108.

Venkata Ratnam, C. and Jain, H. (2002) 'Women in trade union in India', *International Journal of Manpower*, 23(3): 277–292.

Voydanoff, P. (2007) *Work, Family, and Community: Exploring Interconnections*, Applied Psychology Series. New York: Psychology Press.

Wang, J. and Verma, A. (2012) 'Explaining organizational responsiveness to work–life balance issues: the role of business strategy and high performance work systems', *Human Resource Management*, 51(3): 407–432.

Williams, K. and O'Reilly, C. (1998) 'Demography and diversity in organizations: a review of 40 years of research', in B.M. Staw and L.L. Cummings (eds), *Research in Organizational Behaviour*, 20. Greenwich, CT: JAI Press, pp. 77–140.

Wise, L.R. and Tsehirhart, M. (2000) 'Examining empirical evidence on diversity effects: How useful is diversity research for public sector managers?', *Public Administration Review*, 60(5): 386–394.

Wöcke, A. and Sutherland, M. (2008) 'The impact of employment equity regulations on psychological contracts in South Africa', *International Journal of Human Resource Management*, 19(4): 528–542.

World Bank (2006) *India Country Data 2014*, http://data.worldbank.org/country/india (accessed 16 June 2014).

Xiao, Y.C. and Cooke, F.L. (2012) 'Work–life balance in China? Social policy, employer strategy and individual coping mechanisms', *Asia-Pacific Journal of Human Resources*, 50(1): 6–12.

Yukongdi, V. and Benson, J. (eds) (2006) *Women in Asian Management*. London: Routledge.

Corporate Social Responsibility and Sustainability through Ethical HRM Practices

Fang Lee Cooke

15

Contents

Learning objectives

After reading this chapter you will be able to:

- Understand the concepts of ethics, labour standards and corporate social responsibility
- Differentiate perspectives of ethics and corporate social responsibility
- Explain how ethical employment practices can contribute to sustainable business success and social development
- Critically evaluate the gaps between the aspirations of corporate social responsibility and actual practices in workplaces
- Understand competing demands on multinational corporations in sustaining their businesses and justifying their behaviour to different stakeholders

Chapter outline

This chapter provides an overview of the emergence of the concepts of ethics, labour standards and corporate social responsibility. It examines driving forces, from national and international bodies, for promoting ethical employment and labour standards as important areas of corporate social responsibility. It provides examples to illustrate how different societal contexts may affect firms' level of motivation and accountability in fulfilling their social responsibility through ethical HRM practices.

1 Introduction

> Corporate social responsibility is a concept whereby companies integrate social and environmental concerns in their business operations and in their interaction with their stakeholders on a voluntary basis. (European Commission, 2008)

Labour standards, employment ethics, equal opportunities and diversity management are key concerns of human resource management in the global context. While international labour standards have attracted much attention as part of the corporate social responsibility, relatively few studies have looked at these issues from the CSR perspective within the IHRM context. Meanwhile, firms are facing increasing pressure to act in a socially responsive way towards their stakeholders, including their investors, shareholders, employees, trade unions, customers and the local community (e.g. Bhattacharya and Sen, 2004; Brammer et al., 2007).

Due to space constraints and for clarity, we have discussed EO and DM in detail in Chapter 14. In this chapter, we examine various theoretical perspectives and organizational practices related to employment ethics, labour standards and CSR in the international context. We begin the chapter with a section that discusses corporate ethical and social responsibility generally and employment ethics, specifically. This is followed by a section that examines international labour standards as a pertinent issue of CSR. Finally, the chapter draws together employment ethics, labour standards, EO and DM, as building blocks of CSR, by providing an integrated framework within which the relationships of these dimensions can be understood and their implications for HRM and organizational outcomes assessed. In particular, the chapter highlights two related aspects of HRM in CSR. One is how HR initiatives, such as employee involvement (EI), may facilitate firms' fulfilment of their CSR tasks. The other is how firms may adopt ethical or socially responsible HR practices as part of their CSR governance. It argues that the integration of HR policy with CSR policy will contribute to the sustainability of businesses and the social and economic development of nations, particularly the less developed countries.

2 Ethics and corporate social responsibility

Issues related to business ethics and CSR have been the subject of growing debate across an increasingly wide range of disciplines in the social sciences and business and management studies (see Egri and Ralston (2008) for a comprehensive review). Business ethics and CSR are distinctive concepts, but they share in common a concern for the ethical dimension (Cacioppe et al., 2008). CSR has an expanding focus in both academic studies and business practices in different parts of the world, with some countries advancing at a more rapid pace than others. The 2008 global financial crisis has triggered a new wave of interest in the topic that has resulted in a bourgeoning body of literature that has extended both the intellectual and empirical frontiers (e.g. Brammer et al., 2012).

Theoretical perspectives of CSR

The study of CSR is often traced back to the 1950s when it focused primarily on philanthropy (see Carroll, 1979; Garriga and Melé, 2004 for more detailed reviews). Despite more than four decades of debate, there is still no consensus on the concept of CSR and what it really means (e.g. Carroll, 1979, 1999; Bhattacharya and Sen, 2004; Crowther and Capaldi, 2008). Corporate responsibility, corporate citizenship, responsible business, social responsibility and corporate social opportunity are some of its variant terms. Carroll (1991: 42) argued that CSR is a multi-dimensional construct embracing four sets of responsibilities: economic, legal, ethical and philanthropic. Through representing the four components of total CSR in a pyramid (see Figure 15.1),

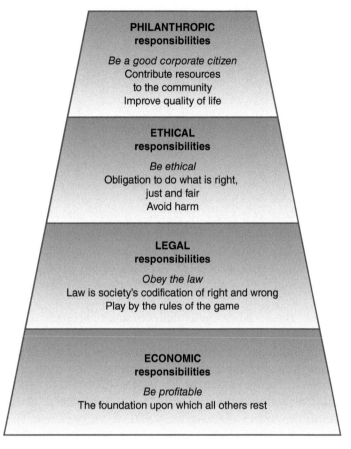

Figure 15.1   The pyramid of CSR

Source: Carroll (1991: 42)

Carroll (1991) proposed that each of these responsibilities should be fulfilled together and in parallel rather than within a sequence.

The growing interest in corporate ethical and social responsibility in recent years has led to the proliferation of theoretical perspectives. Two commonly debated ethical theories (see Ackers, 2006) are Utilitarianism and Kantianism. Proponents of Utilitarianism hold the view that whichever action gives the greatest happiness or utility is to be preferred. In other words, if one follows solely the principle of utility, then the end justifies the means. By contrast, proponents of Kantianism believe that the imperative to respect everybody is the means as well as the end and that what is right for one person is right for everyone (see Table 15.1).

Table 15.1   Means and ends in ethical theories

Consequentialist	Non-consequentialist
Utilitarianism	Kantianism
Happiness of the greatest number	Human dignity an end in itself
The end justifies the means	Universal moral rules
Language of economic utility	Language of human rights

Source: adapted from Ackers (2006: 429)

Garriga and Melé (2004: 52–53) divide CSR theories into four groups:

1. *Instrumental theories*: This group of theories understands CSR as a mere means to the end, which is profit. It is assumed that the corporation is an instrument for wealth creation and that this is its sole social responsibility. Only the economic aspect of the interactions between business and society is considered. So any social value or activity is accepted if, and only if, it is consistent with wealth creation.
2. *Political theories*: The social power of the corporation is emphasized in this group of theories, specifically in its relationship with society and its responsibility in the political arena. This leads the corporation to accept social duties and rights or participate in activities requiring social cooperation.
3. *Integrative theories*: This group of theories argues that business depends on society for its continuity and growth and even for the existence of business itself. Therefore, business ought to be integrated with social demands.
4. *Ethical theories*: A fourth group of theories understands that the relationship between business and society is embedded with ethical values. This leads to a vision of CSR from an ethical perspective which implies that firms ought to accept social responsibilities as an ethical obligation above any other consideration.

While acknowledging the comprehensiveness of Garriga and Melé's (2004) review, Secchi (2007) pointed out a number of weaknesses in their analysis. Secchi (2007: 347) proposed an alternative way of categorizing the CSR literature into three major groups based on their theoretical perspectives, each consisting of some sub-groups (see Figure 15.2):

1. The Utilitarian group, in which the corporation is intended as a maximizing 'black box' where problems of externalities and social costs emerge.
2. The managerial category, where problems of responsibility are approached from inside the firm (internal perspective).
3. Relational theories, in which the type of relations between the firm and the environment are at the centre of the analysis.

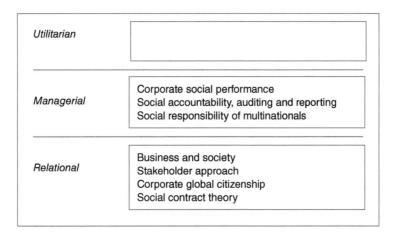

Utilitarian	
Managerial	Corporate social performance Social accountability, auditing and reporting Social responsibility of multinationals
Relational	Business and society Stakeholder approach Corporate global citizenship Social contract theory

Figure 15.2   Utilitarian, managerial and relational theories of CSR

Source: Secchi (2007: 350)

Two schools of thought have been influential in the debate on corporate ethical and social responsibility: the efficiency theory and the social responsibility theory. The efficiency perspective, as represented by Milton Friedman, has a utilitarian and narrow focus on shareholder value. According to Friedman (1962: 133):

> There is one and only one social responsibility of business – to use its resources and engage in activities designed to increase its profits so long as it stays within the rules of the game, which is to say, engages in open and free competition, without deception or fraud.

By contrast, the social responsibility theory, or the integrated-strategy perspective (Baron, 2001), adopts a much broader focus that emphasizes stakeholder value (e.g. Freeman, 1984). It argues that corporations should take into account the interests of different stakeholders, such as employees, customers, suppliers and communities when making business decisions:

> Socially responsible companies not only try to be economically sustainable and profitable, but also endeavour to work with their employees, families, local communities and nation states to improve the quality of life in ways that are both ethical and sustainable in relation to society and the environment. (Cacioppe et al., 2008: 684)

The stakeholder concept is highly relevant to HRM, since looking after employees' welfare and well-being is an important part of a company's social responsibility. As employers, firms have the responsibility to ensure the quality of their employees' working life, which includes job quality, work–life quality and personal well-being associated with work. This calls for an approach that promotes EI and participation in organizational decision making. It also requires firms to take employees' interests into account when formulating HR policy.

CSR in practice

Companies may adopt different approaches to CSR in practice. Table 15.2 summarizes some of the issues on which companies may choose to focus their CSR activities, dependent on the nature of the business, operational environment, management cognition and business priorities.

Table 15.2 Issues covered by CSR

• Environmental	• Concern for human rights
• Fair trade	• Philanthropic history
• Organic produce	• Cooperative principles
• Not tested on animals	• Support for education
• Community involvement	• Participates in local business initiatives
• Cause related marketing	• Supports national business initiatives
• Charitable giving	• Commitment to reporting
• Religious foundation	• Employee schemes
• Support for social cause	• Refusal to trade in certain markets

Source: Howard and Willmott (2001), cited in Sachdev (2006: 264)

Firms may be influenced to adopt CSR practices by several driving forces, some of which are related. One is the rising awareness of ethical consumerism, particularly related to environmental issues, health concerns, and human and animal rights. Another driving force comes from international and domestic pressure groups. As business competition intensifies globally, MNCs are under increasing pressure to reduce their costs and simultaneously face growing demand to review their labour standards, sourcing strategy, environment policy and their wider role in the economic and social development of less developed countries. Many MNCs now have an espoused CSR policy and publish it on their corporate websites. As part of CSR initiatives, employees are encouraged to participate in community projects and charity activities, and may be supported by their employer through sponsorship and time off.

CSR and business benefits

Opinions on the perceived benefits of CSR activities differ widely. Some argue that there is a strong business case for CSR and that adopting a proactive CSR approach can help companies to:

- avoid business risks such as corruption scandals or environmental accidents
- have greater access to capital through distinctive ethical values that appeal to particular types of investors
- attract and retain customers through enhanced brand image and corporate reputation
- legitimize business and profit levels and avoid government intervention or public criticism
- manage human resources more effectively through attraction and retention of talent and enhanced motivation and commitment of the workforce, and
- gain acceptance in local communities and support from host country governments, including favourable policy treatment.

Indeed, a number of empirical studies have provided evidence to support these claims, though sometimes they are conditional on other additional factors (e.g. Hillman and Keim, 2001; Sen and Bhattacharya, 2001; Zinkin, 2004). For example, Baron (2001: 7) argued, based on his economic modelling, that CSR not only has 'a direct effect on the costs of the firm', but also has 'a strategic effect by altering the competitive positions of firms in an industry'. Cacioppe et al.'s (2008: 681) study found that well-educated managers and professionals are likely to take into account 'the ethical and social responsibility reputations of companies when deciding whether to work for them, use their services or buy shares in their companies'. Roozen et al.'s (2001) study found that employees who work for firms that behave in an ethical way to their stakeholders are more likely to accept and be committed to ethical behaviour and suppress their self-interest for the greater good of the organization and the community. Zinkin's (2004) study of BP's activities in China and Malaysia illustrates how an MNC can rebuild its image and maximize the 'licence to operate' in host countries through the engagement of the 'right' type of CSR activities.

Other studies have shown that socially responsible corporations may have a competitive advantage because they are more attractive to potential employees and therefore benefit from a larger talent pool of job candidates (e.g. Turban and Greening, 1997; Albinger and Freeman, 2000). They are also thought to be more likely to have a more committed workforce because employees will be proud to work for companies with favourable reputations through acting in socially and environmentally responsible ways (e.g. Brammer et al., 2007). Similarly, CSR activities have been found to be positively associated with job satisfaction (Brammer et al., 2007; Valentine and Fleischman, 2008). Furthermore, CSR programmes introduced by firms may lead to 'the development of leadership skills and a high level of motivation among employees who are inspired to become involved in CSR programmes' (Cacioppe et al., 2008: 689). Involving employees in CSR initiatives enables firms to identify talent and develop new skills and competences which may not be demonstrated in routine work situations (Cacioppe et al., 2008).

It should be noted, however, that existing studies on the payoffs of improved social responsibility remain inconclusive. For example, Sen and Bhattacharya's (2001) study found that consumers can react to companies' CSR initiatives in different ways and that CSR does not always positively influence consumers' purchasing behaviour. Similarly, Hillman and Keim's (2001) study showed that strategic stakeholder management contributes to the financial performance of the firm, whereas participation in wider social issues (i.e. an altruistic approach to CSR) does not. In addition, good corporate social performance (CSP) only has positive impact on job seekers with high levels of job choice and awareness of CSR issues, but no impact on those who have limited job choice and are unaware of or less concerned with CSR issues (Albinger and Freeman, 2000). Shen and Zhu's (2011) study of 784 managers and employees in two large aluminium manufacturing companies in southwest China also found that socially responsible (i.e. employee-oriented) HRM has a significant positive relationship with employees' affective and normative commitment but not continuance commitment.

A number of concerns have been raised by critics of CSR. Some see CSR as a distraction from the fundamental purpose of the business, as noted above (e.g. Friedman, 1962). Others question firms' motives for engaging in CSR, interpreting it as a public relations exercise and attempt to pre-empt interventions from governments and pressure groups (e.g. Rodriguez et al., 2006). Those who are concerned with companies' genuine willingness to take on CSR argue that better regulation and enforcement at national and international levels, instead of voluntary measures, are necessary to ensure that MNCs behave in an ethical and socially responsible manner (e.g. Chan and Ross, 2003).

Box 15.1 shows how the CSR activities adopted by an MNC may be a pragmatic outcome emerging from strategic business intent when faced with political pressure from the host country and the capacity of the MNC to overcome or diffuse the situation. As such, a company's CSR portfolio may not contain a coherent set of policy statements and activities.

Box 15.1   Stop and reflect

CSR of retail global giant Wal-Mart (China)

Wal-Mart opened its first store in China in 1996. After a low-key entry for the first few years, War-Mart decided in 2000 to launch a major expansion in a bid to catch up with Carrefour of France. In 2001, the State Council of China approved Wal-Mart's expansion plan of developing 60 supermarkets in 20 major cities in China, with a sales revenue target of 18 billion yuan. By March 2005, Wal-Mart had 44 stores with over 23,000 employees in China.

In November 2004, Wal-Mart China announced a US$1 million commitment to establish the China Retail Research Centre at the School of Economics and

Management of Tsinghua University. This is the first academic institution in China dedicated to the research of China's fast growing retail industry. China's rapidly growing economy continues to create unprecedented opportunities for retail corporations like Wal-Mart. The US$1 million donation for establishing the China Retail Research Centre is an example of Wal-Mart's long-term commitment to China. It is believed that Wal-Mart's support for the centre will facilitate China's participation and cooperation in the international retail field and drive the healthy development of the country's retail sector. It is hoped that the China Retail Research Centre will develop into a world-class research institute and boost the theoretical research and management of China's retail industry.

Interestingly, Wal-Mart's enthusiasm in advancing the retail knowledge in China was not extended to support of trade unionism. For years, Wal-Mart has been resistant to China's request to establish a trade union for its workforce, claiming that it was its global corporate HR policy to have a non-unionized workforce. Wal-Mart was publicly criticized by the All-China Federation of Trade Unions (ACFTU) in the early 2000s for its refusal to recognize the trade union. It was not until 2006 that Wal-Mart softened its stance towards union recognition, resulting in the establishment of its first store-level union in July 2006. Within months, more store-level union organizations were set up among Wal-Mart's 50-plus stores.

However, union recognition has not brought true bargaining power or voice to the workforce. On 14 July 2008, the ACFTU concluded the first collective union contract with Wal-Mart in Shenyang city, Liaoning Province in northern China. Wal-Mart has subsequently applied this one single collective contract template to all of its stores nationwide, without allowing individual store's unions to bargain. Many individual store unions were not even given the chance to sign the contract template themselves, as some store unions had been asked to sign a collective contract on behalf of other outlets in the surrounding areas. Given the significant economic disparity and labour market conditions across different regions in China, it is clear that a single nation-wide collective contract is too broad to reflect local needs. However, Wal-Mart held the view that there was no need to amend what had already been approved by the ACFTU. Requests from local union representatives for collective bargaining at store level were ignored by store managers. Wal-Mart's refusal to enter into genuine collective bargaining has attracted public criticism.

Sources: Compiled from *China Business*, 7 August 2006; China Labor News Translations, 2008; Cooke, 2008.

Tensions in ethical HRM and business

As noted earlier, the business case for CSR may not have a sufficient appeal for firms to adopt an ethical and socially responsible employment policy. Instead, moral and legal sanctions remain the main drivers for ethical HRM. The ethical dimension of HRM is a complex issue attracting considerable academic debate and is a source of tension in business decisions (e.g. Bolton et al., 2012).

Employment ethics is a subdivision of business ethics, which according to Ackers (2006: 427) 'involves the application of general moral disciplines to the management of employees' wages and conditions'. The focus is on human relationships at inter-personal and organizational levels. At the individual level, the issue of concern is how individual employees should behave responsibly towards others including their co-workers, employer and customers. An increasing number of companies have intro-duced codes of conduct to ensure their employees behave in a professional and ethical way, although some critics (e.g. Winstanley and Woodall, 2000) argue that this may be a disguised attempt by the company to shift at least some of its corporate responsibility on to individuals through disciplinary action. Some companies introduce HR initiatives, such as appraisal and pay schemes, 'to encourage responsible behav-iour by their staff' (Sachdev, 2006: 266). Since the behaviour of individual employees affects the image, as well as the productivity, of the firm, it is therefore in the firm's interest to ensure that all of its employees act responsibly.

At the organizational level, the issue of concern relates to the ethical dimension of the company's employment or HR policies and practices. There are a number of potential tensions and dilemmas in socially responsible HR policies and practices and their wider business concerns (see Winstanley and Woodall, 2000; Pinnington et al., 2007 for more detailed discussions).

Box 15.2   Stop and reflect

Tensions and dilemmas in CSR and HR practices

Consider the following questions:

- Should companies hire cheap labour, including children, women and agency workers who may be the least protected in the labour market, in order to reduce employment costs?
- Should companies hire the best and most able candidates to maximize productivity at the risk of excluding socially disadvantaged groups?
- Should companies invest in training and development of their employees to enhance their productivity and employability at the risk of losing them to their competitors?

- Should companies economize on their health and safety provisions in the workplace to gain cost advantage?
- Should companies increase their organizational flexibility to gain competitive advantage by requesting their employees to work flexibly including working unsocial hours and overtime at short notice to the detriment of their work–life balance?
- Should international non-governmental organizations operating in deprived areas adopt a performance-related pay scheme to incentivize performance that may be at odds with the norms and culture of the employees and the local community?

These issues are particularly pertinent for Western MNCs that operate in less developed countries where the unemployment rate may be high and labour standards may be generally low and non-compliant with few legal consequences (e.g. Cooke, 2015). The difficulty in formulating and implementing corporate HR strategy for MNCs has been widely noted as a result of variations in ethical codes, moral standards, social values, laws and other institutional settings across different countries (see Chapters 1 and 2 in this volume, for example). Issues related to labour standards, equal opportunity and workforce diversity are even more challenging as they are often central to the debate on corporate ethical and social responsibility (also see Janssens and Steyaert (2012) for a conceptual discussion of ethics and IHRM in three cosmopolitan – political, cultural and social – perspectives). In the following sections, we will discuss issues related to labour standards in more detail (see Chapter 14 for equal opportunity and diversity management).

3 International labour standards and decent work

The role of MNCs in disseminating good practice has been noted, albeit a process often constrained by institutional and cultural challenges (e.g. Bartlett and Ghoshal, 1989; Briscoe and Schuler, 2004; Harzing and Ruysseveldt, 2004; Yu, 2012). However, it has been argued that intensifying competition at the global level has exerted pressure on MNCs 'to enhance their competitiveness through ongoing rounds of cost-cutting' that are centred on labour cost (Wood, 2006: 265). This is often achieved by worsening employment terms and conditions that are typically manifested in low standards of health and safety, extremely poor pay and long working hours, suppression of labour organization, and withdrawal of workplace training, employment benefits and job security (e.g. Rodgers, 2002; Chan and Ross, 2003; Kalleberg, 2009; Bolton et al., 2012). Evidence from around the world has shown that the neo-classical model that relies on market forces to determine labour market outcomes is not in the interest of many, especially communities from deprived regions. Global capitalism with its associated proliferation and expansion of MNCs in developing countries has so far aggravated income and spatial inequalities and reinforced the dependency of the poor on the rich and of the less developed on the developed countries (Stiglitz, 2002).

The development of international labour standards is a response to the growing number of needs and challenges faced by workers and employers in the global economy. International labour standards are the norms or rules that regulate or govern working conditions and labour relations. Box 15.3 provides an indication of the scope of labour protection set by the International Labour Organization. The ILO is one of the main actors involved in establishing international labour standards (see Rubery and Grimshaw, 2003). Founded in 1919 with an initial 42 member states, ILO had 182 member states by May 2008. The labour standards are not imposed upon member states as the ILO has little power to implement them. Rather, the ILO works with member states 'to promote labour standards through technical assistance and development policy' (Rubery and Grimshaw, 2003: 247).

The primary goal of the ILO is to promote opportunities for women and men to obtain decent and productive work in conditions of freedom, equity, security and human dignity. 'Decent work' was defined in the 1999 report by the Director General of the ILO as productive work in which rights are protected, which generates an adequate income, with adequate social protection. It also means sufficient work, in the sense that all should have full access to income-earning opportunities. It marks the high road to economic and social development, a road in which employment, income and social protection are achieved without compromising workers' rights and social standards. 'Decent work' is at the centre of all its four strategic objectives: promote rights at work, encourage decent employment opportunities, enhance social protection and strengthen dialogue on work-related issues (ILO, 1999).

Box 15.3   Stop and reflect

International labour standards

ILO international labour standards embrace numerous aspects of labour markets, ranging from minimum wages and equal pay to health and safety regulations. These standards can be classified into six main categories:

- respect for fundamental human rights
- protection of wages

- employment security
- working conditions
- labour market and social policies
- industrial relations.

How can these standards be applied to garment factories in Bangladesh to improve the working terms and conditions for the workers, many of whom are women?

Source: OECD, 1994: 138.

Proponents of the enforcement of labour standards in developing countries argue that such standards are necessary to provide a minimum level of protection to workers in these countries who otherwise are likely to be exploited by their employers due to the large size of the informal sector and the intense competition for wage employment in the formal sector (e.g. Standing, 1997; Rodgers, 2002). At the most basic level, paying a living wage by local standards is important as it is not only a human rights issue for the individuals and their families concerned, but also a mechanism to prevent less developed countries from competing against each other in a race to the bottom with widening inequality and declining labour standards (Chan and Ross, 2003).

There are three key arguments for labour standards: the human rights, social justice and economic case arguments. The human rights argument sees certain labour standards, such as no forced labour, as a matter of human rights universal to all societies. The social justice argument of labour standards is dependent upon the wealth and living standards of specific countries, once the principle of human rights is in place. The economic case argument suggests that the provision of labour standards may create pressure on employers to enhance their labour productivity through skill upgrading and better health and safety protection (see Rubery and Grimshaw (2003) for a more detailed discussion).

However, what constitutes a fair level of labour standards changes with time and is, in part, contingent upon the state of economic development of specific societies. In poor societies, relatively high labour standards may actually be detrimental to the economic development and expansion of employment opportunities and may encourage the growth of an informal sector that is largely, if not entirely, unregulated (Rubery and Grimshaw, 2003). Over-regulation also reduces the competitiveness of firms and industries where the flexible deployment of labour constitutes an important part of their competitive strategy. The promotion of labour standards therefore needs to take into consideration the promotion of the twin objectives of efficiency and equity (e.g. Buchanan and Callus, 1993; Fudge and Vosco, 2001).

It is important to note that a cost-benefit analysis of employment should not be based solely on financial considerations. Instead, it should take into account the psychological well-being of the workers and emotional return to investment. Here, the concept of moral economy, which 'views economies as socially, politically and economically embedded systems, fuelled by norms and values', is highly relevant (Bolton et al., 2012: 121). According to Bolton et al. (2012: 121), 'at the heart of moral economy is a normative understanding of mutual reciprocality' and interdependence between the employer and the worker (see Islam (2013) on the care perspective of HRM advocating an employee-centred management philosophy).

4 Sustainability through the integration of CSR and HR policy

In Chapter 14 and this chapter so far, we have discussed some of the different societal contexts for and challenges to the implementation of international labour standards, EO legislation and DM initiatives. These are issues central to the IHRM aspects of CSR. Two major objectives are consistent with the argument for active engagement with CSR, labour standards, EO and DM: (a) to identify and eliminate discriminatory practices in workplaces, and (b) to enable organizations to gain competitive advantage through ethical and strategic HR practices. This line of argument is summarized in Figure 15.3.

The adoption of CSR activities has unique implications for MNCs, particularly those operating in less developed countries where the ideas of business ethics and CSR may take on different meaning, the enforcement of legislation may be precarious and the

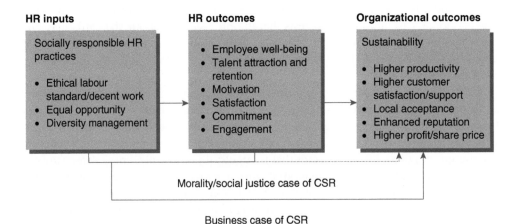

Figure 15.3   Socially responsible HR practices and business sustainability

majority of people still live in poverty. Here, HR professionals have a crucial role to play in assisting organizations to develop their CSR agendas effectively through the integration of CSR and HR policy (see Dubois and Dubois (2012) for a summary of how HR functions can be designed to support environmental sustainability initiatives; also see Gond et al. (2011) on how the role of HR can contribute to CSR through responsible leadership).

CSR through employee involvement

There are two aspects of CSR that are linked to employees, either directly through HR practices or indirectly through the participation of employees in CSR activities. One aspect is the non-HRM related CSR activities that firms adopt to demonstrate their commitment to, for example, environmental protection and the development of local communities. These activities may help to attract, develop, retain and motivate employees who share similar values enshrined in these activities. It is believed that the positive HR outcomes obtained will lead to enhanced organizational performance. While there is now growing awareness of CSR by MNCs, research evidence suggests that they are not engaging their employees sufficiently to gain the full benefit of their strategic commitments and CSR investments.

For example, Pless et al. (2012) observed that there are only a small number of companies in which HRM plays a crucial role in CSR and sustainability. Nevertheless, an increasing number of MNCs are using leadership development programmes as the driver to develop their managers' cognitive understanding of social, ecological and ethical issues confronting companies and their competence in dealing with these issues. Bhattacharya et al.'s (2008) study concluded that most companies take a top-down approach to designing, implementing and managing CSR programmes. Few firms communicate systematically with their employees on the firm's CSR efforts. They rarely consider the needs and values of employees and how these can be fulfilled by developing CSR programmes that align the values of employees with the firm. Most firms do not have a clear understanding of the positive impact that CSR activities may have on employee productivity through enhanced organizational identification and commitment. It follows that better understanding of employees' needs and greater involvement of employees in CSR initiatives will help to improve the return on investment.

Indeed, tensions may arise between CSR efforts and employees' perception, where the interests of the two are seen to diverge. For example, corporate donation of large sums of money to charity work may not be appreciated by employees who are lowly paid and work in harsh environments. This altruistic act may be seen as a hypocritical gesture and may create the impression that the firm is treating outsiders better than its own employees, therefore de-motivating its staff. Kostova (1999: 313) argued that the regulatory, normative and cognitive institutions between the parent country and the host countries of an MNC may be very different ('institutional distance'). A normative institution refers to group or societal beliefs, values and norms, whereas a cognitive institution refers to people's shared knowledge and understanding. Institutional differences can make it more difficult to transfer organizational practices. Understanding local employees' attitude towards CSR will help the MNC make informed decisions as to what initiatives it can or should take at the local level, which may be significantly different from what is considered appropriate in the parent country.

Box 15.4 gives an example of how a Chinese company uses its EI scheme to help the company achieve its environmental protection target.

Box 15.4   Stop and reflect

Environment protection through employee involvement

Dongcheng Ltd is a privately owned textile dye works established in 1994 in southern China. It employs about 600 people who are mainly migrant workers from rural China. The education level is generally low among these workers and earning a reasonable wage to support the family is their main concern.

Due to the nature of the business, the cost of energy and waste (waste water and exhaust) discharge has been high each month. In recent years, environmental protection has ascended in the Chinese government's agenda. Dongcheng was increasingly being fined by the local government for its excessive waste discharge. The company had initially taken different measures in an attempt to reduce the cost. These included educating the workers and imposing energy consumption quotas on production departments. But the result had been negligible. In 2006, Mr Guan, the owner CEO of the company, decided to introduce the 'efficiency gains-sharing scheme'. Each month, a certain percentage of the company's financial gain from energy saving and reduced waste discharge was shared by its employees as a bonus. A small amount of additional fund was allocated to the subsidized staff canteen to provide extra dishes on top of the normal menu twice a month. In addition, a small amount of capital fund was also allocated from the efficiency gain to improve the working environment in the factory.

This scheme was well received by employees and a significant saving was made by the company through reduced cost of energy consumption and waste treatment. Undoubtedly, financial cost, rather than a strong sense of social responsibility, was the main motive of the company in its action to protect the environment. Nevertheless, there was tangible achievement made by the EI scheme which was attentive to employees' welfare and well-being. On this occasion, material incentives, rather than moral education, appears to have been a more effective motivator for employees to help the company achieve its environmental protection target.

Consider how initiatives like this can be sustained when efficiency is increased to the maximum level.

Source: interview with the CEO by the author in 2008.

Building blocks of socially responsible HR practices

The other employee-related aspect of CSR concerns the adoption of socially responsible HR practices to fulfil a firm's social responsibility (fundamental obligation) and to attract and retain talent (competitive advantage). As we have discussed in Chapter 14 and earlier in this chapter, labour standards, EO and DM are three important building blocks of an ethical HR strategy (see Figure 15.4). At the minimum level, firms need to observe labour standards and EO legislation to ensure demonstrable legal compliance. Beyond that, firms have the moral obligation to look after the well-being of their employees and contribute to the economic and social development of less developed countries (Perlmutter, 1969; Bolton et al., 2012). Legal compliance and social justice are the primary concerns of employment ethics. The business case perspective, which appears to be the dominant discourse of CSR and diversity, advances the argument further by suggesting that implementing labour standards, EO legislation and DM programmes not only fulfils firms' legal and social justice obligations, but also creates business benefits through ethical behaviour and valuing people (see Figures 15.3 and 15.4).

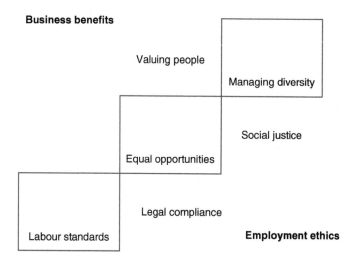

Figure 15.4   An integrated framework for socially responsible employment and HR practices

Alignment of CSR values and the delivery of the HR function

The importance of MNCs maintaining a coherent set of values and corporate culture while leveraging the diversity of the global workforce has been widely noted (e.g. Rosenzweig, 1998; Evans et al., 2002; Sparrow et al., 2004; Brewster et al., 2005). The highly contextual nature of labour standards, EO and workforce diversity is likely to be even more challenging to manage due to societal differences and varying management priorities, as we have discussed in this chapter. Where specific HR functions are outsourced to local firms in the host country, as is increasingly the practice in MNC subsidiaries, the ability of the MNC to ensure a consistent corporate approach to socially responsible HRM may be further compromised. For example, recruitment is an HR function that is often outsourced in host countries (Cooke and Budhwar, 2009). It is also an area of HRM where discrimination is most likely to take place in less developed countries (see Box 15.5 for example). Outsourcing HRM functions therefore raises a question: How should MNCs collaborate with their local HR agency firms to ensure their corporate ethical standards are adhered to? In a way, this is a similar issue to how MNCs should ensure that their suppliers behave in a socially responsible way in an era of global sourcing and production.

Box 15.5   Stop and reflect

Outsourcing recruitment by an MNC and its impact on gender equality in China

A highly reputable pharmaceutical MNC outsourced the recruitment function of its subsidiary in China to a local recruitment agency firm. The HR regional director who monitored the HR function in the Asia region found out that the recruitment agency firm systematically rejected female graduate job candidates, even though during the screening process their CVs were as good as, and in some cases better than, those of their male counterparts. The MNC had a global corporate policy of equal opportunities and imposed a gender ratio in its recruitment targets. As a result, the Chinese subsidiary's gender ratio statistics consistently fell below the corporate target. When this discriminatory practice of the recruitment agency firm was discovered, the HR director drew the attention of the staff from the agency firm to the corporate policy and requested them not to discriminate against female candidates. This request was dismissed by the Chinese recruitment agency staff. Instead, they tried to convince the HR director that this was a common practice in China as women employees were deemed to be less productive due to their family commitments. By rejecting female candidates, they argued, they were actually acting in the interest of the MNC by ensuring that only the most 'productive' staff were recruited.

Now contemplate discussion question 3 below.

Source: interview with the HR regional director by the author in 2007.

5 Summary and conclusions

This chapter has provided an overview of the conceptual debates concerning employment ethics and labour standards as central issues of CSR. Evidence of organizational practices has demonstrated the immense challenges, as well as the moral and economic imperatives, for global firms to act as socially responsible employers to sustain their business growth and the economic and social development of the host countries in which they operate. The impact of CSR is multifaceted, but the important role of ethical HRM in CSR has been largely overlooked (Shen and Zhu, 2011). While national legislation and soft regulations at national and international levels, such as labour standards, may provide a minimum level of protection to workers when effectively enforced, intensive global competition may undermine incentives for firms to take on a higher level of social responsibility. Nevertheless, there is still much more that firms can do to integrate their efforts in HRM and CSR to achieve better results for all concerned.

More importantly, in the multinational context, a liberal notion of voluntary engagement and sharing of social responsibility that has largely been the approach adopted in CSR and corporate engagement may be inadequate to capture the diverse views of CSR informed by various societal values and constraints. Instead, an institutional perspective sensitive to local contexts will be a more promising avenue 'to explore how the boundaries between business and society are constructed in different ways' (Brammer et al., 2012: 3) and to design more effective CSR interventions.

Discussion questions

1. 'In the context of intensifying global competition, firms that observe international labour standards voluntarily will lose out to those that do not.' Do you agree with this statement? Provide evidence to support your answer.
2. Imagine you are an HR manager of a European MNC in the mining industry. The company already has operations in several African countries. As part of its expansion plan, you have been asked to provide an audit report on the company's CSR activities in African countries and provide suggestions on how the company can use CSR to help its expansion. How will you go about the task?
3. Imagine you were the HR regional director of the pharmaceutical MNC reported in Box 15.5. How are you going to work with the recruitment agency firm to ensure their recruitment practices are fair and conform to the company's corporate values? In view of this discovery, do you think it will be necessary to review other HR outsourcing services in the Chinese subsidiary and those in other countries in Asia? What actions will you propose at the regional level to influence your HR outsourcing providers' business ethics?

CASE STUDY

Contract labour and industrial conflicts at Maruti Suzuki (Manesar), a Japanese-funded automotive plant in India

Company background

Maruti Suzuki India Ltd (MSIL) is a Japanese funded multi-plant car manufacturing firm. It is the largest passenger carmaker in India. MSIL was established as a joint venture between the Government of India and Suzuki Motor Corporation (54.2 per cent) in 1982 in Gurgaon, Haryana State near Delhi. The company dominated the Indian passenger car market from the beginning – about 35 per cent of the cars sold in India were produced by MSIL. The company was listed on the Indian stock market in 2003. In 2007, the Government of India sold its complete share to Indian financial institutions and no longer has any stake in the company. According to the Annual Report of the Suzuki Motor Corporation, MSIL's sales accounted for 62 per cent of Suzuki's overseas sales (outside Japan) and 48 per cent of its total global sales in 2010–11. Between 2009–10 and 2010–11, Suzuki's car sales fell by 5.4 per cent in Japan while its overseas sales increased by 18.8 per cent. MSIL contributed the most to this by registering sales growth of 24.8 per cent between 2009–10 and 2010–11.

Maruti Suzuki's Manesar plant, based in the Haryana State, is one of the major factories of MSIL. The plant employs some 3,000 workers (see Table 15.3). Up until the end of 2012, the majority of the shopfloor workers were non-permanent workers whose pay package is substantially less than that of the permanent workers (see Table 15.6). In addition, MSIL is reported to have a strict code of conduct for

Table 15.3   Staffing information at Maruti Suzuki Manesar Plant (2012)

	Permanent	Trainee	Contract	Apprentice
No. of workers	970	400–500	1,100	200–300
Monthly wage rate (in Rs)	8,000+	6,500+	[235 per day + 75 per day (v)] x 23 working days a month	3000+
	8,000(v)*	2,250 (v)		1,000 (v)

* v = variable compensation component (productivity incentive), depending on the number of days of leave the worker takes in a month. Rs 1,500 per day of leave is deducted for a permanent worker; Rs 800 per day of leave is deducted for a trainee. For contract workers and apprentices, two days of leave in a month exhaust the entire (v) component.

Source: Bose and Ghosh (2012)

its workers, including specifying the amount of time one can spend visiting the toilet.

The outburst of mass labour violence – an account of workers' grievances

In spite of the continuous growth of output and sales of MSIL, industrial relations at the Manesar plant over the last decade have been increasingly confrontational. Demands for job security and better employment conditions to reflect a fairer share of the company's profit have been the main reason for the ongoing workers struggle. In 2011, in an attempt to improve their working conditions, the Maruti workers held staggered strikes for 59 days that had led to a revenue loss of about Rs 25 billion and 100,000 cars in output to Maruti. The company had to pay about Rs 1.6 million to each of the 30 workers whose services were terminated by the company and had to re-instate all the permanent workers along with 1,100 contract workers at its Manesar plant. As part of the dispute settlement agreement, the Haryana Labour Department had initiated prosecution proceedings against Maruti for violating the agreement with the workers in 2011. MSIL had committed to form a statutory 'Grievance Redressal Committee' and 'Labour Welfare Committee' at its Manesar plant to help workers settle their grievances with the management. However, this had not been implemented when labour disputes occurred again in 2012, because the company allegedly held the view that the demand from the Labour Department was 'sub-judice'.

Labour disputes escalated in 2012 and turned violent in July. Since April 2012, the Manesar union had been demanding a three-fold increase in basic pay, a monthly conveyance of Rs 10,000, a laundry allowance of Rs 3,000, a gift for every new car launch, and housing for every worker who wants one or cheaper home loans for those want to build their own house. In addition, contract workers and temporary employees want the company to offer them a permanent job so that they can enjoy the same terms and conditions for doing similar work. On 18 July, some 3,000 workers at the plant turned to violence. Armed with steel rods, tools and car components, they went for the bones of the managers and supervisors. They set fire to buildings in the plant. The half-hour riot led to the killing of a general manager (HR) who could not escape the fire due to heavy injuries to his limbs, another 100 plus managers and supervisors were injured, some in a critical condition, and 88 workers were arrested by the police. In the process of controlling the riot, nine policemen were also injured.

(Continued)

(Continued)

There are different versions as to how the violence was ignited. It appears that a supervisor insulted a worker with discriminatory remarks about his caste. The worker then assaulted the supervisor and was subsequently suspended by the company without pay. Union leaders (the plant union was set up in 2011 after the labour disputes) went to see the management on behalf of the workers to ask for the suspension to be lifted, in addition to demands for wage increases. The management displayed indifference to the demands and the union leaders went back to the workers empty handed. Outraged, violence then broke out.

Reasons for the labour–management conflict

The growing use of contingency employment in the form of agency employment, internship and fixed-term contracts is a key source of industrial conflict. A major reason for using contract labour is the highly restrictive labour laws of India, including the Industrial Disputes Act (also see Chapter 14). As a result, casual and contract labour are an attractive option for employers, because workers in these employment categories (also known as informal employment) are normally not covered by the labour laws. Contract workers are offered a three-to-six-months employment contract which then may be rolling for several years. They also receive lower terms and conditions than their permanent counterparts in similar work. Although the Contract Labour Act mandates that contract labour engaging in the same work as permanent workers should receive equal pay, non-compliance remains the norm. Some companies may employ young workers as trainees for several years. It is not unusual for a trainee to be working four days a week doing regular work in their 'placement' company. Overtime may be worked but seldom paid accordingly. The company claims this 'training' as corporate social responsibility to make these young workers employable.

Another reason for using contingency employment is to avoid workers' collectivism and trade union involvement. For example, companies may hire employees under a fixed-term contract, often one year term. The contract will not be renewed if the worker proves troublesome. This is a strategy to prevent workers from joining the trade union and taking industrial action. Although the proportion of workers in the Indian formal sector is relatively small (less than 10 per cent), they are often organized by relatively strong unions which had an adversarial tradition until recent years (Cooke, 2012).

In addition to avoiding legal constraints and circumventing collective actions, contingent employment contracts offer employers substantial savings in wages and benefits. This is especially so whenever wage hikes occur, which are relatively common in India. For example, in representing permanent workers in their (annual) wage negotiation with the management, trade unions traditionally adopt a hard nose approach with a negotiation tactic of starting with high demands. In the Maruti Suzuki case, the wage increase demand presented to the management by the Maruti Suzuki Workers' Union at Manesar in April 2012, if granted, would have meant a four-fold increase in gross pay. Temporary and contract workers typically earn less than half of what the permanent workers earn doing similar work and enjoy little job security, social security provision and company benefits. As a result, 'super contractors' have emerged in the Indian labour market where an employment agency firm may have thousands of workers on their book, supplying them and rotating them in different firms in the same industry doing similar jobs year after year.

'Indisciplined workforce' the cause of the problem – views from the management

According to the general manager (corporate) of MSIL, at the heart of the problem was the indiscipline of a small section of misguided workers at the Manesar plant for over a period of two months. They refused to follow instructions of supervisors and managers, resorted to go-slows, violated processes and systems and even manhandled a supervisor. They also sabotaged car products. When the culprits were identified, they were asked to sign a good conduct bond before resuming work. The good conduct bond is derived from the Certified Standing Orders, and requires workers to reaffirm that they will follow discipline on the shop floor.

The company also maintains that Maruti Suzuki workers are among the best paid for their category of skill, qualification and experience. A Maruti Suzuki worker who has served for five years earns Rs 300,000 per year. Those with ten years' experience receive Rs 450,000. Workers who have served since the founding of the company could be earning about Rs 680,000 per annum. All of them are entitled to medical cover which is comprehensive and high quality. Among those who have served for a certain length of time, nearly 90 per cent own a home. Nearly 70 per cent own a car. This, and also quality education for children, has been facilitated by the company. Most children of workers are pursuing professional courses in reputed institutes.

(Continued)

(Continued)

This, the company claims, has been possible because the management and workers at the company have moved together as one team. There are robust systems, including a recognized union of employees, to address workers' interests. The workers have reciprocated by aligning themselves to the interests of the company and the business. Many of the company's manufacturing and quality processes have been evolved by the workers, by organizing themselves into quality circles and other participative forums. They have shunned the rhetoric of the self-styled guardians of workers, and focused on what is good for them and their company. The management further maintains that the large majority of workers are committed and hard working.

Management response in the aftermath of the labour protest tragedy

On 19 July 2012, Maruti Suzuki issued a statement, which says: 'By any account, this is not an "industrial relations" problem in the nature of management–worker differences over issues of wages or working conditions. Rather, it is an orchestrated act of mob violence at a time when operations had been normal over the past many months' (www.marutisuzuki.com/Maruti-Suzuki-statement-on-Manesar.aspx, accessed 16 August 2012).

In August 2012, the company announced that it would cease using contract workers on the direct production line by March 2013; that its HR department would be doing the hiring; and that priority would be given to contract workers when vacancies for permanent jobs arise. From September 2012, the existing 1,869 contract workers were screened for permanent positions.

MSIL also claimed that the wage difference between contract workers and permanent workers had been much smaller than was reported by the media. According to the company, a contract worker at Maruti received about Rs 11,500 per month, while a permanent worker received about Rs 12,500 per month at the start, which increased in three years to Rs 21,000–22,000 per month.

Mr Shinzo Nakanishi, the managing director and CEO of MSIL, was reported to have said that this kind of violence had never happened in Suzuki Motor Corp's entire global operations spread across Hungary, Indonesia, Spain, Pakistan, Thailand, Malaysia, China and the Philippines. Mr Nakanishi visited each victim and apologized, on behalf of the company, for the suffering inflicted upon them by fellow workers. In a press interview, the CEO requested the central and Haryana state governments to help stop this kind of violence by legislating decisive rules to restore corporate confidence in the light of the emergence of this new 'militant workforce' in Indian factories. He announced, 'we are going to de-recognize Maruti Suzuki Workers' Union and dismiss all workers named in connection with the incident. We will not compromise at all in such instances of barbaric, unprovoked violence.' The company dismissed 500 workers accused of causing the violence and re-opened the plant on 21 August.

Summary

The Maruti Suzuki labour dispute is by no means an isolated incident in contemporary industrial relations in India. The cause of ongoing labour–management tensions is multi-fold. While inferior terms and conditions may be the fuse that has ignited the violent protest, institutional and cultural issues are at the heart of the worsening industrial relations climate in the liberalized Indian economy, as manifested by the Maruti Suzuki dispute. The recurrence of labour unrest in Maruti Suzuki Manesar plant since the early 1990s has caused substantial losses to the company in productivity, property damage and corporate reputation. The July 2012 violence at the Manesar plant took the management by surprise as they thought labour–management relations were improving following the industrial disputes resolution in 2011.

Sources

Bhattacharya, R. (2012) 'Maruti Suzuki continues to walk the labour tight rope' (November), www.thehindubusinessline.com/companies/article2606953.ece (accessed 25 May 2014).

Chauhan, C.P. (2012) 'Labour department moves court against Maruti Suzuki', http://articles.economictimes.indiatimes.com/2012-06-20/news/32335997_1_manesar-plant-haryana-government-maruti-haryana-labour-department (accessed 25 May 2014).

Hindu Business Line (2012) 'Maruti shuts Manesar plant; 88 workers arrested' (July), www.thehindubusinessline.com/companies/article3656659.ece (accessed 25 May 2014).

Kashyap, G.K. and Saikia, R. (2012) 'Shame: labour violence – a blot on modern India', *People Matters* (2 August), http://peoplematters.in/articles/learning-curve/shame-labor-violence-a-blot-on-modern-india (accessed 25 May 2014).

Maruti Suzuki company website: www.marutisuzuki.com (accessed 25 May 2014).

(Continued)

(Continued)

Murthy, K. (2012) 'Restrictive terms of Industrial Disputes Act leads to contract labour', http://forbesindia.com/article/web-special/restrictive-terms-of-industrial-disputes-act-leads-to-contract-labour/33682/1#ixzz2EWgIsQAz (accessed 25 May 2014).

Singh, K. (2012) 'Maruti Suzuki management's response to article on workers' struggle' (September), www.thehindu.com/opinion/op-ed/maruti-suzuki-managements-response-to-article-on-workers-struggle/article2494317.ece (accessed 25 May 2014).

Wikipedia: http://en.wikipedia.org/wiki/Maruti_Suzuki (accessed 25 May 2014).

Case study questions

1. What do you think are the main causes of the recurrence of labour disputes in Maruti Suzuki?
2. How would you develop training programmes to help managers and supervisors in the company develop their competence in managing industrial relations?
3. To what extent do you think the workers are responsible, and should be held accountable, for the incident?

Further reading

- Crowther, D. and Capaldi, N. (eds) (2008) *The Ashgate Research Companion to Corporate Social Responsibility*. Aldershot: Ashgate.
  This edited volume contains 20 chapters authored by scholars from around the world. Each chapter focuses on a different aspect of CSR, offering a variety of theoretical lenses and a wide range of perspectives from different countries and experiences. In particular, Part II of the volume contains three chapters related to CSR and the employment relationship.

- Janssens, M. and Steyaert, C. (2012) 'Towards an ethical research agenda for international HRM: the possibilities of a plural cosmopolitan framework', *Journal of Business Ethics*, 111: 61–72.
  This conceptual article develops an agenda for ethical research in IHRM against a context of changing geo-political dynamics and the political role of MNCs. The authors turn to cosmopolitanism and distinguish three main perspectives – political, cultural and social. Each of them implies a different understanding of the self–other relation in the context of the global world and has different ethical implications for MNCs.

- Islam, G. (2013) 'Implementing care in organizations: recognizing employees: reification, dignity and promoting care in management', *Cross Cultural Management*, 20(2): 235–250.
  This article discusses the care perspective in HRM. Instead of treating employees as human capital to be exploited, an 'ethic of care' views individuals as fundamentally situated in a relational community. The author proposes that the organizing principles of caring organizations are centred on fulfilling employees' needs, promoting their best interest and valuing their contributions. Caring organizations, therefore, increase the well-being of the workforce by generating their positive self-views.

Internet resources

- www.ilo.org. The International Labour Organization (ILO) is a tripartite United Nations agency that brings together governments, employers and workers of its member states in common action to promote decent work throughout the world. The ILO is the global body responsible for drawing up and overseeing international labour standards. Working with its member states, the ILO seeks to ensure that labour standards are respected in practice as well as in principle.
- http://ec.europa.eu/enterprise/csr/index_en.htm. The CSR website of the European Commission's Directorate-General for Enterprise and Industry provides insight into what CSR is, why it is important, and what the European Commission is doing to promote it, with a particular interest in links between CSR and competitiveness.
- www.corporatewatch.org.uk. Corporate Watch is a small independent not-for-profit research and publishing group based in the UK. It undertakes research and analysis on the social and environmental impact of large corporations, particularly multinationals, raises awareness and contributes to public debate and education.
- www.sustainability-indexes.com. The Dow Jones Sustainability Indexes, launched in 1999, track the financial performance of the leading sustainability-driven companies worldwide.
- www.wbcsd.org. The World Business Council for Sustainable Development (WBCSD) is a CEO-led global association of some 200 companies dealing exclusively with business and sustainable development. The Council provides a platform for companies to explore sustainable development, share knowledge, experiences and best practices, and to advocate business positions on these issues in a variety of forums, working with governments, non-governmental and intergovernmental organizations.

Self-assessment questions

Indicative answers to these questions can be found on the companion website at study.sagepub.com/harzing4e.

1. Employee involvement and consultation has been promoted by many Japanese firms and modelled by Western firms in the 1990s as a progressive HRM practice. How can Maruti Suzuki management develop a cooperative labour–management relationship by adopting/adapting some of the Japanese management philosophy that made the Japanese economy a success in the 1980s?
2. How may the demographic profile of the Indian workforce have changed? And what may be the aspirations and expectations of the younger generation of the Indian workers? What do you think should be the social responsibility of the workers as a corporate and society citizen?
3. 'Agency employment only benefits agency firms and nobody else.' Do you agree with this statement?
4. How can the trade unions in Maruti Suzuki develop a new strategy to help fulfil the workers' expectations on the one hand, and to help the company remain competitive on the other?
5. What do you think may be the major issues in the industrial relations system in India? What should the Indian government do to address the issues?

References

Ackers, P. (2006) 'Employment ethics', in T. Redman and A. Wilkinson (eds), *Contemporary Human Resource Management: Text and Cases*. London: Financial Times Prentice Hall, pp. 427–449.

Albinger, H. and Freeman, S. (2000) 'Corporate social performance and attractiveness as an employer to different job seeking populations', *Journal of Business Ethics*, 28(3): 243–253.

Baron, D. (2001) 'Private politics, corporate social responsibility, and integrated strategy', *Journal of Economics and Management Strategy*, 10(1): 7–45.

Bartlett, C. and Ghoshal, S. (1989) *Managing Across Borders: The Transnational Solution*. Boston, MA: Harvard Business School Press.

Bhattacharya, C. and Sen, S. (2004) 'Doing better at doing good: when, why, and how consumers respond to corporate social initiatives', *California Management Review*, 47(1): 9–24.

Bhattacharya, C., Sen, S. and Korschun, D. (2008) 'Using corporate social responsibility to win the war for talent', *MIT Sloan Management Review*, 49(2): 37–44.

Bolton, S., Houlihan, M. and Laaser, K. (2012) 'Contingent work and its contradictions: towards a moral economy framework', *Journal of Business Ethics*, 11(1): 121–132.

Bose, P. and Ghosh, S. (2012) 'Workers' struggle in Maruti Suzuki', www.thehindu.com/opinion/op-ed/article2490903.ece (accessed 26 May 2014).

Brammer, S, Jackson, G. and Matten, D. (2012) 'Corporate social responsibility and institutional theory: new perspectives on private governance', *Socio-Economic Review*, 10(1): 3–28.

Brammer, S., Millington, A. and Rayton, B. (2007) 'The contribution of corporate social responsibility to organizational commitment', *International Journal of Human Resource Management*, 18(10): 1701–1719.

Brewster, C., Sparrow, P. and Harris, H. (2005) 'Towards a new model of globalising HRM', *International Journal of Human Resource Management*, 16(6): 949–970.

Briscoe, D. and Schuler, R. (2004) *International Human Resource Management: Policy and Practice for the Global Enterprise*, 2nd edn. London: Routledge.

Buchanan, J. and Callus, R. (1993) 'Efficiency and equity at work: the need for labour market regulation in Australia', *Journal of Industrial Relations*, 35(5): 515–537.

Cacioppe, R., Forster, N. and Fox, M. (2008) 'A survey of managers' perceptions of corporate ethics and social responsibility and actions that may affect companies' success', *Journal of Business Ethics*, 82(3): 681–700.

Carroll, A. (1979) 'A three-dimensional conceptual model of corporate performance', *Academy of Management Review*, 4(4): 497–505.

Carroll, A. (1991) 'The pyramid of corporate social responsibility: toward the moral management of organizational stakeholders', *Business Horizons*, 34(4): 39–48.

Carroll, A. (1999) 'Corporate social responsibility', *Business and Society*, 38(3): 268–296.

Chan, A. and Ross, R. (2003) 'Racing to the bottom: international trade without a social clause', *Third World Quarterly*, 24(6): 1011–1028.

China Labor News Translations (2008) 'Promising Wal-Mart trade union chair resigns over collective contract negotiations', September, www.clntranslations.org/article/34/promising-wal-mart-trade-union-chair-resigns-over-collective-contract-negotiations (accessed 24 September 2008).

Cooke, F.L. (2008) *Competition, Strategy and Management in China*. Basingstoke: Palgrave Macmillan.

Cooke, F.L. (2012) 'Employment relations in China and India', in M. Barry and A. Wilkinson (eds), *Edward Elgar Handbook of Comparative Employment Relations*. Cheltenham: Edward Elgar, pp.184–213.

Cooke, F.L. (2015) 'The role of international HRM in offshoring and managing contingent workers', in D. Collings, G. Wood and P. Caligiuri (eds), *The Routledge Companion to International Human Resource Management*. London: Routledge, pp 496–510.

Cooke, F.L. and Budhwar, P. (2009) 'HR offshoring and outsourcing: research issues for IHRM', in P. Sparrow (ed.), *Handbook of International Human Resource Management*. Chichester: John Wiley, pp. 341–361.

Crowther, D. and Capaldi, N. (eds) (2008) *The Ashgate Research Companion to Corporate Social Responsibility*. Aldershot: Ashgate.

Dubois, C. and Dubois, D. (2012) 'Strategic HRM as social design for environmental sustainability in organization', *Human Resource Management*, 51(6): 799–826.

Egri, C. and Ralston, D. (2008) 'Corporate responsibility: a review of international management research from 1998 to 2007', *Journal of International Management*, 14(4): 319–339.

European Commission (2008) The Corporate Social Responsibility (CSR) website of the European Commission's Directorate-General for Enterprise and Industry http://ec.europa.eu/enterprise/csr/index_en.htm (accessed 21 December 2008).

Evans, P., Pucik, V. and Barsoux, J. (2002) *The Global Challenge: Frameworks for International Human Resource Management*. London: McGraw-Hill.

Freeman, E. (1984) *Strategic Management: A Stakeholder Approach*. Boston, MA: Pitman.

Friedman, M. (1962) *Capitalism and Freedom*. Chicago: The University of Chicago Press.

Fudge, J. and Vosko, L. (2001) 'By whose standards? Reregulating the Canadian labour market', *Economic and Industrial Democracy*, 22(3): 327–356.

Garriga, E. and Melé, D. (2004) 'Corporate social responsibility theories: mapping the territory', *Journal of Business Ethics*, 53(1–2): 51–71.

Gond, J., Igalens, J., Swaen, V. and El Akremi, A. (2011) 'The human resources contribution to responsible leadership: an exploration of the CSR–HR interface', *Journal of Business Ethics*, 98: 115–132.

Harzing, A. and Ruysseveldt, J. (eds) (2004) *International Human Resource Management*. London: Sage.

Hillman, A. and Keim, G. (2001) 'Shareholder value, stakeholder management, and social issues: what's the bottom line?', *Strategic Management Journal*, 22(2): 125–139.

Howard, M. and Willmott, M. (2001) 'Ethical consumption in the twenty-first century', in T. Bentley and D. Stedman Jones (eds) *The Moral Universe*, pp. 1–8. London: Demos.

ILO (International Labour Organization) (1999) *Report of the Director-General: Decent Work*. International Labour Conference, 87th Session. Geneva: International Labour Organization, www.ilo.org/public/english/standards/relm/ilc/ilc87/rep-i.htm (accessed 20 December 2008).

Islam, G. (2013) 'Implementing care in organizations: recognizing employees: reification, dignity and promoting care in management', *Cross Cultural Management*, 20(2): 235–250.

Janssens, M. and Steyaert, C. (2012) 'Towards an ethical research agenda for international HRM: the possibilities of a plural cosmopolitan framework', *Journal of Business Ethics*, 111: 61–72.

Kalleberg, A. (2009) 'Precarious work, insecure workers: employment relations in transition', *American Sociological Review*, 74(1): 1–22.

Kostova, T. (1999) 'Transnational transfer of strategic organizational practices: a contextual perspective', *Academy of Management Review*, 24(2): 308–324.

OECD (Organisation for Economic Co-operation and Development) (1994) Employment Outlook, Chapter 4, 'Labour standards and economic integration'. Paris: OECD, pp. 137–166, www.oecd.org/els/emp/2409984.pdf (accessed 26 May 2014).

Perlmutter, H.V. (1969) 'The tortuous evolution of the multinational corporation', *Columbia Journal of World Business*, 4(1): 9–18.

Pinnington, A.H., Macklin, R. and Campbell, T. (eds) (2007) *Human Resource Management: Ethics and Employment*. Oxford: Oxford University Press.

Pless, N., Maak, T. and Stahl, G. (2012) 'Promoting corporate social responsibility and sustainable development through management development: what can be learned from international service learning programmes?', *Human Resource Management*, 51(6): 873–904.

Rodgers, J. (2002) *Decent Work and the Informal Economy*. International Labour Conference, 90th Session. Geneva: International Labour Organization.

Rodriguez, P., Siegel, D., Hillman, A. and Eden, L. (2006) 'Three lenses on the multinational enterprise: politics, corruption, and corporate social responsibility', *Journal of International Business Studies*, 37(6): 733–746.

Roozen, I., Pelsmacker, P. and Bostyn, F. (2001) 'The ethical dimensions of decision processes of employees', *Journal of Business Ethics*, 33(2): 87–100.

Rosenzweig, P. (1998) 'Managing the new global workforce: fostering diversity, forging consistency', *European Management Journal*, 16(6): 644–652.

Rubery, J. and Grimshaw, D. (2003) *The Organisation of Employment: An International Perspective*. Basingstoke: Palgrave Macmillan.

Sachdev, S. (2006) 'International corporate social responsibility and employment relations', in T. Edwards and C. Rees (eds), *International Human Resource Management: Globalization, National Systems and Multinational Companies*. Essex: Pearson Education Ltd., pp. 262–284.

Secchi, D. (2007) 'Utilitarian, managerial and relational theories of corporate social responsibility', *International Journal of Management Reviews*, 9(4): 347–373.

Sen, S. and Bhattacharya, C. (2001) 'Does doing good always lead to doing better? Consumer reactions to corporate social responsibility', *Journal of Marketing Research*, 38(2): 225–243.

Shen, J. and Zhu, C. (2011) 'Effects of socially responsible human resource management on employee organizational commitment', *International Journal of Human Resource Management*, 22(15): 3020–3035.

Sparrow, P., Brewster, C. and Harris, H. (2004) *Globalizing Human Resource Management*. London: Routledge.

Standing, G. (1997) 'Globalization, labour flexibility and insecurity: the era of market regulation', *European Journal of Industrial Relations*, 3(1): 7–37.

Stiglitz, J. (2002) *Globalization and Its Discontent*. London: Penguin Books.

Turban, D. and Greening, D. (1997) 'Corporate social performance and organizational attractiveness to prospective employees', *Academy of Management Journal*, 40(3): 658–672.

Valentine, S. and Fleischman, G. (2008) 'Ethics programs, perceived corporate social responsibility and job satisfaction', *Journal of Business Ethics*, 77(2): 159–172.

Winstanley, D. and Woodall, J. (eds) (2000) *Ethical Issues in Contemporary Human Resource Management*. London: Macmillan Business.

Wood, G. (2006) 'International human resource management', in T. Redman and A. Wilkinson (eds), *Contemporary Human Resource Management: Text and Cases*. London: Financial Times Prentice Hall, pp. 263–277.

Yu, Z. (2012) *Managing Human Resource in China: The View from Inside MNCs*. Cambridge: Cambridge University Press.

Zinkin, J. (2004) 'Maximizing the "Licence to Operate": CSR from an Asian perspective', *Journal of Corporate Citizenship*, 14 (Summer): 67–80.

Index

NB: numbers in italics indicate figures; numbers in bold indicate tables